Character *and*
Moral Education

This book is part of the Peter Lang Education list.
Every volume is peer reviewed and meets
the highest quality standards for content and production.

PETER LANG
New York • Washington, D.C./Baltimore • Bern
Frankfurt • Berlin • Brussels • Vienna • Oxford

Character *and* Moral Education

A READER

EDITED BY
Joseph L. DeVitis *and* Tianlong Yu

PETER LANG
New York • Washington, D.C./Baltimore • Bern
Frankfurt • Berlin • Brussels • Vienna • Oxford

Library of Congress Cataloging-in-Publication Data

Character and moral education: a reader /
edited by Joseph L. DeVitis, Tianlong Yu.
p. cm.
Includes bibliographical references.
1. Moral education—United States. 2. Character.
3. Students—United States—Conduct of life.
I. DeVitis, Joseph L. II. Yu, Tianlong.
LC268.C335   370.11'40973—dc23   2011021144
ISBN 978-1-4331-1100-6 (hardcover)
ISBN 978-1-4331-1099-3 (paperback)
ISBN 978-1-4539-0140-3 (e-book)

Bibliographic information published by **Die Deutsche Nationalbibliothek**.
Die Deutsche Nationalbibliothek lists this publication in the "Deutsche
Nationalbibliografie"; detailed bibliographic data is available
on the Internet at http://dnb.d-nb.de/.

The paper in this book meets the guidelines for permanence and durability
of the Committee on Production Guidelines for Book Longevity
of the Council of Library Resources.

© 2011 Peter Lang Publishing, Inc., New York
29 Broadway, 18th floor, New York, NY 10006
www.peterlang.com

Printed in the United States of America

To Nel Noddings and John Martin Rich—
who taught us to search for deeper meanings in moral education

Contents

PART TWO: MORAL EDUCATION

Introduction

JOSEPH L. DEVITIS & TIANLONG YU

> The test of the morality of a society is what it does for its children.
> DIETRICH BONHOEFFER

Perhaps there has never been a better time to talk about character and moral education than now, especially in light of the critical need to better serve our nation, our world, and our children. At the end of the first decade of the twenty-first century, we continue to witness the unprecedented emphasis on accountability and standardization in national policies on education. Among the many unfortunate results produced by this school reform movement is an erosion of the moral mission of schooling. As economic objectives increasingly drive the reform movement, the moral purpose of education is forsaken. Education is projected only to transmit knowledge and traditions, not to transform individuals and their cultures by engaging their thinking, feeling, and action, both personally and collectively. Forced into a uniform, standardized curriculum that evaluates learning according to standardized tests, students are denied their right to a well-rounded education that should necessarily address their moral development and character formation. A moral hypocrisy is well at work when children's worth is assessed on a four-point scale and education becomes equivalent with training and transporting everyone to the same destination. The top-down and one-size-fits-all approach to schooling also ignores the issues of cultural diversity, educational equality, and social justice. The continuing marginalization of minority and poor children by the reform movement reflects a betrayal of democratic and moral principles of education. Instead, education for democracy seeks the development of critical thinking and moral deliberation. That kind of learning mode is vitally present in many essays in this book.

With this book, we hope to add a collective voice to this urgent call: Educational reform must be guided by moral principles, and moral education must become a priority of schools. Authors of all the chapters in this volume, both previously published and originally written for this book, share this common concern, albeit from divergent philosophical, political, and academic perspectives. We are well aware and fully respectful of that diversity in the scholarship on moral education and intend to reflect and further promote it through this book.

It is necessary to explain the central terms we utilize in this volume, as indicated in the title. For many today, the term "character education" has become an umbrella one, used to refer to a varied array of approaches to moral education; thus, it has become synonymous with "moral education." Several authors in this book may have used "character education" in this broad sense. However, it seems that more scholars today tend to identify character education as a special approach to moral education. For example, some prominent proponents and critics of character education have defined character education as virtue-centered moral education informed by particular philosophical, political and educational frameworks (Lickona, 1991; McClellan, 1999; Noddings, 2002). On the other hand, "moral education" is understood as a "larger" concept. Following Dewey, we use "moral education" in two ways: educating people to be moral and providing an education that is moral. We applied that conceptual distinction in our selection of articles and contributors.

Accordingly, we divide the book into two sections. The first section, devoted to "character education," includes mostly previously published pieces (with two original chapters by Boyd and DeVitis & Yu). Though hardly comprehensive, these chapters offer a significant overview of the national movement in character education. With some very different, even opposing, treatments of the topic, they provide readers with a number of penetrating analyses of character education—its history, politics, conceptual underpinnings, and pedagogical ramifications. After thirty years in the limelight and dominating the national conversation on moral education, character education is undergoing a much needed careful scrutiny.

Grouped under the title of "moral education," the chapters in the second section are largely original contributions for this volume. Our inclusion of these chapters is based on several considerations. First, we seek to look beyond character education as the prevailing model of moral education. In addition to the many theoretical and educational problems pinpointed in the book's first section, we are concerned with character education's dominance in today's school practices, especially when its emphasis has been politically driven (which certainly appears to be the case). The explicit inculcation of character through federal legislation (such as the No Child Left Behind Act) and other state laws warrants grave reservations and, more importantly, a serious search for alternatives. Therefore, we hope to generate an extensive and intensive debate on moral education in order to promote new, diverse, and more vibrant dialogue and action.

Second, we hope this new scholarship on moral education will challenge the normalcy in the field, deconstruct the master narratives, and break through some established paradigms. For example, few of the chapters in this section follow the pre-established and historically significant models of moral education such as the Kohlbergian cognitive-developmental approach. We may still acknowledge their influences on the new thinking, but we seek new ways of knowing and feeling about difficult, often ambiguous, moral matters. We especially strive to challenge the "scientific," positivist treatment of teaching and learning so evident in the current reform agenda as well as in research on moral development and education. Instead, we attempt to advance contextualized examination with keen attention to the social, cultural, political issues surrounding moral education. The chapters indeed cover a wide range of issues relevant to moral education, including governance and politics, democracy and citizenship, religious influences, peace and social justice, gender identity, sexual orientation, race relations, feminism, globalization, environmental concerns, media and popular culture, and classroom strategies. Writings across these chapters demonstrate both thoughtful theoretical understanding and practical wisdom. A "public intellectual" worldview guides these writings. That is to say, our contributors write not for specialized, circumscribed scholarly circles only but also for the wider public. Moral education *is* in the public interest, and this book represents an effort toward its renewal and enhancement.

If we are not successful in restoring the moral mission to schools and developing our children in genuinely moral ways, our culture will rightly be judged a "sick society." Granted, our journey toward authentic moral growth presents few easy destination points. To paraphrase Mark Twain, physical courage is much more common than moral courage. Yet, we must all attempt to engage the moral imagination as intensely as possible. If we do so, we will have at least satisfied our moral conscience. And, in today's troubled and uncertain landscape, that feat itself constitutes a large step in the direction of a better world. The next step will be to act, in concert, with our fellow human beings for the good of us all.

References

Lickona, T. (1991). *Educating for character: How our schools can teach respect and responsibility.* New York: Bantam Books.

McClellan, B. E. (1999). *Moral education in America: Schools and the shaping of character from colonial times to the present.* New York: Teachers College Press.

Noddings, N. (2002). *Educating moral people: A caring alternative to character education.* New York: Teachers College Press.

PART ONE

Character Education

CHAPTER ONE

Moral Education in the Schools

WILLIAM J. BENNETT & EDWIN J. DELATTRE

The belief that moral values should be taught to young Americans in the schools is at least as old as the nation itself. Thomas Jefferson's *Bill for the More General Diffusion of Knowledge* argued for an educational system that would fortify citizens with moral probity to resist the schemes of the enemies of liberty. In his *Proposals Relating to the Education of Youth in Pennsylvania*, Benjamin Franklin prescribed the study of ethics in an instructional program that would seek to instill "benignity of mind." Perhaps the most explicit embodiment of this drive to inculcate the young with moral lessons is to be found in *McGuffey's Readers*. On another level, John Dewey's forceful and highly influential writings concerning the interdependence of democracy, education, and moral character are a modern reformulation of the old belief that "virtue" can and should be taught in the schools. To be sure, an opposite belief—that the schools should teach *no* values, but should stick to imparting skills and basic knowledge—also has its adherents among educators and social theorists. But more and more in recent years, and especially now, in the aftermath of Watergate and accounts of corruption in government and business, there has been a call for reemphasizing moral education in the schools.

At the moment the entire discussion is dominated by two figures: Sidney Simon, of the School of Education at the University of Massachusetts, who advocates "values clarification," and Lawrence Kohlberg, of Harvard and the Center for Moral Education, who calls for "cognitive moral development." Although they differ in important ways, and although their respective followings are in different segments of the educational community, Simon and Kohlberg share an enormous popularity. Both are widely sought after for "workshops" in their methods, and their programs have gained broad support among the nation's teachers and are increasingly used in the classroom. Simon and Kohlberg agree in rejecting what they regard as the fundamental error of traditional approaches to moral education in this country—what they call "indoctrination." In their shared opinion, moral education has amounted in the past to little more than an attempt by elders to "impose" values upon the young. They claim to offer something different, and better. In fact, what they offer is different, but certainly no better.

"Values Clarification"

Sidney Simon's approach is the most widely used new method of moral education in elementary and secondary schools (though less well known in college circles). The theory behind it begins by criticizing traditional moral "indoctrination" as useless for making sense out of life: Traditional moral education is irrelevant today because the modern world is uniquely difficult and complex, and young people are confused as never before. "The children of today," Simon writes, "are confronted by many more choices than in previous generations":

> Areas of confusion and conflict abound: politics, religion, love and sex, family, friends, drugs, materialism, race, work, aging and death, leisure time, school, and health. Each area demands decisions that yesterday's children were rarely called upon to make.

Even more troubling than the ineffectiveness of "indoctrination" is the traditional principle that there are right and wrong ways of acting, right and wrong ways of thinking. In fact, Simon asserts, "none of us has the 'right' set of values to pass on to other people's children." Thus there is a need for a new approach-values clarification.

Values clarification is concerned not with "the *content* of people's values, but with the *process of valuing*." Its aims are to promote growth, freedom, and ethical maturity and to enable children to know "how to negotiate the lovely banquet of life ahead of them.'" These stated aims will be furthered if teachers, parents, and other adults commit themselves to the view that "there's no right or wrong answer" to any question of value. The process of values clarification is taught in classroom "simulations" in which students arc offered various choices and taken through exercises (called "strategies") designed to encourage them to make a conscious effort to discover their "own" values. Simon describes the value of this process in these words:

> Each of you who is a parent could leave your own children no legacy more precious than for them to have years of experience in knowing what they want, having learned to set their priorities and rank order the marvelous items in life's cafeteria.

Much of Simon's writing consists of specific "strategies" designed for use in the school and home. In a typical exercise a student might be asked to answer the following:

1. Which do you think is the most religious thing to do on a Sunday morning?
   a. Go to church to hear a very good preacher
   b. Listen to some classical music on the radio
   c. Have a big breakfast with the family
2. Which do you like least?
   a. An uptight indoctrinator
   b. A cynical debunker
   c. A dull, boring fact giver
3. During a campus protest where would you be most likely, to be found?
   a. In the midst of it
   b. Gaping at it from across the street
   c. In the library minding your own business

In making these and other similar choices, the student supposedly moves toward fulfillment of the Socratic ideal of self-knowledge. By answering and *knowing* his answer, according to Simon, he gains insight into himself, which in time brings clarity about his values. The student is then prepared to move freely and confidently in the world.

Other values-clarification exercises are more extensive. One "strategy" is called *Who are all those others? And what are they doing in my life?* A diagram dominates one page of the text: "ME" is at the center, with lines extending to blocks representing other people, e.g., "important teacher, a parent-guardian, best friend." The student is asked:

> Essentially, what do they count on you for? What demands do they place on you? What do they want you to be, to do, to think? What do they want you to value?…Consider the similarities and differences between what the various people in your life want from you . . .

In another "strategy," called *Who Comes to My House?,* the student is to consider "an inventory of the symbolic warehouse of your life." He is told to ask, "How many people are invited to your house only because you feel obligated to them?" Simon comments on this "strategy":

> When you come to think of it, there is something silly, certainly something nonessential, about paying off obligations, about spending too much precious leisure time with people who are millstones. . . .
>
> There are, of course, "Responsibility People," those toward whom we have an important personal obligation; perhaps an elderly relative or infirm "other." These are responsibilities that, for the most part, we bear graciously, keeping in mind the inevitability of the aging process. To be kind and to help those who need us demonstrates a personal value we respect.
>
> On the other hand, we can choose to spend our time with those who give as they take, who offer at least as much as they receive.

In *Priorities,* Simon "asks you and your family at the dinner table, or your friends across the lunch table, to rank choices and to defend those choices in friendly discussion." One example of Simon's "delightful possibilities" for mealtime discussion is this:

> Your husband or wife is a very attractive person. Your best friend is very attracted to him or her. How would you want them to behave?
>   a. Maintain a clandestine relationship so you wouldn't know about it
>   b. Be honest and accept the reality of the relationship
>   c. Proceed with a divorce

Values-clarification strategies, says Simon, enable the student to achieve knowledge about values, free from the inhibitory inculcation of adults. Despite an admitted shortage of empirical evidence, Simon claims positive results: "Students have become less apathetic, less flighty, less conforming as well as less overdissenting."[1]

"Simulations" or Indoctrination?

Values-clarification "strategies" are supposed to give students the greatest possible freedom of choice and knowledge of themselves and the world. By accepting the idea that there are no right or wrong answers to questions of morality and conduct, students learn that being clear about what one wants is all that is required to live well. But do such "strategies" really provide knowledge about the world and freedom of choice? Do they actually make for self-knowledge and ethical maturity and autonomy? Or do they encourage something else? Simon's examples are instructive in more ways than one.

The first exercise, about the most religious thing to do on a Sunday morning, asks the student to think about what he wants and likes to do on Sunday mornings. Yet it introduces no other considerations and implies that whatever the student thinks is religious thereby is religious.

The second exercise asks the student to say which of three unattractive choices he likes least—an uptight indoctrinator, a cynical debunker, or a dull, boring fact-giver. Here again, the student is asked to consider only what he likes and dislikes. Moreover, it is assumed that these three are all meaningful choices to the students. No other possibilities or greater descriptions of these people are offered for consideration before a choice is made. The suggestion is clearly that factual information is necessarily boring, debunking necessarily cynical, indoctrination necessarily uptight.

In the exercise on campus protest, the student again answers on the basis of his immediate likes and dislikes, without any knowledge of the circumstances and other germane information about the protest. In this "strategy," it is not relevant whether the protest is a violent, illegal take-over of a university building, or a peaceful, legal demonstration against such an action.

The first of the longer exercises, *Who are all those others? And what are they doing, in my life?* centers on the student and instructs him to consider other people only in terms of his and their wants and demands. Any larger aspects of their relationship to him—what they really are doing in his life—are not included in this "strategy."

In *Who Comes to My House*, the student is asked to think of people who are invited to his home only because he "feels obligated to them." The student is then told that "paying off obligations" is "silly" and "non-essential." He is also told that while he may graciously bear responsibilities toward elderly relatives, he can choose instead to spend time with people "who offer at least as much as they receive." The student's "precious leisure time" and what he wants to do with it are, again, the main considerations in the exercise. Elderly and infirm people are presented, *a priori*, as "millstones," and the exercise assumes that the student will not want to spend time with them. Further, in the options offered, the student is treated as if his wants always conflicted with his obligations. Note that it is never assumed that the student wants to be decent.

The last exercise asks the student how he would want his spouse and best friend to behave if they were attracted to each other. Typically, the spouse and best friend are presented as having desires they will eventually satisfy anyway: The student is offered only choices that presuppose their relationship. All possibilities for self-restraint, fidelity, regard for others, or respect for mutual relationships and commitments are ignored.

All these examples attest to the failure of Simon's approach to live up to his claims. They involve not "values" but only desires and self-gratification; they do little more than glorify a doctrine of the primacy of wants—the wants, likes, and dislikes of the student and of others. The "strategies" thus offer severely limited and misleading options for conduct. Moreover, the exercises are indifferent throughout to relevant facts—except those that Simon *wants* the student to consider. Absent in all the examples are many considerations—circumstances, context, history—to which moral judgment must be attentive. As a result, these exercises seem more likely to promote hasty, ill-informed, ignorant, and precipitous judgment than any kind of informed free choice. The student is hardly free to make creative choices, since he is closed in by the narrow options Simon gives him. Since the student is taught that clarity about one's desires is the only thing that matters, the importance of knowledgeable, informed, and conscientious judgment in life is entirely obscured. The "strategies" thus reveal the moral content of Simon's approach. People are bundles of wants; the world is a battlefield of conflicting wants; and no one has room for goodness, decency, or the capacity for a positive exercise of will. Moral maturity is certainly not to be found in the clarification of values, which is cast solely in the language of narrow self-gratification and is devoid of any considerations of decency whatsoever. Finally and ironically, Simon's approach emphatically indoctrinates—by encouraging and even exhorting the student to narcissistic self-gratification.

"Cognitive Moral Development"

Kohlberg's work is also gaining in influence and popularity; but although its impact and following in the schools is increasing, Kohlbert's highest standing is among his colleagues in the university community—particularly in departments of psychology and philosophy, and in schools of education. Kohlberg regards values clarification as useful to some degree, but ultimately of limited value:

Besides leaving unsolved problems, "a firm restriction to values clarification merges into an actual teaching that ethical relativity is true." Kohlberg believes that relativism is philosophically and scientifically false, and claims to offer instead a version of a long-standing account of objective moral truth: a "reassertion of the Platonic faith in the power of the rational good."

Kohlberg's position emerges from a much more extensive and complicated theoretical background than Simon's. Relying on a series of cultural and anthropological studies, Kohlberg contends that there is a universal and invariant series of six stages of cognitive moral development; that reaching any stage requires passing through the preceding sequence; and that each successive stage is morally superior to those preceding it. Although human beings may stop at any stage in the invariant sequence, they can be stimulated to ascend the scale.

Kohlberg agrees with Simon that moral education has, up to this time, been dominated by "indoctrination." He says that "traditional moral education…[is] undemocratic and unconstitutional." Kohlberg stresses the need for a new psychology and a new philosophy that recognizes "the child's right to freedom from indoctrination."

Adults are to view the child not as a pupil but as a "moral philosopher" in his own right. Claiming to follow a tradition running from Socrates through Dewey and Piaget, Kohlberg argues that the sole justifiable end of moral education is cognitive moral development and that only exercises involving moral dilemmas and conflicts can promote such development. This strategy, Kohlberg says, reflects a "progressive ideology" with a "liberal, democratic, and non-indoctrinative" notion of education. Kohlberg sometimes even stresses the "revolutionary nature" of his program.

Kohlberg's six stages of cognitive moral development, in order of temporal sequence and moral value, are as follows. Stage One is *"The punishment and obedience orientation,"* in which the child defers to the superior position or power of the parent, teacher, or authority figure: "The physical consequences of action determine its goodness or badness regardless of the human meaning or value of these consequences." Stage Two is *"The instrumental relativist orientation,"* in which right action consists of instrumentally satisfying one's own needs and occasionally the needs of others. Stage Three is *"The inter-personal concordance or 'good boy-nice girl'" orientation,"* in which the child seeks the approval of others and conforms to stereotypes concerning good behavior and the value of helping others. Stage Four, where Kohlberg claims most citizens peak and most civilized societies dwell, is *"The law and order orientation,"* involving obedience to authority, fixed rules, and the maintenance of the social order. Stage Five is *"'The social contract-legalistic orientation,'"* which recognizes the importance of an arbitrary element of, or starting point for, rules or expectations, for the utilitarian purpose of agreement. Stage Six is "*The universal ethical principle orientation,*" the apex of morality:

> Right is defined by the decision of conscience in accord with self-chosen *ethical principles* appealing to logical comprehensiveness, universality, and consistency....At heart, these are universal principles of *justice,* of the *reciprocity* and *equality* of human *rights,* and of respect for the dignity of human beings as *individual persons* [italics in the original].

According to Kohlberg, "There is only one principled basis for resolving claims: justice or equality. Treat every man's claim impartially regardless of the man." With an approving nod toward John Rawls, whose philosophical position also fundamentally emphasizes equality, Kohlberg describes Stage Six in the following terms:

> To summarize, I have found a no more recent summary statement of the implications of our studies than that made by Socrates: First, virtue is ultimately one, not many, and it is always the same ideal form regardless of climate or culture. Second, the name of this ideal form is justice. Third, not only is the good one, but virtue is knowledge of the good. He who knows the good chooses the good. Fourth, the kind of knowledge of the good which is virtue is philosophical knowledge or intuition of the ideal form of the good, not correct opinion or acceptance of conventional beliefs. Most psychologists have never believed any of these ideas of Socrates. Is it so surprising that psychologists have never understood Socrates? It is hard to understand if you are not Stage Six.

In Kohlberg's view, "the basic referent of the term 'moral' is a type of *judgment* or a type of *decision-making process,* not a type of behavior, emotion, or social institution," "Morality is a unique *sui generis* realm." His account of morality includes a disclaimer:

> We make no direct claims about the ultimate aims of men, about the good life....These are problems beyond the scope of the sphere of morality or moral principles, which we define as principles of choice for resolving conflicts of obligation.

Moral education must therefore be non-indoctrinating, democratic, and directed toward justice and equality. The effective teacher who employs the materials provided by Kohlberg and his followers is "something of a revolutionary, rather than an instiller of virtues." He is expected to be neutral, not imposing his own or other values on the students, but providing a stimulus for students to move through the stages of moral development on their own. Kohlberg says, with another authority (Israel Sheffler), that "to teach...is...to submit oneself to the understanding and independent judgment of the pupil, to his demand for reasons, to his sense of what constitutes an adequate explanation." The presentation of dilemmas creates internal cognitive conflict, inspiring the student "to see things previously invisible to him"; thus "the whole idea is to encourage students...to argue with each other." Students vote on dilemmas in class, to insure that there is sufficient disagreement to create conflict, but they must close their eyes so that none will be influenced by the others.

Examples of simple dilemmas are provided which, along with a standard scoring manual, set forth a series of "criterion judgments" that enable teachers to see where students are on the moral-development continuum. The teacher's responsibility is to use the dilemmas to show the child the insufficiency of his present stage of reasoning in comparison with the reasoning of the next stage. The teacher scores the child by matching student responses with the responses given in the manual for the different stages, by keeping track of the number of Stage One responses, Stage Two responses, and so on, and by noting progress from one level to the next. The teacher is instructed to establish a "non-judgmental atmosphere," and not to be "the enforcer of demands"; the teacher is advised "to relax and enjoy it," even to "swing with it."

Dealing with Dilemmas

An example of a dilemma is presented in *Affiliative Roles and Relationships*. A mother promises her 12-year-old daughter, Judy, that she may go to a rock concert if she saves enough money. Judy saves $5 for the ticket and $3 more. But her mother then changes her mind and tells Judy she must spend the money for new school clothes. Judy goes to the rock concert anyway, after telling her mother that she saved only $3 and went to her friend's house for the day. Later, Judy confesses her lie to her older sister, Louise. In the *Standard Scoring Manual*, the main question about this dilemma is, "Should a daughter [Louise] help her mother exercise authority even if doing so means that her sister's contract or property rights will be violated?" Then for the teacher's use, subsidiary questions are offered:

1. In wondering whether to tell, Louise thinks of the fact that Judy is her sister. Should that make a difference in Louise's decision?
2. What do you think is the most important thing for a good daughter to be concerned about in her relationship to her mother in this or other situations?

At Stage One, or more precisely at Stage One-A, the "bottom level," the student responds that Louise should tell because "Louise *or* Judy will be punished when their mother finds out." A Stage One-B answer is that "Louise should tell *or* a daughter should obey her mother; since the mother is older, she knows more, is smarter, knows what's best, etc." An "Optimal Example" answer of reasoning at the bottom level comes in response to questions about what is most important in the relationship between mother and daughter. The dialogue supposedly goes like this:

[Student:] Be honest.
[Teacher:] Why?
[Student:] Because it is her mother and she should keep promises to her because she is older.
[Teacher:] Why?
[Student:] She knows more and knows what's best.

From this "low" point the student should progress upward to Stage Two (Louise tells because of concern that Judy "might try to get away with lying or deceiving her mother all the time"); to Stage Three ("A good daughter should recognize that her mother loves her and has her best interests at heart"); to Stage Four ("Louise should tell her mother about Judy's lying out of respect for her mother's authority and in recognition of the fact that the mother is responsible for making decisions concerning her daughter's conduct and welfare.") This particular dilemma only goes as far as Stage Five, where the manual presents a fairly elaborate articulation of "Role Norm Obligations" and "Fairness and Equity." The answer at this level is, "The mother had no right to forbid Judy to go to the concert because Judy is an individual with rights equal to her mother's." At this stage, the answer to the second subsidiary question is this:

The most important thing the mother should recognize in the mother-daughter relationship is that her daughter is a free and unique individual who should be treated as such.

The manual describes this peak of moral reasoning:

> This judgment focuses on the obligation to respect each person's individuality or right to autonomy without imposition upon that person of one's own expectations. . . .

The "Optimal Example" is characterized as follows:

> A good mother should early respect her daughter as a person, as an individual with needs, and rights and emotions. If possible she should always deal directly and straightforwardly with her daughter; not condescendingly or authoritarianly.
>
> The mother had no right to forbid Judy to go to the concert because Judy is an individual with rights equal to her mother's. [Students] may say that Judy's youth or ostensibly subordinate role as daughter should not be regarded as a morally relevant consideration....The mother's authority is legitimate only insofar as it is based on mutual respect, is just, and could be freely accepted by all parties with informed consent.

And other examples of Stage-Five sophistication are offered:

> What is a daughter but a person, and should be treated as such. Double standards should not exist for a sub-person-children, over whom you have "power" and others over whom you don't....A mother may guide or suggest the most advantageous use of property, but must not impose herself on her children, and accept their decisions and properties, as she must for other people as well, and may not use the excuse that they are too young to manage such things, to rule two lives and consciences....When people are reacted to as people not as threats to one's self, or as an instrument for your power, but as people, is the only way harmony will ever begin to exist in the conscience and the world.

A full book of such dilemmas, *Hypothetical Dilemmas for Use in Moral Discussions*, has been prepared and distributed by the Moral Education and Research Foundation at Harvard. This is a typical dilemma found in the book:

> *Sex as a Need:* The Johnson family (with four children) was a very happy and close one. Mr. and Mrs. Johnson were in their 30's. One day Mr. Johnson fell from a third-story building where he was working. He broke his back in this accident and was totally paralyzed from his waist down. The accident did not result in economic hardship because of workmen's compensation. Three months after the accident, when Mr. Johnson came home, the problem began. Ms. [*sic*] Johnson, who was a young person, realized that she would have to give up sexual intercourse with her husband. If she did not want to give up her sex life, she had the following choices: either get a divorce, or to have extramarital affairs.

> 1. Is it possible to separate sex from affection? What do you think she should do? Give reasons.
> 2. Do you think this woman should remain married to the husband? Why or why not?
> 3. What do you think would happen to the family if she had an affair?
> 4. If she decides to have an affair, should she tell her husband or keep it a secret? Why?

The remaining 50 dilemmas deal with similar crises. Twenty-one are related to sexual conflicts—homosexuality, swapping, extramarital sex. There are simple one-or two-page statements about the dilemmas of My Lai, Daniel Berrigan, Daniel Ellsberg, women's liberation, kidney transplants, Mayor Daley, draft evasion, abortion, and choosing one child over another.

A Curious Libertarianism

Kohlberg purports to have advanced far beyond the relativism and glorified idiosyncrasy of the Simon approach.[2] He claims to be returning to a rich philosophical tradition—that of Socrates, Plato, and Dewey—which has justifiably long been regarded as powerful and insightful. Moral education, in Kohlberg's account, does have an intellectual core: The exchange of ideas between teacher and student suggests a process that is an improvement over Simon's method. Kohlberg's belief that students can become more rational through education does indeed reaffirm, in principle, the faith of this tradition.

Kohlberg says his approach is designed to lead students through stages of moral development to greater and greater objectivity in their moral judgments. The ideal perspective, Stage Six, involves viewing the claims of others with "justice," that is, treating "every man's claim impartially regardless of the man." As the examples amply demonstrate, in Kohlberg's view, moral claims are to be decided by considering individual "rights." Presumably, the student progresses to an ever more impartial evaluation of respective claims to "rights." There is thus a distinct libertarian emphasis in Kohlberg, revealing his dislike of what he regards as the imposition of authority—by parents, rules, or traditional forms of indoctrination. Kohlberg's libertarianism is intended to remind the student that the rights of all must be respected equally: Moral judgment to a very large extent involves assessing competing claims of individuals about their rights.

The example of Judy and her mother, for example, is discussed in the language of the rights of each—Judy's right to go to the concert with "her" money (her contract and property rights) and her mother's alleged right to exercise authority. (The mother's "right" to have her daughter tell her the truth is never mentioned.) But in the progress up Kohlberg's scale, as the child supposedly gains in moral perspicuity, the mother's rights and her claims to rights get dimmer and dimmer, while Judy's rights seem to grow and to dominate the discussion. In the "enlightened" Stage Five, the mother has no right to forbid Judy to go to the concert, because Judy has "equal" rights. In fact, however, the mother's rights at this level have almost evaporated; Judy's "equal rights" appear to be more than equal to her mother's. The mother's rights are subordinated to her obligations, specifically the obligation to respect her daughter's rights. It is as if Judy is assumed to be disadvantaged; Kohlberg takes Judy, as a daughter, to be a victim of parental authority. In the progress upward through the stages, Judy increasingly gains support for her claims. The "optimal answers" stress that "a good mother should early respect her daughter as a person" and that "the mother had no right to forbid Judy." Reciprocity—real equality of claims to rights—seems to be absent.

According to Kohlberg's *theory*, students should impartially consider the rights of all the people involved in the example about the Johnson family. But in the narrative and the questions, the emphasis is entirely on Ms. Johnson's rights, desires, and rights to her desires. The student is invited to consider and focus on her choices, divorce or extramarital affairs, and whether she has the right to these things. Mr. Johnson's and the children's choices and rights are not discussed. With all the theoretical emphasis on the importance and value of impartiality, this example clearly seems sympathetic toward the "predicament" of Ms. Johnson and uncaring toward that of Mr. Johnson and the children. It is as if Mr. Johnson and the children lost their rights, including their right to consideration, when Mr. Johnson fell from the building. Again, paradoxically, only one person in a complex relationship seems to be entitled to "equal consideration in the matter": Ms. Johnson is taken to be *the* disadvantaged individual. The example ignores justice, reciprocity, and the equality and equal rights of all the persons involved.

The "Hidden Curriculum"

An additional and increasingly dominant thread in Kohlberg's thinking is that treating the child as a "moral philosopher" and stimulating moral development require a commitment by educators to create a "just community" in the school, because of what Kohlberg calls the "hidden curriculum" in most schools. This "hidden curriculum" embodies the values of the teachers and administrators, which are never made explicit to students but are ultimately used to evaluate them, and which express "the moral atmosphere of the school." The function of the "hidden curriculum," according to Kohlberg, is "moral education or perhaps miseducation." He gives an example of some of its dangers:

> To make the point I took a trivial episode. My son, then in the second grade, came home from school one day saying, "I don't want to be one of the bad boys at school." I asked, "Who are they," and he answered, "They are the boys who don't put their books away, and they get yelled at"...[The] guts of the hidden curriculum are the praise, the teacher's use of rewards or punishment; the crowd, or the life in a crowded group; and the teacher's power.

Kohlberg believes that his vision of moral education will do away with the "hidden curriculum." He concludes that the moral development of students depends upon a sense of working together for a just society in schools, "based on concepts of justice and participatory democracy."

Kohlberg offers an example of a real-life dilemma arising in an actual "just school": the experience of one of his disciples, Elsa Wasserman, at the Cluster School in Cambridge. There, according to Wasserman's description, "black and white students argue about a decision to correct racial injustice as they see it in their school community"; this suggests the benefits of a "just community" to Kohlberg—"that a school based on concepts of justice and participatory democracy can be a community which operates close to the level of its highest members and continues to progress upward." Wasserman offers the following example to show the "viable democracy," "moral growth," and "consideration for fairness" found at the school:

> This year a difficult issue of fairness focused on the admission of students for six remaining openings in the school. There were 47 white students in the school and 18 black students. The black students wanted more equal representation in the community. But there were already six students on the waiting list, only one of whom was black. The democracy class proposed that all six openings be filled by blacks.

Here is the student dialogue. A white student responded to the proposal:

> Does that mean that there's only one black on it now, but you want to get five more blacks to jump in front of the rest of the waiting line?

A black student replied:

> I'm one of the people that wants some black people to come in....From what I see I feel I would be more comfortable with them here. I want them here. . . .

Another white countered:

> If they were all black people [on the waiting list], it would be fair to let them in. I don't care if there were six black people on the waiting list, they could come in, but these five white people, they were first, right?

Still another white student asked:

But why can't everybody accept the fact that the blacks would feel more comfortable and get a better education with more blacks in school?

Another black student asked:

Can I ask all you white people something? I 'm not prejudiced, but is it going to make that much difference if there 's six more black people instead of white? Is it? There's 47 of you whites now. There 's 18 blacks. Six more blacks isn't going to make one difference.

Still another black student concluded:

Never in my life have I seen as many of you who have outnumbered me and mine, anyway. O.K., then I get to know them. I say, these whites are all right.…And then I came back here and I try to get some of my brothers and sisters at this school so they can be helped like I'm being helped. And what do I hear? No. Because they don't want to hear it. Why can't they just give us 18 blacks a little personal satisfaction with ourselves to have some more of us so we can be together? All right. (Applause.)

Following this the community voted. A majority was in favor of the proposal. One student in opposition asked:

The reason I voted against the proposal was that I wanted to hear more reasons from the black kids but I'm also feeling a little guilty because I want six black kids to come in, but I don 't know what to say about the five white kids on the waiting list. What are we going to tell them?

Wasserman writes that the following justification for the decision was offered:

All you have to do is explain to them that the community decided that it was the best idea to take all blacks this time for the community 's sake and from now on, every June we're going to admit more kids, we 'll admit half-black, half-white. By then eventually, it will be fairer and we can accept blacks and whites the same way.

The "viable democracy" then voted "almost unanimously" to adopt the proposal. The reasoning of the students and the outcome of their vote are celebrated as an example of a community moving upward through stages of moral development to respect for justice. Yet the facts suggest something else. The one student concerned to treat the whites on the waiting list impartially—in Kohlberg's words, "to treat every man's claim impartially regardless of the man"—is never answered. His request for reasons that would show that something is wrong with the colorblind admissions policy and the rules of the school, and his clear willingness to listen to the arguments of other students despite their indifference to his, are answered with *a priori* assertions clearly favoring the other point of view without offering reasons. In fact, the entire discussion is weighted against reasons. "I want them here," says one student; "Blacks would feel more comfortable and get a better education," says another; "Give us blacks a little personal satisfaction," says a third. These responses—fairly characterized in Kohlberg's own terms as primarily the kind of instrumental relativism found in lower Stage Two—are not arguments; they are not reasons; and they clearly treat color and personal desires as overriding other factors, ignoring justice and impartiality and the questions of troubled students.

Kohlberg treats the discourse and the solution as exemplary of moral progress and objectivity, even though the teachers and the majority of the students do not consider claims, questions, or rights objectively. If this "just community" is to be praised, it cannot be in terms of justice and impartiality. At the end, the result is a pronunciamento of a "general will" of the "democracy class" a tyranny of a particular majority over the students who ask questions (and over their rights), and over those on the waiting list who have a reasonable expectation to have themselves and their rights "treated equally." With chilling arrogance, the democracy class informs its opposition, "All you have to do is explain that the community decided that it was the best idea. . . ." This is very far from Kohlberg's libertarian celebration of Stage Six morality, and far from deciding questions on the basis of a "'universal, ethical principle orientation."

The Dismal Science of Pedagogy

As these and other examples suggest, practice does not square with theory in Kohlberg's universe. His theory appears to be transformed in practice into a particular ideology giving certain individuals and groups of individuals rights more than equal to those of others. The claims of those in authority and the claims of rules always yield to the claims of the "disadvantaged," or those whom Kohlberg takes to be disadvantaged. In this way, the examples belie the theory of impartial justice, suggesting *progress* less toward impartial justice—an appreciation of the power of the rational good—than toward sharing his sympathies and dispositions regarding the special claims of those victims of authority.

Whether or not this is a reasonable approach to moral education, it certainly conflicts with Kohlberg's theoretical edifice and its claims of impartiality. In this respect, Kohlberg himself conceals what can fairly be called a "hidden curriculum" of instruction in partial justice. This is not a program for justice as fairness to all parties regardless of the man, or for promoting principled, objective moral development.

In fact, it must be doubted whether what Kohlberg describes is really morality at all. Morality takes place among human beings and not among disembodied bearers of "rights," who are incessantly engaged in squabbling about them. Morality is concerned with doing good, with sacrifice, altruism, love, courage, honor, and compassion, and with fidelity and large-mindedness regarding one's station, commitments, family, friends, colleagues, and society in general. Morality among men is not merely legalistic and formalistic; it does not consist merely of so many non-negotiable demands.

Both Simon and Kohlberg also fail to avoid indoctrination. Both of their programs offer indoctrination in the "values" they take to be important—the celebration of wants and desires, the exhortation to self-gratification, and a particular ideology of rights and "special justice." Although they both claim to disavow traditional moral education because it indoctrinates, Simon and Kohlberg dearly do not oppose indoctrination per se, but the indoctrination of traditional values.

Yet Simon and Kohlberg's view of the world—the message they deliver, the values they recommend—is worth a good deal less than much of what they oppose. To them, goodness simply does not exist: People press for their wants or their rights and are continually at each other's throats. Although Simon and Kohlberg dislike authority, each offers a program that would impose on students an authority much more malevolent in its consequences than any traditional form of authority or "indoctrination." The tyranny of the passions and of minorities and majorities—the arbitrary exercise of power by special groups, be they advantaged or disadvantaged—offers not more freedom, but less, and a far less attractive world. Subjected only to one's wants or to the whims of special groups wielding arbitrary power, the individual and his life and moral relations are much bleaker than they actually are, or than they have traditionally been represented to be by the old to the young. In Simon and Kohlberg, responsibility and love are missing; life and man are oppressive; and the world is cold, ugly, brutish, and lonely. In this distorted view of life and morality, they fail to recognize the significance of what is possible among people across generations.

The barren world Simon and Kohlberg offer to students, teachers, and parents allows room for only an endless succession of conflicts and dilemmas. "Values clarification" and "cognitive moral development" neglect and deny precious and important features of morally mature life—friendship, love, fidelity, regard for work, care for home and family—which are, for the most part, not morally problematic. Finally, according to Simon and Kohlberg, there is no place for stories and lessons, no place for the passing on of knowledge and experience. Children are invited to a world where it is a travesty and an imposition for anyone to tell them the truth.

Notes

1. In defense of his methods against what he regards as powerful dogmatic and political traditions of indoctrination, Simon sometimes disparages his opponents in authoritarian terms, thus avoiding the need to consider the merits or shortcomings of their arguments. For example, when the school district in Great Neck, New York, cut from its budget funds for training teachers in values clarification, Simon was quoted as saying, "An orthodox Jewish, right-wing group got hold of it and just raised hell."
2. This difference of opinion should not be exaggerated, however. In the Great Neck controversy, Kohlberg testified on behalf of Simon. Kohlberg commented that the "protestors" insisted that values should not be dealt with in the school, but should be left for the church and home.

(This chapter originally appeared in *The Public Interest*, Vol. 50 (Winter, 1978): 81–98. Published with permission of National Affairs, Inc.)

CHAPTER TWO

The Great Tradition in Education

Transmitting Moral Values

EDWARD A. WYNNE

Within the recent past, American education substantially disassociated itself from what may be called the great tradition in education, the deliberate transmission of moral values to students. Despite this separation, many education reforms are being considered or are under way to increase the academic demands made on students. These reforms can be generally helpful, however, unless they are sensitive to the implications of our break with the great tradition, their effect on student conduct and morality may be transitory or even harmful. To understand the significance of the great tradition, we must engage in a form of consciousness-raising by enriching our understanding of the past and by understanding the misperceptions that pervade contemporary education.

The transmission of moral values has been the dominant educational concern of most cultures throughout history. Most educational systems have been simultaneously concerned with the transmission of cognitive knowledge—skills, information, and techniques of intellectual analysis—but these admittedly important educational aims, have rarely been given priority over moral education. The current policies in American education that give secondary priority to transmitting morality represent a sharp fracture with the great tradition.

Our break with the past is especially significant in view of the increase since the early 1950s of youth disorder, suicide, homicide, and out-of-wedlock births. Patterns revealed by statistics coincide with popular conceptions about these behaviors. For instance, in 16 of the past 17 Gallup Polls on education, pupil discipline has been the most frequent criticism leveled against public schools. One may wonder if better discipline codes and more homework are adequate remedies for our current school problems, or whether these dysfunctions are more profound and should be treated with more sensitive and complex remedies. Although literacy and student diligence are unquestionably worthy of pursuit, they are only a part of the process of communicating serious morality. If we want to improve the ways we are now transmitting morality, it makes sense to recall the way morality was transmitted before youth disorder became such a distressing issue.

Some Definitions

The term "moral values" is ambiguous and requires some definition. It signifies the specific values that particular cultures generally hold in regard. Such values vary among cultures; during World War II, a Japanese who loved his homeland was likely to be hostile to Americans, and vice versa. Value conflicts along national or ethnic lines are common, although most cultures treat the characteristic we call "patriotism" as a moral value and treat "treason" with opprobrium. Comparable patterns of value govern interpersonal relations in cultures beliefs about proper family conduct or the nature of reciprocal relationships. Such beliefs are laden with strong moral components.

In sum, common "moral values" are the vital common beliefs that shape human relations in each culture. Often these values—as in the Ten Commandments—have what is popularly called a religious base. Whether their base is religious, traditional, or secular, however, such values are expected to be widely affirmed under most circumstances.

The term "educational systems" also is somewhat obscure. Contemporary Americans naturally think in terms of formal public or private schools and colleges. But for most history, and all prehistory, formal agencies were a minute part of children's and adolescents' education. In traditional cultures, education was largely transmitted by various formal and informal nonschool agencies nuclear and extended families, religious institutions, "societies" for the young organized and monitored by adults. In addition, the complex incidental life of preindustrial rural and urban societies, and the demands of work in and out of the family socialized young persons into adult life. Many of these agencies still play important educational roles in contemporary America, nonetheless, in the modern period, the gradual replacement of such agencies by schools has been a strong trend.

Transmitting Moral Values

Whether the dominant educational system has been formal or informal, the transmission of moral values has persistently played a central role. This role has been necessary and universal for two reasons.

1. Human beings are uniquely adaptable animals and live in nearly all climates and in diverse cultural systems. But, as the anthropologist Yehudi Cohen (1964) put it, "No society allows for the random and promiscuous expression of emotions to just anyone. Rather, one may communicate those feelings, either verbally, physically, or materially, to certain people." Because our means of communicating emotions are socially specific, slow maturing young persons must be socialized gradually to the right—or moral—practices appropriate to their special environment.

2. Without effective moral formation, the human propensity for selfishness—or simply the advancement of self-interest—can destructively affect adult institutions. Thus, moral formation is necessary to cultivate our inherent, but moderate, propensity for disinterested sacrifice. The institutions of any persisting society must be organized to ensure that people's "unselfish genes" are adequately reinforced.

The general modes of moral formation have remained relatively stable throughout all cultures. To be sure, social class and sex-related differences have influenced the quantity and nature of moral formation delivered to the young, for instance, in many environments, limited resources have restricted the extent and intensity of the education provided to lower-class youths. Furthermore, the substance of the moral training transmitted to older youths has varied among cultures according to

Plato, Socrates was put to death because the Athenians disapproved of the moral training he was offering to Athenian young men. But such variations do not lessen the strength of the general model. . Despite his affection for Socrates, Plato, in *The Republic* (circa 390 B.C.) emphasized the importance of constraining the learning influences on children and youths, to ensure appropriate moral outcomes.

Although secular and church-related educators have disputed the *means* of moral formation since the nineteenth century both, until comparatively recently, have agreed on their programs' behavioral *ends*. Children should be moral: honest, diligent, obedient, and patriotic. Thus, after the American Revolution, deists and secularists such as Thomas Jefferson and John Adams felt democracy would fail unless citizens acquired an unusually high degree of self-discipline and public spiritedness. They termed this medley of values "republican virtue." After the Revolution many of the original 13 states framed constitutions with provisions such as "…no government can be preserved to any people, but by a firm adherence to justice, moderation, temperance, frugality, and virtue."[1]

The founders believed that popular education would be a means of developing such precious traits. As the social historians David J. and Sheila Rothman have written, "The business of schools [in our early history] was not reading and writing but citizenship, not education but social control." The term "social control" may have a pejorative sound to our modern ears, but it simply and correctly means that schools were concerned with affecting conduct, rather than transmitting information or affecting states of mind.

Characteristics of the Great Tradition

Although issues in moral formation posed some conflicts in traditional societies, there were great areas of congruence around the great tradition of transmitting moral values. Documents generated in historical societies as well as ethnographic studies of many ancient and primitive cultures reveal through anecdote and insight the principles that characterize the tradition. Since the principles are too often ignored in contemporary education, we should consider them in some detail.

- *The tradition was concerned with good habits of conduct as contrasted with moral concepts or moral rationales.* Thus, the tradition emphasized visible courtesy and deference. In the moral mandate, "Honor thy father and mother," the act of *honoring* can be seen. It is easier to observe people *honoring* their parents than *loving* them. Loving, a state of mind, usually must be inferred.
- *The tradition focused on day-to-day moral issues telling the truth in the face of evident temptation, being polite, or obeying legitimate authority.* It assumed that most moral challenges arose in mundane situations, and that people were often prone to act improperly.
- *The great tradition assumed that no single agency in society had the sole responsibility for moral education.* The varieties of moral problems confronting adults and youths were innumerable. Thus, youths had to be taught to practice morality in many environments. One agency, for example, the nuclear family or the neighborhood, might be deficient, so considerable redundancy was needed. In other words, there could be no neutrality about educating the young in morality; youth-serving agencies were either actively promoral or indifferent.
- *The tradition assumed that moral conduct, especially of the young, needed persistent and pervasive reinforcement.* To advance this end, literature, proverbs, legends, drama, ritual, and

folk tales were used for cautionary purposes. Systems of symbolic and real rewards were developed and sustained; schools used ribbons, awards, and other signs of moral merit; noneducational agencies used praise and criticism as well as many symbolic forms of recognition.

* *The tradition saw an important relationship between the advancement of moral learning and the suppression of wrong conduct.* Wrong acts, especially in the presence of the young, were to be aggressively punished, as punishment not only suppressed bad examples, but also corrected particular wrongdoers. The tradition also developed concepts such as "scandal," a public, immoral act that also lowered the prestige of a person or institution. Conversely, since secret immoral acts were less likely to confuse or misdirect innocent persons, they received less disapproval.

* *The tradition was not hostile to the intellectual analysis of moral problems.* Adults recognized that life occasionally generates moral dilemmas. In the Jewish religious tradition, learned men were expected to analyze and debate Talmudic moral issues. Other cultures have displayed similar patterns. But such analyses typically relied on a strong foundation of habit oriented, mundane moral instruction and practice. Instruction in exegetical analysis commenced only after the selected neophyte had undergone long periods of testing, memorized large portions of semididactic classics, and displayed appropriate deference to exegetical experts.

* *The great tradition assumed that the most important and complex moral values were transmitted through persistent and intimate person-to-person interaction.* In many cases, adult mentors were assigned to develop close and significant relationships with particular youths. The youths might serve as apprentices to such persons, or the mentors might accept significant responsibilities for a young relative. In either case, constructive moral shaping required a comparatively high level of engagement.

* *The tradition usually treated "learners," who were sometimes students, as members of vital groups, such as teams, classes, or clubs.* These groups were important reference points for communicating values, among them, group loyalty, and the diverse incidents of group life provided occasions for object lessons. The emphasis on collective life contrasts sharply with the individualism that pervades contemporary American education and which is often mistaken for "humanism."

* *The tradition had a pessimistic opinion about the perfectibility of human beings, and about the feasibility or value of breaking with previous socialization patterns.* The tradition did not contend that whatever "is" is necessarily right, but it did assume that the persistence of certain conduct over hundreds of years suggested that careful deliberation should precede any modification or rejection.

As schooling spread, the tendency was to present the formal curriculum in a manner consistent with the tradition, and thus to focus on the transmission of correct habits and values. We should not assume that the interjection of moral concern was necessarily cumbersome. The famous *McGuffey's Reader* series featured stories and essays by substantial writers, such as Walter Scott and Charles Dickens. The literary quality of such writings was appropriate to the age of the student. Significantly, both the materials and their authors supported the development of certain desired traits.

Character Education

The most recent efflorescence of the great tradition in America can be found in the "character education" movement in our public schools between 1880 and about 1930. That movement attempted to make public schools more efficient transmitters of appropriate moral values.

The efforts to foster character education assumed schools had to operate from a purely secular basis, which posed special challenges for moral formation. Whereas some earlier education reformers had semisecular sympathies, in previous eras their impact had been tempered by the proreligious forces concurrently affecting schools. Before 1900, for example, probably 15–25 percent of American elementary and secondary school pupils attended either private or public schools that were explicitly religious, another 25–50 percent attended public schools that were tacitly religious. For example, they used readings from the King James Bible.

The character education movement articulated numerous traditional moral aims promptness, truthfulness, courtesy, and obedience. The movement strove to develop elementary and secondary school programs to foster such conduct. It emphasized techniques such as appropriately structured materials in history and literature, school clubs and other extracurricular activities, rigorous pupil discipline codes, and daily flag salutes and frequent assemblies. Many relatively elaborate character education plans were designed and disseminated to schools and school districts. Often the plans were adopted through the mandate of state legislatures or state boards of education. Some modern authorities, such as James Q> Wilson (1973), have perceived a strong relationship between the character education movement and the relatively high levels of youth order in America during the nineteenth century.

An Unfavorable Evaluation

From the first, the supporters of character education emphasized rational organization and research. Despite such attempts, much of the research was superficial. Nonetheless, the research persisted because of the importance attributed to character, and gradually its quality improved. During the mid-1920s, researchers led by Hugh Hartschorne and Mark A. May concluded that the relationship between pupil good conduct and the application of formal character education approach was slight. Good conduct appeared to be relatively situation-specific a person might routinely act correctly in one situation and incorrectly in another. slightly different one. A person could cheat on exams, for example, but not steal money from the class fund. This situational specificity meant that good character was not a unified trait that could be cultivated by any single approach.

Despite this research, character education was never formally abandoned. Few educators or researchers have ever said publicly that schools should *not* be concerned with the morality or character of their pupils. Indeed, recent research and statistical reanalysis of earlier data has contended that Hartschorne and May's findings were excessively negative. Still, their research was a turning point in the relationship between American public education and the great tradition of moral values. Before the research many schools were fully concerned with carrying forward that tradition, and the intellectual forces affecting schools were in sympathy with such efforts. Even after the 1930s, many schools still reflexively maintained their former commitment to moral formation; the prevailing intellectual climate among researchers and academics, however, was indifferent or hostile to such efforts. Gradually, a disjunction arose between what some educators and many parents thought was appropriate (and what some of them applied), and what was favored by a smaller, more formally trained group of experts.

Ironically, the research findings of Hanschorne and May did not refute conflict with the major intellectual themes of the great tradition. The tradition emphasized that moral formation was complex. To be effective, it had to be incremental, diverse, pervasive, persistent, and rigorous. Essentially, it relied on probalistic principles: the more frequent and more diverse techniques applied, the more likely that more youths would be properly formed, but even if all techniques were applied, some youths would be "missed." Given such principles, it logically follows that the measured long-term effect of any limited program of "moral instruction" would be minute.

The Hartschorne and May findings demonstrated that American expectations for character education were unrealistic, a proposition not inconsistent with expectations we seem to have for *any* education technique. This does not mean that education's effects are inconsequential, but that Americans often approach education from a semi-utopian perspective. We have trouble realizing that many things happen slowly, and that not all problems are solvable.

New Approaches to Moral Instruction

During the 1930s, 1940s, and 1950s, there was little intellectual or research concern with moral formation in America. Schools continued to be engaged in moral instruction, both deliberately or incidentally, but the inschool process relied on momentum stimulated by earlier perspectives. In other words, moral instruction went on but without substantial intellectual underpinning.

Since the 1960s, a number of different—perhaps more scientific—approaches to moral instruction have evolved. Many of these approaches have been described by the term "moral education." Among these have been values clarification, identified with Louis L. Raths and Sidney B. Simon, and the moral development approach identified with Lawrence Kohlberg and his colleagues. Despite the variations among contemporary approaches, almost all the more recent techniques have had certain common elements. Their developers were not school teachers, ministers, or education administrators, but college professors who sought to emphasize the scientific base for their efforts. But, most important, the approaches disavowed the great tradition's persistent concern with affecting *conduct*. The moral dilemmas used in some exercises were highly abstract and probably would never arise in real life. Their aim was to cause students to feel or reason in particular ways rather than to practice right conduct immediately.

The developers of the new systems were conscious of Hartschorne and May's research. They recognized the difficulty of shaping conduct and presumably felt that shaping patterns of reasoning was more feasible. Furthermore, many of the moral education approaches were designed as curriculum materials that could be taught through lectures and class discussion. Such designs facilitated their adoption by teachers and schools. Had the approaches aimed to pervasively affect pupil day-to-day conduct, they would have been more difficult to disseminate. Finally, both the researchers and the proponents of the new approaches felt it was morally unjustifiable to apply the vital pressures needed to actually shape pupils' conduct, feeling such pressures would constitute "indoctrination." On the other hand, methods of moral reasoning apparently might be taught as routine school subjects with the tacit consent of the pupils involved.

The anti-indoctrination stance central to the new approaches invites amplification. Obviously, the great tradition regarded the issue of indoctrination as a specious question. Proponents of the great tradition say, "Of course indoctrination happens. It is ridiculous to believe children are capable of objectively assessing most of the beliefs and values they must absorb to be effective adults. They must learn a certain body of 'doctrine' to function on a day-to-day basis in society. There is good and bad doctrine, and thus things must be weighed and assessed. But such assessment is largely the responsibility of parents and other appropriate adults."

It is hard to articulate fairly the position of the anti-indoctrinators. Although they are against indoctrination, they provide no clear answer as to how children are given many real choices in a relatively immutable world necessarily maintained by adults. The anti-indoctrinators also do not say what adults are to do when children's value choices and resulting potential conduct are clearly harmful to them or others. After all, punishments for bad value choices are, in effect, forms of indoctrination. And the idea of presenting pupils with any particular approach to moral education in a school is inherently indoctrinative: the pupils are not allowed to refuse to come to school, or to hear seriously the pros and cons articulated by sympathetic spokespersons (or critics) for moral education or to freely choose among various approaches to them. Providing such choices is antithetical to the operation of any school.

To consider another perspective, the secular nature of the typical public school obviously indoctrinates pupils against practicing religion in that environment, although most religions contend that some religious practices of a public nature are inextricably related to day-to-day life. This "reality" of separating religion and public education is understandable. However, it is disingenuous to call this policy nonindoctrinative. Thus, it is specious to talk about student choices. The point is that, *on the whole, school is and should and must be inherently indoctrinative.* The only significant questions are will the indoctrination be overt or covert, and what will be indoctrinated?

The great tradition has never died. Many administrators and teachers in public and private schools have continued practices consistent with its principles.

1. The Virginia Constitution

References

Cohen, Y. *The Transition from Childhood to Adolescence.* Chicago: Aldine, 1964.

Hartschorne, H., and May, M. A. *Studies in Deceit, Studies in Service and Self-Control,* and *Studies in the Organization of Character.* New York: Macmillan, 1928, 1929, 1930.

Klapp, O. *The Collective Search for Identity.* New York: Holt, Rinehart, and Winston, 1969.

Meyers, E. *Education in the Perspective of History.* New York: Harper & Row, 1960.

Rothman, D. J., and Rothman, S. M. *Sources of American Social Tradition.* New York: Basic, 1975.

Wilkinson, R. *Governing Elites.* New York: Oxford University Press, 1969.

Wilson, J. Q. Crime and American Culture. *The Public Interest* 70 (Winter 1973) 22–48.

Wynne, E. A. *Looking at Schools.* Lexington, MA: Heath/Lexington, 1980.

Yulish, S. M. *The Search for a Civic Religion.* Lanham, MD: University Press of America, 1980.

Note: Partial support for the research underlying this article was received from NIE Grant No G-83–0012.

(This chapter originally appeared in *Educational Leadership*, Vol. 43, No. 4 [December-January, 1985–1986]: 4–9. Published with permission of the Association for Supervision and Curriculum Development [ASCD].)

CHAPTER THREE

Character Education

Seven Crucial Issues

THOMAS LICKONA

One of the most important ethical developments of recent times has been a renewed concern for character. This is nowhere more evident than in the national character education movement, arguably the most rapidly growing school reform initiative in the country today. To fulfill its potential, however, the character education movement must coherently address basic philosophical and pedagogical questions. I would like to address seven such issues.

1. What Is the Relationship Between Character and Virtue?

Good character consists of the virtues we possess. The more virtues we possess and the more fully we possess them, the stronger our character.

Virtues are objectively good human qualities such as wisdom, honesty, kindness, and self-discipline. Virtues are good for the individual in that they are needed to lead a fulfilling life, to be in harmony with ourselves. They are good for the whole human community in that they enable us to live together harmoniously and productively.

Virtues provide a standard for defining good character. Because they are intrinsically good, virtues don't change. Prudence, patience, perseverance, and courage always have been and always will be virtues. In this sense, virtues transcend time and culture, although their expression may vary culturally (with one culture giving more emphasis to respect for elders, for example, and another more emphasis to egalitarian relationships).

To speak of virtues and good character is to believe that there is objective moral truth. Objective truth—whether it is scientific truth, historical truth, or moral truth—is truth that is independent of the knower (Kreeft & Tacelli, 1994). Although objective truth must always be grasped by a subjective knower, and therefore is often imperfectly known (a fact that should keep us humble), there is an objective reality outside of, and independent of, the mind. That Lincoln was president during the Civil War is objectively true, whether I know it or not.

In the moral realm, this philosophy of objective truth asserts that some things are truly right and others truly wrong. Some ways of behaving are truly better than others: It's better to be generous than selfish, better to be faithful than unfaithful, better to be self-controlled than reckless. Thus our life task in developing our personal character (and for all of us, our character is a work in progress) is to learn what is true and right and good, and then conform our conscience and conduct to that high standard.

It is a cultural cliche that we should each "follow our conscience," but that is a dangerous half-truth. Charles Manson, Adolf Hitler, and American slaveholders may have all been following their consciences. A malformed conscience has historically been the source of much evil. If following our conscience is to have any moral worth, we must first form our conscience correctly, in accord with what is truly right.

2. What Is the Nature of Character Education?

Character education is the deliberate effort to cultivate virtue. The school stands for virtues such as respect and responsibility and promotes them explicitly at every turn. Thinking and discussing are important, but the bottom line is behavior, taken to be the ultimate measure of character.

A core theoretical principle is Aristotle's: Virtues are not mere thoughts but habits we develop by performing virtuous actions. Acting on that principle, character educators seek to help students to perform kind, courteous, and self-disciplined acts repeatedly—until it becomes relatively easy for them to do so and relatively unnatural for them to do the opposite.

3. What Are the Goals of Character Education?

Character education has three goals: good people, good schools, and a good society.

The first goal asserts that we need good character to be fully human. We need strengths of mind, heart, and will to be capable of love and work, two of the hallmarks of human maturity.

The second goal asserts that we need character education in order to have good schools. Schools are much more conducive to teaching and learning when they are civil, caring, and purposeful communities.

The third goal asserts that character education is essential to the task of building a moral society. Societal problems—such as violence, dishonesty, greed, family disintegration, growing numbers of children living in poverty, and disrespect for life born and preborn—have deep roots and require systemic solutions. But it is not possible to build a virtuous society if virtue does not exist in the minds, hearts, and souls of individual human beings.

4. What Are the Psychological Components of Character?

Character must be broadly conceived to encompass the cognitive, affective, and behavioral aspects of morality: moral knowing, moral feeling, and moral action. Good character consists of knowing the good, desiring the good, and doing the good—habits of the mind, habits of the heart, and habits of behavior. We want young people to be able to judge what is right, care deeply about what is right, and then do what is right—even in the face of pressure from without and temptation from within.

The cognitive side of character includes at least six components: moral alertness (does the situation at hand involve a moral issue requiring moral judgment?), understanding the virtues and what they require of us in specific situations, perspective-taking, moral reasoning, thoughtful decision-making, and moral self-knowledge—all the powers of rational moral thought required for moral maturity.

The emotional side of character serves as the bridge between moral judgment and moral action. It includes at least five components: conscience (the felt obligation to do what one judges to be right), self-respect, empathy, loving the good, and humility (a willingness to both recognize and correct our moral failings).

There are times when we know what we should do, feel strongly that we should do it, and yet still fail to translate moral judgment and feeling into effective moral behavior. Moral action, the third part of character, involves three additional components: moral competence (including skills such as communicating, cooperating, and solving conflicts); moral will (which mobilizes our judgment and energy and is at the core of self-control and courage); and moral habit (a reliable inner disposition to respond to situations in a morally good way).

5. What Is the Content of Character?

Which virtues should a school use to define "the good"—the content of character?

The ancient Greeks named four "cardinal virtues": prudence (which enables us to judge what we ought to do), justice (which enables us to give other persons their due), fortitude (which enables us to do what is right in the face of difficulties), and temperance (which enables us to control our desires and avoid abuse of even legitimate pleasures). In his book *Character Building: A Guide for Parents and Teacher*s, British psychologist David Isaacs (1976) offers a developmental scheme: 24 virtues, grouped according to developmental periods during which the different virtues should be given special emphasis: (1) Up to 7 years: obedience (respecting legitimate authority and rules), sincerity (truth-telling with charity and prudence), and orderliness (being organized and using time well); (2) From 8 to 12 years: fortitude, perseverance, industriousness, patience, responsibility, justice, and generosity; (3) From 13 to 15 years: modesty (respect for one's own privacy and dignity and that of others), moderation (self-control), simplicity (genuineness), sociability (ability to communicate with and get along with others), friendship, respect, patriotism (service to one's country and affirmation of what is noble in all countries); and (4) From 16 to 18 years: prudence, flexibility, understanding, loyalty, audacity (taking risks for good), humility (self-knowledge), and optimism (confidence). A recent book, *The Heart of Virtue* by Donald DeMarco (1996), recommends 28 virtues, from care and chastity through temperance and wisdom.

The choice of which virtues to teach is influenced by context. In democratic societies, for example, character education would logically include "democratic virtues" such as respect for individual rights, concern for the common good, reasoned dialogue, regard for due process, tolerance of dissent, and voluntary participation in public life—virtues that are important to the kind of character needed for democratic citizenship.

In a similar way, a religious context profoundly affects how the virtuous life is conceived. The proper aim of character education in a Catholic school, for example, is nothing less than to develop the character of Christ. That would include the natural moral virtues that can be taught in the public school, but it would also include spiritual virtues that public schools can't teach: faith in God, obedience to God's will, prayer, a sacrificial Christ-like love of others, sorrow for sin, and a humility that acknowledges our total dependence on God and is grateful for all our blessings. From this perspective, Jesus is both the example and the source of virtue; it is through our relationship with Him that we die to self and are transformed in Christ.

Public schools obviously can only study such worldviews, not teach them as truth. But even public schools do well to challenge students—drawing on their full intellectual and cultural resources, including their faith traditions if they have one—to develop a vision of the purpose of life that will guide them in the task of developing their personal character. Without this larger vision, the quest for character lacks a philosophical rudder.

6. What Is a Comprehensive Approach to Character Development?

In order to develop character in its cognitive, emotional, and behavior dimensions, schools need a comprehensive approach. At the State University of New York at Cortland, our Center for the 4th and 5th Rs (Respect and Responsibility) (www.cortland.edu/character) defines a comprehensive approach in terms of twelve mutually supportive strategies, nine that are classroom-based and three that are schoolwide.

These twelve strategies are both direct and explicit (e.g., explaining the virtues, studying them, and intentionally practicing them) and indirect and implicit (e.g., setting a good examples and providing a good moral environment that enables students to experience the virtues in their day-to-day relationships). A comprehensive approach regards adults' moral authority and leadership as an essential part of character education, but also values students' taking responsibility for constructing their own characters. There is an effort to transmit a moral heritage of tested virtues but also to equip students to think critically about how to apply the virtues to future moral challenges (e.g., combating the destruction of the environment and solving the problem of abortion in a way that both respects preborn life and supports women). Let me briefly explain and illustrate each of the twelve strategies in this comprehensive model. (See *Educating for Character*, Lickona, 1991, and *Character Matters*, Lickona, 2004, for a fuller discussion.)

Classroom Strategies

In classroom practice, a comprehensive approach to character-building calls upon *the individual teacher* to do nine things:

- *Act as caregiver, model, and mentor:* Treat students with love and respect, setting a good example, supporting prosocial behavior, and correcting hurtful actions through one-on-one guidance and whole-class discussion.
- *Create a moral community:* Help students know each other as persons, respect and care about each other, and feel valued membership in, and responsibility to, the group.
- *Practice moral discipline:* Use the creation and enforcement of rules as opportunities to foster moral reasoning, voluntary compliance with rules, and a generalized respect for others.
- *Create a democratic classroom environment:* Involve students in collaborative decision making and shared responsibility for making the classroom a good place to be and learn.
- *Teach character through the curriculum:* Use the ethically rich content of academic subjects (such as literature, history, and science) as a vehicle for studying the virtues; ensure that the sex, drugs, and

alcohol education programs promote self-control and other high character standards taught elsewhere in the curriculum (see, for example, Napier, 1996, and *National Guidelines for Sexuality and Character Education*, 1996).

- *Use cooperative learning:* Through collaborative work, develop students' appreciation of others, perspective-taking, and ability to work toward common goals.
- *Develop the "conscience of craft":* Foster students' valuing of learning, capacity for working hard, commitment to excellence, and public sense of work as affecting the lives of others.
- *Encourage moral reflection:* Foster moral thinking and thoughtful decision-making through reading, research, essay writing, journaling, discussion, and debate.
- *Teach conflict resolution:* Help students acquire the moral skills of solving conflicts fairly and without force.

Schoolwide Strategies

Besides making full use of the moral life of classrooms, a comprehensive approach calls upon *the school as a whole* to do three things:

- *Foster service learning beyond the classroom:* Use positive role models to inspire altruistic behavior and provide opportunities at every grade level for service learning.
- *Create a positive moral culture in the school:* Develop a total moral environment (through the leadership of the principal, schoolwide discipline, a schoolwide sense of community, meaningful student government, a moral community among adults, and making time for discussing moral concerns) that supports and amplifies the virtues taught in classrooms.
- *Recruit parents and the community as partners in character education*: Inform parents that the school considers them their child's first and most important moral teacher; give parents specific ways they can reinforce the character expectations the school is trying to promote; and seek the help of the community (including faith communities, businesses, local government, and the media) in promoting the core virtues.

7. How Can Schools of Education Prepare Effective Character Educators?

At the State University of New York at Cortland, we have about 1,000 undergraduates in our N-9 teacher certification programs and another 300-plus in our Master's programs in education. We integrate character education into teacher preparation in the following ways:

- *An annual 4-day K-12 Summer Institute in Character Education (K-12).* Initially supported by two small foundation grants but now self-supported (through registration fees of $300 per person), our Summer Institute features national experts on character education and local practitioners—principals and teachers who describe their schools' character education initiatives. Enrolling 200 to 400 persons a year, the Institute recruits school teams of 3–6 persons (e.g., a building administrator and several faculty) and teaches them our Center's comprehensive approach. During the week, these teams develop an action plan that they later propose to their home school.
- *One-Day Character Education Conference*. To stimulate and respond to broader interest in character education, we make Day 3 of our Summer Institute a one-day conference option. Each summer, more than 100 educators have taken advantage of that option; many have gone on to start character education efforts in their schools.
- *Two-Day High School Character Education Conference.* Besides including sessions relevant to high school educators in our 4-day Institute, we also offer a two-day conference just for high school peo-

ple. Seventy to 100 persons have attended that each year. The high school component focuses on the model emerging from *Smart & Good High Schools* (Lickona & Davidson, 2005), our two-year study of 24 award-winning high schools (available on our website).

- *Follow-up Seminars.* We invite all participants in our Summer Institutes and summer conferences to come back to campus for a day in the fall and a day in the spring to share what's working and to brainstorm solutions to problems in implementation.

- *Graduate course in character education.* Each semester, for the past 12 years, I have taught an elective, 3-credit, Master's-level course in character education. This course examines contemporary approaches to character education, with an emphasis on a comprehensive approach.

- *Newsletter.* With the help of a small grant, our Center publishes a newsletter (originally *The Fourth and Fifth Rs*, now *excellence & ethics*, that publishes practitioner-written articles recounting character education success stories. Many of these come from schools and teachers that have attended our summer programs. We post our newsletter on our website, distribute it to all Cortland College faculty, and mail it to more than 700 schools of education around the country.

- *The integration of character education into undergraduate courses.* Our undergraduate elementary education major includes a required course titled Classroom Discipline. Education faculty who teach that course typically include character education as an important classroom and schoolwide approach to preventing and dealing with discipline problems. Methods courses in reading and social studies are other ready-made opportunities for incorporating character-relevant materials such as value-rich children's literature and outstanding published curricula such as *Facing History and Ourselves* (Facing History and Ourselves National Foundation, 1994).

- *The informal dissemination of character education information to interested students and faculty.* On the wall outside our Center, we have a nine-compartment "take-one" rack with assorted articles on the theory and practice of character education. Both undergraduate and graduate students regularly help themselves to this literature; we have probably reached more students in this way than in any other way. We also have a small library of books and other resources that students can borrow for a paper or project on character education they are doing for a course. We make videotapes on character education available to faculty, some of whom have begun to show them in their courses.

- We have invited faculty teaching summer school to bring their classes to some of the keynote lectures in our Summer Institute. We have also asked faculty in our School of Professional Studies to offer workshops (e.g., "Fostering Virtue Through Children's Literature" and "Building Character Through Sports") for our Summer Institute—still another way to bring more people into the character education effort.

- *Collaboration with teacher inservice programs.* In New York State, most teacher professional development is carried out by Boards of Cooperative Educational Services. We have begun to work with two such groups in our region to co-sponsor breakfast meetings on character education for school administrators. We have also offered a free seat at our Summer Institute to several BOCES staff developers and have invited them to conduct Summer Institute workshops on aspects of character development such as cooperative learning and the Responsive Classroom. When people in schools of education notice that character education is beginning to appear on the menu of educational innovations offered by these leading-edge professional development agencies, character education will take on more importance in the minds of higher educators.

Not all of these approaches will work in all settings. But multiple approaches—combining undergraduate, graduate, and inservice education—are needed if the character education movement hopes to be a major influence in forming the next generation of teachers.

References

Isaacs, D. (1976). *Character-building: A guide for parents and teachers*. Dublin, Ireland: Four Courts Press.

DeMarco, D. (1996). *The heart of virtue*. San Francisco: Ignatius Press.

Facing History and Ourselves National Foundation. (1994). *Facing history and ourselves: The Holocaust and human behavior*. Brookline, MA: Author.

Kreeft, P., & Tacelli, R.K. (1994). *Handbook of Christian apologetics*. Downers Grove, IL: InterVarsity Press.

Lickona, T. (1991). *Educating for character*. New York: Bantam.

Lickona, T. (2004). *Character matters*. New York: Touchstone.

Lickona, T., & Davidson, M. *Smart & Good High Schools*. New York: Center for the 4th and 5th Rs/Washington, DC: Character Education Partnership.

Napier, K. (1996). *The power of abstinence*. New York: Avon Books.

National guidelines for sexuality and character education. (1996). Austin, TX: Medical Institute (800/892–9484).

(This chapter originally appeared in *Action in Teacher Education*, Vol. 20, No. 4 [Winter, 1998]: 77–84. Publlished with permission of The Association of Teacher Educators [ATE].)

CHAPTER FOUR

Eleven Principles of Effective Character Education

THOMAS LICKONA, ERIC SCHAPS, & CATHERINE LEWIS

What Is Character Education?

Character education is the intentional effort to develop in young people core ethical and performance values that are widely affirmed across all cultures. To be effective, character education must include all stakeholders in a school community and must permeate school climate and curriculum.

Character education includes a broad range of concepts such as positive school culture, moral education, just communities, caring school communities, social-emotional learning, positive youth development, civic education, and service learning. All of these approaches promote the intellectual, social, emotional, and ethical development of young people and share a commitment to help young people become responsible, caring, and contributing citizens.

Character education so conceived helps students to develop important human qualities such as justice, diligence, compassion, respect, and courage, and to understand why it is important to live by them. Quality character education creates an integrated culture of character that supports and challenges students and adults to strive for excellence.

No single script for effective character education exists, but there are some important guiding principles. Based on the practices of effective schools, the *Eleven Principles of Effective Character Education* form the cornerstone of Character Education Partnership's philosophy on how best to develop and implement high-quality character education initiatives. As broad principles that define excellence in character education, the eleven Principles serve as guideposts that schools and others responsible for youth character development can use to plan and evaluate their programs.

Principle 1: The school community promotes core ethical and performance values as the foundation of good character.

Schools that effectively promote good character come to agreement on the core ethical and performance values they most wish to instill in their students. Some schools use other terms such as virtues, traits, pillars, or expectations to refer to the desirable character qualities they wish to foster. Whatever the terminology, the core values promoted by quality character education are ones which affirm human dignity, promote the development and welfare of the individual, serve the common good, define our rights and responsibilities in a democratic society, and meet the classical tests of *universality* (i.e., Would you want all persons to act this way in a similar situation?) and *reversibility* (i.e., Would you want to be treated this way?).

The school makes clear that these basic human values transcend religious and cultural differences and express our common humanity. Examples of core ethical values are caring, honesty, fairness, responsibility, and respect for self and others. Examples of performance values include diligence, best effort, perseverance, critical thinking, and positive attitude. The school community selects and commits to its core values as the foundation for how people interact and do their best work in the school. A school committed to its students' character development treats its core values as essential to its mission and often refers to them in its code of conduct or "touchstone."

Principle 2: The school defines "character" comprehensively to include thinking, feeling, and doing.

Good character involves understanding, caring about, and acting upon core ethical and performance values. A holistic approach to character development therefore seeks to develop the cognitive, emotional, and behavioral dispositions required to do the right thing and do one's best work. Students grow to understand core values by studying and discussing them, observing behavioral models, and resolving problems involving the values. Students learn to care about core values by developing empathy skills, forming caring relationships, developing good work habits, taking on meaningful responsibilities, helping to create community, hearing inspirational stories, and reflecting on life experiences. And they learn to act upon core values by striving to do their best and be their best in all areas of school life. As children grow in character, they develop an increasingly refined understanding of the core ethical and performance values, a deeper commitment to living according to those values, and a stronger capacity and tendency to behave in accordance with them.

Principle 3: The school uses a comprehensive, intentional, and proactive approach to character development.

Schools committed to character development look at themselves through a character lens to assess how virtually everything that goes on in school affects the character of students. A comprehensive approach uses all aspects of schooling as opportunities for character development. This includes the formal academic curriculum and extracurricular activities, as well as what is sometimes called the hidden or informal curriculum (e.g., how school procedures reflect core values, how adults model good character, how the instructional process respects students, how student diversity is addressed, and how the discipline policy encourages student reflection and growth).

"Stand-alone" character education programs can be useful first steps or helpful elements of a comprehensive effort but are not an adequate substitute for a holistic approach that integrates character development into every aspect of school life. With an intentional and proactive approach, school staff do more than react to "teachable moments" to integrate character lessons. They take deliberate steps to create opportunities for character development.

Principle 4: The school creates a caring community.

A school committed to character strives to become a microcosm of a civil, caring, and just society. It does this by creating a community that helps all its members form respectful relationships that lead to caring attachments to and responsibility for one another. This involves developing caring relationships between students and staff, among students (within and across grade levels), among staff, and between staff and families. These caring relationships foster both the desire to learn and the desire to be a good person. All children and adolescents have needs for safety, belonging, and the experience of contributing, and they are more likely to internalize the values and expectations of groups that meet these needs. Likewise, if staff members and parents experience mutual respect, fairness, and cooperation in their relationships with each other, they are more likely to develop the capacity to promote those values in students. In a caring school community, the daily life of classrooms and all other parts of the school environment (e.g., hallways, cafeteria, playground, sports fields, buses, front office, and teachers' lounge) are imbued with a climate of concern and respect for others.

Principle 5: The school provides students with opportunities for moral action.

In the ethical as in the intellectual domain, students are constructive learners—they learn best by doing. To develop the cognitive, emotional, and behavioral aspects of their character, students need many and varied opportunities to grapple with real-life challenges (e.g., how to plan and carry out an important responsibility, work as part of a team, negotiate for peaceable solutions, recognize and resolve ethical dilemmas, and identify and meet school and community needs). Through repeated experiences and reflection, students develop appreciation for and commitment to acting on their ethical and performance values. When providing service to others, the school follows guidelines for effective service learning to include student voice and choice, integration of service into the curriculum, and reflection.

In addition to service learning, moral action can include conflict resolution, bully resistance, academic integrity, and sportsmanship.

Principle 6: The school offers a meaningful and challenging academic curriculum that respects all learners, develops their character, and helps them to succeed.

Because students come to school with diverse skills, interests, backgrounds, and learning needs, an academic program that helps all students succeed will be one in which the content and pedagogy engage all learners and meet their individual needs. This means providing a curriculum that is inherently interesting and meaningful to students and teaching in a manner that respects and cares for students as individuals. Effective character educators model persistence, responsibility, and caring as they differentiate instruction, employ a variety of active teaching and learning strategies, and look for ways that character is potentially developed *in and through* everyday teaching and learning. When teachers bring to the fore the character dimension of their classes, they enhance the relevance of subject matter and content area skills to students' natural interests and questions, and in the process, increase student engagement and achievement. When teachers highlight models of excellence and ethics and promote social-emotional skills, such as self-awareness and self-management, and ethical decision-making, students are able to access the curriculum with greater focus. When teachers promote moral and performance values such as academic integrity, intellectual curiosity, critical thinking, and diligence, students are better able to do their best work and gain greater autonomy, competence, and self-confidence.

Principle 7: The school fosters students' self-motivation.

Character means doing the right thing and doing our best work "even when no one is looking." The best underlying ethical reason for following rules, for example, is respect for the rights and needs of others—not fear of punishment nor desire for reward. We want students to be kind to others because of an inner belief that kindness is good and an inner desire to be a kind person. We want them to do a good job—work that applies and further develops their best abilities—because they take pride in quality work, not just because they want a good grade. Becoming more self-motivated is a developmental process that schools of character are careful not to undermine by an emphasis on extrinsic incentives. Intensive focus on rewards and behavior modification is consciously limited.

Schools of character work with students to develop their understanding of rules, their awareness of how their behavior affects others, and the character strengths—such as self-control, perspective taking, and conflict resolution skills—needed to act responsibly in the future. Rather than settle for mere compliance, these schools seek to help students benefit from their mistakes by providing meaningful opportunities for reflection, problem solving, and restitution.

Principle 8: The school staff is an ethical learning community that shares responsibility for character education and adheres to the same core values that guide the students.

All school staff—teachers, administrators, counselors, paraprofessionals, resource teachers, school psychologists and social workers, nurses, coaches, secretaries, cafeteria workers, playground and classroom aides, bus drivers—need to be involved in learning about, discussing, and taking owner-ship of the school's character education effort. First and foremost, staff members assume this respon-sibility by modeling the core values in their own behavior and taking advantage of opportunities to positively influence the students with whom they interact. Second, the same values and norms that govern the life of students serve to govern the collective life of adult members in the school com-munity. Third, a school devotes time to staff reflection on issues that affect their collective pursuit of excellence and ethics. Through faculty meetings and smaller support groups, a reflective staff reg-ularly asks questions such as: What character building experiences is the school already providing for its students? How effective and comprehensive are these? What negative moral behaviors is the school currently failing to address? What school practices are at odds with its professed core values and desire to develop a school of character? Reflection of this nature is an indispensable condition for developing an all-encompassing culture of character.

Principle 9: The school fosters shared leadership and long-range support of the character education initiative.

Schools that are engaged in effective character education have leaders who visibly champion the effort and share leadership with all stakeholders. Many schools and districts establish a character educa-tion committee—often composed of staff, students, parents, and community members—that takes responsibility for planning, implementation, and support. Over time, the regular governing bodies of the school or district may take on the functions of this committee—or, as character education goals become well-known and fully shared, formal organizational structures may no longer be necessary. The leadership also takes steps to provide for the long-range support (e.g., adequate staff develop-ment, time to plan) of the character education initiative, including, ideally, support at the district and state levels. In addition, within the school, students assume developmentally appropriate roles in lead-ing the character education effort through, for example, class meetings, student government, peer mediation, cross-age tutoring, service clubs, task forces, and student-led initiatives.

Principle 10: The school engages families and community members as partners in the character-building effort.

Schools that reach out to families and include them in character-building efforts greatly enhance their chances for success with students. They communicate with families—via newsletters, e-mails, fam-ily nights, the school website, and parent conferences—about goals and activities regarding charac-ter education. To build greater trust between home and school, parents are represented on the character education committee or through whatever decision-making structures exist. These schools also make a special effort to reach out to subgroups of parents who may not feel part of the school community. Finally, schools and families enhance the effectiveness of their partnership by recruit-ing the help of the wider community (i.e., businesses, youth organizations, religious institutions, the government, and the media) in promoting character development.

Principle 11: The school regularly assesses its culture and climate, the functioning of its staff as character educators, and the extent to which its students manifest good character.

Effective character education includes ongoing assessment of progress and outcomes using both qualitative and quantitative measures. The school uses a variety of assessment data (e.g., academic test scores, focus groups, survey results) that include the perceptions of students, teachers, and parents. Schools report on this data and use it to determine next steps. Schools administer questionnaires to stakeholders early in their character education initiative and again later to assess progress.

Three outcomes merit attention. First, schools assess the culture and climate of the school in light of the core values by asking stakeholders questions about the extent to which members of the school community demonstrate the core values and thereby function as an ethical learning community. For example, schools might administer climate surveys in which they ask students whether they agree with statements such as, "Students in this school (classroom) respect and care about each other." Second, the school assesses the staff's growth as character educators by examining the extent to which they model the core values and integrate these values into their teaching and other interactions with students. Schools ask teachers to reflect upon their character education practices, survey students about their perceptions of their teachers as role models, and have administrative procedures in place to monitor desired teacher behaviors. Third, the school assesses student character by examining the degree to which students manifest understanding of, commitment to, and action upon the core ethical values. Schools can, for example, gather data on various character-related behaviors (e.g., attendance, suspensions, vandalism, service hours, drug incidents, and cheating). Effective schools collect data on desired outcomes in student attitudes and behaviors and report to parents on students' growth in character just as they report academic progress (e.g., on report cards, during parent/teacher conferences).

(Excerpts from *The Eleven Principles of Effective Character Education*, revised ed.[2010]. Published with permission of the Character Education Partnership.)

CHAPTER FIVE

Character and Acdemics

What Good Schools Do

JACQUES S. BENNINGA, MARVIN W. BERKOWITZ,
PHYLLIS KUEHN, & KAREN SMITH

The growth of character education programs in the United States has coincided with the rise in high-stakes testing of student achievement. The No Child Left Behind Act asks schools to contribute not only to students' academic performance but also to their character. Both the federal government and the National Education Association (NEA) agree that schools have this dual responsibility. In a statement introducing a new U.S. Department of Education character education website, then Secretary of Education Rod Paige outlined the need for such programs:

> Sadly, we live in a culture without role models, where millions of students are taught the wrong values—or no values at all. This culture of callousness has led to a staggering achievement gap, poor health status, overweight students, crime, violence, teenage pregnancy, and tobacco and alcohol abuse.…Good character is the product of good judgments made every day.[1]

And Bob Chase, the former president of the NEA, issued his own forceful call to action:

> We must make an explicit commitment to formal character education. We must integrate character education into the fabric of the curriculum and into extracurricular activities. We must train teachers in character education—both preservice and inservice. And we must consciously set about creating a moral climate within our schools.[2]

Despite the clear national interest in character education, many schools are leery of engaging in supplementary initiatives that, although worthy, might detract from what they see as their primary focus: increasing academic achievement. Moreover, many schools lack the resources to create new curricular initiatives. Yet the enhancement of student character is a bipartisan mandate that derives from the very core of public education. The purpose of public schooling requires that schools seek to improve both academic and character education.

If it could be demonstrated that implementing character education programs is compatible with efforts to improve school achievement, then perhaps more schools would accept the challenge of doing both. But until now there has been little solid evidence of such successful coexistence.

Definitions and Research

Character education is the responsibility of adults. While the term *character education* has historically referred to the duty of the older generation to form the character of the young through experiences affecting their attitudes, knowledge, and behaviors, more recent definitions include such developmental outcomes as a positive perception of school, emotional literacy, and social justice activism.[3]

There are sweeping definitions of character education (e.g., Character Counts' six pillars, Community of Caring's five values, or the Character Education Partnership's eleven principles) and more narrow ones. Character education can be defined in terms of relationship virtues (e.g., respect, fairness, civility, tolerance), self-oriented virtues (e.g., fortitude, self-discipline, effort, perseverance) or a combination of the two. The state of California has incorporated character education criteria into the application process for its statewide distinguished school recognition program and, in the process, has created its own definition of character education. Each definition directs the practice of character education somewhat differently, so that programs calling themselves "character education" vary in purpose and scope.

There is some research evidence that character education programs enhance academic achievement. For example, an evaluation of the Peaceful Schools Project and research on the Responsive Classroom found that students in schools that implemented these programs had greater gains on standardized test scores than did students in comparison schools.[4] The Child Development Project (CDP) conducted follow-up studies of middle school students (through eighth grade) who had attended CDP elementary schools and found that they had higher course grades and higher achievement test scores than comparison middle school students.[5] Longitudinal studies have reported similar effects for middle school and high school students who had participated as elementary school students in the Seattle Social Development Project.[6]

A growing body of research supports the notion that high-quality character education can promote academic achievement. For example, Marvin Berkowitz and Melinda Bier have identified character education programs for elementary, middle, and high school students that enhance academic achievement.[7] These findings, however, are based on prepackaged curricular programs, and most schools do not rely on such programs. Instead, they create their own customized character education initiatives. It remains to be seen whether such initiatives also lead to academic gains.

Toward an Operational Definition of Character Education

We decided to see if we could determine a relationship between character education and academic achievement across a range of elementary schools. For our sample we used the elementary schools that applied in 2000 to the California Department of Education for recognition as distinguished elementary schools, California's highest level of school attainment. Eligibility to submit an application for the California School Recognition Program (CSRP) in 2000 was based on the previous year's academic performance index (API) results.

However, 1999 was the first year for California's Public School Accountability Act (PSAA), which created the API. Thus, while the state department stated that growth on the API was the central focus of the PSAA, schools applying for the CSRP in 1999–2000 did not receive their 1999 API scores until January 2000, after they had already written and submitted their award applications.

Approximately 12.7% of California elementary schools (681 of 5,368 schools) submitted a full application for the award in 2000. The average API of these schools was higher than the average for the schools that did not apply, but both were below the state expectancy score of 800. The mean API for applicant schools was 751; for non-applicant schools, 612. The API range for applicant schools was 365–957; for non-applicant schools, 302–958. Hence the sample for this study is not representative of all California elementary schools. It is a sample of more academically successful schools, but it does represent a broad range of achievement from quite low to very high.

Specific wording related to character education was included for the first time in the CSRP application in 2000. Schools were asked to describe what they were doing to meet a set of nine standards. Of these, the one that most clearly pertained to character education was Standard 1 (Vision and Standards). For this standard, schools were required to include "specific examples and other evidence" of "expectations that promote positive character traits in students."[8] Other standards could also be seen as related to character education. For these, schools were asked to document activities and programs that ensured opportunities for students to contribute to the school, to others, and to the community.

We chose for our study a stratified random sample of 120 elementary schools that submitted applications. These 120 schools were not significantly different from the other 561 applicant schools on a variety of academic and demographic indicators. For the schools in our sample, we correlated the extent of their character education implementation with their API and SAT-9 scores—the academic scale and test used by California at that time.[9]

The first problem we needed to grapple with was how to define a character education program. We spent considerable time discussing an operational definition to use for this project. After conferring with experts, we chose our final set of character education criteria, drawn from both the standards used by the California Department of Education and the *Character Education Quality Standards* developed by the Character Education Partnership.[10] Six criteria emerged from this process:

- This school promotes core ethical values as the basis of good character.
- In this school, parents and other community members are active participants in the character education initiative.
- In this school, character education entails intentional promotion of core values in all phases of school life.
- Staff members share responsibility for and attempt to model character education.
- This school fosters an overall caring community.
- This school provides opportunities for most students to practice moral action.

Each of the six criteria addresses one important component of character education. We created a rubric encompassing these six criteria and listing indicators for each, along with a scoring scale.

Character Education and Academic Achievement

Our study of these high-performing California schools added further evidence of a relationship between academic achievement and the implementation of specific character education programs. In our sample, elementary schools with solid character education programs showed positive relationships between the extent of character education implementation and academic achievement not only in a single year but also across the next two academic years. Over a multi-year period from 1999 to 2002, higher rankings on the API and higher scores on the SAT-9 were significantly and positively correlated with four of our character education indicators: a school's ability to ensure a clean and safe physical environment; evidence that a school's parents and teachers modeled and promoted good character; high-quality opportunities at the school for students to contribute in meaningful ways to the school and its community; and promoting a caring community and positive social relationships.

These are promising results, particularly because the *total character education score* for the year of the school's application was significantly correlated with every language and mathematics achievement score on the SAT-9 for a period of three years. In two of those years, the same was true for reading achievement scores. In other words, good-quality character education was positively associated with academic achievement, both across academic domains and over time.

What Good Schools Do

From our research we derived principles—the four indicators mentioned above—that are common across schools with both thoughtful character education programs and high levels of academic achievement.

• *Good schools ensure a clean and secure physical environment.* Although all schools in our sample fit this description, the higher-scoring character education schools expressed great pride in keeping their buildings and grounds in good shape. This is consistent with what is reported about the virtues of clean and safe learning environments. For example, the Center for Prevention of School Violence notes that "the physical appearance of a school and its campus communicates a lot about the school and its people. Paying attention to appearance so that the facilities are inviting can create a sense of security."[11]

One school in our sample reported that its buildings "are maintained well above district standards.…The custodial crew prides themselves in achieving a monthly cleaning score that has exceeded standards in 9 out of 12 months." And another noted, "A daily grounds check is performed to ensure continual safety and cleanliness." Each of the higher-scoring schools in our sample explicitly noted its success in keeping its campus in top shape and mentioned that parents were satisfied that their children were attending school in a physically and psychologically safe environment.

All schools in California are required to have on file a written Safe School Plan, but the emphases in these plans vary. While some schools limited their safety plans to regulations controlling access to the building and defined procedures for violations and intrusions, the schools with better character education programs defined "safety" more broadly and deeply. For example, one school scoring high on our character education rubric explained that the mission of its Safe School Plan was "to provide all students with educational and personal opportunities in a positive and nurturing environment which will enable them to achieve current and future goals, and for all students to be accepted at their own social, emotional, and academic level of development." Another high-scoring school addressed three concerns in its Safe School Plan: identification of visitors on campus, cultural/ethnic harmony, and safe ingress and egress from school. To support these areas of focus, this school's teachers were all trained to conduct classroom meetings, to implement the Community of Caring core values, and to handle issues related to cultural diversity and communication.

• *Good schools promote and model fairness, equity, caring, and respect.* In schools with good character education programs and high academic achievement, adults model and promote the values and attitudes they wish the students to embrace, and they infuse character education throughout the school and across the curriculum. Rick Weissbourd drove home this point in a recent essay: "The moral development of students does not depend primarily on explicit character education efforts but on the maturity and ethical capacities of the adults with whom they interact....Educators influence students' moral development not simply by being good role models—important as that is—but also by what they bring to their relationships with students day to day."[12] The staff of excellent character education schools in our sample tended to see themselves as involved, concerned professional educators, and others see them that way as well.

Thus one school described its teachers as "pivotal in the [curriculum] development process; there is a high level of [teacher] ownership in the curriculum....Fifty percent of our staff currently serves on district curriculum committees." Another school stated that it "fosters the belief that it takes an entire community pulling together to provide the best education for every child; that is best accomplished through communication, trust, and collaboration on ideas that reflect the needs of our school and the community....Teachers are continually empowered and given opportunities to voice their convictions and shape the outcome of what the school represents." A third school described its teachers as "continually encouraged" to grow professionally and to use best practices based on research. In the best character education schools, teachers are recognized by their peers, by district personnel, and by professional organizations for their instructional prowess and their professionalism. They model the academic and prosocial characteristics that show their deep concern for the well-being of children.

• ***In good schools students contribute in meaningful ways.*** We found that academically excellent character education schools provided opportunities for students to contribute to their school and their community. These schools encouraged students to participate in volunteer activities, such as cross-age tutoring, recycling, fund-raising for charities, community cleanup programs, food drives, visitations to local senior centers, and so on.

One elementary school required 20 hours of community service, a program coordinated entirely by parent volunteers. Students in that school volunteered in community gardens and at convalescent hospitals, and they took part in community cleanup days. Such activities, while not directly connected to students' academic programs, were viewed as mechanisms to promote the development of healthy moral character. According to William Damon, a crucial component of moral education is engaging children in positive activities—community service, sports, music, theater, or anything else that inspires them and gives them a sense of purpose.[13]

• ***Good schools promote a caring community and positive social relationships.*** One school in our sample that exemplified this principle was a school of choice in its community. The district had opened enrollment to students outside district boundaries, and this school not only provided an excellent academic program for its multilingual student population but also worked hard to include parents and community members in significant ways. Its Family Math Night attracted 250 family members, and its Family Literacy Night educated parents about read-aloud methods. Parents, grandparents, and friends were recruited to become classroom volunteers and donated thousands of hours.

This particular school also rented its classrooms to an after-school Chinese educational program. The two sets of teachers have become professional colleagues, and insights from such cultural interaction have led both groups to a better understanding of the Chinese and American systems of education. One result has been that more English-speaking students are enrolling in the Chinese after-school program. And teachers in both programs now engage in dialogue about the specific needs of children. One parent wrote a letter to the principal that said in part, "It seems you are anxious to build up our young generation more healthy and successful....I am so proud you are not only our children's principal, but also parents' principal."

Other schools with strong social relationship programs provide meaningful opportunities for parent involvement and establish significant partnerships with local businesses. They encourage parents and teachers to work alongside students in service projects, to incorporate diverse communities into the school curriculum, and to partner with high school students who serve as physical education and academic mentors. As one such school put it, all stakeholders "must play an important and active role in the education of the child to ensure the future success of that child."

Conclusion

It is clear that well-conceived programs of character education can and should exist side by side with strong academic programs. It is no surprise that students need physically secure and psychologically safe schools, staffed by teachers who model professionalism and caring behaviors and who ask students to demonstrate caring for others. That students who attend such schools achieve academically makes intuitive sense as well. It is in schools with this dual emphasis that adults understand their role in preparing students for future citizenship in a democratic and diverse society. The behaviors and attitudes they model communicate important messages to the young people in their charge.

Future research on the relationship between character education and academic achievement should include a greater representation of schools in the average and below-average achievement categories. In particular, a study of the extent of the implementation of character education in schools that may have test scores at the low end of the spectrum—but are nevertheless performing higher than their socioeconomic characteristics would predict—would be an important contribution to our understanding of the relationship between character education and academic achievement.

While this was our initial attempt to explore the relationship between these two important school purposes, we learned a good deal about what makes up a good character education curriculum in academically strong schools. We know that such a curriculum in such schools is positively related to academic outcomes over time and across content areas. We also know that, to be effective, character education requires adults to act like adults in an environment where children are respected and feel physically and psychologically safe to engage in the academic and social activities that prepare them best for later adult decision making.

At a time when resources are scarce, we see schools cutting programs and narrowing curricula to concentrate on skills measured by standardized tests. Our research suggests that school goals and activities that are associated with good character education programs are also associated with academic achievement. Thus our results argue for maintaining a rich curriculum with support for all aspects of student development and growth.

Notes

1. U.S. Department of Education, "ED Launches Character Education Web Site," www.thechallenge. org/15-v12n04/v12n4-communitiesandschools. htm.
2. Bob Chase, quoted in "Is Character Education the Answer?" *Education World*, 1999, www. education-world.com/a_admin/admin097. shtml.
3. Marvin W. Berkowitz, "The Science of Character Education," in William Damon, ed., *Bringing in a New Era in Character Education* (Stanford, Calif.: Hoover Institution Press, 2002), pp. 43–63.
4. Stuart W. Twemlow et al., "Creating a Peaceful School Learning Environment: A Controlled Study of an Elementary School Intervention to Reduce Violence," *American Journal of Psychiatry*, vol. 158, 2001, pp.

808–10; and Stephen N. Elliott, "Does a Classroom Promoting Social Skills Development Enable Higher Academic Functioning Among Its Students over Time?," Northeast Foundation for Children, Greenfield, Mass., 1998.

5. Victor Battistich and Sehee Hong, "Enduring Effects of the Child Development Project: Second-Order Latent Linear Growth Modeling of Students' 'Connectedness' to School, Academic Performance, and Social Adjustment During Middle School," unpublished manuscript, Developmental Studies Center, Oakland, Calif., 2003.

6. J. David Hawkins et al., "Long-Term Effects of the Seattle Social Development Intervention on School Bonding Trajectories," *Applied Developmental Science*, vol. 5, 2001, pp. 225–36.

7. Marvin W. Berkowitz and Melinda C. Bier, *What Works in Character Education?* (Washington, D.C.: Character Education Partnership, 2005).

8. "California School Recognition Program, 2000 Elementary Schools Program, Elementary School Rubric," California Department of Education, 2001. (Data are available from Jacques Benninga.)

9. For more detail on the design of the study, see Jacques S. Benninga, Marvin W. Berkowitz, Phyllis Kuehn, and Karen Smith, "The Relationship of Character Education Implementation and Academic Achievement in Elementary Schools," *Journal of Research in Character Education*, vol. 1, 2003, pp. 17–30.

10. *Character Education Quality Standards: A Self-Assessment Tool for Schools and Districts* (Washington, D.C.: Character Education Partnership, 2001).

11. "What Is Character Education?," Center for the Fourth and Fifth Rs, 2003, www.cortland. edu/c4n5rs/ce_iv.asp.

12. Rick Weissbourd, "Moral Teachers, Moral Students," *Educational Leadership*, March 2003, pp. 6–7.

13. Damon is quoted in Susan Gilbert, "Scientists Explore the Molding of Children's Morals," *New York Times*, 18 March 2003.

(This chapter originally appeared in *Phi Delta Kappan*, Vol. 87, No. 6 (February, 2006): 448–452. Published with permission of Phi Delta Kappa International.)

CHAPTER SIX

The Politics of
Character Education

DAVID E. PURPEL

Background

The current debate on moral and character education is one of the few instances where there is as much, if not more, public as professional debate and discussion. Indeed, the public discussion of character education has come to the point where it has become an overtly partisan political issue, serving as metaphor and code for those interested in pursuing the neoconservative social and cultural agenda. Part of the strategy of neoconservatives is to create a discourse in which the schools are blamed for not "teaching values" and families are blamed for teaching the wrong ones. Implicit in such a discourse is the assumption that our social problems are *not* so much rooted in the failures of our social, economic, and political structures as they are in the personal attitudes and behaviors of individuals. The thrust of this approach is to move the discussion away from the extremely controversial realm of ideological dispute toward the safer and presumably more consensual realm of desirable personal traits, to convert social and political issues into educational and pedagogical ones, and to focus on stability rather than transformation.

We would all be better served by recognizing that the current so-called Character Education Movement essentially represents an *ideological and political* movement rather than a debate about curricular and instructional matters. My basic criticisms of this approach are elaborated in this chapter and briefly, have to do with the naivete and/ or disingenousness of the discourse and of the inadequacies of its political and social assumptions. I will also try to show how this movement, far from being innovative and reforming, represents instead a long-standing tradition of using schools as agents of social stability, political stasis, and cultural preservation. It is also my hope that this analysis will shed light on the more general issues of moral education and the moral nature of education.

The Politics of the Discourse: An Historical Perspective

The matter of deliberately intervening into the behavior and character of students is a central if not dominating theme in the history of public schooling in the United States. Indeed, our early colonial experience with formal education not only foreshadows this emphasis, but much of its agenda and orientation continues to have an important influence on current views, policies, and practices. We can speculate further and posit the claim that basic to the entire colonization project were two obsessions that are fundamental to the subsequent and continuing development of American culture (and hence a critical dimension of public education)—the drive to make the community morally good and the individual materially rich. The attempts to reconcile these two projects with Christianity and, later, with democracy has led to a highly complex, ingenious, and compelling, if not contradictory, ambiguous, and controversial social and cultural system, or, if you will, mythos. This mythos represents an attempt to create a vision of America which seemingly integrates moral, religious, political, economic, social, and cultural perspectives seamlessly. The broad effort involved in creating, promoting, enforcing, and sustaining this vision has, of course, a very important *political* dimension, i.e., issues regarding who is to be involved in this process, who is privileged by this process, and who benefits from the substance of the vision.

It is clear that public schooling has always been considered an important resource in this political task from colonial times (Bailyn 1962) to the Common School movement (Kaestle 1983) to the present (Purpel 1995). The establishment of the early Puritan schools was in response to fears that families were increasingly unable or unwilling to adequately inculcate their children with the spiritual beliefs and moral virtues of the Puritan Commonwealth. The battle for compulsory education in the nineteenth century was led by members of the establishment who strongly believed that a system of schools with a common curriculum was the answer to the worries over national solidarity, social stability, and cultural purity. The current revival of interest in character education represents merely a revival of awareness of issues and concerns that have been a constant in our educational discourse, which should not be especially surprising given the essentially moral character of education. However, what is surprising about this revival is that, in its present discourse, character education is characterized as innovative and/or controversial. What is also surprising is how little the political and ideological substance of this particular discourse has changed over the past 300 years.

One of the important changes in the current broader educational discourse relates to the matter of explicitness; whereas the language of colonial and nineteenth-century education is overtly and aggressively moral in content, contemporary educational discourse tends to be circumspect and wary when it comes to moral issues. This is partly a function of a politics of legal fairness and impartiality that emerges from the constitutional separation of Church and State and a politics of accommodation that reflects the realities of a pluralistic society. Another dimension of the coyness about the moral aspects of education is intellectual, i.e., the dominant position of positivism has produced a consciousness of the primacy and necessity of objectivity and neutrality in which moral issues are seen as necessarily "subjective" and hence irrelevant and distracting. The confluence of constitutional limits, political expediency, and positivistic paradigm has produced an orientation in which education becomes a process of learning information and gaining intellectual insights that are presumed to be independent of moral and political consideration. This has allowed the phenomenon of a "new" field of moral or character education, which has been able to transform what used to be assumed as inevitable and inherent aspects of educational dialogue into a problematic and controversial agenda issue. The question changed over time from, "What should be the moral orientation of education?" to "Should education have a moral orientation?," thereby allowing the notion of moral education to be seen as a possibility rather than an inevitability.

However, one of the anomalies of much recent literature in moral education is that many of the writers easily and quickly accept and postulate that moral education *is* always present, inevitably and inherently *and yet* go on to urge that the schools develop moral/character education programs! Thomas Lickona titles a section of his book *Educating for Character*, "The Case for Values Education" (1991), a title that suggests that we have a choice of whether or not there needs to be values education. He goes on to list "at least ten good reasons why schools should be making a clear-headed and wholehearted commitment to teaching moral values and developing good character" (p. 20). On the very same page, good reason number 6 turns out to be, "There is no such thing as value-free education." Lickona sums up this view this way: "In short, the relevant issue is never 'Should schools teach values?' but rather 'Which values will they teach?' and 'How well will they teach them?'" (21).

There are some troublesome issues here. If the schools are already engaged in values education, then why a discourse (as so much of the Character Education literature stresses strongly) on the necessity of schools doing what they are already doing. Much of the discourse in both the political and educational realms has been framed in such a way that values, morality, and ethics are seen as notoriously absent from the schools and must be reintroduced, as represented by the theme "Our nation needs to return to family values." If, as Lickona puts it so acutely, "the relevant issue is never 'Should schools teach values?'" then why does he begin his book with a whole chapter titled, "The Case for Values Education" (Lickona, 1991)?

The effect of such a discourse is to mischievously polarize education (and other social and cultural institutions) into those which are concerned with moral issues and those which are not. Furthermore, this absurdity has a way of giving aid and comfort to those educators and theorists who are extremely wary and nervous about concepts like *moral* and *character* and who are loathe to get involved in such a discourse. It is difficult to attribute naïveté to those in Character Education who actually affirm the inevitability of moral education but perhaps easier to interpret their coyness as an attempt to seize the territory as their own. The political issue at hand then has to do with who is to control the current discourse on the moral and ethical dimensions of education? I believe, regrettably, that the answer to this question has to be that it is controlled largely by those who have been able to reify the concept of moral/character education into something distinct and separable from the broader curriculum and social-cultural context. This control is especially troublesome when this is exercised by those who seem to have a particularly sophisticated understanding of how values impinge powerfully and pervasively on all aspects of schooling.

This separation has allowed some politicians (and educators) to claim a monopoly on a concern for the moral character of society and individuals. When such people call for putting values "back" into the classroom, we might get some satisfaction from knowing that this is tautological and absurd thinking. However, such rhetoric has been used effectively in the public arena and has enhanced the political and literary ambitions of many. More importantly, in the wake of serving the narrow political interests of the Right it has also blurred and distorted the extraordinarily important issues involved. The reality that this reductive and misleading discourse has gone almost unchallenged only adds to the tragedy of the near impossibility of engaging the public in serious and thoughtful debate and dialogue on such complex, sensitive, and vital matters. If the question before the House becomes "Should we or should we not have values education in the schools?" then it seems to me that the appropriate response ought to be either (politely) "Yes"; or (impertinently) "That's a silly question." How then can we account for the persistence of such silly questions?

One explanation that is persuasive to me is that there is a code operating here and that the masked issue is really not a demand for raising public awareness and moral sensitivity nor an attempt to promote the development of ethical consciousness. Rather, it is that the call for moral/character education that comes from the Character Education movement and, by its parallels in the political arena, turns out to be a call on behalf of a *particular and specific moral and ethical system*. It is one thing to advocate that educators and the public seriously address the moral and ethical implications of educational policies and practices and to urge us to ground our education in a moral framework; it is altogether different to urge that we buy into a distinct and particular moral orientation. Either one or both of these discourses is to me perfectly valid, but what I find irresponsible is to blur them in such a way that to favor moral discourse on education equates to having a particular moral point of view and cultural vision.

Not only is such an approach disingenuous, but it serves to further alienate those who have always suspected that discussion of moral issues is, at best, the equivalent to Sunday School and at worst, to sectarian indoctrination. Furthermore, such a discourse can serve to create an artificial and destructive distinction between those who are pure of heart and those who are not, which, of course, tends to exacerbate existing suspicion, divisiveness, and distrust. Unfortunately, much of the professional discourse in this area mirrors the political rhetoric of those who seek to claim for themselves the mantle of moral righteousness in distinction to those whose morals are of an uncertain if not dubious nature. Again, Lickona has put it trenchantly: "The relevant question is…which values will they [the schools] teach and how well will they teach them?" (1991). In other words, let us end this absurdity of framing the debate over whether or not schools should be involved in moral/character issues and get on with the much more compelling questions regarding the question of what moral orientation(s) ought to ground our educational policies and principles (Purpel 1991). It is also time that those educators who have had the courage to engage in the often thankless task of addressing these challenging and daunting issues—but who have insisted on blurring the questions with the answers—acknowledge that these are public issues requiring very wide participation by the public and the profession. Hence, they have a responsibility to frame the issues in such a way as to invite and promote the reluctant, the confused, the conflicted, and the squeamish to become involved in the dialogue. By the same token, those who have luxuriated in their detachment and non-commitment must not leave the struggle to those who have particular if not narrow moral orientations and therefore need to give up their ennui and extend their responsibility beyond claiming that dialogue on the moral dimensions of education amounts to the return of the Spanish Inquisition. We owe the moral educators our gratitude for their questions; we need to be thankful to the skeptical for their criticality; and we should respect the reluctant and uncommitted for their hesitation. Yet we must all be mindful of the insufficiency of separating criticality and affirmation from each other. Criticism without affirmation can easily lead us to the emptiness and despair of cynicism, while affirmation without criticism can just as easily lead us to the distracting and self-serving blandness of sentimentality.

Character Education and Ideology

Let us then indeed move to the question of which values are actually being taught in the public schools. We can perhaps illumine this issue (as well as reiterate the prior point of the inevitability of moral education) by offering examples of values that are more or less uniformly imparted by way of general public and professional consensus on what constitutes good values and proper character. Schools teach that work and effort are good; that learning as well as imagination and creativity are valuable. Students are urged to be polite, respectful, and obedient to adults in general and school personnel in particular. They are taught that achievement is extremely important and that competition is inevitable if not salubrious; that those who do well in school merit certain advantages and that those who flout the rules and expectations deserve to be punished. Generally speaking, students are expected to talk, write, move, and go to the bathroom when they are given permission. Schools teach that time is valuable—tardiness, absences, and missed deadlines are considered offenses that require forgiveness. Students are required to do things they may not wish to do and are taught that this is a good thing.

Even though I basically agree with Herbert Kliebard's (1986) thesis that the public school curriculum represents a mélange of conflicting orientations, I am able to perceive some recognizable ideological shape to such moral emphases. My sense is that the values taught in the schools are very much in the line of Puritan traditions of obedience, hierarchy, and hard work, values which overlap nicely with the requirements of an economic system that values a compliant and industrious work force, and a social system that demands stability and order. There is an ideology here that puts very strong emphasis on control—adult control of children is mandated and legitimated, and children's self-control of their bodies and minds is demanded. Moreover, the state, acting as surrogate for the economic and cultural systems, exercises its power to impose this ideology by requiring children to attend institutions that the state establishes and controls and which are financed by mandatory taxation.

This cursory interpretation is not meant in any way to pass for a complete ideological analysis of the curriculum but only to indicate that it is possible (and valuable) to discern larger political and cultural meaning in school practice and to emphasize the ideological nature of moral/character education. Clearly, one can find other, sometimes conflicting ideological forces at work in the public schools (e.g., concerns for democracy and/or individualism), for the point is that schools are important public arenas of ideological debate and struggle. The concerns I want to raise here have to do with the ideological nature of moral/character education proposals and with my assumption that any such program is necessarily embedded in some larger social, political, cultural, economic vision. Moral issues are by definition socially and culturally situated and any dialogue on proper character is based on some communal notion of propriety.

Unfortunately, one of the characteristics of the recent professional literature in this area has been the near absence of ideological analysis, never mind ideological affirmation. This again seems extraordinarily anomalous, particularly for those who write in a context of responding to a sense of cultural and moral crisis, since it would seem that a thoughtful response to crisis inevitably requires some interpretation of its etiology and nature. It is interesting that virtually all of the recent researchers in this field tend to provide some social and cultural perspective to their work but their programs are largely, if not entirely, psychologically oriented—the problems are acknowledged to be largely social but the proposed solutions are largely personal! The anomaly is a discourse that seemingly recognizes the interpenetration of social, historical, cultural, economic, and personal forces, yet it fails to acknowledge its own ideological assumptions and tends consequently to focus only on personal intervention.

This anomaly is especially apparent in the work of those who are closely identified with the current Character Education Movement (e.g., Lickona 1991; Wynne and Ryan 1993). These writers identify a series of serious social and cultural problems that they characterize as reflecting moral and character deterioration. Included in these phenomena are such matters as the rates of divorce, unwed parents, teenage pregnancies, substance abuse, crime, school violence, classroom cheating, and child abuse. There tends to be very little in the way of close examination of the data used to substantiate their claim that we are in the midst of moral degeneration, and about the only interpretation that they offer for this state of affairs is a rise in a consciousness of personalism and individualistic hedonism. There is no serious effort, for example, to examine the complex issues regarding teenage pregnancies—first of all there are data that suggest that the rate of teen-age pregnancies tends to fluctuate and that current rates are not unprecedented (Rhode and Lawson 1993). Even if there has been a significant increase, there still is a question of why this is considered to be a moral transgression? Is it wrong because the parents will be economically or psychologically unable to provide appropriate child care? If the problems are economic in origin then we have to ask why we have an economy that makes it so difficult to raise children at times that Nature seems to indicate are close to optimal? Or is the problem here one of morality? Do the writers believe that teenagers simply shouldn't be sexually active at this age. What is the grounding for such a morality? Community convention? Part of a larger religious framework? Personal opinion? Moreover, why is this issue lumped together with certain other issues like substance abuse and school violence and not with others like social inequality and multinational capitalism? Surely these writers ought to have some reasonably comprehensive framework that gives order and meaning to their critique and program, but alas, what they offer is skimpy and thin. The reluctance or inability of the Character Education Movement to elaborate and clarify its larger worldview is unfortunate for at least two reasons. First of all, it represents a truncated dialogue which deprives us of a chance to recognize the way in which educational and social/cultural/political issues are interrelated and thus significantly weakens the opportunity for a more thorough and comprehensive public discussion. Secondly, it allows others (like me) to attempt to fill in the missing links, which may or may not do justice to their orientation. However, this is a vacuum that needs to be filled as long as those in the movement fail to fully own up to their prior political, spiritual, and theoretical assumptions.

As it stands, the Character Education movement seems to me to have an uncanny resemblance to certain historical traditions as well as to particular strains of contemporary political ideology. Historically, the emphasis on the maintenance of the status quo, order, hard work, obedience, sexual restraint, stability, and hierarchy represent the continuation of the Puritan tradition, minus the explicit affirmation of Christianity. Its rhetoric of fear and trembling of rapid moral and social deterioration, and its insistence on a return to an ethic of communal responsibility, sobriety, delay of gratification, respect for authority, industriousness, and conventional morality can hardly be differentiated from the pietistic language of nineteenth century advocates of the common school.

Carl Kaestle, in his book *Pillars of the Republic* (1983), has interpreted the common school movement as a triumph of an "ideology centered on republicanism, Protestantism, and capitalism, three sources of social belief that were intertwined and mutually supporting." He goes on to delineate several of what he terms to be "major propositions of native Protestant ideology" (76). The presence as well the absence of these themes in the current Character Education movement is revealing and instructive. Briefly these themes are a concern for the "fragility of the republican polity"; the importance of individual character in maintaining social morality; the critical importance of "personal industry" as determinants of merit; a respected but limited domestic role for women; the critical importance of a strong and appropriate family and social environment (in contrast to those of certain ethnic and racial groups) to character building; the superiority of white American Protestant culture; the equality and abundance of economic opportunity; the grandeur of American destiny; and the "necessity of a determined public effort to unify America's polyglot population, chiefly through education'" (76–77). This nineteenth-century ideology clearly bears striking resemblance to the rhetoric and program of the neoconservative movement of the past two decades, as exemplified currently in the political arena by the likes of Newt Gingrich and Pat Buchanan and culturally by people like William Bennett and Pat Robertson. It is surely not the same—the conditions are very different and the language has a very different resonance with present historical circumstances. However, it is also clear (and reasonable to expect) that the culture continues to passionately engage in issues that confronted the nation in its early history. It is also apparent that the orientation towards these issues that Kaestle describes as the native Protestant ideology of the mid-nineteenth century overlaps substantially with perhaps the dominant political ideology of the 1990s, and more to the point, has significant resonance with the Character Education movement.

I want to make it clear that I am not suggesting that there is collusion and conspiracy between the professional and political figures of the Character Education Movement or even that the professional movement is totally congruent with the agenda of the political Right. I am saying, however, that at the very least there is an implicit, fairly consistent and coherent political orientation embedded within the message of Character Education and that the message has strong and vital resonance with the neoconservative political and cultural program.

Edward Wynne, for example, in advocating schools promoting "traditional values," which he defines as "the panoply of virtues connoted by phrases such as the work ethic and obedience to legitimate authority and by the important nonreligious themes articulated by the Ten Commandments" (Wynne 1989, 19). Note the attempt to define the concept of "traditional values" as unproblematic and to focus on work and obedience. He goes on to make a case for the close connection between character development and academic performance, claiming, "Academics and character are coincident, since persons with character are, by definition, industrious" (31). In a discussion of teacher-student relations, he asserts that, "Adults who routinely deal with children and adolescents are gradually driven to recognize that adult-child relations in schools cannot and should not be governed by so-called democratic theories" (34). This is hardly an affirmation of the traditional values of democracy and autonomy.

Another major figure in Character Education, Thomas Lickona, lists ten current "signs of a moral decline" to be "violence and vandalism, stealing, cheating, disrespect for authority, peer cruelty, bigotry, bad language, sexual precocity and abuse, increasing self-centeredness and declining civic responsibility, and self-destructive behavior" (Lickona 1991, 12–18). This is hardly distinguishable from what would come in a Dan Quayle speech in its focus on individual behavior and its absence of structural criticism.

We also can gain further insight into Character Education's ideology by reflecting on what is not considered, that is, by what is presumably not a "sign of moral decline." There is, for example, and in this case in sharp contrast to the nineteenth century ideology, only token mention of the importance of sustaining a democratic consciousness. The references seem to be mostly concerned with procedural issues like voting rather than notions of social democracy, and there certainly is no sense of a crisis in the vitality of democratic institutions. Clearly, there is no mention or even an implied affirmation of the American tradition of revolutionary democracy as an expression of resistance to authoritarianism nor of the spiritual traditions that command us to afford human dignity to all as an expression of divine will.

Nor is there a concern for the harshness and cruelty of an increasingly unbridled free market economy, of growing economic inequality, of the systemic nature of poverty, of the enormous disparity in the quality of medical care, of ecological devastation, of the ever-increasing desperation of have-not nations, or of the continuing dangers of international conflicts. The basic theory the Character Education Movement offers for moral decline is a psychological one, that the problems are rooted in an inflated sense of personalism and self-centeredness rather than rooted in social economic, and cultural institutions. The Character Education Movement therefore, takes on, at least implicitly, the ideology of the struggle to preserve the social and political status quo; there are serious problems out there and what we have to do is not make structural changes (the economic system, the social class structure, the political hierarchy) but instead insist that individuals change. In this ideology, society is being victimized by unvirtuous (lazy, selfish, indulgent, and indolent) individuals rather than an ideology which posits individuals as being victimized by an unvirtuous (rapacious, callous, competitive, and heartless) society.

The politics of the preservation of the status quo involves the privileging of those already in positions of power, influence, and advantage and maintaining the barriers to those who are relatively powerless and disadvantaged. In our present social reality we find ourselves in a particularly divisive situation in which virtually all the major social, political, and cultural institutions and traditions have been seriously challenged, if not threatened, by dramatic changes in consciousness. The most visible of these changes can be seen not only in such phenomena as the civil rights, anti-war, multiculturalism, women's liberation, gay rights movements but also in the more pervasive mood of growing alienation, disenchantment, and frustration. Much of the energy behind the conservative movement is in counterreaction to the challenge to and disaffection with the status quo, and it is in this context that the Character Education movement can best be understood. The context is like the one in which an army that is winning but has not yet won the war, calls for peace, i.e., the conservative call for an increase in such admirable qualities as civility, deference to the community, stability, and orderliness also serves to consolidate the gains and authority of those already in power. It also serves to distract attention from the potentially disruptive substantive critique of established social institutions to the more emotionally charged issues of personal morality and conduct. Better to discuss poverty in terms of personal laziness and moral flabbiness than as an inevitable and structured consequence of our economic system; better to discuss the alienation of youth in terms of school violence than as aspects of a culture drowning in dispiriting materialism and consumerism. This is not to say that we should ignore the real dangers inherent in a doctrine of social and cultural determinism or forget that individuals have important responsibilities and opportunities for agency. It strikes me, however, that we would be better served by an analysis that accepts a dynamic dialectic between the social and the individual, between the forces of social realities and the possibilities of individual responsiveness, and between individual rights and social responsibility.

It is also extremely important to point out that this body of work does not exhaust by any means the literature on moral/character education, and by the same token to note that all other such orientations require political and ideological examination, analysis, and interpretation. For example, my work has focused on the necessity to ground education in a commitment to pursue a vision of a just and loving community within a consciousness of moral outrage and personal responsibility (Purpel 1989). In addition, there are other major orientations such as the program for democratic schools, reflected in the work of Ralph Mosher (1994), and the notions of teaching for compassion, nurturance, and caring, as reflected in the work of Nel Noddings (1992) and Jane Roland Martin (1992), which carry with them quite different but equally strong ideological. political, and cultural assumptions in varying degrees of explicitness. We simply cannot allow those in the Character Education movement to monopolize and control the moral discourse of education. Conservatives, like any other political group, not only have the right but have the responsibility to lay out the educational implications of their ideology, but they, like other groups, have a corresponding responsibility to engage in good faith dialogue on the realities of divergent viewpoints.

It is also vital to remember that this realm is not exhausted by those who write explicitly about moral/character education, for we must also examine work that impinges directly and indirectly on efforts to develop particular moral values and behaviors, such as material on school discipline, instructional theory, school counseling, attendance policies, curriculum development, and just about everything else. In a word, to talk of education is to inevitably talk of personal character and a moral community, and to talk of personal character and a moral community is inevitably to speak of political, social, cultural, and economic structures.

Problematics of the Field

I believe very strongly that the most important aspects of education are moral and that the term *moral education* is largely redundant. Because of this, I have argued that we would be better off without a field of moral/character education (Purpel 1991) on the basis that such a discourse is distracting and misleading. As I have maintained above, this discourse tends toward reification as it ignores and separates itself from the moral aspects of the larger school and social settings. A major anomaly in much of this field is its tendency to base its program on broad diagnosis and narrow treatment, on locating the problems in the society and culture and the responses to be located in schools and classrooms. Those who work in this field have made a very important contribution by drawing our attention to these problems and issues, for the reality is that mainstream educators have allowed moral discourse to atrophy, perhaps out of a naive faith in the possibility of so-called value-free education. In addition, they have provided a much needed balance to the theories of social and economic determinists in stressing the importance and possibilities of individual responsibility. Moral/character educators also provide much needed energy and hope, and, perhaps most importantly, remind us of our responsibility to honor our moral commitments. Our quest for the morally good society and for becoming good persons cannot be limited to compiling lists of attractive characteristics but must be extended to a serious examination of the conditions under which these contradictions continue to persist. Our task as educators is not limited to striving for morally sound schools and to improving the character of its students but also involves participation in the broader task of creating a just and loving society and a culture of joy and fulfillment for all. This task requires that we embrace a politics that does not privilege, exclude, or demean but rather one that includes, affirms, and empowers everyone. Whatever advances that vision is sound moral/character education.

References

Bailyn, Bernard. 1962. *Education in the Forming of American Society: Needs and Opportunities for Study.* New York: W.W. Norton.

Educational Freedom for a Democratic Society: A Critique of *National Goals, Standards, and Curriculum.* Brandon, VT: Resource Center for Redesigning Education.

Kaestle, Carl. 1983. *Pillars of the Republic: Common Schools and American Society.* New York: Hill and Wang.

Kliebard, Herbert. 1986. *The Struggle for the American Curriculum 1893–1958* . Boston: Routledge and Kegan Paul.

Lickona, Thomas. 1991. *Educating for Character: How Our School Can Teach Respect and Responsibility.* New York: Bantam.

Mosher, Ralph and Robert A. Kenny. 1994. *Preparing for Citizenship: Teaching Youth to Live Democratically.* Westport: Praeger.

Noddings, Nel, 1992. *The Challenge to Care in Schools: An Alternative to Education.* New York: Teachers College Press.

Purpel, David E. "Goals 2000, The Triumph of Vulgarity and The Legitimation of Social Justice" in Ron Miller (ed.), 1995.

Purpel, David E. "Moral Education: An Idea Whose Time Has Gone," *Clearing House*, 64, (May/June 1991): 309–312.

Purpel, David E. 1989. *The Moral and Spiritual Crisis in Education.* Granby, MA.: Bergin and Garvey.

Rhode, Deborah and Annette Lawson. *The Politics of Pregnancy: Adolescent Sexuality and Public Policy.* New.Haven: Yale University Press.

Roland Martin, Jane. 1992. *The Schoolhome: Rethinking Schools for Changing Families* Cambridge: Harvard University Press.

Wynne, Edward A. "Transmitting Traditional Values in Contemporary Schools" in Larry B. Nucci (ed.), *Moral Development and Character Education: A Dialogue.* Berkeley: McCutchan.

Wynne, Edward A. and Kevin Ryan. *Reclaiming Our Schools: A Handbook on Teaching Character, Academics, and Discipline.* N.Y., N.Y.: Merrill.

(This chapter originally appeared in David E. Purpel, *Moral Outrage in Education* [New York: Peter Lang, 1999].)

CHAPTER SEVEN

The "Moral Poverty" of Character Education

JOSEPH L. DEVITIS & TIANLONG YU

> Poverty…is very good in maxims and sermons, but it is very bad in practical life.
> HENRY WARD BEECHER

In our several decades of studying character and moral education, we have come across only two persons who use the term "moral poverty" as a major concept in their analysis of American culture and education. Those individuals are the arch-conservative icons William Bennett and Robert Schuller. The object of this chapter is to explicate how and why they employ "moral poverty" and to characterize how it skews their treatment of character education. In the process, we will raise questions about the appropriateness of their claims for today's schools and society and contend that they are long on pithy verbiage and sermonizing but short on substantial evidence and sustained argument. We will also explore the implications of their recommendations for educational policy and practice.

William Bennett: Moral Poverty and a Very Grim View of Society, Education, and Children

Former Secretary of Education under Ronald Reagan, "drug czar" under George H. W. Bush, and ubiquitous television and radio commentator, William Bennett has been among the most notable modern-day proponents of character education. Most importantly, he has connected his arguments to other vital aspects of the conservative agenda, thus providing ideological rationales for its overall sustenance. Bennett (1992) believes that the condition of American culture is indeed "troubling." He claims that there has long been an all-out assault on the common sense and values of the American public by a so-called "liberal elite" among academics and intellectuals, in the artistic community, and in the mainstream media. According to Bennett, the liberal elite questions the very nature of the "American dream" and advocates an "adversary culture" that contradicts the "common culture" and the more "traditional values of the American people." He bemoans a supposed "cultural breakdown…in areas like education, family life, crime, drug use, as well as in our attitudes toward sex, individual responsibility, civic duty, and public service" (p. 33).

Embracing a grim view of education and attaching "low academic standards" to declining morality, Bennett derides what he characterizes as the "entire mediocre enterprise in America" (p. 47). To buttress his case, he draws upon many national education reports, most particularly *A Nation at Risk* (National Commission on Excellence in Education, 1983). How does Bennett respond to the militaristic tone of that report? He calls for a concerted emphasis on "Three C's—content, character, and choice." At the same time, he urges schools to teach a "sound common curriculum," stressing traditional academic subjects in the liberal arts, moral character, and standards of right and wrong.

Harkening back to the common school movement of the 19th century, Bennett (1992) contends that "improving American education requires not doing new things but doing (and remembering) some good old things" (p. 56). He urges that today's schools be committed to the "faith that public education could teach good moral and civic character from a common ground of American values" (p. 58), i.e., an insistence on "values that all American citizens share." Thus, he believes that "enculturation, the passing on of our values, in an often hostile atmosphere" is a critical task for schools (p. 35). Bennett envisions schools as beacons of a single, unified high culture, transmitting the "best" that is known and thought in the traditional canon, e.g., the Bible and other "great books" of the Western world.

In brief, Bennett systematically describes what he sees as a serious "moral decline" in our society, claiming that our overall moral, socio-cultural, and behavioral conditions are impoverished. He contends that moral decline is at the root of our social problems, and he blames failures in moral education for our presumed "regression" as a nation. For Bennett, so-called "pathologies" in our cultural and ideological predilections clearly reflect moral decay. Why? We have not educated our youth properly to practice moral behavior. Virtue-centered character education is Bennett's panacea for all our dilemmas.

To further manifest moral poverty in the United States, Bennett compiled *The Index of Leading Cultural Indicators: Facts and Figures on the State of American Society* (1994), which provides statistical and numerical data, charts, and graphs on crime, family and children, youth behavior and deviance, popular culture, and religion. According to Bennett, we have experienced drastic upsurges in total violent crimes, including violent juvenile crimes. In addition, he laments that family stability and child-rearing practices have deteriorated while illegitimate births, single-parent households, and divorce rates have increased. In fact, he calls illegitimacy "the single most important social problem of our time—more important than crime, drugs, poverty, illiteracy, welfare or homelessness because it drives everything else" (p. 48).

Bennett's (1994) portrait of American schools is similarly bleak: SAT scores have plummeted and discipline problems have skyrocketed. Furthermore, his statistics show that our children watch far too much TV and that sex and violence are pervasive in it, film, and music. All the while, the churches are losing their grip on believers. Bennett is indeed a major doomsayer: "Unless these exploding social pathologies are reversed, they will lead to the decline and perhaps even to the fall of the American republic" (p. 8). Though he does not overtly claim that all of our problems are moral in nature, he does emphasize their moral implications by mixing them together in such phrases as "the moral, social, and behavioral conditions" of our cultural fabric. For Bennett, then, assumed social pathologies plainly mirror moral decay and moral poverty. When addressing the paucity of moral education as the underlying cause of many of these problems, Bennett is clearly stressing the link between them and individual morality.

Although Bennett (1994) is pessimistic about our moral condition, he is decidedly enthusiastic about what he views as our exceptional status as a nation: "The United States has the strongest economy in the world, a healthy entrepreneurial spirit, a still-healthy work ethic, and a generous attitude—good signs all" (p. 8). For him, the capitalist production machine is a thing of beauty; social resources are fairly distributed; and the political system is effective and just. In a word, the social structure has only a few inconsequential deficiencies. Yet his general prognosis for the future is dim because of our alleged social pathologies. Once again, Bennett falls back upon the loss of morality and the lack of moral education as the prime malefactors of social regression. Indeed, Bennett et al.'s *Body Count* (1996) explicitly employs the term "moral poverty" and isolates it as the root cause of those so-called social pathologies.

Bennett is not alone in using the rhetoric of moral poverty. Other character education leaders have frequently addressed the same concerns about the so-called moral decline in American society and its schools (Kilpatrick, 1992; Lickona, 1996; Ryan, 1989; Wynne, 1989a, 1989b). They, too, draw upon similar statistics to support their arguments. While emphasizing the latter, they often fail to check the validity of the figures in the statistics and neglect to examine their crucial meanings, underlying assumptions, and implications. For instance, none of the critics seriously explore how morality could be involved in those problems (e. g., the decline in SAT scores or the rising rates of out-of-wedlock births). Indeed, none of them question whether such problems really represent a moral regression. That they could be part and parcel of larger social questions never sees the light of day in their analysis. (See Yu, 2004 for a more detailed critical analysis of the political rationale for character education constructed by Bennett and others.)

Robert Schuller: Moral Poverty and "Be (Happy) Attitudes"

From the 1980s until his recent retirement from the pulpit (but not the lucrative lecture circuit), Reverend Robert Schuller telecast "The Hour of Power" worldwide at the Crystal Cathedral in Garden Grove, California. In fact, the road from Bennett to Schuller makes for a very short trip. In contrast to the bleak and grim image Bennett often represented on television and in the lecture halls, Schuller has relentlessly appeared as a smiling sword carrier for blissful righteousness and the healing balm of the Christian Beatitudes.

Schuller's (1985) *The Be (Happy) Attitudes* sets forth a full menu of positive principles for effective living in light of precepts gleaned from the Sermon on the Mount. At bottom, he is a direct descendant of the practical ideas and prescriptions of Dr. Norman Vincent Peale, one of the all-time most influential proponents of commercial idealism. Peale (1952) was the author of one of the largest-selling self-help books in the history of trade publishing, *The Power of Positive Thinking*.

Like Peale, Schuller (1985) insists that external social factors have little to do with achieving personal happiness. Indeed, he skirts over any problems related to financial poverty in order to concentrate instead on issues of occupational, intellectual, and emotional poverty. To avoid occupational poverty, one must chart goals toward professional success and strive to reach those aspirations. To ward off intellectual poverty, one must acknowledge that one is not an expert on everything, i.e., that one will someday need help from other sources besides oneself. To suppress emotional poverty, we all "need to be needed," and we must grant that "success starts when I dare to admit I need help." In a soothing, if questionable, rendering of financial poverty via a softened version of Social Darwinism, Schuller muses: "Poverty handled in a pleasant, positive manner is an opportunity to involve good and generous people in our dreams, for often the strong welcome an opportunity to help the weak" (pp. 21–25).

Along with seeking help for their problems, Schuller (1985) recommends that human beings take on the humble cloak of the poor in spirit, for they are blessed in their openness to their predicament. In a real way, he is beseeching us to convert our problems into success through the sheer force of will (p. 39). Thus, only errors in human judgment forestall us from the ultimate fulfillment of our dreams of happiness and success, i.e., we can change our lives if we but change our attitudes. Given the possibilities of such great expectations, Schuller (1985) continues to smile down upon those still in grimness: "…that's why the people that mourn are really comforted. Believe it or not, they're happy" (p. 71).

Of course, not everyone believes (at least not in the way Schuller does) and, presumably, that is why they are not happy. Relentlessly, but sweetly, Schuller (1985, p. 76) urges those with unhappy consciousnesses to unravel the potential riches in the simple, yet powerful, word "meek": M (mighty), E (emotionally stable), E (educable), and K (kind). If one does not succeed on that sure-fire formula, the problem is either a failure due to personal pride or perhaps an inability to be corrigible. For Schuller, both are doubtless one and the same. In his sermonizing therapeutic style, Schuller seems disingenuous to at least some of his readers and listeners.

Those who find Schuller a difficult mentor have evidently not "moved ahead with possibility thinking" (Schuller, 1978). They have failed to discover life's promise and rewards. They have been too impulsive. They have lagged in energy, patience, and, above all, faith. In brief, they have not been positive thinkers (Schuller, 1978). In some of his pleading for possibility thinking, Schuller takes on an emphatic, even cartoonish, posture, admonishing his flock to partake of: "Positive stress! Work! Dream! Hold on! Never give up! Keep on believing! Set goals beyond goals! Think bigger! Think longer!" (Schuller, 2005, p. 4).

Thus, Schuller strongly ties the Protestant Ethic, especially its capitalist ideology, to his philosophy of earthly success. He is eager to tell his audience to "turn problems into profitable projects" and to "turn opportunities into rich enterprises" (Schuller, 1978, p. 16).

Their World Views: Character and Mind Power Ethics

Although their perspectives on moral poverty are strikingly similar, Bennett and Schuller spawn their treatments from somewhat differing worldviews. We will argue that Bennett's ideas emerge from the character ethic tradition and that Schuller's precepts are enmeshed in a kind of mind power ethic. Both models share a long history in the main currents of American culture. (For a fuller discussion of the character and mind power ethics, see DeVitis & Rich, 1996.)

At least since the days of Benjamin Franklin's image of the "self-made man," the character ethic has been a mainstay of the American Dream. It represents a group of traits and a way of life considered by many to have significance and moral quality. Certain key words are associated with the concept of character: citizenship, duty, work, honor, morals, manners, and integrity. Its desirable connotations include perseverance, industry, frugality, sobriety, punctuality, reliability, thoroughness, and initiative (Susman, 1979). The character ethic has been part of Western tradition from ancient

Greece, through the Protestant Ethic and common schools, to Boy Scout pledges today.

Bennett (1992) implicitly extols the character ethic in his recommendations for education. He urges educators not only to state the difference between right and wrong but also exemplify right conduct. For instance, if we expect students to respect the law, they should know why Socrates submitted to the decree of Athens. If we seek to teach honesty, we could teach about such moral exemplars as Joan of Arc, Horace, and the like.

On the other hand, Schuller's brand of "enlightenment" invokes mind power as the ultimate bridge to happiness and success. He emphasizes the sheer force of will and mental exertion as the panacea for all that plagues us. According to Schuller, faith through prayer and imaging power can eventually conquer our fleshly incapacities. We need to think positively, create our own happiness, and ride toward the Lord's glory:

> God particularly pours out His blessings upon those who know how much they need Him. The *promise* is joy. The *principle* is to ask God for help, admit we cannot do it alone. The *problem,* of course, that stands in the way of our crying out to God is the problem of an *unholy pride.* (Schuller, 1985, p. 33)

Though the mind-power ethic provides the fulcrum for Schuller's moral scaffolding, his recommendations are filled with explicit references to the power of the character ethic: "Character is the definition of your personhood. It is the essential core that defines and describes your reputation. Character is conceived and born in the arena where your life's principles are Chosen" (Schuller, 2005, p. 65). Indeed, for Schuller, the modeling of character is crucial for how individuals make everyday decisions, set their goals, and commit to "noble and honorable values" (Schuller, 2005, p. 66).

Intrinsically linked to character are religious values and what Schuller refers to as the "deepening" of tradition, which he likens to "the root system of a plant." Schuller contends that evil external forces can invade that system in "toxic" ways. Only tradition and Judaic-Christian teachings can protect us from such invasion (Schuller, 2005, pp. 67–70).

The worldviews of Bennett and Schuller are surely in need of careful scrutiny. Both perspectives lack any kind of fair and full assessment of existing socio-cultural conditions. Neither of them provides an evaluation of those social forces and factors that necessarily impede most of our vision and progress. Bennett and Schuller simply stress the individual's own efforts as the primary impetus for any change. If those efforts fail, they blame the victim for failing to scale the heights of success in American life. Thus, both merely pour sour wine into the old bottle of "rugged individualism" as a policy solution for far more complex and contentious societal issues.

What do Bennett and Schuller lose or forget in their analysis? For one, they submerge such root causes as economic poverty, racism, and lack of governmental action to solve larger social problems. In their spiritual fervor, they want to save individual souls, but neglect the communitarian possibility of social salvation. In the end, they concoct a set of false circumstances in which morality is played out as somehow independent of wider social conditions. Bennett, Dilulio, and Walters (1996) state their position in bold terms that blend both religion and the character ethic:

> Social regeneration depends on *individual* (italics added) citizens living better, more committed, more devoted lives...just lives that reflect the basic and modest character traits—self-discipline, civic-mindedness, fidelity to commitments, honesty, responsibility, and perseverance...and to accomplish these things, it would be no small help...to remember God. (p. 207)

Finally, Bennett and Schuller, especially Bennett, tend to frame their reality in metaphors and discourse alien to the idea of developing people in fully humane, life-generating fashion. Instead, their agendas are filled with shrill calls for duty and discipline based on fear, what George Lakoff (2002) terms the "strict father" model of child-rearing. Largely missing from their analysis is any attachment to more nurturing forms of empathy, equity, caring, mutual respect, and, above all, the willingness to question authority.

Moral Poverty: The Politics of Rhetoric

In the world of politics, religion, and education, there is no scarcity of sloganeering and public relations propaganda. Bennett and Schuller provide major models for how public figures can overstate problems and sometimes fool the larger public. (Because Schuller does not write explicitly on education, much of our argument in this section will be limited to a critique of Bennett's claims about public schools and social concerns.)

Bennett's 1994 book on social indicators (e.g., crime, drugs, family structure, and religion) hardly offers exclusive and exhaustive indicators of the complexities of societal forces and factors. Statistics on each of the indicators are limited and do not express the depth and breadth of any one particular issue. For instance, his data on education are restricted to changes in SAT scores, several samples of subject-based international assessments, and an informal teachers' survey on discipline problems. Yet he relies on such limited data to conclude that the entire educational system has failed.

More flagrantly, Bennett is far from completely honest about his statistics. For example, *The Statistical Abstracts of the United States* (the major source in the index to his book on social indicators) clearly shows that overall crime rates have steadily *decreased* over the last several decades. Bennett uses eye-catching charts to draw our eyes away from reality. He also forgets to mention that the nation's general population has increased as well. In writing his 1994 book, Bennett does admit that "overall drug use among Americans is down more than 50 percent from its peak in the late 1970s" and that "among adolescents, drug and alcohol use is at its lowest since monitoring began in 1975" (Bennett, 1994, pp. 38–40).

Does Bennett ask critical questions about similar statistics that contribute to his labeling of "social pathologies," "moral decline," and "moral poverty"? He does not. Consider his treatment of SAT data in his 1994 book. Bennett reports that SAT scores have dipped 73 points from 1960 to 1993. He neglects to note the shifting demographics of the test-takers. In the 1960s, a select, elite, and more affluent group of college preparatory students took the SAT. More equal opportunity and the testing of students from more varied walks of life appeared only later in the testing game. Rothstein (2001) also notes that the SAT and ACT are voluntary tests. The number of students taking them has, in fact, increased greatly over the past several decades. Thus, the decline can largely be traced to the huge increase in test-takers, a different population of them, and the increasing percentage of students who apply to college. Given that set of circumstances (which Bennett hides), one could argue that it is indeed amazing that the scores have held as well as they have.

In addition, some critics claim that the SAT is a poor barometer of general school performance. According to Stedman (1993), "The most serious limitation of the SAT data…is their lack of relevance as a measure of school quality" (p. 218). The SAT is designed to predict a selective group's future college performance but ignores most of the high school curriculum in its assessment structure. Such irrelevance is acknowledged by Lynne Cheney, one of Bennett's political allies. Cheney points out that "looming over our educational landscape is an examination that, in its verbal component, carefully avoids assessing substantive knowledge gained from course work" (in Stedman, p. 219).

While Bennett stresses SAT scores, he does little in the way of mapping out an outline for educational opportunity. He does not want to admit that the change in SAT outcomes is less a measure of educational decline and more a sign of at least some growth in equal opportunities. Instead, Bennett would rather recall the "good old days" that never were. As Stedman (1993) puts it, "We should all have serious doubts about a so-called golden age of education and be leery of solutions to today's problems that are justified primarily by wistful references to the past" (p. 216). Of course, Bennett has never been known to advocate for equitable expenditures for education. Indeed, he has said, "There is no systematic correlation between spending on education and student performance" (Bennett, 1994 p. 83).

Meanwhile some educational researchers have perceptively shown that the recent "crisis" in public schools has been largely "manufactured." They depict a less dismal picture of student attainment (see Berliner & Biddle, 1995, for example). Some scholars have sifted through the evidence more carefully and have taken a more evenhanded approach to the issues (see Stedman, 1995, for instance). They have found that student achievement in U.S. schools has historically been low, suggesting a serious long-standing concern that certainly needs addressing, but they also note that Bennett and others like him have exploited the evidence and exaggerated any educational decline.

Bennett has also misled the public by overstating youth behavioral problems. Fear and exaggeration have played prime roles in his depiction of the degree of youth violence. Studies reveal no widespread expansion of such violence, but the level of trepidation has risen because of a relatively few major school shootings since Columbine (Spina, 2000). These incidents have produced an abnormal fear of youth deviance, and critics like Bennett have been more than willing to gain exposure from them. Without saying they are morally right, the more sober among us have been able to accept the existence of such behaviors in some form. We have not panicked nor predicted the fall of our republic or that of any civilization across the globe.

Since Bennett cherishes the "great thinkers" of the Western world, we recommend that he reread Emile Durkheim (2000) and his modern-day interpreter, Kai Erikson, on the matter of deviance in society. Deviance can serve useful functions, as Erikson sees it: "Deviant forms of behavior, by making the outer edges of group life, give the inner structure its special character and thus supply the framework within which the people of the group develop an orderly sense of their own cultural identity" (in Adler & Adler, 2000, p. 14).

Furthermore, there is really nothing deviant in any particular act until powerful groups define the act as "deviant." That is to say, concepts such as "deviance," "moral decline," and "moral decay" are socially constructed. Few people in our society have had the privilege of sitting in as many seats of power as William Bennett. He has clearly represented some of the most potent political, economic, and cultural groups in the United States. As such, he has been permitted to act as a kind of "moral entrepreneur" (Adler & Adler, 2000) in staking out the definition of "public morality." In the process, Bennett has been allowed to justify and disseminate his ideology (and those of other conservative allies) on such crucial questions as crime, deviance, and morality. He has thus painted a horrific picture of youth problems for public consumption. He has inspired adult fear and loathing. He has created moral panic.

Moral entrepreneurs like Bennett and Schuller crusade to transform certain behaviors into deviant acts. If one looks slightly beyond the surface, s/he will usually find that they are basing their thought and action on their own ideological predilections. In the foreground, they claim their positions are essential to protect and preserve the moral fabric of society. They are self-righteous, but they are savvy enough to employ humanitarian overtones: "The crusader is not only interested in seeing to it that other people do what he thinks is right. He believes that if they do what is right it will be good for them" (Becker, 2000, p. 139). Because of their grim view of human nature, character educators like Bennett and Schuller emphasize moral training and control. That sense of ownership includes control of social, political, economic, and moral resources. For that reason, the overarching term "moral poverty" is both apt and rewarding to their eyes and ears. Moral poverty has become their instrument of power.

Has moral poverty really caused our social problems? By inflaming the public and making it more responsive to emotional than rational argument, Bennett and Schuller have jettisoned efforts to examine the root causes of actual economic poverty. The latter is widely accepted as perhaps the primary factor in crime. Yet our policy analyses rarely face that fact head on. William Luksetich and Michael White (1982) argue that empirical evidence strongly supports the economic theory of crime:

> There is significant relationship between economic conditions and the amount of crime. Increases in the unemployment rate are predicted to be associated with increases in the amount of crime….The relationship between income and the amount of crime is predicted to be inverse; that is, the lower an individual's income, the greater is the likelihood of involvement in criminal activity. (p. 144)

Instead, Bennett takes on the role of a moralizer who would prod people to "know the good and do the Good." Meanwhile Schuller's more therapeutic stance allows individuals to "feel the good" as well—so long as it corresponds with his sermonizing aims. Both Bennett and Schuller rather ignore the social contexts of individual struggles in their recommendations.

For Schuller, the blaming-the-victim mentality is alive and well in assessing human failures. He claims that "there are no rules" in our secular culture, and only the Bible and Jesus Christ can save criminal elements in our society (Schuller, 2005, p. 85). Schuller blames America's educational institutions for what he views as the inculcation of false assumptions and "negative thinking." Not surprisingly, his antidote to such "miseducation" lies in religious instruction and a huge spiritual leap of faith: "*Faith is a fact, not a fantasy* [Schuller's italics]. Individuals who live with faith are allowing their positive assumptions to drive their lives. Faith is not a myth. It is a scientific reality operating in human personality and human behavior" (Schuller, 2005, p. 187). That none of his faith argument is susceptible to actual proof or real scientific investigation appears to cause Schuller no sleepless nights.

In the social realm, Bennett and Schuller argue against almost all forms of "social investment" in human life, i.e., provision of social cushions for those without adequate resources. As Henry Giroux (1997) puts it, "An emphasis on social failing in the society (leads to) questions of individual character, social policy moves from the language of social investment—creating safety nets for children—to the language of containment and blame" (p. 17).

The educational implications become obvious. Character education, as propounded by Bennett, Schuller, and others, is a major vehicle for knowledge and values transmission—of those values and knowledge that support existing political and economic systems. And who benefits from such socialization of the citizenry? Those already in power do, and Bennett and Schuller enjoy their unique status in the established power structure.

In the hands of character educators like them, civic education is thus promoted as mere socialization. The role of the informed, active citizen is generally ignored. According to Kevin Ryan, a prominent voice in the contemporary character education movement: "Character development puts a heavy emphasis on culture….It places more emphasis on the traditional role of the school as transmitter of the culture" (Ryan, 1989, p. 14). In the "good feeling" bromides of Schuller, we can recall President George W. Bush's allegiance to character education: "Americans believe in character education because we want more for our children than apathy and cynicism."

Conclusion

In the end, neither Bennett nor Schuller affords a genuinely dialogic approach to educational and ethical understanding. Their acknowledgment of external constraints is truly subterranean in their own curious versions of "reality." Though their words might offer solace to some religious adherents, the earthly effects of their discourse are much less discernible in the daily phenomenological course of human events. They are both guardians of tradition and culture and critics of the ways of society as lived by those they disagree with (whose legions are many).

Like some other churchmen, Bennett and Schuller seek "to repress new ideas and usages" and want to forestall change as much as possible—unless it is change that suits their own ideological perspectives. In a word, they tend to be authoritarian, intolerant, and obsessive about social control. In a very real sense, Bennett and Schuller indoctrinate, i.e., they intentionally inculcate a certain belief system. Their approach is hardly reflective, interpretive, or integrative. Any form of autonomous reflection is sadly lacking, thus mitigating against authentic moral education. The ethical agent must be aware of, and understand, those considerations that surround her moral decision-making. The kind of "true believers" that Bennett and Schuller would like to mold do not possess the opportunity for such awareness and understanding (Rich & DeVitis, 1994, pp. 12–15).

Whereas Bennett uses fear and hatred to massage his message, Schuller beseeches his brethren and sisters in more soothing, optimistic tones. Yet, in essence, they tend to beat the same moralistic drum, one that targets the individual for ultimate blame while safeguarding the status quo. In the form of character education, their priorities are seen in schools that emphasize behavioral techniques to train children to accept their role and place in the social order. In the process, Bennett and Schuller seek to avoid controversial and complex learning about life's social realities and autonomous decision-making.

With both character and mind-power ethics, Bennett and Schuller curiously de-value critical thinking and the abilities and skills needed to make ethical choices. They purposely conceal the political and economic nature of social problems. They preach that there is only something wrong with the nature of individuals and *their* morality. Consequently, Bennett and Schuller are crude sculptors of *individual* morality who reinforce the interests of those in power. Ultimately, they can be seen as handmaidens for the destruction of democratic vitality.

References

Adler, P. A. & Adler, P. (Eds.) (2000). *Constructions of deviance: Social power, contexts, and interaction* (3rd ed.). Belmont, CA: Wadsworth.

Becker, H. (2000). Labeling theory. In P. A. Adler & P. Adler (Eds.). *Constructions of deviance* (pp. 78–82). Belmont, CA: Wadsworth.

Bennett, W. J. (1992). *The de-valuing of America: The fight for our culture and our children.* New York: Summit Books.

_____. (1994). *The index of leading cultural indicators: Facts and figures on the state of American society.* New York: Simon & Schuster.

_____, Dilulio, J. J. Jr., & Walters, J. P. (1996). *Body count: Moral poverty…and how to win America's war against crime and drugs.* New York: Simon & Schuster.

Berliner, D. & Biddle, B. (1995). *The manufactured crisis: Myths, fraud, and the attack on America's public schools.* New York: Addison-Wesley.

DeVitis, J. L. & Rich, J. M. (1996). *The success ethic, education, and the American dream.* Albany, NY: State University of New York Press.

Durkheim, E. (2000). The normal and the pathological. In P. Adler & P. Adler (Eds.), *Constructions of deviance* (pp. 53–57). Belmont, CA: Wadsworth.

Giroux, H. (1997). *Channel surfing: Racism, the media, and the destruction of today's youth.* New York: St. Martin's Griffin.

Kilpatrick, W. K. (1992). *Why Johnny can't tell right from wrong.* New York: Simon & Schuster.

Lakoff, G. (2002). *Moral politics: How liberals and conservatives think.* Chicago: Universityof Chicago Press.

Lickona, T. (1996, June). The decline and fall of American civilization: Can character education reverse the slide? *Currents in Modern Thoughts*, 285–307.

Luksetich, W. A. & White, M. D. (1982). *Crime and public policy: An economic approach.* Boston: Little, Brown.

Moberg, D. (1962). *The church as a social institution: The sociology of American religion.* Englewood Cliffs, NJ: Prentice-Hall.

National Commission on Excellence in Education (1983). *A nation at risk.* Cambridge, MA: SA Research.

Peale, N. V. (1952).*The power of positive thinking.* New York: Prentice-Hall.

Rich, J. M. & DeVitis, J. L. (1994). *Theories of moral development* (2nd ed.). Springfield, IL: Charles C. Thomas.

Rothstein, R. (2001, August 29). SAT scores aren't up. Not bad, not bad at all. *The New York Times*, p. B8.

Ryan, K. (1989). In defense of character education. In L. Nucci (Ed.), *Moral Development and character education* (pp. 3–17). Berkeley, CA: McCutchan.

Schuller, R. H. (1978). *Move ahead with possibility thinking.* New York: Jove.

_____. (1985). *The be(happy) attitudes.* Waco, TX: Word Books.

_____. (2005). *Don't throw away tomorrow: Living God's dream for your life.* San Francisco: HarperCollins.

Spina, S. U. (2000). Introduction: Violence in schools: Expanding the dialogue. In S. U. Spina (Ed.), *Smoke and mirrors: The hidden context of violence in schools and society* (p 1–39). Lanham, MD: Rowman & Littlefield.

Stedman, L. C. (1993). The condition of education: Why school reformers are on the right track. *Phi Delta Kappan*, 75(3), 215–225.

_____. (1995, November 5). Putting the system to the test. *The Washington Post, pp.* 16–17.

Susman, W. I. (1979). Personality and twentieth century culture. In J. Higham & P. L. Conkin (Eds.), *New directions in intellectual history* (pp. 212–226). Baltimore: Johns Hopkins University Press.

Wynne, E. A. (1989a). Transmitting traditional values in contemporary schools. In L. Nucci (Ed.), *Moral development and character education* (pp. 19–36). Berkeley, CA: McCutchan.

_____. (1989b). Managing effective schools: The moral element. In M. Holmes, K. Leithword, & D. Musella (Eds.), *Educational policy for effective schools* (pp. 128–142). Toronto: OISE Press.

Yu, T. (2004). *In the name of morality: Character education and political control.* New York: Peter Lang.

CHAPTER EIGHT

Legislating Character

Moral Education in North Carolina's Public Schools

AARON COOLEY

The young men who follow me around of their own free will, those who have the most leisure, the sons of the very rich, take pleasure in hearing people questioned; they themselves often imitate me and try to question others. I think they find an abundance of men who believe they have some knowledge but know little or nothing. The result is that those whom they question are angry not with themselves but with me. They say: "That man Socrates is a pestilential fellow who corrupts the young." If one asks them what he does and what he teaches to corrupt them, they are silent, as they do not know. (Plato trans. 1975)

SOCRATES FROM THE *APOLOGY*

Character education cannot be covered in ten minutes a day. It must be at the heart of the entire education program...Character can't be taught as a course, it is a way of living. As President Bush has said, "Our children must learn to make a living, but even more, they must learn to live." (Paige 2003, 3)

ROD PAIGE, UNITED STATES SECRETARY OF EDUCATION

Living to Learn

Despite the tremendous differences between the present day United States and ancient Athens, these cultures share a common trait of concern about character and morality—especially in their society's youth (Euben 1997). This chapter illustrates that the public and its representatives continue to be concerned about how young citizens act in society and what they learn in school about morality. The paper pays particular interest in specific and articulated attempts to shape the moral attitudes of students through character education. Specifically, it will look at legislative efforts concerning character education undertaken by the North Carolina General Assembly to set guidelines for what is taught to students throughout the state. From all accounts, the program passed in North Carolina is indicative of the nationwide movement towards character education (Spring 2002).

The first section of the chapter will look at the background and history of the character education movement, from its idealistic philosophical basis to its conservative policy agendas. The next section will discuss the precise aspects of the relevant legislation of the "Student Citizen Act of 2001" as well as North Carolina's broader commitment to education beyond mere vocational training. The third part will delve into philosophical questions raised by the legislation. Here, it will draw on the work of Richard Rorty for a philosophic policy analysis. The conclusion will assert that a reorientation of North Carolina's character education policy is needed if in fact the articulated legislative intent of a more just and moral society is to be achieved. At its heart, this alteration would focus on increased emphasis on a shared commitment to public service in our nation's democratic arenas (Barber 1992).

The Foundations of Character Education

Education of any sort can be thought of as a moral enterprise. As American public education has become increasingly secular, there have been several attempts to replace the religious nature of moral education that was common in public schools. Most initiatives regarding character education have common roots. These connections come from an adherence to a psychological and philosophical paradigm that believes virtues can be simply taught and learned.

Beginning in the 1970s, moral development and value clarification theories were beginning to be seen as a possible replacement and a potential secular remedy to the void left by removing religion from moral education. Instead of being taught that an external (and omnipotent) authority judges the rightness of human actions, young people were encouraged to develop their own, personal frameworks for moral and ethical judgment. Many of these notions have their historical roots in the line of psychologists that includes Abraham Maslow (1954, 1959) and Jean Piaget (1965, 1977). These trends in humanistic psychology continued to gain influence in the works of Howard Kirschenbaum (1977) and Lawrence Kohlberg (1981, 1984, 1987). Also, there were a number of other authors who shaped and expanded these theories, including Doyle (1975), Damon (1978), and Power (1989). What is interesting at this point is that the introduction of a set of conservative values and a right-leaning social agenda were not a part of this discourse. In fact, the most influential writers in character education would come to disparage this earlier work.

As diverse as these individuals' interpretations were, their commonalities strongly focused on the notion of what can be described as the quantification and labeling of human ethical judgment. The graphing of morality, the creation of pyramid charts of development, and the rigidity of ethical stages rose quickly in popularity throughout this time period. In short, many of these psychological theories stressed individual choice and development in moral decisions. The overriding perception that ethics of this type was mere relativism and that "anything goes" gave character educators ample fodder to attack the supposed moral laxity and relativism of the era and, then, to call for a change of course in moral education.

As such, a majority of the ideas of moral stages and development have been critiqued and the ideas have fallen out of favor in many circles. Additionally, serious questions have been raised about the universality of such research across cultures and among different ethnic groups; questions regarding embedded gender biases within these theories have also emerged (Gilligan 1993). Yet, despite the criticisms from all sides, work is still being done in moral development. A particularly disturbing offshoot is *Building Moral Intelligence: The Seven Essential Virtues That Teach Kids to Do the Right Thing* by Michele Borba (2001), which links moral development to the realm of intelligence.

Having mentioned the deep background on moral development, the next step is to discuss the origins of the movement that became the modern character education initiative. This process of creation took place during the tenure of William J. Bennett (1993, 1995, 2000, 2001) as Secretary of Education in the mid-1980s. Bennett's high-profile and elevated platform gave great emphasis to reforms in education. In a well-known speech, published in *Our Country, Our Children: Improving America's Schools and Affirming the Common Culture* (1988), he proclaimed a need for the "3 C's" of education. Namely, content, character, and choice needed to move to the forefront of American public education in order to save the schools. Bennett's call was heard by a sympathetic and well-financed audience. His work galvanized interest in combating the deficiency of moral clarity in society through a secular moral education program. Thomas Lickona (1983, 1992) expanded upon the type of sentiment advanced by Bennett. He placed character as the primary objective of education. In particular, his *Educating for Character* (1991) became a virtual template for the traits pushed by the most influential conservative policy organizations and for character education legislation, including that of North Carolina.

With these intellectual foundations, two lobbying and advocacy groups rose to prominence seeking a secular character education program in public schools. The Character Counts! Coalition and The Character Education Partnership began to have remarkable success in convincing legislators at the state and federal levels to begin funding pilot programs in the early to mid-nineties to combat the litany of problems (violence, teen pregnancy, dropping out) in public schools that they saw as coming from a lack of character education. Central to these programs was the desire to rebut the moral relativism of earlier efforts on moral development that character education's supporters saw as having contributed to the present moral crisis.

Bipartisan support for character education continued to grow and Congress declared a national Character Counts! week in 1994. In the years following this initial legislative program, states began to explore broader use of character education across the curriculum as a tool of educational reform. With pilot programs coming to an end, many states sought to permanently codify character education into the curriculum through legislative means.

Before leaving this context, two preliminary points must be made to describe what might be the possible motivations for this movement. First, it appears that the movement is an attempt to intervene in the demographic and cultural changes occurring in the United States' population. E.D. Hirsch's *Cultural Literacy* (1993) and Allan Bloom's *The Closing of the American Mind* (1987) are the intellectual progenitors of a change-resistant type of domestic policy that is at best socially conservative and at worst xenophobic. Clearly, this movement is central to the conservative political restoration; it plays a strong role in the larger landscape of education as a political issue (Apple 1996; Shor 1986; Spring 1972, 1998a, 1998b, 2002). Careful observers cannot miss the ethnocentrism that pervades the call to reform our youth based on character education.

Second, the rise of interest in the morality of students must be seen as a product of an increasingly pan-optic culture (Foucault 1977; Rabinow 1984). Specifically, the increased acuity of the social sciences to quantify and track the rates and prevalence of any number of illicit behaviors among young people has fed the impression that there are more "traditionally" immoral actions occurring now than in the past among the nation's youth. In fact, we may just be more accurate in our data collection about our ubiquitous social problems. Therefore, we may be suffering from hyper-empiricism and an over-reliance on malleable statistics—not necessarily seeing a precipitous increase in "immoral" behaviors. The point here is that certain behaviors have become the objects of statistical knowledge that were unquantifiable in previous times (Hacking 1975, 1990, 1995, 1999; Rose 1999) and that are now understood in ways that would have been incomprehensible to previous moral paragons. These new modes of knowledge have transformed the way in which we are able to think about morality; data sets, percentages, risk factors, causes, and correlation have altered our ability to comprehend moral problems as an issue that can be affected by legislation, public policy, and social tinkering.

It is within this larger cultural framework of negative reactions to the changes in America's demographics and the refinement of our ability to "know" the facts of immorality that this inquiry proceeds. North Carolina's attempt to legislate traits of good character to its young citizens fits squarely within this framework.

North Carolina's Character Education Initiative and Its Constitutional Foundation

The primary vehicle to legislate character education in North Carolina's public schools is the "Student Citizen Act of 2001" and several related statutory provisions. Supporting these mandates is a handbook issued by the Department of Public Instruction meant to aid local school districts in crafting their individual district plans, which is entitled *Character Education: Informational Handbook & Guide for the Support and Implementation of the Student Citizen Act of 2001 (Character and Civic Education)* (hereinafter *Character Education*). Before moving to discuss the specifics of this legislation, it is instructive to look at the constitutional foundation for moral education in North Carolina.

Following the Civil War, several sections were added to North Carolina's Reconstruction Constitution of 1868 that reaffirmed the responsibility of the state for public education. Article 1, Section 15 stated: "**Education**. The people have a right to the privilege of education, and it is the duty of the State to guard and maintain that right" (Orth 1993, 51). Further, Article IX, Section 1 added: "**Education encouraged**. Religion, morality, and knowledge being necessary to good government and the happiness of mankind, schools, libraries, and the means of education shall forever be encouraged" (Orth 1993,144). The essence of these words might well underlie the highest aspirations of a democracy aiming to develop an informed and character-laden citizenry. Significantly, this section emphasized the state's institutions and their processes as vehicles for realizing the educational mandate. The present extension of this state responsibility for religion, morality, and knowledge comes through the public schools in the form of a character education initiative.

North Carolina's effort to fulfill this constitutional mandate came through a legislative action in Section 28.36 of Senate Bill 1005, The Appropriations Act of 2001, in the Long Session of the 2001 North Carolina General Assembly. That section describes the public policy designed to meet the state's constitutional obligation as follows: "The State Board of Education shall use funds appropriated in this act for character education to develop a model character education curriculum for the public schools" (S.L. 2001–424). The main thrust of the accompanying "Student Citizen Act of 2001" is the involvement of students in the mechanics of democracy and the addition of character education.

The act's two foci are these: "*Modifications to the social studies curriculum to instruct students on participation in the democratic process and to give them hands-on experience in participating in the democratic process*" (S.L 2001–363). On face value, these are unequivocally positive goals, but, as I will discuss in a later section of this chapter, it will become clear why positive aims are not enough for the program to succeed.

The state often sets educational policies and then gives local school districts some choice in coming up with its own way of meeting the requirements; the character education legislation follows this general mold. Generally, the element of statutory choice is fairly minimal in that districts usually adopt extremely similar plans to meet state standards; character education falls prey to this common policy outcome. As one can imagine, there is not very much room for variation when the state mandates that the list of traits below be put into the curriculum.

In North Carolina, the law states: "Character Education.—*Each local board of education shall develop and implement character education instruction with input from the local community. The instruction shall be incorporated into the standard curriculum and should address the following traits*" (S.L. 2001–363). It does not specify what type of input would be welcome or incorporated from the local community, but one can imagine anything too controversial or that questions the purpose of the entire enterprise would not be of great concern to the local administrators. Regardless, the law moves quickly to listing the most important traits that need to be taught in North Carolina's schools. Again, there is no mention of why these traits have not been taught previously or why reading a novel in a literature course should provide exposure to these traits without having to resort to didactic lecturing. These complications are obviously not a concern for the policymakers as the list of the most important traits includes:

1. Courage.—Having the determination to do the right thing even when others don't and the strength to follow your conscience rather than the crowd; and attempting difficult things that are worthwhile.
2. Good judgment.—Choosing worthy goals and setting proper priorities; thinking through the consequences of your actions; and basing decisions on practical wisdom and good sense.
3. Integrity.—Having the inner strength to be truthful, trustworthy, and honest in all things; acting justly and honorably.
4. Kindness.—Being considerate, courteous, helpful, and understanding of others; showing care, compassion, friendship, and generosity; and treating others as you would like to be treated.
5. Perseverance.—Being persistent in the pursuit of worthy objectives in spite of difficulty, opposition, or discouragement; and exhibiting patience and having the fortitude to try again when confronted with delays, mistakes, or failures.
6. Respect.—Showing high regard for authority, for other people, for self, for property, and for country; and understanding that all people have value as human beings.
7. Responsibility.—Being dependable in carrying out obligations and duties; showing reliability and consistency in words and conduct; being accountable for your own actions; and being committed to active involvement in your community.
8. Self-Discipline.—Demonstrating hard work and commitment to purpose; regulating yourself for improvement and restraining from inappropriate behaviors; being in proper control of your words, actions, impulses, and desires; choosing abstinence from pre-

marital sex, drugs, alcohol, and other harmful substances and behaviors; and doing your best in all situations.
(S.L. 2001–363)

Again on face value, these traits can be social positives for individuals and larger social communities. However, the program's asserted claims to universal values, conservative social agenda, and possibly intolerant interpretations come through and will be a part of my later critique of the law and character education policy.

There is also a handbook provided by the Department of Public Instruction to help the educational communities across the state to implement this legislation across the curriculum. It makes sense to briefly mention several parts of the manual to provide a full picture of North Carolina's character education discourse. The manual begins with a central question: "WHAT IS CHARACTER EDUCATION?...Character Education is a national movement creating schools that foster ethical, responsible, and caring young people by modeling and teaching good character through an emphasis on universal values we all share" (Character Education 2002, 2). It continues: "Character education may address such critical concerns as student absenteeism, discipline problems, drug abuse, gang violence, teen pregnancy and poor academic performance" (Character Education 2002, 2). Despite warnings that "it is not a 'quick fix' or silver-bullet cure-all" (Character Education 2002, 2), the implication of the manual content is that character education can cure societal ills, that character education needs to be taught, and that the whole program is easy to start.

To implement a character education program, the handbook provides extensions of the codified character traits and expands on them for use by local school boards as well as serving as a resource for teachers. An example of an extension the handbook makes from the standards to the beginnings of a curricular unit follows:

> **5. Diversity.** Reverend Martin Luther King, Jr. had a dream that one day his children would be judged, "not by the color of their skin, but by the content of their character." That dream becomes a real possibility when we realize that nearly all cultures, world religions and schools of thought have their most basic tenet in common—TREAT OTHERS THE WAY THAT YOU WANT TO BE TREATED. Many refer to this as the "Golden Rule." Words and languages may change; in Judaism it is stated as "What you hate, do not do to anyone" and in Hindu as "Do nothing to thy neighbors which thou wouldst not have them do to thee," but they all yield the most common character trait of RESPECT. Appreciating diversity begins with knowing and understanding those things we have most in common. (Character Education 2002, 5)

I see this conflation of difference among social groups as sealing the fate of the character education regime by reverting to such simplistic answers. This fundamental misunderstanding of cultural difference is just another complication in the mounting problems associated with the present character education initiative.

Problems with Character: The Need for a Critical Perspective

It would be politically expedient and popular to uncritically accept this character education initiative as it currently stands. Unfortunately, there are several problems with the legislation and the accompanying handbook in their aims, justification, and scope. I must question if the program is really geared towards achieving North Carolina's constitutional mandate and if it is providing a social environment that is hospitable to increasing access to education with its requisite focus on religion, moral-ity, and knowledge. These concerns are distressing as they counter the stated objectives of the leg-islation and inhibit the true fulfillment of the state's responsibility to its citizens.

I will suggest some preliminary problems with the initiative. Then, I will discuss the major errors that frame the most fundamental problems with the legislation, which prompts my use of Richard Rorty's theoretical work on community and democracy. I end the section by foreshadowing the pol-icy suggestions that would reorient the aims and outcomes of the program. It should be clear that my comments are on the epistemological aims and justifications of the character education effort. In this theoretical arena, I forgo an analysis of the practical struggles of working character into an already overloaded curriculum. My critique proceeds at a deeper level that suggests that structural problems with the initiative and the chronic social ills within the society engendered by it will still exist even if character education was flawlessly taught and the entire program was well funded—both of which are certainly not guaranteed.

The first troublesome aspect of the character education program is its claim to universal values and universal applicability. Many authors have suggested that all people around the world share a common set of ethical commitments. However, works such as Samuel Huntington's *The Clash of Civilizations and the Remaking of the World Order* (1997) assert that there are stark differences among cultures and that their values and goals are incommensurable. Differences within a culture, such as the United States, are less strong but, nonetheless, universalism in values among all groups and all people in our diverse country glosses over profound differences. Regardless, there must be move-ment beyond the relativism vs. universalism debate, as it hampers the creation of a more democra-tic, pragmatic, and realistically ethical country. As such, in contrast to the assertion of universalism in character education, there needs to be a focus on developing shared values in school and society. However, it would be a mistake to assume that these ethical values exist in students' minds *a priori*. Instead, these values must be developed through democratic agreement and relevant teaching and not through fallacious appeals to a set of universal values that are merely posted on the wall or read out of a textbook.

Another preliminary point must be emphasized here, as it goes to the legitimacy of the state's ability to inculcate students with virtues and character traits that the state itself has yet to fully estab-lish. Essentially, the failure to achieve a just and equal society outside of school must be confront-ed in schools, especially when addressing the character of children. It is difficult to demand that students believe in this program that values high ideals, when, at the same time, their lives are being affected by economic, tax, and social policies that do not reflect the beneficence of the character traits that are to be required of them in their lives as students and budding citizens. Students are aware of the palpable injustice they are confronted by when they enter deteriorating schools and are taught by overburdened and under-prepared teachers. "Do as we say, not as we do" should not become the nation's domestic and social policy.

Further, the above point hints at the lack of a coherent message to promote equality in the leg-islation. Without promoting equality among all of North Carolina's citizens as a central focus of a character program, too much ethical action can fall through the cracks. There must be an emphasis on ethics leading to greater equality if a character education initiative is to be fundamentally success-ful and change the social and political landscape of the state and, eventually, the nation.

While there are sections of the initiative that suggest a link between character in schools and character in society, these efforts are not strong enough. A society bereft of character, one that only emphasizes values in school and does not reflect them in the public square (or in its government's public policy), is setting children up to fail in meeting their parents' and society's ethical expectations. My thesis, here, is that the character education program needs a sustained effort beyond classroom instruction that overlaps with and extends the lessons of school to support—and not undercut—students' ethical choices.

Having addressed these initial concerns, I will continue with the two main issues that set up my discussion of Rorty. The issues I address can be categorized in two ways. One is a logical dilemma and the other is a political predicament. Unfortunately, in the end, they are interrelated in their likely negative outcomes.

The logical error in the current character education plans exists in its insistence on a developmental path from character traits to a fully formed and developed moral student/citizen. In this presently asserted conception of morality, growth in ethics is first linked to a sense of political citizenship, which implies a tie to a greater polity. The next step is to advance a reinvigorated social studies curriculum that stresses involvement with democracy. Again, this implies a discussion of issues within a larger social sphere. It suggests a highly social and interactive sense of moral action with others. Next, this policy package uses character education as the vehicle for carrying out the state constitutional mandate of providing education beyond mere vocational training.

This is the point at which the logic falls apart and the path to moral clarity becomes cloudier. In the first two instances, there is a collective and democratic sense of morality that entwines the individual to the larger polis. Then, the focus changes from this active, reciprocal relationship of the citizen among citizens to the notion of a moral actor looking out for his or her individual best interests. This stems from the individualistic language of the traits. Certainly, a successful moral education program for youth should not be partial in its scope, and it should certainly not lack a coherent emphasis geared towards greater democratic action. To reiterate, the logical problem is in moving from individual ethical action to the interaction with a larger social group. It seems that at present the character education program fails to address this fundamentally important ethical paradox.

The second problem is a political one. It centers on what problems would still exist in a school filled with students who exemplified all these traits. I would suggest that even in this utopian atmosphere, there would inevitably be social problems that would reveal the epistemological failure of the program. The neo-liberal aim of the program—to teach students a billiard ball sense of individualistic morality—is reflected in it being titled the "Student Citizen Act." By not including a greater sense of collective action to the polity, the individual nature of the program is stressed and the larger social sphere is neglected. Serving individual interests at the expense of the greater polity amounts to a marketization of ethics and, in a market of any sort, there are capital losses and bankruptcies, neither of which should be acceptable in the moral education of students.

In conclusion, the preceding section and this section of the chapter have provided an outline of North Carolina's commitment to character and moral education. The analysis of the text of the bills and the handbook hints at my larger philosophical critique. Although I commend the North Carolina General Assembly for its effort, I wish that the program went further, as it is presently too individualistic in thinking about the nature of character and ethical action. Further, statements that promote good character are only effective if they promote good character in practice. Just getting everyone to think that they have the traits of good character does not make them act in accordance with their claimed knowledge. The lesson is simple—ethical action should come before an epistemology of what is thought to be right action.

My primary suggestion for reform is to include a more egalitarian frame for notions of character education—that is, the discussion of character in the discourse of creating a more just democracy that fulfills its commitment to its most disadvantaged citizens, not merely inculcating students with claimed universal values. Leaving the specifics of the democratic action, public interest, and social welfare on the table undercuts the legislation's full potential and hampers its efficacy. I will proceed with my critique by applying the work of Richard Rorty to the issues raised by character education. Rorty's writing is relevant because of its insistence on a sense of ethical action in the context of a larger political structure, especially his notion of social hope. Therefore, his work is vital to the critique I have mounted against the individualistic program.

Pragmatism, Rorty, and Character Education

This section will utilize the thought and work of neo-pragmatist Richard Rorty to suggest a reorientation of the character education program in North Carolina and similar programs around the country. Rorty is useful to this project because he is hopeful about the chances for positive and democratic social change through a greater sense of ethical and political solidarity. His work is extremely pertinent to the character education initiative because it provides a framework for positive ethical action that holds all members of a democratic community accountable for the ethical actions that citizens take. Stressing the social significance of ethical and democratic action would certainly improve the current character education program. Before reaching this conclusion, however, a brief look at the roots of American pragmatism is warranted to fully understand Rorty's views and their use in helping to achieve a better program.

The philosophical currents that developed into what would become pragmatism were strongly anchored in the liberal tradition of political philosophy. Compared to European philosophy of the period, pragmatism with its American provenance was considered provincial and unsophisticated. Pragmatism was considered by many foreign philosophers even to be unphilosophical because of its practicality when compared to other established traditions in philosophy. The lectures given by C.S. Peirce at Harvard University garnered initial attention to this budding philosophy and were collected in *Pragmatism as Principle and Method of Right Thinking* (1997). Peirce had selected pragmatism over practicalism as the name for this new group of ideas based on its positive English language impression (much the same way that Comte picked the name positivism for his new philosophy).

The commonality between Peirce and William James, another early pragmatist and author of *Pragmatism* (1975), comes from the instrumentality of their ideas. That is, Peirce and James stressed the evaluation of the rightness or wrongness of an idea on how well it worked. Their work can also be linked to the English utilitarians as it also brought philosophy down from the stars (metaphysics) and focused it on the social realm (ethics). Indeed, James' connection to J. S. Mill is made evident by the dedication of his *Pragmatism* to the famed utilitarian. This displacing of metaphysics in the early period of pragmatism links us to a similar and much more recent tectonic shift in philosophy.

This change in modern philosophy came in Richard Rorty's *Philosophy and the Mirror of Nature* (1979). In it, Rorty argues that philosophy as a method should be removed from its high pedestal and should eschew its role as the adjudicator and arbiter of disputes among other intellectual disciplines. This momentous volume's conclusions were largely ignored by many of Rorty's former analytical colleagues; however, to other scholars searching for a different view of philosophy, his work was a revelation. The work demarcates a line in Rorty's own work that mirrors the break pragmatism made with metaphysics. It also marks Rorty's emancipation from the analytical tradition and sets up his many fruitful years exploring both old and new pragmatism.

With this background on pragmatism and on Rorty, I can move to discussing why Rorty's work is particularly useful in looking at how character education could be altered. Specifically, his *Philosophy and Social Hope* (1999) is of immense utility—in part, because this work lends insight to Rorty's views on Peirce, James, and his intellectual idol, John Dewey (1981). Rorty's version of pragmatism draws on the work of these three authors (although his interpretations of their work continues to be critiqued), as well as his own wide-ranging knowledge of literary sources and continental philosophy.

I suggest that character education programs be altered to reflect the philosophic progress made by Rorty's version of pragmatism. The first part of this change is related to his anti-Platonic stance. Rorty characterized his views on moving away from metaphysics in the following way:

> The title 'Hope in Place of Knowledge' [a chapter from *Philosophy and Social Hope*] is a way of suggesting that Plato and Aristotle were wrong in thinking that humankind's most distinctive and praiseworthy capacity is to know things as they really are—to penetrate behind appearance to reality. That claim saddles us with the unfortunate appearance—reality distinction and with meta-physics: a distinction, and a discipline, which pragmatism shows us how to do without. I want to demote the quest for knowledge from the status of end-in-itself to that of one more means towards greater human happiness. (Rorty 1999, xiii)

Building from Rorty's anti-metaphysical assertion and his Deweyan roots, I suggest a change of direction for the character education program that rejects the metaphysics implicit in the present regime.

Rorty's work is fundamentally democratic in spirit and here his connection to Dewey is at its strongest. Hence, when confronted with difficult questions Rorty puts the question back to the people and asserts that the most essential elements of democracy such as debate and cooperation will assist us in having the best decision emerge. In the following passage, he describes several of the benefits of democracy and the connection to character education should become clear:

> My candidate for the most distinctive and praiseworthy human capacity is our ability to trust and to cooperate with other people, and in particular work together so as to improve the future…These projects aim at improving our institutions in such a way that our descendants will be still better able to trust and cooperate, and will be more decent people than we ourselves have managed to be. In our century, the most plausible project of this sort has been the one to which Dewey devoted his political efforts: the creation of a social democracy; that is, a classless, casteless, egalitarian society. (Rorty 1999, xiv)

The goals Rorty articulates are essential to social progress. The current character education program, in not adopting these types of goals, missed an opportunity to direct the state's youth towards growing into a more benevolent populace. Without the framework offered by Rorty, I fear that we risk future generations of young people who will only act with a myopic sense of self-interest derived from the most puerile elements of popular culture (Barber 2007).

Also central to reorientation of the present character education program is accepting a different paradigm for understanding moral truth and ethical knowledge. This is a preeminent problem for character education in its current form as it appeals to an abstract universalism and an un-tethered rationality. I suggest replacing the "foundational" type of character education that elusively searches for certainty in truth and ethics with pragmatic goals that might actually be achieved. Rorty's suggestion for replacing certainty with social hope is the inspiration for my proposal to reorient North

Carolina's character education program in this manner. The change would move from developing decontextualized traits in individual students to guiding students to an ever greater sense of empathy for their fellow citizens.

To more fully extrapolate this point, it is instructive to analyze Rorty's view on reason and the need to develop shared values in a democratic community. He explains:

> The idea of a universally shared source of truth called 'reason' or 'human nature' is, for us pragmatists, just the idea that such discussion *ought* to be capable of being made conclusive. We see this idea as a misleading way of expressing the hope, which we share, that the human race as a whole should gradually come together in a global community, a community which incorporates most of the thick morality of the European industrialized democracies. It is misleading because it suggests that the aspiration to such a community is somehow built into every member of the biological species. (Rorty 1999, xxxii)

This sentiment is certainly at odds with the current program. Giving up the search for universal moral truth in this case is not a relativist position—it is a pragmatic one. As such, Rorty is reiterating a necessary point on the fundamental notion that differences among social populations exist and that these differences are reflective of substantial disagreements over values and sources of truth.

Rorty continues describing the benefits of pragmatism, which also has positive implications for my suggestions in altering the character education program:

> Pragmatists—both classical and 'neo'—do not believe that there is a way things really are. So they want to replace the appearance—reality distinction by that between descriptions of the world and of ourselves which are less useful and those which are more useful. When the question 'useful for what?' is pressed, they have nothing to say except 'useful to create a better future.' (Rorty 1999, 27)

This should not be seen as moral turpitude, but instead as acknowledgment of history, culture, and change. Pragmatism gives you the ability to hit moving ethical targets while still acknowledging that you, too, are moving. That moral standards and cultural norms change is not acknowledged by the current character education program, which is a substantial flaw even though its proponents see it as a fundamental guiding beacon of strength.

Further, Rorty provides direction on distinguishing good ethical actions from bad ones. If these were heeded in character education, it would certainly make the program more useful. He states: "When asked, 'And what exactly do you consider good?,' pragmatists can only say, with Whitman, 'variety and freedom,' or, with Dewey, 'growth.' 'Growth itself,' Dewey said, 'is the only moral end'" (Rorty 1999, 28). It is inconceivable to think that this would be a satisfactory answer in many arenas. However, with the framework offered earlier, this notion of growth would occur in a system geared towards the common good and not the individual interests of singular citizens as in the present character education program.

Central to this process of change in the character program would be the expansion of our sense and notion of humanity. This must be taken seriously as it is key to character education. Rorty describes here what he sees as the importance of expanding this concept of humanity:

> But you *can* aim at ever more sensitivity to pain, and ever greater satisfaction of ever more various needs. Pragmatists think that the idea of something nonhuman luring us human beings on should be replaced with the idea of getting more and more human beings into our community—of taking the needs and interests and view of more and more diverse human beings into account. (Rorty 1999, 82)

Attempts to initiate Rorty's notion into public policy could have profoundly positive effects on students' evolving or "growing" character. Rorty's novel American vision of philosophy must be vitalized. In the schools of North Carolina and elsewhere, programs of character education, positive as policymakers may think they might be, require significant reorientation that recognizes this philosophical growth. The wisdom of Rorty comes in his utility and sympathetic notion of social hope. Giving up the quest for certainty in favor of hope will provide us the best chance for a future character education program that allows students to grow in a moral framework that fits with real life and their backgrounds.

Character Education in a Moral Society

In seeking character education in public schools, the focus must be on the process of improving social progress through the actions of young citizens, especially in conjunction with each other. We must stress the social nature of ethics and morality and move away from the individualistic ethics that are asserted and supported by the legislation. This would counterbalance one of the frailties of the current program—that it does not necessitate critical self or group analysis of moral action. When thoughts about ethical actions become unreflective, they cease to be moral.

Without reflection on the inequalities of the country, democracy will cease to have its positive meaning and our civic participation will wither (see Callan 1997; Shapiro 1999; Macedo 2000). It is essential to interlock character and civics to connect right personal action with right group and public action. We must extend the benefits of economic, technological, and social progress to all of the country's citizens. If some in our society are doomed to poor schools, unfair tax policies, and limited opportunity, then the character of the nation will need much more than the alteration to the curriculum I am suggesting. Additionally, social foundations scholars must work to alter this character education regime both in our classrooms and in the educational policy arena. Much future work is needed to frame theoretical and practical paths on these fronts.

In closing, we should remember Rorty's prediction for the future, written as if he were looking back from the year 2096:

> Until the last 50 years, moral instruction in America had inculcated personal responsibility, and most sermons had focused on salvation. Today morality is thought of neither as a matter of applying the moral law nor as the acquisition of virtues but as fellow feeling, the ability to sympathize with the plight of others. (Rorty 1999, 249)

This sense of solidarity should be heeded. If steps are taken currently, we can avoid the disastrous predictions Rorty provides in the remainder of his hypothetical retrospective. In essence, we must use efforts for character education to emphasize "that everything depends on keeping our fragile sense of American fraternity intact" (Rorty 1999, 251).

We must use policy initiatives such as character education as engines of social change. We must use current social and economic inequalities in our nation and the world, as well as the misdeeds in history, as examples of errors in character of individuals and groups. Further, we must demonstrate that often inequalities were considered by many people at the time to be taken for granted necessities and thought to be morally correct. This intellectual honesty and recognition of roadblocks to social betterment and improvement of the human condition must be communicated to students. The motto and the imperative statement of a reoriented character education program must be that "much is left to be done." Hence, the addressing of problems that confront students outside of school within the framework of character education will begin to make critical links between the lessons of greater social sympathy in the classroom and benevolent action in life.

References

Apple, Michael. 1996. *Cultural Politics and Education*. New York: Teachers College Press.

Ball, Stephen (Ed.). 1990. *Foucault and Education: Discipline and Knowledge*. London, England: Routledge.

Bar-On, Revuen and James Parker (Eds.). 2000. *The Handbook of Emotional Intelligence: Theory, Development, Assessment, and Application at Home, School, and in the Workplace*. San Francisco: Jossey-Bass.

Barber, Benjamin. 1992. *An Aristocracy of Everyone: The Politics of Education and the Future of America*. New York: Oxford University Press.

_____. 2007. *Consumed: How Markets Corrupt Children, Infantilize Adults, and Swallow Citizens Whole*. New York: Norton.

Barry, Brian. 2001. *Culture and Equality: An Egalitarian Critique of Multiculturalism*. Cambridge: Harvard University Press.

Bennett, William. 1988. *Our Children and Our Country: Improving America's Schools and Affirming the Common Culture*. New York: Simon & Schuster.

_____. 1993. *The Book of Virtues: A Treasury of Great Moral Stories*. New York: Simon & Schuster.

_____. 1995. *The Moral Compass: Stories for a Life's Journey*. New York: Simon & Schuster.

_____. 2000. *The Policies for and the Promise of an American Education*. Washington, DC: Heritage Foundation.

_____. 2001. *The Broken Hearth: Reversing the Moral Collapse of the American Family*. New York: Doubleday.

Borba, Michele. 2001. *Building Moral Intelligence: The Seven Essential Virtues That Teach Kids to Do the Right Thing*. San Francisco: Jossey-Bass.

Callan, Eammonn. 1997. *Creating Citizens: Political Education and Liberal Democracy*. New York: Clarendon Press.

Casteel, Doyle. 1975. *Value Clarification in the Classroom: A Primer*. Pacific Palisades: Goodyear Publishing Company.

Character Education Information Handbook & Guide for Support and Implementation of the Student Citizen Act of 2001 (Character and Civic Education). 2002. Raleigh, NC: North Carolina Department of Public Instruction, Character Education Office.

Damon, Williams (Ed.). 1978. *Moral Development*. San Francisco: Jossey-Bass.

Dewey, John. 1981. *The Philosophy of John Dewey: Two Volumes in One* (Ed. John McDermott). Chicago: Chicago University Press.

Esipov, B. P. 1947. "I Want to Be Like Stalin" (Trans. George Counts and Nucia Lodge). From a Russian text on pedagogy. New York: Day.

Euben, Peter J. 1997. *Corrupting Youth: Political Education, Democratic Culture, and Political Theory*. Princeton, NJ: Princeton University Press.

Feyerabend, Paul. 1993. *Against Method*. New York: Verso.

Friedman, Milton. 1962. *Freedom and Capitalism*. Chicago: Chicago University Press.

Gardner, Howard. 1999. *Intelligence Reframed: Multiple Intelligences for the 21st Century*. New York: Basic Books.

Gilligan, Carol. 1993. *In a Different Voice: Psychological Theory and Women's Development*. Cambridge: Harvard University Press.

Gordon, David. (Ed.). 2003. *A Nation Reformed: American Education 20 Years after A Nation at Risk*. Cambridge: Harvard Education Press.

Gutmann, Amy. 1999. *Democratic Education with New Preface and Epilogue*. (Rev. ed.). Princeton, NJ: Princeton University Press.

Hacking, Ian. 1990. *The Taming of Chance*. Cambridge, England: Cambridge University Press.

Hawkins, John. 1974. *Mao Tse-Tung and Education: His Thought and Teachings*. New York: Shoe String Press.

Hirsch, E.D. 1993. *The Dictionary of Cultural Literacy* (2nd ed.). Boston: Houghton Mifflin.

Huntington, Samuel. 1997. *The Clash of Civilizations and the Remaking of the World Order*. New York: Touchstone Books.

James, William. 1975. *Pragmatism*. Cambridge, MA: Harvard University Press.

Kirschenbaum, Howard. 1977. *Advanced Value Clarification*. La Jolla, CA: University Associates.

Kohlberg, Lawrence. 1981. *The Philosophy of Moral Development: Moral Stages and the Idea of Justice*. San Francisco: Harper & Row.

_____. 1984. *The Psychology of Moral Development: The Nature and Validity of Moral Stages*. San Francisco: Harper & Row.

_____. 1987. *Child Psychology and Childhood Education: A Cognitive-Development View*. New York: Longman.

Kuhn, Thomas. 1996. *The Structures of Scientific Revolutions* (3rd ed.). Chicago: University of Chicago Press.

Levin-Waldman, Oren. 1996. *Reconceiving Liberalism: Dilemmas of Contemporary Public Policy*. Pittsburgh, PA: Pittsburgh University Press.

Lickona, Thomas. 1983. *Raising Good Children: Helping Your Child through the Stages of Moral Development*. New York: Bantam Books

_____. 1991. Educating for Character: How Our Schools Can Teach Respect and Responsibility. New York: Bantam.

_____. 1992. *Character Development in Schools and Beyond*. (2nd ed.) Washington, DC: Council for Research in Values and Philosophy.

Macedo, Stephen. 2000. *Diversity and Distrust: Civic Education in a Multicultural Democracy*. Cambridge, MA: Harvard University Press.

Marx, Karl. 1974. *Capital*. (3rd ed.) (Samuel Moore and Edward Aveling,, Trans.) London, England: Lawrence and Wishart.

Maslow, Abraham. 1954. *Motivation and Personality*. New York: Harper.

_____. 1959. *New Knowledge in Human Values*. New York: Harper.

Nozick, Robert. 1974. *Anarchy, Utopia and State*. New York: Basic.

Orth, John. 1993. *The North Carolina State Constitution with History and Commentary*. Chapel Hill, NC: University of North Carolina Press.

Paige, Rod. 2003. "Paige Announces New Character Education Effort." In *Education Grants Alert*. 13 no. 46, (pp.1–3).

_____. 1997. *Pragmatism as Principle and Method of Right Thinking: The 1903 Harvard Lectures on Pragmatism*. Albany, NY: State University of New York.

Peirce, Charles S. 1972. *Charles S. Peirce: The Essential Writings*. New York: Harper & Row.

Piaget, Jean. 1965. *The Moral Judgment of the Child* (Trans. Marjorie Gabain). New York: Free Press.

_____. 1977. *The Essential Piaget*. New York: Basic Books.

Plato. 1975. *The Trial and Death of Socrates* (Trans. G.M.A. Grube). Indianapolis, IN: Hackett Publishing.

Power, Clark. 1989. *Lawrence Kohlberg's Approach to Moral Education*. New York: Columbia University Press.

Rawls, John. 1971. *A Theory of Justice*. Cambridge, MA: Harvard University Press.

_____. 1993. *Political Liberalism*. New York: Columbia University Press.

_____. 1999. *A Theory of Justice* (Rev. ed.). Cambridge, MA: Harvard University Press.

Rorty, Richard. 1979. *Philosophy and the Mirror of Nature*. Princeton, NJ: Princeton University Press.

_____. 1998. *Achieving Our Country: Leftist Thought in Twentieth-Century America*. Cambridge, MA: Harvard University Press.

_____. 1999. *Philosophy and Social Hope*. New York: Penguin.

Session Law 2001–363. Enacted by the North Carolina General Assembly. Raleigh, NC: Legislative Services Office.

Session Law 2001–424. Enacted by the North Carolina General Assembly. Raleigh, NC: Legislative Services Office.

Session Law 2003–284. Enacted by the North Carolina General Assembly. Raleigh, NC: Legislative Services Office.

Shapiro, Ian. 1999. *Democratic Justice*. New Haven, CT: Yale University Press.

Shor, Ira. 1986. *Culture Wars: School and Society in the Conservative Restoration, 1969–1984*. Boston, MA:

Routledge & K. Paul.

Spring, Joel. 1972. *Education and the Rise of the Corporate State*. Boston, MA: Beacon Press.

_____. 1998a. *American Education* (8th ed.) Boston, MA: McGraw-Hill.

_____. 1998b. *Education and the Rise of the Global Economy*. Mahwah, NJ: Erlbaum.

_____. 2002. *Political Agendas for Education: From the Religious right to the Green Party* (2nd ed.) Mahwah, NJ: Lawrence Erlbaum Associates.

(This chapter originally appeared in *Educational Studies*, Vol. 43, No. 3 [2008]: 188–205. Published with permission of the American Educational Studies Association [AESA] and Lawrence Erlbaum Associates, Inc.)

CHAPTER NINE

Character Education in Contemporary America

McMorals?

SUZANNE S. HUDD

Character education, the instruction of core ethical values and cultivation of good conduct in the classroom (McClellan, 1999), is increasingly being incorporated in public school curricula across the country. Over the last few years, schools in 48 states have introduced programs in character education as a means to nurture moral behavior among our youth (Gilbert, 2003). Public support for the addition of character education to school curricula is the strongest it has been since the 1950s (McClellan, 1999), and it is bolstered by a variety of statistics related to moral decline. An often-cited survey of 12,000 high school students conducted by the Josephson Institute of Ethics (2002) suggests that children are more likely to steal, cheat, shoplift, and lie to their teacher and parents than they were only a decade ago. Character educators contend that we are experiencing a national "crisis of character" that necessitates the inclusion of formalized curricula in character in public schools. Among the trends they identify are: rising youth violence, growing disrespect for parents, teachers and authority figures, the deterioration of language and increased levels of "self-destructive" behavior such as premature sexual activity, substance abuse and suicide are all presented by (Lickona, 1996; Josephson Institute for Ethics, 2002).

In this era of purported moral decline, the federal government has taken up character education as a cause. Nothing can energize an academic field so strongly as a societal crisis revolving around the field's area of inquiry (Damon & Colby, 1996). So it is with character education. On January 8, 2002, President Bush signed into law the *No Child Left Behind Act of 2001* (NCLB). Much has been written about the strict academic achievement standards imposed in NCLB and their effect within schools across the country. Less frequently noted, however, is the fact that NCLB has tripled federal funding for character education, to nearly $25 million. The funding is being used to both expand the implementation of character education programs, as well as to evaluate their effectiveness.

Thus, for many children, the "hidden curriculum" (Jackson, 1968) is being shifted to a central, more structured place in their daily lives. In this essay, I will explore the extent to which contemporary character education programs are being provided through a "McDonaldization" model. My thesis is that federal sponsorship of character education programs through NCLB has the potential to lead us to what I define as an era of "McMorals." Increasing pressure to fit character education into the national standards movement in education and to employ and fund only "effective" techniques poses a great risk because it ignores the complexity of character development and the importance of acknowledging and working within situational constraints and cultural complexities that naturally affect the process of character development.

Ritzer (2000) defines "McDonaldization" as:

> The process by which the principles of the fast-food restaurant are coming to dominate more and more sectors of American society as well as the rest of the world. (Ritzer, 2000: 1)

He argues that the effects of McDonaldization on our culture have been profound, and that the fast-food operating principles of efficiency, calculability, predictability, and control have become cultural values around which much of our lives are centered. The movement to integrate character education in public school in more formal ways is, in fact, characterized by many of the advantages common to McDonaldization in other industries, including: goods and services are more widely available; the availability of goods and services is not location dependent; people can get what they want instantaneously; goods and services acquire a more uniform quality; fast, efficient goods and services are available to a population with less hours to spare; because of quantification, consumers can more easily compare competing products; and goods and services are of a more uniform quality (Ritzer, 2000, 15–16).

I must preface this analysis by noting that I am a proponent of character education. The literature on college students suggests they exist in a culture where "wrong is right." Surveys demonstrate that college students cheat regularly and that they perceive that faculty do not notice or do not care (McCabe, 1999). Similar trends have been documented at the high school level. A recent study of 4,500 students in public and private high schools across the country found that 72 percent reported one or more instance of "serious cheating" on written work (McCaffrey, 2001). As both an educator and a parent, I support the movement to put discussions of character at the center of our national educational agenda. Although the statistics on moral decline are questioned by some (Kohn, 1998; Hunter, 2000), it is essentially impossible to avoid issues of character in the classroom. Therefore, we must be explicit in our decisions about the ways in which we will provide it.

With this said, I write this essay from a position of great concern. In essence, the introduction of formalized character education into public school curricula alters the educational process. What are the effects of making the "hidden curriculum" visible? Much has been written and discussed about the curricular content of character education programs. I will not address these concerns here. Rather, I will focus on the *process* by which we have chosen to provide instruction in character "for the masses." What are the long-term consequences of altering the processes by which our children learn character? Is it possible that the outcome of school-based character education instills our children with a view of character that is situation-specific? Does school-based character education supplant or support moral conversations in the home? What will the implications be as our schools increasingly provide character education through models that emphasize efficiency, calculability, predictability and control? These are some of the important questions I will address in this essay.

By incorporating funding for character education in NCLB, we have taken the amorphous concept of character and allied it with legislation that emphasizes achievement, quantitative outcome assessment and penalties for schools that fail to perform. There is a long history of measuring academic outcomes. Not so for the "hidden curriculum." We are entering new territory, and I am fearful that the temptation to simplify character will be too great. We are increasingly looking to schools to serve as "surrogate parents" when it comes to moral education (Wilson, 1995: 2). The provision of funds for character education in NCLB, with its orientation to "proven methods" suggests that the expectations for outcomes with respect to character education will be high. The character education "industry," as this seems to be what it is rapidly becoming, is increasingly orienting itself to a McDonaldization model. The development of character, when it is driven by principles of efficiency, control, predictability, and calculability, is a dangerous undertaking. Here, I will consider the many potential pitfalls we may encounter as we move into this uncharted territory.

Efficiency

A primary principle of McDonaldization is efficiency: using the optimum method for getting from one point to the other (Ritzer, 2000: 12). The goal of efficiency is evident in contemporary approaches to incorporating character education into public school curricula. The increased demand for school-based instruction in character has led to the development of standard curricular packages offered by a plethora of organizations and institutes. As Rusnack and Ribich (1997) note:

> A teacher need only open the professionally assembled box and follow the study guide. Occasionally it is necessary to distribute a few pre-made handouts, sprinkle in some wholesome conversation about honesty, respect and responsibility, and reinforce the lesson with a scattered story or two about values. All is right with the world! It's quick, efficient, simple, and easy to use. (11)

Such "pre-packaged" curricula in character offer the advantage of making character education programs accessible to a wider audience. The development of character is a complex process, no doubt made easier by the provision of a common curriculum which can be used as the basis for the creation of a shared language that is utilized throughout the school. Yet, as Lickona (1993) argues virtually everything that goes on in the classroom affects the values and character of students.

Thus, one possible outcome is that formalized instruction in character education may intrude upon the "hidden curriculum," the more subtle instruction in values that teachers provide. Schools that emphasize instruction in a specific list of traits and values, for example, may experience a concurrent reduction in attention to issues such as role modeling and the creation of school climate which also serve to foster character (Milson, 2000). Likewise, "efficient" character education may destroy the complex interrelationship of factors that enhances moral development. This is not to say teachers will no longer serve as good role models, but rather that the shift to formalized character instruction will leave students with less time for informal observation and processing that are essential elements in character development. Even the most ardent proponents of formalized character education argue that isolated character education programs must be reinforced throughout the school because research demonstrates that curricular instruction in character does not build a child's deep understanding of values or provide occasions to act upon these values (Schaeffer, 2003).

Ironically, our current emphasis on efficient character education may ultimately encourage a kind of character development that is rooted in rote behavior. Some proponents of moral character argue that habit forms an important basis for moral behavior (Cole & Kiss, 2000). However, others have noted that morality is similar to language in that it changes with use, and there are many different languages or dialects that can be spoken (Shropshire, 1997). What are the consequences if the character education our children receive at school is never integrated into their daily lives? One possible response: they may come to perceive character as a commodity that is temporal and responsive to the setting in which they find themselves, rather than deeply engrained in their way of being. There are numerous examples in the media that might serve to reinforce this view, e.g., athletes and politicians who routinely practice dishonesty in their private lives but who retain their professional roles. These broader observations, concurrent with what Rusnack and Ribich (1997) refer to as the "character in a box" (p. 11) approach to providing character education may ultimately foster an alternative mindset among our youth: that ethics takes on a new and different meaning outside school walls.

Another potential backlash related to the proliferation of efficient school-based character education programs is the possibility that formalized character education will be perceived as *the solution,* rather than as an important *part* of the solution. Programs funded through the NCLB legislation must incorporate a parental component. This becomes increasingly difficult, however, with the growing number of dual-career and single-parent families. While the involvement of parents is optimal, it is definitely *not* efficient. Thus, the school may come to supplant a portion of the parents' role, rather than support it. Parental approval of character education has been documented (Josephson Institute for Ethics, 2000). However, scholars of character education have yet to examine the implications of these programs for both the quality and quantity of moral conversation at home. While the NCLB legislation stresses parental integration, busy parents may perceive that they have fulfilled their role by attending a school meeting on character. Potentially more detrimental than neglect, however, is inconsistency. What happens when parents actively disagree with a specific value or "lesson" that has been taught in the school setting and, in essence, contradict school-based instruction at home? The answer to this question is complex, and may certainly prove disruptive to 'efficient' instruction in character.

Calculability

It is noteworthy that federal funding for character education has been incorporated within the NCLB legislation, with its primary emphasis on establishing standards for academic achievement. Concurrent with this funding, there has arisen a growing interest in assessing the effects of character education through formalized, largely quantitative evaluation studies (Berkowitz & Bier, 2003, 2004). NCLB prescribes that only programs that are based on scientific research will be eligible for federal funding (No Child Left Behind Act of 2001). Researchers and educators in character education have responded promptly. The Character Education Partnership has received $350,000 in grant funds from the Department of Education to create an online resource for character education (Character Education Partnership, 2003). The web-based clearinghouse provides descriptions of curricula, assessment tools, and information on the latest research.

Few would argue against the need for scientific studies to assess the effectiveness of character education. This will be difficult, however, given the complex array of programs and varied effects they purport to yield. Congressional testimony in support of character education suggests it can be linked to: reductions in violence and school suspensions, increased academic achievement, school reform and an improved understanding of democratic values (House Subcommittee on Early

Childhood, Youth and Families, 2000). This despite the fact that:

> ... educational experts have not yet been given the opportunity to develop these sound scientific conclusions. It is not even known where and how character education has found its greatest success. (*Congressional Record* 2001 March 28: E475)

Others have concurred, describing evidence on the effectiveness of character education as "scant" and "anecdotal" (Hunter, 2000: 154).

If there is one point of consensus in the community of scholars researching character education it is this: character is a complex concept. Research designed to determine whether character education programs create fundamental changes in reasoning and behavior must then, in accordance with the goals of these programs, be multi-faceted. Simple measurements of behavioral disruptions, tardiness, and school expulsions do not, in and of themselves, demonstrate changes in character.

Yet the vast majority of scientific research on character education outcomes has been quantitative (Berkowitz & Bier, 2003).

Policy makers in character education have expressed a particular interest in documenting the relationship between character education and academic outcomes (Fink & McKay, 1999; Schaeffer, 2003). This trend is clearly rooted in the theme of "calculability," as it will provide a potential mechanism for sustained federal interest and funding. There are inherent risks, however, in creating a link between character education and academic achievement in an NCLB framework that is founded on "scientific methods" and rooted in quantitative assessment. Several studies have documented that the burden to meet achievement standards has given rise to a new phenomenon in the classroom: teacher cheating (Kantrowitz & McGinn, 2000; Jacob & Levitt, 2002). While such cases are limited, it will certainly be ironic if formal assessment of character education outcomes produces similar results.

Assessing the effectiveness of character education is a complex process. It is difficult to know whether students who behave well in school will make the "right" choices in the world at large. To truly document the effects of character education on students' character, assessment must be longitudinal and it must examine behaviors that occur both in and out of school. Observations of "real world" behaviors will be necessary in order to fully understand whether the lessons of character taught in the classroom have been fully incorporated into students' behavioral repertoires. Although Fink and McKay (1999) note that 'paper and pencil' tests cannot be used to assess aspects of character, it is questionable whether federal or local authorities will be willing to make the financial and time commitments necessary to fully analyze the effects of character education in these ways.

Of course, my comments presume that the agenda for character education is, in fact, to produce such long-term and fundamental changes in character. There is an alternative scenario: that demonstrating short-term, immediate behavioral change (e.g., a reduction in school violence during the year) will be enough to sustain the character education movement. This seems possible since funding for character education has already been increased in the absence of hard data. While reductions in school violence are certainly worth pursuing, they are not indicative that character education is fulfilling its broader mandate. Perhaps we are simply deferring problems to other settings, or later time points. Despite these unknowns, the perpetuation of a "one size fits all" approach to implementing and assessing character education looms increasingly likely in an era where the future of character education is tied to academic achievement in a model that emphasizes quantitative results.

Predictability

Our "McDonaldized" culture strives for predictability: the assurance that products and services will be the same over time and in all locations. "The success of the McDonald's model suggests that many people have come to prefer a world in which there are few surprises" (Ritzer, 2000: 13). It seems odd to expect predictability in character. Yet despite the many organizations that offer curricular programs for character education in schools (Rusnak & Ribich, 1997), and the wide array of outcomes they arguably produce, the lack of variability among character education curricula is striking. The various templates through which programs in character education are provided all share one commonality: they reduce character to a set of limited principles or values that can be modeled and taught through classroom exercises and procedures. As we read through short lists of values and virtues and the processes for instilling them in our children and classrooms, the solution to our "moral crisis" is, on the surface, simplified.

> Community is different from consensus. To have community, there must be struggles, trials, successes and failures...These are the things that give values their depth and separate them from mere opinion, (Noblit et al., 1996: 206)

Since programs in character education are necessarily rooted in our culture, they are ultimately designed to legitimate it rather than transform it (Hunter, 2000).

Many public school character education programs operate using a system of rewards and punishments. Assemblies are held, and children are publicly acknowledged for positive behaviors. In the real world, however, the rewards of positive behavior are often intrinsic, rather than extrinsic. Likewise, "doing the right thing" (e.g., whistle blowing) often entails going *against* the prevailing organizational wisdom, rather than dutiful compliance with organizational mandates. Kohn (1998) argues that there is considerable body of research indicating that children who are rewarded for prosocial choices such as helping someone, are less likely than other children to repeat the behavior. In sum, our striving for 'predictability' in character may not necessarily produce consistent results because of our tendency to disregard the complex of interrelationship between moral thought social actions.

Again, however, we must return to a discussion of the goals of character education. Kohn (1998) notes that character education can essentially be narrowed down to a set of behavioral guidelines that is intended to create compliant children. He argues that the purpose of many character education programs is to drill students in specific behaviors. Thus, rather than providing them with opportunities for deep thought and reflection on moral choices, children are inspired to act in accordance with prescribed guidelines as a kind of "reflex" reaction to the training they have received.

If we emphasize predictability of outcomes in the development of character education programs, we can almost be assured that our children will not experience opportunities for moral growth through formalized character education. Our society is characterized by what Wilson (1995) describes as "moral dualisms": what we define as 'right' and 'wrong' is not necessarily what we put into practice. Outside the school setting, where social norms sometimes do not function as effectively as "school rules" to constrain behavior, children are left to make sense of which set of morals they should act upon and when. If they have not been given the chance to practice moral decision making in the absence of institutional constraints, they may lack the ability to make "good choices" because their "bad behaviors" have simply been inhibited. Hunter (2000) notes the ultimate aim of moral education is to liberate students from the constraints of social order, rather than to teach adaptation or conformity. However, to a large extent, our public schools have always rewarded conventionality. The consequences of moral predictability are certainly advantageous for teachers and schools. But will they be beneficial to society?

Control

Perhaps the most pivotal question in relation to the implementation of school-based character education is this: whose behavior is it intended to control? Our "McDonaldized" model for creating character has the potential to restrict conduct in many ways. Behaviors and interactions between students, teachers and families are all potentially affected. I will elaborate on the possible consequences for each of these constituent groups below.

The most obvious goal of formalized character education programs is to alter the thinking and behavior of students. Through McDonaldization, customers are controlled in various ways: they receive cues that indicate what is expected of them; structural constraints force them to behave in certain ways, and thus, they come to exhibit internalized taken-for-granted norms which they follow when they enter the fast-food restaurant (Ritzer, 2000: 113). In essence, these principles encourage a reduction in complex thought on the customers' part: I observe a prompt, and I respond automatically.

Standardized programs in character education employ these same strategies. Many pre-packaged character education curricula are accompanied by bright posters and educational pamphlets which can be posted throughout the school. A large sign, emblazoned with the word "respect" certainly provides a distinct behavioral cue. The Character Counts! program (Josephson Institute for Ethics, 2004) offers "gotcha tickets" which can be awarded to students as they are witnessed demonstrating behaviors consistent with one of the desired "pillars of character." Each of these tangible items is designed to reinforce values that are reiterated in the curriculum and to reward desirable behaviors in such a way that they become almost automatic.

The McDonaldization principle of control can also be applied to teachers who are charged with putting character education into practice in the classroom. As "employees," teachers in schools where formal character education curricula are implemented may be asked to both teach character education differently, and to document its effects. These added responsibilities may produce increased stress related to a lack of clarity regarding obligations, rights, objectives, status or accountability (Byrne, 1999). Likewise, teachers may experience at least some uncertainty in terms of their disciplinary role as the school moves toward a system where responses to both good and bad behaviors must be standardized throughout the school to a certain extent, if the program is to be effective.

While the literature suggests that teachers tend to support character education, they also express different opinions about what it should include, and how it should be taught (Mathison, 1998). The effect of character education on teachers may ultimately be analogous to the infusion of technology in the fast-food restaurant. At McDonald's, the cook is not charged with determining when the French fries are ready; rather the computer is programmed to lift them from the oil at a predetermined time. For teachers, the emphasis on standardization and measurable outcomes in character education may lead to reductions in autonomy. To a certain extent, control of the "hidden curriculum" is shifted to administrators who assume responsibility for imparting *THE* character education program to faculty. We know that worker deskilling in the industrial setting can lead to alienation and increased dissatisfaction with work (Braverman, 1974). It will be important to observe and understand the experiences of teachers implementing formal character education programs over time in order to ensure that they do not become estranged from this important part of their role.

People are the greatest threat to the predictability and control inherent in McDonaldization (Ritzer, 2000). While character educators describe their primary audience as children, some have acknowledged, "We do not have a youth problem in our country; we have an adult problem" (Hearing before the Subcommittee on Early Childhood, Youth and Families, 2000: 7). NCLB incorporates parental involvement as an essential element of effective character education, and consequently, many schools seek to foster the commitment of parents and to engage them in an ongoing dialogue on character. Is the goal of parent involvement policies, however, to include parents or to alter their attitudes towards character as well? If we truly have an "adult problem," it seems unlikely that school-based programs will be adequate to counteract the causes of moral decline. Yet it is plausible that the language of character provided in school-based programs will naturally find its way home and perhaps gradually, as this generation comes of age, into our social institutions in such a way that it will ultimately provide a framework for national conversations of character.

Conclusion: McMorals?

The proliferation of character education may stem from the fact that it offers "something for everyone." The proponents of character education outline an expansive set of goals. On March 1, 2000, as he opened the Subcommittee Hearing on the "Role of Character Education in America's Schools," Congressman Michael N. Castle noted:

> . . . some children lack basic values that would not only help them to avoid unwanted pregnancies, drugs, alcohol and violence, but also teach them the importance of being respectful and honest. Today every teacher and every student can articulate the consequences of this neglect. The recent rash of school shootings is one example, but so is the low voter turn-out among young people and their lack of involvement in community organizations. As a result, many Americans are looking to character education as one possible solution to the problems that plague our classrooms and communities. (House Subcommittee on Early Childhood, Youth and Families, 2)

Castle's comments demonstrate the range of expectations that character education programs are typically designed to fulfill. Recurring themes that emerge during Congressional consideration of character education include reducing school violence, providing discipline, increasing academic achievement, and instilling the values of civic mindedness and citizenship. Thus, not only is character education charged with instilling moral habits, it must enhance classroom performance and be comprehensive enough to create good citizens and a sense of community. These goals are multifaceted and complex. However, policy makers continue to look to character education as a panacea for restoring social order.

The provision of funds for character education in NCLB, with its orientation to scientific methods suggests that the expectations for quantifiable outcomes in character will be high. Will we enter an era where educators are held accountable for the "character performance" of their students? In a time when schools must produce annual report cards to document academic progress, to what degree will character education become another important outcome to be measured? The contemporary shift to school-based moral education, coupled with the ongoing emphasis on standards and assessment in our national educational policy has created a ripe set of circumstances for the evolution of "McMorals": character development that is guided by the principles of efficiency, predictability, calculability and control. The extent to which this system will simultaneously foster critical thinking skills that form the basis for complex moral reasoning remains unclear.

A "McDonaldized" approach to character education, with efficient methods, calculable products, predictable programming and controlled results is imbued with great risk. Schwartz (1999) argues that our society suffers from a loss of family structure as a guiding force. We are increasingly turning to social institutions to replace functions once fulfilled in the family.

> The general wail of being overwhelmed and emotionally isolated transcends class, income and ideology...Several cultural trends are converging: the fear of family failure, disconnection and disorder, the recognition that extended family help and interaction has been greatly modified for everyone except first or second generation Americans in some poorer communities....The loss of neighborhood, city and even regional community remains mostly unmeasured, but I believe it has had a huge impact on American society. (Schwartz, 1999: 3)

Proponents of character education will no doubt argue that it is a vehicle through which we might re-establish important connections between family and school. Research has demonstrated that there can be positive effects when parents, teachers, and students are jointly involved in conversations around complex topics such as social justice and prejudice (Jennings et al., 2002). A consensus between parent, child, and teacher on such issues is clearly optimal. Yet, legislators and policy makers appear to be more focused on reaching an agreement on *what* is taught in character education curricula, rather than *how* it is taught. In the end, the process may detrimentally affect the product.

My primary concern is this: recognizing that creativity is thwarted in systems characterized by repetitive and externally imposed demands (Ritzer, 2000), will standardized character education impose upon us a generation of children who prefer habitual moral action over thoughtful moral reasoning? Certainly, this is a potentially devastating outcome in an era where we face a growing number of issues characterized by high levels of moral complexity. It is these 'unintended consequences' (Hunter, 2000) of character education—its impact on the development of moral thinking and the quality of moral conversations in the home—that warrant our immediate attention. That character education can produce positive behavioral changes in school is good, but it is not good enough. If we fail to comprehensively assess whether formalized character education affects the ways in which our children develop character and make ethical decisions in the real world, we risk displacing parents from the process of moral education, and worse, creating a generation of children who lack the skills to process complex moral problems. While this is not the goal of character educators, it may become an inevitable consequence of a movement designed to rationalize and quantify character development.

References

Berkowitz, Marvin & Melinda Bier. 2003, October. "What Works in Character Education." Paper presented at the Annual Conference of the Character Education Partnership.

Berkowitz, Marvin & Melinda Bier. 2004. Research-Based Character Education. *Annals of the American Academy of Political and Social Science* 591: 72–85.

Braverman, Harry. 1974. *Labor and Monopoly Capital.* New York: Monthly Review Press.

Byrne, Barbara M. 1999. The Nomological Network of Teacher Burnout: A Literature Review and Empirically Validated Model." Pp. 15–37 in *Understanding and Preventing Teacher Burnout: A Sourcebook of International and Research Practice,* edited by Roland Vandenberghe and A. Michael Huberman. London, UK: Cambridge University Press.

Character Education Partnership. 2003. "Character Education News: CEP Awarded Grant to Develop Character Education Resource Center." Retrieved November 20, 2003 from http://www.character.org.

Cole, Sally & Elizabeth Kiss. 2000. What Can We Do About Student Cheating? *About Campus* 5 (2): 5–12.

Damon, William & Anne Colby. 1996. Education and Moral Commitment. *Journal of Moral Education* 25: 31–37.

Fink, Kristin & Linda McKay. 1999. *Making Character Education a Standard Part of Education.* Washington, DC: Character Education Partnership.

Gilbert, Susan. 2003 March 18. Scientists Explore the Molding of Children's Morals. *The New York Times* F: 5.

House Subcommittee on Early Childhood, Youth and Families. 2000, March 1.*The Role of Character Education in America's Schools.* Washington, DC: U.S. Government Printing Office.

Hunter, James Davison. 2000. *The Death of Character: Moral Education in an Age Without Good or Evil.* New York: Basic Books.

Jackson, P. 1968. *Life in Classrooms.* Chicago: University of Chicago Press.

Jacob, Brian A. & Steven D. Levitt. 2002 December. Catching Cheating Teachers: The Results of an Unusual Experiment in Implementing Theory. Working Paper 9414. National Bureau of Economic Research.

Jennings, Louise B., Ruth Shagoury Hubbard, & Brenda Miller Power. 2002. Parents and Children Inquiring Together: Written Conversations about Social Justice.*Language Arts*79: 404–415.

Josephson Institute for Ethics. 2004. *Character Counts!* http://www.charactercounts.org.

Josephson Institute for Ethics. 2002. 2002 Report Card: The Ethics of American Youth: Press Release and Data Summary. Retrieved September 3, 2003 from http:// www.josephsoninstitute.org/Survey2002/.

Kantrowitz, Barbara & Daniel McGinn with Ellise Pierce & Erika Check. 2000 June 19. When Teachers Are Cheaters. *Newsweek*: 48.

Kohn, Alfie. 1998. *What to Look for in a Classroom and Other Essays.* San Francisco: Jossey-Bass.

Lickona, Thomas. 1996. Eleven Principles of Effective Character Education. *Journal of Moral Education* 25: 93–100.

Lickona, Thomas. 1993. The Return of Character Education. *Educational Leadership* 51 (3): 6–11.

Mathison, Carla. 1998. How Teachers Feel About Character Education. *Action in Teacher Education* 20 (4): 29–38.

McCabe, Donald L. 1999. Toward a Culture of Academic Honesty. *The Chronicle of Higher Education* 46 (8): B7.

McCaffrey, Meg. 2001. Kids and Cheating, 2001. *School Library Journal* 47 (8): 30.

McClellan, B. Edward. 1999. *Moral Education in America: Schools and the Shaping of Character from Colonial Times to the Present.* New York: Teachers College Press.

Milson, Andrew. 2000. Social Studies Teacher Educators' Perceptions of Character Education. *Theory and Research in Social Education* 28 (2): 144–169.

Noblit, George W. & Van O. Dempsey with Belmira Bueno, Peter Hessling, Doris Kendrick & Reeda Toppin. 1996. *The Social Construction of Virtue: The Moral Life of Schools.* Albany, NY: State University of New York Press.

No Child Left Behind Act of 2001, Pub. L. No. 107–110, 115 Stat. 1425 (2002).

Ritzer, George. 2000.*The McDonaldization of Society.* Thousand Oaks, CA: Pine Forge Press.

Rusnak, Timothy & Frank Ribich. 1997. The Death of Character Education. *Educational Horizons.* 76: 10–13.

Schaeffer, Esther F. 2003. Character Education Makes a Big Difference. *Principal* 82: 36–39.

Schwartz, Pepper. 1999. Quality of Life in the Coming Decades. *Society* 36: 55–60.

Shropshire, William O. 1997. Of Being and Getting: Academic Honesty. *Liberal Education* 83 (4): 24–31.

Wilson, J. Andrew. 1995. Livin' on the Edge: A Look at the Need for Moral Education. Paper submitted to the Educational Resources Information Center, May 10.

(This chapter originally appeared in *Taboo,* Vol. 8, No. 2 [Fall–Winter, 2004]: 113–124. Published with permission of Caddo Gap Press.)

CHAPTER TEN

Would You Like Values with That?

Chick-fil-A and Character Education

DERON BOYLES

"Character education" represents a long-standing staple of U.S. schools. From the "Old Deluder Satan" Law of 1647 to *The New England Primer* in the eighteenth century to McGuffey Readers from the late 1830s (and well into the 1920s), the idea of transmitting core values to the young is so deeply rooted in the history of schooling that "morals" is often assumed to be a "given."[1] Over time, various social and religious concerns melded into a taken-for-granted presupposition that schools should play a major role in transmitting "good character" and fostering character development. In contemporary schools, state curricula often include character education, and a series of organizations have been established to advance the idea that character education is fundamental to schools.

National programs that currently exist include, among others, "Character Counts!" from the Josephson Institute and "A 12-Point Comprehensive Approach to Character Education" from The Center for the 4th and 5th Rs (respect and responsibility). Other national and international organizations include the Character Education Partnership (CEP) and the Institute for Global Ethics.[2] These organizations proclaim themselves to be nonpartisan, and each identifies universal values that should be adopted, though the number of values vary. Michael Josephson developed "Character Counts!," the most widely used character education program in the U.S. Josephson retired from careers in law, business, and education to run the Joseph and Edna Josephson Institute, named for his parents. He serves the organization without a salary, and all proceeds from speaking engagements and written work are stated as going directly back into the nonprofit institute.[3] The Center for the 4th and 5th Rs is led by Thomas Lickona, a professor of educational psychology at the State University of New York-Cortland. The Center for the 4th and 5th Rs is a university bureau committed to "building a moral society and developing schools which are civil and caring communities."[4] Lickona is a widely published author who also serves on the board of the CEP. Josephson and Lickona, however, are not the only ones influencing character education programs. Truett Cathy also influences character education curriculum in the U.S.

Cathy is the founder and CEO of Chick-fil-A, the fast food restaurant headquartered in Georgia. Cathy is also an avowed Christian fundamentalist.[5] Accordingly, he donated an "age-appropriate" (Protestant) Bible to every school library in the state of Georgia in 2003. He is also the financial resource behind the national "Core Essentials " character education initiative based in Georgia, and through his financing, Chick-fil-A sponsors the teacher's guides sent to each school.[6] In addition, Cathy teamed with William Bennett to offer wristbands and cassettes as part of "kid's meals" at various Chick-fil-A stores. The wristbands and cassettes tout such values as "respect," "courage," and "honesty." This essay explores three main lines of inquiry: (1) the specifics of "Core Essentials" as a strategy for teaching character; (2) the role (and ironies) of private businesses influencing public school curricula; and (3) the assumptions inherent in the kind of teaching of character outlined by Core Essentials. Girding this inquiry is a concern about the problematic enterprise of teaching character itself as if it were an unquestionable domain. Further, the larger contexts of childhood obesity findings and Christian influences on and in public spheres will be considered along with Theodore Brameld's *Ends and Means in Education*, John Dewey's *Moral Principles in Education*, and Pierre Bourdieu's *Acts of Resistance* and *Firing Back*.[7] Ultimately, this article offers a critique and raises questions that may be helpful when considering character education and school-business partnerships.

Since Truett Cathy is a fundamentalist Christian as well as a private businessman, this chapter questions the understanding demonstrated by the Georgia state superintendent of schools, Kathy Cox, in a July 1, 2003, letter to Georgia school principals. She wrote that Truett Cathy is "a pioneering businessman" whose "generosity" allowed for an "age-appropriate Bible" to be placed in every school library in the state. She also wrote that Truett Cathy 's "initiative has been completely funded by Mr. Cathy. No state funds have been used to supply this book to your school. Mr. Cathy has a passion for helping children, [sic] and he sees this as another way to encourage the youth of our great state."[8] What does the distinction between state and private funds for Bible purchases and placement mean? Does the fact that a Christian fundamentalist funded a character education program represent any challenges or concerns for, say, students who are Jewish or agnostic or Muslim? Is there any connection between Kathy Cox's endorsement, nay, praise of Truett Cathy and Cox's claim that the term "evolution" is a "buzzword" that should be replaced in the state curriculum of Georgia?[9] If Truett Cathy were actually interested in the welfare of children, why would he promote unhealthy fast-food as part of a character education program that touts "honesty" as a virtue? Indeed, what assumptions are made by Truett Cathy, furthered by the state, and pushed into the hands of teachers by the private, nonprofit Core Essentials organization that Cathy's profits from Chick-fil-A support?

The Program Itself: An Overview of Various Aspects

A visit to the Chick-fil-A website reveals an interesting phenomenon. On the page displaying information regarding Chick-fil-A's support of "Core Essentials," the company also notes the following: "Amid our nation's growing concern for children's character development, Chick-fil-A has found a way to help. Since 2000 we've been a national sponsor of Core Essentials, an educational program that gives teachers and parents tools for imparting key values to elementary-age boys and girls. By teaching inner beliefs and attitudes such as honesty, patience, respect, orderliness and courage, Core Essentials helps children treat others right, make smart decisions, and maximize their potential. The entire program teaches 27 values over a three-year period. To learn more about Core Essentials, contact a Chick-fil-A franchisee in your area."[10]

When you go to the website page and begin reading the paragraph just cited, you are interrupted by the cartoon image of the back of a cow's head. The image then scrawls "eat mor chikin'" across the screen, the very screen that includes the words "character development." It seems inconsistent, at least, to (1) have "more" and "chicken" spelled incorrectly on the page devoted to children's schooling, and (2) for those who would support the general notion of character education and the ensuing lists that accompany the phrase, where do "graffiti" and "interruption" appear on those lists?

Once past the website interruption, however, one can find more information about the program, and it does not take long to understand the underlying point. The website indicates that there is a booklet for teachers to help in the teaching of character. In *Core Essentials: A Strategy for Teaching Character*, the first page of the booklet *qua* teachers' guide outlines three main elements of the program: Identifying Basic Components, Preparation, and Establishing a Routine. Each of the three main elements has subheadings identifying key features indicative of the main elements as well as the overall intent of the larger program. Under "Identify the Basic Components" exists "teacher's guide, bookmarks/tablecards, value-able card, and posters." The teacher's guide is the booklet and tells teachers what to do, when to do it, and how to do it. The subsection that explains elements in the teacher's guide notes that "each month you have age-appropriate materials at two academic levels, K-2 and 3–5. Included in the guide are literature and video suggestions which may be displayed in the library by the media specialist."[11] For the bookmarks/tablecards, the booklet instructs that "the bookmark is perforated and should be separated from the tablecard, which is designed to be folded and placed in a convenient location at home (kitchen counter or table). The parents of each child may then use this tool to emphasize the value through family discussions and activities." For the value-able card, importantly, the booklet reveals that the "...card is a key component which leads to successful implementation of the program. It is designed as the incentive for children who are caught [sic] displaying the value. Each month you will see suggestions in the Teacher's Guide for 'Catching Kids.' Use these ideas to help you choose students who show they understand the value. The card rewards them with a FREE Chick-fil-A Kid's Meal. *Ideally, you should have enough cards to reward each student every month (if earned)*."[12]

Good, Old-Fashioned Character

With this overview, consider what happens to the students in classes that adopt the Core Essentials program. What I intend to do here is outline the specific instructions that are included in the teacher's guide and underscore the elements that make this character education plan a traditional, and thereby restrictive and troubling, approach to teaching children. One may argue that a traditional approach to character education is what is needed. Core Essentials relies heavily on the idea that values are to be "imparted," thus reinforcing a banking approach to teaching and learning whereby the teacher deposits data into the students' "empty vaults" (or minds).[13] This essay intends to problematize the banking approach and show that there are underlying ironies that make the program highly questionable. There are also elements of hypocrisy that make the entire enterprise suspect.

There is a different value for each month of the year represented by the guidelines in question. They include, beginning in September and ending in May: initiative, respect, uniqueness, peace, orderliness, kindness, courage, joy, and patience. For each month, the teacher's guide begins with the exact same formula: a definition of the term, a list of suggested books that represent the value, a list of quotes, a story about an animal that illustrates the value, and directions for teachers. Consider the directions for October. The value is "respect" and the teacher is given the definition: "responding with words and actions that show others they are important."[14] One of the "famous person" quotes given in the booklet is "Always respect your parents…Do whatever your parents say. They are your best friends in life." Aside from the obvious parallel to one of the Ten Commandments (Honor thy father and mother), there is also an irony in having the quote signify "respect." The quote is attributed to George Steinbrenner, the notorious baseball owner whose fights with managers and team members are legendary.

For December, the value is peace and is defined as "proving that you care more about each other than winning an argument." The booklet also indicates that "the first step toward living peaceably is one made quietly inside ourselves. We must decide that other people are worth more to us than our own selfish desires, and that the value of agreement is greater than the satisfaction of defeating an opponent."[15] While the moralistic sentiment may sound nice, I wonder about a possible hidden agenda. Much like the "always respect your parents…do whatever they say" quote from the October lesson, I wonder about the degree to which students are actually being subjugated under a logic of hegemony. As though a sexually abusive parent's directions are always to be followed, the underbelly of universalism may reveal itself given careful analysis. That a corporate fast-food chain arguably interested in increasing market share via competition supports a program that appears to want to produce docile, unquestioning students goes to the heart of the school-business intersection as well. To wit, are schools about producing unquestioning consumers via a character education program that appears to elevate passivity and dogma? This concern does not only apply to the students subjected to the program, however. Teachers, too, are under a hegemonic rationale that subjugates and marginalizes their expertise and professionalism under pre-ordained scripts.

Each week in December, for example, has a corresponding paragraph that begins "Our value this month is peace. The definition of peace is 'proving that you care more about each other than winning an argument.'"[16] Forget that the vast majority of schools are not in session for a full four weeks in December; the four-week script nevertheless reflects a kind of proletarianization or de-skilling of teaching at the same time that it seems to mimic catechism-like recitations from Christian churches. For the "bulletin board" aspect of the teacher's guide for December, teachers are told to "design a bulletin board with a chimney made of craft paper. Give each child a stocking made out of construction paper. On the stocking, have the students write how they care for other people. The children may decorate their stockings afterwards. Hang their stockings on the chimney that you have made." The title given to the bulletin board assignment is "The Stockings Were Hung by the Chimney with Peace." Aside from the overly prescriptive directions that devalue teachers' autonomy and professionalism, stockings are typically hung by chimneys in Christian homes, not Jewish or Muslim homes. Furthermore, if stockings are hung in homes for the Christmas holidays, is the point of young children hanging the stockings to "care for other people" or to receive presents?

A Christian theme is able to be discerned in other parts of the Core Essentials handbook as well. For January, orderliness is the value, and while the paragraph begins with "a study of nature," the teacher is supposed to explain to the students that "the constellations are a beautiful example of the order which exists in the skies."[17] Given the recent controversy in Georgia concerning Kathy Cox and evolution, the "order in the skies" reference sounds eerily like creationist "grand design" assertions.[18] For February, the value is kindness, and the teacher is supposed to explain that a wise saying is "do to others as you would have them do to you."[19] Fine as far as it goes, the *un*hidden "Golden Rule" taken together with other religious themes raises concerns in my mind. Should elementary students hassle their parents into taking them to Chick-fil-A for their "free" meal during the month of

X, they would receive a cassette and/or a bracelet/watch-type band that has a compartment to hold more information from the Core Essentials program. For "responsibility" the plastic holder on the wristband is a sheep dog and the insert of stickers includes statements like "guard sheep dogs are responsible for protecting sheep" and "shepherds trust their sheep dogs to do what is expected of them." While my intent is not to make too much of these points, it does seem to me to be another Christian theme. Sheep? Shepherds? Further, married with the religious and overwhelmingly Christian themes are themes about work and capitalism. For the month of April, for example, students read quotes from Dale Carnegie and Henry Ford Carnegie's quote is "when fate hands you a lemon, make lemonade" and Ford's is "there is joy in work."[20]

What these and other quotes within the curriculum arguably indicate is the nexus of Christianity and capitalism. By weaving a language of accommodation with a language of economics, contrived optimism becomes an unquestioned foundation for docile, naïve workers. The nexus results in a kind of confused nationalist mythology that takes Christian values for granted while accommodating the lauding of individualism and pretenses of participating in a democracy. The mythology of "anyone can be anything they want" given "free markets," "hard work," and entrepreneurialism masks the reality faced by increasing numbers of workers. As Bourdieu points out,

> there are more and more low-level service jobs that are underpaid and low-productivity, unskilled or underskilled (based on hasty on-the-job training), with no career prospects—in short, the *throwaway jobs* of what André Gorz calls a 'society of servants.' According to economist Jean Gadrey, quoting an American study, of the thirty jobs that will grow fastest in the next decade, seventeen require no skills and only eight require higher education and qualification. At the other end of social space, the *dominated dominant*, that is, the managers, are experiencing a new form of alienation. They occupy an ambiguous position, equivalent to that of the petty bourgeois at another historical stage in the structure, which leads to forms of organized self-exploitation.[21]

Part of the historical stage to which Bourdieu refers was outlined in 1926 by Richard Henry Tawney. In his classic text, *Religion and the Rise of Capitalism*, Tawney presaged that "rightly or wrongly, with wisdom or its opposite, not only in England but on the Continent and in America, not in one denomination but among Roman Catholics, Anglicans, and Nonconformists, an attempt is being made to restate the practical implications of the social ethics of the Christian faith, in a form sufficiently comprehensive to provide a standard by which to judge the collective actions and institutions of mankind [sic], in the sphere both of international politics and of social organizations."[22]

The scenario goes something like this: inculcate the youngest and most impressionable with externally contrived religious values and increasingly mold the docile congregation of followers into workers who honor authority. In the process, remove opportunities for critique and questioning by championing *a priori* notions of consensus and the status quo. According to Lindblom, corporations are intimately tied to this very process and set up the nexus of and integration between capitalism and Christian moral codes at the expense of public debate and authentic democratic governance. He notes the key features in business terms and calls them "the grand issues of politico-economic organization: private enterprise, a high degree of corporate autonomy, protection of the status quo on distribution of income and wealth, close consultation between business and government, and restriction of union demands to those consistent with business profitability....They try, through indoctrination, to keep all these issues from coming to the agenda of government."[23] For the parallel to schools, I am reminded of Theodore Brameld's discussion of indoctrination when he was attempting to defend the notion of "partiality" in schools in his *Ends and Means in Education*.[24]

Brameld defined indoctrination as a "method of learning by communication which proceeds primarily in one direction…for the purpose of inculcating in the mind and behavior of the latter a firm acceptance of some one doctrine or systematic body of beliefs—a doctrine assumed in advance by its exponents to be so supremely true, so good, or so beautiful as to justify no need for critical, scrupulous, thoroughgoing comparison with alternative doctrines."[25] Brameld's concern was that schools practiced indoctrination at the expense of the society. For the purpose of this essay, however, he went even further. He indicted "the Church" for establishing the very conditions that promoted learning of the kind he deplored (and this essay challenges). "For many centuries," Brameld wrote, "the Church has deliberately and frankly inculcated its own doctrine as alone true and good, its chief indoctrinators being priests vested with authority to communicate its tenets to receptive minds.…this kind of education flourishes oftener than not: inculcation of moral codes or social folklore, and especially of attitudes and programs identified with the traditional economic-political system, simply means that public schools, far more often than most of their personnel themselves realize, are under the heavy influence of the dominant ideology."[26]

When specifically looking carefully at the text of the Core Essentials teacher's guide, to link and illustrate Brameld's point, a series of questions comes to mind. When, in March, the theme is courage, teachers are told that "courage is the foundation of our democracy. Discover the courage of the young citizens in your class by using a few of these ideas: Watch for students who do the right thing even when it has consequences; Observe students who stand up for their beliefs; Notice those students who do not give in to peer pressure; and Let students write or discuss what courage means to them. Allow them to make a pledge about their courage and watch to see who lives up to that pledge."[27] Given the preceding months that privileged meekness and obedience to authority, what should be "discovered" about the "young citizens" in the class? If citizenship has been crafted in a hierarchical and externally imposed fashion, with the teacher at the center—or more accurately, the Core Essentials program at the center—how serious are teachers supposed to take the task laid out for them? Further, in terms of power, if the teachers are the ones "allowing" students to make a pledge and "letting" students write and discuss what courage means to them, the idea of students as courageous citizens is further subjugated under the power and authority of the teacher via the Core Essentials curriculum.

Values and the Drive-Thru

Throughout the Core Essentials teacher's guide there are sections called "Catching Kids." These sections are ostensibly intended to "catch" children "doing good," so as to turn the idea of "catching" a student doing something into a positive rather than a negative action. Unique to the Core Essentials program, however, is that, because the program is underwritten by Truett Cathy and his Chick-fil-A fast-food chain, the "Catching Kids" sections have "value-able cards." These cards are considered "rewards" by the program and, when given out by the teacher to the student, enable the student to get a free "kid's meal" at Chick-fil-A. A couple of issues converge around this point. First, the students who "earn" the reward are specifically within grades K-2 and 3–5. What we have are the youngest and most impressionable students in schools being bribed to act in particular ways in order to get a meal that is unhealthy. As Carolyn Vander Schee has pointed out, childhood obesity is a concern that has direct links to schools and programs they sponsor (both via in-school food services and out-of-school connections like Core Essentials).[28] Other studies also conclude that fast-food intake among school children is part of a growing obesity epidemic.[29]

By using an unhealthy meal as a reward for complying with a "character education" program, one wonders about the hypocrisy. Where in the program, for example, are students instructed to demonstrate courage by questioning the corporate underwriting of the program itself? When are the students encouraged to consider the fact that, in order for them to redeem their "kid's meal" voucher, they will have to be accompanied by an adult who most likely will purchase food and provide profit for Chick-fil-A? Indeed, recall the direct quote from the teacher's guide noted toward the beginning of this chapter. The guide encourages teachers to "use these ideas to help…choose students who show they understand the value…*Ideally, you should have enough cards to reward each student every month (if earned)*." The point may not be to reward students for good character, even if we could agree on what good character means. The point is to get as many children from grades K-5 into a fast-food chain to eat greasy food with their parents. Can we imagine that the marketing department at Chick-fil-A has not surmised the amount of business they would generate over a three-year period of time? Differently, but related, when are students asked about honesty in disclosing complete calorie and fat content in the food that is being used to lure them to behave in particular ways? Chick-fil-A does have a section on its website where it lists the nutritional value of *items* on their menu.[30] But even the way the documentation is presented is misleading. To consider the amount of fat and calories in a "kid's meal," you have to know what actually comprises a "kid's meal." On the website, for example, both 4- and 6-ounce servings of chicken nuggets are provided on separate lines. A "kid's meal," however, includes more than just the chicken nuggets. The meal includes waffle fries and a drink. Why not be "honest" and include the combined caloric value of the entire meal (allowing for variants like whether the drink is a soda, lemonade, or water)? Is it easier to differentiate and parse the particulars so the whole is not easily discernible? Perhaps the most extreme evidence of Chick-fil-A's Janus-faced approach to the issue of caloric intake and nutrition is their stance that eating plenty of their fast food is not really the problem. The problem is lack of exercise. Indeed, and incredibly, Chick-fil-A offers a "Chick-fil-A 10-Second Tip" in the Children's Hospital's (Knoxville, TN) "Healthy Kids" newsletter. The tip is, "Rather than only focusing on decreasing a big eater's intake, try to increase activity and exercise."[31]

To illustrate the link between the previous claims concerning the problems with externally imposed ideology and health issues associated with fast-food intake, consider that students in the Core Essentials program are structurally inhibited from exploring the issue of healthy eating. The subject does not fall under any of the categories that are pre-ordained for and imposed on teachers. Furthermore, teachers are "sold" the idea that the program will "only take 15 minutes," so when would teachers find the time to go beyond the pre-packaged approach anyway? Missing is the kind of approach developed by Janet Cundiff. She suggests a general structure through which students can answer the question, "Can you 'eat healthy' by frequenting fast food restaurants?"[32] Her approach uses Web links and teams of students to investigate food pyramids and food facts. Teams are asked to learn more about various fast-food restaurants, including, among others, Taco Bell, Burger King, and Chick-fil-A. Teams search for healthy meals, and individuals have roles regarding the various aspects of nutrition to be found on the various websites. Students then synthesize the information, present it to others, and reconsider, according to Cundiff, their own decisions, opinions, and arguments. Accordingly, the students are actively engaged in developing questions and critiques. The Core Essentials program does not foster these postures, as its primary concern is with external imposition of pre-ordained assumptions about character.

I wonder what it would be like if, during the month of October (when "respect" is the value of the month), students would be encouraged to ask whether they, as a group, are actually being shown "respect" via the very program touting the value. Said differently, when is respect for the children shown by the teachers, Core Essentials executives, and Truett Cathy? What role did they have in determining whether they should be subjected to the overtly Christian themes embedded in the program? I also wonder whether the lessons being taught—regardless of whether they are ultimately valid—are also being demonstrated by the people who are promoting the program? How patient would Truett Cathy be of students demonstrating against his company? How respectful of students would Kathy Cox be if they refused to engage in surveillance of one another as the "catching kids" section of the program encourages?

Implications and Further Considerations

One point, then, is to discern the ironies and to tease out the inconsistencies related to the Core Essentials program. We have, in short, a program funded by a fundamentalist Christian whose company uses "kid's meals" as a bribe for behaving in docile, disempowered, uncritical ways. Might this actually be the motive for the program? That is, might it be the case that imposing hierarchy, developing non-questioning students, and privileging Christian-corporate values are intentional acts perpetrated by those wishing to maintain and increase their power, even at the expense of the very students to which they preach equality and kindness? To have Core Essentials and Chick-fil-A work in tandem with William Bennett's *Book of Virtues* raises an obvious question about hypocrisy. Bennett, of course, was revealed to have gambled away millions of dollars at the same time he was loudly proclaiming the vital importance of teaching "virtues" in schools. Is this a "do as I say, not as I do" quagmire? What does it mean that universalists like Bennett actually represent particularist and contextual realities that are not easy to generalize? What does it mean when the Georgia State Superintendent of Schools, Kathy Cox, wishes to delete "evolution" from the curriculum, but applauds Truett Cathy's donation of protestant versions of the Bible to all of the public schools in the state?

Beyond critique of those in power and control of the program, one has to consider the reality of classroom life. Teachers, in a perversely thankful way, simply do not have the time to spare to "add-on" the "curriculum" represented by Core Essentials. The state of Georgia already has a character education component. It also has a core curriculum that, given No Child Left Behind, is raising the degree to which teachers teach to end-of-year tests. Teachers simply do not have the time to alter their bulletin boards, monitor the Chick-fil-A vouchers, and "catch" students behaving in ways the authors of the program do not conduct themselves anyway. So, beyond exploiting the youngest students in schools, beyond the attempt to further proletarianize teaching, beyond attempting to mold obedient and subservient future workers, and beyond the irony and hypocrisy, is there anything valuable about the values valued by Core Essentials? Maybe.

If "Core Essentials" would be used as an object lesson itself, we might be able to reveal a kind of criticality that teaches about values while not externally imposing them without critique. Values exist in schools. Students bring values to the classroom just like their teachers. The question is whether those values are to be explored or whether they are to be assumed. Dewey makes it clear that "morals" are an important part of being a citizen (or any part of a group). He differs greatly from "Core Essentials," though, in that he is not interested in externally imposed, "specialist-"developed terms and themes spread out over three years as part of a preparation plan for future work or future citizenship. In *Moral Principles in Education*, Dewey puts it this way: "We need to see that moral principles are not arbitrary, that they are not 'transcendental'; that the term 'moral' does not designate a special region or portion of life. We need to translate the moral into the conditions and forces of our community life, and into the impulses and habits of the individual. All the rest is mint, anise, and cumin."[33] In another passage, Dewey writes that "the emphasis then falls upon construction...rather than upon absorption and mere learning."[34] As though he is aware of Core Essentials and other such programs, Dewey argues that children are rarely emergent and constructive creatures in classroom settings. Their intellectual life is stunted by the proceduralism of traditional expectations and methods. So, too, says Dewey, of morals in schools:

> The child knows perfectly well that the teacher and all his fellow pupils have exactly the same facts and ideas before them that he [sic] has; he is not *giving* them anything at all. And it may be questioned whether the moral lack is not as great as the intellectual. The child is born with a natural desire to give out, to do, to serve. When this tendency is not used, when conditions are such that other motives are substituted, the accumulation of an influence working against the social spirit is much larger than we have any idea of— especially when the burden of work, week after week, and year after year, falls upon this side.[35]

Three years worth of value-able "kid's meal" cards externally dangled for Pavlovian results strikes me as the very thing Dewey would argue against. Importantly, Dewey is not arguing against morals. Instead, he is arguing against morals "in the air...something set off by themselves...[morals] that are so *very* 'moral' that they have no working contact with the average affairs of everyday life."[36] As a pragmatist and fallibilist, however, he argues that the utility that various values might have get their worth in their organic growth and development in context. Dewey again:

> Here, then, is the moral standard, by which to test the work of the school upon the side of what it does directly for individuals....Does the school as a system...attach sufficient importance to the spontaneous instincts and impulses? Does it afford sufficient opportunity for these to assert themselves and work out their own results? Can we even say that the school in principle attaches itself...to the active constructive powers rather than to processes of absorption and learning?[37]

I submit that the answers to Dewey's questions are "no," "no," and "no." Far too often in far too many schools, far too many teachers fall back on methods of teaching that are comfortable, traditional. Accordingly, students' natural tendencies to inquire become stifled in rooms that are organized (physically and in terms of curriculum) for convenience and platoon-style management.[38] While teachers are not primarily to blame for the external imposition of No Child Left Behind mandates and high-stakes testing that structure their lives, the very frustration they often feel with such external imposition is not recognized when they, in turn, impose upon their students. Core Essentials is simply another in a long line of impositions that teachers and students must navigate. The difference is the degree to which the program represents corporate infiltration under the guide of character education and the universalism it entails.

Extending Dewey, Bourdieu challenges the rhetoric of universalism that sets up the structures within which schools operate as stifling places for external imposition. For Bourdieu, "the effect of shared belief...removes from discussion ideas which are perfectly worth discussing."[39]

Indeed, Bourdieu envisions a kind of collective intellectualism that challenges deeply held beliefs. Long-standing assumptions become the focus of renewed critique and action. He is specifically interested in examining the major power brokers in modern society. As he puts it, "the power of the agents and mechanisms that dominate the economic and social world today rests on the extraordinary concentration of all the species of capital—economic, political, military, cultural, scientific, and technological—as the foundation of a symbolic domination without precedent. . . ."[40] This symbolic domination is difficult to critique, however, because of the power it has over members of society. For Bourdieu, students are also a direct target and engage in hegemonic practices that further subjugate them to the influence of the market. He claims, for example, "that the 'civilization' of jeans, Coca-Cola, and McDonald's [Chick-fil-A] has not only economic power on its side but also the symbolic power exerted through a seduction to which the victims themselves contribute. By taking as their chief targets children and adolescents, particularly those most shorn of specific immune defenses, with the support of advertising and the media which are both constrained and complicit, the big cultural production and distribution companies gain an extraordinary, unprecedented hold over all contemporary societies—societies that, as a result, find themselves virtually infantilized."[41]

Recall that Core Essentials is imposed on students in grades K-5. Bourdieu's suggestion that the larger society is infantilized by the hold corporate interests have over it is even more striking when we consider that the project of disempowerment literally begins with infants. Organic growth of student interests, for Dewey, paired with sociological critique of business influences, for Bourdieu, make for heady prospects when envisioning what schools—and their curricula—might look like during reformation. It would take, however, a sober reconsideration of the roles of students and teachers in schools to engage in substantive reconstruction of schools. It would require a collective "intellectualization" of various roles and, in order to do so, a sloughing off of the dead skin of corporate- and fundamentalist-sponsored, universalist edicts in the form of, among others, character education programs like Core Essentials.

What is not being advocated is a substitution of one kind of pre-ordained morality for another. There should not exist, in other words, a revised script that suggests "The value of the month is criticality. Criticality is defined as . . ." This sort of "bait and switch" game has been played for too long in the history of curriculum. The function of indoctrination is the same, even though the forms may morph. Instead, students and teachers should develop their own versions of criticality as those versions emerge (and change) through the natural curiosity of students in K-5. In this way, a singular (Christian) view of character education is replaced with a pluralistic understanding of character and students, taking a cue from Dewey, would utilize their instincts and impulses to explore that variety with one another. No fries are necessary.

References

Blanchard, Ken and S. Truett Cathy. 2002. *The Generosity Factor*. Grand Rapids, MI: Zondervan.

Bourdieu, Pierre. 1998. *Acts of Resistance: Against the Tyranny of the Market*. New York: The New Press. Trans. Richard Nice.

Bourdieu, Pierre. 2003. *Firing Back: Against the Tyranny of the Market 2*. New York: The New Press. Trans. Loïc Wacquant.

Bowman, Shanthy A., Steven L. Gortmaker, Cara B. Ebbeling, Mark A. Pereira, and David S. Ludwig. 2004. "Effects of Fast-Food Consumption on Energy Intake and Diet Quality Among Children in a National Household Survey." *Pediatrics* 113, no. 1, January.

Brameld, Theodore. 1950. *Ends and Means in Education: A Midcentury Appraisal*. New York: Harper and Row Publishers.

Cathy, S. Truett. 2002. *Eat MOR Chikin: Inspire More People Doing Business the Chick-fil-A Way*. Nashville: Cumberland House Publishing.

Cathy, S. Truett. 1989. *It's Easier to Succeed Than Fail*. Nashville: Thomas Nelson Publishers.

Chick-fil-A. 2003. "Chick-fil-A 10-Second Tip." *Children's Hospital's Healthy Kids: A Quarterly Publication for Parents Preschoolers* [sic]. IX. Knoxville, TN: Children's Hospital. Winter.

Core Essentials. 2001. *Core Essentials: A Strategy for Teaching Character*. Alpharetta, GA: Core Essentials, Inc.

Cundiff, Janet. 2004. "Living in the Fast (Food) Lane!" www.web-and-flow.com/members/jcundiff/fastfoods/webquest.htm.

Deckelbaum, Richard J., and Christine A. Williams. 2001. "Childhood Obesity: The Health Issue." *Obesity Research* 9, suppl. 4. November.

Dewey, John. 1909. *Moral Principles in Education*. Carbondale, IL: Southern Illinois University Press.

Freire, Paulo. 1970. *Pedagogy of the Oppressed*. New York: Continuum.

Josephson, Michael. 2002. "Character Education Is Back in Our Public Schools," *The State Education Standard*. Autumn.

Kaestle, Carl F. 1983. *Pillars of the Republic: Common Schools and American Society, 1780–1860*. New York: Hill and Wang.

Kliebard, Herbert. 1995. *The Struggle for the American Curriculum, 1893–1958*. New York: Routledge.

Lickona, Thomas. 2004. *Character Matters: How to Help Our Children Develop Good Judgment, Integrity, and Other Essential Virtues*. New York: Simon and Schuster.

Linblom, Charles E. 1977. *Politics and Markets: The World's Political-Economic Systems*. New York: Basic Books.

Ludwig, David S., Karen E. Peterson, and Steven Gortmaker. 2001. "Relation between Consumption of Sugar-Sweetened Drinks and Childhood Obesity: A Prospective, Observational Analysis." *The Lancet* 357. February 17.

MacDonald, Mary. 2004. "Evolution Furor Heats Up." *The Atlanta Journal-Constitution*. January 31. A1.

MacDonald, Mary. 2004. "Georgia May Shun 'Evolution' in Schools: Revised Curriculum Plan Outrages Science Teachers." *The Atlanta Journal-Constitution*. January 29. A1.

Marty, Martin E. and R. Scott Appleby. 1997. *Fundamentalism and Society: Reclaiming the Science, the Family, and Education*. Chicago: The University of Chicago Press.

Mosier, Richard. 1965. *Making the American Mind: Social and Moral Ideas in the McGuffey Readers*. New York: Russell & Russell.

Nestle, Marion. 2003. *Food Politics: How the Food Industry Influences Nutrition and Health*. Berkeley, CA: University of California Press.

Spring, Joel. 2005. *The American School, 1642–2004*. Boston: McGraw-Hill.

Tawney, Richard Henry. 1926. *Religion and the Rise of Capitalism*. New York: Harcourt, Brace, and Company.

Vander Schee, Carolyn. 2005. "Food Services and Schooling." *Schools or Markets?: Commercialism, Privatization, and School-Business Partnerships*. Ed. Deron Boyles. Mahwah, NJ: Lawrence Erlbaum.

Williams, Mary M. 2000. "Models of Character Education: Perspectives and Developmental Issues," *Journal of Humanistic Counseling, Education, and Development* 39, no. 1, September.

www.character.org

www.charactercounts.org

www.chickfila.com/CoreEssentials.asp

www.chickfila.com/MenuTable.asp?Category=specialties

www.cortland.edu/c4n5rs/

Zarra, Ernest J. 2000. "Pinning Down Character Education," *Kappa Delta Pi Record* 36, no. 4, Summer.

Notes

1. See, for example, Richard Mosier, *Making the American Mind: Social and Moral Ideas in the McGuffey Readers* (New York: Russell & Russell, 1965); Carl F. Kaestle, *Pillars of the Republic: Common Schools and American Society, 1780–1860* (New York: Hill and Wang, 1983); Joel Spring, *The American School, 1642–2004* (Boston: McGraw-Hill, 2005), sixth edition; and Thomas Lickona, *Character Matters: How to Help Our Children*

Develop Good Judgement, Integrity, and Other Essential Virtues (New York: Simon and Schuster, 2004); Ernest J. Zarra, "Pinning Down Character Education," *Kappa Delta Pi Record* 36, no. 4 (Summer 2000): 154–157; and Mary M. Williams, "Models of Character Education: Perspectives and Development Issues," *Journal of Humanistic Counseling, Education and Development* 39, no. 1 (September 2000): 32–40. See also Martin E. Marty and R. Scott Appleby, eds., *Fundamentalism and Society: Reclaiming the Science, the Family, and Education* (Chicago: The University of Chicago Press, 1997).

2. See, for example, http://www.character.org, http://www.charactercounts.org, and http:// www.cortland.edu /c4n5rs/.

3. See http://www.charactercounts.org. See also Michael Josephson, "Character Education Is Back in Our Public Schools," *The State Education Standard* (Autumn 2002): 41–45.

4. See also Thomas Lickona, *Character Matters: How to Help Our Children Develop Good Judgment, Integrity, and Other Essential Virtues* (New York: Simon and Schuster, 2004).

5. See S. Truett Cathy, *Eat MOR Chikin: Inspire More People Doing Business the Chick-fil-A Way* (Nashville: Cumberland House Publishing, 2002); S. Truett Cathy, *It's Easier to Succeed Than Fail* (Nashville: Thomas Nelson Publishers, 1989); and Ken Blanchard and S. Truett Cathy, *The Generosity Factor* (Grand Rapids, MI: Zondervan, 2002). Both Thomas Nelson and Zondervan are Christian publishing houses.

6. Core Essentials, *Core Essentials: A Strategy for Teaching Character* (Alpharetta, GA: Core Essentials, Inc., 2001).

7. Theodore Brameld, *Means and Ends in Education: A Midcentury Appraisal* (New York: Harper and Row Publishers, 1950); John Dewey, *Moral Principles in Education* (Carbondale, IL: Southern Illinois University Press, 1909); Pierre Bourdieu, *Acts of Resistance: Against the Tyranny of the Market* (New York: The New Press, 1998), trans. Richard Nice; and Pierre Bourdieu, *Firing Back: Against the Tyranny of the Market 2* (New York: The New Press, 2003), trans., Loïc Wacquant.

8. Kathy Cox, letter to school principals, July 1, 2003.

9. See Mary MacDonald, "Georgia May Shun 'Evolution' in Schools: Revised Curriculum Plan Outrages Science Teachers," *The Atlanta Journal-Constitution* (29 January 2004): A1.

10. See http://www.chick-fil-a.com/CoreEssentials.asp. Accessed 21 January 2004.

11. Core Essentials, p.1.

12. Ibid., italics in the original.

13. See Paulo Freire, *Pedagogy of the Oppressed* (New York: Continuum, 1970).

14. Core Essentials, 5.

15. Ibid., 11.

16. Ibid., 12.

17. Ibid., 14.

18. See Mary MacDonald, "Evolution Furor Heats Up," *The Atlanta Journal-Constitution* (31 January 2004): A1.

19. Core Essentials, 17.

20. Ibid., 23.

21. Bourdieu, *Firing Back*, 31. Italics in original.

22. Richard Henry Tawney, *Religion and the Rise of Capitalism* (New York: Harcourt, Brace, and Company, 1926), 5.

23. Charles E. Lindblom, *Politics and Markets: The World's Political-Economic Systems* (New York: Basic Books, 1977), 205.

24. Brameld, *Means and Ends in Education*, 65ff.

25. Ibid., 66.

26. Ibid., 67.

27. Core Essentials, 20.

28. See Carolyn Vander Schee, "Food Services and Schooling," in *Schools or Markets?: Commercialism, Privatization, and School-Business Partnerships*, ed. Deron Boyles (Mahwah, NJ: LEA, 2005), 1–30.

29. Shanthy A. Bowman, Steven L. Gortmaker, Cara B. Ebbeling, Mark A. Pereira, and David S. Ludwig, "Effects of Fast-Food Consumption on Energy Intake and Diet Quality Among Children in a National Household

Survey," *Pediatrics* 113, no. 1 (January, 2004): 112–118; Richard J. Deckelbaum and Christine A. Williams, "Childhood Obesity: The Health Issue," *Obesity Research* 9, suppl. 4 (November, 2001): 239S-243S; David S. Ludwig, Karen E. Peterson, and Steven Gortmaker, "Relation between Consumption of Sugar-Sweetened Drinks and Childhood Obesity: A Prospective, Observational Analysis," *The Lancet* vol. 357 (17 February 2001): 505–508. See also Marion Nestle, *Food Politics: How the Food Industry Influences Nutrition and Health* (Berkeley, CA: University of California Press, 2003).

30. See http://www.chickfila.com/MenuTable.asp?Category=specialties. Accessed June 10, 2004.

31. "Chick-fil-A 10-Second Tip," *Children's Hospital's Healthy Kids: A Quarterly Publication for Parents Preschoolers* [sic] (Knoxville, TN), volume IX (Winter, 2003): 3. That the hospital condones (and promotes) this kind of logic is fodder for further investigation.

32. Janet Cundiff, "Living in the Fast (Food) Lane!" http://www.web-and-flow.com/members/jcundiff/fastfoods /webquest.htm. Accessed June 10, 2004. The movie *Supersize It!* also explores issues relating to and resulting from eating fast food.

33. Dewey, *Moral Principles in Education*, 58.

34. Ibid., 21.

35. Ibid., 22.

36. Ibid., 57.

37. Ibid., 53.

38. Herbert Kliebard, *The Struggle for the American Curriculum*, 1893–1958 (New York: Routledge, 1995), 84, 162.

39. Bourdieu, *Acts of Resistance*, 6.

40. Bourdieu, *Firing Back*, 39.

41. Ibid., 71.

(This chapter originally appeared in Deron Boyles [ed.]. *The Corporate Assault on Youth: Commercialism, Exploitation, and the End of Innocence* [New York: Peter Lang, 2008].)

CHAPTER ELEVEN

Does Character Education *Really* Support Citizenship Education?

Examining the Claims of an Ontario Policy

SUE WINTON

Introduction

Character education may become commonplace in public schools in Canada (Ontario Ministry of Education, 2006; Alberta Education, 2005) as it has in the USA (Hamilton Fish Institute, 2005) and Britain (Arthur, 2005). Character education is the explicit attempt by schools to teach values to students. Advocates claim that character education increases academic achievement, improves student behaviour, and supports citizenship education (Benninga, 1997; Character Education Partnership, 2003; Ontario Ministry of Education, 2006).

In this article I consider the claim that character education supports citizenship education and identify the approach(es) to citizenship education, if any, supported by character education. Approaches to citizenship education vary and reflect different and opposing beliefs about the purpose of citizenship education (Clark & Case, 1999). I focus on the character education policy of a school district in Southern Ontario, Canada, and examine the ways the policy supports and/or undermines the national consensus goal of citizenship education to prepare to become "knowledgeable individuals committed to active participation in a pluralist society" (Sears, Clarke, and Hughes, 2000, p. 153).

Purposes of Citizenship Education

The purposes of citizenship education are debatable (Clark & Case, 1999) . Should it enable students to fit into society or prepare them to change it? Should citizenship education emphasize social cohesion, students' personal characteristics, or the methods of academic disciplines? Each of these purposes has served as a rationale for citizenship education in North America (Clark & Case, 1999), and each gives rise to different conceptions of citizenship education.

Approaches to citizenship education that adopt social *initiation* as their purpose believe citizenship education should pass on "the understandings, abilities, and values that students require if they are to fit into and be productive members of society" (Clark & Case, 1999, p. 18). These approaches imply that society is functioning well and is worthy of reproduction. Citizenship education for social *reformation*, on the other hand, assumes that society is in need of improvement and aims to empower students "with the understandings, abilities, and values necessary to critique and ultimately improve their society" (Clark & Case, 1999, p.18). These two opposing purposes have given rise to dualist models of citizenship education including elitist/activist (Sears, 1996), minimal/critical (DeJaeghere, 2005), and traditional/progressive (Parker, 1996).

Social initiation models of citizenship education emphasize teaching students a common body of knowledge about history, government institutions and processes (Sears, 1996). They portray history as a narrative of continuous progress, and political institutions are presented as operating in lock step fashion (Sears, 1996). Democratic concepts and values are also taught, but their tensions in society are not considered (DeJaeghere, 2005). These models attribute societal problems to personal deficits rather than structures (Westheimer & Kahne, 2004), and while they may encourage citizen participation, civic actions are limited to those that maintain the status quo (e.g., picking up trash). The highest level of participation demanded of citizens, according to elitist conceptions, is informed voting (Sears, 1996). Thus, citizenship education approaches that adopt social initiation as their purpose encourage students to respect tradition, institutions, authority, and dominant narratives and in so doing perpetuate the status quo.

Alternatively, approaches that adopt social reformation as their purpose aim to prepare students to critique and change society (Clark & Case, 1999; DeJaeghere, 2005). They encourage students to develop a deep commitment to democratic values including "the equal participation of all citizens in discourse where all voices can be heard and power (political, economic, and social)is relatively equally distributed" (Sears, 1996, p. 8). Further, the tensions inherent in democratic society are explored. Social reformation models not only encourage active participation, but they also examine the relationship between an individual's behaviour and social justice (DeJaeghere, 2005). Students also learn how structures and institutions, including schools, textbooks, teachers and curriculum (Clark & Case, 1999), discriminate against some groups while privileging others (DeJaeghere, 2005; Sears, 1996). They are taught to uncover forms of oppression and consider how structures might be changed to become more inclusive and democratic.

Joshee (2004)proposes that a third purpose of citizenship education, social cohesion, is being pursued in Canada. The concern to address and promote social cohesion has arisen as citizens have become increasingly different from one another due to unequal consequences of neoliberal policies that advocate a global market economy with little state intervention (Jenson, 1998).

While it may be reasonable for schools to promote social cohesion, it can be pursued in ways that support democratic principles and in ways that promote assimilation (Bickmore, 2006; Blackmore, 2006). Democratic conceptions of social cohesion, for example, encourage diversity of identities and viewpoints and "significant citizen agency," whereas assimilationist conceptions emphasize social harmony values, individual skills (such as cooperation, communication, appreciation of diversity and generic critical thinking skills), and the marginalization of dissenting viewpoints (Bickmore, 2006, p. 361).

Regardless of the purpose and approach adopted, the very nature of citizenship education, with its goal of creating citizens, is concerned with producing and encouraging certain attitudes, values, and behaviours. Across Canada, developing knowledgeable citizens with commitments to active participation and pluralism are "key elements of citizenship [education] around which there is consensus" (Sears, Clarke, & Hughes, 1998, p. 3).

The first of these three elements, *knowledge*, includes both situated and conceptual knowledge. Situated knowledge is knowledge that is used to enhance and frame thoughtful participation in civic life (Sears et al., 1998). Conceptual knowledge includes understanding of concepts and ideas related to citizenship including justice, freedom, dissent, due process, the rule of law, equality, diversity, loyalty, and due process (Hughes, 1994; Sears et al., 1998). The second element of citizenship education is the preparation of students to *actively participate* in civic life. To do so effectively requires decision-making, conflict resolutions, and communication skills (Sears et al., 1998). Finally, the third element of citizenship education involves encouraging students to develop a *commitment to pluralism*. This commitment is dedicated "to fostering pluralist civic society with wide participation from many different individuals and groups" (Sears et al., 1998, p. 4). Below I examine if and how an Ontario school board's character education policy supports the development of these key elements of citizenship education.

Character *Matters!*

The focus of this study is Character *Matters!*, York Region District School Board's (YRDSB) character education policy. The Board serves York Region, a large geographical area (1,776 square kilometres) located just north of Toronto, Ontario, Canada, with a culturally and economically diverse population of almost one million residents (York Region, n.d.).

Character *Matters*! states that it "is committed to *high academic achievement* as well as *personal, interpersonal and citizenship development*" (emphasis in original, Havercroft, 2002, p. 2). It also claims that character education helps students become "reliable, productive employees and active, responsible participants in community life" (YRDSB, n.d.-j). Finally, the policy promises that "[b]y incorporating character education into existing curriculum in an intentional and systematic manner, our schools can help foster the democratic ideals of citizenship, justice, thoughtful decision-making, and enhanced quality of life" (YRDSB, n.d.-i).

The central component of Character *Matters!* is a list of ten character attributes: respect, responsibility, honesty, empathy, fairness, initiative, perseverance, courage, integrity, and optimism. Character *Matters!* claims these values "are universal and transcend religious, ethnocultural and other demographic distinctions" (YRDSB, 2003, p. 1). The policy also assumes character can be taught and learned through direct teaching of the ten values (YRDSB, 2003).

Character *Matters!*'s assumptions and predominantly traditional approach to character education are shared by popular character education initiatives in the USA (e.g., Character Counts!, The Character Education Partnership). Traditional approaches to character education appeal to neoconservatives who are concerned about moral decline and wish to return to the "good old days" in which students learned important, traditional knowledge and were part of a common culture that held traditional values in high regard (Apple, 2006; Nash, 1997; Smagorinsky & Taxel, 2005).

Traditional character education also serves neoliberalism. It does so by promoting the Protestant work ethic (Kohn, 1997a; Smagorinsky & Taxel, 2005) which addresses neoliberalism's interest in the production of good workers and belief in the value of competition and a free-market economy. This ethic links individual effort with material success and suggests that individuals who do well in the economy have earned it through their hard work and good character.

Data & Analysis

One hundred eighty-one documents served as the data for this study. The documents include "a wide range of written, visual, and physical material relevant to the study at hand" (Merriam, 2001, p. 112) and fall into four sets. The first set includes documents produced by the YRDSB that explicitly focus on Character *Matters!* The second set includes articles from *The Attribute,* "a character based e-newsletter" produced by the YRDSB (YRDSB, 2005, December 14). Documents linked to the Character *Matters!* website or referenced in documents available on the website but are not published by YRDSB comprise the third set. Finally, texts that are not explicitly connected to Character *Matters!* but are related to it through policy webs (Joshee & Johnson, 2005) make up the final set. Each document was analyzed to determine how *Character Matters!* supports or undermines the development of knowledgeable citizens with commitments to active participation and pluralism.

The three elements of citizenship education (knowledge, active participation, and commitment to pluralism) served as the initial categories for the analysis. I read each document and highlighted words, phrases, and passages that drew attention to one or more of these elements and their subcomponents. For example, to understand how and in what ways Character *Matters!* encourages students to acquire *situational knowledge* (knowledge used to frame and enhance participation) I highlighted passages that link students' knowledge with their participation. I then considered the *kind* of knowledge students' were encouraged to use. These kinds of knowledge include knowledge from academic disciplines, knowledge of character attributes, knowledge of current events, and knowledge of interpersonal skills.

To determine how Character *Matters!* encourages students' to develop *conceptual knowledge* I highlighted all references to freedom, justice, loyalty, equality, dissent, and law and due process in the documents. I considered how each concept is discussed and how each is defined and constructed. I also examined how discussions related to pluralism and difference might support or undermine students' understanding of the concepts of equality and diversity. In addition, I considered the definitions of the ten attributes promoted by Character *Matters!* as another possible source of information about the democratic concepts. For example, I considered how the definition of fairness might influence students' understanding of the concepts of justice and due process.

Similarly, to understand how the policy encourages students' *active participation*, I adopted a broad definition of participation and highlighted all extortions to teachers, principals, parents, and the community to encourage students to become actively involved in their community; exhortations to students directly to become involved; descriptions of activities in which students were involved in their classroom, school, community, or beyond; as well as policy statements that addressed the benefits and need for student involvement. I paid particular attention to the ways the texts encourage the development of conflict resolution, communication and decision-making skills and considered each of these as subcomponents of active participation (Sears et al., 1998).

Next, I created subcategories that represent different types of involvement (e.g., service learning, making donations, fundraising, organizing conferences, serving in student government), location of involvement (classroom, school, local community, province, Canada, international), and adjectives used to describe participation (e.g., contributing, effective).

I followed a similar process to identify the policy's support for the development of students' commitment to pluralism. I first highlighted words, phrases, and passages that reflect efforts to influence students' attitudes towards diversity and difference. I included descriptions of activities that focus on diversity, lessons about dealing with differences, and anti-racism initiatives, for example. I also examined the stated goals of activities related to diversity. These goals include encouraging students to recognize, celebrate and value diversity. Finally, I considered the policy's underlying assumptions and claims about differences between people (e.g., claims of universal values) and how they support or undermine efforts to influence students' attitudes towards pluralism.

Findings

Situated Knowledge

Education stakeholders in Canada believe citizenship education should encourage students to develop both situated and conceptual knowledge (Sears et al., 2000). Situated knowledge is knowledge that enhances and frames "thoughtful participation in civic life" (Sears et al., 1998, p. 3). Character *Matters!*'s declaration that "[s]tudents who adopt positive character attributes become reliable, productive employees and active, responsible participants in community life" (Havercroft, 2002, p. 3) suggests that the knowledge students need for civic participation is knowledge of certain character attributes. This idea is furthered in an *Attribute* article linking democracy and character:

> The conditions for democracy exist when all citizens have the potential to participate equally in the work of society. As such, in a democracy, the necessity for character also exists. A democratic people must be committed to principles of respect and empathy for others. They exhibit honesty, fairness and courage, sometimes in the face of adversity. A democratic people educate with a strong sense of optimism for the future of humankind, that kindness and compassion, and a sense of belonging to the family of humankind is paramount to serving the self. (YRDSB, 2005, January 24)

Absent from this discussion is mention of any additional knowledge needed to participate in society beyond knowledge of the character attributes promoted by Character *Matters!*

Instead, Character *Matters!* encourages students to combine their knowledge of the attributes with various interpersonal skills. An *Attribute* article states that "part of the function of schools is to develop the capacity of students to work with others" (YRDSB, 2004, August 23). According to the article, this ability requires social awareness; relationship skills including active listening, empathy, and a willingness to lead or follow according to the group's best interest; conflict resolution and participation skills; and a sense of humour (YRDSB, 2004, August 23). These skills, like the attributes, must be explicitly taught and modeled (YRDSB, 2004, August 23).

Thus, while Character *Matters!* does not argue against teaching students to use other knowledge to enhance their participation in civic life, it does not promote it either. Instead, Character *Matters!* suggests that the knowledge students need for responsible and effective participation is knowledge of Character *Matters!*'s attributes and a variety of interpersonal skills.

Conceptual Knowledge

Character *Matters!* claims that "[b]y incorporating character education into existing curriculum in an intentional and systematic manner, our schools can help foster the democratic ideals of citizenship, justice, thoughtful decision-making, and enhanced quality of life" (YRDSB, n.d.-i). In this section I examine this claim by considering if and how Character *Matters!* promotes teaching and learning core concepts of Canadian democracy: freedom, justice, due process, dissent, the rule of law, equality, diversity, and loyalty (Hughes, 1994).

Character *Matters!* explicitly supports teaching and learning about some but not all of these concepts. As I discuss in detail below, Character *Matters!* encourages students to understand and appreciate diversity, but it adopts a narrow definition and emphasizes similarities rather than differences between individuals and groups.

The policy also offers limited support for teaching and learning about justice in general and social justice in particular. For example, the 2004 Board Report lists "justice orientation discussions" as an example of an approach to character education (York Region District School Board, 2004, p. 7), and a letter to staff identifies social justice issues as part of character education (Hogarth, 2005, p. 1). Thus, while the policy supports teaching and learning about issues of justice, it emphasizes how they can be used as vehicles for developing character rather than facilitating students' understanding of justice as a democratic concept.

Similarly, Character *Matters!* does not explicitly advocate the teaching and learning of loyalty, freedom, due process, dissent, the rule of law, and equality as democratic concepts and ideas. It does, however, construct some of these concepts as character attributes and provides implicit lessons about some of them. For example, the *Family Workbook* (2002) lists loyalty as an attribute that a family might choose to demonstrate. Like all the Character *Matters!* attributes, loyalty is constructed as a behaviour rather than an internal commitment or democratic concept. So while the policy explicitly supports students' demonstrations of loyalty, it does not encourage them to explore its relationship to citizenship. Implicitly, however, the policy emphasizes and encourages loyalty through its emphasis on the responsibility of students to contribute to their communities and enact their community's supposedly shared values (i.e., the ten attributes). The importance of demonstrating this loyalty by acting in accordance with the attributes is reinforced through rewards and celebrations.

The concept of freedom, like loyalty, is discussed in Character *Matters!* but not as a concept that students must come to understand. Instead, Character *Matters!* discusses freedom in terms of its relationship to character. An *Attribute* article explains

> Many people have asked why it is necessary to "teach" character. I think the answer is quite clear. Without character, there is no freedom…no freedom as individuals or as a society…In short, freedom without character does not exist. (YRDSB, 2004, September 20a)

This article positions character and character education as necessary precursors to the attainment and maintenance of freedom.

Thus, Character *Matters!* does not encourage teachers to teach about the concept of freedom directly. Implicitly, however, the policy teaches that individuals are free to act within boundaries set by others. For example, while Character *Matters!* permits teachers to teach the ten attributes in ways that suit their students' needs and teachers' personal styles, their freedom to do is limited by the assumption that the attributes are universal.

Similarly, the policy does not explicitly encourage teachers to teach the concept of dissent. However, by rewarding students who comply with the behavioural expectations of the attributes the policy implicitly teaches that dissent is undesirable. This view is also evident in the *York Region District School Board* Character Matters! *First Annual Review* (Havercroft, 2002) in which "disenfranchised students" are identified as "a particular challenge to Character *Matters!*" (p. 12).

The final two democratic concepts education stakeholders in Canada believe Canadian citizens need to know (Hughes, 1994), the rule of law and due process, are not addressed in Character *Matters!* Their absence, in addition to the relative absence of the concepts of justice, freedom, loyalty, and equality as democratic concepts to be learned by students, suggests that Character *Matters!* offers little support for the development of students' knowledge of democratic concepts.

Active Participation

Ministries and Departments of Education across Canada agree that citizenship education should aim to prepare students to actively participate in civic life (Sears et al., 1998). The abilities to make decisions, resolve conflicts and communicate are believed to be necessary skills for citizens' active participation (Sears et al., 1998). Character *Matters!* supports students' development of these skills and promotes civic participation. However, not all types of participation are equally encouraged.

Below I present Character *Matters!*'s stated commitments to promoting active citizenship. I then examine the ways the policy advocates developing students' skills in decision-making, conflict resolution, and communication. Next, I consider the policy's support for student involvement in charity work, service learning and advocating for social justice to better understand the purpose(s) of citizenship education supported by the policy.

Character *Matters!* explicitly supports active participation. Students are told "It is in your best interests to become the very best that you can be, and becoming involved at the school and community levels can be personally rewarding. Take the challenge . . ." (YRDSB, n.d.-g). Further, the policy claims that "Students who adopt positive character attributes become reliable, productive employees and *active, responsible participants* in community life" (YRDSB, n.d.-j, emphasis added). Importantly, as I show below, Character *Matters!* promotes participation in activities that support the state, its agencies, and the status quo much more frequently and emphatically than it encourages students to participate in activities that challenge social and political systems of inequity.

Decision-Making Skills

Character *Matters!* supports student involvement in decision-making in a variety of ways. First, the policy encourages student involvement in developing classroom and school-wide rules. For example, the *Attribute* encourages teachers to "Have the students think of and share the 'rules' and expectations they've ever had to follow at school. Once their ideas have been recorded, have them vote of the ones that they are willing to live by for the entire school year" (YRDSB, 2004, July 26).

Character *Matters!* also encourages the development of students' decision-making skills through involvement in committees, student councils, and other leadership positions (YRDSB, n.d.-f). In fact, the policy offers strong support for the development of students' leadership skills through their participation in a variety of events and programs. Notably, many of these initiatives involve students explicitly promoting character education to other students. In one program, *LINK*, senior high school students are trained to "deliver Character Education through TAP (Teacher Advisor Program)" (YRDSB, 2004, March 22). At another school students "chair a Character Education Committee and organize two student-led Character Forums each year. [They]…are also responsible for selecting, printing and distributing 'Words of Wisdom' (student issues with positive messages) to the teachers for discussion with their classes. A quote of the week, selected by the committee, is delivered to the school body via the morning announcements" (YRDSB, 2004, February 20).

Thus, while Character *Matters!* does promote the development of students' decision-making skills by providing opportunities for them to be involved in decision-making, these opportunities are often limited and serve ends predetermined by the school. Organizing conferences, choosing classroom rules out of a set of rules followed in previous classrooms, and chairing character committees all provide students with experience making decisions that support rather than possibly challenge the schools' interests.

There are a few instances, however, where the policy offers support for student decision-making without these constraints. For example, the *Attribute* recommends *Meaningful Student Involvement*, a resource that aims to "establish a foundation for an emerging movement that promotes democracy in education by engaging students in researching, planning, teaching, evaluating leading and advocating for schools" (YRDSB, 2004, April 5b). While other similar instances may be found, they are greatly outnumbered by efforts and descriptions of ways to involve students in making decisions within tightly controlled parameters so that the schools' purposes are achieved.

Conflict Resolution

Like decision-making skills, skills in conflict resolution are recognized across Canadian education jurisdictions as necessary for active participation in civic life (Sears et al., 1998). While they receive less emphasis than decision-making skills, Character *Matters!* does support the development of students' ability to resolve conflicts.

The document *Peer Mediation, Peace, Conflict Resolution* (YRDSB, n.d.-i) defines conflict resolution as teaching basic communication and problem solving skills, developing an environment where conflicts do not erupt into violence, promoting opportunities for increased understanding, supporting and affirming diversity, and seeking to establish an overall tone of respect. Essential skills for constructive resolutions include perception, emotional, communication, and creative and critical thinking abilities as well as certain values, beliefs, and attitudes (YRDSB, n.d.-i). This document also suggests a number of Web resources and lists tips for creating a peaceful classroom. These resources define peace narrowly as "the absence of direct violence and conflict" (Joshee, 2004, p. 150) rather than adopting a proactive view of peace that involves understanding and addressing underlying structural causes of violence.

An *Attribute* article encourages teachers to "[i]mplement a school wide peer mediation/conflict resolution programme" (YRDSB, 2004, August 9). In fact, peer mediation is the conflict resolution strategy most frequently advocated in Character *Matters!* The model of peer mediation promoted involves "[teaching] a select group of students advanced intervention and problem solving strategies [and empowering] students to assist other students in resolving conflicts when they occur" (YRDSB, n.d.-i).

The conflict resolution skills promoted in Character *Matters!* and the ways they are discussed in the policy construct conflict as something that should be avoided. While this may often be desirable, conflict is inevitable in pluralist societies (Bickmore, 2004) and can lead to possibilities that might not have otherwise been imagined. Emphasizing conflict resolution and avoidance are not likely to encourage or prepare students to challenge injustice since these challenges will undoubtedly conflict with mainstream thinking.

Communication Skills

Character *Matters!* supports the development of students' communication skills in a variety of ways. First, the policy is explicitly linked to the Board's focus on literacy.

Character Matters! and Literacy states that a "classroom that actively strives for creating a culture where the 10 attributes are actually lived, is one that is free form [sic] negative distractions that prevent learning from taking place; the teaching and learning of literacy skills are enabled" (YRDSB, n.d.-b). Furthermore, the 2004 Board Report argues that "character [is] the very foundation for literacy and instruction" (Havercroft, 2004, p. 1).

Developing writing skills, a component of literacy, is encouraged through the policy's support of an annual essay contest that asks students to write about their core values. Character *Matters!* also suggests integrating writing with character education through themes in Language writing, respect essays in Language class, daily journals in English, and Character Education Acrostic Poem (YRDSB, n.d.-c).

Character *Matters!* encourages the development of oral communication skills through drama, song writing, and public speaking. For example, the "Character Counts" speaking contest at an elementary school required students speak about "the importance of character" and "[t]hey clearly exemplified the character message and its importance in helping all to become responsible and contributing citizens" (YRDSB, 2004, June 1). In the *Literacy through Music* project students and an artist-in-residence "wrote lyrics to effectively convey a character message through song" (YRDSB, 2005, May 17). Finally, the policy encourages teachers to use drama to illustrate and practice the attributes in action.

Reading and responding to stories, other elements of communication, are also supported by Character *Matters!* For example, the *Family Character Workbook* (YRDSB, 2002) encourages families to seek out stories that illustrate selected attributes. Similarly, teaching about the attributes through reading about characters who exemplify them is encouraged.

As described above, the policy encourages students to become involved in student councils, committees, organizing conferences, and providing training and counselling (e.g., peer mediation) to other students. Involvement in any of these activities would require communications skills as the activities demand that students work with one another, educators, and/or community members. However, I have already suggested that these opportunities also help the schools achieve their purposes and predetermined goals. So, too, do essay contests centred on students' core values, speaking contests about the importance of character, and the other communication activities described above. These activities do not encourage students to use their communication skills to achieve their own purposes nor do they provide opportunities for students to advocate for social change.

Another way Character *Matters!* encourages the development of communication skills is its support of cooperative learning. Cooperative learning is cited as an example of the "Hands" component of the "Head, Heart, Hands" paradigm of Character *Matters!* (Havercroft, 2005). An *Attribute* article (YRDSB, 2004, August 23) lists the following communication skills as necessary for cooperative learning: active listening, making a plan, making suggestions, responding to suggestions, asking for reasons, giving reasons, asking for feedback, giving feedback, checking accuracy, checking for understanding, persuading others, paraphrasing, summarizing, body language, reading others, control of one's own voice, seeing the point of view of others, and elaborating. Teachers are explicitly encouraged to teach these skills (YRDSB, 2004, August 23).

While there is considerable evidence that Character *Matters!* supports and encourages students' development of communication skills, it does not connect them to active participation in the way that Canadians do (Sears et al., 2000). That is, while Canadians identify the ability to communicate as necessary for participation in civic life (Sears et al., 2000), Character *Matters!* presents them as ways to achieve the goals of character education, work cooperatively, and support student achievement. I now turn to consider the kinds of participation most frequently advocated by the policy.

Charity and Service

Character *Matters!* strongly encourages students to become actively involved in civic life by donating to others. The *Attribute* is replete with articles honouring students' and teachers' efforts to collect and donate money and items such as food and clothing. Similarly, toy and clothing drives, bake and calendar sales, and other fundraisers are recognized at Board meetings as evidence of empathy and character. Importantly, many of the charity initiatives are designed to assist people in countries other than Canada. While these kinds of initiatives are important and necessary, the emphasis on helping individuals in other countries draws students' attention away from the needs of individuals in their own communities. It teaches students that charity work is a suitable way to be active in civic life without encouraging them to examine the social, political and economic factors that contribute to inequality locally, nationally, and globally.

In addition to being charitable, Character *Matters!* encourages "learning through service to others" (YRDSB, 2004, October 4). Not only does Character *Matters!* consider service learning to be "one of the most meaningful ways to teach responsibility, empathy and understanding," it is also considered "a wonderful way to encourage our students to become caring and responsible members of our community" (YRDSB, 2004, October 4). The underlying assumption is that students will develop character and civic mindedness through their service to others. Service learning is recognized in the 2004 Board Report (YRDSB, 2004) as an example of how Character *Matters!* is embedded in curriculum and instruction, and it is explicitly listed as a valued component of the policy in the 2002 Board Report (Havercroft, 2002).

Social Justice

Character *Matters!* offers limited support for student involvement in activities linked to social or political activism. Support is evident in the policy's definition of fairness; it is defined in part as "stand[ing] up for human rights" (YRDSB, n.d.-a). This statement suggests that students should participate in challenging and changing attitudes, individuals, and institutional structures that promote injustice. A few documents suggest examples of what this might look like or recognize individuals who have become involved in this way. For example, *How to Get Involved: Students* tells students that "[w]hen things go wrong, when you see bullying or racism, don't ignore it. Say something to help turn things around and / or talk to the adults in the building," (YRDSB, n.d.-g). Participating in walks against male violence and racism, breakfast clubs, and posting antiracism posters are a few suggested ways to integrate character education into a school's program. Notably, these activities are part of a much longer list of suggestions, the majority of which are not linked to social justice. Nevertheless, while students' participation in activities linked to social activism receives less emphasis than other types of participation, the policy does offer some degree of support for it.

The "Head, Heart, Hands" paradigm represents the components of character identified by Character *Matters!*: knowledge (head); feeling (heart), and doing (hands) (Havercroft, 2002).

Pluralism

Acceptance, promotion and valuation of diverse people, lifestyles, and perspectives are hallmarks of democracy (Solomon & Portelli, 2001). Citizenship education in a democratic society, then, must be committed to fostering a commitment to pluralism and recognition of its importance. Character

Matters! goes some way to foster this commitment and recognition, but its narrow definition of diversity and emphasis on shared values, behaviour, and language contradict these efforts.

Character *Matters!* explicitly promotes recognition and celebration of diversity. For example, an *Attribute* article describes the events of a Black History Month Celebration which recognized "several distinguished Black Canadian citizens who have made noteworthy contributions to the Markham community" (YRDSB, 2004, March 8). Another article invites students to enter a contest "celebrating and promoting respect for our diverse community" in honour of the International Day for the Elimination of Racial Discrimination (YRDSB, 2004, November 15).

Beyond accepting and celebrating differences, the policy explicitly encourages students to value diversity. For example, The *Attribute* describes and promotes a conference for educators that provides them with "sources 'to develop the skills, attitudes, knowledge and disposition' needed to create learning environments that value diversity" (YRDSB, 2004, April 5a). Another article describes and provides a link to *The Harmony Movement*; this organization promotes "the appreciation and value of human diversity in communities across the country through public education programs . . ." (YRDSB, 2004, September 20).

Character *Matters!*'s concern with diversity is also reflected in its support of antiracism initiatives. School-based and board wide conferences focussed on antiracism are described in the *Attribute* (e.g., YRDSB, 2004, May 3, 2005, February 21, 2005, June 14), and an article encourages readers to "commit to making each day a day dedicated to the elimination of all forms of discrimination" (YRDSB, 2005, March 21a). Further, units on antiracism and discrimination are suggested as ways to integrate character education in the curriculum (YRDSB, n.d.-e).

While the significance of these initiatives must not be overlooked, their focus and the policy's claim that "[i]n Canada and in York Region, all races, religions, and ethno-cultural groups are respected and valued" (YRDSB, n.d.-d) show that Character *Matters!* promotes a narrow concept of diversity. This concept is limited to differences in culture, ethnicity, and religion. Other forms of difference, such as differences in language, sexual orientation, or ability, are not usually part of discussions about diversity in the policy. In fact, the only case in which a wide range of differences *is* recognized is in the claim that "To be Canadian suggests that one holds a perspective that transcends boundaries of race, ethnicity and culture, socioeconomic background, ability, faith, gender, sexual orientation and age" (Hogarth, 2005, p. 4). This claim silences dissenting voices and delegitimizes different perspectives as it defines and essentializes what it means to be Canadian. It also constructs diversity as something that must be transcended—something to get past—rather than something to be valued for itself.

Crucially, while Character *Matters!* encourages recognition and respect for a narrow concept of diversity and the elimination of racism, the policy is much more interested in emphasizing and constructing similarities between individuals. This interest is evident in its emphasis on teaching and adopting shared values and in the policy's concern that everyone uses the same language when discussing character education.

The 2002 Board Report includes multiple statements about using a shared language including "The challenge here is to gather the many related initiatives under the Character *Matters!* umbrella to develop consistent language and principles from Kindergarten through Grade twelve" (Havercroft, 2002, p. 9). Parents are told to "Speak the language of the attributes" (YRDSB, 2002, p. 21), and teachers are encouraged to "Use the language of the character attributes to address 'teachable moments'…Weave the language of character education into the content of your curriculum" (YRDSB, n.d.-h).

The focus on regulation and standardization of language reflects Character *Matters!*'s interest in changing students' behaviour so that it conforms to expectations linked to the policy's ten attributes. For example, the 2002 Board Report explains that the attributes "mark a standard for our behaviour as adults and youth across the system" (Havercroft, 2002, p. 4). Principals and teachers are encouraged to "Correct gently against the character attributes" (YRDSB, n.d.-d; n.d.-h, p. 7). At a school featured in the *Attribute* "the ten character attributes form the cornerstone of student behaviour and expectations" (YRDSB, 2005, March 21b). Students at the school see the attributes in their agendas and hear about them in assemblies and announcements. Students then "earn certificates for displaying these traits through their words and actions" (YRDSB, 2005, March 21b). Moreover, the policy requires that everyone on the board, not just the students, act according to the attributes (YRDSB, 2003), and it encourages administrators to use them as a "focus for discussions about expectations of staff and student behaviour" (Havercroft, Kielven, & Slodovnick, 2004).

Character *Matters!*'s emphasis on conformity to standardized expectations for behaviour, its desire to regulate individuals' language and standardize their values, and its narrow definition of diversity offer little support for the development of students' commitment to pluralism.

Conclusions

These findings show that Character *Matters!* supports conceptions of citizenship education that aim to promote an assimilationist conception of social cohesion and to prepare students to fit into Canadian society rather than change it. These two purposes are not unrelated; I consider their relationship and discuss Character *Matters!*'s support of these purposes below.

While an emphasis on promoting social cohesion through citizenship education is not new, it has re-emerged as a priority in response to increasing differences that have arisen in response to neoliberal policies (Jenson, 1998). Without a socially cohesive society, Canada's neoliberal policies may not be sustainable (Committee on Social Affairs, Science, and Technology, 1999; Jenson, 1998). Canada's Standing Senate Committee on Social Affairs, Science, and Technology (1999) stated that "The most serious challenge for decision-makers is to ensure that economic integration driven by globalising markets does not lead *to domestic social disintegration*" (emphasis in original, Introduction). If, however, social cohesion can be secured, neoliberalism can continue to dominate and impact economic, social (Olssen, 2004), and education policies (Osborne, 2001).

Efforts to promote social cohesion may emphasize assimilation or democratic commitments to pluralism and diversity (Bickmore, 2006). Assimilationist notions of social cohesion emphasize "homogenization through inculcation of unproblematized values [and the] silencing or marginalization of dissenting viewpoints" (Bickmore, 2006, p. 382). Character *Matters!*'s commitments to teaching and learning shared values, its inattention to dissent as a democratic concept, and its celebration of compliance to the behavioural expectations linked to the character attributes show that the policy supports an assimilationist view of social cohesion.

Additional support is evident in Character *Matters!*'s treatment of conflict. Rather than advocating that students learn about the inevitability and potential utility of conflict in pluralist societies (Bickmore, 2006), conflict is instead constructed as something to be avoided. Bickmore (2006) argues that "[w]here curriculum reinforces student passivity and disengagement by marginalizing conflicting viewpoints, it denies those students the opportunities to develop skills and understandings of themselves as social actors (citizens)" (p. 361). Moreover, within this limited social cohesion framework, differences are constructed as things to recognize and ultimately overcome rather than continually address and revisit. This positioning demands that less attention be paid to issues of inequality and the pursuit of social justice since it implies that doing so is divisive (Joshee, 2004).

In addition to promoting an undemocratic notion of citizenship education for social cohesion, Character *Matters!* supports citizenship education that adopts social initiation as its purpose. Evidence of this support is found in the policy's use of the curriculum and students' communication skills as ways to support and further the policy and goals of the school board rather than as means of student advocacy or interrogating injustice.

Furthermore, the predominantly traditional approach to character education advocated by Character *Matters!* (Winton, in press) conflicts with a number of central tenets of citizenship education for social reformation. For example, in addition to discouraging dissent, avoiding conflict, and offering limited support for social justice, Character *Matters!* promotes a deficit view of students by constructing adults as having good character while children do not and suggests that without adult guidance children will not develop it. Students are expected to learn and enact the attributes prescribed by the policy; they are not encouraged to debate the merits of each attribute, suggest others, and modify the list based on their discussions—hallmarks of democratic processes.

Character *Matters!* reproduces inequities in society more generally by paying attention to *individuals'* character rather than encouraging students to investigate how economic, political, or cultural factors affect character and behaviour. This focus allows political, economic, and cultural institutions and ideologies, including neoliberalism, to remain unchallenged (Purpel, 1997). Neoliberalism's commitment to competition and celebration of the individual is also furthered through Character *Matters!* support for contests and rewards as teaching and learning strategies. Thus, Character *Matters!*, like other traditional approaches, takes on the "ideology of the struggle to preserve the *status quo*" (p. 150).

Fortunately, even though Character *Matters!* promotes an undemocratic notion of social cohesion and the status quo, there are many opportunities in the policy for teachers to resist its efforts. For example, while Character *Matters!* defines conflict resolution narrowly as the avoidance of conflict, critically-minded teachers can use the policy's endorsement of conflict resolution to initiate discussions about issues about which there is little consensus. These discussions can form the basis of examinations of ways to work despite unresolved conflicts, the benefits of differing viewpoints, and discussions about the desirability of avoiding conflicts. These examinations will help students see that conflict is part of life and provide them with strategies for dealing with it.

Similarly, Character *Matters!* offers a limited definition of active citizenship that teachers can build upon. For example, they can use the policy's endorsement of active participation to introduce critical examination of policy issues and provide students with opportunities to protest current policy (e.g., through letter writing, awareness campaigns) and imagine other possibilities. Teachers can encourage students to draw on their knowledge of history and current events to identify means of resistance and advocating change. This would provide students with opportunities to develop a sense of their own agency as well as teach students to use their knowledge to enhance and frame their participation.

In sum, Character *Matters!* *does* support citizenship education, but importantly, it supports undemocratic social cohesion and social initiation models of citizenship education rather than a social reformation model. This study shows that individuals committed to social justice and democratic education must approach claims that character education supports citizenship education with caution and ask *"What kind of citizenship education? For what purpose?"* before embracing character education as a means to prepare students to transform society.

References

Bickmore, K. (2004). Education for peacebuilding citizenship:Tteaching the dimensions of conflict resolution in social studies. In *Challenges and prospects for Canadian Social Studies* (pp. 187–201). Vancouver, B.C.: Pacific Educational Press.

Bickmore, K. (2006). Democratic social cohesion (assimilation)? Representations of social conflict in Canadian public school curriculum. *Canadian Journal of Education, 29*(2), 259–386.

Blackmore, J. (2006). Deconstructing diversity discourses in the field of Education Managament and Leadership. *Educational Management, Administration and Leadership, 34*(2), 181–199.

Clark, P., & Case, R. (1999). Four purposes of citizenship education. In P. Clark & R. Case (Eds.), *The Canadian Anthology of Social Studies* (pp. 17–27). Vancouver, B.C.: Simon Fraser University Press.

DeJaeghere, J. G. (2005). Global dimensions of citizenship in the Australian secondary curriculum: Between critical contestations and minimal constructions. In E. D. Stevick (Ed.), *Educating democratic citizens: Sociocultural research on civic education around the globe.* Lanham, MD: Rowman & Littlefield, Inc.

Hamilton Fish Institute. (2005). *Character education.* Retrieved December 27, 2005, from http://www.hamfish.org/topics/character_education.html

Havercroft, J. (2002, October 15). *York Region District School Board Character Matters! First Annual Review,* from http://www.yrdsb.edu.on.ca/pdfs/a/agenda/ms/sc021015/yrdsb-sc021015-p3–54.pdf

Havercroft, J. (2004). *York Region District School Board: Character Matters!* Retrieved August 22, 2005, from http://www.yrdsb.edu.on.ca/pdfs/a/agenda/mp/bd041028/yrdsb-bd041028-p77–78.pdf

Havercroft, J. (2005). *Character Matters! June Newsletter.* Retrieved May 18, 2006, from http://www.yrdsb.edu.on.ca/pdfs/w/charactermatters/junenewsletter.pdf

Havercroft, J., Kielven, J., & Slodovnick, M. (2004). *Building character schools: The York Region experience. The Attribute 2(6).* Retrieved October 31, 2005, from http://yrlc.on.ca/charactermatters/attribute/

Hogarth, B. (2005). *Character Matters!* Retrieved June 26, 2005, from www.yrdsb.edu.on.ca/pdfs/w/charactermatters/junenewsletter.pdf

Hughes, A. S. (1994). Understanding citizenship: A delphi study. *Canadian and International Education, 23*(2), 13–36.

Jenson, J. (1998). *Mapping social cohesion: The state of Canadian research.* Ottawa: Canadian Policy Research Networks.

Joshee, R. (2004). Citizenship and multicultural education in Canada. In J. A. Banks (Ed.), *Diversity and citizenship education: Global perspectives* (pp. 127–156). San Francisco: Jossey-Bass.

Joshee, R., & Johnson, L. (2005). Multicultural education in the United States and Canada: The importance of national policies. In D. W. Livingstone (Ed.), *International Handbook of Educational Policy* (pp. 53–74). London: Springer.

Merriam, S. B. (2001). *Qualitative research and case study applications in education.* San Francisco: Jossey-Bass.

Olssen, M. (2004). Neoliberalism, globalisation, democracy: Challenges for education. *Globalisation, Societies and Education, 2*(2), 231–275.

Osborne, K. (2001). Democracy, democratic citizenship, and education. In J. P. Portelli & R. P. Solomon (Eds.), *The erosion of democracy: From critique to possibility* (pp. 29–62). Calgary, Alberta, Canada: Detselig Enterprises.

Parker, W. C. (1996). "Advanced" ideas about democracy: Toward a pluralist conception of citizen education. *Teachers College Record, 98*, 104–125.

Purpel, D. E. (1997). The politics of character education. In A. Molnar (Ed.), *The construction of children's character* (pp. 140–153). Chicago, IL: University of Chicago Press.

Purpel, D. E., & Shapiro, S. (1995). *Beyond liberation and excellence: Reconstructing the public discourse on education.* Westport: Bergin & Garvey.

Sears, A. (1996). "Something different to everyone": Conceptions of citizenship and citizenship education. *Canadian and International Education, 25*(2), 1–16.

Sears, A., Clarke, G., M., & Hughes, A. S. (1998). Learning democracy in a pluralist society: Building a research base for citizenship education in Canada: A Discussion paper prepared for the Councils of Ministers of Education, Canada.

Solomon, R. P., & Portelli, J. P. (2001). Introduction. In R. P. Solomon & J. P. Portelli (Eds.), *The erosion of democracy in education: Critique to possibilities* (pp. 15–27). Calgary: Detselig Enterprises.

Standing Senate Committee on Social Affairs Science and Technology. (1999). *Final report on social cohesion.* Retrieved 22 December, 2006, from http://www.parl.gc.ca/36/1/parlbus/commbus/senate/Com-e/SOCI-E/rep-e/repfinaljun99part1-e.htm

Westheimer, J., & Kahne, J. (2004). What kind of citizen? The politics of educating for democracy. *American Educational Research Journal, 41*(2), 237–269.

Winton, S. (in press). The appeal(s) of character education. *Comparative Education.*

York Region. (n.d.). *York Region facts.* Retrieved April 30, 2007, from http://www.region.york.on.ca/About+Us/York+Region+Facts/default+York+Region+Facts.htm

York Region District School Board. (2002). *Family Workbook.* Retrieved September 9, 2005, from http://www.yrdsb.edu.on.ca/pdfs/w/charactermatters/FamilyCharacterWorkshop.pdf

York Region District School Board. (2003). *Character education; Policy #380.0.* Retrieved April 26, 2005, from http://www.yrdsb.edu.on.ca/page.cfm?id=TPP3800000

York Region District School Board. (2004). *Character Matters! Board Report 2004 Appendices*: York Region District School Board.

York Region District School Board. (2004, April 5a). Professional Development. *The Attribute 1(4).* Retrieved October 28, 2005, from http://yrlc.on.ca/charactermatters/attribute/

York Region District School Board. (2004, April 5b). Resources. *The Attribute 1(4).* Retrieved October 24, 2005, from http://yrlc.on.ca/charactermatters/attribute/

York Region District School Board. (2004, August 9). Creating opportunities to experience and practice character. *The Attribute 1(13).* Retrieved October 28, 2005, from http://yrlc.on.ca/charactermatters/attribute/

York Region District School Board. (2004, August 23). Cooperative learning and character: Community building in classrooms. *The Attribute 1(14).* Retrieved October 25, 2005, from http://yrlc.on.ca/charactermatters/attribute/

York Region District School Board. (2004, February 20). In the Schools. *The Attribute 1(1).* Retrieved October 28, 2005, from http://yrlc.on.ca/charactermatters/attribute/

York Region District School Board. (2004, July 26). Dissecting discipline. *The Attribute, 1*(12).

York Region District School Board. (2004, June 1). In the schools. *The Attribute 1(8).* Retrieved March 13, 2007, from http://theattribute.ca/archive/

York Region District School Board. (2004, March 8). Character in the community. *The Attribute 1(2).* Retrieved October 28, 2005, from http://yrlc.on.ca/charactermatters/attribute/

York Region District School Board. (2004, March 22). In our schools. *The Attribute 1(3).* Retrieved October 28, 2005, from http://yrlc.on.ca/charactermatters/attribute/

York Region District School Board. (2004, May 3). In the schools. *The Attribute 1(6).* Retrieved October 28, 2005, from http://yrlc.on.ca/charactermatters/attribute/

York Region District School Board. (2004, November 15). Character in the community. *The Attribute 2(5).* Retrieved October 31, 2005, from http://yrlc.on.ca/charactermatters/attribute/

York Region District School Board. (2004, October 4). Service learning and partnerships. *The Attribute 2 (2).* Retrieved July 27, 2006, from http://theattribute.ca/archive/

York Region District School Board. (2004, September 20). Resources. *The Attribute 2(1).* Retrieved October 31, 2005, from http://theattribute.ca/archive/

York Region District School Board. (2005, December 14). *The Attribute 3(5).* Retrieved January 11, 2006, from http://theattribute.ca/index.php?y=05&m=12

York Region District School Board. (2005, February 21). In our schools. *The Attribute 2(12).* Retrieved October 31, 2005, from http://yrlc.on.ca/charactermatters/attribute/

York Region District School Board. (2005, June 14). In our schools. *The Attribute 2(20).* Retrieved March 13, 2007, from http://theattribute.ca/archive/

York Region District School Board. (2005, March 21a). *The Attribute 2(14).* Retrieved November 7, 2005, from http://yrlc.on.ca/charactermatters/attribute/

York Region District School Board. (2005, March 21b). In our schools. *The Attribute 2 (14).* Retrieved November

7, 2005, from http://yrlc.on.ca/charactermatters/attribute/

York Region District School Board. (2005, May 17). In our schools. *The Attribute 1(18)*. Retrieved November 7, 2005, from http://yrlc.on.ca/charactermatters/attribute/

York Region District School Board. (n.d.-a). *Attributes*. Retrieved August 4, 2005, from http://www.yrdsb.edu.on.ca/page.cfm?id=ICM000012

York Region District School Board. (n.d.-b). *Character Matters! and Literacy*. Retrieved August 5, 2005, from http://www.yrdsb.edu.on.ca/page.cfm?id=ICM000013

York Region District School Board. (n.d.-c). *How to get involved: Curriculum*. Retrieved September 1, 2005, from http://www.yrdsb.edu.on.ca/page.cfm?id=ICM200212

York Region District School Board. (n.d.-d). *How to get involved: Principal's role*. Retrieved 1 May, 2006, from http://www.yrdsb.edu.on.ca/page.cfm?id=ICM200207

York Region District School Board. (n.d.-e). *How to get involved: Sample curriculum activities*. Retrieved September 1, 2005, from http://www.yrdsb.edu.on.ca/page.cfm?id=ICM200212

York Region District School Board. (n.d.-f). *How to get involved: Sample programme activities*. Retrieved September 1, 2005, from http://www.yrdsb.edu.on.ca/page.cfm?id=ICM200213

York Region District School Board. (n.d.-g). *How to get involved: Students*. Retrieved September 1, 2005, from http://www.yrdsb.edu.on.ca/page.cfm?id=ICM200210

York Region District School Board. (n.d.-h). *How to get involved: Teachers*. Retrieved September 1, 2005, from http://www.yrdsb.edu.on.ca/page.cfm?id=ICM200211

York Region District School Board. (n.d.-i). *Peer mediation, peace, conflict resolution*. Retrieved September 9, 2005, from http://www.yrdsb.edu.on.ca/page.cfm?id=ICM200670

York Region District School Board. (n.d.-j). *Questions and answers*. Retrieved March 23, 2004, from http://www.yrdsb.edu.on.ca/page.cfm?id=ICM000002#2

(This chapter originally appeared in the *Canadian Journal of Educational Administration and Policy*, No. 66 [December, 2007]: 1–24. Published with permission of the Faculty of Education, University of Manitoba.)

CHAPTER TWELVE

Through the Eyes of Students

High School Students' Perspectives on Character Education

MICHAEL H. ROMANOWSKI

Introduction

Character education is broad in scope and difficult to precisely define. For the purpose of this chapter, character education can best be described "as any school-initiated program, designed in cooperation with other community institutions, to shape directly and systematically the behavior of young people by influencing explicitly the non relativistic values believed directly to bring about that behavior" (Lockwood 1997, p. 179). Character education programs are intentional efforts by schools and teachers to foster good character in students and to help them "acquire a moral compass—that is a sense of right and wrong and the enduring habits necessary to live a good life" (Ryan & Cooper, 2000, p. 451).

Educators can find numerous studies and expert opinions, about character education, but they are seldom given the opportunity to view character education through the eyes of students. This chapter reports findings from a qualitative study conducted at one particular high school. It presents high school students' perspectives and understanding of character education.

Objectives of the study

This study examines one particular high school Character Education Program (CEP) as described by students and asks the question: What do students think about the CEP implemented in their school? The study is descriptive in that it does not evaluate the overall effectiveness of the CEP, but rather describes students' perspectives. The study began by raising the following research questions: 1) What is the purpose of the CEP as described by students? 2) What are the important, exciting, and negative aspects of the CEP as described by students? 3) Do students view the CEP as effective? 4) What do administrators and teachers need to know regarding the students' perspective when implementing a CEP?

The setting

This research centers on the school-wide CEP implemented at Edwardsville High School (the school's name has been changed) located in a rural setting in Northwest Ohio. The school is staffed with five administrators (two principals, two counselors, and an activity director), a coordinator for character education and service learning, and 38 faculty members. The school serves 575 students in grades 9–12. In response to the 1999 Columbine High School massacre, EHS administration and teachers met to discuss ways to better the civility of the school environment, improve academic performance, and increase community involvement. From these meetings, several teachers agreed to investigate and apply to the Ohio Department of Education's Partners in Character Education grant program. EHS received a $25,000 grant that was renewed for the 2001 school year. Additional funds were provided in order to examine a service learning option.

EHS formed a character education committee consisting of administrators, teachers, parents, selected students, community members, and local business leaders. Through consensus, the committee developed the following framework served as the basis for the CEP:

- Vision and Mission: to value self and others; to desire, know, and do right; and to serve all.
- Goals: to improve academic performance to develop and maintain a civil school environment to increase and maintain community involvement.
- Objectives: to develop students who know, desire, and do right.
- Nine Monthly Themes: respect, responsibility, citizenship, service, sensitivity, honesty, self-discipline, work ethic, and justice.
- 36 Words of the Week

The Character Education Committee has continued to meet on a monthly basis in order to secure funding and provide program direction.

The CEP consisted of a formal 30 minute class called Team Time for all students every Tuesday and Thursday. Students were assigned to Team Times based on grade levels. The first year lessons were designed to develop the knowing of character. The second year emphasized the desiring of character including conflict resolution and perspective, while the third and fourth years provided students with opportunities to apply various character traits. These lessons used a variety of teaching strategies including reflective questions, short stories, literature, and videotapes. Each team was encouraged to have an ongoing service project.

In addition to Team Times, students we presented with words of the week and various messages on the particular theme of the month. Guest speakers addressed topics such as conflict resolution, anger management, investments, nutrition, and environmental stewardship. The school was filled with posters announcing the trait of the month, the mission statement, and monthly character themes. Classroom walls displayed posters such as "the Golden Rule Rules" and "Save Sex for Marriage."

Faculty development included seven teachers attending Thomas Lickona's Summer Institute for the study of Character Education at the State College of New York at Cortland in the summer of 2000. Upon their return, these teachers became the leaders for the CEP and developed a three-year action plan. Throughout the year, several national advocates for character education were invited to the school in order to provide workshops for faculty and administration. Several teachers received mini-grants that enabled them to attend character education conferences and workshops throughout the United States.

The character education committee developed an assessment plan that used Lickona's 30 question School as a Caring Community Profile (SCCP)₁. The questionnaire was administered to each class at the beginning and end of each school year. Attitude improvements of 15 to 20% were recorded for the junior and senior classes over the first two years of the program.

Methods of investigation

Data collected in this qualitative study included semi-structured interviews and spontaneous conversations with students. The purpose of these interviews was to listen to students as they described their experiences, feelings, and thoughts about the CEP. All interviews were tape-recorded and transcribed, while notes were taken during spontaneous conversations. The interviews took place prior to the start of each school day and during lunch periods. Focus group interviews ranging from six to fourteen students with four of the Team Times classes (two senior, one junior, and one sophomore team time) were conducted, and students from seven classes were taken from class and interviewed in groups of three. A total of 144 students (over 25 percent of the EHS student body) were interviewed; 33 seniors, 47 juniors, 26 sophomores, and 38 freshmen. Through inductive analysis, various themes emerged from the data. The information was categorized according to topics and categories that were predominantly derived from the data itself. Pertinent examples and quotes were identified and added to the relevant categories. The findings discussed below were similar throughout the four grade levels and consistent in one-on-one, three-on-one and large group interviews.

Findings

This study presents the students' perspectives and understandings of the CEP implemented in their school. The following themes emerged from the data analysis.

Why Do We Need This Character Education Stuff?

Regarding the purpose of the CEP, the large majority of the EHS students that were interviewed understood and agreed with the good intentions of the administration's rationale. They saw the purpose for character education to be "to make us better people." Students' responses seemed to accept the basic premise that society, the school climate, and individuals in general need improvement regarding character issues, and they agreed that the administration had "good intentions." Although most students believed that character education was important, they questioned the need for it in their own lives and the appropriateness of teaching character at the high school level:

> There is no need for this program…I think more or less we are already comfortable with our values and have decided how we are going to act. (Senior)

> I think it should be taught in elementary and junior high because no one is going to change their ways in high school they already are set in their ways. (Junior)

> By high school we already have our minds made up on what we are going to be like regardless of what teachers say. (Sophomore)

> What they are trying to teach is important but not at our level. We already know this. (Freshman)

These student comments support results from the Josephson Institute's 1998 Report Card on the Ethics of American Youth. This study presents findings that the majority of students believe "character was important, and 91 percent were satisfied with their own ethics and character."

Important to this perspective is not that students believe they fully understood character traits such as honesty, but rather they already knew the superficial level at which these traits are taught within the CEP program. For example, several students disputed a Team Time lesson where a videotaped scenario poses a question concerning if students should return a dollar bill that was found in a parking lot. One student sarcastically commented that the videotapes "are like if Bobby found a dollar on the playground would you turn it into the teacher or keep it…who cares it just a dollar. They are kind of cheesy…there is more to honesty than that." Because of what students perceived as a simplistic presentation of character traits, they were quick to dismiss the program or their need for character education citing their prior knowledge and experiences.

Students were satisfied with their character. Their concern centered on the idea that some students chose not to act on their morals. For example, during interviews when students discussed that they already knew values such as honesty, they were asked why there was cheating at their school. The following response sums the majority of EHS students' views:

> Everyone knows what honesty is it is; just that many don't want to be honest. We know what is right and wrong we just don't do it…it is too late to teach these [character traits] (Sophomore)

The argument that they know these character traits and that it is too late to teach character in high school served as the foundation for the vast majority of students' argument that the CEP should be used in the elementary or middle school where the program would be more effective.

Don't Teach Down to Us.

Not only did students question whether values can be taught, but they were also concerned with the pedagogical aspects of the CEP. One Senior commented that, "The way it (CEP) is taught right now, it should be for middle and elementary school. They teach us like little kids." This quote exemplifies the frustrating climate at EHS because of what students perceived as inappropriate teaching, better suited for elementary or middle school students. In one particular Team Time, Juniors created acrostic poems describing the various characteristics of being honest. Students argued that they simply went through the motions because the strategy to teach honest behavior was childlike and demeaning.

From the students' standpoint, Kohn (1997) rightly argues that most strategies used in CEP programs are limited to simple memory level thinking skills with minimum instructional time spent on developing the more complex understanding of character traits and their application:

> The great majority of character education programs consist largely of exhortation and directed recitation. The leading providers of curriculum materials walk teachers through highly structured lessons in which character related concepts are described and then students are drilled until they can produce the right answers. (p. 158)

Student contention surfaced when curriculum and teaching were regarded as demeaning, ineffective, and the traits themselves were reduced to what students perceived as a simplistic level. The following student comments described this disagreement and frustration toward this aspect of the CEP:

> The worksheets are kind of a drag. They are teaching us how to be nice to people so they give us a word search. You don't learn how to be nice to people by doing a word search. Some of this stuff is just ineffective…a lot of true and false stuff. I don't think you can teach character with busy work. It just doesn't work. (Sophomore)

> I don't think writing a 150 word essay is going to make me a better person. (Sophomore)

This discontent about teaching strategies was closely related to the curriculum. One student commented that the CEP needs "to address the real problems not these petty things." The curriculum and teaching strategies left little room for discussion or alternative opinions. Students indicated that discussion was limited because there was only one acceptable answer to the "ethical dilemmas."

Another teaching tool used in the CEP was posters. Classrooms walls and hallways were pasted with posters that displayed the words of the week, the nine character traits, and an assortment of character traits and motivational messages. Some of these were made by students, but most were supplied with the character education curriculum. Were these posters effective? Did students notice and read the posters? Citing Berkowitz and McDonnell, professors of character education at the University of St. Louis, Berreth and Ernst (2001) argue that there is "no research that suggests that posters, signs, and trinkets foster human development." Several students expressed similar concerns:

> Posters are never read. They look like things I would see in my fifth grade class…they are not affecting anyone and if they do it is not a very big impact.

> The posters are dumb! No one reads them and they are not real!

Although these posters contained clever slogans and had very important messages about character and behavior, it seems that they are irrelevant to students and the overall CEP when simply displayed on walls.

In contrast, when teachers used posters in class and modeled the desired behavior, there seemed to be somewhat greater impact on students. For example, one poster titled "Insert Here" encouraged students to discover the roots to the problems in their lives. Instead of blaming others for late homework, missed assignments or an array of other problems, the poster encouraged students to realize that they are in control of particular situations and are responsible for their behavior and related consequences. Several students commented that one teacher used this poster in an effort to demonstrate that students had the responsibility for their homework and that she would no longer "nag" and "pester" them for their homework. The students believed that this teacher changed her behavior by applying the poster to her own life and forced them to "own up" to their responsibilities.

Finally, Berreth and Ernst (2001) argued that the shallowness of character education is a concern. In particular, "words of the week" programs where students are exposed to a term describing a character trait are superficial and overly simplistic. Students interviewed at EHS support this perspective. When asked, students seldom recalled the word of the day or week without looking around the room to locate posters that would provide them with this information.

Student Resistance to Character Education

It is clear that EHS students have conflict with the CEP, and this conflict often surfaces as a form of resistance. The concept of resistance can best be described as a "principled, conscious, ideological nonconformity which has its philosophical differences between the individual and the institution" (Bennet deMarrais & LeCompte, 1999, p. 138). Resistance to institutional constraints is more than simple student misbehavior. Rather, resistance involves withholding assent from school authorities such as administrators or teachers and resistive behaviors manifest themselves in school in a variety of forms. All forms of student resistance become problematic for teachers and schools and serve to undermine the CEP. It is important to note that students' resistive actions were in no way directed at the specific character traits that were being promoted. Student resistance focused on their belief that they already knew the character traits, on the simplistic strategies used to teach character education, and on their judgment that the traits were being "forced" or "jammed down their throats." Student resistance took many forms. First, students ridiculed the character education program.

> We mock the program. Like if Mrs. Smith tells us that we should do something then we will exaggerate it times ten. We will beat it to death. If we are learning compassion or something we will be so nice to each other until it is over and out of her sight. We just make fun of it. (Sophomore)

This form of resistance was an extremely effective way for students to cope and deal with imposed school knowledge. They used humor to endure what they saw as unnecessary knowledge that was being forced upon them.

Second, students indicated that they engaged in some of the traditional types of resistance. Students chose to ignore the teacher and talk with other students about "more important things" during Team Times. Others chose behaviors such as sending notes to one another, sleeping, goofing off, or trying to "get the teacher going" as their responses to the character education program that they perceived as being forced upon them.

Finally, because students viewed the CEP material as meaningless or imposed, they often engaged in intellectual resistance. This type of resistance represented a decision on the part of the student not to engage the material in any meaningful way. Instead of some of the traditional forms of resistance that emerge as a student who stops studying engages in "smart-aleck" misbehavior, commits vandalism, or drops out of school, intellectual resistance occurred in the form of vocal questioning or a conscious nonparticipation in classroom activities and assignments.

Some students openly questioned or challenged the place of character education. Others reported: "I do the assignments just to get them done," "I just go through the motions," and "We just play along, do the stupid work and move onto other more important things."

There were also students who resisted by completely withdrawing from all aspects of the classroom because they did not want to engage the material or openly challenge the authority.

Teacher Resistance to Character Education

EHS students were not the only ones who engaged in resistive behavior. Based on their Team Time experiences, students suggested that some faculty members also were resistive to the CEP. Because of messages transmitted through the hidden curriculum, students were able to articulate how various teacher behavior suggested faculty opposition to the CEP. The inconsistency of Team Times suggested teacher opposition. Students pointed out some team times strictly followed the CEP, other teachers rushed through the lessons, and some Team Times were used as study halls or free time.

There were teachers who bashed and made fun of the CEP by verbally attacking and labeling the CEP activities as "stupid" or "dumb." This indicated to students that it was all right for students to criticize and oppose character education. Because of the "authority" of teachers, teacher resistance does not legitimize the value or worth of the CEP and justified students' negative views, nonparticipation, and their own resistance.

Finally, students believed that the teacher opposition was not directed toward the character traits but rather teachers argued that character could not be taught in a separate class, the CEP teaching strategies were problematic, and that it was very difficult to change students' behavior at this point in their education. Students often cited teacher resistive behaviors as a main reason for the ineffectiveness of the CEP.

Students' Perceptions of Problems with CEP

EHS students discussed the effectiveness of the CEP in terms of what they believed hampered the program. For most students, student and faculty apathy was cited as a significant indicator of the CEP's ineffectiveness. Students also believed that high school students were already too set in their values for the CEP to change their behavior. There were numerous comments to this effect:

> I think we know what honesty is, and it teaches what honesty is about but it's not going to make us be honest. Just because we know what the right thing to do is, doing the right thing is a personal decision, and it can't be affected by a character education program like this. (Sophomore)

> Honestly, I doubt that you can make it any more effective. I am 15 years old and nothing Mrs. Smith says to me or any stupid worksheet or videotape about how sensitive or how many random acts of kindness I should do is going to help me or change me…I think my character can change but not the way they are doing it. (Sophomore)

Students voiced a concern that, even though there were many students in the school who needed character education, it was doubtful that these students would be willing to learn and change. One student's comment describes this view "there is no possibility for change in some people" and few, if any, students believed there was a need for change in their own lives.

An important element of character education is that the selected values are embraced and consistently modeled by the faculty (Character Education Partnership, 1999). Williams (1993) argues that, according to students, one of the most effective aspects of teaching values is that teachers themselves follow the rules and model the traits. EHS students also saw this as an important issue. They cited the lack of faculty change and consistent role modeling as evidence of the CEP's ineffectiveness. These student comments illustrate this perspective:

> Teachers who are trying to teach character education don't have the character traits that they are trying to teach. Things that teachers say are rude and shouldn't be said, but they are. Then they tell us to respect others? (Sophomore)

> They want us to get excited and fired up about it (the CEP) but when we don't, they get mad and upset. That seems to contradict the whole character education thing. (Junior)

This demonstrates the need for a change in faculty behavior that is in harmony with the traits of the CEP.

What Works and Why: Student Thoughts and Suggestions

For students, what worked really meant what was interesting, entertaining, and worthwhile. Throughout the interviews, not only were students' negative voices heard, but these same students offered suggestions as to how to improve the quality and effectiveness of the CEP. Students believed that any CEP must use a relevant and interesting curriculum that was not isolated but rather integrated within the existing school curriculum. Included in this curriculum was class discussion. For example, one student stated that class discussion proved both interesting and effective:

> Last year our teacher was gone and we had Mr. Smith come in and we put the green book away and we sat around like this (semicircle) and had a class discussion about the value we were on and how it was used in our everyday life. That was so much more productive than reading out of a book.

Relevant class discussion was important not only because of its interest value but also because students heard their peers' thoughts about various traits and issues.

Second, there were numerous students who made positive comments about one guest speaker they had the opportunity to hear. He was a Vietnam veteran who was considered interesting because of his real life experiences. Interesting and effective guest speakers who have had relevant stories seem to have been enjoyed by students; however, there was an uncertainty as to their effectiveness in changing student behavior.

Finally, students indicated that popular culture can be an affective tool to engage character traits and offered several examples where teachers used popular culture to develop particular character traits. For example, a freshman Team Time group analyzed the Disney film *Mulan* and discussed issues dealing with citizenship and gender roles.

Another example of an effective use of popular media was the use of the sitcom *The Simpsons*. One student described how her teacher showed a segment of a *Simpsons* episode during Team Time, and the class analyzed Bart's disrespectful behavior toward his parents, peers, and others. The teacher and the ensuing class discussion pointed out the negative aspects of disrespect, how others view disrespectful individuals, and why Bart's behavior was inappropriate. Suggestions for change were also discussed. The use of relevant popular media is viewed by students as "an improvement from the character education videos."

Summary of Students' Perspectives

The following is a brief summary of findings regarding students' perspectives regarding the Character Education Program at EHS:

1. There was little need for character education because students already know the superficial level of character traits that are being taught in the CEP.
2. Topics were irrelevant to their lives and too simplistic.

Students viewed CEP teaching strategies as inappropriate and better suited for elementary or middle school.

1. Students engaged in various forms of resistance because they viewed character education as being forced upon them.
2. Students cited teacher resistance, lack of faculty involvement, and poor faculty role modeling as reasons for the CEP's ineffectiveness.
3. Students suggested relevant topics, interesting guest speakers, class discussion and the use of popular culture as effective CEP tools.

Discussion

The study raised several fundamental issues regarding character education. First, one of the primary goals of this CEP was to create an awareness in students about character issues. From student conversations, it is clear that the EHS student body seemed more aware of the character traits and issues that were being taught by the school. Most students interviewed had some insight into issues concerning character traits, were quick to provide relevant examples, and were capable to articulate their view on character education. Several students mentioned that the program would have some benefits after their graduation such as helping them raise their own children. Second, with any CEP we must be concerned about the failure to address social and cultural influences that may play a major role in the development of character. Character education often centers on individual behavior exclusive from the many cultural, economic and social factors that influence individual behavior. Kohn (1997) argues that "when character education programs attempt to 'fix the kids,' they ignore the accumulated evidence from the files of social psychology demonstrating that much of how we act, and who we are, reflects the situation in which we find ourselves" (pp. 155–156). The assumption is that children can simply be "fixed" by adding character education without ever addressing the causes of "character deficiency." Before addressing a lack of self-control, an individual's social environment must be considered and included in character education. Finally, the encouraging results from the School as a Caring Community Profile (SCCP) assessment tool cannot be overlooked. EHS spring (2002) SCCP results indicated that EHS juniors improved in 26 of 30 areas that are assessed. In particular, all four grade levels improved in areas such as "refraining from put downs" and "not fighting as a way to resolve conflict." Although EHS lacked a control group for comparison purposes, the administration viewed these results as positive.

Any assessment of the program must be skeptical because EHS students viewed the CEP as one more requirement that must be learned and then given back to teachers in one form or another in order to meet the requirement. For example from interviews, students clearly knew that cheating was unacceptable, and they would likely respond in that manner when answering a given survey. However, these students also acknowledged that cheating was still a part of their school experience.

Suggestions for Schools and Teachers

According to these findings, students presented a unified viewpoint regarding their attitudes toward the EHS character education program. Not only did they express a variety of concerns but also offered valuable suggestions as to how character education could be improved.

1. *Character education must be taught at appropriate levels with appropriate teaching strategies.* High school CEPs must provide a more mature approach to character education by providing opportunities

for students to engage in discussion of relevant and complicated character traits and dilemmas. CEP curriculum should include opportunities for implementing character traits when making decisions and topics must be "more relevant," "interesting," "realistic," and "hard hitting." Suggestions from students included issues such as teenage pregnancy, premarital sex, school problems, personal student problems, drugs, alcohol,"real problems addressed and taught in a realistic way." The administration and faculty should not only use student suggestions but consult sources like Kessler (2000) in order to gain insight into the questions that concern students at different grade levels.

2. Faculty and students must develop accurate understandings of church and state in order to better address controversial topics.

This concern was prompted by several student comments regarding the school's role dealing with moral or value laden issues.

> I think that if they can't teach religion they shouldn't be able to teach character education because in my mind they go hand-in-hand. You know church and state. (Sophomore)

Because this uninformed perspective is common among students, faculty must be able to articulate accurate understandings of church and state issues and how this is relevant to character education. This will prove helpful in reducing student resistance and will encourage students and faculty to be more open to dealing with these issues.

3. *Character traits should be integrated into the existing curriculum.* Williams (1993) argues that students believed that teaching morals fails "if teachers try to make it a big deal or have a separate class" (p. 22). This view was articulated by several EHS students who were frustrated that they had to spend time in the extra CEP class, time that could be used to prepare academically and get ready for college. If this is the case, then administrators and teachers must consider writing the core values into the existing K12 curriculum. This approach will prove to be more acceptable and meaningful for students and teachers. For example, the use of current issues might be worthwhile in addressing specific character traits.

4. *Administrators and teachers must develop complex understandings of the workings of student resistance.* They must move beyond simplistic explanations of student misbehavior as laziness, apathy, and seekers of attention. Instead, they must realize that resistance is a powerful force that shapes classrooms. Included in this understanding is an awareness and concern for how resistance influences classroom climate.

    One possibility is for students to write a letter to the superintendent, or school board member regarding why character education should or should not be introduced into their school. The assignment should require students to support their positions with examples, consequences, their own personal thoughts and any problems they see with character education. This information will provide teachers with insight into the class climate, their students' views and struggles with character education, and can be used to better implement appropriate teaching strategies.

5. *Administrators must gain faculty support.* Etzioni suggests that administrators hold a faculty retreat to discuss issues and concerns about character education (Berreth & Scherer, 1993). Questions such as: What are the value messages being sent to our students explicitly and implicitly? Are those the messages the faculty wants to transmit? How can the faculty structure teaching, the classroom, and school to bring the messages sent closer to the messages they want to send? The retreat can be used to discuss the CEP, and selected traits, to develop an awareness of the assumptions about character education, and discuss the faculty's concerns about implementing such a program. The results of these discussions cannot be cosmetic. The ideas and thoughts of the faculty must be used as a productive tool in planning a character education program in order to increase faculty support. This time can also be used to discuss effectiveness and encourage teachers to model these traits and to be flexible in order

to increase a comfortable feeling about particular lessons while meeting students' needs.

6. *Administrators should use students' ideas and input.* These findings suggest that not only is there a need for administrators and teachers to initially acquire the students' perspective prior to developing a character education program, but also that it is important to continually assess the students' thoughts and feelings regarding character education. There is no question that the use of ideas and input from a variety students, when they have the appropriate background, will certainly aid in the acceptance and success of any CEP.

References

Bennet deMarrais, K., & LeCompte, M. (1998). *The way schools work: A sociological analysis of education* (3rd ed.). New York: Addison Wesley Longman.

Berreth, D. G., & Ernst, D. (2001). *Character education: A common goal.* ASCD Infobrief, Issue 25. Alexandria, VA: Association for Supervision and Curriculum Development.

Berreth, D., & Scherer, M. (1993). On transmitting values: A conversation with Amitai Etzioni. *Educational Leadership, 51* (3), 12–15.

Character Education Partnership. (1999). *Character education: Questions and answers.* Washington, DC: Author.

Kessler, R. (2000). *The soul of education: Helping students find connection, compassion, and character at school.* Alexandria, VA: Association for Supervision and Curriculum Development.

Kohn, A. (1997). The trouble with character education. In A. Molnar (ed.), *The construction of children's character* (pp. 154–162). Chicago, IL: The University of Chicago Press.

Lockwood, A. L. (1997). What is character education? In A. Molnar (ed.), *The construction of children's character* (pp. 174–185). Chicago, IL: The National Society for the Study of Education.

Ryan, K., & Cooper, J. M. (2000). *Those who can, teach.* Boston, MA: Houghton Mifflin Company.

Williams, M. M. (1993). Actions speak louder than words: What students think. *Educational Leadership, 51* (3), 22–23.

(This chapter originally appeared in *American Secondary Education,* Vol. 32, No. 1 [Fall, 2003]: 3–20. Published with permission of The Dwight Schar College of Education, Ashland University.)

CHAPTER THIRTEEN

How Not to Teach Values

A Critical Look at Character Education

ALFIE KOHN

Teachers and schools tend to mistake good behavior for good character. What they prize is docility, suggestibility; the child who will do what he is told; or even better, the child who will do what is wanted without even having to be told. They value most in children what children least value in themselves. Small wonder that their effort to build character is such a failure; they don't know it when they see it.

JOHN HOLT, *HOW CHILDREN FAIL*

Were you to stand somewhere in the continental United States and announce, "I'm going to Hawaii," it would be understood that you were heading for those islands in the Pacific that collectively constitute the 50th state. Were you to stand in Honolulu and make the same statement, however, you would probably be talking about one specific island in the chain—namely, the big one to your southeast. The word *Hawaii* would seem to have two meanings, a broad one and a narrow one; we depend on context to tell them apart.

The phrase *character education* also has two meanings. In the broad sense, it refers to almost anything that schools might try to provide outside of academics, especially when the purpose is to help children grow into good people. In the narrow sense, it denotes a particular style of moral training, one that reflects particular values as well as particular assumptions about the nature of children and how they learn.

Unfortunately, the two meanings of the term have become blurred, with the narrow version of character education dominating the field to the point that it is frequently mistaken for the broader concept. Thus educators who are keen to support children's social and moral development may turn, by default, to a program with a certain set of methods and a specific agenda that, on reflection, they might very well find objectionable.

My purpose in this article is to subject these programs to careful scrutiny and, in so doing, to highlight the possibility that there are other ways to achieve our broader objectives. I address myself not so much to those readers who are avid proponents of character education (in the narrow sense) but to those who simply want to help children become decent human beings and may not have thought carefully about what they are being offered.

***

Let me get straight to the point. What goes by the name of character education nowadays is, for the most part, a collection of exhortations and extrinsic inducements designed to make children work harder and do what they're told. Even when other values are also promoted—caring or fairness, say—the preferred method of instruction is tantamount to indoctrination. The point is to drill students in specific behaviors rather than to engage them in deep, critical reflection about certain ways of being. This is the impression one gets from reading articles and books by contemporary proponents of character education as well as the curriculum materials sold by the leading national programs. The impression is only strengthened by visiting schools that have been singled out for their commitment to character education. To wit:

A huge, multiethnic elementary school in Southern California uses a framework created by the Jefferson Center for Character Education. Classes that the principal declares "well behaved" are awarded Bonus Bucks, which can eventually be redeemed for an ice cream party. On an enormous wall near the cafeteria, professionally painted *Peanuts* characters instruct children: "Never talk in line." A visitor is led to a fifth-grade classroom to observe an exemplary lesson on the current character education topic. The teacher is telling students to write down the name of the person they regard as the "toughest worker" in school. The teacher then asks them, "How many of you are going to be tough workers?" (Hands go up.) "Can you be a tough worker at home, too?" (Yes.)

A small, almost entirely African American school in Chicago uses a framework created by the Character Education Institute. Periodic motivational assemblies are used to "give children a good pep talk," as the principal puts it, and to reinforce the values that determine who will be picked as Student of the Month. Rule number one posted on the wall of a kindergarten room is "We will obey the teachers." Today, students in this class are listening to the story of "Lazy Lion," who orders each of the other animals to build him a house, only to find each effort unacceptable. At the end, the teacher drives home the lesson: "Did you ever hear Lion say thank you?" (No.) "Did you ever hear Lion say please?" (No.) "It's good to always say…what?" (Please.) The reason for using these words, she points out, is that by doing so we are more likely to get what we want.

A charter school near Boston has been established specifically to offer an intensive, homegrown character education curriculum to its overwhelmingly white, middle-class student body. At weekly public ceremonies, certain children receive a leaf that will then be hung in the Forest of Virtue. The virtues themselves are "not open to debate," the headmaster insists, since moral precepts in his view enjoy the same status as mathematical truths. In a first-grade classroom, a teacher is observing that "it's very hard to be obedient when you want something. I want you to ask yourself 'Can I have it—and why not?'" She proceeds to ask the students, "What kinds of things show obedience?" and, after collecting a few suggestions, announces that she's "not going to call on anyone else now. We could go on forever but we have to have a moment of silence and then a spelling test."

***

Some of the most popular schoolwide strategies for improving students' character seem dubious on their face. When President Clinton mentioned the importance of character education in his 1996 State of the Union address, the only specific practice he recommended was requiring students to wear uniforms. The premises here are, first, that children's character can be improved by forcing them to dress alike, and second, that if adults object to students' clothing, the best solution is not to invite them to reflect together about how this problem might be solved, but instead to compel them all to wear the same thing.

A second strategy, also consistent with the dominant philosophy of character education, is an exercise that might be called "If It's Tuesday, This Must Be Honesty." Here, one value after another is targeted, with each assigned its own day, week, or month. This seriatim approach is unlikely to result in a lasting commitment to any of these values, much less a feeling for how they may be related. Nevertheless, such programs are taken very seriously by some of the same people who are quick to dismiss other educational programs, such as those intended to promote self-esteem as silly and ineffective.

Then there is the strategy of offering students rewards when they are "caught" being good, an approach favored by right-wing religious groups[1] and orthodox behaviorists but also by leaders of— and curriculum suppliers for—the character education movement.[2] Because of its popularity and because a sizable body of psychological evidence germane to the topic is available, it is worth lingering on this particular practice for a moment.

In general terms, what the evidence suggests is this: the more we reward people for doing something, the more likely they are to lose interest in whatever they had to do to get the reward. Extrinsic motivation, in other words, is not only quite different from intrinsic motivation but actually tends to erode it.[3] This effect has been demonstrated under many different circumstances and with respect to many different attitudes and behaviors. Most relevant to character education is a series of studies showing that individuals who have been rewarded for doing something nice become less likely to think of themselves as caring or helpful people and more likely to attribute their behavior to the reward.

"Extrinsic incentives can, by undermining self-perceived altruism, decrease intrinsic motivation to help others," one group of researchers concluded on the basis of several studies. "A person's kindness, it seems, cannot be bought."[4] The same applies to a person's sense of responsibility, fairness, perseverance, and so on. The lesson a child learns from Skinnerian tactics is that the point of being good is to get rewards. No wonder researchers have found that children who are frequently rewarded—or, in another study, children who receive positive reinforcement for caring, sharing, and helping—are less likely than other children to keep doing those things.[5]

In short, it makes no sense to dangle goodies in front of children for being virtuous. But even worse than rewards are *a*wards—certificates, plaques, trophies, and other tokens of recognition whose numbers have been artificially limited, so only a few can get them. When some children are singled out as "winners," the central message that every child learns is this: "Other people are potential obstacles to my success.[6] Thus the likely result of making students beat out their peers for the distinction of being the most virtuous is not only less intrinsic commitment to virtue but also a disruption of relationships and, ironically, of the experience of community that is so vital to the development of children's character.

Unhappily, the problems with character education (in the narrow sense, which is how I'll be using the term unless otherwise indicated) are not restricted to such strategies as enforcing sartorial uniformity, scheduling a value of the week, or offering students a "doggie biscuit" for being good. More deeply troubling are the fundamental assumptions, both explicit and implicit, that inform character education programs. Let us consider five basic questions that might be asked of any such program: At what level are problems addressed? What is the underlying theory of human nature? What is the ultimate goal? Which values are promoted? And finally, How is learning thought to take place?

1. At what level are problems addressed?

One of the major purveyors of materials in this field, the Jefferson Center for Character Education in Pasadena, California, has produced a video that begins with some arresting images—quite literally. Young people are shown being led away in handcuffs, the point being that crime can be explained on the basis of an "erosion of American core values," as the narrator intones ominously. The idea that social problems can be explained by the fact that traditional virtues are no longer taken seriously is offered by many proponents of character education as though it were just plain common sense.

But if people steal or rape or kill solely because they possess bad values—that is, because of their personal characteristics—the implication is that political and economic realities are irrelevant and need not be addressed. Never mind staggering levels of unemployment in the inner cities or a system in which more and more of the nation's wealth is concentrated in fewer and fewer hands; just place the blame on individuals whose characters are deficient. A key tenet of the "Character Counts!" Coalition, which bills itself as a nonpartisan umbrella group devoid of any political agenda, is the highly debatable proposition that "negative social influences can [be] and usually are overcome by the exercise of free will and character."[7] What is presented as common sense is, in fact, conservative ideology.

Let's put politics aside, though. If a program proceeds by trying to "fix the kids"—as do almost all brands of character education—it ignores the accumulated evidence from the field of social psychology demonstrating that much of how we act and who we are reflects the situations in which we find ourselves. Virtually all the landmark studies in this discipline have been variations on this theme. Set up children in an extended team competition at summer camp and you will elicit unprecedented levels of aggression. Assign adults to the roles of prisoners or guards in a mock jail, and they will start to become their roles. Move people to a small town, and they will be more likely to rescue a stranger in need. In fact, so common is the tendency to attribute to an individual's personality or character what is actually a function of the social environment that social psychologists have dubbed this the "fundamental attribution error."

A similar lesson comes to us from the movement concerned with Total Quality Management associated with the ideas of the late W. Edwards Deming. At the heart of Deming's teaching is the notion that the "system" of an organization largely determines the results. The problems experienced in a corporation, therefore, are almost always due to systemic flaws rather than to a lack of effort or ability on the part of individuals in that organization. Thus, if we are troubled by the way students are acting, Deming, along with most social psychologists, would presumably have us transform the structure of the classroom rather than try to remake the students themselves—precisely the opposite of the character education approach.

2. What is the view of human nature?

Character education's "fix-the-kids" orientation follows logically from the belief that kids need fixing. Indeed, the movement seems to be driven by a stunningly dark view of children—and, for that matter, of people in general. A "comprehensive approach [to character education] is based on a somewhat dim view of human nature," acknowledges William Kilpatrick, whose book *Why Johnny Can't*

Tell Right from Wrong contains such assertions as: "Most behavior problems are the result of sheer 'willfulness' on the part of children."[8]

Despite—or more likely because of—statements like that, Kilpatrick has frequently been invited to speak at character education conferences.[9] But that shouldn't be surprising in light of how many prominent proponents of character education share his views. Edward Wynne says his own work is grounded in a tradition of thought that takes a "somewhat pessimistic view of human nature."[10] The idea of character development "sees children as self-centered," in the opinion of Kevin Ryan, who directs the Center for the Advancement of Ethics and Character at Boston University as well as heading up the character education network of the Association for Supervision and Curriculum Development.[11] Yet another writer approvingly traces the whole field back to the bleak worldview of Thomas Hobbes: it is "an obvious assumption of character education," writes Louis Goldman, that people lack the instinct to work together. Without laws to compel us to get along, "our natural egoism would lead us into 'a condition of warre one against another.'"[12] This sentiment is echoed by F. Washington Jarvis, headmaster of the Roxbury Latin School in Boston, one of Ryan's favorite examples of what character education should look like in practice. Jarvis sees human nature as "mean, nasty, brutish, selfish, and capable of great cruelty and meanness. We have to hold a mirror up to the students and say, 'This is who you are. Stop it.'"[13]

Even when proponents of character education don't express such sentiments explicitly, they give themselves away by framing their mission as a campaign for self-control. Amitai Etzioni, for example, does not merely include this attribute on a list of good character traits, but he *defines* character principally in terms of the capacity "to control impulses and defer gratification."[14] This is noteworthy because the virtue of self-restraint—or at least the decision to give special emphasis to it—has historically been preached by those, from St. Augustine to the present, who see people as basically sinful.

In fact, at least three assumptions seem to be at work when the need for self-control is stressed: first, that we are all at war not only with others but with ourselves, torn between our desires and our reason (or social norms); second, that these desires are fundamentally selfish, aggressive, or otherwise unpleasant; and third, that these desires are very strong, constantly threatening to overpower us if we don't rein them in. Collectively, these statements describe religious dogma, not scientific fact. Indeed, the evidence from several disciplines converges to cast doubt on this sour view of human beings and, instead, supports the idea that it is as "natural" for children to help as to hurt. I will not rehearse that evidence here, partly because I have done so elsewhere at some length.[15] Suffice it to say that even the most hardheaded empiricist might well conclude that the promotion of prosocial values consists to some extent of supporting (rather than restraining or controlling) many facets of the self. Any educator who adopts this more balanced position might think twice before joining an educational movement that is finally inseparable from the doctrine of original sin.

3. What is the ultimate goal?

It may seem odd even to inquire about someone's reasons for trying to improve children's character. But it is worth mentioning that the whole enterprise—not merely the particular values that are favored—is often animated by a profoundly conservative, if not reactionary, agenda. Character education based on "acculturating students to conventional norms of 'good' behavior...resonates with neoconservative concerns for social stability," observed David Purpel.[16] The movement has been described by another critic as a "yearning for some halcyon days of moral niceties and social tranquility."[17] But it is not merely a social order that some are anxious to preserve (or recover): character education is vital, according to one vocal proponent, because "the development of character is the backbone of the economic system" now in place.[18]

Character education, or any kind of education, would look very different if we began with other objectives—if, for example, we were principally concerned with helping children become active participants in a democratic society (or agents for transforming a society into one that is authentically democratic). It would look different if our top priority were to help students develop into principled and caring members of a community or advocates for social justice. To be sure, these objectives are not inconsistent with the desire to preserve certain traditions, but the point would then be to help children decide which traditions are worth preserving and why, based on these other considerations. That is not at all the same as endorsing anything that is traditional or making the preservation of tradition our primary concern. In short, we want to ask character education proponents what goals they emphasize—and ponder whether their broad vision is compatible with our own.

4. Which values?

Should we allow values to be taught in school? The question is about as sensible as asking whether our bodies should be allowed to contain bacteria. Just as humans are teeming with microorganisms, so schools are teeming with values. We can't see the former because they're too small; we don't notice the latter because they're too similar to the values of the culture at large. Whether or not we deliberately adopt a character or moral education program, we are always teaching values. Even people who insist that they are opposed to values in school usually mean that they are opposed to values other than their own.[19]

And that raises the inevitable question: Which values, or whose, should we teach? It has already become a cliche to reply that this question should not trouble us because, while there may be disagreement on certain issues, such as abortion, all of us can agree on a list of basic values that children ought to have. Therefore, schools can vigorously and unapologetically set about teaching all of those values.

But not so fast. Look at the way character education programs have been designed and you will discover, alongside such unobjectionable items as "fairness" or "honesty," an emphasis on values that are, again, distinctly conservative—and, to that extent, potentially controversial. To begin with, the famous Protestant work ethic is prominent: children should learn to "work hard and complete their tasks well and promptly, even when they do not want to," says Ryan.[20] Here the Latin question *Cui bono?* comes to mind. Who benefits when people are trained not to question the value of what they have been told to do but simply to toil away at it—and to regard this as virtuous?[21] Similarly, when Wynne defines the moral individual as someone who is not only honest but also "diligent, obedient, and patriotic,"[22] readers may find themselves wondering whether these traits really qualify as moral—as well as reflecting on the virtues that are missing from this list.

Character education curricula also stress the importance of things like "respect," "responsibility," and "citizenship." But these are slippery terms, frequently used as euphemisms for uncritical deference to authority. Under the headline "The Return of the 'Fourth R'"—referring to "respect, responsibility, or rules"—a news magazine recently described the growing popularity of such practices as requiring uniforms, paddling disobedient students, rewarding those who are compliant, and "throwing disruptive kids out of the classroom."[23] Indeed, William Glasser observed some time ago that many educators "teach thoughtless conformity to school rules and call the conforming child 'responsible.'"[24] I once taught at a high school where the principal frequently exhorted students to "take responsibility." By this he meant specifically that they should turn in their friends who used drugs.

Exhorting students to be "respectful" or rewarding them if they are caught being "good" may likewise mean nothing more than getting them to do whatever the adults demand. Following a lengthy article about character education in the *New York Times Magazine,* a reader mused, "Do you suppose that if Germany had had character education at the time, it would have encouraged children to fight Nazism or to support it?"[25] The more time I spend in schools that are enthusiastically implementing character education programs, the more I am haunted by that question.

In place of the traditional attributes associated with character education, Deborah Meier and Paul Schwarz of the Central Park East Secondary School in New York nominated two core values that a school might try to promote: "empathy and skepticism: the ability to see a situation from the eyes of another and the tendency to wonder about the validity of what we encountered."[26] Anyone who brushes away the question "Which values should be taught?" might speculate on the concrete differences between a school dedicated to turning out students who are empathic and skeptical and a school dedicated to turning out students who are loyal, patriotic, obedient, and so on.

Meanwhile, in place of such personal qualities as punctuality or perseverance, we might emphasize the cultivation of autonomy so that children come to experience themselves as "origins" rather than "pawns," as one researcher put it.[27] We might, in other words, stress self-determination at least as much as self-control. With such an agenda, it would be crucial to give students the chance to participate in making decisions about their learning and about how they want their classroom to be.[28] This stands in sharp contrast to a philosophy of character education like Wynne's, which decrees that "it is specious to talk about student choices" and offers students no real power except for when we give "some students authority over other students (for example, hall guard, class monitor)."[29]

Even with values that are widely shared, a superficial consensus may dissolve when we take a closer look. Educators across the spectrum are concerned about excessive attention to self-interest and are committed to helping students transcend a preoccupation with their own needs. But how does this concern play out in practice? For some of us, it takes the form of an emphasis on compassion; for the dominant character education approach, the alternative value to be stressed is loyalty, which is, of course, altogether different.[30] Moreover, as John Dewey remarked at the turn of the century, anyone seriously troubled about rampant individualism among children would promptly target for extinction the "drill-and-skill" approach to instruction: "The mere absorbing of facts and truths is so exclusively individual an affair that it tends very naturally to pass into selfishness."[31] Yet conservative champions of character education are often among the most outspoken supporters of a model of teaching that emphasizes rote memorization and the sequential acquisition of decontextualized skills.

Or take another example: all of us may say we endorse the idea of "cooperation," but what do we make of the practice of setting groups against one another in a quest for triumph, such that cooperation becomes the means and victory is the end? On the one hand, we might find this even more objectionable than individual competition. (Indeed, we might regard a "We're Number One!" ethic as a reason for schools to undertake something like character education in the first place.) On the other hand, "school-to-school, class-to-class, or row-to-row academic competitions" actually have been endorsed as part of a character education program,[32] along with contests that lead to awards for things like good citizenship.

The point, once again, is that it is entirely appropriate to ask which values a character education program is attempting to foster, notwithstanding the ostensible lack of controversy about a list of core values. It is equally appropriate to put such a discussion in context—specifically, in the context of which values are *currently* promoted in schools. The fact is that schools are already powerful social-izers of traditional values—although, as noted above, we may fail to appreciate the extent to which this is true because we have come to take these values for granted. In most schools, for example, students are taught—indeed, compelled—to follow the rules regardless of whether the rules are reason-able and to respect authority regardless of whether that respect has been earned. (This process isn't always successful, of course, but that is a different matter.) Students are led to accept competition as natural and desirable, and to see themselves more as discrete individuals than as members of a com-munity. Children in American schools are even expected to begin each day by reciting a loyalty oath to the Fatherland, although we call it by a different name. In short, the question is not whether to adopt the conservative values offered by most character education programs, but whether we want to con-solidate the conservative values that are already in place.

5. What is the theory of learning?

We come now to what may be the most significant, and yet the least remarked on, feature of char-acter education: the way values are taught and the way learning is thought to take place.

The character education coordinator for the small Chicago elementary school also teaches second grade. In her classroom, where one boy has been forced to sit by himself for the last two weeks ("He's kind of pesty"), she is asking the children to define tolerance. When the teacher gets the specific answers she is fishing for, she exclaims, "Say that again," and writes down only those responses. Later comes the moral: "If somebody doesn't think the way you think, should you turn them off?" (No.)

Down the hall, the first-grade teacher is fishing for answers on a different subject. "When we play games, we try to understand the—what?" (Rules.) A moment later, the children scramble to get into place, so she will pick them to tell a visitor their carefully rehearsed stories about conflict res-olution. Almost every child's account, narrated with considerable prompting by the teacher, concerns name-calling or some other unpleasant incident that was "correctly" resolved by finding an adult. The teacher never asks the children how they felt about what happened or invites them to reflect on what else might have been done. She wraps up the activity by telling the children, "What we need to do all the time is clarify—make it clear—to the adult what you did."

The schools with character education programs that I have visited are engaged largely in exhor-tation and directed recitation. At first one might assume this is due to poor implementation of the pro-grams on the part of individual educators. But the program themselves—and the theorists who promote them—really do seem to regard teaching as a matter of telling and compelling. For exam-ple, the broad-based "Character Counts!" Coalition offers a framework of six core character traits and then asserts that "young people should be specifically and repeatedly told what is expected of them." The leading providers of curriculum materials walk teachers through highly structured lessons in which character-related concepts are described and then students are drilled until they can produce the right answers.

Teachers are encouraged to praise children who respond correctly, and some programs actually include multiple-choice tests to ensure that students have learned their values. For example, here are two sample test questions prepared for teachers by the Character Education Institute, based in San Antonio, Texas: "Having to obey rules and regulations (a) gives everyone the same right to be an individual, (b) forces everyone to do the same thing at all times, (c) prevents persons from expressing their individually [sic]"; and "One reason why parents might not allow their children freedom of choice is (a) children are always happier when they are told what to do and when to do it, (b) parents aren't given a freedom of choice; therefore, children should not be given a choice either, (c) children do not always demonstrate that they are responsible enough to be given a choice." The correct answers, according to the answer key, are (a) and (c) respectively.

The Character Education Institute recommends "engaging the students in discussions," but only discussions of a particular sort: "Since the lessons have been designed to logically guide the students to the right answers, the teacher should allow the students to draw their own conclusions. However, if the students draw the wrong conclusion, the teacher is instructed to tell them why their conclusion is *wrong*."[33]

Students are told what to think and do, not only by their teachers but by highly didactic stories, such as those in the Character Education Institute's "Happy Life" series, which end with characters saying things like "I am glad that I did not cheat," or "Next time I will be helpful," or "I will never be selfish again." Most character education programs also deliver homilies by way of posters and banners and murals displayed throughout the school. Children who do as they are told are presented with all manner of rewards, typically in front of their peers.

Does all of this amount to indoctrination? Absolutely, says Wynne, who declares that "school is and should and must be inherently indoctrinative."[34] Even when character education proponents tiptoe around that word, their model of instruction is clear: good character and values are *instilled in* or *transmitted to* students. We are "planting the ideas of virtue, of good traits in the young," says William Bennett.[35] The virtues or values in question are fully formed, and, in the minds of many character education proponents, divinely ordained. The children are—pick your favorite metaphor—so many passive receptacles to be filled, lumps of clay to be molded, pets to be trained, or computers to be programmed.

Thus, when we see Citizen-of-the-Month certificates and "Be a good sport!" posters, when we find teachers assigning preachy stories and principals telling students what to wear, it is important that we understand what is going on. These techniques may appear merely innocuous or gimmicky; they may strike us as evidence of a scattershot, let's-try-anything approach. But the truth is that these are elements of a systematic pedagogical philosophy. They are manifestations of a model that sees children as objects to be manipulated rather than as learners to be engaged.

Ironically, some people who accept character education without a second thought are quite articulate about the bankruptcy of this model when it comes to teaching academic subjects. Plenty of teachers have abandoned the use of worksheets, textbooks, and lectures that fill children full of disconnected facts and skills. Plenty of administrators are working to create schools where students can actively construct meaning around scientific and historical and literary concepts. Plenty of educators, in short, realize that memorizing right answers and algorithms doesn't help anyone to arrive at a deep understanding of ideas.

And so we are left scratching our heads. Why would all these people, who know that the "transmission" model fails to facilitate intellectual development, uncritically accept the very same model to promote ethical development? How could they understand that mathematical truths cannot be shoved down students' throats but then participate in a program that essentially tries to shove moral truths down the same throats? In the case of individual educators, the simple answer may be that they missed the connection. Perhaps they just failed to recognize that "a classroom cannot foster the development of autonomy in the intellectual realm while suppressing it in the social and moral realms," as Constance Kamii and her colleagues put it not long ago.[36]

In the case of the proponents of character education, I believe the answer to this riddle is quite different. The reason they are promoting techniques that seem strikingly ineffective at fostering autonomy or ethical development is that, as a rule, they are not *trying* to foster autonomy or ethical development. The goal is not to support or facilitate children's social and moral growth, but simply to "demand good behavior from students" in Ryan's words.[37] The idea is to get compliance, to *make* children act the way we want them to.

Indeed, if these are the goals, then the methods make perfect sense—the lectures and pseudo-discussions, the slogans and the stories that conk students on the head with their morals. David Brooks, who heads the Jefferson Center for Character Education, frankly states, "We're in the advertising business." The way you get people to do something, whether it's buying Rice Krispies or becoming trustworthy, is to "encourage conformity through repeated messages."[38] The idea of selling virtues like cereal nearly reaches the point of self-parody in the Jefferson Center's curriculum, which includes the following activity: "There's a new product on the market! It's Considerate Cereal. Eating it can make a person more considerate. Design a label for the box. Tell why someone should buy and eat this cereal. Then list the ingredients."[39]

If "repeated messages" don't work, then you simply force students to conform: "Sometimes compulsion is what is needed to get a habit started," says William Kilpatrick.[40] We may recoil from the word "compulsion," but it is the premise of that sentence that really ought to give us pause. When education is construed as the process of inculcating *habits*—which is to say, unreflective actions—then it scarcely deserves to be called education at all. It is really, as Alan Lockwood saw, an attempt to get "mindless conformity to externally imposed standards of conduct."[41]

Notice how naturally this goal follows from a dark view of human nature. If you begin with the premise that "good conduct is not our natural first choice," then the best you can hope for is "the development of good habits"[42]—that is, a system that gets people to act unthinkingly in the manner that someone else has deemed appropriate. This connection recently became clear to Ann Medlock, whose Giraffe Project was designed to evoke "students' own courage and compassion" in thinking about altruism, but which, in some schools, was being turned into a traditional, authoritarian program in which students were simply told how to act and what to believe. Medlock recalls suddenly realizing what was going on with these educators: "Oh, *I* see where you're coming from. You believe kids are no damn good!"[43]

The character education movement's emphasis on habit, then, is consistent with its view of children. Likewise, its process matches its product. The transmission model, along with the use of rewards and punishments to secure compliance, seems entirely appropriate if the values you are trying to transmit are things like obedience and loyalty and respect for authority. But this approach overlooks an important distinction between product and process. When we argue about which traits to emphasize—compassion or loyalty, cooperation or competition, skepticism or obedience—we are trafficking in value judgments. When we talk about how best to teach these things, however, we are being descriptive rather than just prescriptive. Even if you like the sort of virtues that appear in character education programs, and even if you regard the need to implement those virtues as urgent, the attempt to transmit or instill them dooms the project because that is just not consistent with the best theory and research on how people learn. (Of course, if you have reservations about many of the values that the character educators wish to instill, you may be *relieved* that their favored method is unlikely to be successful.)

I don't wish to be misunderstood. The techniques of character education may succeed in temporarily buying a particular behavior. But they are unlikely to leave children with a *commitment* to that behavior, a reason to continue acting that way in the future. You can turn out automatons who utter the desired words or maybe even "emit" (to use the curious verb favored by behaviorists) the desired actions. But the words and actions are unlikely to continue—much less transfer to new situations—because the child has not been invited to integrate them into his or her value structure. As Dewey observed, "The required beliefs cannot be hammered in; the needed attitudes cannot be plastered on."[44] Yet watch a character education lesson in any part of the country and you will almost surely be observing a strenuous exercise in hammering and plastering.

For traditional moralists, the constructivist approach is a waste of time. If values and traditions and the stories that embody them already exist, then surely "we don't have to reinvent the wheel," remarks Bennett.[45] Likewise an exasperated Wynne: "Must each generation try to completely reinvent society?"[46] The answer is no—and yes. It is not as though everything that now exists must be discarded and entirely new values fashioned from scratch. But the process of learning does indeed require that meaning, ethical or otherwise, be actively invented and reinvented, from the inside out. It requires that children be given the opportunity to make sense of such concepts as fairness or courage, regardless of how long the concepts themselves have been around. Children must be invited to reflect on complex issues, to recast them in light of their own experiences and questions, to figure out for themselves—and with one another—what kind of person one ought to be, which traditions are worth keeping, and how to proceed when two basic values seem to be in conflict.[47]

In this sense, reinvention is necessary if we want to help children become moral people, as opposed to people who merely do what they are told—or reflexively rebel against what they are told. In fact, as Rheta DeVries and Betty Zan add (in a recent book that offers a useful antidote to traditional character education), "If we want children to resist [peer pressure] and not be victims of others' ideas, we have to educate children to think for themselves about all ideas, including those of adults."[48]

Traditionalists are even more likely to offer another objection to the constructivist approach, one that boils down to a single epithet: *relativism!* If we do anything other than insert moral absolutes in students, if we let them construct their own meanings, then we are saying that anything goes, that morality collapses into personal preferences. Without character education, our schools will just offer programs such as Values Clarification, in which adults are allegedly prohibited from taking a stand.

In response, I would offer several observations. First, the Values Clarification model of moral education, popular in some circles a generation ago, survives today mostly in the polemics of conservatives anxious to justify an indoctrinative approach. Naturally, no statistics are ever cited as to the number of school districts still telling students that any value is as good as any other—assuming the program actually said that in the first place.[49] Second, conservative critics tendentiously try to connect constructivism to relativism, lumping together the work of the late Lawrence Kohlberg with programs like Values Clarification.[50] The truth is that Kohlberg, while opposed to what he called the "bag of virtues" approach to moral education, was not much enamored of Values Clarification either, and he spent a fair amount of time arguing against relativism in general.[51]

If Kohlberg can fairly be criticized, it is for emphasizing moral reasoning, a cognitive process, to the extent that he may have slighted the affective components of morality, such as caring. But the traditionalists are not much for the latter either: caring is seen as an easy or soft virtue (Ryan) that isn't sufficiently "binding or absolute" (Kilpatrick). The objection to constructivism is not that empathy is eclipsed by justice, but that children—or even adults—should not have an active role to play in making decisions and reflecting on how to live. They should be led instead to an uncritical acceptance of ready-made truths. The character educator's job, remember, is to elicit the right answer from students and tell those who see things differently "why their conclusion is *wrong.*" Any deviation from this approach is regarded as indistinguishable from full-blown relativism; we must "plant" traditional values in each child or else morality is nothing more than a matter of individual taste. Such either/or thinking, long since discarded by serious moral philosophers,[52] continues to fuel character education and to perpetuate the confusion of education with indoctrination.

To say that students must construct meaning around moral concepts is not to deny that adults have a crucial role to play. The romantic view that children can basically educate themselves so long as grownups don't interfere is not taken seriously by any constructivists I know of—certainly not by Dewey, Piaget, Kohlberg, or their followers. Rather, like Values Clarification, this view seems to exist principally as a straw man in the arguments of conservatives. Let there be no question, then: educators, parents, and other adults are desperately needed to offer guidance, to act as models (we hope), to pose challenges that promote moral growth, and to help children understand the effects of their actions on other people, thereby tapping and nurturing a concern for others that is present in children from a very young age.[53]

***

Character education rests on three ideological legs: behaviorism, conservatism, and religion. Of these, the third raises the most delicate issues for a critic; it is here that the charge of *ad hominem* argument is most likely to be raised. So let us be clear: it is of no relevance that almost all of the leading proponents of character education are devout Catholics. But it is entirely relevant that, in the shadows of their writings, there lurks the assumption that only religion can serve as the foundation for good character. (William Bennett, for example, has flatly asserted that the difference between right and wrong cannot be taught "without reference to religion.")[54] It is appropriate to consider the personal beliefs of these individuals if those beliefs are ensconced in the movement they have defined and directed. What they do on Sundays is their own business, but if they are trying to turn our public schools into Sunday schools, that becomes everybody's business.

Even putting aside the theological underpinnings of the character education movement, the five questions presented in this article can help us describe the natural constituency of that movement. Logically, its supporters should be those who firmly believe that we should focus our efforts on repairing the characters of children rather than on transforming the environments in which they learn, those who assume the worst about human nature, those who are more committed to preserving than to changing our society, those who favor such values as obedience to authority, and those who define learning as the process of swallowing whole a set of preexisting truths. It stands to reason that readers who recognize themselves in this description would enthusiastically endorse character education in its present form.

The rest of us have a decision to make. Either we define our efforts to promote children's social and moral development as an *alternative* to "character education," thereby ceding that label to the people who have already appropriated it, or we try to *reclaim* the wider meaning of the term by billing what we are doing as a different kind of character education.

The first choice—opting out—seems logical: it strains the language to use a single phrase to describe practices as different as engaging students in reflecting about fairness, on the one hand, and making students dress alike, on the other. It seems foolish to pretend that these are just different versions of the same thing, and thus it may be unreasonable to expect someone with a constructivist or progressive vision to endorse what is now called character education. The problem with abandoning this label, however, is that it holds considerable appeal for politicians and members of the public at large. It will be challenging to explain that "character education" is not synonymous with helping children to grow into good people and, indeed, that the movement associated with the term is a good deal more controversial than it first appears.

The second choice, meanwhile, presents its own set of practical difficulties. Given that the individuals and organizations mentioned in this article have succeeded in putting their own stamp on character education, it will not be easy to redefine the phrase so that it can also signify a very different approach. It will not be easy, that is, to organize conferences, publish books and articles, and develop curricular materials that rescue the broad meaning of "character education."

Whether we relinquish or retain the nomenclature, though, it is vital that we work to decouple most of what takes place under the banner of "character education" from the enterprise of helping students become ethically sophisticated decision makers and caring human beings. Wanting young people to turn out that way doesn't require us to adopt traditional character education programs any more than wanting them to be physically fit requires us to turn schools into Marine boot camps.

What does the alternative look like? Return once more to those five questions: in each case, an answer different from that given by traditional character education will help us to sketch the broad contours of a divergent approach. More specifically, we should probably target certain practices for elimination, add some new ones, and reconfigure still others that already exist. I have already offered a catalogue of examples of what to eliminate, from Skinnerian reinforcers to lesson plans that resemble sermons. As examples of what to add, we might suggest holding regular class meetings in which students can share, plan, decide, and reflect together.[55] We might also provide children with explicit opportunities to practice "perspective taking"—that is, imagining how the world looks from someone else's point of view. Activities that promote an understanding of how others think and feel, that support the impulse to imaginatively reach beyond the self, can provide the same benefits realized by holding democratic class meetings—namely, helping students become more ethical and compassionate while simultaneously fostering intellectual growth.[56]

A good example of an existing practice that might be reconfigured is the use of literature to teach values. In principle, the idea is splendid: it makes perfect sense to select stories that not only help students develop reading skills (and an appreciation for good writing) but also raise moral issues. The trouble is that many programs use simplistic little morality tales in place of rich, complex literature. Naturally, the texts should be developmentally appropriate, but some character educators fail to give children credit for being able to grapple with ambiguity. (Imagine the sort of stories likely to be assigned by someone who maintains that "it is ridiculous to believe children are capable of objectively assessing most of the beliefs and values they must absorb to be effective adults."[57])

Perhaps the concern is not that students will be unable to make sense of challenging literature, but that they will not derive the "correct" moral. This would account for the fact that even when character education curricula include impressive pieces of writing, the works tend to be used for the purpose of drumming in simple lessons. As Kilpatrick sees it, a story "points to these [characters] and says in effect, 'Act like this; don't act like that.'"[58] This kind of lesson often takes the form of hero worship, with larger-than-life characters—or real historical figures presented with their foibles airbrushed away—held up to students to encourage imitation of their actions.

Rather than employ literature to indoctrinate or induce mere conformity, we can use it to spur reflection. Whether the students are 6-year-olds or 16-year-olds, the discussion of stories should be open-ended rather than relentlessly didactic. Teachers who refrain from tightly controlling such conversations are impressed again and again by the levels of meaning students prove capable of exploring and the moral growth they exhibit in such an environment. Instead of announcing, "This man is a hero; do what he did," such teachers may involve the students in *deciding* who (if anyone) is heroic in a given story—or in contemporary culture[59]—and why. They may even invite students to reflect on the larger issue of whether it is desirable to have heroes. (Consider the quality of discussion that might be generated by asking older students to respond to the declaration of playwright Bertolt Brecht: "Unhappy is the land that needs a hero.")

***

More than specific practices that might be added, subtracted, or changed, a program to help children grow into good people begins with a commitment to change the way classrooms and schools are structured—and this brings us back to the idea of transcending a fix-the-kid approach. Consider the format of classroom discussions. A proponent of character education, invoking such traditional virtues as patience or self-control, might remind students that they must wait to be recognized by the teacher. But what if we invited students to think about the best way to conduct a discussion? Must we raise our hands? Is there another way to avoid having everyone talk at once? How can we be fair to those who aren't as assertive or as fast on their feet? Should the power to decide who can speak always rest with the teacher? Perhaps the problem is not with students who need to be more self-disciplined, but with the whole instructional design that has students waiting to be recognized to answer someone else's questions. And perhaps the real learning comes only when students have the chance to grapple with such issues.

One more example. A proponent of character education says we must make students understand that it is wrong to lie; we need to teach them about the importance of being honest. But why do people lie? Usually because they don't feel safe enough to tell the truth. The real challenge for us as educators is to examine that precept in terms of what is going on in our classrooms, to ask how we and the students together can make sure that even unpleasant truths can be told and heard. Does pursuing this line of inquiry mean that it's acceptable to fib? No. It means the problem has to be dissected and solved from the inside out. It means behaviors occur in a context that teachers have helped to establish; therefore, teachers have to examine (and consider modifying) that context even at the risk of some discomfort to themselves. In short, if we want to help children grow into compassionate and responsible people, we have to change the way the classroom works and feels, not just the way each separate member of that class acts. Our emphasis should not be on forming individual characters so much as on transforming educational structures.

Happily, programs do exist whose promotion of children's social and moral development is grounded in a commitment to change the culture of schools. The best example of which I am aware is the Child Development Project, an elementary school program designed, implemented, and researched by the Developmental Studies Center in Oakland, California. The CDP's premise is that, by meeting children's needs, we increase the likelihood that they will care about others. Meeting their needs entails, among other things, turning schools into caring communities. The CDP offers the additional advantages of a constructivist vision of learning, a positive view of human nature, a balance of cognitive and affective concerns, and a program that is integrated into all aspects of school life (including the curriculum).[60]

Is the CDP an example of what character education ought to be—or of what ought to replace character education? The answer to that question will depend on tactical, and even semantic, considerations. Far more compelling is the need to reevaluate the practices and premises of contemporary character education. To realize a humane and progressive vision for children's development, we may need to look elsewhere.

Notes

1. See, for example, Linda Page, "A Conservative Christian View on Values," *School Administrator*, September 1995, p. 22.
2. See, for example, Kevin Ryan, "The Ten Commandments of Character Education," *School Administrator*, September 1995, p. 19; and program materials from the Character Education Institute and the Jefferson Center for Character Education.
3. See Alfie Kohn, *Punished by Rewards: The Trouble with Gold Stars, Incentive Plans, A's, Praise, and Other Bribes* (Boston: Houghton Mifflin, 1993); and Edward L. Deci and Richard M. Ryan, *Intrinsic Motivation and Self-Determination in Human Behavior* (New York: Plenum, 1985).
4. See C. Daniel Batson et al., "Buying Kindness: Effect of an Extrinsic Incentive for Helping on Perceived Altruism," *Personality and Social Psychology Bulletin*, vol. 4, 1978, p. 90; Cathleen L. Smith et al., "Children's Causal Attributions Regarding Help Giving," *Child Development*, vol. 50, 1979, pp. 203–10; and William Edward Upton III, "Altruism, Attribution, and Intrinsic Motivation in the Recruitment of Blood Donors," *Dissertation Abstracts International* 34B, vol. 12, 1974. p. 6260.
5. Richard A. Fabes et al., "Effects of Rewards on Children's Prosocial Motivation: A Socialization Study," *Developmental Psychology*, vol. 25, 1989, pp. 509–15; and Joan Grusec, "Socializing Concern for Others in the Home," *Developmental Psychology*, vol. 27, 1991, pp. 338–42.
6. See Alfie Kohn, *No Contest: The Case Against Competition*, rev. ed. (Boston: Houghton Mifflin, 1992).
7. This statement is taken from an eight-page brochure produced by the "Character Counts!" Coalition, a project of the Josephson Institute of Ethics. Members of the coalition include the American Federation of Teachers, the National Association of Secondary School Principals, the American Red Cross, the YMCA, and many other organizations.
8. William Kilpatrick, *Why Johnny Can't Tell Right from Wrong* (New York: Simon & Schuster, 1992), pp. 96, 249.
9. For example, Kilpatrick was selected in 1995 to keynote the first in a series of summer institutes on character education sponsored by Thomas Lickona.
10. Edward Wynne, "Transmitting Traditional Values in Contemporary Schools," in Larry P. Nucci, ed., *Moral Development* and *Character Education: A Dialogue* (Berkeley, Calif.: McCutchan, 1989), p. 25.
11. Kevin Ryan, "In Defense of Character Education," in Nucci, p. 16.
12. Louis Goldman, "Mind, Character, and the Deferral of Gratification," *Educational Forum*, vol. 60, 1996, p. 136. As part of "educational reconstruction," he goes on to say, we must "connect the lower social classes to the middle classes who may provide role models for self-discipline" (p. 139).
13. Jarvis is quoted in Wray Herbert, "The Moral Child," *U.S. News & World Report*, 3 June 1996, p. 58.
14. Amitai Etzioni, *The Spirit of Community: The Reinvention of American Society* (New York: Simon & Schuster, 1993), p. 91.
15. See Alfie Kohn, *The Brighter Side of Human Nature: Altruism and Empathy in Everyday Life* (New York: Basic Books, 1990); and "Caring Kids: The Role of the Schools," *Phi Delta Kappan*, March 1991, pp. 496–506.
16. David E. Purpel, "Moral Education: An Idea Whose Time Has Gone," *The Clearing House*, vol. 64, 1991, p. 311.
17. This description of the character education movement is offered by Alan L. Lockwood in "Character Education: The Ten Percent Solution," *Social Education*, April/May 1991, p. 246. It is a particularly apt characterization of a book like *Why Johnny Can't Tell Right from Wrong*, which invokes an age of "chivalry" and sexual absti-

nence, a time when moral truths were uncomplicated and unchallenged. The author's tone, however, is not so much wistful about the past as angry about the present: he denounces everything from rock music (which occupies an entire chapter in a book about morality) and feminism to the "multiculturalists" who dare to remove "homosexuality from the universe of moral judgment" (p. 126).

18. Kevin Walsh of the University of Alabama is quoted in Eric N. Berg, "Argument Grows That Teaching of Values Should Rank with Lessons," *New York Times*, 1 January 1992, p. 32.

19. I am reminded of a woman in a Houston audience who heatedly informed me that she doesn't send her child to school "to learn to be nice." That, she declared, would be "social engineering." But a moment later this woman added that her child ought to be "taught to respect authority." Since this would seem to be at least as apposite an example of social engineering, one is led to conclude that the woman's real objection was to the teaching of particular topics or values.

20. Kevin Ryan, "Mining the Values in the Curriculum," *Educational Leadership,* November 1993, p. 16.

21. Telling students to "try hard" and "do their best" begs the important questions. *How,* exactly, do they do their best? Surely it is not just a matter of blind effort. And *why* should they do so, particularly if the task is not engaging or meaningful to them, or if it has simply been imposed on them? Research has found that the attitudes students take toward learning are heavily influenced by whether they have been led to attribute their success (or failure) to innate ability, to effort, or to other factors—and that traditional classroom practices such as grading and competition lead them to explain the results in terms of ability (or its absence) and to minimize effort whenever possible. What looks like "laziness" or insufficient perseverance, in other words, often turns out to be a rational decision to avoid challenge; it is rational because this route proves most expedient for performing well or maintaining an image of oneself as smart. These systemic factors, of course, are complex and often threatening for educators to address; it is much easier just to impress on children the importance of doing their best and then blame them for lacking perseverance if they seem not to do so.

22. Edward A. Wynne, "The Great Tradition in Education: Transmitting Moral Values," *Educational Leadership,* December 1985/January 1986, p. 6.

23. Mary Lord, "The Return of the 'Fourth R,'" *U.S. News & World Report,* 11 September 1995, p. 58.

24. William Glasser, *Schools Without Failure* (New York: Harper & Row, 1969), p. 22.

25. Marc Desmond's letter appeared in the *New York Times Magazine,* 21 May 1995, p. 14. The same point was made by Robert Primack, "No Substitute for Critical Thinking: A Response to Wynne," *Educational Leadership,* December 1985/January 1986, p. 12.

26. Deborah Meier and Paul Schwarz, "Central Park East Secondary School," in Michael W. Apple and James A. Beane, eds., *Democratic Schools* (Alexandria, Va.: Association for Supervision and Curriculum Development, 1995), pp. 29–30.

27. See Richard de Charms, *Personal Causation: The Internal Affective Determinants of Behavior* (Hillsdale, N.J.: Erlbaum, 1983). See also the many publications of Edward Deci and Richard Ryan.

28. See, for example, Alfie Kohn, "Choices for Children: Why and How to Let Students Decide," *Phi Delta Kappan,* September 1993, pp. 8–20; and Child Development Project, *Ways We Want Our Class to Be: Class Meetings That Build Commitment to Kindness and Learning* (Oakland, Calif.: Developmental Studies Center, 1996).

29. The quotations are from Wynne, "The Great Tradition," p. 9; and Edward A. Wynne and Herbert J. Walberg, "The Complementary Goals of Character Development and Academic Excellence," *Educational Leadership,* December 1985/January 1986, p. 17. William Kilpatrick is equally averse to including students in decision making; he speaks longingly of the days when "schools were unapologetically authoritarian," declaring that "schools can learn a lot from the Army," which is a "hierarchial [sic], authoritarian, and undemocratic institution" (see *Why Johnny Can't,* p. 228).

30. The sort of compassion I have in mind is akin to what the psychologist Ervin Staub described as a "prosocial orientation" (see his *Positive Social Behavior and Morality,* vols. 1 and 2 [New York: Academic Press, 1978 and 1979])—a generalized inclination to care, share, and help across different situations and with different people, including those we don't know, don't like, and don't look like. Loyally lending a hand to a close friend is one thing; going out of one's way for a stranger is something else.

31. John Dewey, *The School and Society* (Chicago: University of Chicago Press, 1900; reprint, 1990), p. 15.

32. Wynne and Walberg, p. 17. For another endorsement of competition among students, see Kevin Ryan, "In Defense," p. 15.

33. This passage is taken from page 21 of an undated 28-page "Character Education Curriculum" produced by the Character Education Institute. Emphasis in original.

34. Wynne, "Great Tradition," p. 9. Wynne and other figures in the character education movement acknowledge their debt to the French social scientist Emile Durkheim, who believed that "all education is a continuous effort to impose on the child ways of seeing, feeling, and acting which he could not have arrived at spontaneously…We exert pressure upon him in order that he may learn proper consideration for others, respect for customs and conventions, the need for work, etc." (See Durkheim, *The Rules of Sociological Method* [New York: Free Press, 1938], p. 6.)

35. This is from Bennett's introduction to *The Book of Virtues* (New York: Simon & Schuster, 1993), pp. 12–13.

36. Constance Kamii, Faye B. Clark, and Ann Dominick, "The Six National Goals: A Road to Disappointment," *Phi Delta Kappan,* May 1994, p. 677.

37. Kevin Ryan, "Character and Coffee Mugs," *Education Week,* 17 May 1995, p. 48.

38. The second quotation is a reporter's paraphrase of Brooks. Both it and the direct quotation preceding it appear in Philip Cohen, "The Content of Their Character: Educators Find New Ways to Tackle Values and Morality," *ASCD Curriculum Update,* Spring 1995, p. 4.

39. See B. David Brooks, *Young People's Lessons in Character: Student Activity Workbook* (San Diego: Young People's Press, 1996), p. 12.

40. Kilpatrick, p. 231.

41. To advocate this sort of enterprise, he adds, is to "caricature the moral life." See Alan L. Lockwood, "Keeping Them in the Courtyard: A Response to Wynne," *Educational Leadership,* December 1985/January 1986, p. 10.

42. Kilpatrick, p. 97.

43. Personal communication with Ann Medlock, May 1996.

44. John Dewey, *Democracy and Education* (New York: Free Press, 1916; reprint, 1966), p. 11.

45. Bennett, p. 11.

46. Wynne, "Character and Academics," p. 142.

47. For a discussion of how traditional character education fails to offer guidance when values come into conflict, see Lockwood, "Character Education."

48. Rheta DeVries and Betty Zan, *Moral Classrooms, Moral Children: Creating a Constructivist Atmosphere in Early Education* (New York: Teachers College Press, 1994), p. 253.

49. For an argument that critics tend to misrepresent what Values Clarification was about, see James A. Beane, *Affect in the Curriculum* (New York: Teachers College Press, 1990), pp. 104–6.

50. Wynne, for example, refers to the developers of Values Clarification as "popularizers" of Kohlberg's research (see "Character and Academics," p. 141), while Amitai Etzioni, in the course of criticizing Piaget's and Kohlberg's work, asserts that "a typical course on moral reasoning starts with something called 'values clarification'" (see *The Spirit of Community,* p. 98).

51. Kohlberg's model, which holds that people across cultures progress predictably through six stages of successively more sophisticated styles of moral reasoning, is based on the decidedly nonrelativistic premise that the last stages are superior to the first ones. See his *Essays on Moral Development, Vol. 1: The Philosophy of Moral Development* (San Francisco: Harper & Row, 1981), especially the essays titled "Indoctrination Versus Relativity in Value Education" and "From Is to *Ought.*"

52. See, for example, James S. Fishkin, *Beyond Subjective Morality* (New Haven, Conn.: Yale University Press, 1984); and David B. Wong, *Moral Relativity* (Berkeley: University of California Press, 1984).

53. Researchers at the National Institute of Mental Health have summarized the available research as follows: "Even children as young as 2 years old have (a) the cognitive capacity to interpret the physical and psychological states of others, (b) the emotional capacity to effectively experience the other's state, and (c) the behavioral repertoire that permits the possibility of trying to alleviate discomfort in others. These are the capabilities that, we believe, underlie children's caring behavior in the presence of another person's distress.…Young children seem to show patterns of moral internalization that are not simply fear based or solely responsive to parental com-

mands. Rather, there are signs that children feel responsible for (as well as connected to and dependent on) others at a very young age." (See Carolyn Zahn-Waxler et al., "Development of Concern for Others," *Developmental Psychology,* vol. 28, 1992, pp. 127, 135. For more on the adult's role in light of these facts, see Kohn, *The Brighter Side.*)

54. "Education Secretary Backs Teaching of Religious Values," *New York Times,* 12 November 1985, p. B-4.

55. For more on class meetings, see Glasser, chaps. 10- 12; Thomas Gordon, *T.E.T. Teacher Effectiveness Training* (New York: David McKay Co., 1974), chaps. 8–9; Jane Nelsen, Lynn Lott, and H. Stephen Glenn, *Positive Discipline in the Classroom* (Rocklin, Calif.: Prima, 1993); and Child Development Project, op. cit.

56. For more on the theory and research of perspective taking, see Kohn, *The Brighter Side,* chaps. 4–5; for practical classroom activities for promoting perspective-taking skills, see Norma Deitch Feshbach et al., *Learning to Care: Classroom Activities for Social and Affective Development* (Glenview, Ill.: Scott, Foresman, 1983). While specialists in the field distinguish between perspective taking (imagining what others see, think, or feel) and empathy (*feeling* what others feel), most educators who talk about the importance of helping children become empathic really seem to be talking about perspective taking.

57. Wynne, "Great Tradition," p. 9.

58. Kilpatrick, p. 141.

59. It is informative to discover whom the proponents of a hero-based approach to character education themselves regard as heroic. For example, William Bennett's nominee for "possibly our greatest living American" is Rush Limbaugh. (See Terry Eastland, "Rush Limbaugh: Talking Back," *American Spectator,* September 1992, p. 23.)

60. See Victor Battistich et al., "The Child Development Project: A Comprehensive Program for the Development of Prosocial Character," in William M. Kurtines and Jacob L. Gewirtz, eds., *Moral Behavior and Development: Advances in Theory, Research, and Applications* (Hillsdale, N.J.: Erlbaum, 1989); and Daniel Solomon et al., "Creating a Caring Community: Educational Practices That Promote Children's Prosocial Development," in Fritz K. Oser, Andreas Dick, and Jean-Luc Patry, eds., *Effective and Responsible Teaching* (San Francisco: Jossey-Bass, 1992). For more information about the CDP program or about the research substantiating its effects, write the Developmental Studies Center at 2000 Embarcadero, Suite 305, Oakland, CA 94606.

(This chapter originally appeared in *Phi Delta Kappan*, Vol. 78, No. 6 [February, 1997]: 429–439. Published with permission of Phi Delta Kappa International.)

CHAPTER FOURTEEN

Character Education from the Left Field

DWIGHT BOYD

Titles carry considerable connotative weight, appropriately so in my view. Thus I want to antic-ipate here my aims in this chapter by noting some of the differing connotations of "from the left field" and explaining which of them I willingly own, and in what way. Sometimes "from the left field" suggests something close to "bizarre," so out of the ordinary that whatever is so characterized can be rejected out of hand. I do not want to be heard in this way. But if some of the terminology that I use to identify new kinds of virtues at the end of this chapter seems bizarre, so be it...as long as you consider what it is meant to do. Another, more common, meaning is "unexpected," given normal ways of thinking. This definition I will comfortably claim. What I say in this chapter will indeed likely be unexpected because no one seems to be saying anything of this sort, despite the fact that I think it should be clear that it is badly needed. In fact, the field broadly identified as "moral education" tends generally to shy away from facing up to social difference and conflict, especially from that rep-resented in macro moral/political problems of oppression such as racism, sexism, and classism. Further, to those in the field who prefer to identify their concern in terms of the arguably narrower phrase "character education" my arguments will likely be even more unexpected. I say this because they tend to think about character education in such a way that the systemic and deep nature of these moral/political problems simply disappears. In political terms, I submit there is a highly conserva-tive nature to almost all contemporary character education discourse. Thus, finally, I also want to own the description connoted by "from the left field," as *contrasted* to the conservative right in terms of squarely facing such problems with a focus on social justice.

Introduction

A particular take on character education has now achieved the status of a movement in the U.S.[1] However, it is clearly *not* a movement for social justice. It is commonplace for papers and books about character education to start from a litany of putatively worrisome social problems that character education will supposedly alleviate—problems such as high crime rates, high divorce rates, teenage sexual activity, and percentage of out of wedlock births. But seldom if ever do these problems include the forms of systemic oppression faced by women, members of the working class, or those in racialized and sexually marginalized groups. By ignoring these deeper, more insidious social conditions, this movement becomes politically conservative by default, if not by design. However, it can also be shown that aspects of the design itself are productive of a conservative political orientation, with significant and negative implications for social problems in a liberal democratic society in general.

In this chapter, I will first explain why this movement should be seen as essentially conservative. To do so I explore the nature of four discursive aspects of this approach to character education, with a focus on their implications for the recognition and accommodation of difference and conflict in society. Finding this approach woefully inadequate in these terms, I will then turn to two alternative ways of thinking about virtues that are not vulnerable to this criticism. In contrast to the currently popular approach to character education, both focus on the more refined question of what virtues *citizens* would in fact need if they were to be able to recognize and take action to challenge social injustice. The first alternative will be explored in section two as an important step in the correct direction. This alternative is grounded in John Rawls' highly respected theory of justice. Rawls' work presents a systematically developed and, in many ways, very progressive liberal perspective on how justice should function to organize a democratic society that will accommodate diversity. It also identifies specific virtues that citizens would need to exhibit (and thus should be part of character education) if a society so organized were to remain stable over generations. These are indeed important virtues, and, properly understood, provide some antidote to the view presented by the contemporary character education movement. However, in the third section I will argue that, in the end, they fail to provide adequate dispositional leverage to face the more systemic, oppressive relations within which actual citizens are formed and interact. For this purpose, we need to think more creatively, even further "from the left field." I thus propose some particular virtues of the citizen that come into view when this more critical perspective is assumed.

Why the Character Education Movement Should Be Seen as Essentially Conservative

Again, my motivation for this work is grounded in my observation that the character education movement as currently constituted is shaped by a conservative political perspective. For some, the credibility of this claim might seem easily established by noting that George W. Bush actively supported it throughout his presidency. Moreover, he did so with millions of dollars given to institutions that seemed to be promoting this viewpoint. Others might be persuaded by the fact that very little attention is given to the kind of systemic social problems that call for a perspective from the left field. Although there are some exceptions, this is largely true of work published in the pre-eminent academic journal in this field, the *Journal of Moral Education*, and the books that have garnered the most public attention, such as Damon's (2002) well-received *Bringing in a New Era in Character Education* and Lickona's (2004) *Character Matters*. However, beyond pointing out these general observations, it is also possible to *show* how the pull to a conservative political position *works* in this particular conceptualization of character education. In this section I will do exactly that to demonstrate the need for deeper and more satisfactorily conceptualized approaches.

To establish the basis of my criticism of character education as essentially conservative, I must identify several working assumptions. First of all, I am using "conservative" here in a *political* sense (in contrast to the economic sense, for example). To refer to something as "political" as I will use it in this chapter entails a number of assumptions:

- It means that a view so characterized provides some sort of practical perspective on the status quo and change.
- In particular, it will include the balancing of the preservation of the status quo vs. change with regard to how individuals and groups of people relate to each other and to the state in terms of opportunities and power to effect their desired ends that differ.
- Any morally legitimate political view must thus include attention to social justice as the core normative lens for viewing this balancing.

Then, a "conservative" perspective, understood in this political sense, is one that does not rock the boat, one that either actively—or by default through lack of attention—supports the relationships among individuals and groups as they currently exist (or did so in some putatively ideal past period). In contemporary North American society a good test case can be found in how relations between racialized individuals and groups are dealt with (or by any such relation that is formally similar, e.g., gender, class, sexual orientation, etc.).

In addition to these assumptions about the meaning of "political," I must identify a set of further assumptions pertaining to different kinds of boundaries within which my critical observations apply. First, although there is a range of interpretations as to how character education might be approached, I will narrow my focus to just one, albeit major, part of that range. I will be concerned only with the approach that currently seems most popular in both the United States and Canada. This approach is identified primarily by its stipulation of a finite list of particular character traits or virtues that are said to be common property of all concerned, and thus should form the core of all educational activities in this area. Second, I will assume the social context within which the criticism applies is that of shared commitments to the maintenance and improvement of a liberal democracy and to the role of education in these efforts. Third, and most importantly, I will also assume that a central aspect of a "liberal democracy" is a shared commitment among its citizens to seek reasonable and fair adjudication of inevitable *differences* and the *conflicts* they engender and that this orientation is manifested, in part, through the learning and practice of particular virtues. Indeed, it is primarily character education's failure to recognize and accommodate this essential characteristic of a liberal democracy that drives my critique.

In this section, this failure will be exposed in terms of four particular discursive aspects of this approach to character education. Each aspect can be commonly found, often in combination with one or more others. For heuristic purposes, however, I will treat them individually to show how that particular aspect discursively *works* to produce a conservative orientation toward social problems.

Conflict Ruled Out Dictatorially

In describing this first discursive aspect pertaining to difference and conflict commonly found in character education, I will refer to the work of Thomas Lickona. There are three reasons for this focus. First, Lickona was one of its originators, at least in contemporary times. Second, although there were other influential early promoters of character education, notably Edward Wynne, Kevin Ryan, and

William Bennett (a former U.S. Secretary of Education), I think Lickona has had the most impact. Moreover, if anything, Lickona's impact seems to be increasing, in both Canada and the United States. Third, although this discursive aspect can be identified in the work of other major promoters of this approach to character education, it shows up in such clean, unabashed form in Lickona's work that he serves well as its spokesperson.

The anchoring point of everything Lickona has to say about character education lies unwaveringly in an epistemological arrogance, in what he claims that "we" know *with certainty* about morality. In *Character Matters* Lickona (2004) makes this claim quite explicitly:

> The content of good character is virtue. Virtues—such as honesty, justice, courage, and compassion—are dispositions to behave in a morally good way. They are objectively good human qualities, good for us whether we know it or not. (p. 7)

He then identifies 10 "essential" virtues, each with multiple "sub-virtues," that fit this bill. He does stick in a totally unexplained parenthetical qualifier, ("although their cultural expression may vary"), but there is clearly no room for epistemological waffling on the content of this list. Rather, it is just an asserted *fact* that, as he puts it, "They are affirmed by societies and religions around the world" (p. 7).

The implication of these claims seems clear to me: if someone disagrees with any item on the list—or even has an interpretation of an item that differs from the one offered in the many practical suggestions of how to teach to the list—they are just simply *wrong*. And note that this is not just a purely factual mistake, like an error in addition or a mistaken belief about a foreign capital, but a *moral* wrongness. After all, those 10 virtues are what enable us to be morally good, and they are "good for us whether we know it or not." Disagreeing with the list amounts to a contemporary form of what used to be called "heresy" when someone attempted to dissent from some Catholic Church doctrine, only now it is a moral heresy. But, in contrast to medieval society, contemporary North American society contains many different beliefs among its citizens. For example, I live in a city that has over 500 ethno-cultural groups, each with 5,000 or more members! I am not willing to just assert that the same simple list of virtues will accommodate all 500. In fact, I doubt it very much. Some epistemological humility is warranted here, not the arrogance of certainty.

When the context is public schools and the development of the next generation of liberal citizens, failure to exhibit appropriate epistemological humility in conceptualizing character education is tantamount to disenfranchising a significant portion of the body politic. It does this by letting some citizens' views of what constitutes the "correct" interpretation of the "good person" override those of others. Since one of the strengths of liberalism is facing the conflicts that can arise from the fact that citizens often differ on exactly this kind of question, it amounts to a dictatorial denial of difference. Moreover, this denial is not politically neutral. On the contrary, it serves to protect the status quo in relationships among citizens. Naming things, especially those that are seen as being of ultimate importance, is one of the strongest powers that humans have. But restricting the opportunity to exercise this power means that only a select few will be privileged to exercise it. Character education that supports this restriction thus works *against* the aim of improving social interaction in the direction of enabling the voices of marginalized individuals and groups to be heard and accommodated.

The other three discursive aspects of this approach to character education that produce a conservative political orientation to difference and conflict may in the end come to the same thing as that located in Lickona's views. But they are not as openly dictatorial, and thus harder to detect. In fact, on the surface they may sound much better. They are, however, more deceptive, just more subtle ways of propping up the status quo. Since each can be easily found in a local, Ontario-based program of character education, I will use that particular approach to illustrate them. It is important to note, however, that these particular aspects are not limited to this one local initiative; instead, they can be found quite widely in North American schools. It is perhaps even more important to emphasize here that, with this strong criticism, I am *not* characterizing those individuals who have designed, or are implementing, such programs (nor is it my intention to judge Lickona's character in the above comments). On the contrary, my contacts with these individuals have supported the view that they are usually nice, well-meaning people. My critique is of the program they advocate in terms of the political impact it has, whatever their intentions.

Conflict Ruled out Methodologically

"Character Matters!" is the name given to the approach to character education originating in York Region, a large, culturally diverse suburb of Toronto. The administrators and teachers who designed the program explicitly acknowledge their indebtedness to Lickona. What it adds to my reading of Lickona, however, is the appearance of a more democratic than dictatorial tone. "Character Matters!" (CM) claims to be a firmly and widely community-based approach. Educational leaders in the district speak proudly of their extensive consultation during the initial stages of development. To support this claim, they refer to a wide range of activities involving different kinds of community members. Clearly, the most important of these consists of the series of "community forums" from which emerged their list of chosen virtues that is the backbone of the program. (I should note that they refer to the items on this list by the less politically charged designation of "attributes." But I think it is easily shown that this just amounts to window dressing…or camouflage.) Since they also claim that these forums consisted of a cross-section of the community at large (Glaze, Hogarth, & McLean, 2003, p. 2), what happened in them is crucial to my concern. In short, given their apparent democratic leanings in their efforts to design the program, this is the context in which one might legitimately expect to find some recognition of difference and conflict among the involved citizens and some attempt to incorporate those concerns into the program. The fact that one does *not* find this has definite political implications.

As the promoters of this approach note, the main task of the participants of these Forums was that they "identified the attributes upon which we gained consensus," i.e., the list of character attributes that would be subsequently promoted as the content of the program system-wide after a "Work Group later developed definitions for the attributes" (Glaze, Hogarth, & McLean, p. 2). But, how did this actually work? On the basis of my discussion with the York Region Superintendent of Education, my understanding is the following. After some general discussion of character education, participants were invited to suggest attributes that they thought should be the focus of the program. These were listed on a flip chart. The procedure then was to see if everyone agreed with the suggestion of each attribute in turn. If anyone *disagreed*, it was removed from the list. The resulting list thus consisted of those attributes upon which there was "consensus." The winners of this popularity contest were respect, responsibility, honesty, empathy, fairness, initiative, perseverance, integrity, courage, and optimism. However, as already noted, it should be kept in mind this consensus was reached *before* the "Work Group" provided definitions of the items on the list.

Most people tend to think of consensus as an unqualified good thing. Certainly it is often something worth striving for. However, this is not always the case, especially when the manner of seeking consensus vitiates its meaning. I think this is one of those contexts. The problem is that a character education program is being built on a foundation that methodologically *rules out disagreement*. If someone disagrees with the list, that very fact disappears from view. (Indeed the Superintendent of Education spoke only of the fact that apparently everyone agrees with this list—but not at all about what might have been suggested but did not make the "consensus" list.) Moreover, it is especially notable to me—given its central importance in liberal theory—that justice did not end up on the list. This absence is crucial, since justice is arguably the core virtue that grounds how citizens in a liberal democracy seek to deal with difference and conflict.

But even if justice were on the list (and it often is in other examples of this approach), there still remains the fact that disagreement about both the meaning and the relative weighting of the different items that do make the list is also ruled out of order: consensus was reached *before* a small team developed the interpretations that would be attached to the items. If we recall that a liberal democracy thrives only when its citizens learn how to deal with difference and conflict and to practice the virtues that enable this orientation, the discursive absence of any awareness of these social and educational needs may be even more insidiously dangerous than what I find in Lickona's views. The method of (supposed) consensus-seeking through hiding disagreement promotes a kind of "willful difference blindness" and unwarranted certainty that in the end looks very much like Lickona's dictatorial denial of difference. But because this end is achieved through activities that look (but *only* look) democratic, it provides even stronger support for propping up the status quo. Those citizens who do in fact disagree with the list or the interpretations given to items on the list are methodologically marginalized, deemed too different to matter. Even worse, if they complain, the charge of being anti-democratic can be used as a political/moral trump. Thus, again, any political change in the direction of giving them more voice for expression of difference is blocked—all in the name of producing better democratic citizens, as we will see below.

Two different but related kinds of conceptual confusion compound the methodological problem of not noticing difference and conflict. The first concerns a failure to recognize a distinction between two different normative questions that lie at the heart of dominant liberal theories and thus the heart of a liberal society's view of how people should interact with each other in social organization. The second type of confusion involves the failure to recognize a distinction that liberal theory then makes between two different perspectives from which that interaction might be viewed. Each by itself would serve to protect the status quo, but working together they multiply this effect.

Conflict Not Recognized Conceptually: No Differentiation of the "Good" vs. the "Right"

Mainstream liberal theories, in the sense of those having had the most influence in how liberal democracies are conceptualized today, rest on a basic distinction between two kinds of normative questions that people worry (or should worry) about: "What kind of ultimate ends should I pursue in my life?" and "How ought I to act in regard to other people?" The first question is said to center on the concept of the "good," and the second, on the concept of the "right." As identifying concepts, these terms pick out qualitatively different ways of making meaning about different kinds of concerns that matter ultimately in the context of human flourishing and interaction. Moreover, it is the contrast between the work done by the "good" versus the "right" that is so crucial to liberal political theory, particularly in its aim of addressing the inevitability of difference and conflict among citizens.

Although this distinction may seem a commonplace to most philosophers (even those who disagree with it), non-philosophers often have difficulty keeping it clearly in mind. Furthermore, recognized academic experts who in the character education movement that I am addressing in this chapter regularly blur the distinction when it serves their rhetorical purposes (e.g., Howard, Berkowitz, & Schaeffer, 2004). So, to make my criticism of CM on this point as clear as possible, I see the basic conceptual distinction as follows.

The concept of the "good" is utilized when attention is turned to those kinds of activities, states of mind, and states of affairs that are deemed ultimately worth pursuing as *ends* in human experience. Some of these will be important because they enable other ends; some will be thought to be the anchoring points to "why?" questions and thus considered intrinsically worthwhile. Both, however, might be considered valuable enough to be passed on to the next generation as aspects of how individuals can flourish as human persons (for example, through forms of "liberal education"). In contrast, within this tradition, the concept of the "right" is brought into play to *regulate* the interaction of individuals as they seek to pursue their various conceptions of the "good." How the concept of the "right" is expressed and used determines the shape of social cooperation. In particular, some of the uses of this concept are positive, aiming at individuals' furthering the interests of the other(s); other uses, probably the most salient in this tradition, function in the context of the kinds of possible conflict between and among persons that arise *because* they have differing and competing conceptions of the "good."

As far as I have been able to determine, this crucial conceptual distinction—and the work that it is meant to do with regard to difference and conflict—simply is not recognized by the CM approach. CM offers a view of the make up of good character that sounds good because it is simple and easy to understand—and to sell. (It has discursive connotations to my mind something like "We've got our list and checked it twice. Now we know who's naughty and nice.") But matters of character are not that simple, conceptually speaking. Failing to accommodate crucial conceptual distinctions, as that between the "right" and the "good" can have real-life consequences. This particular conceptual failure functions significantly to support the status quo by effectively undermining the capacity to recognize one fundamental kind of difference that any liberal society must address. The tools have been hidden. Anyone wishing to take issue with the existing dominant views of the "good"—e.g., rampant consumerism, anti-intellectual orientations, and neo-conservative worship of competition—are left to flounder. Even worse, for those who do have conceptions of the "good" that challenge the dominant status quo view, the failure of a character education program to provide them with an effective understanding of the regulatory function of principles of the "right" undermines their capacity to argue for political room to pursue those conceptions. Thus, again, the possibility of change is blocked politically.

Perspectives on Conflict Conceptually Conflated: No Differentiation of the "Good Person" vs. the "Good Citizen"

An additional, related conceptual confusion significantly deepens this undermining. The first distinction just outlined, and the way it is explained, is indeed central to liberal *moral* theories. But it is even more important when the context is more *political*, as it is in this chapter. In the former, the interaction of persons and the social cooperation they are seeking are seen from the perspective of individuals in their relatively private and limited social worlds. Here we are concerned with what needs to be true to be able to say that someone is a "good person." But when the concern is located more in the political realm, i.e., how individuals interact with each other in society at large and through structures of the state, it changes to a focus on the "good citizen." Within mainstream liberal political theories a central tenet is then that the "good citizen" is a distinct *role*, not to be confused with the more general one of the "good person" (or other roles such as the "good parent" or the "good teacher"). But it is exactly this confusion that we find permeating CM. In fact, the proponents of this approach explicitly conflate character education and citizenship education—and apparently see no problem in doing so (Glaze, Hogarth, & McLean, 2003, p. 2).

This distinction is crucial because it opens up public space for consideration of how individuals and the collectivities they choose to belong to are being dealt with by those of differing and conflicting views about the "good." This public space takes many forms, but one most easily recognized is that of the courts at all levels, especially that of the Supreme Court when it rules on claimed violations of constitutionally encoded rights of citizens. In other words, when the context is the interaction of individuals *qua citizens*, certain kinds of public, shared reasons are said to hold sway, to be the grounds for adjudication of conflicts. An example here would be a case in which a collective of individuals are bound together by a shared aim of pursuing and developing a way of life organized around a particular, and not generally shared, set of beliefs about how best to flourish as humans. But some other group, or even some state agency, disagrees with this aim and seeks to impede or prevent them from congregating for the purpose of furthering this aim. In principle, it is at this point that public appeals to shared conceptions of what makes a good democratic citizen are said to be overriding concerns for the courts in their effort to resolve the conflict fairly. They do not, cannot, appeal to a particular view of the "good person" to adjudicate the conflict because this difference is the source of the conflict. By ignoring this distinction between the perspective of the "good person" and the perspective of the "good citizen"—indeed, by explicitly conflating the two perspectives—CM again offers a simple, easy to sell view: two educational goals can apparently be achieved by this one approach. (To my mind this has the discursive connotations of a "two-for-one sale.") With this move CM even more effectively eliminates this public space for expressing difference from the mainstream status quo beliefs about the "good" *and* the "good person" and its crucial function in a liberal democracy of adjudicating conflict. When the difference *is* expressed, there turns out to be no public leverage to seek redress in cases of conflict with the status quo. Thus it is protected by a conservative character education program—in the name of good citizenship.

To sum up, it must be observed that all of the above criticisms would apply even in a society that was homogenous in terms of the cultural identification of its citizens. But the location of both Lickona's work and that of CM is decidedly different from anything like homogeneity. In fact, both the United States and Canada are now societies of remarkable diversity. Indeed, the proponents of the CM program speak proudly of the diversity in their region. (Recall the earlier statistic of the existence in Toronto of 500 ethno-cultural groups with at least 5,000 members each. The figure for York Region might be slightly different but probably not in any major way.) As far as I know, there never has been a society that is completely multicultural, i.e., one where all cultural groups enter public discourse on an equal playing field. On the contrary, one culture, or a small set of similar cultures, will be seen to have the most power, at the expense of others that are marginalized. Character education approaches that depend on identifying a set, finite list of virtues about which everything revolves are inevitably politically conservative in nature. Whether by dictatorial fiat, by methodological means, or by conceptual inadequacies, when difference and conflict are avoided the essential liberal concern with "justice" will also disappear, either actually or in some more subtle manner. And when "justice" disappears, its absence will always serve the status quo—instead of change—with regard to how individuals and groups of people relate to each other and to the state in terms of opportunities and power to effect their desired ends and ways of life that differ from the dominant view.

As we will see in the last section of this chapter, culturally based difference and conflict are not the only sources of conflict that matter. Nor are they the most politically problematic for a society supposedly based on liberal political beliefs. However, they are politically important and easier to pin down. The next section summarizes one way this can be done by avoiding the discursive problems of character education as currently promoted. It may be taken, in short, as one step in the direction of "left field," one that clearly challenges some of the conservative orientation.

Character Education When Difference, Conflict, and Justice Are Taken Seriously: What We Get with John Rawls' Theory of Justice

If my arguments are assumed to be correct, where do we go? What are the alternatives? What do they enable that is politically different from current character education theory?

Actually, there could be, at least in principle, many alternatives, many of them quite different from the current view, and even from each other. Making this case, however, is an aim far beyond what can be accommodated in this chapter. So, again, I will restrict my focus in terms of the boundaries outlined above by turning to two prominent philosophical views that take justice to be the central concern of a liberal democratic society. The first, in this section, is that of John Rawls; the second, in the following section, that of Iris Marion Young. I have chosen these two, however, not just because of their prominence. Rather, it is the contrast between them that enables my move toward "left field" and my thoughts about what some of the content of character education might look like from that political perspective. In particular, it is the *kinds* of difference and conflict that function centrally in their theories that drive my move in this direction.

A Brief Overview of Rawls

So, why do I start with Rawls? My motivation for doing so is that he provides a particularly apt and robust springboard for launching the discussion in the direction of left field. There are several reasons for this assessment:

- His focus is directly on justice, claiming on the first page of *A Theory of Justice* that "Justice is the first virtue of social institutions as truth is of systems of thought" (Rawls, 1971, p. 3).
- He further restricts his attention to the *political* arena, in the sense of how citizens in a democratic society should seek to regulate their interactions over time.
- He starts with an appreciation of the need to respect, and make political room for, *differences* among individuals.
- He recognizes, contrary to the conservative view, that our deep intuitions include the insight that justice must allow and facilitate the questioning of aspects of the status quo in terms of existing social conditions.
- Finally, he explicitly recognizes that for any just society to remain stable over generations the citizens within it would need to manifest the appropriate virtues in relating to each other.

To uncover the kind of virtues that Rawls views as necessary for good citizenship in a liberal democracy characterized by diversity, it is necessary to identify some of the key assumptions and claims that form the substance of his theory. The five reasons just outlined for my choice Rawls are for the most part formal, without much content. To get as fast as possible to the question of what *virtues* citizens need to exhibit if society were to be organized according to Rawls' theory, I will simply add to this formal framework what I see as the essential normative elements of his theory. (Warning: this should be seen as something like an abbreviated "Coles Notes" on a remarkably complex and nuanced theory of justice, based on the many major works of Rawls over his career of more than 35 years. If the reader is not familiar with Rawls, the references provided will provide needed clarification and support.) Again, to save space, I will do this in a bulleted list:

- Locating himself solidly in the liberal tradition, Rawls' primary focus is on the discrete individual and how that entity fares in efforts of social cooperation (1971, p. viii).
- For any legitimate political regulation of those efforts, Rawls then insists that individuals must be conceived as "free and equal citizens" (1993, p. 19).
- What qualifies individuals for this role is that they are assumed to share two basic capacities: (i) the capacity for a sense of justice, and (ii) the capacity for a conception of the good (1993, p. 19).
- As a deontological theorist of the social contract school, Rawls is concerned to identify the basic structure of an ideal society in which the "right" is prior to the "good," thus protecting individuals' equal chance at pursuing differing conceptions of the good life. Thus, his favorite phrase, "justice as fairness." (1971, p. 3)
- In his later work, particularly *Political Liberalism,* the kind of diversity that justice must seek to deal with is not just that of differing conceptions of the "good" but, in addition, how these are often based in much more fundamental, systematically developed, and historically stable conceptions of what it means, ideally, to be human and to engage with each other and all aspects of reality from a particular overarching normative perspective—what he calls "comprehensive doctrines" (1993, p. xviii).
- The picture of justice Rawls paints throughout his work is captured for him in his expression of, and systematic argument for, two principles of justice:

  a. Each person has an equal right to a fully adequate scheme of equal basic liberties which is compatible with a similar scheme of liberties for all.

  b. Social and economic inequalities are to satisfy two conditions. First, they must be attached to offices and positions open to all under conditions of fair equality of opportunity; and second, they must be to the greatest benefit of the least advantaged members of society (1993, p. 291).

The Virtues of "Justice as Fairness"

So, what would character education look like from a Rawlsian perspective? What virtues of the citizen would be necessary for "justice as fairness" to characterize a society? And how much of an improvement would it be over what passes for character education today? I submit that it represents a perspective that would be a *huge* improvement. The main reason for this positive assessment is that it places justice at the core of character and then identifies supportive virtues that make critical, reasonable engagement of difference and conflict possible—rather than hiding it as unnecessary under a false, dominating unity. I want to briefly point to these advantages as they are manifested in particular political virtues. However, in the next section I want then to argue that there are still major kinds of moral/political work that cannot be done from this perspective. That work requires the addition of a radically different set of virtues, at least for some people.

Several papers by Ben Spiecker and Jan Steutel are helpful in clarifying the picture that Rawls has of virtues. Central to their interpretation of Rawls are the implications of the two moral capacities of Rawls crediting persons as "free and equal" citizens. With this in mind, they argue that the primary focus in considering what virtues must be exhibited by the liberal citizen is grounded in the "*cardinal virtue*" entailed by the two principles of justice.

When the formal capacity for a sense of justice is provided with the content of these basic liberal princi-ples, we may speak of the *virtue* of justice. Given the correspondence with the two principles of justice, Rawls considers this trait of character as a *political* virtue. In addition to this he sums up a number of other political virtues, which are in fact incorporated in the virtue of justice, among which are tolerance, rea-sonableness, the disposition to compromise, mutual respect and mutual trust. (Spiecker & Steutel, 1995, p. 390)

It is important to keep in mind what is meant by designating these virtues as "political." Although there may very well be overlap with the character traits of a moral person in general, any argument for them as such would necessarily depend on some grounding in a particular "comprehensive doc-trine." But this is ruled out in the kind of political liberalism that Rawls seeks to develop. Thus, they should be seen as legitimated only by what is required by this kind of political social cooperation. As these authors put it quite succinctly,

Generally, we can say that people who have not acquired these qualities lack the intrinsic willingness to support and uphold fair cooperation between free and equal citizens. These virtues make up the ideal of the good citizen of a democratic state. (p. 390)

In short, this picture of the "sense of justice" as the *cardinal virtue* means not only that justice is now front and center as the most important (or, in Rawls' terms "first") virtue, but also that it gives the other noted virtues their core interpretation. Thus, the sense of justice, together with its various "incor-porated" manifestations in citizens' efforts to practice it, constitutes what is needed from the *politi-cal* perspective for citizens to be virtuous in their dealings with each other.

But the picture is not yet complete. What should be added to this basic picture is also important. In short, Steutel and Spiecker argue that parallel to the cardinal virtue of a "sense of justice" is anoth-er necessary cardinal virtue of "concern and respect for the truth" (Steutel & Spiecker, 2000, pp. 247–248). They identify examples of the various lesser, but constitutive, intellectual virtues that are "based on and unified by" this generalized virtue, such as "open-mindedness, respect for evidence, intellectual honesty, tolerance towards rival views, intellectual fairness, a concern for accuracy in observation and inference, clarity, thoroughness and intellectual modesty" (p. 247). Again, as these authors are careful to note, it is important to keep in mind that the argument for these additional virtues is not based on their being characteristics of a virtuous person according to some comprehensive moral/religious doctrine, but only what is needed for a person in the role of a good liberal citizen, especially as he/she seeks to accommodate the two kinds of difference and conflict identified above that characterize contemporary Western society.

These intellectual virtues are seen as necessary requirements of citizens who are committed to engaging each other in the public arena in ways that respect, express, and maintain the sense of jus-tice identified by "justice as fairness." "In short, a flourishing democracy needs citizens who are char-acterized by *political* autonomy—that is, by 'a critical, questioning attitude toward official decisions, and self-critical participation in public debate'(Macedo 1992, 217…)" (Steutel & Spiecker, 1999, p. 64). Steutel and Spiecker then identify two particular aspects of the need for this critical, political autonomy. The first aspect concerns citizens' critical stance toward political authority: this "requires citizens who are able and disposed to evaluate critically the performance of…[elected] officials" (p. 64). The second reason political autonomy is deemed necessary is said to be grounded in the fact that "a striking feature of a liberal democracy is the so-called ideal of public justification" (p. 64). This ideal then requires "the exchange of reasons that are openly accessible and widely acceptable to reasonable citizens, even though these citizens may disagree fundamentally among themselves about what sorts of life are choiceworthy" (p. 64). The intellectual virtues identified earlier are then, from this perspective, dimensions of the character of good liberal citizens that enable them to engage each other respectful of the shared sense of justice, to understand as much as possible the different kinds of positions taken on issues and policies as grounded in different comprehensive doctrines, and to fairly utilize the institutions of a liberal democracy to negotiate and actively construct the means of social cooperation congruent with all being "free and equal citizens."

Rawls presents a remarkably systematic, coherent, and compelling normative vision of justice within a liberal democratic state, one designed to deal with individual and cultural aspects of diversity. We see in Rawls' theory something quite different from the kind of politically conservative perspective of the contemporary character education movement. Through his focus on justice as the "first virtue of social institutions" and his clear recognition of the political reasons to differentiate the role of the citizen from tradition-based views of the good person, his theory gives us a perspective from which different kinds of difference and conflict can be addressed in social cooperation. Further, we also get a clear picture of what is so glaringly missing in character education, namely, a focus on some political and intellectual virtues that citizens need to exhibit in order to interact with each other fairly in the face of this difference and conflict.

However, I do not think that Rawls' theory of justice is, in the end, adequate for dealing with all kinds of difference and conflict that characterize contemporary society in North America. Beyond the fair distribution of liberties and opportunities for enhancing individuals' welfare, contemporary society is shot through with deeper, structural, systemic injustices, such as racism, sexism, and classism. On my reading of Rawls, his account falls short in recognizing and dealing with these egregious forms of injustice. Rawls does see one of his central concerns as using justice as leverage to counter the inequalities that accrue from the effects of being born into different positions in society (1971, p. 7). However, it seems to me that there are significant limitations to how he interprets this fact. His theory does deal explicitly with some aspects of class differences, particularly in the last part of his second principle of justice. However, his account seems insufficiently group based, systemic, and relational. (One might say, then, that he heads in the direction of "left field," but, as we will see in the next section, building these characteristics into one's theory is a necessary condition for a full appreciation of the perspective "from the left field.") Moreover, attention to gender fares even worse, being acknowledged as important only late in his work, and with very little change in the theory to better accommodate this concern. Much worse than even this weakness is his handling of racism. As a significant and potentially different kind of political problem, racism is barely acknowledged—and never dealt with in a substantive manner. When these kinds of problems come to the forefront, a different kind of justice concern becomes salient. Along with it I believe a different kind of concern needing attention in character education also comes into view. In the next section of this chapter, I outline how these concerns might take shape.

A View of Justice and Related Virtues beyond Rawls

Young's Focus on Social Groups and Oppression

There are alternative perspectives on justice, some of which seem to offer a better grip on some of the more difficult and intransient political kinds of difference and conflict, in particular, those that are properly seen as forms of oppression, such as racism. Among those I find the work of Iris Marion Young (1990, 1997) most helpful. It is her work that provides me with a perspective to imagine some of what character education might look like—what new virtues would be needed more clearly "from the left field"—for a fuller picture of social justice.

First, it is important to emphasize that Young is quite clear that she does not wish to reject distributive justice concerns (such as Rawls') as unimportant. Instead, as she says,

> I wish rather to displace talk of justice that regards persons as primarily possessors and consumers of goods to a wider context that also includes action, decisions about action, and provision of the means to develop and exercise capacities. The concept of social justice includes all aspects of institutional rules and relations insofar as they are subject to potential collective decision. The concepts of domination and oppression, rather than the concept of distribution, should be the starting point. (Young, 1990, p. 16)

At first glance, this might not seem much of a departure, but that impression is wrong. At the bottom lies a fundamentally different social ontology, one that, I will argue, brings to light the need for different, or at least additional, political virtues of the citizen. The difference hangs on how individuals are perceived as they enter the public arena of democratic discourse and politics. And from this difference emerges a significant change in terms of what kind of social difference and conflict comes to the forefront of attention.

As I have argued elsewhere (Boyd, 2004), a first step—the most crucial step—toward identifying this difference, is that it must be recognized that some harmful relations in the social world are not primarily between or among individuals, nor properly conceptualized as moral/political matters that can be addressed solely from the perspective of the ideal of everyone on the level playing field as "free and equal." Racism is one example. In contrast, in such cases, the social entity that comes to the forefront is a particular kind of group and a relationship of "oppression."

From this point of view, it is insofar as individuals are identified as members of such groups that they can be said to be oppressed, i.e., to "suffer some inhibition of their ability to develop and exercise their capacities and express their needs, thoughts, and feelings" (Young, 1990, p. 40). This interpretation moves us away from the common understanding of oppression as necessarily involving the coercion of a tyrannical power and toward structural and systemic concerns:

> Oppression in this sense is structural, rather than the result of a few people's choices or policies. Its causes are embedded in unquestioned norms, habits, and symbols, in the assumptions underlying institutional rules and the collective consequences of following those rules. It names, as Marilyn Frye puts it, "an enclosing structure of forces and barriers which tends to the immobilization and reduction of a group or category of people." (Young, 1990, p. 41)

It is especially important to understand here that the reference to a "group or category" does not mean just *any* group of *any* description.

Instead, both Frye and Young mean to refer here to a particular kind of social group. These are the kind of socially constructed groupings that (for the most part) we are born into, and thus "thrown" into independently of our intentions, and that form a large part of our identities as a result. (In Young's philosophically technical terms, these kinds of groups—in contrast to the kind that a Rawlsian liberalism can recognize—are "ontologically prior" to individuals, not the other way around (Young, 1990, p. 45). They are categories of ways in which difference is socially constructed that are remarkably stable over time and close to cultural universals—even when the actual content description of the category changes culturally or historically. Further, and particularly important for understanding the full meaning of "oppression," they are categories that can only be understood when seen *in relation to* each other; they are not stand-alone categories. Examples of such groups in contemporary societies are masculine/feminine, black/white, and upper class/working class. Finally, "oppression" picks out not just this relationality but also instances in which it is not one of equality, but one in which one side asymmetrically and systemically dominates the other in many, related ways (as is the case in all of the above examples).

The full harms of racism as oppression, then, come into view only when groups are seen to be defined in relation to each other and this relation is systemically manifested through structures of unequal power. What then matters is not just "horizontal" difference such as differing conceptions of the good or differing comprehensive doctrines (as in Rawls), but also the "vertical" difference of hierarchical relationships in terms of the possibility and ease of developing and exercising one's capacities, and having an effective voice in public decision making. In contrast, I submit that the perspective provided by focusing on the discrete individual as the only relevant entry point into conceptualizing justice, as in all forms of liberalism, occludes coming to grips with the reality of this kind of moral/political relationship.

Some Truly "Left Field" Asymmetrical Virtues Needed for Some Good Citizens

Although the commitment to persons as "free and equal" *qua* democratic citizenship is a powerful political ideal, it is clearly counterfactual: as racialized, they are, in fact, not free and equal. The problem with the account of virtues provided by Rawls (and Spiecker and Steutel) seems to me to be found in the tendency to see the needed virtues of *actual* citizens as if they were still symmetrically positioned relative to each other, as in ideal theory. For example, it is only citizens so positioned relative to each other who can exhibit the virtue of "tolerance" (whether conceived morally or intellectually) toward others—if reciprocity is assumed, as I think it must be from the perspective of "justice as fairness." In this sense, tolerance depends on having some power, in fact, to change what/who is being tolerated (Mendus, 1989)—but this is what is missing on the part of those who are in fact oppressed when facing those who (and whose views) are dominant (Boyd, 1996b). Similarly, it is only citizens who are on a level playing field of power who should be thought of as virtuous in respect to exhibiting the "disposition to compromise." Indeed, in one crucial passage in *Political Liberalism* in which he is at pains to identify the "very great virtues" of political cooperation "that make a constitutional regime possible," Rawls explicitly notes the virtue of "being ready to meet others halfway" (1993, p. 157). It stretches the moral imagination to the breaking point to assume that the racially oppressed should be thought of as virtuous only if they seek to be citizens who would meet their oppressors halfway.

If, on the other hand, we take seriously the kind of oppressive hierarchical relationships in which actual contemporary citizens find themselves, the picture of needed virtues changes in important ways. The broader conception of justice requires different virtues, or at least additional ones that are arguably different in kind. Elsewhere (Boyd, 1996a) I have argued that development of aims in moral education adequate to the task of addressing contemporary forms of oppressive relationships depends on critical assessment of how predominant views of both responsibility and objectivity function to protect the privilege of some, e.g., people who are deemed white and/or masculine. Similarly, I submit that some revision in the way virtues are thought of is also warranted. In fact, I would argue that recognition of this fact is the first step toward fuller responsibility and better objectivity.

But what would these other virtues look like? And where might we start in thinking about how to conceptualize them? For reasons of space my answers to these questions must be suggestive only, though, I hope, *provocatively* so. I say "provocative" because the seeming tendency of virtue talk toward conservatism, especially when this tendency can affect how racism is approached, must be challenged sharply. And one way to do so is by disrupting normal discourse concerning virtues.

A possible entry point into this disruption can be found in one of the "intellectual virtues" pointed to by Steutel and Spiecker, namely, the requirement that the citizen be disposed toward "self-critical participation in public debate." Despite the fact that they do not develop it in this way, this characteristic can be interpreted in a direction that opens up different virtues in the context of taking racism seriously in the way I have suggested. But immediately I will depart in a significant way from the assumption of symmetrical positioning in this work. Although this assumption is perhaps supported by the fact that within virtue theory in general any acceptable virtue is supposedly available to anyone, there is good reason in this case to think otherwise. Racism *depends* on a fundamental asymmetry in how individuals—as members of racialized groups—are located politically with respect to each other. Thus it is unlikely that they could be properly characterized in terms of the same virtues. In particular, I submit that those individuals on the dominant side should bear more of the burden of challenging their participation in this form of social relationship. Moreover, I would then argue that the virtues that would facilitate social stability—in the sense of manifesting the promotion of social justice in the broader sense—will be quite different than those needed for just *any* citizen, however located.

To make this case, I must also restrict my attention to racism as it is found in a particular social milieu, namely, that of North America. Racism takes many different forms in different societies, and how one would appropriately characterize the relevant asymmetry would differ accordingly. With that in mind, I submit that any attempt to identify political virtues that would not run the risk of doing more harm than good in the context of contemporary North American society *must* start with deep appreciation of the implications of the historical construction of whiteness-in-relation-to-Blackness within which any virtue must work. In short, I think those characterized by whiteness would need to be "self-critical" about how they are oriented in the world vis-à-vis others deemed non-white. A major part of the performative meaning of being white in this society is an understanding of oneself as legitimately claiming the center-in-relation-to-Blackness in myriad ways. And the center, by definition, is not the margin, not suspect, not guilty. Thus conceptualizing virtues in this context must start with some kind of cognitive gestalt switch that involves a variety of kinds of "off-centering" of one's understanding of oneself for white people. And a large part of this off-centering would be more self-reflexive openness to complicity in oppressive race relations and, in Larry May's words, to "moral taint" and shame (May, 1992).

If this kind of self-critical "off-centering" is legitimately called a kind of intellectual virtue that white citizens should endeavor to cultivate, it can then be seen as necessitating other moral/political virtues that are then also required in the face of racism. The first of these would be the character expression of the acceptance of what Young (1997) has called the aim of "asymmetrical reciprocity." She has argued persuasively that the kind of symmetrical reciprocity—the belief that one can and should seek the ideal of complete, reciprocal role-taking in moral deliberation—that is at the heart of liberal moral and political theory is in principle impossible. Indeed, as suggested above, in the context of oppressive group relations such as racism not only is it impossible, but it can also do active harm when mistakenly thought to be the default position for all citizens. In fact, a racially privileged citizen who seeks to exhibit this intellectual virtue of "off-centering" seriously would then seem to exhibit a kind of political virtue that might be called "symmetrical reciprocity suspicion" or the appreciation that there will always be hidden remainders to the experience and meaning of oppression not accessible to the privileged, however sincere or well meaning they are.

Then two other related virtues come more clearly into view, both of which also contest basic assumptions of Rawlsian liberalism. As noted above, one of the central assumptions of liberalism is the belief that the discrete individual must be the starting point of any legitimate moral and political theorizing. Further, as I have argued elsewhere (Boyd, 2004), the assumption is that all individuals are "ontologically unique." This is the fundamental basis of the emphasis on "respect for persons" that grounds so much of liberal moral and political theory, including that of Rawls. However, in contrast, one of the characteristics of individuals when seen in terms of their membership in racialized groups is the fact that they are essentially interchangeable as placeholders in the historical project of racial oppression. They are, in other words, "fungible." If this is the case, then another virtue that white people should cultivate is something like "fungibility sensitivity," a sensitivity to how racialized institutions function to benefit any and all place holders who can qualify as "white."

This sensitivity, however, must not be limited to simple awareness of differential receipt of benefits from racism. Rather, there is a second, concomitant virtue that effects a deeper acceptance of the complicity noted above. From the perspective of liberalism, not only are individuals considered ontologically unique, they are also the only possible source of agency in the social world. Though they may join together to be more effective, ultimately anything that will count as action in the world derives from the intentional choice and will of discrete individuals. In contrast, insofar as individuals are interchangeable as racialized white, action in the world is possible through the agency of others similarly located. When action is taken by a person *qua* white, it is in effect done in the name of *anyone* similarly located in the project of racial oppression regardless of his or her agreement or intentions. This possibility is part of the insidious systemic nature of how racism "works," and it does not come into view from a standard or Rawlsian liberal perspective. Surely, then, to counter it something like a virtue of "acceptance of proxy-action responsibility" is also desirable in racially privileged white people if justice is to have a chance in the face of the kind of difference and conflict that racism represents in a democratic society.

Conclusion

In this chapter I have explored from a political point of view three different ways of thinking about character education. Starting from the assumption that reasonable and fair adjudication of difference and conflict lies at the heart of the ideal of a liberal democracy, each way thinking about character education is examined in terms of how well it addresses this goal. I first assess a currently popular form of character education that endeavors to produce better people through the promotion of a finite list of virtues said to be common to all. I find this approach to be woefully inadequate, even harmful, and show how it is discursively productive of a very conservative political perspective that serves to protect the status quo of social relations. In particular, I demonstrate this through exposure of its various ways of ignoring or hiding difference and conflict, and see this as especially problematic when compounded by its blurring the crucial distinction between educating for the "good person" and educating for the "good citizen." I then turn to John Rawls' well known theory of justice to identify one kind of alternative perspective on what virtues would come to the forefront of attention if one starts from this distinction and focuses on the inevitability of difference and conflict among citizens. I see this alternative as a huge improvement over the essentially conservative nature of contemporary character education, especially in its centering of justice as the cardinal virtue that gives substance and meaning to a set of moral virtues that are constitutive of this core political virtue, and then in terms of the kind of intellectual virtues that enable citizens to effectively manifest them. Finally, although not rejecting all of the Rawlsian liberal perspective, I then seek to introduce to the character education discourse a new perspective, one in contrast to both the current view and to that derived from Rawls. Through engaging Iris Young's work, I argue that for some of the more egregious moral/political problems in contemporary North American society we need to utilize her focus on oppressive relations between relationally defined groups, not just on the interactions of individuals. Using racism as one such example, I then suggest some new—and definitely new-sounding—virtues that white people need to practice to mitigate the harm in which they are complicit as a result of the status quo of race relations. These I think of as "from the left field" in terms of their emergence from a perspective on social justice that is in sharp contrast to the other alternatives.

Note

1. Portions of the next section of this chapter have appeared in "The Virtues of Educating for Justice in a Diverse Society." In Leendert F. Groenendijk and Jan W. Steutel (Eds). *Analytisch Filosoferen over Opvoeding en Onderwijs: Liber Amicorum voor Ben Spiecker*. (*Philosophical Explorations of Education: Festschrift for Ben Spiecker*). Amsterdam: SWP, 2004, pp. 139–150. Portions of the second and third sections have appeared in "Character Education, Citizenship Education, and Conflict: A Cancerous Relationship." In Gert Biesta (Ed.) *Philosophy of Education 2010*. Urbana-Champaign, IL: Philosophy of Education Society, (In Press).

References

Boyd, D. (1996a). A question of adequate aims. *Journal of Moral Education*, 25 (1), 21–29.

Boyd, D. (1996b). Dominance concealed through diversity: Implications of inadequate perspectives on cultural pluralism. *Harvard Educational Review* 66 (3), 609–630.

Boyd. D. (2004). The legacies of liberalism and oppressive relations: Facing a dilemma for the subject of moral education. *Journal of Moral Education* 33 (4), 3–22.

Damon, W. (Ed.). (2002). *Bringing in a New Era in Character Education*. Stanford: Hoover Institution Press.

Glaze, A., Hogarth, B., & McLean, B. (2003). Can schools create citizens? *Orbit* 33 (2), 1–3.

Howard, R., Berkowitz, M., & Schaeffer, E. (2004). Politics of character education. *Educational Policy*. 18 (1), 188–215.

Lickona, T. (2004). *Character matters*. New York: Touchstone.

Macedo, S. (1992). Charting liberal virtues. In J. Chapman and W. Galston (Eds.) *Virtue. Nomos* XXXIV(204 -232). New York: New York University Press.

May, L. (1992). *Sharing responsibility*. Chicago: University of Chicago Press.

Mendus, S. (1989). *Toleration and the limits of liberalism*. London: Macmillan Education Ltd.

Rawls, J. (1971). *A theory of justice*. Cambridge: Harvard University Press.

Rawls, J. (1993). *Political liberalism*. New York: Columbia University Press.

Spiecker, B., & Steutel, J. (1995). Political liberalism, civic education and the Dutch government. *Journal of Moral Education*, 24 (4), 383–394.

Steutel, J., & Spiecker, B. (1999). Liberalism and critical thinking: On the relation between a political ideal and an aim of education. In R. Marples (Ed.) *The aims of education* (pp. 61–73). New York: Routledge.

Steutel, J., & Spiecker, B. (2000). The aims of civic education in a multi-cultural democracy. In M. Leicester, C. Modgil, & S. Modgil (Eds.) *Education, culture and values. Vol. VI: Politics, education, and citizenship* (pp. 243–252). London: Falmer. .

Young, I. M. (1990). *Justice and the politics of difference*. Princeton: Princeton University Press.

Young, I. M. (1997). *Intersecting voices: Dilemmas of gender, political philosophy, and policy*. Princeton: Princeton University Press.

PART TWO

Moral Education

CHAPTER FIFTEEN

Morality, Virtue, and Democratic Life

JOHN F. COVALESKIE

The Problem of Generations

Humans, from the moment of their birth, are social beings. As such, they are also moral beings, concerned with right and wrong and anxious to be judged good by the standards of the normative community in which they find themselves. Those standards can vary widely, and we often belong to several moral communities that are not always mutually compatible. For example, the political party to which I might belong may take positions that are not completely consistent with the moral norms of my religious community. The personal morality of a parent who is also a business executive may not be at all consistent with the actions taken to maximize profits for one's corporations (Jackalls, 1988). As children mature within their normative community (communities, but for simplicity's sake I will speak as though there is just one), they develop a sense of right and wrong, good and evil. They develop a sense of the sort of person they should become. Indeed, what they develop is a sense of what sort of person they *want* to become—the standards of right and wrong of their community become their own standards.

What we are describing is the formation of conscience to membership in a specific normative community. By "conscience," what I mean is that inner voice that passes judgment on our own actions and thoughts. It is more than a narrow sense of right and wrong; it also evaluates the products one produces and the skill with which one performs. It is conscience that tells me whether I am doing a good job as a teacher, and it is my conscience that judges when (if) the paper I am working on is ready to be sent out for review. Relative to this chapter, conscience is the inner voice that tells me that I must attend to the needs and interests of others when I am making decisions in the privacy of the voting booth, where there is no other judge of my vote than my own conscience. At a deeper level, conscience is the part of us that passes judgment on the sort of person one is.

Karl Mannheim (1928) first described the significance of the nature of human generations. To make clear what he called the "problem of generations," and what can be more properly called the "problem of education across generations," Mannheim made his point about the essentially social and cultural nature of human life by comparing humans to butterflies. With butterflies, a new generation is a new event; the old generation is dead. The young come into the world as a unit, programmed with the skills they need to survive. Two things are different about humans: (1) they need culture, and (2) humans do not have discrete generations in the sense that butterflies do; we are not all born at once, and we do not all die at once. These facts mean we must provide culture for our offspring—what we call education—and this is an ongoing, perpetual task. Children are always being born, and they must always be brought into the culture.

And that is a key point: being born into a society does not make one a member. Membership in a social group—what I will be calling a "normative community"—is a process and achievement. It is something virtually everyone does, but the fact that it is common—virtually universal—should not mislead us into thinking it is easy. The more complex the society into which one is born, the more difficult it is. The implications for complex industrial societies with a great deal of diversity, then, are significant.

Democracy, the Public, Norms, and Virtue

Democracy is a way of life that is governed by norms, and which relies on the virtue of its citizens, who govern themselves by forming and acting as a public. In this section I want to lay out what I mean by each of these terms. "Democracy" and "virtue" are ambiguous terms, "public" has a wide variety of common meanings, and "norm" is a word we do not use much. Democracy first.

Often we speak of the essence of democracy as being "one man, one vote." And while majority rule is part of democracy, it cannot be the whole. The very existence of a Constitution that defines and limits what the majority acting thtough its government can do is evidence that rule was not to be simply of the majority. The Bill of Rights made this even more clear.

The view of democracy assumed in this paper is that constructed by John Dewey (1916/1944, 1976/1980, 1927/1954). Democratic life is a great deal more than the procedures and institutions of majority rule. Such procedures are what philosophers call necessary conditions, but they are not sufficient. Dewey sees democratic life as desirable because it allows for the collective consideration of the best public policy that can lead to the best outcomes for the public, not just for the individual or the majority—if we are willing to do the work for bring it about. In a democracy we can form ourselves into a public that makes decisions with the common good in mind, but this is hard work and does not come naturally to us. However, this is not the same as saying it is unnatural.

It is often said that democracy is a government of laws, not of men. And there is some truth in that, if we mean that democracy is not governed by the whim or will of any individual and that there is a consistency in democratic polity that binds all equally—that no one is "above the law." But it is incorrect if what we mean is that we are governed by laws imposed upon us. In a democracy, laws are an expression of our norms. There are two ways this matters. First, the laws must be ones by which we are inclined to live voluntarily. Any society that would even pretend to be democratic must be so governed that its laws are ones we endorse and voluntarily abide by. We must not be merely compliant: a police officer on every corner could do as much, but that would not be democratic. The population of Oceania in *1984* (Orwell 1949/2003) was obedient enough but only because of coercion. Government by coercion is the death of democracy, even if the forms remain.

Second, even willing compliance is not enough: the population of Huxley's *Brave New World*

(1950) was compliant enough, but only because there was no reflection, no thought about doing otherwise. The essence of democratic life is that we are governed by laws to which we willingly and mindfully assent. Democratic laws govern—must govern—from inside, not from outside. They must be not just society's laws, but *our* laws. This is what I mean when I speak of "norms."

And the mindless compliance of *Brave New World* is the danger that we appear to face today as we run the risk of being entertained into compliance and out of democracy. Our media do not do a good job of educating us regarding the issues that face the public. This "miseducation" (Martin, 2002) of the public is a true threat to democratic life, and one that schools and other agents of public education must counter by a mindful preparation for citizenship—a deliberate and deliberative effort to foster the virtues of character and intellect that democracy requires of its citizens.

Norms are not fully identified by our actions, for we sometimes do fail to live up to what we believe to be right. Norms define not so much what we do as what we believe we should do. Of course, if we truly think we should do X, then most of the time we will. It is not that norms do not guide conduct: they do. But they do in a certain way. There is always a temptation to break rules that stand in our way when they are just rules. If I think I can get away with being dishonest, and if there is a good profit in doing so, and if I typically avoid lying only because I know I get punished when I get caught, I am likely to be seriously tempted to lie. If I mostly tell the truth out of fear of punishment, I am not an honest person, merely one who usually tells the truth.

On the other hand, an honest person will tell the truth even when there is no reason to do so other than that it is what honest people do, and I am an honest person. This is what a norm means: it is the thing itself that matters, not the consequences: an honest person feels bad after telling a lie, even a successful one. And it is this that means that democracy is governed by norms, not rules and not laws. It is collective government by self-governing members. In a functioning democracy, it is the individual conscience of each member that protects the individual rights of all other members. Without a conscience well formed to democratic life restraining our pursuit of our own good, the majority will trample the rights of the minority.

This observation brings us to a consideration of what we mean when we speak of a "public." As I am talking about what goes on in public schools, it is important to consider the meaning of public. In relation to schools, the adjective "public" is multiple in meaning: it means the schools are open to the public, answer to the public, are funded by the public, reflect the public will, and create the future public. None of this tells us, however, what a "public" is.

In *The Public and Its Problems*, John Dewey (1927/1954) argues that a democracy is governed not by individuals but by a public, the criteria for which are both specific and stringent. A public is not a mere gathering. It is neither a crowd nor a mob nor an audience. It is an intentional collection of people. A public forms in response to some perceived or felt problem, a problem that is collective and communal, not just individual.

If an individual is poor, that is an individual problem, often in our current culture explained by attributes and failures of the individual. The cure for poverty so explained is reform of the individual: education, better work habits, etc. However, if the public comes to believe that poverty and our acceptance of it result from social, political, and economic structures and arrangements that can be changed, then poverty can also become a public problem, a problem of and for the public (while also and obviously remaining a particular problem for the individual so afflicted). When poverty becomes a public problem, it is no longer a problem of each individual poor person—or not just so; it becomes a problem of all members of the public, rich and poor alike. But that requires a moral transformation of the rich, and of the poor as well. As long as our conscience tells us that we have no positive obligations to others, it is difficult for us to conceive of, let alone perform as, a public with respect to the problem of poverty or anything else. One measure of our failure in this regard is the utter lack of policy proposals to address the large and growing gap between the rich and the poor as well as the growing number of poor. We know this is a problem, and it is addressed in news media as well as dinner-table conversation, but we do not seriously discuss how we might address what is a quintessential problem of the public. We have done little to help those who have been hurt by the economic collapse of 2008, and we do even less (nothing, actually) to deal with the structural causes of the collapse in particular and unimaginable inequality in general.

A public is the organization of a democratic polity. It does the work of democratic governance when it (1) recognizes the existence of a common problem; (2) communally discusses the nature of the problem, taking into account the voices and concerns of all; (3) considers the solutions, again taking into account the voices and concerns of all; (4) plans the appropriate response to the problem; and (5) works to implement that response. In this process the proper relationship between the public and the government is that the government is one means the public has to do its work. Communal organizations, formal and informal, institutionalized and *ad hoc* are others. For problems widespread and deep, government will be the most effective vehicle for public action.

While an individual (if there really is such a thing as a person disconnected from the concerns of others) may pursue self-interest and advantage, even over others, a citizen, a member of a public, is not free to do so. "Citizen" is an office with responsibility for the common good. This is the meaning of Barber's (1998) reminder that "…we may be natural consumers and born narcissists, but citizens have to be made.…Public schools are how a public—a citizenry—is forged and how young, selfish individuals turn into conscientious, community-minded individuals" (220). Barber's point is that this sort of consideration does not come naturally, which does not mean that it is unnatural or against our nature. It is a potential but one that must be mindfully nurtured and fostered. The virtue that makes democratic life realizable is something we must mindfully and deliberately foster in each new member of each new generation. Democracy is something that must be constantly renewed and sustained. It is always a new achievement; and the democratic conscience is always a work of the public.

Finally, a word about virtue. We often think of virtues as being items on a list (Bennett, 1996), which is often the case when people talk about educating for virtue with the "virtue of the month" approach (Lickona, 1991). I would like to suggest a slightly broader view of virtue, one rooted in an understanding that virtues are relative to a given time, place, and culture. That is, virtue is defined by the norms of a culture and reflected in the context of a member's conscience. It is not some universal idea of goodness that defines virtue but local moral norms. Virtue is the ability to live the norms of one's culture well. Although it is not particularly useful for fashioning a list of virtues, Aristotle's (1985) definition is probably as good as anything anyone has come up with since: virtue is the settled disposition to do the right thing, in the right way, at the right time, and for the right reasons. Critical to note in this definition is that virtue is an attribute of character (the disposition to do the right thing, for the right reasons), judgment (doing the right thing at the right time and knowing what the right thing is in the first place), and skill (doing it in the right way). A modern version of this Aristotelian view is presented by Pincoffs (1986) who defines virtues as the attributes of a person that give others reason to think well of him or her (82).

Moderns following Kant generally do not count skill as part of virtue, seeing it as a matter of judgment and will. If one knows the right things to do, and if doing the right thing matters, then one will do the right thing. This is very much the image of morality on display in the work of Kohlberg

(1971): moral development is the development of one's ability to reason about moral problems. This is not incorrect, but it is incomplete: knowing the right thing to do is relatively easy most of the time. Teaching rules of behavior to children is also relatively easy. Shaping conscience is something quite different. That children know that sneaking a cookie before dinner or hitting a sibling is wrong is shown by the fact that they are likely to lie about having done these things. Knowing right from wrong is easy. Having it matter is the important thing (which brings us back to the discussion of norms: when the rules become our norms, we are more likely to live by them even when no one is looking). This is the central problem of moral/character education: whatever we mean by "good," how does anyone get to be that way?

And moral/character education is necessary for democratic life because a public requires that its members—citizens—do the right thing not just in public but also in the privacy of the voting booth, where there is no one to monitor except the individual's conscience. And beyond that, much work required of citizens is difficult—it demands skill, judgment, and a properly formed conscience. One must study the issues, keep informed, take the time to go to meetings and consider the *things of the public* (the English translation of *res publica*, from which we get "republic," the formal name for our sort of government). And then when it comes to decide, a member of a public is frequently called upon to do that which is in the common good, not necessarily what is in one's own best interest.

Thus is virtue required for the citizens to act so as to call a public into being. There are many specific skills that are required in this formation of a public, but in broad terms we can see that citizens, when they act as members of a public, are both speaking and listening in a particular way. When speaking in the creation of a public, citizens must do so honestly and forthrightly. In *The Gorgias*, Plato says one of the traits of a democratic citizen is *parrhesia*, which Tarnopolsky (2010) describes as speaking "frankly and boldly...[one's] own sincere thoughts on a subject without flattering or deceiving the audience by tailoring his remarks to their views" (98). In addition to the intellectual and moral virtues that lead us to hold the right opinions on public issues, speaking as Plato exhorts requires both honesty and courage.

Virtue is also required to listen so as to create a public. As Green (1994) describes what he calls the Auditory Principle, one's speech becomes public speech—that is, speech that creates a public—when it is heard in a certain way: "*public speech occurs when what is said in one person's speech is heard by others as candidates for their own speech*" (375; italics in original). That is, it is not the act of speaking in a public space that makes speech public; it is the act of hearing the speech of the other in such a way that the listener works to take the speaker's perspective so that forms a public of which they are two members. We thus grant (or deny) each other citizenship by how we hear each other, and in so doing we help to create (or to prevent) a public.

This is what Barber means when he tells us that citizens must be made; their consciences must guide them into certain ways of acting and away from others. Without the sort of virtuous citizenship willing and able to enact a public, democratic governance can be no more than an illusion at best.

The Problem of Governance

For most of our history we have understood that education is properly and primarily a matter of formation of conscience. *Education is that process by which any society transforms its children into fully participating members.* That this is the point of public education is obvious on even the briefest reflection. If education is about merely the pursuit of individual advantage in a capitalist economy, that is, if education were to be seen as a personal rather than a communal good, or if the communal good were merely about national economic development and competitive advantage, then there would be no need to educate for citizenship. More precisely, citizenship would be defined as mindless docility in the civil sphere coupled with an equally mindless pursuit of economic wealth and security. Clearly, no one would take *that* seriously as the goal of public education in a democracy! Education for citizenship is by definition an education in virtue, because it is an education for civic responsibility.

The focus of this chapter is on the public school because it is in the public school that the public supposedly decides mindfully how its children will be formed. This is in no way to suggest that private schools cannot or do not also serve the public will and the public good. Many of them do. But the difference is significant: public schools serve a *public* vision of the public good, while private schools, whether secular or sectarian, serve a *private* vision of the public good. Who decides matters in a democracy and the quality of the decisions are equally central to the essence of democratic life. However benevolent a philosopher-ruler would be, a society so ruled would not be democratic. Similarly, however "democratic" the procedures by which a decision is reached, if the decision does not respond to the welfare and interest of all, it is not democratic either.

It is only very recently that the claim that education is centrally about formation of the citizen seems odd. I dated myself in a class discussion recently by telling my students that I remembered when there was a clear and sharp distinction maintained between "education" and "training." Over time, "training" became "vocational education" and is now simply "education." What used to be called "education" is hardly a memory. It is certainly not a common practice in public schools today.

It must be noted that the project of fostering virtue is a dangerous one that can go horribly wrong: Germany in the 1930s did a very good job of teaching very bad moral norms. For much of our own history, there is also much that we got wrong and got wrong well, teaching the young a vicious set of moral norms and reinforcing the same in adults. The results included slavery, genocide, racial discrimination, and misogyny as but a partial list. One does wonder what comparable failings our great-grandchildren will perceive in us.

As a result, it seems sometimes that we fear doing moral formation of the young badly and so decide not to do it at all. Attempts at moral neutrality and development of pedagogical technique have to some degree replaced the project of thoughtful moral formation. However, even in such a regime, we do teach morality, even if not very thoughtfully: we teach children it is good to compete with others, to come in first, to be better, faster, brighter than others, and, perhaps most significantly, to not care much about the losers. We teach children to be individuals, not members, and we actively erode both the public and democratic life.

John Dewey (1976/1980) presents us with a very challenging notion of what it means to be a member of a public:

> What the best and wisest parent wants for his own child, that must the community want for all of its children. Any other ideal for our schools is narrow and unlovely; acted upon, it destroys our democracy. (5)

This is a moral claim, not an empirical one. It expresses Dewey's preference for democracy over other forms of government and his preference for a specific form of democracy over others (e.g., simple majoritarian forms, Madison's idea that it is a competitive balancing of individual and communal interests, or Jefferson's idea of a system allowing the people to select their leaders from among the natural aristocracy). And we should make no mistake about this: "Preference" in this context is a *moral* preference, not just a taste. Dewey is not only claiming that *he* prefers this sort of democratic life, but that we all should do so precisely because it is morally superior to available alternatives.

Democracy and Morality

So democracy is a form of *moral public life*, not just a form of government (Dewey, 1916/1944). Given the responsibilities of citizenship, one's conscience must be properly formed before one can fully participate as a member. Without a well-formed private conscience, one is not prepared to take on the obligations of citizenship. If it is correct that democratic citizenship requires virtue, and if it is correct that education is supposed to prepare one for citizenship, then it follows that education must inform the content of conscience. It seems beyond obvious that we are not doing so.

This is not to say that there is no moral formation going on. The formation that is happening willy-nilly amid the instrumentalism and accountability that pervades educational discourse is differentially preparing students to be worker-drones, unemployed, or masters of the universe—almost anything but citizens. In the 1960s when I was a young teacher, educators used to take seriously the notion of "citizenship education" or teaching "civics," however badly this might have been done in practice. Today we no longer even pretend to be interested in preparing children to be citizens, and we seem to give little if any thought to the meaning or consequences of that loss.[1]

Nor are schools the only institutions involved in the process of formation: entertainment media, news media, religious institutions, and politics all also play a part in the formation of the young as citizens. The range of these "mediating institutions" (Putnam, 1995) working as "multiple educational agencies" (Martin, 2002) is very broad. In addition to the obvious ones mentioned above, there are street gangs, labor unions, corporations, civic organizations like Kiwanis and Owls and Rotary, the military, book clubs, and quite literally too many others to mention. What is missing and prevents the formation of a public is the lack of institutions that connect the various local mediating institutions and allow for the perspective-taking across local publics that makes what Aristotle called "civic friendship" possible.

The assumption of this chapter is that the proper unit of analysis for this sort of question is not the individual, but the member. That is, moral or character education is essentially and intrinsically a work of and for the commons, a properly formed conscience is always and unavoidably the work of and for some particular morally normative community. It is an individual achievement, but a communal project, done within and according to the norms of some specific community. This does not mean there is no ultimate Good or Ground of The Good—some objective moral order. The existence of such an order would not affect the claim that morality is, as a matter of lived fact, defined by some local normative community. That is, there may be a God's-eye view of moral norms, but that view is not, and never will be ours in this life. The best we can do is to discern within the moral landscape in which we find ourselves the moral standards that are most conducive human thriving and a good life, while admitting that these, too, are locally and socially defined. Children are likely to become adults who share the moral norms of the group into which they were born and in which they were raised; culture has us before we have culture. However, this is hard work and easily undone. Schools were intended as the primary institution for preserving whatever gains we make in the direction of a public, and they are failing to do the work required.

Citizens as Officeholders

Democracy requires active participation not only from office-holders and lobbyists, but also from citizens—who are themselves officeholders. Citizens who do not vote, or vote without being fully informed, or vote and then treat politics as a spectator sport until the next election are failing in their responsibilities as citizens. When that becomes common, a society may retain the forms and institutions of democratic society, but will be left as only a simulacrum of democratic life.

Democratic life, with its commitment to both the common good and government as the institutionalization of the will of the people, seeks to dissolve the ages-old antipathy between rulers and ruled by the simple, or, as it turns out, the not-so-simple, expedient of making the people the rulers. Or, more precisely and which amounts to the same thing, of reversing the relationship so that government does the work of "We, the people." If government of, by, and for the people is the democratic ideal, then when we fail to join together in pursuit of the common good, we abandon the democratic experiment. We should be clear on this: to define government as an enemy of the people is to give up on the possibility of democratic life. On the other hand, to accept that government is the repository of the agent of the common will and the common weal means that (1) citizens must act so that is true, and (2) this common will and weal must both represent and respect the interests of the public (Dewey 1927/1954). That is, government is not automatically the instrument of the public will, nor will wishing make it so: it requires effort and skill, virtue and wisdom. These are, of course, the products of education worthy of the name, but there is no other way for the public to enact its will.

In that sort of democracy, there is a "general welfare" that "We the people" are supposed to pursue. True, we are also unalienably entitled to pursue our individual happiness, but that must be balanced against the common, or public, good. There will always be differences about the precise point of proper balance as well as about the content of that common good, but the normative content of democracy commits us to certain standards of public life, one of which is to seek that balance and understanding in common with others. As individuals we are entitled to pursue our own well-being, but as citizens we must be also concerned with the well-being of our fellow citizens, of the polity as a whole. That is just part of the job description.

This notion that we "must" be so concerned is not a "must" enforced on us by others. We must be concerned about others because that is the sort of people we are collectively; we are unlikely to be that sort of a people collectively if we are not first that sort of people individually. The sort of citizen I am is almost purely a function of the sort of person I am: my conscience is personal—it is mine—but it is not private: it affects the public and those with whom I share its civic space. And, if Dewey is right about what democracy demands of us as citizens, democracy depends on its members, conscience being formed in this way. Public education as the formation of conscience is the means by which democracy sustains itself. If we let public education become merely an exercise in economic preparation or self-gratification, we must seriously question whether we will be capable of sustaining self-government.

Implications for Public Education

If schools are supposed to foster certain forms of virtue in our children in preparation for their role in a democratic polity, what does that mean in practical terms?

Consider as one answer to that question a story Deborah Meier (1995) tells in *The Power of Their Ideas:*

> I recently had a conversation that gave me a good deal to think about. Two students had gotten into one of those stupid quarrels. The origins were silly. But what became clear was that one of the kids was a "victim"—over and over he was the subject of teasing and other minor cruelties on the part of his classmates. Everyone knows about it, including we adults. We worry, feel bad, get angry and end up doing very little good.
>
> I asked the student about it and he agreed that the other student was indeed the target of a lot of peer cruelty, and also that the reasons were silly, petty, and unkind. "Which side are you on?" I asked. "His side or his tormentors'?"
>
> We were both startled by my question. He said he wasn't really on any side.
>
> I didn't stop, because I was busy thinking about it myself. So I pushed. If someone is being cruel to someone else, if someone is the victimizer and someone the victim, rapist and raped, abused and abuser—can you really be neutral?"
>
> He paused. "No," he said, "I'm never with the abusers."
>
> What we realized was that there were two questions here and they were getting mixed up together. (1) Whose side am I on? And (2) what am I prepared to do about it. (86–87)

Note that Meier does not refer to any rules against bullying, harassing, or abusing other students. It is probably safe to say that there are such rules in Central Park East Middle School (where this incident takes place). But the rules are not the point: Meier is, in effect, asking this young man, this young member of this community, "What sort of person are you? Give some thought to your answer. Are you the sort of person you should be, the sort of person you want to be? The sort of person the community needs you to be?"

Meier has spent her professional life trying to put into educational practice the thought of John Dewey—the idea that public education must be one of the institutions that does the work of forming an actual public in the pursuit of democratic life. In doing that work, schools must consciously foster those virtues, both moral and intellectual (not only whose side are you on, but what are you going to *do* about it?) on which democracy depends. Knowing right from wrong is simpler than knowing what to *do* in a given situation (wisdom is needed), and knowing what to do does not automatically mean that we have the will or skill to do it (the adults do nothing about the bullying, in part, because they are afraid their intervention will make things worse). Virtue is not only the inclination or disposition to do the right thing: it is the wisdom to know what that is and the skill to do it.

In the Central Park East (CPE) Schools—public charter schools in New York City—Meier has mindfully planned and put together a K-12 program that is committed to small size and the development of the sort of community small schools allow (but do not automatically create: there is nothing magical about school size, but there is potential in them). This is a student-centered institution but not in the shallow sense that children get to do what they want. Meier is clear that this is an institution where adults are frequently "in students' faces," in ways the children do not always like, but which make sure that the program is centered on them. Adults are mentors here, not just teachers. Or, more precisely, what they are teaching is how to live democratically, not just economically or selfishly. The children are not only taught that the common good matters: they see that belief lived and are called to live it themselves.

Meier takes seriously the idea that public schools should be and can be that which they were created and originally funded to be: places where democracy is modeled for, taught to, and fostered in the young. The school is *not* democratic in the sense that is sometimes meant when people talk about "democratic education." That is, decisions in the school are not made by a vote of all present. The adults govern the institution, but they do so not just to maintain order but to develop in the young a certain sort of public consciousness and public conscience. They do, furthermore, engage in public thoughtful discussions about their common life. The size of the school is important for the goals Meier has in mind because it means no one is anonymous, no one can hide, no one gets lost. All the students know each other; all the teachers know each other; all the students know all the teachers, and vice versa. Such knowledge makes community possibility.

In such a community we *see* virtue lived and modeled. It is expected. It is also treated as a complex accomplishment, and one continually being developed, in part through discussion and communal reflection. In such a community, members hold each other accountable to the norms that define the community. In the event described above, Meier is working to make clear to the young man she is talking with the meaning of the norms in practice and wants the young man to reflect on the meaning of being one sort of person rather than another: "whose side are you on?" she is engaging the young man's conscience in an act of self-assessment.

Meier believes that if the sort of attention to the well-being of others taught and modeled at CPE becomes habitual, it will also carry into the civic square as a similar attention to the well-being of those whom I do not know and with whom I do not have direct contact.

Or consider the work of Vivian Paley, who taught kindergarten for many years in Chicago. Each year she recorded the progress of her students and her own development as a teacher. In *You Can't Say, You Can't Play* (1992) she tells about the year she set out to end the exclusion and minor social cruelties that most adults take for granted among young children. She, like any kindergarten teacher, is aware that some students are regularly excluded, and others regularly exclude. This, of course, echoes Meier's observation that the victim in the incident she describes is often victimized, and the adults have known about the situation but not done anything about it.

One year, Paley sees this tendency to exclude not simply as "the way things are" or "the way children are," but as a social problem that must be surfaced and explored, discussed in an ongoing democratic conversation. Exclusion ceased to be an individual problem and becomes a problem of that small public. As was the case with Meier, Paley was facilitating a public exploring their common life together, and learning how to take account both of the needs of others and the kind of person they wanted to be. Her students were learning to be members, not just individuals. She was actively shaping their consciences to prepare them for democratic life.

Paley realized that year that the tendency to treat others as inferiors or as superiors is a real threat to democracy. Some of Paley's students claimed that the inclusion rule would be nice for the students being excluded, but that it would not be fair to those with the power to exclude. Those who had been doing the rejecting felt they had a right to do so. In reflecting on the issues being raised, Paley draws an important distinction between private spaces and public spaces. While students have the right to invite whom they want over to their homes, the public school is a public space, where everyone is equal and no one has the right to exclude anyone else.

We often face similar disputes in our society, and they are similarly construed as a conflict of rights: the right of free speech versus the right of people to be safe from harassment in public spaces; the right of African Americans to be treated equally versus the right of segregationists to reserve the best public spaces for whites; or the right of some straight people to marginalize people who are lesbian, gay, bisexual, and transgendered, against the right of those LGBT people to be fully members of the public square and civil society. Paley's view was that there is no conflict of rights in any of these cases: there is no right to discriminate in public spaces, regardless of one's prejudices or preferences.

As with Meier, an action by a member of the community that violated the norms of the community was dealt with by conversation and consideration, not simple punishment. Paley was not simply teaching the students to be obedient; like Meier, she was working to make democracy possible by forming democratic consciences in her students.

Conclusion

In this chapter I have argued that if we desire to prepare the young for civic membership and civic responsibility, it will be necessary for us to recognize that schooling is about more and more important than the mere acquisition of knowledge, however much it is also about that. It is the task of adults—teachers at least as much as parents—to mindfully work for the moral formation of the young. Without the proper moral formation, it is unlikely that children will grow up to have the virtues necessary for democratic citizens.

Nor, as I show by a consideration of the work of Meier and Paley, does this moral formation need to be dogmatic, rigid, or exclusive, a mere "bag of virtues" (Kohlberg, 1971). The way we teach virtue is by living virtuously in the sight of our students (Sizer and Sizer, 1999). If we do not begin doing this more mindfully than has been the case for the last few decades, we will be left with a population, no longer citizens, no longer a public, incapable of conceiving of such a thing as a common good.

Note

1. "We" here refers to us as a society. There are plenty of mediating institutions that do this work, but we have lost or broken the means by which they can communicate and form a broader social consensus (Putman, 1995).

References

Aristotle. 1985. *Nichomachean ethics*. Trans. Terence Irwin. Indianapolis, IN: Hackett.

Barber, Benjamin. 1998. Education for democracy. In *Passion for democracy*. Princeton, NJ: Princeton University Press.

Bennett, William J. 1996. *A book of virtues: A treasury of great moral stories*. New York: Simon and Schuster.

Canter, Lee, and Marlene Canter.1976. *Assertive discipline*. Los Angeles: Lee Canter and Associates.

Dewey, John. 1916/1944. *Democracy and education: An introduction to the philosophy of education*. New York: The Free Press.

Dewey, John. 1976/1980. *The school and society*. Carbondale, IL: Southern Illinois University Press.

Dewey, John. 1927/1954. *The public and its problems*. Athens, OH: Swallow.

Green, Thomas F. 1994. Public speech. *Teachers College Record* 95 (3): 369–388.

Huxley, Aldous. 1950. *Brave New World*. New York: Harper.

Jackalls, Robert. 1988. *Moral mazes: The world of corporate managers*. New York: Oxford University Press.

Kohlberg, Lawrence. 1971. Education for justice: A modern statement of the Platonic views. In *Moral education*, ed. Nancy Sizer and Theodore Sizer. Cambridge, MA: Harvard University Press.

Lickona, Thomas. 1991. *Educating for character: How our schools can teach respect and responsibility*. New York: Bantam.

Manheim, Karl. 1928. The problem of generations. In *Essays on the sociology of knowledge*, ed. Paul Kecskemeti. New York: Oxford University Press.

Martin, Jane Roland. 2002. *Cultural miseducation: In search of a democratic solution*. New York: Teachers College Press.

Meier, Deborah. 1995. *The power of their ideas: Lessons for America from a small school in Harlem*. Boston, MA: Beacon.

Orwell, George. 1949/2003. *1984*. New York: Plume.

Paley, Vivian Gussin. 1992. *You can't say, you can't play*. Cambridge, MA: Harvard University Press.

Pincoffs, Edmund L. 1986. *Quandaries and virtues: Against reductivism in ethics*. Lawrence, KS: University Press of Kansas.

Putnam, Robert D. 1995. Tuning in, tuning out: The strange disappearance of social capital in America. *PS: Political Science and Politics 24* (4): 664–683.

Sizer, Theodore R. and Nancy Faust Sizer. 1999. *The students are watching: Schools and the moral contract*. Boston, MA: Beacon.

Tarnopolsky, Christina H. (2010). *Prudes, perverts, and tyrants: Plato's* Gorgias *and the politics of shame*. Princeton, NJ: Princeton University Press

CHAPTER SIXTEEN

Liberal Education and Moral Education

DANIEL R. DENICOLA

My intent is to advance two claims: the first is that liberal education entails moral education; the second is that moral education must ultimately engage liberal learning. These two assertions may be regarded simply as descriptive: so, for example, the first claim may be read as "*any* liberal education entails *some sort of* moral education," which wouldn't imply that the entailed moral education is adequate or proper, let alone optimal—it might in fact be objectionable. But these claims may also be taken normatively: the first proposition would then be read, for example, as "an *excellent* liberal education entails a *sound* moral education." I mean to assert these claims in the stronger, normative sense. This is *not* to say that the two forms of education are identical (I will claim they are not), and I certainly do not contend that one must have a liberal arts degree to be a moral person.[1]

Given the current scene—the barrage of "narratives of decline"[2] regarding liberal education and the "hermeneutics of suspicion"[3] regarding moral education—my claims may seem rather rosy and retro. That is no argument against them, of course, but simply ignoring this climate would be blinkered. Clearly, I have some explaining to do.

Critiques of Liberal Education

There are two sorts of critiques of liberal education, both of which have made publishers happy since at least the 1980s; together they have created a discouraging miasma. The first sort focuses on performance gaps. Now any normative practice, especially one that is complex and institutionalized, frequently displays regrettable performance gaps; my view is not so rosy as to claim that liberal education is a flawless exception. (Alas! Not even John Dewey's assault on the theory/practice dichotomy has made it possible to elicit and assure excellent practice just by articulating sound theory.) Pointing out such failures, degradations, and corruptions of practice is, however, a call to mend, correct, and reform, not a strike against liberal learning itself (just as deploring the problems in our criminal justice system would not *per se* discredit the ideal of justice). On the contrary, to decry a performance gap is often to *endorse* the value of the ideal. The jeremiads that fall into this category, however, typically bemoan *widespread* and *systemic* degradation of performance, and they often elevate a *particular* conception of liberal education as the salvational ideal.[4] I usually find myself reluctant to embrace such friends of liberal learning, because I often disagree with their characterization or the alleged scope of the claimed decadence, or with the conception of liberal education they advocate as redemptive—or with all three.

The second sort of critique is more worrisome, because it argues that the very ideal of liberal education itself is problematic.[5] Those critics in this group who go on to offer constructive proposals advocate a spectrum of changes that range from significant supplement to radical reform to the outright replacement of liberal education with a distinctly different paradigm. Such vigorous lines of criticism come from many directions, but although aimed truly, most of them seem to miss the mark. Given my goals for this essay, it is impossible to address even the most cogent of these critiques in deserved detail; instead, I will describe three generic ways such critiques fall short and hope that these adumbrations will intimate the outline of a fuller, more adequate response.

1. Critics frequently take (or mistake) a particular conception for the concept[6]: they find fault with an influential conception of liberal education (say, that of John Henry Cardinal Newman or Robert Hutchins) or with a particular historical institutionalization (say, the Victorian university or the modern research university) and then conclude expansively that the concept of liberal education is thereby on the ropes. It is as though one were to criticize the theories of justice developed by Aristotle and Rawls and summarily conclude that the concept of justice itself is defective. To use a biological analogy, this mistakes the phenotype for the genotype.[7] If it is wrong to equate the concept of liberal education with one of its iterations, it is also egregious to reduce it to a specific curriculum or pedagogy—or even to a theory of curriculum or pedagogy. Liberal education is more than the trivium and quadrivium, Oxbridge tutorials, or the Great Books Program. How then do we get at the ideal itself? My preference is, in fact, not to construe liberal education as an abstract ideal, which would ignore or problematize its dynamism but rather to understand it as a tradition that remains interactive and open. Liberal education comprises a rich, complex, and live tradition of educational theory and practice, traceable to the classical cultures of Greece and Rome; it has evolved over the ages in mutual cause-effect interactions with other aspects of Western cultures—especially socio-political, intellectual, and technological aspects.[8] Responsive to its day, it has had a multitude of interpreters and appeared in varying manifestations, and it has been a dependable and bounteous fount of intellectual life, flowing for centuries as the mainstream in places of higher learning. It is this venerable and still-evolving tradition that grounds the concept and merits our attention.

2. Perhaps because of the first error, critics are often led to a second: they restrict liberal education to the classroom only—to what is ordained by the teacher—and ignore other aspects of the educational situation. But liberal education is always situational, shaded by place and time, and its educational impact is shaped by a community of learners, a co-curriculum, and an institutional context—as well as by what transpires in classrooms and laboratories. Any adequate theory must comprehend these typical aspects of practice. These elements are not fixed ideals either; they too have particular iterations and change in response to many factors—but they are relevant, even indispensable, to a holistic understanding of liberal education. Recent developments such as the encouragement and expansion of experiential, collaborative, and service learning, should be understood to be as integral to contemporary liberal education as the globalization of the curriculum. (This point is especially salient when considering the ways in which liberal education involves moral education.) Indeed the boundaries of the classroom are increasingly porous as courses become more like twenty-four-hour learning communities, incorporating a variety of experiential modes of learning.

3. Most disturbing, I find many critiques of liberal education to be self-refuting—not in a formal, logical sense but in an existential sense: a refutation of the self. Most critics of liberal education are drawing upon their own liberal learning—it seems undeniable—to attack the ideal of liberal education; truly, it is their own liberal education that enables the substance, acuity, and eloquence of their complaints— and thereby belies them. More than a disheartening ingratitude, more than a sophisticated self-deception, this amounts to an educated refutation of one's own education, an *alma matricide*.

These quickly sketched responses will have to suffice so that I may return to my present claims. Any argument for my two assertions of strong relations between liberal and moral education crucially turns on what is meant by the two terms. Not only are both terms controversial, but their component terms— "liberal," "moral," and "education"—are individually contested also; indeed, they abide in a thicket of contested concepts. To attempt to clear that thicket would be folly. Rather, by understanding liberal education as a tradition that accommodates various competing conceptions (and later, of moral education as a range of practices), I will accept its contested status as natural or appropriate, give due regard to context, and interpret many controversies over meaning as internal to the tradition. Perhaps we can at least tiptoe through the thicket without losing our way.

Liberal Education and the Good Life

How are we to characterize this perdurable yet contested tradition, distinguishing it from other forms of education? And why does it entail moral education? I prefer the Aristotelian approach: let's look to its aims.

Liberal education is distinctive in having as its supreme purpose *the discernment of and preparation for the good life*. It is, therefore, both descriptively and in its aspirations, fundamentally a moral education. The "breadth" so often associated with liberal education is not, in the first instance, breadth of content (*that* is derivative); rather it is the breadth of its normative concern: the activity of living as a human being and one's life as a whole. Insofar as the pursuit of a liberal education is an intentional action, its purpose is transformative; that is, it is an action intended to improve the agent *as an agent*. These are quite different aims from those of, say, vocational, military, or professional education.

There are some who will interrupt at this early point to declare that, performance gaps aside, such an education is not *normatively* moral, that what it provides is a *deficient* or *misguided* moral education. The so-called "good life," they might say, reeks of an elitist, aristocratic life; or, it is an impractical and arid intellectualist existence, without passion or the warmth of caring relationships; or, it is presented as *the* good life—a single, homogeneous, hegemonic, sexist vision of what life should be; or, it presumes not only the moral authority of the educators but the righteousness of their teachings and methods.[9] Some of these arguments, and others like them, are compelling when applied to some versions of liberal education—indeed, all of them are probably apt critiques of a few versions— but they do not engage the underlying and fundamental ideas that have inspired the tradition. To explain why, I need to refine the three key terms in my account. First, the guiding phrase, "the good life," need not designate a singular, pre-existing ideal; there is no reason why, in principle, we might not anticipate diverse, individual, and contrasting visions of the good life (having correlative implications for educational content). Second, the learner's effort to lay claim to such a vision and to understand what it requires, for which I have used the term "discernment," is an intrinsic part of liberal learning; and the vision thus claimed is both found and formulated, always open-ended, and under continual refinement. Third, my word "preparation" might wrongly imply that the good life commences when learning ends; rather, living and learning come to permeate and cultivate each other throughout a lifetime. Thus refined, the unfolded and explicit (but infelicitous) statement of liberal education's aim would become: *the continual discernment and (re-)synthesis of, as well as commitment to, preparation for, and cultivation of, a flourishing and moral life.* So understood, we might have conceptions of liberal education that are democratic rather than aristocratic; that require the cultivation of emotions and personal relationships as well as intellect; that include experiential learning and encourage practical engagement; that are gender sensitive and culturally pluralistic; that are alert to issues of race and class; and that avoid morally egregious indoctrination. (In fact, these very possibilities are prominent among contemporary trends in liberal education.) Indeed the ultimate concerns of liberal education are not confined to situations of privilege and comfort; concern for one's life and its best prospects arise amidst poverty, in despair, when shining ideals of the good life are shattered—even after great horror.[10]

How does one come to understand what a flourishing and fulfilled life—a good life—is? And how does one prepare for such a life? It is natural that different approaches to these questions would develop in the tradition, strands of thought that express a vision of liberal education, each interpreting the supreme aim, each initially quite expansive but letting loose a cascade of conceptions and ideas in increasing specificity reaching from goals to curriculum and pedagogy.[11] Four such strands, which may be identified by their announced educational aim, are dominant and intertwined in the tradition. The four I have in mind are:

1. Education is for the transmission of cultural inheritance across generations.
2. Education is for self-actualization, leading to a normative individuality.
3. Education is for understanding the world and the forces that shape one's life.
4. Education is for engagement with and action in the world.

These strands represent polarities in the philosophy of education, create forms of educational discourse, and establish perspectives from which theories of curriculum and pedagogy may be developed; they each accommodate clusters of variant conceptions of liberal education. (In fact, they are so capacious that one might easily forget their subsidiary connection to the cultivation of a good life.) All four are detectable in robust conceptions of liberal education (and also in most mission statements of institutions devoted to liberal education), but it is the variation in the weaving of these strands that gives such conceptions (and institutions) their particular distinctiveness. Indeed, the dynamics of liberal education's history may be ascribed largely to the shifting relationship, balance, and blend of these strands. I will draw abbreviated sketches of them, trusting in their familiarity to suggest something of their larger visions.

1. *Education is for the transmission of cultural inheritance across generations.* Humans are born into helplessness and ignorance; parents cannot convey what they have learned through their genes. Learning is imperative for survival, but every generation must start to learn anew. Our ancestors, however, produced two innovations that transformed the possibilities for learning: the development of complex symbol systems to encode experience, and the techniques of preserving these codes in durable artifacts. Thus we are able to articulate, accumulate, and preserve the human experience, creating a legacy of learning that grows with each generation and can be passed along to the next. It is the urgent imperative of education to conserve and bequeath this cultural treasure, our intellectual heritage: sophisticated languages, whole disciplines of knowledge, a profusion of great texts and works of art, historical narratives, and unsolved but intriguing problems—along with the keys to understanding them.[12]

The appreciation and assimilation of that legacy (what we have come to call "the canon") are averred to be indispensable to the aim of discerning and living a good life. This education-as-transmission strain has claimed several well-known moral dimensions: a significant portion of any such cultural legacy is moral in content, explicitly or implicitly; it portrays moral exemplars; it may also stimulate and serve salient moral capacities, such as moral imagination or judgment; more subtly, moral considerations are involved in the evaluation of this heritage, the principles of selection employed, and in the implications conveyed regarding the uses and value of this legacy.

2. *Education is for self-actualization, leading to a normative individuality.* In this view, education is focused on the actualization of valued potentials in the learner, the awakening and development of capacities, dispositions, and skills. This strand draws on a desire for fulfillment or completion and is perfectionist in that it links particular conceptions of the good life to the cultivation and exercise of certain elements of human nature or of individual character (or both), the perfection of oneself in what I am calling "a normative individuality." The picture of the self-actualized person may be drawn from social mores or roles, from naturalistic indices of well-being and flourishing or from the unique potential and perceived promise of the individual student (or from a blend of these). Hinting at differing metaphysical commitments, the process itself may be described variously as finding or forming a self; as self-creation, self-definition, self-realization, or self-actualization. But all interpretations presume that liberal learning individuates, that it shapes and fulfills character, and that such an education offers individuals a better version of themselves that would likely be unattainable through simply growing up and older. Thus self-actualization entails moralization.[13]

3. *Education is for understanding the world and the forces that shape one's life.* In this strand, by contrast, the focus is on the actuality of this world and the human predicament. To comprehend our context is to grasp not only the physical world but also the social, cultural, and psychological factors in play.[14] The prescribed means for understanding the world—the disciplines and techniques of inquiry—vary in different versions, and the list of salient "forces" changes over time. Proponents may even debate to what extent we discover or create the "world" we inhabit, what it is to "dwell" in a world, and what limits there are to our knowledge of our situation. Yet among these versions there is unity in the aim of making sense of things, in the value of wonder or curiosity; achieving understanding is always tied to making the phenomena meaningful. The assumption in the background is that understanding our world is indispensable to a good life, either in the strong sense that such understanding (and contemplation of the understood world) *is* the good life, or in the weaker (and more common) sense that understanding the world is conducive to or a component of a good life.[15] To know myself and others; to understand my situation and its possibilities; to grasp the risks and consequences of my actions—these all are surely relevant to my moral action. Moreover, the imperative to understand may itself be seen as a moral obligation in the spirit of Alfred North Whitehead's observation, "Where attainable knowledge could have changed the issue, ignorance has the guilt of vice."[16]

4. *Education is for engagement with and action in the world.* Liberal education, on this view, may bring us to cope with the world, to serve it nobly, to critique it trenchantly, or to reform it. Under different interpretations of "the world" and our prospects in it, the engagement and action may include civic engagement, public service, moral action, policy analysis (as an aspect of *praxis*), social criticism—even a principled withdrawal from the world. It may seem surprising that I include this strand within liberal education, since the latter is often portrayed as elevating theory and disdaining practice; but as far back as classical Athens, Isocrates—whose school rivaled Plato's and may be considered a prototype of a liberal arts institution—sought to prepare students to be wise and active citizens, to train them in dialectic and rhetoric, a power to articulate and persuade grounded in deep and sound moral commitments.[17] Living a good life requires practical wisdom, sound judgment and reflective action; a good community must be constructed and sustained by the continual efforts of virtuous and competent people. Even in those marginal versions that advocate withdrawing from the world's dizzying arena, education (on this account) is interpreted as readying the student for effective and appropriate moral action.[18]

Through these various strands, the learner confronts primal questions: Who am I? What may I become? What is our story? What sort of place and situation am I in? What should I do? What may I hope? Tied to the ultimate concern for living a good life, these four strands, though distinct, are throughout the tradition of liberal education shown to be related necessarily: sometimes, one aim is subsumed as means to another's ends; often the elaboration of one leads to another; and at other times, more than one strand, even all four, are declared boldly as pluralistic ends of equal status—leaving to the learner the task of discovering their relationship. For example, one might see self-actualization as requiring engagement with the world: Aristotle is identified primarily with the educational aim of self-actualization, of developing and exercising virtuous traits in a flourishing or eudaimonistic life; but Aristotle thought such a life was expressed through understanding one's world (*sophia*, or theoretical wisdom) and engaging in action with virtue (*phronesis,* or practical wisdom).[19] Or, one might see the assimilation of transmitted culture as a path to self-realization: Michael Oakeshott is known for valuing the transmission of culture, interpreting our intellectual heritage in the image of a grand conversation, in which we must "learn the voices"; yet Oakeshott also asserts that entering this conversation, "our common inheritance…is the only way of becoming a human being, and to inhabit it is to be a human being"—expressing thereby an ultimate, motivating hope for self-actualization.[20]

There are, in addition, noteworthy continuities or themes that thread through and bind the strands of liberal education, and that are morally salient. One such theme (reflected in the often misunderstood term "liberal") is freedom.[21] The original terms commonly translated as "liberal arts" (*eleutheriai technai* in Greek, *artes liberales* in Latin), could be rendered equally well as "the skills of freedom." Liberal education proceeds from and for freedom, and each of the four strands offers its particular form of liberation: (1) the cultural transmission ideal offers liberation from a timeless, meaningless, unconstructed present; (2) self-actualization offers liberation from confused and imposed identities, liberating one's authentic self in the realization of one's own possibilities; (3) understanding the world delivers a liberation from superstition, ignorance, and error; and (4) and effective engagement in the world yields a liberation from powerlessness, false constraints, and social entropy. Together, they free us (and burden us) to be morally mature persons together.

Related to the theme of freedom are the ties to autonomy and to democracy—all terms with moral bearing. Autonomy, willing and making one's own choices, is enshrined both as a goal of and an ethical constraint on the educational process (indoctrination is condemned as a violation of this constraint). In postmodern times, autonomy is sometimes derided as a relic of the Enlightenment (despite its ancient roots and perennial blossoms), reflecting atomistic individualism and celebrating self-sufficiency—charges that are sometimes apt. But autonomy may also grace the "situated self" when understood in other ways—for example, as what enables the exercise of human capabilities in response to one's situation, or as a condition of moral agency that shapes relationships.[22] Having the capacity to influence one's own life in response to critical reflection may even be essential to the concept of a developed self—situated and related, or not. That there is a link between liberal education and democracy, on the other hand, may seem an odd claim, since one striking historical change in liberal education is its metamorphosis from the classical model of an exclusive education suitable only for leaders—free, aristocratic, leisured men—to the contemporary vision of an education required of all for effective democratic citizenship. But the connection was there at the outset: after all, though citizenship was usually limited to free and propertied males, it was the emergence of democracy and the correlative threat to aristocratic values that provoked consideration of the best education for such citizens and the establishment of competing schools to offer it. Through the fits and starts of a punctuated social evolution, our collective sense of who is capable of and entitled to such citizenship has become increasingly inclusive—and the need for liberal education more widespread. The moral climate of democracy, in which each individual's experience is valued as relevant to the construction of the good, a society in which virtually all adults may shape their own lives—and therefore the lives of others—depends on liberal education for its very survival as well as its thriving. In such a climate, the concern for the one's life as a whole and for what it is to live a flourishing life becomes a live issue for all.

Finally, liberal education presents learning as continuous with living, as a *lifelong* endeavor. Schooling may end, but the liberal learner is never finished. We learn how to learn because life keeps surprising us, we age and change, and we may grow continually in our ability to derive meaning from experience, reflect critically, and respond wisely. The transformation of liberal learning may be dramatic, but it is never completed: the four strands—individually and together—set infinite tasks.

Let me take stock at this point. I have presented liberal education as a live and evolving tradition, characterized by the dynamism of four interrelated strands of thought, and unified by normative concern for the activity of living as a human being and one's life as a whole. I hope to have shown that in its supreme aim, in the visions of subsidiary strands, in its themes and the questions that motivate its learners, and in its effects, it is a profoundly moral education. It's well past time to turn to my second claim: moral education ultimately and inexorably leads us to liberal learning.

Moral Education and the Moral Person

Moral education is the range of practices aimed at moralizing individuals and rectifying social arrangements through structured learning.[23] As with educational processes in general, it anticipates hopefully both an individual and a social good: it is good to become a moral person; and a society is better if it is just and composed of moral individuals. We should mark the contrast between incidental and purposeful learning. Learning is inevitable and continuous throughout our lives, although much is learned incidentally—and a good deal of that is below the threshold of our consciousness. But we may also pursue learning purposefully and reflectively; learning in that way requires intention and attention, as well as self-awareness and reflection on experience—though incidental and unnoticed learning always accompanies it as well. Moral *education* implies purposeful and reflective learning.[24] Although humans have evolved neural capacities that enable a moral life and perhaps even preferences or dispositions that tilt or direct our values and although we develop, mature, and surely acquire some sense of morality through normal socialization, a moral education claims to offer "value-added" outcomes: in other words, moral education "goes beyond" whatever morality is hardwired in our biology and unfurled by simply growing up human—in fact, it may even resist, redirect, or attempt to undo these presentments.

The content of moral education—the intended "value-added outcomes"—may be derived from theory or from practice (or both). Every moral theory contains an embedded image of the moral person from which the content of a moral education may be drawn. Cultural relativists, for example, seek to develop people who understand and embrace the values of their society—and perhaps display tolerance to the differing judgments of other societies; Kantians strive to produce persons of good will, individuals who have strong reasoning skills, a keen sense of duty, and a profound respect for every human being; and virtues theorists focus on the development of persons who have moral character, interpreted as a configuration of specific traits. These examples are stated roughly, of course, and each may be dilated into ideals of burnished detail, but the point here is simply that different ethical theories impart different models of the moral person—different senses of what is required for moral agency; of what motives, actions, traits, principles, and practices are morally worthy (and unworthy); of what outcomes or relationships or experiences are good—and that these images guide the practices of moral education.[25] Similarly, implicit theoretical models of the ethical community or moral society may yield content for moral education projects of social reform. Frequently, however, the practices of moral education, instead of being drawn from rarified moral theory, are developed from practice, from shared experience or cultural custom. In that case, the programmatic content may be derived from considering such pre-theoretic questions as: How must we act in order to get along together? What traits and actions are inevitably self-destructive or harmful to others? What is expected of a decent citizen in our society?[26]

These moral education projects may also have varying levels of aspiration: moral education may take a minimalist approach, aiming modestly at preventing egregious immorality and producing people who are generally decent; or it may be more ambitious, trying to moralize students as far as possible toward *eudaimonia*, supererogation, or some other perfectionist ideal. The primary "value-added outcome" is then one that governs all others: it is the provision of a considered and compelling ideal of moral personhood and a moral community. Yes, this ideal may be more or less implicit and inchoate or explicit and polished, open and pluralistic or closed and singular, minimal or maximal—but it serves to define the intentionality and structure that make the experience of moral learning a moral education.

Typically, moral education will aim to produce the following outcomes, each made specific by the particular model of the moral person it enshrines or its answers to pre-theoretic questions:

1. *The development of morally relevant capacities.* It will seek to awaken and expand the range, sensitivity, and effectiveness of such capacities as, for example, practical reason or judgment, empathy, moral imagination, or the capacity to form caring relationships.

2. *The acquisition of morally relevant skills.* Moral persons are competent in certain morally salient skills, proficiency in which is an aim of moral education—for example, the application of principles to cases, consequentialist reasoning, participation in ethically structured discourse and deliberation, techniques of values clarification, or skills of nurturance.

3. *The development of moral character.*[27] Moral education nurtures virtuous traits and eliminates vicious or morally dysfunctional traits: for example, to develop honesty, courage, persistence, compassion, or tolerance, as settled dispositions, while reducing patterns of deceptiveness, cowardice, giving up easily, carelessness, or stinginess.

4. *The development of moral agency.* Moral education will try to develop various second-order traits relevant to moral agency, metacognitive dispositions that allow a person to monitor conduct and improve as a moral agent, such as: self-reflectiveness, open-mindedness, sensitivity to particulars, emotional integrity, and acceptance of responsibility.

5. *The making of moral commitments and the alteration of conduct.* Success in achieving the previous outcomes should produce a final outcome: students will embrace certain values (and reject others) and act morally (in acts characterized by decency, compassion, utility, care, good will, or supererogation, etc.). In short, they should more closely approach the model of a moral person.

These objectives are inseparably intertwined; they are complementary perspectives on morality. For example, displaying a virtuous character surely engages morally relevant capacities; and character education, which views the third and perhaps fourth elements as foundational, nevertheless cannot dismiss the others, though it may interpret them as derivative. Seriously pursuing these outcomes—

from the moment such education becomes purposeful and self-reflective—will inevitably engage liberal learning.[28] Moreover, my list so far is, I believe, incomplete; there is an essential element missing, one that is deeply connected to liberal learning: moral understanding.

From Moral Education to Liberal Learning

Why does moral education lead to liberal learning? In the first place, the concept of a moral person is ineluctably tied to the concept of a good life; giving color to one, shades the other. Asking "How should I act?" or "What should I value?" really projects the question "How should I live?" with a shorter focal length. There are, moreover, clear connections to the various four strands of liberal education described earlier. The "moralization" of a person is a form of self-actualization, the realization of "a normative individuality." If we are concerned to trigger value commitments and encourage moral conduct, we are led to prepare for a normative engagement with the world. And surely, we must have a basic understanding of our world if we are to be effective moral agents. These relationships seem obvious, requiring only articulation; more needs to be said, however, regarding the link between moral education and the education-as-transmission-of-culture approach.

Traditionally, the study of encoded human experience is used in moral education to convey cultural norms and to provide compelling portrayals of moral exemplars. But perhaps more significant are the claims that, in all its blends of reasoning, speculation, fact and fiction, such study demands and develops various moral capacities and skills—enlarging the moral imagination, encouraging empathy through vicarious subjectivity, increasing sensitivity to salient particulars. These are much-debated empirical claims, difficult to prove. In the recent past, many educators accepted these claims but used them to critique the curriculum: they said, in effect, that in order to truly enlarge a student's moral imagination in a global society, the range of cultures whose legacy was transmitted should be expanded—more different voices from the vast body of distilled human experience should be heard. Those critics (with whom I identify) have largely succeeded, and the heritage of human works students typically encounter is now much more inclusive. Other critics claim, however, that this is neither efficient nor productive; a more effective strategy to achieve these desired outcomes—developing capacities and increasing first- and second-order moral skills—is experiential education. Direct experience, not mediated or vicarious experience, has the real impact in, for example, developing the capacity to care, or inculcating a tolerant attitude. We all understand the pull of this argument, but no experience is pure and unmediated, and what meaning we may derive from an experience depends upon what we bring to it. This argument points us toward the issue of moral understanding, the desired outcome of moral education that was missing from my list. Let's now add:

6. *The deepening of moral understanding.* Moral education strives to provide the relevant knowledge, perspectives, or understanding that a moral person requires, such as an understanding of oneself and other people, of the implications of social practices, of cultural values, of the moral point of view or aspects of moral theory.

How important to moral education is the goal of deepening moral understanding? Most philosophers and educators have had doubts about the radical Socratic position that understanding is everything: virtue is knowledge. Aristotle spearheaded that response by showing (convincingly, for most of us) that intellectual and moral virtues differ, that morality requires practical wisdom (*phronesis*) or the art of good judgment, and is threatened by weakness of will and other factors.[29] But Aristotle never claimed that knowledge is irrelevant to virtue; that right action is altogether divorced from understanding. Yet, as Australian philosopher Jean Curthoys has written, "astonishingly few philosophers have reconsidered the extent to which moral questions may be questions of understanding. But without some such notion, morality will not have depth and nor, therefore, will the moral philosophy that purports to elucidate it." Her comment occurs in a review of Christopher Cordner's beautiful and evocative work, *Ethical Encounter*. She states that Cordner traces our deepest moral intuitions to a "sensitive understanding, which is the core of our moral life." In Cordner's vision, this requires a deep, empathic knowledge of the other people and transformative emotional experiences, as of love, awe, disgust, and reverence. As Curthoys notes, "The understanding involved, however, is not of the purely cognitive kind, and is accessible to all, whatever their educational level."[30] These observations might lead one to conclude that even if we grant understanding a significant place in moral education, it is an understanding that won't be achieved through liberal learning. But let's not be too hasty. First, there may be an old, dubious assumption at work in this interchange that says emotions are non-cognitive, though Curthoys does note that the understanding required is "not of the *purely* cognitive kind."[31] Second, in a sustained analysis of one case of moral understanding, Cordner focuses on the agent's "seeing [another person and her situation] in the light of" a "web of meaning." One person can understand another's situation "only so far as he or she can imaginatively participate in that web of human meaning."[32] So once again, we are led to the need to develop moral imagination and a web of meaning, and it is precisely for these tasks and that sense of moral depth that we turn to liberal education. It isn't that lived experience is irrelevant or even unnecessary; the point is rather that our lived experience and liberal learning—learning that focuses on our life and living it well; learning that dwells in the full range of human experience; that helps us become who we are, understand ourselves and our situation, grasp the forces that shape our lives, and act effectively in the world—enhance and sustain each other.

Concluding Thoughts

Both liberal and moral education aim to be (and often are) transformative—not merely in the sense that we come to possess more knowledge, acquire more skills, and know better how to fulfill our desires, etc.; but also in the deeper sense that we acquire different perspectives, find our desires reformed, and activate new second-order desires. They profoundly affect our identity. There is no fool-proof recipe, no algorithm, for educating a moral person, and often the best efforts at both liberal and moral education are tragically double-edged.[33] Both are life-long processes. But the two are not identical.

Liberal education is wider in scope than moral education: the concept of a good life that it addresses is more comprehensive than the concept of a moral life; it responds to additional sources of normativity, recognizing that there are more values in a flourishing and effective life than the moral—though "living morally" is an essential element. That is how liberal education can provide a critical perspective on moral education and its content. After all, the risks of "performance gaps" in moral education are many: the inculcation of judgmental attitudes, often without understanding; the over-reaching of moral claims; the caricaturing of moral exemplars; institutional indoctrination; the equation of moral commitment with closure of the mind; lopsided character development, such as a conscientiousness that lacks imagination, or a courage that lacks compassion—among others. Liberal learning is a significant, and sometimes essential, monitor of and corrective for these failures and of assurance that moral learning is lifelong and placed in the larger "web of meaning" of one's life.

These are expansive claims for liberal learning, I know. Even those sympathetic readers who are willing to abandon stilted conceptions of liberal education in favor of the rich and evolving educational tradition I have described may reply sadly that such an educational experience simply is nowhere to be found. What I have described is, for them, if not an educational unicorn, then an ivory-billed woodpecker—once vibrant, now extinct or appearing only in rare, disputed sightings. In fact, the tradition of liberal education thrives in many places today (most clearly, in my experience, in strong liberal arts colleges): its recent evolutionary adaptations—innovations in curriculum, pedagogy, and the co-curriculum—are, as ever, responsive to social, intellectual, and technological developments. As a recent report of the Association of American Colleges & Universities put it: there has emerged a "strong trend toward pluralistic, collaborative, experiential, and integrative modes of learning."[34] The language of "morality" may be shifting to a preferred language of "ethics," but the activities and mission statements of these colleges show a continuing concern for "character" and a focus on the quality of life. And there is some hopeful, empirical documentation of success.[35]

Although this evolution is as it should be—each age needs to shape a contemporary conception of liberal education—there are in fact significant threats to the tradition. At this late point, I will mention only one, the one that seems the most serious: it is the multifaceted phenomenon of specialization, academic tribalism, and the cult of the major. The major was introduced to provide flexibility and the opportunity to pursue subjects of special, individual interest,[36] but it quickly (and ironically) became a requirement at most institutions. Today, it is widely taken to be the defining aspect of a degree (one gets a bachelor's degree *in psychology*, for example); other components may be seen at best as simply supportive of the major, or at worst as extraneous requirements to be gotten out of the way. This is a result of several mutually reinforcing factors: the explosion of knowledge resulting in a profusion of new disciplines and a dramatic increase in the specialization required to achieve genuine understanding; the increase in scale of institutions of higher learning, and the rise of the department as a unit of academic administration; and increasingly elaborated academic tribalism that discourages dialogue about matters outside the specialization. What is threatening, of course, is that the concern for the life one is to live and the discernment of a good life are pale, absent, irrelevant, or considered beyond the reach of serious scholarship. Rampant at research universities, these phenomena are incursive at liberal arts colleges as well.

It is, however, too early for despair. The boundaries of disciplines are eroding daily: disciplinary scholarship and research increasingly borrow intellectual tools, models, and techniques from other disciplines, and new interdisciplinary fields of study mushroom. The very terms "discipline" and "interdisciplinary" seem outmoded, but we have as yet no good language to replace them. (Academic departments do patrol their borders effectively: I suspect they may outlive the disciplines that once defined them rather like the historic but arbitrary borders of nation states that no longer bound a culture or a people.) Moreover, concern for ethical issues—both for issues internal to the field and for the larger set of public issues which the field addresses—still resonates in these institutions of learning. And finally, the educational trends and innovations I alluded to earlier work to reduce disciplinary insularity.

Despite my optimism, I believe it is important not merely to celebrate, but to reclaim effectively the supreme purpose of liberal education. It is natural for faculty to see their courses as the units of educational meaning; some can grasp the major as a unit, a coherent whole to which their individual course makes a contribution. It is difficult for today's faculty to grasp a degree as a unit of educational meaning, let alone the key unit. They may be the master of their own courses, only a competent contributor to the major, and simply flummoxed in debates about general education and graduation requirements. A profound educational paradox underlies this situation: one cannot put the supreme purpose of discerning and preparing for a good life as the direct and immediate objective of teaching without distorting the process and likely missing the mark. It is not likely to appear as a learning objective on any course syllabus. One works directly on subsidiary purposes—the study of the cultural legacy or the understanding of the world—or on contributory skills like critical thinking and effective communication. But it is also a mistake to forget about the supreme purpose altogether. When that happens, subsidiary aims rule: education becomes simply about knowing great works, engaging in political action, gaining a particular body of knowledge, developing a career, or acquiring a skill; moral education may become vestigial, and liberal education fades. The ultimate aim of liberal education—the normative concern for one's life as a whole and for living a human life well—needs to be a felt presence in our educational efforts. At the proper distance and height, yes, but tethered securely, and a felt presence nonetheless. It is the recognition of such a presence that guides the learner and makes a teacher truly an educator.[37]

Notes

1. Perhaps I should also be clear about terms: by "education" I mean a formal, sequenced, and purposeful program of learning; "learning," both as a process and as an achievement, has a wider range and may occur within and without education. "Schooling" is institutionalized education.
2. The phrase is widely attributed to Francis Oakley, President Emeritus of Williams College, as introduced in various conference speeches. For analysis of such narratives, see his "Against Nostalgia: Reflections on Our Present Discontents in American Higher Education" in *The Politics of Liberal Education,* edited by Darryl J. Gless and Barbara Herrnstein Smith (Duke, 1992)
3. This vivid phrase of Paul Ricoeur's is used in this context by Elizabeth Kiss and L. Peter Euben in the introductory essay (p. 10) to their anthology, *Debating Moral Education: Rethinking the Role of the Modern University* (Duke, 2010).
4. This argument that the ideal of liberal education is sound, but we are everywhere failing to live up to it has produced a large, polemical, and provocative literature. Examples range from Alan Bloom's *The Closing of the American Mind: How Higher Education Has Failed Democracy and Impoverished the Minds of Today's Students* (Simon & Schuster, 1987) to A. T. Kronman's *Education's End: Why Our Colleges and Universities Have Given up on the Meaning of Life* (Yale, 2007).
5. Examples of this expanding genre include Jean-Francoise Lyotard, *The Postmodern Condition: A Report on Knowledge,* trans. by G. B. Massumi (Minnesota, 1979, 1984); Jane Roland Martin, *Changing the Educational Landscape: Philosophy, Women, and Curriculum* (Routledge, 1994); and Nel Noddings, *The Challenge to Care in Schools: An Alternative Approach to Education* (Teachers College Press, second edition, 2005).
6. This distinction between "concept" and "conception" gained traction, I believe, when used by John Rawls in *A Theory of Justice* (Harvard, 1971) to distinguish the idea of justice from the various competing theories of justice. He modestly claimed to have borrowed it from H. L. A. Hart's *The Concept of Law* (Oxford, 1961). While Hart does explicate "law" in a similar way, he does not use the contrasting terms "concept" and "conception."
7. One *may*, of course, make the more ambitious argument and argue that the concept itself is flawed—by showing it to be incoherent, for example, or claiming that no workable conception is possible, or that it has inherent moral deficiencies. In making such an argument, one might even need to adduce prominent examples—"particular conceptions"—as cases in point. But such arguments need to have a different structure and import.

8. One of the most highly regarded histories of this tradition is Bruce A. Kimball's *Orators & Philosophers: A History of the Idea of Liberal Education* (Columbia, 1986). My necessarily brief account of the liberal education tradition employs a different conceptual frame from Kimball's; they are not, however, in opposition. I would also claim that although the tradition is clearly identified with Western cultures, elements of liberal education are part of the traditions of Eastern educational philosophy and practice as well, notably in the heritage of Confucianism. See for example, John Israel, "The Idea of Liberal Education in China," in R. Morse, *The Limits of Reform in China* (Westview, 1983).

9. There is a large literature of such criticism, prominent examples of which include: Jean-Francoise Lyotard, *op. cit.*; Nel Noddings, *Educating Moral People* (Teachers College Press, 2002); Jane Roland Martin, *Changing the Educational Landscape: Philosophy, Women, and Curriculum* (Routledge, 1994); and D. G. Mulcahy, *The Educated Person: Toward a New Paradigm for Liberal Education* (Rowman & Littlefield, 2008).

10. Compare Theodor Adorno's essay, "Education After Auschwitz," published in Adorno's *Critical Models: Interventions and Catchwords* (Columbia, 1998). My thanks to Gary Mullen for calling this essay to my attention.

11. The process I describe here is intended to be conceptual not precisely chronological. There is no significance intended by the order in which I present these four strands of liberal education, nor do I claim they are exhaustive.

12. Versions of this strand differ on the principle of selection by which worthy elements of the legacy are determined, but most agree that: (a) the whole must be reviewed, reorganized, and refined by successor generations; and (b) the legacy long ago became too vast for any one learner, so a division of labor (some level of specialization) is clearly required. Among theorists in whose work this strand predominates, I would include Alan Bloom, Robert Hutchins, Mortimer Adler, and E. D. Hirsch.

13. Theorists for whom self-actualization predominates include: Plato, Aristotle, Rousseau, Nietzsche, and David Norton. Even in versions like Nietzsche's that self-consciously reject conventional moral standards, there is a normative individuality (for Nietzsche, the *Übermensch)* that is to be achieved through self-actualization.

14. Including the world of abstract ideas, what Karl Popper (after Gottlob Frege) termed "World 3," in distinction from "World 1" (physical objects and events) and "World 2" (subjective mental states) in several works, including *Objective Knowledge* (Clarendon, Oxford, 1972, 1979).

15. These are exemplified in, e.g., Aristotle's account of theoretical wisdom (*sophia*) in the *Nicomachean Ethics* and Mill's concept of activities that yield "higher order" pleasures, in *Utilitarianism*.

16. Alfred N. Whitehead, *The Aims of Education and Other Essays* (Free Press, 1929, 1957, 1967), p. 14.

17. An excellent account of Isocrates in relation to the tradition of liberal education may be found in Takis Poulakos, *Speaking for the Polis: Isocrates' Rhetorical Education* (University of South Carolina, 1997) and Janet M. Atwill, *Rhetoric Reclaimed: Aristotle and the Liberal Arts Tradition* (Cornell, 1998).

18. Among theorists who emphasize this strand I would include, in addition to Isocrates, John Stuart Mill, William James, and Paulo Freire. Recent trends in liberal education (see note 33) suggest it is resurgent.

19. Aristotle, *Nicomachean Ethics.*

20. Michael Oakeshott, "Learning and Teaching," reprinted in Timothy Fuller (ed.), *The Voice of Liberal Learning: Michael Oakeshott on Education* (Yale, 1989), p. 45.

21. This claim of continuity does not deny the evolution in the concept of freedom, ranging widely as it has from an achievement of self-determination to a natural condition of autonomy to a basic human right.

22. The "capabilities" approach was famously developed by Amartya Sen in *Commodities and Capabilities* (Oxford, 1985) and applied by Martha C. Nussbaum in *Women and Moral Development: The Capabilities Approach* (Cambridge, 2000).

23. I use the verb "moralize" here to mean "to improve the morals of, to make moral." It is a sign of social change as well as evolving usage that "moralize" now commonly connotes "to make moral pronouncements, to preach." By "rectify," I mean to align with moral values, such as justice, fairness, or compassion. See also note 1.

24. No doubt, the sense of purposefulness may often be stronger and clearer for the educator than the student; their purposes may in fact be disjoint. The terms I am using here are analyzed by Peter Jarvis in *Towards a Comprehensive Theory of Human Learning* (Routledge, 2006).

25. I do not mean to suggest that every moral theory presents its conception of a moral person in a singular pro-file. The theory-derived concept of a moral person may be quite open, comprehending many different qualities and characters with minimal constraints; it may even focus on achieving a society in which different moral perspectives are balanced in a moral ecology; or it may be quite restrictive and homogeneous in its prescription.

26. The authority of moral theory is likely to be required for more formal, institutionalized practices; the moral education conducted in families, by organized youth activities like sports and scouting, is more likely to be drawn from shared experience (except perhaps in the families of some resolute philosophers or psychologists, where theory may reign).

27. This is an implication of nearly all programs of moral education, whether they are drawn from "virtue ethics" and "character education" theories or not.

28. Note that I am using "liberal learning," not "liberal education." See note 1.

29. Aristotle, *op. cit.*

30. All quoted material is from her piece, "Understanding Others" in *Australian Book Review*, 2002, p. 47. I have adopted her way of framing the issue.

31. Italics are mine.

32. Christopher Cordner, *Ethical Encounter: The Depth of Moral Meaning* (Palgrave, 2002), p. 170.

33. For a compelling portrayal and analysis of bittersweet educational transformations, see Jane Roland Martin, *Educational Metamorphoses: Philosophical Reflections on Identity and Culture* (Rowman & Littlefield, 2006).

34. Quoted from a report by Carol G. Schneider and Robert Schoenberg, *Contemporary Understandings of Liberal Education* (AAC&U, 1998). See also the report by Hart Research Associates, *Trends and Emerging Practices in Liberal Education* (AAC&U, 2009) accessed in July 2010 at: http://www.aacu.org/membership/documents/2009MemberSurvey_Part2.pdf.

35. The trends I cite are described in Kiss and Euben, *op. cit.*, pp. 3ff. The life-long research led by Alexander Astin at UCLA is perhaps the most widely recognized on the effects of the practices of liberal education—though sometimes longitudinal, it is mostly survey based, not behavioral. His work (with various partners and teams) has appeared in various works, from *Four Critical Years: Effects of College on Beliefs, Attitudes, and Knowledge* (Jossey-Bass, 1977) to *Cultivating the Spirit: How College Can Enhance Students' Inner Lives* (Jossey-Bass, 2010).

36. President Charles William Eliot of Harvard University introduced the "elective" system of courses in 1885. See his speech, "How to Transform a College with One Uniform Curriculum into a University," at http://www.higher-ed.org/resources/Charles_Eliot.htm *(accessed July 2010)*.

37. My thanks to John C. Hill, whose impressive work as undergraduate research assistant was invaluable during the writing of this article; and to my colleagues, Lisa Portmess and GailAnn Ricket, who read an earlier version and generously offered perceptive comments.

CHAPTER SEVENTEEN

Democracy in a Cosmopolitan Age

Moral Education for the Global Citizen

SCOTT FLETCHER & PETER J. NELSEN

Introduction

Contemporary discussions abound with descriptions of the increasingly intertwined nature of our lives; we find evidence of myriad social, political, and economic connections that cross geopolitical boundaries in virtually all domains of public discourse. Within the United States, such observations have taken on even more urgency since the terrorist attacks on the World Trade Center on September 11, 2001, two subsequent and ongoing wars in the Middle East, the deepening environmental crisis, and the global economic recession that began in 2008. Pronouncements like, "the world is flat" (Friedman, 2006) or, perhaps more bluntly, "hot, flat and crowded" (Friedman, 2008) capture both important fears and hopes in this global context. Even those who live, or seek to live, in relative cultural isolation find their daily lives impacted by global events and their decisions influenced deeply by fears of violence, environmental catastrophe, and economic ruin.

In education, we find increasing calls for curricular responses that help students situate themselves among the shifting political, economic, technological, and social dynamics that shape our shared experience (cf. Gewertz, 2008). We also see a wide variety of attempts to envision new possibilities for schooling and the educational goals that are appropriate to pursue under these emerging conditions. In this chapter, we trace one thread of response to the increasing globalization of our thinking about the goals of education and, in particular, the forms of moral judgment and deliberation that might guide our response to the often bewildering cultural heterogeneity presented in this context. The thread we explore here is one that begins in contemporary discussions of democratic education and moves (necessarily quickly, given the constraints of the chapter) to the possibilities that recent work on cosmopolitanism brings to the challenges these theories face. Our hope is to show the continuity between work in these two traditions and to shine a light on some of the possibilities of moving forward with the crucial task of educating students in a way that prepares them both to understand and shape the forces that will ultimately determine the trajectory of our global community. This requires a consideration of the moral foundations of democratic education and the kinds of moral education that are directed at preparing citizens for life in a democracy.

Democratic Education and the Challenge Of Globalization

Democratic theories of education invariably look at schools as one of many social institutions whose functioning may impede or advance democratic social relations. Theories of democratic education also focus on the specific qualities, often closely related to moral reasoning and judgment but not exclusively so, which students should acquire in schools as part of their preparation to participate with others in democratic deliberation. As David Sehr notes, public schools are "the one public institution specifically charged with preparing young people to become full members of society, [they] can play a central role in the formation of young people's understanding of democracy, and of themselves as citizens in a democracy" (Sehr, 1997, p. 28). Here we consider how globalization places increasing pressure both on the way we define the role of schools in society, as part of a system of collective responsibilities and obligations, and on the particular forms of moral reasoning that democratic schools help students to develop.

Democratic theories of education embrace the assumption that society is constituted by citizens with a great diversity of life plans and that individuals' efforts to pursue these life plans can lead to conflict or, at a minimum, questions about the relative distribution of opportunities or resources to pursue them. Thus, democratic theories of education concern themselves both with authority over the ways schools function, as institutions with great socializing power, and with the capacities for moral judgment that individuals need to develop in order to sustain democratic social relations from one generation to the next. Globalization challenges democratic theories at both levels: it questions the boundaries of moral authority over social institutions like schools, and it suggests the need for a revised view of the deliberative qualities that democratic education seeks to cultivate in students (and thus citizens).

Most work on democratic educational theory assumes, or at least appears to assume, that deliberation over such practices and policies will be undertaken in a national context or one nested within it (e.g., a state or school district). The fact that such boundaries lie at the heart of democratic theories of education is made apparent in one of the most powerful contemporary works in the field, Amy Gutmann's *Democratic Education* (1987, 1999). She argues that, rather than developing a theory to answer the dilemmas posed by our conflicting views over specific educational issues, we are better served by a theory that determines the nature and boundaries of moral authority in explaining how democratic schools should work:

> The primary aim of a democratic theory of education is not to offer solutions to all the problems plaguing our educational institutions, but to consider ways of resolving those problems that are compatible with a commitment to democratic values. A democratic theory of education provides principles that, in the face of our social disagreements, help us judge (a) who should have authority to make decisions about education, and (b) what the moral boundaries of that authority are. (p. 11)

Such an approach offers the further benefit, Gutmann argues, of engaging citizens in just the kind of moral deliberation (here over educational practices and policies) that life in a democratic society requires more broadly and that is required for its reproduction over time. Gutmann (1987, 1999) writes, "the most distinctive feature of a democratic theory of education is that it makes a democratic virtue out of our inevitable disagreement over educational problems" (p. 11). Gutmann sees the resolution of these conflicts as itself part of our moral education, undertaken in the process of learning to live together.

Democratic educational theory has also concerned itself deeply with the qualities of deliberative thinking and moral judgment that schools should help students to develop. A prominent theme that emerges in this work is that schooling should aim, to one degree or another, at helping students to develop the capacity and desire to bridge parochial interests in favor of a more thickly conceived conception of collective citizenship. Characteristic work in this area includes the vast literature on multicultural education and the pedagogical means by which difference can be explored through dialogic and collaborative classroom practices. Rob Reich (2002), for example, argues that, "The pedagogy of liberal multicultural education aims at a hermeneutical process of reciprocal interpretation and understanding in which students attempt to understand different cultural values and take up the position of culturally different others" (p. 184). While the recommendations of Reich and others diverge at various points, often substantively, the point that moral education in a democracy requires both an expanded cultural perspective and the capacity to engage with others in collaboration rooted in mutual recognition is fundamental (see also Howe, 1997).

Globalization challenges our conception of the boundaries of moral obligation and the roles of schools in society. Because we share humanity with others across the globe, and because the solutions to global problems require collaboration across state boundaries, should we transform our vision of democratic education to a global scale? To travel such a path requires that we consider what it means to be a "global citizen" and whether or how this might change our relationships (including our moral obligations) to members of our families, local communities, and nation. Rather than seeing schools as mainly acculturating students to become U.S. citizens and preparing them to assume roles within their local communities, there are increasing calls under the banner of cosmopolitan education for schools to promote cross-cultural understanding and even to help students see themselves primarily as citizens of the world. In considering this movement and the resources and challenges it provides for democratic theories of education, we find both possibility and risk.

Cosmopolitan Education and the Rise of the Global Citizen

In this section, we explore cosmopolitanism by tracing a central debate about the moral obligations of democratic citizens and the educational implications that arise from viewing these commitments from a global perspective. We begin with a sketch of Martha Nussbaum's depiction of cosmopolitanism (Nussbaum, 1997; Nussbaum & Cohen, 1996), as well as some key criticisms of this view captured in the robust dialogue about her work. We then trace an approach that attempts to strike a middle path between Nussbaum and her critics, as we believe there is much to be gained from such an exploration.

One of the fundamental questions facing moral education, especially as it is understood in the context of democratic schooling, concerns the question of moral commitment: *To whom do we owe moral obligations?* Put another way, in situations where it is impossible to prevent harm, *To whom do we owe our strongest allegiance?* For example, should we promote economic policies that benefit workers in the United States at the expense of others outside our borders? Should we promote a curriculum in schools that emphasizes the achievements of U.S. citizens and advances the view that the U.S. has a special role in history? The answers to these sorts of questions draw in part on how we conceive of our relatedness—our affinity—to others, and thus our commitment to aiding, or at least not harming, them. The boundaries of this sense of relatedness or affinity are just the ones that the cosmopolitan project seeks to explore. As we will see, however, even cosmopolitan theorists differ in the weight they give to what appear to be "natural" affinities to family, community, and nation, and the way this shapes our sense of moral obligation.

There is little question that public education in the U.S. has focused historically on building the political, economic, and social infrastructure of the nation (Kaestle, 1983; Kliebard, 2004; Tyack, 1974). There is equally little question that such efforts have also been explicitly directed at the nation's global preeminence, especially economically, as is evident in national education policy statements such as *A Nation at Risk* (National Commission on Excellence in Education, 1983), "Goals 2000" (Goals 2000: Educate America Act, 1994), and No Child Left Behind (No Child Left Behind Act, 2001). There is evidence that this is also frequently the case at the level of classroom instruction. Anatoli Rapoport (2009) argues that teachers in the United States feel significant pressure to teach a curriculum in which students come to understand their moral obligations to other citizens of the nation to be of paramount importance. When teachers explore themes that may challenge the primacy of this national identity or when teachers are critical of political or economic policies that might impact others in the world negatively, they are accused of being unpatriotic and sometimes censored (Rapoport, 2009). The idea that the public school curriculum should promote patriotic pride while tempering, or even omitting, criticism of the history of U.S. social or economic policies (Galston, 1991; Rorty, 1998) has been the focus of spirited debate.

Cosmopolitanism is perhaps the most significant challenge to a view of education that places significant value on national (or even more local) boundaries in understanding moral obligation. Martha Nussbaum, one of the most influential writers in the growing cosmopolitan literature (writing with Joshua Cohen in the following passages), begins by rejecting such national boundaries as "morally irrelevant" (Nussbaum & Cohen, 1996, p. 5). In contrast, Nussbaum advocates schooling that helps students understand themselves as cosmopolitans, people who situate themselves fundamentally within the "worldwide community of human beings" (Nussbaum & Cohen, 1996, p. 4). This moral orientation, she argues, "asks us to give our first allegiance to what is morally good—and that which, being good, I can commend as such to all human beings" (Nussbaum & Cohen, 1996, p. 5).

The work of Nussbaum and other cosmopolitans grows (to varying degrees) from a belief in the possibility that one's identity may be expressed, first and foremost, as a citizen of the world. The concept of the world citizen, or *kosmou polites*, first championed by ancient Greeks of the Cynic school, nests identity within outwardly expanding spheres of attachment, beginning with the family, then neighborhood, city, and nation; however, identification with the global community remains the primary source of self-definition. In this way, Nussbaum pursues and elaborates the claim that our strongest ties of moral responsibility should be focused at this global level, which she follows the Greek philosopher Seneca in describing as "the community of human argument and aspiration" (Nussbaum & Cohen, 1996, p. 7).

Thus, for Nussbaum, one of the primary goals of cosmopolitan moral education is to reduce the distance between our innermost experiences of affinity and the outermost circle of global awareness; "we should work to make all human beings part of our community of dialogue and concern, base our political deliberations on that interlocking commonality, and give the circle that defines our humanity a special attention and respect" (Nussbaum & Cohen, 1996, p. 9). In a subsequent series of books and articles (cf. Nussbaum, 1997; Nussbaum & Cohen, 1996), Nussbaum argues that a cosmopolitan view of education suggests the cultivation of four related capacities. All four capacities have relational or dispositional qualities as well as those related to inquiry and the weighing of arguments or evidence. On Nussbaum's view, cosmopolitan citizens should develop the capacity to see their own well-being as substantively connected to others at a global scale, to imagine the perspectives and experiences of others as fully as possible, to assess the implications of any particular action across the breadth of the global community, and to participate in a form of inquiry that incorporates ongoing scientific discovery in the process of moral deliberation (Nussbaum, 1997; Nussbaum & Cohen, 1996).

To pursue these goals in schools would require a fundamental change in the way we frame our understanding of global issues and, indeed, what we take moral education itself to mean. To take cosmopolitanism seriously in the classroom would not simply redirect our attention in the topical sense of a "global studies" curriculum; it suggests a Copernican shift in how we identify "problems" in the first place, who might be included or consulted in search of a solution, and what responsibility we hold as members of the global community to see such an endeavor through. Likewise, multicultural education would be transformed by cosmopolitanism, making self-reflection, reciprocity, and mutual recognition across national boundaries central to the experiences offered to all students and likely for quite different reasons than we frequently see given for such practices today. And, finally, to presage a later section of the chapter, such an approach would no doubt be a catalyst for discussions of power and privilege on a global scale, an opportunity, as Mitchell and Parker (2008) suggest, to help students confront their

> relative privilege among the peoples of Earth and make them question their moral obligation to the rest of humanity. Such a curriculum would emphasize the choice that wealthy Americans face between our worldwide brothers and sisters—humankind—and a self-serving hypocrisy that allows us to circle the wagons around an arbitrary slice of brothers and sisters who happen to live within the same national borders. (p. 782)

But before proceeding in this direction, we would do well to consider the objections that have been raised against Nussbaum's view and the cosmopolitan approach to moral education in general.

Finding a home for the global citizen

Perhaps the most significant objection to cosmopolitanism is that it promotes a view of moral development and identity that appears to run counter to our deepest feelings about the responsibility we feel to those who are closest to us or those with whom we share the deepest cultural commonalities. This criticism is most commonly articulated by communitarians (but not exclusively by them), who argue that Nussbaum fails to understand the importance of primary cultural attachments both for the creation of individual identity and for the pursuit of a life plan enriched by the presence of others who share similar beliefs. As Eduard Jordaan (2009) argues, communitarianism is committed to the premise that we should preserve "the context and the boundaries in which an individual's moral outlook was formed" (p. 742). Likewise, Benjamin Barber argues that our communal attachments are the starting point in our moral development and that our growth is deeply shaped by those initial relationships: "Our attachments start parochially and only then grow outward" (Barber, 1996, p. 34). For communitarians like Jordaan and Barber, cosmopolitanism fails to grip "the heart, the viscera, the vitals of the body that houses the brain in which Nussbaum would like us to dwell" (Barber, 1996, pp. 33–34). The related pedagogical challenge is equally vexing for cosmopolitans; it questions whether students will be able to take up the cosmopolitan perspective in a meaningful way and make effective use of the moral insights it is presumed to offer.

In answering these critiques, Nussbaum observes that even the ancient advocates of cosmopolitanism rejected the view that adopting this global perspective required one to dismiss the power and attraction of local communities in shaping our moral development and identity: "To be a citizen of the world, one does not, the Stoics stress, need to give up local affiliations, which can frequently be a source of great richness in life" (Nussbaum, 1997, p. 60; cf. Nussbaum & Cohen, 1996, pp. 9 and 141–143). Because the inner circle of our attachments to family and friends matter so much to us, we could not lead rich or fulfilling lives without them. Furthermore, Nussbaum recognizes that we cannot do without the complex web of social relations that constitute the nation state or the framework it offers for our moral lives. Despite her rejection of nationalism, she accepts that the "nation-state sets up the basic terms for most of our daily conduct" (Nussbaum, 1997, pp. 60–61).

The key, however, to Nussbaum's response is that she refuses to cede the argument regarding the ultimate source of our moral obligations. Despite our dependence on the state for the actual conduct of our daily lives, and despite the power and richness of local affinities in shaping our sense of self-identity, these are neither the source of our moral obligations nor a sound basis on which to determine the outcome of our moral deliberations. This more local context is "the only sensible way to do good" (Nussbaum, 1997, pp. 135–136), but it is not a reason to give preference to obligations established in this context over those that have more universal application. As Marilyn Friedman (2000) argues:

> Duties to humanity thus limit the extent to which we are entitled to give preference to 'our own' even on justified grounds of moral expediency. Metaphorically speaking, our citizenly duties are primarily to those with whom we compose the 'state' that has highest moral worth, the state in which all human beings are joined as cocitizens in the common enterprise of instantiating moral law as the law of our common life: the kingdom of ends. (p. 590)

Nussbaum's response (indirectly) to the pedagogical critique cedes even less ground, though the detachment she suggests in our moral deliberation seems somewhat more familiar in a kind of ethnographic sense, urging us "to become, to a certain extent, philosophical exiles from our own way of life, seeing them from the vantage point of the outsider and asking the questions an outsider is likely to ask about their meaning and function" (Nussbaum, 1997, pp. 59–60).

It is worth asking the question at this point whether this is the only or best way that the debate over cosmopolitanism might be framed. It is possible that the distinction between our moral development and responsibilities at the local or nation-state level and what we might envision as citizens of the world, has been drawn too starkly. We believe this is indeed the case and that, to some extent, the vigor of the debate between Nussbaum and her critics has obscured the possibility of a middle path. We see a profitable start in this direction in Kwame Anthony Appiah's work on cosmopolitanism and the effort to bind the elements of the debate together by deepening our focus on moral deliberation.

Instead of embracing the stark choice between global and local perspectives that appear to be offered in the arguments of cosmopolitans like Martha Nussbaum, on the one hand, and those of her communitarian critics on the other, Appiah offers what might be described as a middle path in his conception of "rooted cosmopolitanism" (Appiah, 2006). Appiah begins just where we left the debate between cosmopolitans and communitarians, trying to find the line that connects the obvious power of the affinities we experience in our daily lives with the claims made on us by a much broad-er moral community. Appiah, in his book on cosmopolitanism instructively subtitled, *Ethics in a World of Strangers*, acknowledges the power of both elements from the onset:

> So, there are two strands that intertwine in the notion of cosmopolitanism. One is the idea that we have oblig-ations to others, obligations that stretch beyond those to whom we are related by the ties of kith and kind, or even the more formal ties of a shared citizenship. The other is that we take seriously the value not just of human life but of particular human lives, which means taking an interest in the practices and beliefs that lend them significance. (Appiah, 2006, p. xv)

So, our question for the moment is whether Appiah's approach can balance and integrate these two strands in a way that moves the cosmopolitan project forward on both levels.

Appiah confronts the challenge of envisioning moral obligation at the global level by arguing that this relationship depends on our mutual capacity for giving and exchanging reasons for our moral judgments, not a metaphorical expansion of the kind of affinity we experience in more local relation-ships. Appiah holds that the critics of cosmopolitanism who argue that, as a general category of belonging, "humanity isn't, in the relevant sense, an identity at all" (Appiah, 2006, p. 98), have failed to recognize the potential for finding this mutuality within the very conflicts that occur within and among different communities. We can start to understand this, Appiah argues, by attending to the dis-agreements that take place *within* cultural communities. The intensity of these conflicts arises, he argues, from the different moral arguments we offer based on the *same* cultural values, not the incom-mensurability of conflicting moral perspectives. For example, in the United States, conflicts about abortion and gay marriage are so intense, Appiah suggests, because

> they are battles over the meaning of the *same* values, not that they oppose one value, held exclusively by one side, with another, held exclusively by their antagonists. It is, in part, because we have shared horizons of meaning, because these are debates between people who share so many other values and so much else in the way of belief and of habit, that they are as sharp and as painful as they are. (Appiah, 2006, p. 81)

What are we to do, however, when we reach the boundaries of these shared horizons and the limits of such cultural perspectives? What guides moral education after this point?

Here Appiah suggests a somewhat different approach for the cosmopolitan. While he ultimate-ly believes in the existence of universal moral principles that apply across cultural boundaries, Appiah argues that coming to final agreement in moral matters is not ultimately necessary for peace-able discourse or productive cooperation across these divisions. Instead of seeking universal agree-ment, he argues that we need to embrace an openness regarding the potential value of other moral systems to help us address intractable cross-cultural problems. Indeed, Appiah recognizes that "There will be times when these two ideals—universal concern and respect for legitimate difference—clash. There's a sense in which cosmopolitanism is the name not of the solution but of the challenge" (2006, p. xv).

In response to this challenge, and absent a shared horizon of cultural values, Appiah argues that we are more likely to develop a mutual understanding of the moral commitments we share across such boundaries through dialogue and mutual exploration. Appiah thus argues in support of a kind of cosmopolitan conversation, a

> metaphor for engagement with the experience and the ideas of others. And I stress the role of the imagina-tion here because the encounters, properly conducted, are valuable in themselves. Conversation does not

have to lead to consensus about anything, especially not values; it's enough that it helps people get used to one another. (Appiah, 2006, p. 85)

The shift here toward dialogue and imaginative exploration as key elements of cosmopolitan moral education is reminiscent of Amy Gutmann's earlier claim that "the most distinctive feature of a democratic theory of education is that it makes a democratic virtue out of our inevitable disagreement over educational problems" (Gutmann, 1987, 1999, p. 11). Here, the tension between the local and the global is itself productive and necessary for even the hope of mutual understanding. Appiah concludes, "The world is getting more crowded: in the next half a century the population of our once foraging species will approach nine billion. Depending on the circumstances, conversations across boundaries can be delightful, or just vexing: what they mainly are, though, is inevitable" (Appiah, 2006, p. xxi).

Cosmopolitanism and the Perils of Globalization

So far in this analysis we have treated cosmopolitanism as a strategy for addressing the challenges of globalization as these are posed to democratic theories of education and the forms of moral education they promote. But what of the challenges that globalization poses to cosmopolitan theories themselves, especially insofar as they aim to provide "a morally compelling view of how our many worlds may meet, as they inevitably will, on terms of humanity, justice and tolerance" (Abdelhalim, 2010, p. 64). This terrain is contested mightily on a global scale, not least among the economic structures and institutions that have long preceded educational efforts to cross national borders. Here we raise concerns that an unreflective or unsophisticated cosmopolitanism might actually worsen rather than mitigate the harms of a global economy that has already exacerbated the divisions between rich and poor (Lu, 2000; Mignolo, 2000, 2010). If these criticisms are accurate, one would be hard pressed to view cosmopolitanism as a worthy candidate for reconstructing moral education for democratic citizenship in a global age.

The first of these concerns involves the pitfalls of understanding cosmopolitanism as a disposition or even lifestyle rather than a more thorough going moral commitment. While nothing in discussions of moral cosmopolitanism requires such a globalized lifestyle, the worry is that its focus could be trivialized and commodified in the context of our currently hyper-commodified culture of production and consumption. This "Wal-Mart cosmopolitanism" (Pieterse, 2006) involves acquiring 'global' goods, international travel, or displaying tastes that extend beyond national boundaries. Others note the "banal globalism" (Urry, 2002) that is reflected in listening to 'world' music and watching international sports or cultural events on television or via the internet. Regardless of the means, cosmopolitanism is reduced to a kind of status symbol (fetish), depending on the public display of particular goods and behavior that draw on extra-national cultural frameworks of meaning (see also Strand, 2010). The ability to possess such goods and have access to these opportunities is clearly connected to existing class distinctions and often depends on the availability of educational or other resources that are distributed along class lines. Technology has blurred some of these class lines, but barriers and limitations remain.

Other concerns about globalization as a lens through which cosmopolitanism might be viewed arise from a deeper consideration of the economic structures it would necessarily confront. The broadest way to express this concern is to point out the potential for cosmopolitan efforts to cross national boundaries in pursuit of moral dialogue to be construed as both similar to, and even perhaps a rationale for, the economic policies that likewise seek to facilitate transactions across these borders. From this perspective, cosmopolitanism is a dangerous ally of the globalized free market capitalism associated with the work of Milton Friedman, the political polices that supported its emergence in the era of Ronald Reagan and Margaret Thatcher (Mignolo, 2000, 2010), and current international trade agreements such as the North American Free Trade Agreement (NAFTA), Central American Free Trade Agreement (CAFTA), and the expansion of the European Union. In this context, the growth of a global free trade market is facilitated by removing political or economic impediments to international commerce, and thus helping to usher in a new age of "empire" (Hardt & Negri, 2000) where non-G8 nations are in many ways less powerful than transnational corporations. Thus associated with Western colonial economic expansionism, cosmopolitanism threatens to support increasing global inequality rather than being a democratizing force for positive change (Flikschuh, 2004; Mignolo, 2000, 2010); it is "an ethical doctrine that too easily plays into the hands of the powerful, be they states, cultures or multinational corporations, providing an ideological basis for the maintenance or enhancement of their dominance" (Lu, 2000, p. 252).

It could also be argued that cosmopolitan approaches, under existing conditions of a globalized economy, may undermine the struggles of marginalized non-Westerners to establish solidarity within their own nation-states and thus gain economic and political stability (Cheah, 2006). For example, a cosmopolitan approach of the kind suggested by Nussbaum may fail to account for the local political or cultural structures needed to sustain the moral principles that she advocates on a more universal scale (Skrbis & Woodward, 2004; Turner, 2002). While motivated by sentiments grounded in social justice, those who struggle for global recognition, political rights, and economic justice may find the cost of 'thinking globally' too great if it means that they must sacrifice the distinctive cultural and nationalist resources that might be deployed in more local emancipatory projects. Conversely, as labor is globalized, the power of the political and cultural resources that workers might carry across national borders in their search for economic opportunity might be diminished in relation to the managerial or capitalist classes who eventually employ them. Richard Sennett (Sennett, 2002), for example, argues that when displaced or economically marginalized workers move into unfamiliar places out of economic necessity, their lack of local knowledge and limited ties to insiders render them more exploitable. As Marinus Ossewarde (2007) concludes: "Without knowledge of acquaintance, the locals are thrown back upon themselves, on their own subjectivity, where they are confronted with their own alienation, from which they must dredge up the meaning and stability that they require to exist" (p. 373).

Finally, there is the concern that the very moral foundation of cosmopolitanism rests on unexamined cultural biases and, in particular, an overdependence on western conceptions of the role of rationality in moral theory. On this view, cosmopolitanism has a similar trajectory and purpose as the forms of economic globalization discussed above: to eliminate national and cultural boundaries in the service of a single dominant worldview (Doyal, 2010). Cosmopolitanism thus represents the latest iteration of a world order that preserves Western global economic and political hegemony by suppressing our understanding of the depth of difference in human experience and the gaps that rational engagement may fail to bridge (Lu, 2000). The fear that cosmopolitanism can be a tool of contemporary (if unwitting) colonization animates Ulf Hannerz's (2005) characterization of cosmopolitanism as having a "streak of narcissism" (p. 200) as well as Michael Walzer's (1996) more radical rejection: "The crimes of the twentieth century have been committed alternatively, as it were, by perverted patriots and perverted cosmopolitans" (p. 126).

To our minds, these concerns and critiques of cosmopolitanism clearly suggest the need for an approach that draws more deeply on the critical tradition from which many (but not all) of them come. Such a critical cosmopolitanism would retain a commitment to transnational moral principles in the spirit of Martha Nussbaum's work, along with Kwame Anthony Appiah's advocacy for creative and dialogic exchange, considered in a framework that allows issues of social class politics, cultural hegemony, and economic alienation to be considered. A first step in this direction is to separate as clearly as possible cosmopolitanism as a moral theory from globalization as an economic movement. Mignolo (2010), for example, suggests recognizing that "globalization is a set of designs to manage the world while cosmopolitanism is a set of projects toward planetary conviviality" (p. 157). To inform moral education in this way, cosmopolitanism would need to engage in the kind of structural analysis of power, status, and identity (across national borders) that is the hallmark of the critical tradition; the extent to which these approaches are deeply compatible is a question we must leave for another day, but we are optimistic about the possibilities and comment on some of these in the following section.

Cosmopolitanism and the Future of Democratic Education

Our foray into the world of cosmopolitanism has covered considerable ground quickly. In this last section, we look briefly at the opportunities we see for moral education in a democratic society to take a cosmopolitan turn, not only in response to the extraordinary changes that globalization has wrought but also as the foundation for a profound shift in the way we think about the relationship between diversity and identity. This cosmopolitan turn challenges us to reconsider our roles as citizens of one nation and simultaneously as members of the broader world community. Our hope is that a cosmopolitan approach to moral education in a democracy might better prepare citizens to find solutions to problems, from disquieting to catastrophic, which require coordination and collaboration across national boundaries.

In contrast to the now-dominant approach that mobilizes school curricula in the service of enhancing our nation's global economic competitiveness, along with the often explicit goal of sustaining American exceptionalism, we wish to consider the benefits of a cosmopolitan curriculum that embraces the contradictions and opportunities that have always been a part of our nation's heritage. We believe that such a cosmopolitan education would aim at building a variety of capacities related to moral reasoning and judgment, including the capacity to engage in meaningful inquiry, dialogue, and collaboration across national and cultural boundaries; the capacity for inquiry directed at the fundamental social, political, and cultural structures that shape our self-understanding and our understanding of others; and the disposition to seek reciprocity with others through perspective taking and mutual recognition of others' life plans. We also believe that this perspective challenges schools to provide more authentic opportunities for students to engage in these practices and to take up the perspective of the cosmopolitan wherever they find themselves.

At its roots, a cosmopolitan education would necessarily be guided by a commitment to engaging deeply with the histories, cultural practices, and moral beliefs of groups within and outside our national borders. While it is obvious that such study could never be comprehensive, the skills and dispositions associated with cross-cultural exploration would take center stage among the most important elements of the school curriculum. Such an education would emphasize the process of meaning making within culture and history, and promote a dynamic approach to learning (literally) about the world rather than a static checklist of material to be covered. Such a curriculum would favor depth over breadth and interdisciplinary study over the traditional location of such topics in social studies or world history courses. David Hansen describes this transformation as an engagement with our "cosmopolitan inheritance." He explains: "The cosmopolitan ideal invites the teacher to draw out from curriculum, whether in art or zoology, the ways in which subject matter expresses the human quest for meaning" (Hansen, 2008, p. 296). The effect of shifting our educational focus from meaning to meaning making cannot be underestimated, not least for the contrast it provides to accountability mechanisms that increasingly seek to regulate, standardize, and assess the curriculum in the context of specific, mandated subject matter.

The cosmopolitan turn in democratic moral education also requires a shift from engaging in global study as a "world traveler," or one who visits exotic locales out of curiosity or the pursuit of exciting experiences, to a form of study that challenges students to understand other cultures (within or outside the borders of their home nation) as systems of meaning making and identity. This requires a moral sensibility that welcomes the other not simply as different or as the object of study, but rather as a potential source of new ways of being in the world that might be useful for us to consider or adopt. Such a disposition goes beyond tolerance, surely, but beyond recognition as well; it suggests co-exploration and hybridization as profound forms of educational inquiry. Hansen (2008) recognizes this element of a cosmopolitan education as well when he suggests that it

> . . . embodies respect for the reality of self, other, and world. It propels persons to communicate with others and with other traditions and inheritances. It disposes people not only to be open to new values and ideas but to consider them as addresses from the world, as potential candidates for guiding their own lives. Through an educational, reconstructive engagement between them and the familiar, they can become lights to illuminate the way. (p. 306)

Again, cosmopolitanism expands and deepens an aspect of moral education that, while present in democratic theories, is not generally explored in a global context. This is the kind of educational approach that will be necessary to address global challenges like climate change, sustainable resource management, and poverty.

Incorporating some of the insights of what might be called critical cosmopolitanism opens up further opportunities for exploring new approaches to moral education in democratic societies. Perhaps the most important of these implications is the necessary connection it suggests between the practice of moral education within nation states and the global context in which all such efforts are embedded. Judith Green, in her advocacy of "deep democracy" as a grounding for cosmopolitanism, argues that because "cross-cultural value strife can never be ended without *global transformation in economic and political relations*" (Green, 1999, p. 130 emphasis in original), we must widen the "community of shared democratic struggle to a global scope" (Green, 2008, p. 41). These demands include not only the kind of cross-cultural knowledge that spans state boundaries but an understanding of the underlying social and economic structures that shape exchanges of meaning and value.

Another avenue of inquiry opened up by critical cosmopolitanism concerns the importance of "borders" themselves in the thinking about cross-cultural study and the implications of globalization for schooling. While long a staple in the critical tradition (Giroux, 1992; Giroux & McLaren, 1994; McLaren, 1995), the idea that borders provide a fertile landscape for provocative examples of hybridization and the co-construction of meaning utilizing multiple cultural systems is also central to the cosmopolitan turn. Borders are also the kinds of places where we can sometimes see especially clearly how the historical trajectories of economic, political, and social dimensions of globalization shape the lives of individuals and communities. Of particular importance here is the opportunity for students with relative privilege to somehow experience the realities of those who live in these borderlands and the way their lives are shaped by this experience: "Cosmopolitanism today has to become border thinking, critical and dialogic, from the perspective of those local histories that had to deal all along with global designs" (Mignolo, 2000, p. 744). A cosmopolitan curriculum challenges teachers and students to examine the complex moral choices we face in these cultural intersections and the implications of our choices for social, economic, and environmental justice. It also challenges teachers and students to search for potential solutions to these problems with insights, moral and otherwise, that will not come from a single cultural perspective.

Conclusion

Cosmopolitanism challenges our understanding of moral education for democratic citizenship: it pushes the boundaries of our sense of moral responsibility and questions the primacy of our most powerfully felt affinities. It also suggests that nothing less will work in an age where national boundaries are at best irrelevant, and at worst actual impediments, to meeting the gravest challenges we face as humans on this planet. To solve our most vexing global problems we must educate citizens with the skills and dispositions they need to engage in conversations that challenge existing boundaries and their definitions. We believe cosmopolitanism offers democratic moral education both a broader conceptual landscape and a wider range of philosophical tools to move this project forward. We return, at last, to Kwame Anthony Appiah's recognition that "cosmopolitanism is the name not of the solution but of the challenge" (2006, p. xv).

References

Abdelhalim, J. (2010). Cosmopolitanism and the right to be Legal: The practical poverty of concepts. *Transcience Journal, 1*(1), 63–86.

Appiah, A. (2006). *Cosmopolitanism: Ethics in a world of strangers*. London: Allen Lane.

Barber, B. R. (1996). Constitutional Faith. In J. Cohen (Ed.), *For love of country: Debating the limits of patriotism* (pp. 30–37). Boston: Beacon.

Cheah, P. (2006). *Inhuman conditions: On cosmopolitanism and human Rights*. Cambridge, MA: Harvard University Press.

Doyal, L. (2010). Review of global justice: A cosmopolitan account. *The Philosophical Quarterly, 60*(241), 886–890.

Flikschuh, K. (2004). The Limits of Liberal Cosmopolitanism. *Res Publica, 10*(2), 175–192.

Friedman, M. (2000). Educating for World Citizenship. *Ethics, 110*, 586–601.

Friedman, T. (2006). *The world is flat: A brief history of the twenty-first century* (1st updated and expanded ed.). New York: Farrar, Straus and Giroux.

Friedman, T. (2008). *Hot, flat, and crowded: Why we need a green revolution, and how it can renew America*. New York: Farrar, Straus and Giroux.

Galston, W. A. (1991). *Liberal purposes: Goods, virtues, and diversity in the liberal state*. Cambridge; New York: Cambridge University Press.

Gewertz, C. (2008). States press ahead on 21st century skills. *Education Week, 28*, (8), 21–23.

Giroux, H. (1992). *Border crossings: Cultural workers and the politics of education*. New York: Routledge.

Giroux, H., & McLaren, P. (Eds.). (1994). *Between borders: Pedagogy and the politics of cultural studies*. New York: Routledge.

Goals 2000: Educate America Act. (1994). Pub. L. No. 103–227 (1994).

Green, J. M. (1999). *Deep democracy: Community, diversity, and transformation*. Lanham, MD: Rowman & Littlefield.

Green, J. M. (2008). *Pragmatism and social hope*. New York: Columbia University Press.

Gutmann, A. (1987, 1999). *Democratic education*. Princeton, NJ: Princeton University Press.

Hannerz, U. (2005). Two Faces of Cosmopolitanism: Culture and Politics. *Statsvetenskaplig Tidskrift, 107*(3), 199–213.

Hansen, D. (2008). Curriculum and the idea of a cosmopolitan inheritance. *Journal of Curriculum Studies, 40*(3), 289–312. DOI: 10.1080/00220270802036643.

Hardt, M., & Negri, A. (2000). *Empire*. Cambridge, MA: Harvard University Press.

Howe, K. R. (1997). *Understanding equal educational opportunity*. New York: Teachers College Press.

Jordaan, E. (2009). Dialogic cosmopolitanism and global justice. *International Studies Review, 11*, 736–748.

Kaestle, C. F. (1983). *Pillars of the republic: Common schools and American society, 1780–1860*. New York: Hill and Wang.

Kliebard, H. M. (2004). *The struggle for the American curriculum, 1893–1958* (3rd ed.). New York: RoutledgeFalmer.

Lu, C. (2000). The one and many faces of cosmopolitanism. *The Journal of Political Philosophy, 8*(2), 244–267.

McLaren, P. (1995). *Critical pedagogy and predatory culture: Oppositional politics in a postmodern era*. New York: Routledge.

Mignolo, W. D. (2000). The many faces of cosmo-polis: Border thinking and critical cosmopolitanism. *Public Culture, 12*(3), 721–748.

Mignolo, W. D. (2010). Cosmopolitanism and the De-colonial Option. *Studies in Philosophy and Education, 29*, 111–127.

Mitchell, K., & Parker, W. C. (2008). I pledge allegiance to…flexible citizenship and shifting scales of belonging. *Teachers College Record, 110*(4), 775–804.

National Commission on Excellence in Education. (1983). *A nation at risk: The imperative for education*. Washington, DC: Government Printing Office.

No Child Left Behind Act. (2001). Pub. L. No. 107–110 (2001).

Nussbaum, M. C. (1997). *Cultivating humanity: A classical defense of reform in liberal education*. Cambridge, MA: Harvard University Press.

Nussbaum, M. C., & Cohen, J. (1996). *For love of country: Debating the limits of patriotism*. Boston: Beacon.

Ossewarde, M. (2007). Cosmopolitanism and the society of strangers. *Current Sociology, 55*(3), 367–388.

Pieterse, J. N. (2006). Emancipatory cosmopolitanism: Towards an agenda. *Development and Change, 37*(6), 1247–1257.

Rapoport, A. (2009). A forgotten concept: Global citizenship education and state social studies standards. *The Journal of Social Studies Research, 33*(1), 91–112.

Reich, R. (2002). *Bridging liberalism and multiculturalism in American education*. Chicago, IL: University of Chicago Press.

Rorty, R. (1998). *Achieving our country: Leftist thought in twentieth-century America*. Cambridge, MA: Harvard University Press.

Sehr, D. T. (1997). *Education for public democracy*. Albany, NY: State University of New York Press.

Sennett, R. (2002). Cosmopolitanism and the social experience of cities. In S. Vertovec & R. C. Cohen (Eds.), *Conceiving cosmopolitanism: Theory, context and practice* (pp. 42–47). London: Macmillan.

Skrbis, Z., & Woodward, I. (2004). Locating cosmopolitanism between humanist ideal and grounded social category. *Theory, Culture & Society, 21*(6), 115–136.

Strand, T. (2010). The making of a new cosmopolitanism. *Studies in Philosophy and Education, 29*, 229–242.

Turner, B. (2002). Cosmopolitan virtue, globalization and patriotism. *Theory, Culture & Society, 19*(1), 45–64.

Tyack, D. B. (1974). *The one best system: A history of American urban education*. Cambridge, MA: Harvard University Press.

Urry, J. (2002). The global complexities of September 11th. *Theory, Culture & Society, 19*(4), 59–69.

Walzer, M. (1996). Spheres of affection. In M. C. Nussbaum & J. Cohen (Eds.), *For love of country: Debating the limits of patriotism* (pp. 125–127). Boston: Beacon.

CHAPTER EIGHTEEN

Neo-Deweyan Moral Education

Douglas J. Simpson

Introduction

In this chapter,[1] I unpack a small portion of John Dewey's theory of moral education.[2] In particular, his view of moral education is examined through an analysis of his curriculum philosophy, especially as it is portrayed in my hermeneutical model.[3] This interpretative model identifies four aspects of Dewey's curriculum theory: epistemological, pedagogical, anthropological, and ecological. These four terms—epistemological, pedagogical, anthropological, and ecological—are used in a casual way to refer to what may be called the conventional, methodological, human, and environmental aspects of curriculum. Collectively, these facets of the school curriculum include all of the unconscious and conscious lessons that are taught and/or learned by students. Of course, embedded in these four aspects of the curriculum are various moral education concerns and opportunities. Among these concerns are questions related to curriculum selections, omissions, prescriptions, and proscriptions. Other concerns regard aims related to desirable and undesirable understandings, skills, appreciations, intentions, attitudes, dispositions, actions, and behaviors. Intrinsically, then, the curriculum is, in part, the outcome of ethical decisions made by educators[4] and others and is packed with ethical challenges.

Given this hermeneutical model, Dewey's theory of moral education is explained under the headings of epistemological moral curriculum (EMC[1]),[5] pedagogical moral curriculum (PMC), anthropological moral curriculum (AMC), and ecological moral curriculum (EMC[2]). While these headings are employed for the sake of clarity and convenience, the series of ideas that are discussed under them are interwoven to construct a glimpse of Dewey's comprehensive theory of moral education. Thus, although the different aspects of his curriculum philosophy and view of moral education are distinguishable, they are ultimately inseparable. This interdependency is seen in each section of this chapter but most clearly observed when Dewey's epistemological and ecological moral curricula are examined. In Dewey's philosophy, there is also an interdependency of school personnel—teachers, administrators, aids, student personnel service staff, volunteers, and so forth—as they work together to provide the multiple dimensions of a moral education.

Epistemological Moral Curriculum

Before examining Dewey's view of the EMC[1], a pause to clarify what is meant by the notion of epistemological curriculum is required. Broadly speaking, the epistemological curriculum refers to the conventional curriculum or any lessons that are learned regarding what is perceived of as the desirable or undesirable nature of inquiry and creativity. Thus, it frequently includes the study of mathematics, art, electronics, physical education, history, construction trades, biology, chemistry, drama, automotive care, music, geography, electrical occupations, language, physics, and so forth. Central to study in these fields is the emphasis that is sometimes placed on claims of knowledge or knowing, e.g., claims to know that certain attitudes, dispositions, choices, acts, and practices are ethically justifiable and that others are not. The epistemological moral curriculum, therefore, is concerned with any moral implications that occur in the process of studying the conventional curriculum.

Noticeably, the conventional curriculum is often concerned with learning facts, information, skills, dispositions, and beliefs that are a part of school activities. But the moral potentiality of the conventional curriculum is broader than a study of these domains; it extends to issues related to the nature of inquiring, analyzing, creating, applying, and evaluating. Moral dimensions of school learning are also concerned with connecting students' knowledge to their behavioral tendencies—"impulses and habits" (MW9.366)[6]—so that they develop qualities that encourage them to work and live more openly and fruitfully with one another. Knowing and acting on the known, therefore, are the two parts of the cycle of learning for Dewey. Character emerges and is built only as a person acts on what is known (LW17.218–222).

Dewey believes that when alternatives exist in or fall within any realm of action—school or otherwise—the moral is potentially present (MW14.192–193). Moral potentiality may become moral reality when an issue regarding better or worse arises (MW14.192) or when a choice affects a broader pattern of behavior, character, and habits (LW7.169–170). Specifically, the moral is present when that which is learned has meaning for human interactions (MW14.192–203) or is considered socially significant (MW9.366). Stated differently, "moral thinking begins when we start asking *should or ought* questions and continues when we reflect on relevant reasons for selecting one option or choice rather than another" (LW7.163–164). For instance, when non-educators and educators deliberate about *what* should be taught, *how* it should be taught, *who* should teach the subject, *whose* educational aims and outcomes should be pursued, and *which* conditions should be provided in a school or classroom, they are engaged in moral thinking and, eventually, moral decision making.

Although he recognizes that there are numerous influences on character[7] development, Dewey divides them into two general categories: indirect and direct. In the former category, he places the influences of homes, neighborhoods, social cliques, entertainment venues, economic ideals, gangs, political decisions, and so forth. In the latter category, he locates schools, youth organizations, places of religious teaching, universities, and so on (LW9.186–193). Dewey also distinguishes between moral instruction and instruction about morals; and he largely dispenses with both as key players in moral or character development. His strongest support is reserved for indirect character development in schools:

> Without discussing…the value of so-called direct moral instruction (or, better, instruction about morals), it may be laid down as fundamental that the influence of direct moral instruction, even at its very best, is comparatively small in amount and slight in influence, when the whole field of moral growth through education is taken into account. This larger field of indirect and vital moral education, the development of character through all the agencies, instrumentalities, and materials of school life is, therefore, the subject of our present discussion. (MW4.268)

So, for Dewey, neither teaching *about* morals (e.g., a course on ethical theory or a course on civic responsibilities) nor teaching *a separate course* in character development is practical or effective (LW9. 189) if moral education and development are the goal. But neither is "occasional moralizing" (LW9. 190). Instead, the full range of indirect moral education is encouraged.

Where, then, should the focus of moral or character education[8] be placed? Strangely, it might seem, Dewey says that character or moral education should begin first with economic change in society (LW9. 191). From his standpoint, the economic emphases of society need to shift away from material wealth to providing "useful work," "security for old age," "a decent home," and "opportunity for education for all children" so that parents—and others—will shift their informal educational emphasis away from pursuing material success (LW9.191). This shift in economic emphases and values will have positive influences in a multiplicity of ways, that include moving society from a predominantly competitive culture to a more cooperative one and from a principally individualistic nation to one that emphasizes common interests and needs. Plus, if there is a shift in society's economic philosophy, the new emphases will complement the emphases of parents, schools, and other institutions. The economic security of people will allow them to reevaluate and change their priorities and grow more as people and workers rather put the majority of their energies into being creators and acquirers of goods (LW9.191).

Second, he recommends that parents receive a better education since they are *a*, not *the*, "dominant factor" in educating their children. Parents need to have their eyes and priorities transferred away from teaching their children to be financially successful as individuals, even at the expense of others. Instead, parents should emphasize humane and common interests, needs, and values. Parental education, among other possibilities, should involve parents working and learning together so that they attend to their own personal development as well as to the overall growth of their children. Actually, parental education can be as broad as interests and resources permit (LW9.191–193). In summary, therefore, Dewey recommends that parental education occur so that they can better educate their own children.

Third, Dewey argues that society should provide children and youth with the kinds of recreational and social activities that satisfy "the two dominant impulses of youth": interests in a wide range of activities and in an assortment of group interactions (LW9.192). Being successful educators in these two general spheres will help society reconstruct youth cultures in rural settings, small towns and cities, and urban contexts. To ignore these realms of indirect education and growth is to naively assume that both unguided individual and group activities and interactions will be principally neutral or positive in their moral influence. This assumption is clearly unfounded.

As Dewey moves beyond ideas regarding nation wide economic security and employment, culture wide family education and opportunities for growth, community-wide social networks for children and youth, he arrives at the school. In other words, he progresses beyond "the concrete state of social relations and activities" of indirect moral education to the direct influence of schools on moral development. Paradoxically, however, he wishes to change the direct possibilities of the school into indirect practices: "This larger field of indirect and vital moral education, the development of character through all the agencies, instrumentalities, and materials of *school life* [emphasis added]" become Dewey's fundamental emphasis (MW4.268). He, then, urges an education that understands the moral influence of all environmental conditions of school, the conventional and the "collateral" curricula (LW13.29). The flow of Dewey's moral thought regarding the school begins with the conventional curriculum and leads to the collateral and ecological curricula.

Returning to his fourfold moral education outline—economic, parental, youth, and school emphases—it seems that Dewey's character education program has serious shortcomings. But these deficiencies are reduced exponentially when it is understood that the surrounding, but unmentioned, conditions of Dewey's highlighted economic change include both formal and informal political and educational changes. Democratic changes are needed at the political and governmental levels as well as in the cultural patterns of society: "A society of free individuals in which all, in doing each his [or her] own work, contribute to the liberation and enrichment of the lives of others is the only environment for the normal growth to full stature" (LW9.202–203).

In this kind of society, all social entities "are educational in the sense that they operate to form attitudes, dispositions, abilities and disabilities that constitute a concrete personality" (LW11.221). In this way, democratic values are indirectly and directly taught in complementary ways by each societal unit. Dewey summarizes his view of moral education this way:

> Every place in which men [and women] habitually meet, shop, club, factory, saloon, church, political caucus is perforce a schoolhouse, even though not so labeled. This intercourse is in turn dependent upon the political organization of society, the relations of classes to one another, the distribution of wealth, the spirit in which family life is conducted, and so on. Public agitations, discussions, propaganda of public meeting and press, political campaigns, legislative deliberations, are in this regard but so many educational agencies. In brief, every condition, arrangement, and institution that forms the emotional and imaginative bent of mind [and] gives meaning to overt action is educational in character. (MW7.304)

Dewey's ideas, once again, move from the EMC[1] to the EMC[2] and, incidentally, to the PMC and AMC. But what details does he provide about the EMC[1]? Several ideas are critical. First, he argues that the heart of epistemological moral education is found in the fact that the "educational centre of gravity" for a curriculum is its human import, its personal, social, and cultural implications (MW9.220). That is to say, he believes that ultimately "the cultural or humane aspects" of a subject (MW9.220) constitute the superglue that draws together subjects and contains intrinsic interest for students. Moreover, "the most humane" of all subjects is morals (MW14.204) whether learned in "physical, biological and historic knowledge [that is] placed in a human context" (MW14.204–205). It is easy to understand why he thinks that a knowledge of the past, an alertness in the present, and an intelligent hypothesizing about the future are invaluable in making ethical judgments about unique matters in the present (MW14.182, 204).

Second, promoting intellectual virtues[9] such as "open-mindedness, single-mindedness, sincerity, breadth of outlook, thoroughness, assumption of responsibility for developing the consequences of ideas which are accepted" is a part of character education (MW9.366). Similarly, fostering self-control and "social efficiency," for Dewey, is a part of character education because the qualities developed are "moral traits" (MW9.369). To illustrate, Dewey suggests reflection on the idea of social efficiency, for it entails "intelligent sympathy or good will" for others (MW9.127). Sympathy, in his mind, is a moving trait and entails developing feelings for others through, among other ways, the power of imagination (MW9.127–128).

Third, the EMC[1] is available when teachers—and other school educators—*consciously* seek to teach important moral concepts and behaviors. This approach may be somewhat effective if students come from cultural backgrounds that already support the values that are taught in a school. But it is largely ineffective in schools that have students who come from morally diverse cultures (MW9.364). The approach is unpromising if moral development is a major purpose of schooling *and* the conventional curriculum is believed to have little to do with character education (MW9.364). Plus, educators need to remember that schools are just one of many institutions that influence moral development and are not nearly as powerful as the twenty-four-hours-per-day informal influences in societies (LW9.187). At a minimum, direct instruction needs to be complemented by a rich experience of the meanings of the values taught so that cognitive understanding is enriched by experiential understanding and emotional attachment (MW9.243). But, lest educators think direct instruction in moral education is always ill advised, he adds, "While personal exhortation, advice and instruction is a feeble stimulus compared with that which steadily proceeds from the impersonal forces and depersonalized habitudes of the environment, yet they may start the latter going" (MW14.20).

Fourth, there are not only intellectual virtues that should be developed and displayed by educators and students, but teachers—as they pursue content aims which are in themselves the result of moral decisions (MW9.369)—ought to manage their classrooms ethically and treat humanely "the impulses of youth" (MW14.69); for, "a truly humane education consists in an intelligent direction of native activities in the light of the possibilities and necessities of the social situation" (MW14.69–70). Rather than suppressing or ignoring the native impulses of youths, Dewey claims that a part of moral education involves treating students respectfully while guiding their native tendencies toward educationally and morally rewarding experiences (LW13.22).

Finally, Dewey implies that teachers have an ethical responsibility to be honest and helpful when it comes to discussing moral matters and teaching their subjects. On the one hand, he avers that teachers need to help students understand the differences between "intellectual certainty of *subject matter* and *our* certainty" (MW9.196–198). Thus, he encourages teachers to note that absolutely certain knowledge in a content area is not possible even though an individual may have a personal certitude about a matter (MW14.163). But, on the other hand, reflective inquiry *and* action can lead to "a reasonable degree of security" (LW4.8ff), and some propositions have such "cumulative verifications" (MW14.165) that a person is "justified in *using* [emphasis added] them as if they were absolutely true" (LW2.12).[10] He cautions, however, that it is regrettable teaching that leaves students thinking that they are entirely on their own when making moral decisions (MW14.74). Equally, he thinks it is a distorted moral education that seeks to separate "warm emotions and cool intelligence" (MW14.177); for there is no significant character formation unless the emotions are connected to ideas and result in desirable moral action (LW9.187).

Pedagogical Moral Curriculum

The previous discussion of Dewey's view of moral education introduced us to more than the EME[1]. It also gave us a glimpse of his entire philosophy of moral education: the epistemological, the pedagogical, the anthropological, and the ecological. Now, it is time to address the second of these realms—pedagogical moral curriculum—in more detail.

A brief overview of the pedagogical curriculum comes first, however. Included in the pedagogical curriculum are any lessons that are taught or learned about the desirable or undesirable nature of how to teach and learn, construct and complete assignments, collaborate and cooperate, manage and guide, and interact and relate to others. Plus, there is the myriad of collateral lessons that are taught while utilizing pedagogical strategies that are designed to nurture learning. The pedagogical curriculum, therefore, may include any messages that are conveyed while using face-to-face or e-learning methodologies, engaging or disengaging students as individuals and groups, developing or inhibiting their cooperation and independence, encouraging or discouraging independent thinking and personal agency, and so on. Moral concerns emerge when human or social issues regarding *should or ought* and *right and wrong* enter the picture (LW7.163–164). The earlier mentioned what, how, who, whose, and which questions may arise in this area too.

An example may illustrate how the pedagogical curriculum or a teacher's teaching and methodology is indeed, first, a curriculum and, second, a moral curriculum. It is widely accepted that teaching methods (e.g., lecturing, questioning, discussing, debating, and grouping) can be examined for their effectiveness and efficiency. Is lecturing, to be ridiculous, an effective and efficient way to teach students how to read? What should be done if a teacher keeps lecturing kindergarten or elementary students on how to read when she knows she is ineffective and that her methodology creates classroom management problems? Should the teacher be assigned a new mentor, provided with professional development opportunities, or released? What corrective action—or what ethical action—should a principal pursue when a teacher is clearly ineffective and, it could be argued, unethical for failing to improve her teaching and classroom management? Circumstances of this sort are the kind that Dewey sees as a part of the pedagogical *negative* moral curriculum. But why? He thinks the collateral lessons that are taught by a teacher's ongoing choices to be ineffective and a principal's repeated decisions to allow her to be ineffective are evidence that they are not behaving as ethical professionals.

In view of the above, it is not unanticipated to learn that Dewey sees pedagogy as differently as he does curriculum. He sees at least four overlapping lenses (Simpson et al., 2005): the pedagogy of school environments, the pedagogy of specific subjects, the pedagogy of scientific thinking, and the pedagogy of individual teachers. Because the pedagogy of environments is an important part of EMC[2] and the pedagogy of individual teachers is included in the AMC, discussion at this juncture will be limited to the pedagogy of specific subjects and the pedagogy of scientific thinking.

The Pedagogy of Specific Subjects

When Dewey discusses the teaching of specific school subjects, he stresses at least four ideas. First, he emphasizes the professional and ethical importance of a teacher's understanding and enjoying a subject that she teaches. As a consequence, teachers have an ethical obligation to be passionate about their fields of inquiry and creativity. If not, they will have an extremely difficult time becoming effective educators and may well teach their students that it is fine to be intellectually indifferent (LW13.342–346). Intersecting with the first idea is a second one. Dewey says that narrowing the curriculum or focusing too much on teaching a specific subject and assessing how much a student understands its content can distract teachers from creating broader and deeper qualities of character, such as intellectual interests and attitudes (LW8.158). His piercing question regarding students' learning just the content of specific courses is relevant:

> What avail is it to win prescribed amounts of information about geography and history, to win ability to read and write, if in the process the individual loses his [her] own soul: loses his [her] appreciation of things worth while, of the values to which these things are relative; if he [she] loses desire to apply what he [she] has learned and, above all, loses the ability to extract meaning from his [her] future experiences as they occur? (LW13.29)

Imagine, for instance, some students who develop almost no appreciation for any school subject, lack interest in applying their knowledge to school and community issues, and see no relevance of their studies to everyday life and their futures. Compare these students with other students who are enthusiastic about learning new ideas and skills, employ what they know to address personal and social challenges, and understand the relationship of what they know to what is going on in their lives. Are the different outcomes just *educational* problems or are they also *moral* problems that researchers, theoreticians, educators, and unions are ethically obligated to address?

Third, Dewey notes that there are effective and ineffective ways of teaching some subjects from a moral perspective. He illustrates this in the field of history where he thinks the field can be used to foster "intelligent sympathetic understanding" of present social challenges and controversies (MW9.225). When history is taught in this fashion rather than being used to instill certain moral prescriptions and proscriptions, it can offer students the opportunity to develop assets that are "permanent and constructive" (MW9.225). Teaching a subject as it is a part of the human experience, then, is important for multiple reasons, for instance, because of its value as a way of thinking and seeing, as a way of developing sympathetic insights, and as a way of solving problems. To knowingly choose to teach in ways that do not develop sympathetic understanding, therefore, raises ethical questions.

Another fertile example of teaching a specific subject is found in the way Dewey views the teaching of ethics or, as he stressed, "the study of *ethical relationships*" or "this complex world of which we are members" (EW4.60). With this view, then, the method or "spirit" (EW4.60) of teaching ethics fits well with literature and history (EW4.61). In this area of teaching, he distances himself from several methodologies. As noted earlier, he rejects moralistic teaching and carefully qualifies direct instructional ways of teaching ethics and desirable behavior. Moreover, he contends that direct efforts to implant even warranted ethical ideas may go astray by creating artificial expectations on the part of educators who assume that students' understanding the importance, say, of the principle of equal respect of persons will cause them to act on the principle. In short, understanding alone does not automatically change behavior. Thus, direct teaching that is based on the belief that knowledge will change behavior and attitudes is faulty both theoretically and practically (EW4.54–55).

But Dewey espouses what he considers a justifiable way of teaching ethics or ethical relationships that is both theoretically sound and practically useful and may be used in some form at all levels of schooling (EW4.54–55). This way of teaching, however, has more do with the "character and spirit of ethical teaching" than it does with pedagogy as narrowly understood (EW4.55). The role and the responsibilities that Dewey gives the teacher are illuminating. She may, by way of illustration, prepare and present a genuinely relevant scenario of human suffering and ask students two questions: Should you do anything to help alleviate the suffering and, if yes, how would you lessen or eliminate it? Answering both questions, however, is to be guided by focusing *on the process of deciding* if they should alleviate the suffering and *on the process of deciding* what they should do (EW4. 56).

From the moment that students begin gathering and examining pertinent information about the case they are examining, the teacher's comments ought to be designed to stimulate imagination, consideration of the specific situation being analyzed, and insight into procedural questions. Ultimately, the teacher should guide students to understand the importance of the "*typical features of every human interaction*" and the importance of acting on this understanding (EW4.58). So—from answering key questions, to studying pertinent data, to examining motives, to seeing the connectedness of people, to gaining imaginative understanding, to making choices—the student has the opportunity to experience the common features of living and solving human problems. Pointedly, Dewey amplifies the importance of ethical thinking and decision making as he concludes that "the subject-matter of ethics must furnish the measure of other studies" because the essential moral curriculum of schools is "human life itself," regardless of the prescribed curriculum (EW4.61).

Teaching ethics, ethical relationships, or human life, however, involves ends that are not easily or accurately measured. Of course, the desirable ends go beyond understanding how to analyze ethical issues, gather and interpret relevant data, and make wise judgments, especially if analytical reasoning is seen as "a bloodless reason" (MW14.136). Instead, the end of the "emotional, passionate phase of action" needs attention. Indeed, "more 'passions,' not fewer, is the answer" (MW14.136).

> To check the influence of hate there must be sympathy, while to rationalize sympathy there are needed emotions of curiosity, caution, respect for the freedom of others—dispositions which evoke objects which balance those called up by sympathy, and prevent its degeneration into maudlin sentiment and meddling interference. Rationality, once more, is not a force to evoke against impulse and habit. It is the attainment of a working harmony among diverse desires. "Reason" as a noun signifies the happy cooperation of a multitude of dispositions, such as sympathy, curiosity, exploration, experimentation, frankness, pursuit—to follow things through—circumspection, to look about at the context, etc., etc. (MW14.136)

For Dewey, therefore, the pedagogy of specific subjects means several things, including the idea that the ethical teacher has a set of passions that enliven professional life and guide interactions with students, a perspective that success is measured in part by the passions students acquire for learning and applying their knowledge to human problems, a way of teaching a subject that focuses on human problem solving in a complex world, and an approach to teaching that moves from understanding to acting in view of the acquired knowledge. Students who study subjects with teachers who have these understandings and passions are studying with moral educators regardless of the subject that is being studied.

The Pedagogy of Reflective Thinking

As seen from prior discussion, it is obvious that the pedagogy of reflective thinking is not a stand-alone methodology but, instead, infuses all educational endeavors, including moral education which, in turn, infuses all education. Scientific or reflective thinking for Dewey involves a number of activities that may be either sequential or serendipitous. He sometimes stresses the stimuli of thought, such as having a doubt about a school rule or deciding on the value of assignments. At other times, he observes the importance of clarifying problems, identifying their causes, compiling a list of their potential solutions, deciding which solution to test first, and reconsidering the reflective process as a new cycle of reflection is begun (MW9.158, 180, 304). In time, this type of reflective thinking leads to the modification and expansion of warranted knowledge claims about human behavior (MW9.158, 180, 304).

In discussing reflective thinking, Dewey offers an interesting means of developing insightful thinking, learning, and feeling that is particularly helpful in moral education, a methodology that is implicit—at least in its possible focus on others—in his view of teaching ethics (EW4.54–61). The method or practice of dramatic rehearsal may be directed in two different directions: inwardly toward ourselves and outwardly toward others. When *personal or inward-oriented student deliberation and imagination* is nourished, students are asked to identify and intellectually experiment with some impulse or inclination (such as wanting to bully a classmate) and follow their thoughts and imaginative actions of bullying until they come to the consequences of their thinking and acting. At this stage, students can be asked to determine whether they approve or disapprove of their own actions, the outcomes for the bullied, and, possibly, repeat the process by selecting alternative ways of responding to the person they bullied (LW7.275). Through such deliberative rehearsal, students may come to understand that they can foresee potential consequences of their proposed actions, the responsibility they bear for their actions, and the probable outcomes for themselves and others. They may even learn to feel deeply about their imagined actions and sympathize with the bullied student. When *social or outward-oriented student deliberation and imagination* is nourished, the process is similar, but the focus is on those students who were bullied. Imagination is used to think and feel as a bullied person may. Insight into the pain and anguish may be gained as well as a reasoned response to them (EW4.57). In both personal- and social-oriented dramatic rehearsal, the kind of person who is being developed raises a question: Who am I becoming by bullying or by being bullied (MW6.185–186)? Naturally, dramatic rehearsal can be used as pedagogy to stimulate public, reflective group thinking about the ethical responsibilities involved by the bully, his or her friends, the bullied, bystanders, teachers, and others. This technique helps clarify that in real life situations, stopping to think is crucial because, once a decision is acted on, there is no chance of withdrawing it (MW14.132). Dramatic rehearsal, then, is a form of pedagogy that projects on "the screen of imagination" a series of possible futures that are easily examined and critiqued (MW14.133). Ideally, the reflection stimulated results in consummated action.

When the EMC[1] and the PMC are combined, then, few question why Dewey concludes that the moral responsibility of the teacher includes ensuring that

> the greatest possible number of ideas acquired by children and youth are acquired in such a vital way that they become *moving ideas, motive-forces* [emphasis added] in the guidance of conduct. This demand and this opportunity make the moral purpose universal and dominant in all instruction—whatsoever the topic [or methodology]. Were it not for this possibility, the familiar statement that the ultimate purpose of all education is character-forming would be hypocritical pretense; for as everyone knows, the direct and immediate attention of teachers and pupils must be, for the greater part of the time, upon intellectual matters. It is out of the question to keep direct moral considerations constantly uppermost. But it is not out of the question to aim at making the methods of learning, of acquiring intellectual power, and of assimilating subject matter, such that they will render behavior more enlightened, more consistent, more vigorous than it otherwise would be. (MW4.267–268)

In the above quotation, Dewey touches upon several important moral education ideas. First, he strikes a blow against poor pedagogy: moral education that is undertaken in a boring, irrelevant, and uncaring fashion is deadly. Students are neither inclined to learn boring ideas nor to act on them. Thus, boring teaching is counterproductive when moral development is assessed. Second, he implies that it is essential that teachers have considerable professional freedom in their teaching so that they can select—serendipitously if necessary—curricular topics, events, and experiences that get beyond a purely cognitive understanding of ethical concerns to an affective grasp of issues that moves them to act on what they learn. Third, he underlines that both pedagogy and content play important roles in moral education. The blend can be beautiful and powerful. Fourth, he clarifies that teachers do not need to—indeed, should not—focus on finding ways to inject moral messages in their teaching of subjects: they are already filled with opportunities for indirect moral education when they are taught from a human perspective.

Anthropological Moral Curriculum

As this heading suggests, the anthropological or human curriculum consists of any lessons learned by students, consciously or unconsciously, from others, including classmates, teachers, aids, principals, counselors, vendors, volunteers, and visitors. Thus, the human curriculum contains lessons that are learned—reflectively and/or thoughtlessly—about desirable or undesirable behaviors, cultures, languages, religions, aesthetics, ideologies, and identities. Moreover, the human curriculum involves students acquiring and/or losing attitudes and behaviors, such as respect and/or disrespect, tolerance and/or ridicule, pride and/or prejudice, friendliness and/or detachment from others. When these matters slip over into questions of good and bad, right and wrong, ought and ought not, the human curriculum evolves into the human moral curriculum. The anthropological curriculum is, then, the personalized and embodied program of study of all who are part of a school community. The AMC of a school or classroom is, consequently, what students learn or absorb from others regarding what is ethical or right and wrong, good and bad. But part of their learning is sometimes confounded because of the tendency of many to collapse several kinds of value judgments—ethical, aesthetic, preferential, prudential, and appraisive—into one, usually describing all values as simply matters of preference. When this occurs, students may conclude that acts of bullying and acts of kindness, attitudes of hate and respect, and motives of resentment and benevolence are purely personal preferences, not concerns that deal with right and wrong. Dewey, to the contrary, thinks that distinguishing among these value domains is an important aspect of moral education (MW13.15; LW15.139).

The human moral curriculum, as Dewey understands it, is set in what he terms the social environment, which is made up of "all the activities [including verbal and behavioral communications] of fellow beings" (MW9.26). He argues that the AMC is especially powerful and effective when students work together on assignments, share in the solving of problems, and collaborate in creative activities. The power of united effort results in educative—or miseducative—experiences in ways that individual assignments do not (MW9.26). But the human or anthropological moral curriculum is broader than its desirable features, for it includes the antisocial ideals and behaviors and exclusions that a student may experience, whether they occur in social, athletic, musical, theatric, or religious activities. Therefore, ignoring hostile behavior is, at a minimum, a questionable practice. At its worst, disregarding antisocial student behavior displays hypocrisy by educators: it suggests, maybe, that only student knowledge, not behavior, is prized or that educators lack the courage to live by their beliefs.

While the AMC can be approached from many sides, only two aspects are analyzed here: the teacher as curriculum and the student as curriculum. Other fruitful points of view on this topic include studying the counselor, custodian, administrative assistant, coach, volunteer, cafeteria worker, and, especially, the principal[11] as curriculum. As expected, the multiplicity of curricula that are offered students both enhance and undermine the kinds of AMC that are desirable. The alignment of these various curricula around desirable aims, however, adds to the potency of the delivered moral education.

The Teacher as Curriculum

The AMC involves the moral lessons—including those that are learned via the collateral curriculum—that teachers impart directly and indirectly and intentionally and unintentionally to students. Although some think otherwise, teachers are so important in Dewey's eyes that he claims "the real course of study [in the school] must come to the child from the teacher" (MW1. 273). His rationale for this claim is that the teacher is the channel for everything that reaches the student (MW 15.183–184). Although his unqualified claim is debatable, the idea that the teacher influences what and how objectives, materials, questions, activities, ideas, and ideals will be pursued is manifestly correct. Understanding this thought, it is clear that the pedagogy of individual teacher, noted earlier, interconnects with the teacher as curriculum. To force home this point, Dewey maintains that the personality, intelligence, and spirit of the teacher are factors that ought never to be discounted:

> You can have very rich, full subject matter laid down on paper, and yet the personality and intelligence of the teacher may be such that the subject matter will shrink, dry up, and become a mere trickle of dull fact when it gets to the pupil. You can have an outline of a course of study, in the form of a bare skeleton on paper, and yet that course of study, as it gets over to the pupils in the classroom, may be very full, rich and alive, because of the spirit that the teacher puts into it; the methods the teacher uses; the assignment of outside study that the teacher gives, and new points of view in the student mind. (MW 15.183–184)

Dewey adds to an understanding the significance of the teacher as moral curriculum when he insists that the acts and actions and the manner and spirit of the teacher influence students' behaviors and attitudes, favorably and unfavorably. So, the teacher affects students' moral thinking, attitudes, dispositions, and actions and, thereby, character development and manners (LW8.159). The last word, *manners*, may seem to be an unusual element to add to a moral discussion, but Dewey claims that manners are "minor morals" and deserve attention (MW9.22). Of course, social interactions—in monocultural, cross-cultural, and multicultural contexts—sometimes suggest that understanding and appreciating manners is much more important than the term *minor* implies. Rich understanding of and caring for others' cultures adds immensely to social relationships. Ignorance of and disregard for others' cultures can be ruinous. Whatever our conclusions regarding the status of manners, Dewey notes that "social stimuli"—whether from a teacher or student—can motivate others to explore environmental riches (LW8. 142). If these social stimuli from the teacher include respect for others' manners and cultures, there is, perhaps, a greater probability that they will also include other democratic values that make up the heart of Deweyan moral education.

Of course, understanding that teachers have a moral influence on others is not a novel claim, although seeing teachers as a part of a designed moral education in a democratic classroom may be somewhat original. From antiquity to the present, parents and publics have been concerned with the moral influence of teachers on children. Sometimes this concern has been articulated in terms of hiring, disciplining, and dismissing teachers. On other occasions, the concern has resulted in both private and parochial schools so that only teachers with particular cultural, religious, moral, and intellectual values teach the students who are enrolled. A difference that Dewey's ideal, but not perfect, school offers is a democratic ethic for all students so that they can be nurtured as a community of diverse learners who discover both intellectually and experientially how to respect and honor one another, regardless of religion, sexual orientation, gender, color, race, ethnicity, nationality, handicap, and other differences. In order for this ideal to be at least partially realized, teachers must use democratic means as they interact with students and guide their activities. This suggests that incidental remarks, body language, verbal cues, and other factors—a part of the collateral curriculum—play a vital role in the AMC. Consider what may or may not be learned by a student hearing the following comments: "*Don't* do that, Fatih!" "*Letitia*, stop pestering Morri!" "Do *you* think it is illegal, Juan?" "Aaron, do you know what Melanie will say when she returns?" "Right and wrong are personal matters, aren't they, Ms. Epstein?" "Heejin, does The Bill of Rights have anything relevant to say about the topic?" Embedded in these and thousands of other so-called unimportant remarks and responses are moral implications, prescriptions, and prohibitions. Each teacher may need to surface a plethora of remarks, words, phrases, and expressions as a source for her or his personal growth as well as her students' growth. Especially important in this regard are discussions about ethical principles that enable teachers and students to reflect more clearly about moral matters (MW14.194).

The Student as Curriculum

The human curriculum also portrays the student as part of the moral education curriculum. In short, the student is a curriculum because she or he influences the thinking, values, and lives of other students. Dewey is particularly concerned that teachers utilize the rich knowledge and experiences that students have when they enter school and that students become not only sources of knowledge and but that they be understood as co-teachers. In a sense, the student as curriculum might be viewed as a part of the collateral curriculum or informal education. In this case, what a student knows can become a part of "the matrix of social intercourse" or communication (MW9.188). As is the case with interactions with teachers, so it is with the interactions of students with one another: this is where we find "the reality of education" (MW 1.268). The "personal contact of child with child" may be any and all of the following: planned or unplanned, fruitful or unfruitful, and superficial or profound (MW 1.268). Whatever the form of contact, student interactions will probably be both positive and negative but can nearly always be guided toward productive growth.

While the teacher needs to reflect on her own incidental behavior and alter it when appropriate, she also needs to study the interactions of students with one another. Reflect on the following scenarios that may or may not need immediate or delayed attention: "I *hate* you!" "What's the matter with *you*, Mohammed?" "Why don't you see a dentist, you zero!" "That's *my* answer. You *stole* it from me!" "Who asked *you* to sit with us?" Read these remarks as you imagine that you are the students' classroom teacher: "I grew up in Puebla, México. My papa worked in the Volkswagen plant. My mother died two years ago. So, we moved here to be close to his sister and her family." "My parents are from the Bronx. We moved here so my mother could attend medical school. She's studying to become a gynecologist." "We moved here from Illinois where my mother was an electrician. She wanted to be near her mother who is sick with lymphoma." Or listen to these comments as if you were a teacher-on-the-wall: "My mother says it is a sin to dislike gays and lesbians. They deserve to be treated as people, too." "Isn't it wrong to say that all Middle Easterners are terrorists?" "How would you feel if somebody said something like that about everybody from California?" "Well, I'm glad to be here now although I didn't like Raleigh when we first came here from Newfoundland and Labrador." Once again, it is clear that these types of comments contain excellent subject matter cues and moral lessons and potentialities. To ignore them, is tantamount to throwing out of the classroom some of the most exciting books, software programs, and teachers.

As if the rationale for learning from others may not be clear, Dewey takes the time to briefly explain his thinking. Believing that everyone is born into geographical and cultural contexts that are by definition not as broad and as rich as the totality of the world's diversity, he says that diverse schools provide excellent opportunities for everyone to "supplement the narrowness of his [or her] immediately personal experiences by utilizing the experiences of others" (MW9.164). Stated differently, he says diverse schools provide the "opportunity [for each student] to escape from the limitations of the social group in which he [or she] was born, and to come into living contact with a broader environment" (MW 9.24–25). Since most dominant cultures denigrate some features of other cultures, the idea of escaping a social group's limitations can be misinterpreted to mean that immigrants and people from lower-socio-economic groups need to escape the limitations of their cultures. But Dewey, instead, wants every student—the economically and politically privileged and the economically and politically disadvantaged—to be able to learn from the dissimilar and fertile ways of life that contribute to the cultures of schools. Of course, he recognizes that some social groups—e.g., gangs and social cliques—can have detrimental influences on students (MW 9.25). Even so, he claims that the "intermingling in the school of youth of different races, differing religions, and unlike customs creates for all a new and broader environment" and is helpful in bringing about educative experiences (MW 9.26–27). His school diversity beliefs are consistent with his assumptions about society as a whole: "the very process of living together educates. It enlarges and enlightens experience; it stimulates and enriches imagination; it creates responsibility for accuracy and vividness of statement and thought" (MW 9.9). Educative and moral potentialities, as a result, are tremendous in a diverse classroom (LW8.76, 102). Indeed, Dewey claims that even measured and guided conflict is important for it "is the gadfly of thought" (MW.14.207).

Dewey realizes, however, that gadflies are not always appreciated. Consequently, he is cautious about children learning as groups even in a democracy. He believes that "the chief ideal" of many, perhaps most, is "uniformity" of thought and behavior (LW9.315). Thus, schools and society must be careful to guard students' individuality and their freedom of intelligence (LW9.314). He insists, therefore, that a democratic society must consider "individual variations as precious [because] it finds in them the means of its own growth. Hence a democratic society must…allow for intellectual freedom and the play of diverse gifts and interests in its educational measures" (MW9.315). To impose values on students and coerce them into accepting even warranted beliefs is to act unethically and results in teaching moral lessons that are contrary to democracy. When schools and teachers are successful in forcing their ideas and ideals on students, the teacher and student as curricula take on negative implications. The undesirable curriculum that students become conveys lessons about conformity, trepidation, timidity, and submission. The teacher as curriculum shifts from one of being educative to miseducative (LW13.17–30). Democracy and education are reduced to quasi-democracy and pseudo-education. Students, of course, should be encouraged to avoid "excessive reliance" on either teachers or on other students (MW9.164). Fortunately, educators' awareness of and caution regarding students' individualities and their need to think and choose for themselves are very important if we are to avoid ideological and value impositions.

Ecological Moral Curriculum

Once again, explaining one concept (the ecological curriculum) in order to gain access to another (the ecological moral curriculum) is necessary. The ecological curriculum encompasses (a) all of the lessons that are learned from or taught by the relations and interactions of students with their physical, technological, and natural environments as well as (b) all the lessons that are taught students through their relationships and interactions with the epistemological, pedagogical, and anthropological dimensions of the curriculum. Moreover, the ecological curriculum includes (c) all the lessons that are taught from school, class, or sub-group ethoses. Oddly, some overlook the ecological curriculum because it is external to the student, and they view curricular experience as something that goes on entirely inside "an individual's body and mind" (LW13.22). But this is not the case, for external stimuli from numerous sources constantly feed experience and serve as educative forces (LW13.22). For this reason, educators should not ignore the school environment any more than they would ignore the diversity found among children of different socio-economical, racial, linguistic, and cultural backgrounds (LW13.22). Undeniably, students are a large part of the environmental curriculum that interconnects with the anthropological curriculum.

Naturally, the desirable ethos or culture that Dewey wants is democratic. To the degree that democratic or opposing values are present in a classroom and school, the ecological curriculum can become a hidden and/or open form of the moral curriculum. Among the many democratic values Dewey treasures are cooperation over competition, social spirit over individualistic ambition, and reflective thinking over intellectual conformity (LW6.97–98). To strongly clarify his ideas regarding social spirit and reflective thinking, he adds that education needs the motto "'Learn to act with and for others while you learn to think and to judge for yourself'" (LW6.98). In Dewey's thinking, then, the environmental moral curriculum is so commingled with the total ecological curriculum that they are largely indistinguishable. In fact, the discussion of EMC[1] demonstrates that the various aspects of his views of moral education are a tapestry woven by educational artists.[12] For obvious reasons, neither the previous discussion of EMC[1] nor the lessons that are taught students by their relations and interactions with the epistemological, pedagogical, and anthropological dimensions of the curriculum are revisited here.

Dewey, obviously, is known for emphasizing that a major responsibility of the teacher is to select and create conditions that lead to educative environments. But only a taste of the details of this thinking can be noted. First of all, it is apparent that the physical, technological, and natural elements of the environment are worthy of attention. The available materials, books, technologies, laboratories, resource centers, school grounds, and e-programs all constitute portions of the conditions and environment that teachers need to employ in order to create fertile and vital learning settings. Thus, the consideration that community and government leaders, the public, and educators give to the aesthetic nature of the classroom, school, and grounds suggests a great deal about their priorities. In combination, these material dimensions of the curriculum can be powerful aspects of aesthetic education. Lamenting, Dewey claims:

> I do not see how any very high popular artistic standard can exist where a great many of the people are living in slums. Such persons cannot get artistic culture simply by going to free concerts or the Metropolitan Museum to look at pictures, or the public library to read books, as long as their immediate surroundings, or what they come into direct contact with, unconsciously habituates them to ugly, sordid things. (LW6.45)

But what does aesthetics education have to do with moral education? A great deal if Dewey is correct. For the moment, one thought must suffice: "The moral function of art itself is to remove prejudice, do away with the scales that keep the eye from seeing, tear away the veils due to wont and custom, perfect the power to perceive" (LW10.328). If Dewey is right, how many prejudices, scales, veils, and imperfections are taught by the "ugly, sordid things" that instruct children and youth?

What Dewey might also have declared is: "I do not see how anyone can walk in the midst of unattended children, stoned teenagers, unemployed adults, dilapidated cars, bankrupted businesses, and gutted neighborhoods, and expect educators and students to believe that moral education is even a possibility. Teachers and children will find moral education a ludicrous suggestion when their political, business, and civic leaders provide them with unsanitary restrooms, out-of-date materials, unusable technology, unsafe school grounds, and fatalistic administrators. Societies almost literally make students educationally and morally hopeless when they show them almost no respect, provide them with ridiculous resources, and daily desert them to the uncaring bureaucrats who escape to their petite urban fortresses and suburban mansions." Dewey's theory of moral education, then, suggests the ecological moral curriculum permeates and surrounds the school and stretches out into neighborhoods, apartments, and businesses. In this regard, he urges that the school EMC² be integrated with the external moral curriculum in communities (L5.299–310). Sadly, his desire—although turned inside out—comes true too often in schools and communities that are neglected and rejected by the broader society.

Second, the ethos of the school is a central concern for Dewey and, to a substantial degree, is a construction of educators and students. In part, the ethos is created and maintained by a common set of democratic values, a pattern of regular interactions and communications, and a set of predictable actions and activities. In a fashioned ethos, a school's organization, management practices, policies, and regulations are constructed and reconstructed as needed along democratic lines. Moreover, educative conditions are selected and environments are cultivated so that the school and classroom are communities. As a democratic ethos is built, restored, and revitalized, the school's activities constitute "a form of social life, a miniature community" (MW9.370). Happily, it is this ethos or "atmosphere and spirit [of a school that] is in the end the chief agent in forming manners [and other morals]" (MW9.22). As the school grows as a community, it needs to be "in close interaction with other modes of associated experience beyond school walls" (MW9.370). As noted above, the school and external communities need to cooperate and act on, as appropriate,[13] democratic values and nourish personal democratic tendencies. In this context, it is understandable why Dewey thinks that schools by themselves cannot build a democratic society. But, with good leadership, schools can develop external community allies with whom they can work toward personal, neighborhood, and political democratic values (LW9.207).

But what is a democratic social group or community and what characterizes its ethos? Perhaps Dewey's claim that a community is a social group that has a common purpose or aim which guides each person's activities is an informative place to begin (MW9.8). A primary idea for him is that a society "is a number of people held together because they are working along common lines, in a common spirit, and with reference to common aims. The common needs and aims demand a growing interchange of thought and growing unity of sympathetic feeling" (MW1.10). On the surface, his emphases may seem undemanding or, alternatively, impossible. Regardless, he stresses that commonalities require deeper and reflective communication about the "aims, beliefs, aspirations, knowledge" of those who are in the process of forming a community because many commonalities do not emerge in the absence of communication (MW9.7). Schools, therefore, must be centers of communication in order to come into being and grow as communities.

A further idea that is buried in Dewey's beliefs about community is that there are at least two overlapping and complementary communities in schools: "*an epistemological community* of inquirers and *a moral community* of citizens."[14] Or, stated differently, members of school communities should be viewed and engaged as inquirers and citizens. For example, the ethos of a school or classroom community ought to be characterized by an open exchange of ideas, sympathetic feelings for one another, equitable opportunities to share ideas, dynamic commonalities and differences. One of his terms may deserve underlining: sympathy.[15] For Dewey, sympathy helps develop in students a social spirit by enabling them to see—understand and feel the importance of—others' viewpoints and, thereby, care for others. So, caring for others and seeing through their eyes can be humbling (LW7.270) and help promote "prudential attitudes" (LW7.211). Likewise, maturing in a community of citizen-learners can promote attitudes and actions that are neither largely impulsive nor merely habitual (LW7.211). Instead, the attitudes and actions are founded on personal and group inquiry, discussion, and reflection. Furthermore, a community of inquiring citizens accelerates learning in what Dewey calls the "hardest lesson," i.e., getting people to value and exhibit cooperativeness (MW8.253, 314).

In the midst of the many school and classroom interactions, moral development is an ordinary consequence of learning sympathy and other virtues. Ideally, to use his terms, honor, fraternal feelings, loyalty, amity, and mutual aid are learned (MW9.88) and, as well, students learn to be conscientious, good, wise, honest, generous, frank, and open (LW7.172–291). Correspondingly, students learn from one another and school staff that sympathy and other qualities lead them to avoid being miserly, careless, obstinate, unscrupulous, cruel, malicious, insensitive, mean, selfish, and corrupt (LW7.174–368). But students are not moral sponges: they learn to analyze and think clearly with key concepts, to identify and use ethical principles, to notice and discuss concealed virtues and vices, to recognize and solve precise problems as they avoid becoming absolutistic and simplistic about moral questions and issues (LW7.273).

While it may be clear why Dewey's school community calls for inquiring teachers and students, it may be less clear why it calls for a moral community of citizens. Perhaps, this lack of clarity is partially rooted in the considerable disregard many in society and institutions have for students as citizens, especially in P-12 schools. To the contrary, Dewey thinks students need to be as highly respected as adults. His rationale is somewhat as follows. First, students are inquirers and citizens[16] in their country and school community and have rights and responsibilities regardless of their ages. Plus, the earlier the two roles—inquirers and citizens—are seen as interrelated and complementary, the greater the probability of a democratic ethic being actualized and made genuine in an "entire educational system" (LW6.98). Manifestly, then, students need both to study and to experience democracy throughout their schooling so that they are knowledgeable in the ways and ideals of democracy before becoming adults. Second, a school or class community is ipso facto a moral community by virtue of the fact that educators and students are a morally responsible social group to one another, to society, and, in the case of educators, to their profession. For school communities to ignore these responsibilities is equivalent to rejecting their duties to nurture respect, promote justice, cultivate freedom, stimulate participation, and foster peace (LW6.94). Third, Dewey believes that a good society is characterized by good people inquiring into and discussing together how they can become a better, more just, free, and humane society. The means of becoming a better society are in "*methods* of inquiry, of observation, experiment, of forming and following working hypotheses" (MW15.7) and realizing that it is in "the quality of *becoming*" or growing that "virtue resides" (LW7.306). Fourth, if an emerging mature citizen understands that she or he has certain rights, privileges, and duties she may be more likely to engage in related activities in school, such as school-related voting, further-ing good student government, enjoying freedoms in constructive and educative ways, and delight-ing in the greatest of freedoms, freedom of intelligence (MW15.167), not to mention being active in their communities in order to encourage voting, community projects, caring for the elderly, and integrity in government.

In the school or classroom community, Dewey expects to see not only a democratic and reflec-tive ethical orientation that fosters the growth of students and educators but also the aesthetic dimen-sions of ethics nurturing an ethos that is characterized by a sense of "symmetry," "proportion," "whole," "grace, rhythm, and harmony" (LW7.271). But, again, what does he mean? Actually, he is building on an ancient belief that there is a "similarity of judgment of good and bad in conduct with the recognition of beauty and ugliness in conduct" (LW7.271). So, it is appropriate to think of stu-dents and educators' acts and behavior creating beautiful, harmonious affections such as compassion, helpfulness, and kindness (LW4.237; LW7.271). In the same way, school officials, classroom teach-ers, and students who show a balanced, properly proportioned fairness and mercifulness when mak-ing moral decisions and taking disciplinary action contribute to an educational ethos that avoids "bleakness and harshness" (LW7.271). A community that is characterized by acting ethically, then, has its own beauty, is fed from the streams of "mental fermentation" (LW7.271–172), personal rela-tionships, and "social spirit" (MW9.368).

Conclusion

Obviously, Dewey's theory of moral education is designed to take full advantage of the opportuni-ties of commonplace and planned societal learning occasions, including but not limited to familial interactions, youth cultures, economic and political philosophies, business practices, government agencies, leisure activities, park surroundings, museum amenities, and recreational facilities. Similarly, it is designed to take full advantage of the opportunities of commonplace and planned school learn-ing occasions, involving but not restricted to athletic programs, school clubs, class trips, school and classroom cultures, volunteer work, lecturettes, group activities, parental and guardian associations, individual assignments, and collateral learning. Doing piecemeal and school-only moral education, therefore, is rarely powerful, frequently ineffective, and nearly always lacking cohesive means and ends that foster democratic values in life's activities and educational institutions. Accordingly, it fol-lows that his theory implies that schools are *a*, not *the* moral force in society. On occasions, howev-er, he partially blames schools for various social and international problems, e.g., racism, classism, and war (LW.9.32). Perhaps, he is inconsistent when he blames schools for these vices. Or, alterna-tively, perhaps he realistically expects more from schools than they are delivering—immediately, fos-tering students who understand that they are part of a series of communities that need them to think reflectively and act sympathetically and, ultimately, promoting mature citizens who look beyond their own welfare to national and international well-being. Clearly, he wants educators to encourage and cultivate democratic values and behavior in schools and in society and thinks they should be held accountable for doing so (MW10.207–208; LW11.416).

Given his overall moral education emphases, it is important to glimpse the tension between Dewey's theories of power, education, change, and morality. Correspondingly, it is worthwhile to keep in mind that his theory of moral education is multifaceted and paradoxical. On the one hand, he claims that moral "concern is with the significance of that slight fraction of total activity which starts from ourselves" (MW14. 143). He believes that—compared with the totality of activity and events in the world, nation, state, community, and, perhaps, school—individual influence is relatively insignificant. He thinks, therefore, the educator needs to be appropriately humble about her or his potential influence while teaching, leading, guiding, coaching, advocating, and befriending. The solitary teacher or administrator needs to recognize that her power in the world as a whole is akin to that of "the mouse [which] is infinitely constricted in comparison with the power of events" (MW14.143). On the other hand, he asserts that what is at stake in any "serious deliberation"—and choosing to teach or become an administrator involves many such occasions—is "what kind of person one is to become, what sort of self is in the making, what kind of world is [in the] making" (MW14.150). The connecting link between these two seemingly contradictory ideas—circumscribed individual action, yet self-creation and world outcomes—is that our individual acts can be "connected with an infinity of events that sustain and support" them (MW14.180). Once again, the individual needs to be humbled—this time in the sense of being awed—by the potential of her or his choices and actions when combined with the energies and intelligence of others in a school community, for she or he has the opportunity to help create a different personal self as well as to help students become different selves as they develop attitudes and disposition to be more "sensitive, generous, imaginative, impartial" and "just, sympathetic" (MW14.144). The educator who sees herself as a part of classroom, school, and neighborhood communities is no longer a solitary self but an engaged member of communities that help change one another and their constituents. In the school, being a part of these events affects the epistemological, pedagogical, anthropological, and ecological moral curricula. In society, the educator helps each segment of it to become "perforce a schoolhouse" (MW7.304), an educational entity that realizes that "learning from all the contacts of life is the essential moral interest" (MW9.370). The educator, thereby, becomes a part of the powerful communities and forces exhibiting and working toward inquiry, intelligence, growth, justice, equality, equity, freedom, sympathy, individuality, and commonalities.

Notes

1. I use the term *neo-Deweyan* to indicate two ideas. First, my interpretation of Dewey no doubt modifies—consciously and unconsciously—his ideas and emphases at times. Second, my ideas in this chapter have been influenced by both experiences and scholars who have extended my thinking beyond Dewey at times.

2. I greatly appreciate the permission of Southern Illinois University Press to use quotations which are taken from *The Collected Works of John Dewey, 1882–1953: The Electronic Edition*, edited by Larry A. Hickman (Charlottesville, VA: InteLex Corp., 1966), which is based on the print edition edited by Jo Ann Boydston (Carbondale: Southern Illinois University Press, 1969–91).

3. For a more complete explanation, see my *John Dewey Primer*.

4. The terms *educator* or *educators* are used to include teachers, administrators, counselors, and others unless the context suggests otherwise.

5. EMC[1] and EMC[2] are used so that the Epistemological Moral Curriculum is not confused with the Ecological Moral Curriculum.

6. References to *The Early Works of John Dewey, 1882–1898; The Middle Works of John Dewey, 1899–1924;* and *The Later Works of John Dewey, 1925–1953* are abbreviated as "EW" (early works), "MW" (middle works)

and "LW" (later works). For instance, (MW9.366) indicates that the material cited or idea noted is in *The Middle Works*, volume 9, page 366.

7. He defines character as "all the desires, purposes, and habits that influence conduct" (LW9.186). Notice that he believes that character influences, but does not necessarily determine, conduct.

8. Although many make legitimate and important distinctions between character education and moral education, I use the terms in this context as approximate synonyms.

9. See, for example, "Open-mindedness, single-mindedness, sincerity, breadth of outlook, thoroughness, assumption of responsibility for developing the consequences of ideas which are accepted, are moral traits" (MW9.366).

10. Important features of Dewey's ethical thinking are found in *Experience and Nature* (LW1), *The Quest for Certainty* (LW4), and *Ethics* (LW7). Among other ideas, he grapples with whether ethical judgments can become secure and how. In the process, he discusses morals as a meaning system that can enrich life, one that is intelligently evaluated by examining experimentally the conditions and consequences of living (LW1.323, 326), a mode of experience which involves affections, meaning, and intelligence (LW4.235–248), and a form of reflective or scientific inquiry drawing on numerous fields, including the natural sciences and aesthetics (LW7.262–283). He criticizes the claims that every aspect of moral experience is a matter of truth or falsity (LW1.307–317), that knowledge ought to be understood as the only means of experiencing reality (LW4.237), and that inquiry and reflection are unrelated to moral theory and decision making (LW7. 262–283). Consequently, his theories of knowledge, ethics, aesthetics, experience, meaning, and judgment intersect and inform moral education. In fact, the quest for knowledge is partly to give meaning or purpose to experience or life. Reasoning is making things meaningful, making sense of things. A science of ethics, then, is a way of thinking about personal and social problems that arrives at a morally secure understanding of rich experiences and meaningful living.

11. For introductory comments and readings regarding Dewey's view of how school leaders should support moral education in schools, see Simpson and Stack's *Teachers, Leaders, and Schools*, pp. 117–160.

12. For a more detailed treatment of the artistry of the teacher and moral education, see Simpson, Jackson, & Aycock's *John Dewey and the Art of Teaching*, pp. 24, 53, 102–105, 109, 182–184.

13. Political or governmental democracy probably cannot be fully practiced in all schools for a variety of reasons, but most democratic values can be exhibited, discussed, learned, practiced, and critiqued in many schools. In addition, schools are well advised to start from the premise that they will become as richly democratic as is possible.

14. For a fuller treatment of these two communities, see Simpson and Jackson's *Educational Reform: A Deweyan Perspective*.

15. Dewey rarely uses the term *empathy*.

16. Obviously, every student in a country is not necessarily a citizen of that country, and every student who is a citizen of a country may not enjoy the full privileges of that country until she or he reaches a certain level of maturity or age. Even so, one of the greatest conceivable pedagogical tragedies would be for teachers to relate to students as non-citizens.

References

Boydston, J. A. (Ed.). (1967–1972). *The early works of John Dewey, 1882–1898*. (Vols. 1–5). Carbondale: Southern Illinois University Press.

_____. (Ed.). (1976–1983). *The middle works of John Dewey, 1899–1924*. (Vols. 1–15). Carbondale: Southern Illinois University Press.

_____. (Ed.). (1981–1991). *The later works of John Dewey, 1925–1953*. (Vols. 1–17). Carbondale: Southern Illinois University Press.

Simpson, D. (2006). *John Dewey primer*. New York: Peter Lang.

Simpson, D., & Jackson, M. (1997). *Educational reform: A Deweyan perspective*. New York: Garland.

Simpson, D., Jackson, M., & Aycock, J. (2005). *John Dewey and the art of teaching: Toward reflective and imaginative practice*. Thousand Oaks, CA: Sage.

Simpson, D., & Stack, Jr., S. (Eds.). (2010). *Teachers, leaders, and schools: Essays by John Dewey*. Carbondale, IL: Southern Illinois University Press.

CHAPTER NINETEEN

Critical Pedagogy and Moral Education

RONALD DAVID GLASS

Beginning with the 1970 publication in English of Paulo Freire's path-setting book, *Pedagogy of the Oppressed*, an extensive literature has emerged in the U.S. that has shaped a discourse often gathered under the rubric of "critical pedagogy." Drawing from its theoretical roots in various streams of Marxism, feminism, and critical theory, this literature has grown branches reaching into more emergent scholarship in critical race theory, postcolonial theories, and other critiques of everyday life that seek to ground emancipatory struggles for a more just and democratic society (Darder, Baltodano, & Torres, 2009). This chapter, rather than reviewing this literature in relation to character education and moral education, sets out three basic frameworks informed by critical pedagogical principles. These frameworks point toward the character and moral attributes required of critical democratic citizens committed to making our institutions and communities more just and participatory and thus provide programmatic guidance for public schooling. The character and moral attributes sketched here resonate with Horace Mann's founding vision for the free, universal public schooling required of a democracy, and with his call to form citizens who would "govern the governors" and use a critical and independent reason to improve society (Cremin, 1957; Mann, 1891).

The theory and practice of character and moral education typically assume that the right thing to do is both discernable and possible to enact in any given situation; they assume that the good person, whose character and moral sensibilities have been shaped and ordered by the most important virtues, will reliably know and do the right thing. Rarely do they consider that doing the right thing might require transgressing the established orders—perhaps repeatedly (Glass, 2002, 2004b). In a similar way, critical pedagogues exhort their compatriots to take moral stands against oppression and exploitation, against racial, gender, class, linguistic and other injustices; they also assert commitments to democratic processes and engaged citizenship. But all too often these exhortations and assertions treat the moral realm as relatively transparent; they assume that those who struggle for justice and democracy personify only the good and that their noble aims cannot embody moral problems of their own (Glass, 2004a, b).

In many ways, however, both theoretical considerations and everyday experience undermine these positions. This does not mean that people do not in fact decide one way or another what the right thing to do is in a particular situation, and, once having made a moral judgment, act in accord with it. Rather it simply means that moral judgments are always susceptible to challenge; moreover, human beings are notoriously lax in following the dictates of those judgments, and this *akrasia* afflicts even virtuous persons of good character. Our dilemmas are daunting, and our rationalizations for our inconsistencies are legion; thus, character and moral education face significant obstacles if they are to honor the truth of the moral domain and prepare people for an ambiguous and psychologically fraught moral life. They must also prepare people for intense social and political conflicts undergirded by moral claims that support as well as critique all sides in the conflicts. Given the disordered terrain on which moral lives must be grounded, what are we to do?

The three frameworks elaborated in this chapter—morality without righteousness; knowledge without certainty; struggle without violence—illuminate these difficulties and identify qualities of character necessary to meet the ethical, epistemic, and political demands of critical citizenship. They also suggest some programmatic requirements for the formation of moral persons with the character and skills essential for the transformation of the unjust and inequitable conditions of the present age.

Morality Without Righteousness

Morality has long sought to provide the answers to the questions: how can we become good persons, and how should we live moral lives? The difficulties in answering these questions have inspired religious leaders and philosophers from antiquity to the present to seek a way to order the human drama of history in a morally satisfactory way. In the search for sound judgments and righteous living, they have established codes and commandments to guide and admonish, created canons of parables for instruction and character formation, called upon reason and logic to ground decision procedures, and cultivated the sentiments to nurture moral understanding. But the moral domain remains unruly and all human characters contain their particular flaws, leaving each of us to face the dilemmas of everyday life without guarantees that our good intentions and best efforts can deliver us from evil.

The population of the United States has been formed from every corner of the globe, bringing into the public sphere a vast array of religious, ethnic, and family traditions, social mores, prized dispositions, conventional norms, and modes of moral reasoning; the questions of how to be good and how one ought to live are debated not only within each particular tradition but also across traditions. Further, these debates occur in dialogue with the legal and institutional frameworks of a democracy. The resultant cacophonous Babel spills into school classrooms, hallways, and boardrooms; at times, the unresolved tensions get taken to the courts as citizens seek adjudication of their claims. The courts themselves have been unsettled in their precedent setting, and questions persist about the place of implicit and explicit religious, moral, and value instruction in schools (Feinberg, 2006).

Character and moral education generally, and critical pedagogy as well, must select what and how to teach when initiating children, youth, or adults into moral conduct. What is not clear is how to justify any particular selection. Further, what does any preferred selection mean in relation to the remaining broad panoply of life shaped through moral language and practices that is not chosen? In the mid-19th century, Horace Mann imagined a set of "universal" values that could provide a foundation for the moral education of democratic citizens; but his unconsciously selective gaze did not see far beyond an ecumenical pan-Protestantism. This prompted resistance from the Catholic Church, which rightly believed public schools marginalized its particular beliefs (NCEA, 2010; Tyack, 1974). It also prompted enduring tensions for the Jewish, Native American, and many other non-Christian communities coping with the psychological stresses and social pressures of assimilation to supposedly universal values (Biale, Galchinsky, & Heschel, 1998; Lomawaima & McCarty, 2006). The debates over values and moral education in U.S. schools have not diminished. Moreover, given the theoretical and practical considerations at the root of the disputes, they are unlikely to be resolved.

Yet critical pedagogy necessitates a satisfactory resolution, if not a kind of certainty, concerning these moral matters since it entails the denunciation of and struggle against injustice as well as the annunciation and practice of more equitable forms of life. How else can oppression, dehumanization, and dominant ideologies be called out as such, be resisted, challenged, and finally transformed? But at the same time, it seems that these committed moral positions must recognize that other possible positions might be justified within a contrasting moral framework. In fact, some of the most unjust historical practices themselves, such as slavery or the inequities faced by women, have been defended precisely on moral and religious grounds. What are we to do if we aim for schools to play a key role in the formation of moral citizens able to navigate these conflicts and both fight against perceived injustices and also work to embody more just and democratic practices?

In complex situations in which multiple forces and moral frameworks interact, making warranted moral judgments and taking committed action against injustice are quite difficult. To deal with this difficulty, we face the challenge of forming a morality without righteousness, forming a commitment to ethical ideals and particular moral judgments that can recognize moral difference and be self-critical and open without losing the force of that committed stance. Sometimes people look to seemingly less complicated settings for guidance about these more difficult moral matters. They imagine that if injustices or immorality reach a certain scale, then any fair-minded person could clearly see the rights and wrongs and see the differences in the characters of the decent and the despicable. Here, they believe, moral judgments are simpler to discern and right actions are clear-cut. Often the heinous Nazi concentration camps are proffered as such an example of obvious demarcations of good and evil. Yet even here, as the Auschwitz survivor Primo Levi movingly argued, moral life is not enacted in blacks and whites but rather in a perpetual gray zone (Levi, 1989).

This is not to say that mass murder is morally ambiguous; it is repulsive and to be condemned and punished in the strongest possible way. Nor is it to say that the victims and survivors somehow share in the guilt of the executioners as if all were on the same moral level. Rather, the point is that the gray zone is the dwelling space of the human character, of the ways in which individual human beings and social collectivities or communities inhabit their morality over time. That is, the human beings carrying out the particular murders of the Nazi state and the social organization developed to enable the murdering to be done were not simply or purely evil. They also demonstrated qualities of character and moral rectitude commonly recognized as admirable; their crimes and moral outrages existed directly within or alongside virtues such as loyalty, courage, cooperation, dedication to tasks done well, love of one's family, etc. This reveals the paradox of the moral qualities of warfare, and it is what led William James to call for a moral equivalent of war as an antidote to war itself (James, 1975; also see Hedges, 2002). The moral domain is never simple.

The gray zone is not just part of the character of war; nor is it only the domain of the banality of evil (Arendt, 1963), although it is that as well. Rather, the gray zone provides the landscape on which the moral contradictions within the character of each individual and every nation or community seem constantly to undermine the ground of morality itself. In the gray zone of Primo Levi's anguish, the devastating quality of his agony was not due to the horrific malevolence so evident in the character of the principal evildoers; rather, it was due to the existential abyss opened up by the evil that resided even within the moral exemplars among the victims. They too might steal from another, perhaps a family member; they might treat another with arrogance and disrespect; they might even collude in the deaths of his or her co-community members and co-victims. The ordinary vices of everyday life (Shklar, 1984), along with the normalization of atrocities, color the character and challenge all claims to righteousness, and also call into question how we should think and teach about goodness, about the possibility and meaning of living a moral life.

Although genocide or mass abominations are not among the moral challenges of our present society, other large-scale harms are; these harms destroy peoples' life chances if not their immediate physical life, and they could be avoided with different institutional and social structures and relationships. For example, in the wealthiest nation on earth, millions of children and adults unnecessarily suffer from poverty and its attendant evils of hunger and malnutrition, of inadequate or nonexistent health and dental care, and of high concentrations of toxins in the environments and housing where they live. Our society, and each of us who has grown up in it, also suffers from particular dominant ideologies—such as racism, sexism, classism, linguicism, and xenophobia—that harm the psychological well-being of millions and undermine their capacity to live fulfilling lives. In fact, public schools themselves, despite the best intentions of their teachers, also perpetuate and enact some of these same harms, turning countless children into 'nobodies' cast to the bottom of the social hierarchy; perhaps the greatest cruelty in which schools are complicit is the way they normalize the suffering and injustices just mentioned and render these social crimes as the outcomes of individual choices in the face of fair opportunities for success (Glass, 2007, 2008, 2009). This is the moral gray zone of everyday life in our schools and society; this is the terrain on which character and moral education, on which critical pedagogy, must operate.

Now we can begin to see the full scale of the challenge presented not just to critical pedagogy but also to public schooling and teachers in general. The evils of the day cannot be kept at bay at the schoolhouse door; the character flaws and virtues that compose the personality of the evildoers are the same as those that compose the personalities of the moral exemplars. The people in the schools, from teachers to students and parents, from administrators to the cafeteria and maintenance staffs, are implicated in the evils of the day, not necessarily because of their intentions but despite them. They are implicated simply by virtue of existing in these systems of gray zones. These are the zones where vast harms are treated as common sense reality, as the "way things are" or even as the way things are meant to be. These are the zones where the myth of personal rectitude salves people's consciences and contributes to the psychological barrier that prevents people from taking full responsibility for their role in the maintenance of the status quo and in the failure to make things better. Because we live in gray zones illuminated only partially by the plurality of moral outlooks and because we have no honest choice but to cling to a morality without righteousness, committing oneself to the struggle to make oneself and the world better also requires a thoroughgoing commitment to humility.

To live with integrity in the gray zone, and to teach others to do the same, requires our awareness of our complicity, and it also requires our awareness of the way that luck and ideology shape the ways we have of being moral, of living lives with moral integrity (Katz, 2009). Those who must contend with the social, economic, and political disadvantages caused by dominant ideologies must also often face greater social risks and pay a higher personal price for living in the morally consistent ways demanded by integrity; for example, gay or lesbian persons may be ostracized or demeaned simply for "being themselves." Similar risks compound the challenges of daily life for those who publicly proclaim their moral critiques of dominant ideologies since those assertions disrupt the established norms of the status quo and position the messenger to be the target of retribution. These threats to living a life of integrity pale in comparison to those from far deeper unconscious motivations and self-deceptions; these threats can obscure the truer meanings and purposes of our judgments, actions, and rationalizations (Blizek, 1999; Katz, 2009). Not only are we shaped by powerful and mysterious sexual drives and survival instincts that often remain unacknowledged and hidden from conscious appraisal, but we also are shaped by dominant ideological systems that similarly inhabit us unawares and affect us in ways that can be nearly impossible to grasp. All of our judgments and actions have multiple layers of moral significance that reach into the most intimate aspects of our character and psychology; at the same time, these layers of moral significance connect outwardly with the historical, social, and cultural meanings of the context of our lives. Thus we dwell at all times in both inner and outer moral gray zones, realms where righteousness has no place and humility must reign.

Critical pedagogy needs to develop the character virtues that make citizens capable of this kind of humble yet committed stance; in addition, it must cultivate other comparably crucial virtues. For example, one must be able to search out and see the limits of one's own judgments, the moral flaws in one's own actions, and the hidden drives and desires in our motivations; one must also be able to hear criticisms of one's own character, outlook, and actions with an open heart and mind. Further, one must understand that complicity in the institutional and ideological evils and harms of the day does not entail a condemnation of guilt; rather, it constitutes a call to responsibility. This requires both a response-ability—a capacity to respond empathetically to the pain and suffering of those who are harmed and suffer innocently—and a conscientious effort to critique and disengage from the structures of oppression or dehumanization. Responsibility also necessitates that we repair the harm being done by dismantling those structures and building more just and humane ones.

At the same time, critical citizens must recognize and respect that others have their own particular moral visions and reasons; thus, one must be capable of listening across differences to discern the virtues present even in those with whom one disagrees. One must develop capacities for shaping the public sphere and social institutions not just to maximize their inclusiveness but also to establish legitimate alternatives for groups that believe that they need them to maintain their integrity. Acknowledging the multiple ways to give content to foundational virtues and moral principles and dialogically engaging these to enrich public discourse, critical citizens manifest character traits and moral sensibilities that foster a democratic way of life. Even so, a critical pedagogical approach offers no escape from the ultimate choice of one way of life and set of moral commitments over another, of critiquing injustice and defending democracy clearly and without equivocation; ultimately, critical pedagogy must still embody a resoluteness that remains open to its own critique, must embody a morality without righteousness.

Knowledge Without Certainty

Even an open resoluteness demands a choice, a commitment to action that assumes a foundation in knowing both the facts of the matter and the rightness of the chosen action. Just as the challenges to knowing the right thing to do in any situation are often more complex and difficult to resolve than we are usually ready to acknowledge, so it is with other forms of knowledge. Knowledge about the natural world warranted through scientific investigations and theorizing cannot entirely escape its historical and perspectival limits (Kuhn, 1962; Lakatos & Musgrave, 1970; Popper, 1963), nor can it escape being shaped by non-neutral human interests (Habermas, 1972). The structure of knowledge about the historical, social, and cultural world in which moral judgments must be made is influenced by the uncertainties underlying scientific ways of knowing as well as by forms of embodied knowing rooted in opaque experience and ideological formations that cloud the clearest vision. Indeed the same constraints and traces seep into the structure of scientific knowledge itself (Alcoff & Potter, 1993; Gergen, 1988). These foundational epistemic limits preclude the very sorts of assurances that many people yearn for and that our everyday common sense assumes. Thus, I will next explore how knowledge without certainty bears on some aspects of the moral domain and on critical pedagogy's insistence on morally committed transformative action that claims to know certain truths about the world and about political and ideological matters.

Some argue that moral outlooks or theories should be considered to be akin to natural languages, each with its own conception of the good, ordering of virtues, favored character traits, and form of life (Hampshire, 1983). Such irreducible plurality presents special challenges since it assures that disagreement and conflict cannot be eliminated from the moral and political realm. Because moral conceptions, like languages, are plural, with no universal way to adjudicate or indisputably translate among them (Quine, 1960), claiming to know some singular right thing to do in a given situation always remains problematic. These difficulties of moral discernment are commonly acknowledged even when people are not casting a philosophic gaze on the issues; they are the stuff of countless dinner table conversations and heart-felt chats among friends, as well as the grist for stories passed down through the generations. Even for a particular person whose outlook and value structure fit squarely within the current predominant modes of moral thinking in the Judeo-Christian, Greco-Roman traditions, competing conceptual frames, tenets, and modes of reasoning can lead to contrary judgments.

Considering only utilitarianism, one family of ethical theories that makes judgments by weighing the consequences of actions, we find that differences in the judgment of the right thing to do still exist and cannot be eliminated. That is, alternative ways of weighing or comparing consequences, and of construing the scope of an action's consequences, lead to contrasting decisions (Mill, 1861/1975; Sen & Williams, 1982). Should only the specific action and its immediate consequences be assessed, or should an assessment include consequences that might result if the rule for that action were a general rule, not just for the decision-maker but also for others? How widely and how far into the future should the causal chain be followed to parse the consequences of an action? How should secondary or unintended effects count in assessing the consequences of a particular action? Can we know the future with sufficient certitude to judge different courses of action and their consequences? In judging actions and consequences, can all forms and amounts of pain or happiness legitimately be compared on a single scale of value? Can happiness experienced by one person offset pain suffered by another person? Can there be negative consequences for one person or for a group of people that are of a type or scale as to be impermissible regardless of the positive consequences for others? Clearly, different responses to one or more of these questions yield very different conclusions about the right thing to do; yet these variant judgments and modes of reasoning all reside within the confines of a single ethical tradition. These complexities readily become visible in our daily lives; they arise in the ordinary practice of listing positive and negative outcomes from an action to decide the right thing to do. They also arise in the frequent public policy debates that construct similar lists at the social level to ascertain what is best for the common good.

Other, quite different, mainstream approaches to knowing the right thing to do exist in the Western tradition, and these pay virtually no attention to the consequences of actions. Immanuel

Kant's categorical imperative, perhaps the most prominent among these other views, seeks to establish universal rules of duty—the right thing to do is the right thing to do for every person in a similar situation, regardless of the consequences for oneself or others—and to insure that human beings are always treated as ends in themselves, and never treated as a means to some other end (Kant, 1785/1959). The Kantian conception of morality can be roughly translated as an absolute prohibition against making an exception for oneself from following a moral rule; it can also be construed as the Biblical Golden Rule of "do unto others as you would have done unto you." The ubiquity of these common lessons taught to children throughout the U.S. belies the frequent conflicts among duties that occur and that then need some further appeal to decide between or among them. This appeal typically finds its resolution in a calculation comparing the differences in the consequences from making one duty rather than another the decisive duty for judging the right thing to do. As in the case of utilitarian or consequentialist theories, we cannot always provide conclusive moral direction even after a careful consideration of the applicable moral rules, and a commitment to treating others as we want to be treated, with respect as a person. Conflicts between duties can emerge, and interpretations of respect can diverge. If we then turn again to weighing the effects of various actions to discover the right thing to do, our pursuit once more can founder on incompatible conclusions. Certainty still eludes moral knowledge.

The uncertainties associated with both consequentialist and Kantian theories are somewhat beside the point according to some other common accounts of morality. Moral perspectives grounded in religion draw upon faith in inspired scriptures and long-standing traditions to inculcate obedience to holy will and divine law; this disciplined obedience shapes moral judgments and the virtues in firm accord with the certain authority of those same scriptures and traditions. In these religious views, any uncertainty comes simply from confusion about the ultimate basis of morality, and once a person achieves clarity on the primacy of the sacred, then knowledge of the right thing to do is revealed. Certainty derives from the dictates of true belief or faith, and other views are merely mistaken. Many people who hold this view of morality have no doubt whatsoever about which are the right character traits and the correct form of moral reasoning, and they similarly have no doubt about the right thing to do in any situation. Yet, as the arguments in this chapter show and the fact of the diversity of religious views demonstrates, this view, however common it might be, is untenable as the foundational framework for character and moral education in the public schools of a pluralistic democracy; at the same time, this view must still be granted some degree of free space within the public sphere.

Feminist thinkers and researchers provide an entirely different account of why we should not be particularly concerned with the uncertainties that persist after careful application of ethical decision procedures. These theorists critique the dominant moral traditions for ignoring women's actual social, psychological, and moral development (Gilligan, 1982). They rethink the moral domain from the perspective of maintaining the caring relationships that concern women as they navigate the moral dynamics of their everyday lives (Noddings, 1984). They argue that human relationships, and not rational arguments about justice and ethics, are central to moral reasoning; and they resurrect and reframe the role of sentiments and emotions in moral life, going beyond the position advocated by Hume (1739/1978) to put a relational self at the core of moral experience. This not only recasts the notions of autonomy and rationality in the dominant moral theories but also calls into question the very aim of attempting to arrive at universal ethical principles by which to order moral life (Kittay & Myers, 1987).

In place of this mistaken and vain goal, feminist theorists seek to discover the right thing to do through attending to specific people located within specific relationships and concrete social, cultural, and historical contexts rather than through envisioning the perspective of some generalized other. Not only does this make knowledge about the right thing to do inescapably particular, it also brings out the ways in which multiple actions and outcomes can be considered good. As we engage the nuances of the moral dilemmas of life and probe the complexities of the lives entangled in the dilemmas, we often can discover a number of ways to resolve the conflicts and restore or establish a moral relationship among the people involved. This approach seeks the moral and overall well-being of each person caught in the knot of the dilemma; its deliberations put care for persons at the center, not decision procedures.

Keeping in mind the diversity of moral standpoints and right choices in situations, many feminist moral theories also emphasize critical political projects as necessary to transform the commonsense understanding of reality even to make their moral concerns stand out as such (Card, 1991). For example, biological explanations of human beings naturalized many forms of male aggression or violence against women; to clarify the moral quality of these actions and provide a basis for changes in custom and law, it became necessary to uncover the explanations as interpretations and not scientific fact. In other words, feminists' de/reconstruction of the moral domain often has to include a similar de/reconstruction of the truth about reality.

We thus see in feminist moral theory that once again neither moral nor 'objective' knowledge can claim certainty, and to live with and through this uncertainty requires the formation of particular character and moral traits. The preferred modes of education would nurture the development of empathy and other emotional sensibilities that comprehend the nuances of interpersonal differences and relationships, and that grasp the social, cultural, and historical forces shaping human communities. Rather than fostering skills in decision procedures, this approach fosters modes of understanding and awareness that enrich engagement with others in moral deliberation and dialogue.

As this discussion of various moral traditions reveals, it is difficult to know the right thing to do because the basis for decision making as well as the very facts of the matter do not necessarily admit of a singular determination. This knowledge without certainty becomes further complicated because the character virtues that imbue moral life reside within specific historical, social, and cultural contexts. Thus, even when they have evolved within a distinct tradition, the virtues find expression in substantively different meanings and embodiments, and they cannot be known independently of those particular manifestations (MacIntyre, 1984). Courage, loyalty, commitment to a job done well, love of family, integrity, honesty, respect for others, empathy, commitment to justice—each can appear in starkly contrasting ways and can be marshaled either in defense of or in critique of particular social, cultural, and political institutions.

In summary, we must be moral under conditions of epistemic uncertainty because: 1) the facts of the situation remain subject to question since they are rooted in particular social and historical contexts, shaped by particular perspectives and interests, and tinged by ideology; 2) the judgment of the right thing to do varies depending on the outcome of a decision calculus that varies both across and within moral traditions, some of which even deny the legitimacy of such a calculus due to emotional, relational, and contextual factors; and, 3) a virtuous character means variant and contradictory things, even within a single moral perspective, which itself is always subject to historical development. So, if we cannot know with certainty the facts, the right decision, or even the virtues to bring to bear in the situation, what are we to do?

Critical pedagogy intentionally constructs its approach precisely on the unsettled but still supportive ground of knowledge without certainty, and it recognizes the ethical qualities of this form of knowing. It understands knowledge-creation as part of the human condition, as a never-ending process that continually re-creates what was known before while striving to know it better and to know it from fresh perspectives (Freire, 1994, 1998). Critical pedagogy embraces truth seeking, not truth. It honors every form of knowing for whatever it brings to a grasp of the 'how' and 'why' of the present situation. This kind of knowledge lacks certainties or guarantees; it embodies a provisional knowing that can always be known better. Knowledge becomes known better through understanding and acknowledging its own historical context, its own susceptibility to ideological distortion, and its own need to be criticized and re-created. To dwell in the openings established by this kind of knowledge requires its own virtues or morally inflected epistemic capacities: to discern and critique contradictions; to grasp multiple simultaneous viewpoints; to accept ambiguity and error as part of the way forward; to encourage criticism of one's own position; to engage in disciplined self-criticism of one's facts, and the ideologies and interests shaping them. More such epistemic virtues could be mentioned, but this list provides a sufficient sketch of how knowledge without certainty figures centrally to the ethical position of critical pedagogy and to the character traits it strives to form through its practices.

Struggle Without Violence

In a social and political context marked by multiple competing versions of both truth and morality and by formal commitments to democracy and justice, conflict and struggle cannot be eliminated from public discourse, policy, and institutions. In fact, when constrained in warranted but minimal ways— by prohibitions against oppression of minority views and groups and against discriminatory policies, institutions, and opportunities—these conflicts and struggles provide the very mechanisms for strengthening democracy and the moral improvement of society (Gutmann & Thompson, 1996). They also guide democratic education and enable citizens to assume their civic duties and responsibilities (Gutmann, 1987). Similarly, these moral conflicts and competing visions of the good life provide a reasonable basis for people to agree on what would constitute a minimal conception of procedural justice, one that insures that individuals and groups have an equal voice in public matters and equal rights to participate in decisions that affect their welfare (Hampshire, 1983).

But of course, concern for the truth, for an equal opportunity to voice positions and participate in decision-making, and for the fair and respectful treatment of all does not particularly hold sway in politics or in the institutions of civil society; here the preeminence of power predominates. Too often today, a coarsened political discourse marked by the ascendancy of propagandistic misinformation and lies reduces candidates and elected officials to vehement denunciations of one another while cloaking themselves in moral rhetoric. Thus, to believe that character and moral education can prepare citizens simply to be virtuous and 'get along nicely' as they strive to work through their disagreements is naïve. The formation of citizens capable of engaging fruitfully with the conflicts of moral and political life must concern itself with still deeper rents in the fabric of the nation. In fact, the institutions of government, including its schools, differentially treat certain citizens unfairly, systematically advantaging some and disadvantaging others; moreover, the government often fails to intervene to remedy structural inequities in other institutions of civil society, such as those involved in health care, that bear directly on its citizens' life chances. Those citizens unjustly treated in these ways not only do not bear the same obligations to the body politic as other citizens, they have good warrants for disobeying and resisting the social and legal orders that oppress them (Walzer, 1970).

That is, governmental and social institutions require substantive transformation in order for all citizens to exercise the more modulated forms of having a voice, participating in decision-making, and working through conflicts that standard notions of democratic institutions and citizenship entail. Critical pedagogy foregoes neutrality and aims precisely at equipping unjustly treated citizens with the intellectual and emotional dispositions, and with the capacities for action, needed in the protracted struggle to achieve an equal ground with other citizens. These struggles for justice aim at the ideological and institutional limits that constrain people's human right to be freely self-determining, by the light of their own reason and sense of moral goodness. Critical pedagogy enables people to create a meaningful life, shaping their culture and becoming subjects in history able to transcend the conditions that make them the objects of the decisions of others (Freire, 1994). Because the ideological frameworks undergirding common sense reinforce social and institutional injustices, critical citizens must often 'behave badly' in conventional terms to overcome oppression; thus, to assert their humanity and basic civil rights, Blacks broke Jim Crow laws and women broke with social and religious norms that kept them subservient. Admittedly, these breaks with the status quo and the struggles against unjust institutions and customs also entail causing some harm, however minimal, to some of those who resist the forward movement of justice. As Frederick Douglass (1857) proclaimed:

> The whole history of the progress of human liberty shows that all concessions yet made to her august claims have been born of earnest struggle....If there is no struggle there is no progress. Those who profess to favor freedom and yet deprecate agitation are men who want crops without plowing up the ground; they want rain without thunder and lightning. They want the ocean without the awful roar of its many waters. This struggle may be a moral one, or it may be a physical one, and it may be both moral and physical, but it must be a struggle. Power concedes nothing without a demand. It never did and it never will.

The necessity of these struggles, and their ensuing harms, whether quiet or thunderous, cannot dissolve the moral bonds that tie critical citizens to one another and also to their political opponents. Unlike those filled with righteous certainty, who often feel morally bound only to their kin and kith and thus are unconstrained in pursuit of their moral ends, critical citizens hold the same moral regard for their adversaries as for their allies. Thus, for critical citizens, morality without righteousness and knowledge without certainty find their realization in struggle without violence. Fortunately, Mahatma Gandhi and Martin Luther King, Jr., provided ample lessons in the theory and practice of nonviolence that reveal how forceful committed action can remain consistent with moral and epistemic constraints and can retain a moral connection even to sworn enemies (Ansbro, 2000; King, 1991). This capacity to maintain a moral stance even within an intense struggle comprises a significant element of the force of nonviolence.

Critical citizens prepared for struggle without violence seek neither heroism nor martyrdom; without righteousness or certainty, their fight against injustice and entrenched powers, against dehumanizing ideologies and economic exploitation, is both more humble and more far-reaching. Moreover, the coercive force required in the confrontations to achieve justice and in the preparation of citizens to engage these battles dirties the hands of critical citizens and educators, prompting an expanded sense of moral responsibility (Glass, 2002; Walzer, 1974). Only people committed to the ongoing moral relationships and struggles that forge democratic polities can maintain a moral position in the crucible of these deep conflicts; the practice of nonviolence makes this possible since it both provides the necessary force to transform calcified structures of injustice and sustains the respect and moral engagement necessary to confront the opponents of change for a more just and democratic future (Glass, 2001). We have no choice but to live in moral gray zones with flawed characters and dirty hands, and we have no choice but to decide and act always on incomplete and uncertain knowledge. Thus, we have the right to struggle for our truths and the good we seek to embody, putting our own lives at risk; thus, without righteousness or certainty available to ground our moral position, we must abandon any claim of a right to risk our opponents' lives or use violence against them.

Concluding Comments

In this chapter, we have seen that a critical pedagogy approach to moral education takes its direction not from a consideration of the virtues that might arise in an ideal world and within a single moral perspective but from the virtues required to transform the actual conditions of injustice that permeate everyday life and from the actual complexities of the moral realm. This path follows difficult terrain and requires critical citizens to carry heavy burdens to traverse it. But perhaps this burden is no greater than that imposed by the denial of these realities, which insures a longer period of suffering from the inequities of the day, and at least the burden well borne offers some promise of a better tomorrow.

Undeniably, critical pedagogy's character and moral requirements entail facing up to the terrifying realities, moral obscurities, and irresolvable uncertainties of everyday life, and entail taking hold of the enormous weight of critical citizenship. If we care about justice and democracy, we can do no more and no less than stake our lives on the moral judgments we make without righteousness, on the truths we discover without certainty, on the struggles we undertake with respect and determination. Then we take our own small place in the ebb and flow of history, assured that the burdens may be heavy, but they are not ours alone to carry. When schools and educators everywhere step up to their own parts and shape character and moral education to the necessities of critical citizenship, then we will have created a public education worthy of its promise. Perhaps then some day after that, we will have created a nation worthy of its citizens.

> It is fundamental for us to know that without certain qualities or virtues, such as a generous loving heart, respect for others, tolerance, humility, a joyful disposition, love of life, openness to what is new, a disposition to welcome change, perseverance in the struggle, a refusal of determinism, a spirit of hope, and openness to justice, progressive pedagogical practice is not possible. (Freire, 1998, p. 108)

Note

I am indebted to Michael Katz, Samara Foster, and Susan Verducci for insightful comments on an earlier draft that enabled me to clarify obscurities, correct errors, and make many substantive improvements to this chapter. I also am indebted to Linnea Beckett for assistance with preparing the references. I solicit the reader's forbearance for all remaining deficiencies in the text.

References

Alcoff L. & Potter, E. (Eds.). (1993). *Feminist Epistemologies*. New York: Routledge.

Ansbro, J. J. (2000). *Martin Luther King Jr.: Nonviolent Strategies and Tactics for Social Change*. Lanham, MD: Madison.

rendt, H. (1963). *Eichmann in Jerusalem: A Report on the Banality of Evil*. New York: Viking.

Aristotle. (1985). *Nicomachean Ethics*. (T. Irwin, Trans.). Indianapolis, IN: Hackett.

Biale, D., Galchinsky, M., & Heschel, S. (Eds.). (1998). *Insider/Outsider: American Jews and Multiculturalism*. Berkeley: University of California Press.

Blizek, W. (1999). Caring, Justice, and Self-Knowledge. In M.S. Katz, N. Noddings, & K.A. Strike (Eds.), *Justice and Caring: The Search for Common Ground in Education* (pp. 93–109). New York: Teachers College Press.

Card, C. (Ed.). (1991). *Feminist Ethics*. Lawrence, KS: University Press of Kansas.

Cremin, L. (Ed.). (1957). *Horace Mann: The Republic and the School*. New York: Teachers College Press.

Darder, A., Baltodano, M. & Torres, R. D. (Eds.). (2009). *The Critical Pedagogy Reader* (2nd ed.). New York: RoutledgeFalmer.

Douglass, F. (1857). Two Speeches by Frederick Douglass. Rochester, NY. Retrieved on October 30, 2010 from: http://www.blackpast.org/

Feinberg, W. (2006). *For Goodness Sake: Religious Schools and Education for Democratic Citizenry*. New York: Routledge.

Freire, P. (1994). *Pedagogy of the Oppressed* (Revised 20th Anniversary Edition). New York: Continuum.

Freire, P. (1998). *Pedagogy of Freedom: Ethics, Democracy, and Civic Courage*. Lanham, MD: Rowman & Littlefield.

Gergen, M. M. (Ed) (1988). *Feminist Thought and the Structure of Knowledge*. New York: New York University Press.

Gilligan, C. (1982). *In a Different Voice: Psychological Theory and Women's Development*. Cambridge, MA: Harvard University Press.

Glass, R. D. (2008). Education and the ethics of democratic citizenship. In S. Verducci, M. Katz, G. Biesta (Eds.), *Education, Democracy, and the Moral Life* (pp. 9–30). Dordrecht, Netherlands: Springer Verlag. (Reprinted from *Studies in Philosophy and Education*. (2000), *19*(3), 275–296.

Glass, R. D. (2007). What is democratic education? In W. Hare & J.P. Portelli (Eds.), *Key Questions for Educators* (105–108). San Francisco, CA: Caddo Gap.

Glass, R. D. (2004a). Moral and political clarity and education as a practice of freedom. In M. Boler (Ed.), *Democratic Dialogue and Education: Troubling Speech, Disturbing Silence* (pp. 15–32). New York, NY: Peter Lang.

Glass, R. D. (2004b). Pluralism, justice, democracy and education: Conflict and citizenship. In K. Alston (Ed), *Philosophy of Education* (pp. 158–166). Urbana, IL: Philosophy of Education Society.

Glass, R. D. (2002). On transgression, moral education, and education as a practice of freedom. In S. Rice (Ed), *Philosophy of Education* (pp. 120–128). Urbana, IL: Philosophy of Education Society.

Glass, R .D. (2001). Paulo Freire's philosophy of praxis and the foundations of liberation education. *Educational Researcher*. American Educational Research Association. *30*(2), 15–25.

Gutmann, A. (1987). *Democratic Education*. Princeton, NJ: Princeton University Press.

Gutmann, A. & Thompson, D. (1996). *Democracy and Disagreement*. Cambridge, MA: Belknap.

Habermas, J. (1972). *Knowledge and Human Interests*. (J.Shapiro, Trans.). Boston, MA: Beacon.

Hampshire, S. (1983). *Morality and Conflict*. Cambridge, MA: Harvard University Press.

Hedges, C. (2002). *War Is a Force That Gives Us Meaning*. New York: Random House.

Horton, M. & Freire, P. (1990). *We Make the Road by Walking: Conversations on Education and Social Change*. Philadelphia, PA: Temple University Press.

Hume, D. (1739/1978). *A Treatise of Human Nature*. Oxford, England: Clarendon.

James, W. (1906/1975). *The Moral Equivalent of War*. Santa Cruz, CA: William James Association and Press.

Kant, E. (/1785/1959). *The Foundations of the Metaphysics of Morals*. (L.W. Beck, Trans). Indianapolis, IN: Bobbs-Merrill.

Katz, M. (2009). Teaching with Integrity. In R. D. Glass (Ed.), *Philosophy of Education* (pp. 1–11). Urbana, IL: Philosophy of Education Society.

King, M. L. Jr. (1991). Letter from Birmingham City Jail. In C. Carson et al. (Eds.), *The Eyes on the Prize: Civil Rights Reader: Documents, Speeches, and Firsthand Accounts from the Black Freedom Struggle, 1954–1990* (pp. 153–158). New York: Penguin.

Kittay, E. F. & Meyers, D. T. (Eds.). (1987). *Women and Moral Theory*. Lanham, MD: Rowman & Littlefield.

Kuhn, T. (1962). *The Structure of Scientific Revolutions*. Chicago, IL: University of Chicago Press.

Lakatos, I. & Musgrave, A. (1970). *Criticism and the Growth of Knowledge*. Cambridge, England: Cambridge

University Press.

Levi, P. (1989). The Gray Zone. In *The Drowned and the Saved* (pp. 36–69). New York: Vintage.

Lomawaima, T. S. & McCarty, T. L. (2006). *To Remain an Indian*. New York: Teachers College Press.

MacIntyre, A. (1984). *After Virtue* (2nd ed.). Notre Dame, IN: Notre Dame University Press.

Mann, H. (1891). On the Purposes of the Common School, from *The Means and Objects of Common School Education* (1836). In M. Mann (Ed.), *Life and Works of Horace Mann*. (pp. 77–86). Boston: Lee and Shepard.

Mill, J. S. (1861/1957). *Utilitarianism*. Indianapolis, IN: Bobbs-Merrill.

NCEA—National Catholic Education Association. (2010). Historical Overview of Catholic Schools in America. Downloaded October 28, 2010. http://www.ncea.org/about/historicaloverviewofcatholicschoolsinamerica.asp.

Noddings, N. (1984). *Caring: A Feminine Approach to Ethics and Moral Education*. Berkeley, CA: University of California Press.

Popper, K. R. (1963). *Conjectures and Refutations*. New York: Harper & Row.

Quine, W. V. O. (1960). *Word and Object*. Cambridge, MA: MIT Press.

Sen, A. & Williams, B. (Eds.). (1982). *Utilitarianism and Beyond*. Cambridge, England: Cambridge University Press.

Shklar, J. (1984). *Ordinary Vices*. Cambridge, MA: Belknap.

Tyack, D. (1974). *The One Best System*. Cambridge, MA: Harvard University Press.

Walzer, M. (1970). *Obligations: Essays on War, Disobedience, and Citizenship*. Cambridge, MA: Harvard University Press.

Walzer, M. (1974). Political Action: The Problem of Dirty Hands. In M. Cohen, T. Nagel & T. Scanlon (Eds.), *War and Moral Responsibility* (pp. 62–84). Princeton, NJ: Princeton University Press.

CHAPTER TWENTY

Feminist Theory and Moral Education

BARBARA J. THAYER-BACON

Introduction

As a professor in a Cultural Studies in Education program, I teach a graduate course every other fall semester titled "Feminist Theory in Education."[1] We begin that course by bringing in various definitions of *feminist* to share and discuss with one another. It is important to begin by defining our terms for we live in a world where media images of feminists as man-hating, bra-burning lesbians are still prevalent, including among right-wing radio talk show hosts such as Rush Limbaugh, who continue to refer to feminists as femi-Nazis. Feminists joke that the concept is "the F word." Many of my students are uncomfortable about claiming they are feminists until we carefully define the term and trouble the propaganda. I have yet to have a student who is in favor of gender discrimination or who thinks women should not have the right to vote, equal access to higher education, or the right to equal pay for equal work. These are the kinds of rights the feminist movement has fought long and hard for. We decide we are all feminists, for we all are opposed to discrimination and oppression on the basis of gender. We are all in agreement that women have been oppressed and unjustly treated throughout time and across cultures, although not by all cultures. Various Native American tribes/nations stand as strong counterexamples of cultures that developed spiritual beliefs and ways of living that honored women and treated them as equals.

Feminism, by definition, is committed to exploring gendered dimensions and the restrictive nature of sex roles, believing that women historically have been oppressed and unjustly treated by human institutions and social relationships. Feminism is concerned with the forms and functions of power and how power has been wielded against women. One of my favorite definitions is Elizabeth Minnich's (1983), who defines feminism, at its most basic level, as having "to do with a cast of mind; a way of thinking, and a movement of heart and spirit; a way of being and acting with and for others. The cast of mind is fundamentally one of critique; the movement of heart is toward friendship"

(p. 317). Elaborating further on the cast of mind, Minnich says: "Feminist thought takes nothing as given or settled for all time. It accepts no truths as revealed and holds none to be directly reflective of what is "natural," and so unquestionable" (p. 318).

In *Feminist Epistemologies*, Linda Alcoff and Elizabeth Potter (1993) note in their introductory essay that feminists began contributing to philosophy from the margins, and they have moved to the center. The margins are the applied fields, in particular applied ethics, which is where feminist work was first published. "Feminist philosophers began work in the applied areas because feminism is, first and last, a political movement concerned with practical issues, and feminist philosophers understood their intellectual work to be a contribution to the public debate on crucial practical issues" (such as the right to equal job opportunities, and to own property) (p. 2). The center, or what Alcoff and Potter call "the 'core' areas" of philosophy are epistemology and metaphysics.

It is important to note right up front that feminists don't all agree with each other. Contrary to popular opinion, which tends to lump all feminists together as if we are all alike, feminists come in many shapes and sizes. Classical liberal feminists, such as Simone de Beauvoir (1952/1989), focus on women achieving the same status and equal treatment as men while Marxist feminists such as Nancy Harstock (1983) place a strong emphasis on economic issues in relation to gender, social feminists such as Alison Jaggar (1983) and myself focus on gender within larger social contexts, and Black feminists such as Patricia Hill Collins (1990) and bell hooks (1984) bring race into the mix with gender in important ways. Radical feminists, such as Mary Daly (1978/1990) and Luce Irigaray (1974/1985a, 1985b) work to get "women" as a basic analytic category out from under male influence altogether. An academic department in higher education cannot hire one feminist and think they have now achieved fair representation of all feminist theory, anymore than a student can take one course with a feminist teacher and think they know what all feminist teachers are like. It's absurd to think we would fall into such an over-generalizing trap, and yet the mistake is made again and again in hiring practices as well as decisions for conference scheduling and journal publishing.

My plan for this chapter is to trace the history of the feminist movement in the USA and further explore various meanings of feminist theory, and then consider what feminist theory contributes to moral education. I write this chapter in a manner that models a feminist style of scholarship, from a first-person perspective in which my voice can be heard and my identity is not hidden. Feminist scholars have argued for the value of this style of writing, a style that acknowledges that scholars are situated knowers, embedded and embodied, and they need to reveal their situatedness to the reader. It is a form of writing/scholarship that breaks down artificial barriers between the public and private, between the knower and knowledge, a point that will be very relevant when we turn to considering feminist theory in moral education.

History of Feminist Theory

In the United States the feminist movement is associated with three waves, or periods of time, with the "first-wave" feminist movement (1848–1920s) representing women's efforts to get the right to vote, to own property, to divorce and receive alimony and child support, and to manage their own bodies (e.g., sexual reproductive rights). First-wave feminism is associated with Seneca Falls, New York, and the sustained agitation for concrete social change of suffragettes such as Lucretia Mott, Elizabeth Cady Stanton, Susan B. Anthony, and Sojourner Truth.

The "second wave" of the feminist movement corresponds to the 1960s–70s and to women's efforts to obtain equal access to higher education in all fields of study and to be free from discrimination in the workplace due to their gender. While second-wave feminists sought equal treatment in the classroom and on the job, they continued the fight for the right to manage their own bodies (e.g., sexual reproductive rights). Second-wave feminism is associated with *Ms. Magazine,* Betty Friedan, Gloria Steinem, and Mary Daly, to name a few. It was during this time that women's studies programs opened on college campuses across the country, and feminist theory began to develop in earnest. This is also when "the pill" became available as a form of birth control and *Roe v. Wade* passed in the Supreme Court.

Starting in the early 1990s, a "third wave" of the feminist movement began to develop. This third wave represents an explosion of multiple, diverse perspectives as Third World, lesbian, Chicana, Indigenous, Black feminists, and others add their voices to the movement. They critique the essentializing of "woman" as a category, one that has privileged heterosexuality, First-World, middle class, and White norms. Third-wave feminism is associated with Audre Lorde, Adrienne Rich, María Lugones, Gloria Anzaldùa, Judith Butler, Luce Irigaray, Donna Haraway, Gayatri Spivak, and Trinh Minh-ha, to name a few.

Beyond a general agreement that women have been oppressed and unjustly treated and that discrimination on the basis of gender is wrong, there is much upon which various feminists do not agree. It is dangerous to assume there is a "female point of view" or that women have special resources available to them due to their experiences as females. It is problematic to think that only women can be feminists. In fact, some postmodern feminist scholars such as Judith Butler and Luce Irigaray recommend that we get rid of "gender" as a general category, because of the false binary it establishes (man/woman) and the androcentric and/or heterosexual norms and standards it imposes on people's shifting sexual identities. The feminist movement, in all its waves, has helped us understand that the personal is political, that what goes on in the home is very much related to how one's larger society defines one's gendered roles, and that those roles need to be critiqued. Feminists have demonstrated that language is not gender neutral, but in fact affects our consciousness, and that social institutions are not natural or given and therefore settled for all time. Feminist theory reveals how gender roles are socially constructed, by showing how they have varied across time and cultures and how they continue to adapt and change. Feminism is concerned with the forms and functions of power and how power is wielded, in particular against girls and women.

Feminist Theory and Education

During the second wave of feminist research, much focus was placed on discrimination issues within educational settings (Frazier & Sadker, 1973; Sadker & Sadker, 1982; Sadker, Sadker & Long, 1989; Sadker & Sadker, 1995; Spender, 1982; Stacey, Bercaud, & Daniels 1974; Stanworth, 1983; Thorne & Henley, 1975). Researchers looked at tracking issues, and why it is that girls were tracked into "traditionally feminine" classes such as childcare, home economics, and nursing, and not honors classes and higher-level math and science classes. Attention was placed on studying what teachers do in schools to discourage girls, such as not calling on them as often as boys or not giving them the opportunity to correct their mistakes before moving on to someone else (usually a boy). Attention was also placed on the curriculum and how girls were presented in pictures and stories in comparison to boys. Researchers looked at ways students are assessed and began to consider the possibility that what was taken to be gender-neutral and unbiased methods of assessment might actually favor boys over girls, given the clear indication that in fact boys do consistently score higher on field-independent, analytically focused material, such as multiple-choice exams, while girls tend to do better on essay-type exams which are field dependent. During this time, curricula became open to both genders, and efforts began to be made to actively encourage girls to achieve at the same levels as boys.

In university settings, with the opening of women's studies programs during the second wave, faculty began to explore gender issues and to consider if there was gender discrimination at the higher education level, with students, faculty, and administrators. Faculty began to critically examine their philosophies of teaching to discover if the way they taught, how they assessed students, their expectations, and their curriculum, for example, were gender biased. They turned a critical eye on their curriculum and discovered that women's contributions as scholars and artists were missing. It was hard to find their work included in texts, and if they were included they were relegated to the margins, as the final chapter in the book that no one seemed to get to, or in boxes on the margins and at the end of chapters. More women were admitted to college than ever before during the second wave, but still not in equal proportions or under the same standards as men.

During the second wave of the feminist movement, much effort was placed on trying to recover women's work from the past, and to protect that earlier work that was rescued from biased male presentations of it, to allow the women to speak for themselves. This work continues today. See, for example, Jane Roland Martin's (1985) *Reclaiming a Conversation* and Charlene Haddock Seigfried's (1996) *Pragmatism and Feminism.* Another example of the gender problem is Simone de Beauvoir's (1952/1989) *The Second Sex,* which was translated into English by a male editor without her permission and with her disapproval in regard to the translation. Also during this period of time, scholars began to realize that most studies that were used to shape the development of fields of study, such as psychology, were based on studies of males with the theories developed assumed to be general and applicable to all human beings, regardless of gender. We began to see research that focused on women and girls, such as Carol Gilligan's (1982) work, *In a Different Voice,* and Belenky, Clinchy, Goldberger, and Tarule's (1986) study, *Women's Ways of Knowing,* that drew attention specifically to women and girls and developed theories based on interviews and observations of them. We also began to find feminist scholars who argued for qualities women have and experiences they have that are specific to their gender and have been devalued and marginalized but need to be recognized and valued in society. Care theories are examples of gender-based theories, such as Nel Noddings' (1984) *Caring,* and Sara Ruddick's (1989) *Maternal Thinking,* as well as Sandra Harding's (1986, 1991) feminist standpoint epistemology.

In women's studies courses, during the second wave, feminist professors began to explore alternative methods of instruction and to critically examine their role as teachers as well as their students' roles. Critiques were developed for standard lecture styles of teaching and the passive role in which they positioned students. It became more common to see chairs organized in circles instead of rows in college classrooms, and to have teachers encouraging their students to share their personal lives in the public classroom space as well as for teachers to break down the public/private split and to soften their role as authorities by sharing with students their personal lives as well in the classroom space. Questions concerning the teacher's role as authority and students' roles as active learners and co-constructors of knowledge were openly discussed in classrooms and written about in feminist theory. Small-group discussions and collaborative approaches to teaching were developed, in contrast to competitive models. Performance and portfolio forms of assessment were developed as well as group grades.

Third-wave feminism has contributed to feminist theory in education by critiquing second-wave feminist theory for its lack of attention to other power issues that influence varied gendered experiences and expressions. Attention is currently being placed on the assumed positions of power with first and second wave feminism. Earlier feminist theory is being critiqued for its lack of awareness or attention to norms of whiteness, property-owning classes, heterosexuality, able-bodiedness, for example. Third World women who have received higher levels of education in First World universities are now able to contribute to the conversation as scholars and have their voices heard. They are offering critiques of First World colonization and their assumptions of arrogance in regards to presuming to know Third World women and their needs. Third-wave feminists offer sharp criticisms of their earlier sisters' work, which is unfortunately causing that earlier work to disappear from conversations and classrooms, setting up again what will become the need for future recovery work of women's contributions to scholarship (Martin, 2000).

In the classroom, third-wave feminists have troubled the idea that a classroom can ever be a safe environment, as second-wave feminists tried to make it, for there are too many power issues involved. Not only is safety an impossibility, it is questionable whether it is even a worthy ideal, as it is through risk and discomfort that we learn to trouble our basic categories we take as given, and we begin to experience the cracks and fissures, and see the faults and weaknesses in our worldviews. In this space of discomfort and un-ease is where education as growth can take place. Third-wave feminists emphasize our plurality and differences as they uncover the hidden colonization of the 1960s melting pot metaphor, that argued for others, strangers, to become assimilated to the norms of White, property-owning, Anglo-Saxon, heterosexual Christians. For women and girls this assimilation process meant that they would be treated equally as long as they could adapt and be like the men and boys. Feminists refer to this assimilation approach as "add women and stir."

Feminist theory in education today refers to models for education that emphasize our diversity and encourage us to maintain and value our plurality. Metaphors such as salads and Chinese hot pots abound, to describe students unique, distinctive qualities as well as their commonality. Feminist scholars emphasize our shifting, changing identities [Judith Butler's (1990) drag, Donna Haraway's (1991) cyborg, and Gloria Anzaldùa's (1990) mestiza metaphors come to mind) and our coming together in cohorts to address particular social/political problems and then disbanding as those problems are addressed [for example, Iris Marion Young's (1990) unoppressive city metaphor or my quilting bee metaphor (Thayer-Bacon, 2000)]. Feminist theory in education offers some of the most exciting, cutting-edge, politically and culturally aware work that contributes to our thinking about education in new ways today.

Feminist Theory and Ethics

Within the philosophical world of ethics, there is a long history of moral theories that have influenced education.[2] Euro-western philosophical discussion usually begins with Plato, as the first systematic philosopher to establish a university in the western world. Plato wrote dialogues for the common citizens of ancient Greece with a focus on moral issues, and Socrates, his teacher, served as the main discussant in these dialogues. In the *Meno* and *Protagoras* dialogues, for example, Plato tackles these questions: What is virtue, and can it be taught to others? By the time Plato wrote the *Republic*, Plato was trying to solve this problem: How do we find our most virtuous citizens and how do we encourage all of our citizens to become as virtuous as they can? Plato's moral theory is important to feminist theory as he is the first Euro-western philosopher to argue for gender equality (women and men are both eligible to become guardians in the *Republic*), even though it is a flawed argument (Martin, 1985).

From Plato and Aristotle, up through Kant, to present-day Rawls, there is a long line of male philosophers who have developed moral theories that can be described as principled approaches to ethics, based on basic rules to help guide human behavior, such as Aristotle's (1970) rules for happiness as a balanced, contemplative life, or Kant's (1956) categorical imperative stated as the principle of universality: "Act only on the maxim whereby thou canst at the same time will that it should become a universal law," or Rawls' (1971) principle of equality of opportunity ("Social and economic inequalities are to be arranged so that they are both (a) to the greatest benefit of the least advantaged and (b) attached to offices and positions open to all under conditions of fair equality of opportunity," p. 302). Today there are feminist moral philosophers who continue to model a principled approach to ethics, such as Seyla Benhabib's (1992) theory of communicative ethics, which builds on Habermas's work. Benhabib shifts the focus of ethics from rational agreement to the process whereby we can sustain practices and relationships in which reasoned agreement can flourish and continue as a way of life. Benhabib suggests that communicative agreement counts on strong ethical assumptions. These ethical assumptions commit us to making sure everyone is included in the moral conversation and has the same rights.

> They require of us: (1) that we recognize the right of all beings capable of speech and action to be participants in the moral conversation—I will call this *the principle of universal moral respect*; (2) these conditions further stipulate that within such conversations each has the same symmetrical rights to various speech acts, to initiate new topics, and to ask for reflection about presuppositions of the conversation, etc. Let me call this *the principle of egalitarian reciprocity*. (p. 29)

Within feminist work on moral theory and moral education there is much discussion of *caring* as a form of moral orientation. Caring is certainly not a new concept in philosophy, feminists can lay no claim to inventing the concept. For example, Aristotle considered caring as friendship and love; Martin Buber described caring in terms of an I-Thou relationship, and John Dewey discussed caring as sympathetic understanding. Feminists can not even lay claim to pioneering the current interest in caring as an ethical approach, for Milton Mayeroff's (1971) *On Caring* was published a decade prior to work by Carol Gilligan (*A Different Voice*, 1982) and Nel Noddings (*Caring*, 1984), now considered classics in feminist care ethics. Feminists can lay claim, however, to exploring care's gendered dimensions, which Mayeroff did not address, nor did the other philosophers previously named.

Milton Mayeroff (1971) initiated current interests in caring by describing caring as a means to individual growth and self-actualization. In his Introduction, Mayeroff is careful to distinguish care from "well-wishing, liking, comforting, maintaining, or having an interest in." Caring is a process, a way of relating that involves development. Care involves an appreciation of the other and respect for the other; it is not something that is imposed on the other. Devotion is essential to caring, being there for the other. According to Mayeroff, a person can care for ideas, not just people or other living beings, but the other is always someone or something specific. To care for another, I must know the other directly and indirectly, explicitly and implicitly. I cannot care by habit. Care requires patience, honesty, trust, courage, humility, and hope. I must be able to be *with* the other and be *for* the other. The process is primary, not the product. According to Mayeroff, I find my place in the world by having my life ordered around caring. In caring for others I find and create myself. Living a life centered around caring is living the meaning of my life.

Notice that while Mayeroff has an individual focus (caring is described as being with a particular other), his focus is on caring as a relation with the other and for the other. Caring is not described as a personal attribute, a personal disposition, like how we describe a person as being an honest person or a trustworthy or courageous person. Caring must involve an other. Nel Noddings (1984) contributes more to this relational definition of caring, as she describes the two involved in the caring relation as the one caring and the one cared for. According to Noddings, I only can describe myself as caring if I have established a caring relationship with another, my caring must be received by the other. The establishment of a caring relationship depends on reciprocity and acknowledgment of caring by the one cared for. For Noddings, caring means "feeling with" an other (receptive rationality), "acquaintance," being present and "engrossed," or "attending" to an other in a generous manner (generous thinking), offering a total presence for the other for the duration of the caring relationship.

In Mayeroff's description of caring, he does not contrast this individual, relational moral orientation to a more distant, generalized, principled approach to ethics. His focus is on how caring helps the one caring become self-actualized, a concept usually credited to Abraham Maslov. The focus on individual development is a common quality of the philosophical period known as the Enlightenment.

Both Carol Gilligan (1982) and Nel Noddings (1984) describe caring as having an individual, relational focus as well, but they clearly contrast an ethic of care to an ethic of justice. Their description of the contrast between caring and justice is placed within the context of gender (women and girl's moral development for Gilligan, and a feminine approach to ethics and moral education for Noddings). Gilligan and Noddings both work within the realm of moral education. However Gilligan focuses on moral development as a psychologist, and Noddings focuses on moral orientation as a philosopher of education. In Gilligan's (1982) ground-breaking work on women's development in psychology, she makes the case that in the past women's moral development has been judged by making the false assumption that all women are like all men (this is actually a commitment of two fallacious assumptions, the other being that all men or all women are alike). Committing these errors results in forcing an essentialized female category into a universal "person" category that is based on schemes developed by males, using males as the subjects of their studies.

Gilligan (1982) found that in terms of ethics, the females she studied develop morality organized around notions of responsibility and care, not rights and rules, as males tend to do. Gilligan stresses that these two views of morality are complementary rather than sequential or opposed. She recognizes the need for both justice and care, and strives for a more integrated approach to moral reasoning and moral judgment.

> The morality of rights is predicated on equality and centered on the understanding of fairness, while the ethic of responsibility relies on the concept of equity, the recognition of differences in need. While the ethic of rights is a manifestation of equal respect, balancing the claims of other and self, the ethic of responsibility rests on an understanding that gives rise to compassion and care. Thus the counterpoint of identity and intimacy that marks the time between childhood and adulthood is articulated through two different moralities whose complementary is the discovery of maturity. (1982, p. 165)

In contrast to Gilligan's complementary, integrative approach to moral reasoning and judgment, Nel Noddings (1984) argues that principled ethics is inadequate, and she rejects such an approach as "ambiguous and unstable. Wherever there is a principle, there is implied its exception and, too often, principles function to separate us from each other" (p. 5). Noddings describes principled ethics as the voice of the father, and caring ethics as the voice of the mother. She presents a caring ethical theory as an *alternative* to a principled ethic.

Many have discussed and criticized Gilligan's and Noddings's work, for they have had great impact. Both have been criticized for essentializing "women" or "feminine" as categories, which can lead to potentially dangerous conclusions. In reality "there is no consensus among women," and "no view of ethical priorities or moral questions that can be seen as female" (Grimshaw, 1986, p. 224). Jean Grimshaw (1986) agrees with Gilligan: "it is true that women commonly see 'caring' relationships for others as having a more central role in their lives than men do" (p. 178). However, she does not think we can assume that because many women are better at understanding others' feelings than many men are, this means we can assume women by nature have different moral approaches. Rather, women are more likely better at understanding others' feelings because they have a greater need and occasion for developing this capacity and they are taught to have and are rewarded for developing this ability. Much of that "need and occasion" develops out of power relationships, where women (and other minorities) develop the ability to read their master's feelings in order to avoid punishment and suffering.

Grimshaw (1986) warns us that associating such concepts as *caring* particularly with women can be used oppressively against women, as has been the case in the past. It is therefore very important that we "recognize the ways in which (these concepts) may need transforming before they can guide any re-evaluation of social policy" (p. 224). Other critics have expressed concerns about "the dangers of valorizing relationships in which carers are seriously abused" (Card, 1990, p. 101), "that the unidirectional nature of the analysis of one-caring reinforces oppressive institutions" (Hoagland, 1990, p. 109), and "that if the one-caring sees her moral worth as wholly dependent upon her capacity to care for others, or contingent upon being in relation, then she may opt to remain in relations which are harmful to her" (Houston, 1990, p. 117). In general, they warn that "caring cannot be insular, and it cannot ignore the political reality, material conditions, and social structures of the world" (Hoagland, 1990, p. 113). They worry that "(c)aring is not an ethic that can stand alone" (Houston, 1990, p. 118). Noddings (1990) takes her critics' advice to heart in agreeing she (we) "should pay far greater attention to historical context and social tradition" (p. 126). She also lets us know she did not intend to reduce everything in moral theory to caring. However, she is not ready to say how justice and care should be combined. According to Alison Jaggar (1995), most proponents of the ethics of care dispute the possibility of an easy synthesis of care with justice. Jaggar notes how both Gilligan and Ruddick (*Maternal Thinking*), in their more recent work, have moved in a direction closer to Noddings's position by further distinguishing care from justice as two non-assimilable moral orientations.

Feminist work on caring has already made significant contributions to moral theory (Jaggar, 1995). It has expanded the moral domain of practical morality to include the private sphere, the home, our personal lives, our relationships with our mothers and fathers, spouses and siblings, as a place for moral scrutiny. Because females have been historically the main actors in the private sphere of home-life, a focus on caring has helped to reveal damaging gendered bias in moral theory. Advocates of caring contend that caring, as a moral orientation, is superior and preferable because the action caring generates is stronger and more accurate. This is because caring relies on the direct perception of particular situations. It is not a distant, abstract form of ethics,but it is up close and personal. Caring is more reliable in motivating right action as well, for it regards the interest of the self as inseparable from those of others. Caring for another does not come at the price of my own self-sacrifice; caring enhances myself. Caring is also morally superior for it encourages a certain degree of moral sensitivity.

However, can caring represent what Minnich refers to as the mental side of feminism, the critique? How can caring respond to what others describe as "severe limitations," its inability to focus on social structures and its lack of theoretical interest in justification (Jaggar, 1995, p. 198)? I think caring *can* serve as critic as well as friend in the form of *caring reasoning*. In fact, scholarship in caring has already revealed limitations of practical reasoning, which does not recognize the epistemic functions of the affective. I have made the case for caring's role as critic in "Caring Reasoning" (2008b), *Transforming Critical Thinking* (2000) and *Relational "(e)pistemologies"* (2003). Let me turn now to caring's role in moral education and point to other contributions feminists are currently making to moral education.

Feminist Theory and Moral Education

I would like to conclude by showing the reader how my discussion relates to moral education. In *Caring*, Noddings (1984) concludes her book by discussing the implications of caring for education. She (1992) has also written a separate book just addressing this topic. Jane Roland Martin's (1994) *The Schoolhome* also addresses this topic, as do Charles Bacon and I in (1998) *Philosophy Applied to Education: Nurturing a Democratic Community in the Classroom* in much greater detail than I can ever hope to accomplish here. What I can do is point to the implications a caring "ethic" has for education in general and then suggest contributions that are on the horizon.

First, and foremost, with a caring moral orientation the aim of education becomes the maintenance and enhancement of caring (Noddings, 1984). Teachers, as ones caring, must seek to treat students as subjects, as ones cared for, not as objects. The students must be viewed as much more important than the subject matter. The teacher's focus must become one of being receptive to students and inclusive. Teachers need to work with students cooperatively and seek to engage students in conversations or dialogues. Teachers must try to understand the student's perspective and be generous in their efforts to understand. It is through practice and confirmation (by being valued and attended to), that students and teachers are able to maintain and enhance caring relationships. Noddings (1992) recommends smaller class sizes and that students have the same teacher for three years as ways to enhance caring in our primary and secondary schools. She recommends that students participate in regular service activities within the school as well as within the larger community. She suggests we de-professionalize education, not to reduce the emphasis on quality, but rather to eliminate the specialized language that separates teachers from other educators in the community, to reduce the narrow specialization of subject matter in order to increase contact time with students, and to remove hierarchical administrative ladders that cause a loss of relationship between teachers and administrators.

The Schoolhome (Martin, 1994) gets its roots from Maria Montessori's Casa dei Bambini, a place where children were respected and made to feel safe and secure, where they were nurtured and cared for and they could grow, in all ways. *The Schoolhome* brings that spirit back to life by rekindling the notion of school as being "a moral equivalent of home" (p. 24). Martin draws from Montessori the importance of including domesticity into the curriculum, as well as "the three C's of care, concern, and connection exhibited in the Casa dei Bambini" (p. 34). Martin is well aware that not all homes are good role models, and that there is a great variety of homes that are good; she has chosen with her model to "assume the best: a home that is warm and loving and neither physically nor psychologically abusive; and a family that believes in and strives for the equality of the sexes" (p. 46).

Martin (1994) notes that students need to find themselves reflected in the curriculum, the curriculum design needs to care enough to include them. She points to the damage caused by a curriculum that is silent on domesticity as well as one that tries to give everyone the same curriculum in the name of equality and the need to unify Americans. Martin discusses how to make curriculum connected and alive, uniting head/heart/hand rather than encouraging students to be spectators, as we do now. Martin's suggestion is to place extracurricular activities such as theatre and the school newspaper at the center of the curriculum. Martin warns us, "It is one thing for school to provide integrative activities that unite mind and body, thought and action, reason and emotion. It is quite another for it to teach each child to interact with every other child—and every adult too—as one fully human being to another. But an education for living can do no less" (p. 104). *The Schoolhome* encourages people in schools to have an experimental attitude and to maintain an overarching aim: "educating children not just for living but for living together" (p. 118). Martin takes a look at our U.S. Constitution's "insure domestic tranquility" phrase and suggests we need to redraw our attention to its importance, to look at the nation as a home and to make the care of it everyone's concern as well as view its inhabitants as kin. She's suggesting we teach "children to be citizens of a nation that is itself a moral equivalent of home" (p. 168).

The suggestions Noddings (1992) and Martin (1994) make in regard to caring as an educational aim remind us that our schools represent a community as well and are possibly as profound of a community experience as our families are. Individual children in classrooms affect their classroom communities just as the classroom community affects them. We find there is a transactional relationship between individuals and the group (Thayer-Bacon with Bacon, 1998; Thayer-Bacon, 2008a). Caring helps us recognize the importance of nurturing a community in our classrooms where students can experience caring, receptivity, attention, confirmation. Where students, as concrete others, can have the opportunity to speak for themselves and be heard. Where students are encouraged to be playful and friendly with each other, traveling to each other's worlds, and learning appreciation for their unique experiences (Lugones, 1987). We need chances to hear one anothers' stories and learn from one anothers' perspectives. We need opportunities to read and be exposed to other cultures and diversities, and to affirm the benefits of widening our circle of friends, thus acknowledging the worth of all people as well as enhancing students abilities to be caring. By widening our circle of friends, we will gain greater comparisons and thus will be better able to critique our own situations as well as others'. Caring is able to serve feminism, in the role of friend and critic.

Other feminists such as Audrey Thompson (1999, 2002, 2004), Cris Mayo (2004), Sharon Todd (1997, 2007), Ann Chinnery (2006, 2007), and Barbara Applebaum (2010) contribute to discussions of moral education by expanding gendered discussions of marginalization and discrimination so that power issues are more overtly addressed at the intersections of race, class, sexual orientation, and cultural context. 'Race' is being more explicitly examined as feminists seek to address the problem of whiteness, recognizing that 'race' is a socially constructed category that implicates all of us as educators who have grown up in raced societies. White women still make up the vast majority of teachers who work in public schools with more and more diverse student populations, and they are still struggling with trying to understand what it means to be 'raced' and the unintended consequences that has on student-teacher relationships as well as students' learning. We are finally having conversations about the assumed norm of heterosexuality in our schools, which is still policed and enforced in schools by teachers, students, and their parents, making our schools places where teachers still don't feel safe coming out as gay or lesbian without fear of losing their jobs, and where students who don't fit the heterosexual norms continually face threats of harassment and violence and struggle with self-esteem issues. International feminist scholars draw our attention to issues such as the imposing of dress codes that outlaw the wearing of head scarves in school as examples of moral issues that single out Muslim girls and treat them as if they were not moral agents capable of making decisions for themselves, but are instead in need of protection and rescuing from their religious customs.

These are but a few examples of the current contributions feminist theory is making to moral education. I hope I have made my case that feminist theory offers some of the most exciting and cutting-edge, politically and culturally aware scholarship that contributes to moral theory and moral education today.

Notes

1. The beginning of this chapter is derived from my (2008c) "Feminist Theory in Education."
2. This section and the next are derived from my (1998) Chapter Three of *Philosophy Applied to Education* and my (2008b) "Caring Reasoning."

References

Alcoff, L. & Potter, E. (1993). *Feminist epistemologies.* New York and London: Routledge.

Applebaum, B. (2010). *Being white, being good: White complicity, white moral responsibility, and social justice pedagogy.* London: Lexington.

Anzaldúa, G. (Ed.). (1990). *Making face, making soul: Haciendo caras.* San Francisco: Aunt Lute.

Aristotle. (1970). Nichomachaen ethics. In S. Cahn (Ed.), *The philosophical foundations of education* (pp. 107–120). New York: Harper & Row.

Belenky, M. F., Clinchy, B. M., Goldberger, N. R., & Tarule, J. M. (1986). *Women's ways of knowing.* New York: Basic Books, Harper Collins.

Benhabib, S. (1992). *Situating the self: Gender, community, and postmodernism.* New York: Routledge.

Butler, J. (1990). *Gender trouble: Feminism and the subversion of identity.* New York: Routledge.

Card, C. (Spring 1990). Caring and evil. Review Symposium of *Caring, Hypatia,* 5(1): 101–108.

Chinnery, A. (2006). Cold case: Reopening the file on tolerance in teaching and learning across difference. In K. Howe (Ed.), *Philosophy of Education, 2005* (pp. 200–208). Urbana-Champaign, IL: Philosophy of Education Society.

Chinnery, A. (2007). On compassion and community without identity: Implications for moral education. In D. Vokey (Ed.), *Philosophy of Education 2006* (pp. 330–338). Urbana-Champaign, IL: Philosophy of Education Society.

Collins, P. H. (1990). *Black feminist thought.* Boston: Unwin Hyman.

Daly, M. (1978/1990). *Gyn/ecology: The metaethics of radical feminism.* Boston: Beacon.

de Beauvoir, S. (1952, 1980, 1989). *The second sex.* H. M. Parshley (Trans. and Ed.). New York: Vantage, Random House.

Frazier, N. & Sadker, M. (1973). *Sexism in school and society.* New York: Harper and Row.

Gilligan, C. (1982). *In a different voice.* Cambridge: Harvard University Press.

Grimshaw, J. (1986). *Philosophy and feminist thinking.* Minneapolis, MN: University of Minnesota Press.

Haraway, D. (1991). *Simians, cyborgs, and women: The reinvention of nature.* New York: Routledge.

Harding, S. (1986). *The science question in feminism.* Ithaca and London: Cornell University Press.

Harding, S. (1991). *Whose science? Whose knowledge? Thinking from women's lives.* Ithaca, NY: Cornell University Press.

Harstock, N. (1983). The feminist standpoint: Developing the grounds for a specifically feminist historical materialism. In S. Harding and M. B. Hintikka (Eds.). *Discovering Reality* (pp. 283–310). Dordrecht, Holland, Boston and London: Reidel.

Hoagland, S. L. (Spring, 1990). Some concerns about Nel Noddings' *Caring.* Review Symposium of *Caring, Hypatia,* 5(1): 109–114.

ooks, b. (1984). *Feminist theory: From the margin to the center*. Boston: South End.

Houston, B. (1990, Spring). Caring and exploitation. Review Symposium of *Caring, Hypatia*, 5(1): 115–119.

Irigaray, L. (1974/1985a). *Speculum of the other woman*. G. Gill (Trans.). Ithaca, NY: Cornell University Press.

Irigaray, L. (1985b). *This sex which is not one*. G. Gill (Trans.). Ithaca, NY: Cornell University Press.

Jaggar, A. (1983). *Feminist politics and human nature*. Sussex: Harvester.

Jaggar, A. (1995). Caring as a feminist practice of moral reason. In *Justice and care: Essential readings in feminist ethics*, V. Held (Ed.). (pp. 179–202). Boulder, CO: Westview, HarperCollins.

Kant, I. (1956). *Critique of practical reason* (L. W. Beck, Trans.). New York: Liberal Arts.

Lugones, M. (1987, Summer). Playfulness, "world" traveling, and loving perception. *Hypatia, 2*, 3–19.

Martin, J. R. (1985). *Reclaiming a conversation*. New Haven, CT: Yale University Press.

Martin, J. R. (1992). *The schoolhome*. Cambridge, MA: Harvard University Press.

Martin, J. R. (2000). *Coming of age in academe: Rekindling women's hopes and reforming the academy*. New York and London: Routledge.

Mayeroff, M. (1971). *On caring*. New York: Harper and Row.

Mayo, Cris. (2004). *Disputing the subject of sex: Sexuality and public school controversies*. Boulder, CO: Rowman & Littlefield.

Minnich, E. K. (1983). Friends and critics: The feminist academy, *Learning our way: Essays in feminist education*, C. Bunch and S. Pollack (Eds.). (pp. 317–329). Trumansburg, NY: The Crossing Press.

Noddings, N. (1984). *Caring*. Berkeley and Los Angeles: University of California Press.

Noddings, N. (1990, Spring). A response. Review Symposium of *Caring, Hypatia*, 5(1): 120–126.

Noddings, N. (1992). *The challenge to care in schools: An alternative approach to education* . New York & London: Teachers College Press.

Plato. (1970a). Meno. In S. Cahn (Ed.), *The philosophical foundations of education* (pp. 7–35). New York: Harper & Row.

Plato. (1970b). Protagoras. In S. Cahn (Ed.), *The philosophical foundations of education* (pp. 35–43). New York: Harper & Row.

Plato. (1979). *Republic* (R. Larson, Ed. & Trans.). Arlington Heights, IL: Harlan University.

Rawls, J. (1971). *A theory of justice*. Cambridge, MA: Harvard University Press.

Ruddick, S. (1989). *Maternal thinking: Toward a politics of peace*. Boston: Beacon Press.

Sadker, M., & Sadker, D. (1982). *Sex equity handbook for schools*. New York: Longman.

Sadker, M., & Sadker, D. (1995). *Failing at fairness*. New York: Touchstone.

Sadker, M., Sadker, D., & Long, L. (1989). Gender and educational equality." In J. A. Banks & C. A. McGee (Eds.), *Multicultural education*. Boston: Allyn & Bacon.

Seigfried, C. H. (1996). *Pragmatism and feminism: Reweaving the social fabric*. Chicago: University of Chicago Press.

Spender, D. (1982). *Invisible women*. London: Writers and Teachers.

Stacey, J., Bercaud, S., & Daniels, J. (Eds.). (1974). *And Jill came tumbling after*. New York: Dell.

Stanworth, M. (1983). *Gender and schooling*. London: Hutchinson.

Thayer-Bacon, B. (2000). *Transforming critical thinking: Constructive thinking*. New York: Teachers College Press.

Thayer-Bacon, B. (2003). *Relational "(e)pistemologies."* New York: Peter Lang.

Thayer-Bacon, B. (2008a). *Beyond liberal democracy in schools: The power of pluralism*. New York: Teachers College Press.

Thayer-Bacon, B. (2008b). Caring reasoning, In D. Fasko, Jr., & W. Willis (Eds.), *Contemporary philosophical and psychological perspectives on moral development and education* (pp. 83–105). Cresskill, NJ: Hampton.

Thayer-Bacon, B. (2008c). Feminist theory in education. In E. Provenzo (Ed.), *Encyclopedia of social and cultural foundations of education*. Thousand Oaks, CA: Sage.

Thayer-Bacon, B. with C. Bacon. (1998). *Philosophy applied to education: Nurturing a democratic community in the classroom*. Upper Saddle River, NJ and Columbus, OH: Prentice Hall, Merrill.

Thompson, A. (1999). Colortalk: Whiteness and *Off White. Educational Studies* 30, (2) 141–160.

Thompson, A. (2002). Entertaining doubts: Enjoyment and ambiguity in white, antiracist classrooms. In E. Mirochnik & D. C. Sherman (Eds.), *Passion and pedagogy: Relation, creation, and transformation in teaching* (pp. 431–452). New York: Peter Lang.

Thompson, A. (2004). Caring and colortalk: Childhood innocence in white and black. In V. Siddle Walker and J. R. Snarey (Eds.), *Race-ing moral formation: African American perspectives on care and justice* (pp. 23–37). New York: Teachers College Press.

Thorne, B., & Henley, N. (Eds.). (1975). *Language and sex: Differences and dominance.* Rowley: Newbury House.

Todd, Sharon. (1997). *Learning desire: Perspectives on pedagogy, culture, and the unsaid.* New York: Routledge.

Todd, Sharon. (2007). Unveiling cross-cultural conflict: Gendered cultural practice in polycultural society. In D. Vokey (Ed.), *Philosophy of Education 2006* (pp. 283–291). Urbana-Champaign, IL: Philosophy of Education Society.

Young, I. M. (1990). *Justice and the politics of difference.* Princeton, NJ: Princeton University Press.

CHAPTER TWENTY-ONE

A Warrior for Justice

Jonathan Kozol's Moral Vision of America's Schools and Society

Richard Ognibene

Launching Jonathan Kozol's Moral Crusade

Nicholas Lemann (2010), a journalist with an interest in educational issues, recently criticized the prevalent theory that the American public school system was failing and that wholesale changes were needed to eliminate some dysfunctional elements. Lemann had a different perspective:

> In education, we would do well to appreciate what our country has built, and try to fix what is undeniably wrong without declaring the entire system to be broken. We have a moral obligation to be precise about what the problems in American education are—like subpar schools for poor and minority children—and to resist heroic ideas about what would solve them, if those ideas don't demonstrably do that. (p. 28)

What Lemann wants us to do is exactly the approach that author and educational activist Jonathan Kozol took in his first book in 1967 and in the eleven books he has written since then. The concept of a moral obligation is strongly implied in Kozol's work even though theories or statements about moral development are absent in his texts. Those texts, however, are filled with examples of circumstances that over time promote or inhibit moral development in citizens, students, and teachers.

There are numerous historical conceptions and contemporary theories related to the concepts of morality and moral development, with the result that definitions of those concepts vary (Rich & DeVitis, 1985; McClellan, 1999). In general, one can say "that which is moral…relates to principles of right conduct in behavior" that are in accord "with accepted principles of what is considered right, virtuous, or just" (Rich & DeVitis, 1985, p. 6). Damon (1988) seeks to expand that definition by delineating specific dimensions of morality. He argues that morality (1) distinguishes the good from the bad and prescribes conduct consistent with the good; (2) implies a sense of obligation to shared social standards; (3) includes a concern for the welfare and rights of others; (4) requires a sense of responsibility for acting on one's concern for others; and (5), presumes a commitment to honesty as the norm in interpersonal relations. Damon also notes that the absence of morality provokes upsetting judgmental and emotional responses such as shame, guilt, outrage, fear, and contempt (p. 5). When we examine Jonathan Kozol's work, we find most of these elements present in his descriptions and assessments of the social issues under review.

Kozol's (1967) first book, *Death at an Early Age,* describes his experience as a substitute teacher in 1964–65 in a segregated Boston public elementary school. It was a grim portrait of a decrepit school in which tyranny, cruelty, racism, and anti-intellectualism reigned. His efforts to introduce attractive art in a dismal place and a curriculum that could interest poor Black children were unacceptable to school administrators and other teachers and got him fired. Parents protested but to no avail. Kozol was not a radical when he began to teach in that Roxbury school, but he was unable to repress the cumulative anger he felt at the beatings he witnessed and the expressed assumptions about the intellectual inferiority of the students. His book, based on his diaries, found a receptive audience in the civil rights milieu of the 1960s, won a National Book Award, and launched Kozol's career as a successful writer and educational and social critic.

In this first foray into educational matters, Kozol modeled what he subsequently advised all teachers to do, witness against injustices wherever he found them.

Then, as now, Kozol is aligned with critics who urge educators to express moral outrage in the face of human suffering despite knowing that schools have been designed to perpetuate and not transform society (Purpel, 1999). Even a critic of Kozol was willing to give him credit for *Death at an Early Age*, a book that offered a look at a racist and complacent urban district: "By exposing the conditions at the ghetto school where he taught," Sara Mosle (1996) noted, "Kozol was able to provoke outrage" (p. 28). His experience in that school was partly responsible for the development of Kozol's unwavering moral vision about overcoming inequality in American life and achieving a more just society through high-quality public education for everyone. As Lemann recommended generally, Kozol, in his subsequent books, was always quite specific about a problem to be addressed and insistent that our nation attempt to remedy those problems.

Kozol and Some Critics

Despite the congruence of his views with the ideals upon which our nation was founded, Kozol has had many critics, especially because the United States entered a conservative ideological cycle in the period following the publication of his first book. Richard Neuhaus (1975), for example, called Kozol's 1975 book, *The Night Is Dark and I Am Far from Home,* "incoherent dribblings of discontents from the sixties" (p. 604). Sol Stern, in 1996, characterized the research in *Savage Inequalities* (1991) as a "thinly disguised (newspaper) clip job," and called Kozol a purposely misleading "ideological tourist" (p.70) when he was observing life in the South Bronx to gather data for *Amazing Grace* (1995).

A decade later, another critic, Marcus Winters (2006), published a negative review of five Kozol books in the conservative journal, *Education Next,* prompted no doubt by the appearance of Kozol's first 21st century work, *Ordinary Resurrections* (2000), and most especially, *The Shame of the Nation,* in 2005. Winters restated the essential conservative argument that money will not make a difference in reducing unequal educational outcomes and characterized Kozol's contrary assertions as "savage exaggerations." Even after Kozol published a book like *Letters to a Young Teacher*

(2007a) that was supportive of public schools and many teachers and principals, conservative critics remain focused on his earlier critiques as proof that Kozol was a "frustrated" person whose purpose in life was to spread resentment (Leaf, 2007–2008). One well-known conservative author, Bernard Goldberg (2005), considered Kozol a dangerous person because of a chapter in *On Being a Teacher* (1981). In that chapter, Kozol urged teachers not to remain neutral when examining significant historical and contemporary issues, and to encourage students directly and by example not to accept everything told them without asking questions (Kozol, 1981, pp. 21–28). This approach is generally called critical thinking, but Goldberg saw it as a threat to our "precious heritage" (p. 274).

Repairing the World

Jonathan Kozol's twelve books span 40 years (1967–2007), and one might suggest that, like his Jewish ancestors, he has also been in search of a promised land, in this case, an America that is just and equitable. In this chapter, I argue that the issues raised by Kozol's body of work constitute a moral imperative and that their resolution is crucial for our society's long-term welfare; specifically, I contend that injustice and inequality in our nation would be substantially lessened if Kozol's perspectives were accepted and his suggestions followed. In making this claim, I concur with author and educator Joseph Featherstone's (1981) view that Kozol is a "teacher-prophet" (p.11), someone whose passion could be sufficient to inspire social change.

A prophetic vision, David Purpel (1989) reminds us, is an appropriate and necessary professional characteristic in educators. As a nation whose founding and early history was influenced by the Judeo-Christian tradition, our attachment to the vision of the biblical prophets is not something that is surprising or needs defending. As Purpel notes, "Prophets were passionate social critics who applied sacred criteria to human conduct and, when they found violations of these criteria, they cried out in anguish and outrage" (p. 80). Kozol's sense of rage was awakened by the murder of three civil rights workers in Mississippi in 1964 shortly after he returned home from several years of post-graduation European travels while trying to become a novelist. That awakening, Kozol tells us, was aided by remembered Bible-reading experiences with his mother and grandmother who "quoted Isaiah and Jeremiah to me when I was a child" (Zimmerman, 1996, p. 2). Kozol credits Reverend James Breeden, a Black Episcopal priest active in civil rights work in Boston for advising him to take action to reduce the injustices that northern segregation perpetuated (Book TV, 2009). After the Mississippi murders, Kozol asked Breeden how he could help. "Become a teacher" was the reply, resulting in Kozol's employment in that segregated Roxbury school he later described in *Death at an Early Age* (1967). As previously indicated, a fully developed moral person not only makes judgments about what is right and just but also takes action to alleviate that which is wrong and unjust. Kozol thus began the pattern of his life's work in 1964 at the behest of a religious advisor.

In his adult life, Kozol embodies "tikkun olam," the Jewish notion that one is literally required to repair the world (Jacobs, 2007). In Kozol's books, we find repeated references to his heroes like Francis of Assisi, Mohandas Gandhi, and Martin Luther King, Jr., spiritual persons committed to social action. In modern times, Kozol lists Martha Overall of the South Bronx, and TV's Mr. (Fred) Rogers as friends who helped to inspire his work, and both individuals were ordained ministers. In the period following *Death at an Early Age* (1967), Kozol had significant personal contact with Ivan Illich and Paulo Freire, educators whose ideas helped to radicalize him (Michalove, 1993). While famous for their contributions to critical pedagogy, it is often forgotten that Illich and Freire also contributed significantly to the praxis orientation of Latin American liberation theology. My view on Kozol's life and work is that it deeply connects with spiritual traditions both old and new. From that perspective, it is ironic that the ideological right in this nation, often proudly connected to religious value systems, has so little use for Kozol's work.

Separate and Unequal Schooling

One area that has elicited continuing "anguish and outrage" from Kozol is his unremitting anger about a public school system that remains still separate and unequal. Schools for those whose parents are financially secure tend to produce good academic outcomes, while children who live in poverty attend schools that are deficient in many ways and achieve the low academic results one would expect. His disgust over the unfairness of this circumstance is Kozol's signature issue and is reflected in his book titles with absolute clarity: *Death at an Early Age: The Destruction of the Hearts and Minds of Negro Children in the Boston Public Schools* (1967); *Savage Inequalities: Children in America's Schools* (1991); and *The Shame of the Nation: The Restoration of Apartheid Schooling in America* (2005). Kozol's critics have a field day pointing out that his criticisms seem repetitive, that his call for equitable school funding is a one-note solution, that he is ideologically incapable of considering recommendations for improvement that rely on school choice mechanisms, and that he does not report data that mitigate the evils his school and neighborhood portraits reveal. My view is that even granting these critiques for the sake of argument, there is mounting irrefutable evidence that Kozol has the big picture right; the separate and unequal school systems in this nation have weakened us in several crucial ways, and this collective consequence is in addition to the psychological and educational harm inflicted on individual students who attend schools in neighborhoods that are poor and of color.

In the late 1960s, the phrase "death at an early age" became code for multiple issues associated with urban education. After the publication of Kozol's 1991 book, its title, *Savage Inequalities,* was and continues to be used as a way to describe the disparity between the financial support given to urban and suburban schools. Kozol's simple strategy for writing *Savage Inequalities* (1991) was to visit poor urban schools and contrast what he saw there with what he saw when visiting nearby schools in affluent suburbs. Kozol's description of the decaying school buildings, the curricular and instructional mediocrity, the pervasive sense of hopelessness, and the specific differences in the per-capita support for students, was compelling evidence that urban schools seemed to be the victims of a "calculated unfairness" (p. 57) and "failure by design" (p. 145). Kozol's proposed solution was a system of financial support by the federal government that would result in a plan for equity funding of schools. This did not happen, but the publicity generated by Kozol's book, and a change in the legal strategy used to challenge unfair funding at the state level began to turn the tide against funding formulas that obviously disadvantaged urban districts. The issue is far from settled, but so far lawsuits contesting education funding mechanisms have been filed in 45 of our 50 states, the vast majority of them coming after the publication of Kozol's persuasive book.

What exactly are the educational and social consequences of our nation's dual school system? First and foremost, an educational achievement gap has remained to the detriment of both the low achievers and the nation's prosperity. The nation's report cards in reading and math show persistent gaps between White, Black and Hispanic scores, even as scores generally tend to rise. Those 30- to 40-point gaps translate into higher dropout rates at the secondary level; in 2008 it was 4.8% for

Whites; 9.9% for Blacks; and 18.3% for Hispanics (NCES, 2010a). SAT results in 2010 followed a similar pattern: the combined reading and math score averages were White, 1064; Black, 857; and Hispanic, 914 (FairTest, 2010). For 2005–07, about 30% of Whites in the United States had a bachelor's degree or higher; for Blacks it was 16.8%, while Hispanics trailed at 12.3% (NCES, 2009). These educational disparities result in lower average incomes for Blacks and Hispanics in comparison to Whites at all levels of educational attainment (U.S. Census Bureau, 2009). They also translate into higher poverty rates: in 2009, the percentage of Whites earning below the poverty level was 9.4%; for Blacks it was 25.8%; and for Hispanics, 25.3% (U.S. Census Bureau, 2010). Given the fact that Blacks and Hispanics account for 38 percent of the current elementary and secondary population (NCES, 2010b), and that the Hispanic numbers are growing and will continue to grow rapidly, these data present what should be a monumental societal concern.

In fact, when poverty data are released, they typically elicit little reaction from politicians in a position to do something about it, most likely because the poor vote less than other groups (Fletcher, 2010). No president in the last forty years has made reducing poverty a top priority (Miller, 2010). This is a contradiction because, as Richard Pratte (1988) has argued, an orientation to the common good was an American ideal inspired by Judeo-Christian values and the humanistic traditions of republican Greece and Rome transmitted to our nation by way of the Enlightenment. What these religious and secular traditions hold in common is the principle of human dignity, a belief in the inherent worth of all citizens requiring each citizen, as a moral obligation, to treat others with respect. According to Pratte, "this means not only respecting everyone's rights, but actively promoting modes of self-help to others, helping them achieve their ends. In short, it means making the quality of social life better by helping and serving others" (p. 59). This theme resonates with ideals expressed in Jonathan Kozol's books and his lifelong effort to encourage others to work to overcome the multiple manifestations of inequality in American life. For both Pratte and Kozol, in a moral democratic community, the disposition to help others is the mark of a good person and a good citizen.

In the 21st century, one effort to reduce poor educational outcomes and the inequalities that result from them was the 2002 No Child Left Behind (NCLB) Act, a law that Kozol viewed as "a racially punitive piece of legislation," whose "poisonous essence…lies in the mania of obsessive testing it has forced on our nation's schools and, in the case of underfunded, overcrowded inner-city schools, the miserable drill-and-kill curriculum of robotic 'teaching to the test' it has imposed on teachers…" (Kozol, 2007b). Large sections of *The Shame of the Nation* and *Letters to a Young Teacher* are devoted to descriptions and critiques of these activities, and, as it turns out, Kozol was right. Despite all the emphasis on reading and math improvement in legislation officially described as "An Act to Close the Achievement Gap," minority students made greater NAEP-measured achievement gains in the pre-NCLB era than since the law was implemented (Dillon, 2009). The 2009 NAEP math results produced a firestorm of criticism with the recognition that there were no achievement gains for fourth-grade math and very little gain at the eight grade level for all students, including Blacks and Hispanics, and that gains for all students were greater before NCLB than after. As Mark Schneider (2009), Commissioner of the National Center for Education Statistics during George Bush's second term wrote when analyzing this data, "the bottom line is clear: NCLB has not worked the way it was intended and the nation is worse off because of it." The more recently released 2009 NAEP reading results were even more disappointing (Gewertz, 2010). Ninety percent of Black students in high poverty schools and 88 percent of Hispanics in similar schools failed to achieve proficiency levels on the reading test ("Analysis Ties," 2010)

Our nation is worse off economically because of these results, according to an April 2009 report prepared by the international consulting firm, McKinsey & Company. The report, "The Economic Impact of the Achievement Gap in America's Schools," examines four distinct achievement gaps: between the U.S. and other nations; between students of different income levels; between similar students schooled in different systems or regions; and, more importantly for this chapter, between White, Black, and Hispanic students. McKinsey created models of analysis based on an approach developed by the economist Eric Hanushek. The reasoning used is that if the U.S. had eliminated the achievement gaps in the fifteen years after *A Nation at Risk* was issued in 1983, "GDP in 2008 would have been between $310 billion and 525 billion higher, or roughly 2 to 4 percent of GDP" (p. 17). Our nation is underutilizing its human potential and producing workers who "are, on average, less able to develop, master, and adapt to new productivity-enhancing technologies and methods . . ." (p. 17). A consequence of this circumstance is that "the educational achievement gaps in the United States have created the equivalent of a permanent, deep recession in terms of the gap between the actual and potential output in the economy" (p.18). And beyond being low earners, individuals with low achievement are more often incarcerated, live more unhealthy lifestyles, and are less civically engaged (pp. 19–20). Furthermore, in difficult economic times, the decline in spending by low-wage earners helps to sustain a recession, yet another negative consequence of the achievement gap (Reich, 2010).

Here again one sees the irony of conservative opposition to Kozol's work. The business and financial communities who embrace conservative political and educational ideologies have been closely associated with demands for strict standards in curriculum, accountability through testing, and the tough teaching methods that are supposed to produce better results and enhance the capacities of the pool of potential employees at their disposal. But looking at achievement statistics like the ones presented earlier, Kozol, in *Letters to a Young Teacher*, writes to Francesca, "These are not just bad statistics; they are plague statistics." Supporters of rigid curricula and frequent testing have had ample time to succeed, Kozol says to her, and "they have been proven wrong" (Kozol, 2007a, p. 122). Kozol wants a balance of teaching content and skills with an equal opportunity to provide activities that foster such qualities as wonder, creativity, aesthetic appreciation, playfulness, and connections to others. In Francesca, he saw a teacher who could successfully function and endure the requirements of the testing world while maintaining an educational environment in which care, creativity, and connection were also present. Both Kozol and Francesca see the whole person and not just students who will be efficiently trained to be producers and consumers.

Kozol has held this balanced view for a long time. In his most radical period in the 1970s, he supported the alternative school movement and even wrote a book, *Free Schools* (1972) that was an advice manual for those in that movement. But in that book, he ridiculed the notion that alternative education should be equated with an "anything goes" approach rather than an emphasis on hard skills that students must acquire to better prepare for a life that included both personal gain and social improvement. "Harlem does not need a new generation of revolutionary basket weavers," he wrote in 1972 (p. 53). What it does need, he argued, are powerful, determined, and socially active physicians, attorneys, technicians, and competent civic employees.

For Kozol, the isolation of poor people of color was an indefensible injustice, so much so that his 2005 book on education used the words "shame" and "apartheid" in the title and subtitle. His desire for a more integrated society that could be an outcome of more integrated public schools made Kozol notably hostile to vouchers and privatization as a solution to educational deficiencies, as indicated by a chapter he entitled "The Single Worst, Most Dangerous Idea" (2007a, pp. 131–150). Kozol does not support charter schools because they increase and not lessen segregation; he continues to be more interested in promoting the school integration practices that are still possible in a nation that is both residentially and socially segregated.

Kozol is right to resist charter schools as a solution. Although some 5,000 charter schools exist in 39 states and the District of Columbia and are promoted by President Bush's NCLB legislation and President Obama's "Race to the Top" initiative, they have not accomplished the achievement gains that are their raison d'etre. Although charter school research is highly politicized and the outcomes predictable once the investigator is identified, studies published by neutral and trustworthy sources continuously demonstrate that charter schools do not raise achievement levels or narrow achievement gaps any more than comparable public schools in the locations under review (Ravitch, 2010, Chapter 7).

Kozol was disheartened by the legal climate and fiscal constraints that threatened voluntary inter-district transfer programs (2005, pp. 229–232), and correctly predicted the demise of the right of school districts to use voluntary race conscious plans to increase school integration which is what happened subsequently when the Supreme Court announced its decision in June 2007 in the Seattle/Louisville cases. Even before that decision, Kozol urged the Gates Foundation to reexamine its emphasis on creating small schools, including charter schools, and instead give funds to integrating urban and suburban districts to aggressively create inter-district programs that would promote integration (Kozol, 2007a, p. 187). Instead, in 2009, Gates gave money to states to apply for "Race to the Top" money, and the application required states to remove caps on charter school development, which many did. It is amazing how oversold the charter solution is when even many of the early supporters of the movement recognize that quality control is a pressing charter school issue (Robelen, 2009).

Here again, one could say that Kozol was right: integrated public schools are a superior educational solution to achievement issues we have yet to solve, one that also has the potential to challenge the racial isolation prevalent in our nation. The research evidence to support this contention is voluminous and summarized in an *amici curiae* brief submitted to the Supreme Court during the 2006–2007 term when it was deliberating the Seattle/Louisville integration cases (*Brief*, 2006). The brief was signed by 553 social science researchers from 42 states representing 201 educational and research institutions. The documented benefits for students in racially integrated classrooms include enhanced complex and critical thinking skills, modest positive effects on achievement levels for Black and Hispanic students, no loss of achievement for White students, and an increased sense of civic engagement (*Brief*, 2006, pp. 7–9 and Appendices 12–20 & 23–24). In addition, students with positive experiences in integrated classrooms have fewer racial stereotypes when they enter the work force or the military. When implemented across large geographic areas, school desegregation can provide the basis for increased residential integration (Brief, 2006, p. 9, and Appendices 24–27). It seems almost unbelievable that these findings would not be sufficient to sustain the voluntary race-conscious programs developed to promote integration in Seattle and Louisville, but the Court disallowed those programs.

In addition to Kozol, those who have a preference for school integration suggest several other strategies beyond race-conscious enrollment that would enhance the possibility of integration happening more than it does currently. Regional partnerships between urban and suburban districts are one suggestion, and high-quality magnet schools that would retain students in the public sector who might otherwise leave are another. In this scenario when an out-of-district student selects such a school, the sending district would open a seat to a student from the urban district (Goldstein, 2009). A *Time* magazine story offers another example with an account of a successful 800-student 7–12 Jesuit school in Detroit, a city whose slow death was hastened by racial conflict that exploded there over forty years ago. This school's reputation for academic excellence and character development through community service is so outstanding that three quarters of the student body come *into* the city to attend it from 50 surrounding communities. One-third of that student body consists of minority students. The school has a near-perfect graduation rate, and virtually all the graduates go to college (Sullivan, 2009). The school is private, but it illustrates the kind of institution Kozol would want to exist in public systems and the kind of potential results he desires for all students. Amartya Sen, an economist and Nobel laureate, has refined the definition of justice to mean the reduction of inequality in the respective capabilities of individuals and guaranteeing that all people have adequate capabilities to function in the midst of real opportunities (Freeman, 2010). Enhancing the capabilities of adults and students to function in a society that minimizes barriers to opportunity is not only a definition of justice but also a description of the goal Kozol has worked toward his entire adult life.

Poverty and Moral Development

As noted above, multiple sources have documented the negative academic and economic results that flow from poorly performing segregated urban public schools. In addition, Kozol describes but does not specifically name the harmful consequences for a more natural process of moral development when one lives in an isolated, high-poverty urban ghetto. Social scientists, including those who work from a developmental perspective, stress that moral development is a consequence of the interaction of an individual's natural inclinations with his or her social environment (Damon, 1995; Murray, 2008). That being the case, what is the effect of living in a location like Mott Haven in the South Bronx, the focus of Kozol's *Amazing Grace* (1995) and *Ordinary Resurrections* (2000)?

William Julius Wilson has identified what life is like for *The Truly Disadvantaged* (1987) and the consequences for the new urban poor *When Work Disappears* (1996). When the economy shifted from production to service, jobs and middle-class minorities disappeared from the inner city. What remained were high concentrations of poverty that made family life untenable, and increases in female-headed households, out-of-wedlock births, higher male incarceration rates, and violence, crime, and drug use were the most observable features of the local environment. When inferior schools and destroyed social networks are added to this mix, it becomes almost impossible for impoverished urban minorities to escape from their surroundings. Under these conditions, the likelihood of developing moral values that promote individual growth and productive social systems is greatly diminished but not impossible.

What is notable about Kozol's portrait of the South Bronx is that he found individuals who continued to demonstrate high moral standards and a desire to promote the well-being of others, even though they lived in a community in which almost all life-affirming institutions had collapsed (Kozol, 1995, p.180). His descriptions of the violent life on the streets and in the housing projects, the rat infestations, the indifference of social service workers and police, poor health caused by a toxic environment, and the scarce and segregated health services are a shock to readers unfamiliar with such conditions. In fact, many of the South Bronx individuals with whom Kozol spoke believed that the separation of the inner city from the larger community produced an unawareness that enabled most Americans to cope with a reality that was in conflict with traditional notions of the American Dream. Many of the inner-city residents who appear in Kozol's texts characterize this separation and indifference as evil. So did the South Bronx Protestant and Catholic religious leaders Kozol admired and consulted during his multi-year investigation of that area. Nevertheless, if moral development is promoted by positive social interactions, we discover that Kozol found and described those kinds of interactions in several places: in a successful female-headed household; in a relationship between a young boy and an influential male role model; and in a neighborhood religious institution that made a positive difference in the lives of several children and youth who could have easily succumbed to the anti-social tendencies in their environment.

Alice Washington was the central subject and Kozol's guide in his exploration of the South Bronx that was detailed in *Amazing Grace* (1995). She was born in 1944, grew up in Harlem, and died in 1997 at the age of 53. Mrs. Washington, an African American, was a high school and secretarial school graduate and worked two jobs for 20 years. In later years, beset with chronic illnesses and unable to work, she and her two children became mired in poverty. Nevertheless, the example she set with her bravery in the face of difficult circumstances, her unbreakable determination to live a moral life, her caring for others, and her belief in education, influenced her children to ward off the negative behaviors that were common in the neighborhood. In fact, both her children became successful college students. The "amazing grace" with which Alice Washington lived her life surely influenced her children in the direction of social and moral competence.

Of course Kozol encountered others in the South Bronx who refused to accept the unjust circumstances of life in that community and were moved to act in ways to mitigate those conditions. Juan Bautista Castro, for example, a 70-year-old Puerto Rican who came to the South Bronx as a young man, had an extraordinary influence on one person, a twelve-year-old neighborhood boy named Anthony. Mr. Castro lived an exemplary life. A young man of 22 when he arrived in New York in 1946, he was already a lover of books, but his own treasured collection had to be left behind. He taught himself English by reading classical English poets, married, took one menial job, then another, and a third. He created a large home library, wrote poetry, and when he retired, wrote a Spanish translation of Milton's *Paradise Lost*.

Like Mr. Castro, Anthony was Puerto Rican, but he lived in an extremely impoverished home. Although failing in school, Anthony was passionate about literature, and under Mr. Castro's tutelage, that passion deepened. His frequent discussions with this mentor opened Anthony to wider world of ideas. As Damon (1988) notes, an authoritative adult-child relationship yields positive results regarding that child's moral judgment and conduct and creates or reinforces a respect for the standards, rules, and conventions of the social order. Growth in this direction is one component of enhanced moral development. Anthony's subsequent academic career in high school flourished, and later he enrolled in college (Kozol, 2000, pp. 168 & 375).

The publication of Kozol's *Ordinary Resurrections* (2000) provided an extended second look at the Mott Haven section of the South Bronx. The key figure in that examination was Rev. Martha Overall, a woman affectionately known in the community as "Mother Martha." Hers is an unusual story. A person of privilege, Martha Overall graduated from Radcliffe, then law school, and took a job at a well-known New York City law firm. In the 1980s, she felt called to do a different kind of work, began theological studies, and was ordained an Episcopal priest in 1991. She accepted an assignment at St. Ann's Episcopal Church in Mott Haven, where she remains today. Shortly after she began that assignment, Kozol started his research for *Amazing Grace* (1995). He met her and became an admirer as he watched her engage in the work of "repairing the world" of the poverty-stricken South Bronx. Rev. Overall organized religious services in both English and Spanish for the Black and Hispanic populations served by her church and was viewed as a person without exaggerated religious pretensions, one whose sermons addressed real problems that impacted her congregation.

As a lawyer and a priest, Rev. Overall was disturbed that the legal pursuit of justice and the spiritual tradition of the equal dignity of all persons seemed not apply to the people who lived in her neighborhood. Once, when driving up Park Avenue with Kozol, she stopped her car between 96th and 97th Streets and spoke with anger about the unjust reality of the wealth, health, and educational differences that become visible as one crossed 96th Street into Harlem (Kozol, 1995, pp. 186–189). These differences were never far from her mind (Kozol, 2000, pp. 246–249). Rev. Overall's approach to diminishing these injustices was to create and expand social programs housed at her church.

The scope of these programs is impressive, especially when one considers that Rev. Overall had to raise funds to support them and coordinate their delivery. There is a food pantry that is open on Wednesdays and Fridays, a soup kitchen on Sundays after services, and nightly dinner for the 100 or so children in the after-school program. These programs feed about 1,000 people a month (Wilson, 2010). Kozol's books describe in detail the quality of the after-school program and the feeling of physical and emotional safety the children experience when they are there. Students from six surrounding schools get homework help, literacy, math, and computer instruction, supervised free time, and dinner. Instruction is provided by volunteer members of congregations and college students from many parts of our country who know about and admire Rev. Overall's social action program.

Kozol visited Mott Haven frequently in the 1990s to observe and interview the individuals who became part of the story he told in his two books about that area. St. Ann's was his headquarters, so to speak, and he had repeated opportunities to watch the after-school program in operation. The stories he tells reveal the unrestrained affection the children had for Mother Martha. They pulled at her clothes to get her attention and she greeted them with hugs. When she was absent, they always wanted to know where she was. She spent time in the garden by design so the children could find her in a peaceful place when they wanted to talk. Her office was always open for longer and perhaps more serious conversations when needed. In short, she was a caring person who had a way of responding that individuals of any age perceived as "good."

As Nel Noddings (1984) argues, "it is our longing for caring—to be in that special relation—that provides the motivation for us to be moral" (p. 5). The caring relationships she established with children, volunteers, and adults go a long way to explain her continued success in altering the behavior of the numerous individuals Kozol cites when describing Rev. Overall's outreach to the Mott Haven community. In recent years, some theorists have argued that the end point of heightened moral development was to rationally choose to act in accordance with universally agreed-upon principles of justice. Others have thought that responding with care to those in need was the most important behavior a fully developed moral person could exhibit. Through his portrait of Martha Overall, Jonathan Kozol has shown us that an unrelenting search for justice can and should be combined with unconditional caring when seeking to describe moral development of the highest order. As a matter of fact, reading Kozol's books suggest that the same description could be applied to Kozol as well.

The Work of Teachers

The conservative preference for teachers to act as conduits for society's dominant values while forced to use inflexible, predetermined curricula, was contrary to Kozol's worldview from his first days as a teacher in Roxbury in 1964. His initial act of poetically assertive curriculum implementation focusing on the work of Langston Hughes got him fired, and in all the years and writing that followed, he has called on teachers to live courageous professional lives. This is not exactly novel but rather an educational ideal as old as Socrates. The value of Kozol's consistency in this matter, however, is that he frames the issue of a teacher's work not simply in professional terms, which has been the strategy since the rise of teacher unions but insists that teaching is a way of being that carries substantial moral obligations. It is uplifting to read Kozol's letter to Francesca in which he says that the kind of new teachers he tries to recruit are those who will be "outspoken warriors for justice" (2007a, p. 208). It is very difficult to develop that kind of focus in high–poverty schools in which virtually all other aspects of school life are set aside in favor of test preparation, a factor that pushes teachers out of the system almost as fast as they enter (Perlstein, 2007; De Vise & Chandler, 2009). That circumstance effectively quashes any inclinations, however slight, to critique causes of the poverty and poor conditions in the community the school serves, and absorbs any energy teachers might have to use to improve those conditions.

In the 1970s, when schools were using low risk values clarification strategies or moral reasoning dilemmas, Kozol wrote *The Night Is Dark and I Am Far from Home* (1975), a blistering critique of American society from the perspective of a critical theorist. He analyzed the elements of schooling designed to foster social reproduction and decried the blandness of curriculum that purposely omitted admired historical rebels, thereby contributing to the stunted moral development of students. This truncated formal curriculum gave almost no time to social justice issues and did little to promote a sense that students can say no to evil. It communicated instead a sense that individuals were impotent to change social trends and structures and encouraged passivity while perpetuating the myth that things will eventually get better because America is a place where progress is inexorable. For Kozol, those school processes and attitudes explain the subsequent ability of adult Americans to be hard-hearted when so many of their fellow citizens require compassion and assistance. Kozol's book was a tirade that may have inspired some loyal readers but did not give direction to teachers who may have been sympathetic. He tried to overcome that limitation with his next book, *On Being a Teacher*.

Like *Free Schools* in the 1970s, *On Being a Teacher* (1981) was designed to provide useful advice; it was a curriculum and instruction guide about how teachers could stir students' interest by introducing them to controversial historical and contemporary issues and figures and using that content to get students to think and act more critically and ethically. Furthermore, Kozol wrote, it was "my own belief, repeated often in this book…that a teacher's stated views and—and more important, the visible actions which that teacher takes during a year in public school—are infinitely more relentless in their impact on the students than a wealth of books of any possible variety" (p. 25).

Although Kozol's views have always offended conservatives, his idea about the teacher's role as a conscious moral example was and continues to be accepted by many. Gary Fenstermacher (1990), for example, echoed both Kozol's themes and words a few years later when he wrote that "What makes teaching a moral endeavor is that it is…human action undertaken in regard to other human beings. Thus, matters of what is fair, right, just, and virtuous are always present" (p. 133). Like Kozol, Fenstermacher believed that one "way to undertake moral education is to act morally, holding oneself up as a possible moral model—at first a model to be imitated, later a model that will be influential in guiding the conduct of one's students" (p. 134). Ted and Nancy Sizer said the same thing with their book: *The Students Are Watching* (1999). As the Sizers note, "Moral education for youth starts with us adults; the lives we lead and thus project.…The students watch us all the time. We must honestly ponder what they see, and what we want them to learn from it" (p. 121). Damon (1995) concurs, and argues that when teachers are perceived as untruthful and uncritical, they lose their power to become a moral influence in the lives of their students (pp. 212–218). These perspectives offered by Kozol, Fenstermacher, the Sizers, and Damon constitute more powerful possibilities for moral development than the tepid character education programs that substitute for moral education efforts in most schools today.

A continuous theme found in Kozol's *Letters* (2007a) to Francesca is his praise for her refusal to follow every rule and her willingness to be outspoken in the face of educational demands she believed were shallow or repressive. Unlike his earlier diatribes that were intended to encourage confrontation, Kozol delights in Francesca's quiet acts of subversion. Because education is never neutral (p. 86), he encourages her to continue to resist, and uses the letters to suggest that teachers should record and speak up when they see injustices done to children, and they should refuse demands for classroom practices that would obliterate the natural tendencies of children. According to Kozol, "We need the teachers who are coming to our classrooms making up their minds, before they even get here, *which side are they on*" (p. 109. Emphasis added).

An Activist for All Seasons

As I have argued, given a list of positive potential outcomes that would occur if Kozol's ideals were realized, it's difficult to reconcile those potential social benefits with the sustained ideological criticism of his work (Stotsky, 2006; McWhorter, 2007). In an earlier period, Kozol investigated and wrote about issues not directly related to K-12 schooling, and in these instances the criticisms tended to be from specialists who believed that his simply written works were insufficiently technical and thus shallow (Harman, 1985; Halpern, 1989). But Kozol has a knack for bringing issues before the public, and if those issues remain problematic, we can at least be grateful that he raised public awareness enabling us to retain hope for improvement in the future. The issues here, illiteracy and homelessness, are not insignificant, and that they are still unresolved problems is bad for our nation, many adult citizens, and their children.

Kozol's interest in literacy was heightened when he met Paulo Freire in 1969 and learned about the 1961 campaign to eliminate illiteracy in Cuba. Kozol visited Cuba twice in the mid-1970s to learn about that campaign and wrote a complimentary book about it in 1978. The Cuban literacy campaign was based on the work of Paulo Freire, a radical Brazilian educator, and implemented by the Cuban communist leader, Fidel Castro. That combination made the book, *Children of the Revolution* (1978), a hard sell when it was published and still provides ammunition for right-wing critics of Kozol. One of the effects of this work on Kozol was that it provided a direction for his activist efforts for the next several years, an ongoing intellectual focus that resulted in his 1985 book, *Illiterate America*.

Kozol viewed the tolerated existence of illiteracy as an injustice, in this case, because it caused those experiencing this problem to be excluded from a basic quality of life that should be available to all. Just imagine all one cannot do in a modern society if one cannot read, and conversely, consider how a society is typically deprived of such a person's vote, civic and cultural participation, and higher level economic productivity. In an especially poignant chapter titled "The Pedagogic Time Bomb: The Children of Nonreaders," Kozol outlined the cognitive deficits for children raised in a nonliterate household, and the inability of illiterate parents to engage the school in ways that would be helpful to their children. A recent study by the National Endowment for the Arts (2007) confirms the continuing correctness of Kozol's earlier analysis and even provides data on the correlation between the number of books in households and the academic achievement of the children who live in them (pp. 11–12).

Kozol did not believe that a national literacy campaign in the style of Cuba or some Third World countries could occur. Instead, he proposed individual community mobilizations against illiteracy in the hope that community-based efforts would spread and eventually merge like Martin Luther King's work for civil rights. Volunteering to work against illiteracy today is a popular idea and does occur, but clearly it is an insufficient response. According to the most recent federal data, about 30 million American adults have "below basic" prose literacy skills which represents about 14 percent of our adult population. Of course, illiteracy is not created equal; White adult illiteracy is at 7 percent; for Blacks, it's 24 percent, and for Hispanics, 44 percent (NCES, 2006). None of this would surprise Kozol who wrote in 1985: "Illiteracy among the poorest people in our population is a logical consequence of the kind of schools we run, the cities that starve them, the demagogues who segregate them, and the wealthy people who escape them altogether . . ." (p. 89).

After illiteracy, Kozol turned his attention to the problem of homelessness with the publication of *Rachel and Her Children* in 1988. The book painted a brutally grim picture of 400 plus families living in a welfare hotel in New York City. Fourteen hundred of the 1,600 people living in that decrepit and roach- and rodent-infested place were children. Kozol's depictions of everyday life made one cringe, but the negative publicity caused by the attention paid to his findings caused the city's mayor to close the welfare hotels. It was only a short-lived victory since the housing projects to which many of the homeless were moved soon developed a social pathology of their own. Both liberal and conservative reviewers had problems with this book (Quindlen, 1988; Main, 1988). The main objection was that the poverty and policy issues central to understanding and contesting the issue of homelessness were not adequately addressed. Jim Miller's comments well represent this criticism but also state a perspective with which this writer concurs, not only about the homeless book in particular but about the value of Kozol's work in general: "For all the weaknesses of his approach, Kozol once again forces us to face a disheartening social dilemma. He knows how to make a reader feel deeply disturbed. Perhaps that is reason enough to welcome this bitterly eloquent attack" (1988, p. 55).

Educators need people like Kozol to carry on the prophetic work of inspiring those among us who desire to respond to George S. Counts' (1932) still-timely plea that we try to create "a vision of a future America immeasurably more just and noble and beautiful than the America of today"... (p. 51). As the current recession hangs on, homeless figures rise and the increased enrollment of homeless children (about 1 million students) burdens local school districts (Gewertz, 2008; Eckholm, 2009). Teachers and schools spend personal money and money that was already budgeted for other purposes to buy clothing and supplies for these children, even though their chances for success in school are minimal. Homeless children have significantly lower proficiency rates on standardized reading and math tests, and only one in four will graduate from high school (National Center on Family Homelessness, 2009). Perhaps one thing we can do to honor the moral vision Jonathan Kozol represents, among the many opportunities that exist, is to express rage that the federal allocation to school districts to fulfill the mandate to enroll homeless children is, on average, $64 per year (National Center on Family Homelessness, 2009). One hopes that this is not just another savage inequality that we have learned to accommodate.

Closing Thought

The common criticism that themes in Kozol's books are repetitive might have more weight if the conditions about which he wrote were diminished. In fact the opposite is true: the trend toward school integration has been halted and reversed; the achievement gap which had been shrinking has become persistent; the income and wealth gaps which had narrowed have dramatically increased; and altered economic structures and hostile financial and urban planning policies have helped to create dysfunctional neighborhoods, leading to the destruction of family life and increased crime, homelessness, and illiteracy. As a result, scholars who want to improve schools in poor neighborhoods, and increase the academic achievement of the students of color who attend them, have argued that attention to schools without equal attention to other factors that influence educational outcomes is an inadequate response that is likely to fail (Rothstein, 2004; Berliner, 2009; Darling-Hammond, 2010). Kozol continues to write with the hope that some day there will be the political will and resources to combat the conditions that prevent many of our citizens from fully participating and benefiting from our democratic way of life. His words invite us to take action, the most important outcome of any sympathetic response his books provoke. Martin Luther King famously said "The arc of the moral universe is long, but it bends toward justice." But this does not happen without help, and one could say that the purpose of Jonathan Kozol's books has been to provide that help.

References

Analysis ties 4th grade reading failure to poverty. (2010, May 17). *Education Week*. Retrieved *from* www.edweek.org

Berliner, D. (2009). *Poverty and potential: Out-of-school factors and school success.* Boulder and Tempe: Education and the Public Interest Center & Education Policy Research Unit.

Book TV. (2009, September 6). *In depth with Jonathan Kozol.* Retrieved from www.c-spanvideo.org/program288721–1

Brief of 553 social scientists as amici curiae in support of respondents Jefferson County Board of Education, et al. (No. 05–915) and Seattle Schools District No. 1, et al. (No. 0–908). (2006, October 6).

Counts, G. S. (1932). *Dare the schools build a new social order?* 1978 ed. Carbondale: Southern Illinois University Press.

Damon, W. (1988). *The moral child.* New York: The Free Press.

Damon, W. (1995). *Greater expectations.* New York: The Free Press.

Darling-Hammond, L. (2010). *The flat world and education.* New York: Teachers College Press.

De Vise, D. & Chandler, M. A. (2009, April 27). Poor neighborhoods, untested teachers. *The Washington Post.* Retrieved from www.washingtonpost.com

Dillon, S. (2009, April 29). 'No Child' law is not closing a racial gap. *The New York Times.* Retrieved from www.nytimes.com

Eckholm, E. (2009, September 6). *Surge in homeless children strains school districts.* Retrieved from www.edweek.org

Fair Test: The National Center for Fair and Open Testing. (2010, September 13). *FairTest reacts to the 2010 SAT scores.* Retrieved from www.fairtest.org

Featherstone, J. (1981, August 9). Review of *On Being a Teacher. The New York Times Book Review,* 10–11, 21.

Fenstermacher, G. (1990). Some moral considerations on teaching as a profession. In J. Goodlad, R. Soder, & K. Sirotnik, (Eds.). *The moral dimensions of teaching.* San Francisco: Jossey-Bass Publishers.

Fletcher, M. (2010, September 19). Rise in poor gets a shrug. *Albany Times Union,* A3.

Freeman, S. (2010, October 14). A new theory of justice. *The New York Review of Books,* 58–56.

Gewertz, C. (2008, November 5). Districts see rising numbers of homeless students. *Education Week.* Retrieved from www.edweek.org

Gewertz, C. (2010, March 25). NAEP Reading results deemed disappointing. *Education Week.* Retrieved from www.edweek.org

Goldberg, B. (2005). *100 people who are screwing up America.* New York: HarperCollins.

Goldstein, D. (2009, May 18). Across district lines. *The American Prospect.* Retrieved from www.prospect.org

Halpern, S. (1989, February 16). The rise of the homeless. *New York Review of Books,* 24–27.

Harman, D. (1985, March 27). Teaching Johnny to read. *The New Republic,* 36–38.

Jacobs, J. (2007, June). A history of "Tikkun Olam." *Zeek Magazine.* Retrieved from www.zeek.net/706tohu/

Kozol, J. (1967). *Death at an early age.* Boston: Houghton Mifflin.

Kozol. J. (1972). *Free schools* (revised ed.). New York: Bantam Books

Kozol, J. (1975). *The night is dark and I am far from home.* Boston: Houghton Mifflin.

Kozol, J. (1978). *Children of the revolution.* New York: Delacorte.

Kozol, J. (1981). *On being a teacher.* 1993 ed. Oxford, UK: Oneworld.

Kozol, J. (1985). *Illiterate America.* 1986 ed. New York: Plume.

Kozol, J. (1988). *Rachel and her children.* 1989 ed. New York: Fawcett Columbine.

Kozol, J. (1991*). Savage inequalities.* New York: Crown.

Kozol, J. (1995). *Amazing grace.* New York: Crown Publishers.

Kozol, J. (2000). *Ordinary resurrections.* New York: Crown Publishers.

Kozol, J. (2005). *The shame of the nation.* New York: Crown Publishers.

Kozol, J. (2007a*). Letters to a young teacher.* New York: Three Rivers Press.

Kozol, J. (2007b), September 10). Why I am fasting: An explanation to my friends. *The Huffington Post.* Retrieved from www.huffingtonpost.com

Leaf, J. (2007–2008). The learning disabled education expert: Jonathan Kozol's crusade to prevent school reform. *The Weekly Standard.* Retrieved from www.weeklystandard.com

Lemann, N. (2010, September 27). School work. *The New Yorker,* 27–28.

Main, T. (1988, May). What we know about the homeless. *Commentary,* 26–31.

McCellan, B. Edward. (1999). *Moral education in America.* New York: Teachers College Press.

McKinsey & Company. (2009). *The economic impact of the achievement gap in America's schools.* Retrieved from www.mckinsey.com

McWhorter, J. (2007, August 23). Kozol-ology obscures the facts. *The New York Sun.* Retrieved from www.nysun.com

Michalove, S. (1993). The educational crusade of Jonathan Kozol. *Educational Forum,* 57, 300–311.

Miller, J. (1988, February 1). The homeless: A horror story. *Newsweek,* 55.

Miller, L. (2010, October 11). Dare to care. *Newsweek, 25*

Mosle, S. (1996, June 17). What we talk about when we talk about education. *The New Republic,* 27–36.

Murray, M. (2008, December 2). *Moral development and moral education: An overview.* Retrieved from www.tigger.uic.edu/~Inucci/MoralEd/overview

National Center for Educational Statistics. (2006). *A first look at the literacy of America's adults in the 21st century.* Retrieved *from* www.nces.ed.gov

National Center for Educational Statistics. (2009). *Educational attainment of persons 25 years old and over, by race/ethnicity and state:2005–07.* Retrieved from www.nces.ed.gov

National Center for Educational Statistics. (2010a). *The condition of education 201:* Indicator 20. Retrieved from www.nces.ed.gov

National Center for Educational Statistics. (2010b). *The condition of education 2010:* Indicator 4. Retrieved from www.nces.ed.gov

National Center on Family Homelessness. (2009). *America's youngest outcasts.* Retrieved from www.homelesschildrenamerica.org

National Endowment for the Arts. (2007). *To read or not to read: A question of national consequence.* Washington, DC: Author. Retrieved from www.arts.gov

Neuhaus. R. (1975, December 5). Book reviews. *Commonweal,* 603–604.

Noddings, N. (1984). *Caring: A feminine approach to ethics and moral education.* Berkeley: University of California Press.

Perlstein, L. (2007). *Tested.* New York: Henry Holt.

Pratte, R. (1988). *The civic imperative.* New York: Teachers College Press.

Purpel, D. (1989). *The moral and spiritual crisis in education.* New York: Bergin & Garvey.

Purpel, D. (1999). *Moral outrage in education.* New York: Peter Lang.

Quindlen, A. (1988, January 31). "Give us a shot at something." *The New York Times, Book Review,* 7.

Ravitch, D. (2010). *The death and life of the great American school system.* New York: Basic Books.

Reich, R, (2010, July19/26). Inequality in America and what to do about it. *The Nation,* 13–15.

Rich, J. M. & DeVitis, J. (1985). *Theories of moral development*. Springfield, IL: Charles C. Thomas.

Robelen, E. (2009, February 25). Quality seen as job one for charters. *Education Week,* 1, 16–18.

Rothstein, R. (2004). *Class and schools*. New York: Teachers College Press.

Schneider, M. (2009, March 14). NAEP math results hold bad news for NCLB. *American.Com.* Retrieved from www.blog.american.com

Sizer, T. & Sizer, N. F. (1999). *The students are watching*. Boston: Beacon Press.

Stern, S. (1996, March). Ideological tourist. *Commentary*, 70–72.

Stotsky, S. (2006, March 19). Savage inconsistencies: Kozol's intellectual confusion. *EdNews.org.* Retrieved from www.ednews.org

Sullivan, A. (2009, November 9). Last one standing. *Time,* 46–47.

U.S. Census Bureau. (2009). *National average earnings by educational attainment.* Retrieved from www.census.gov

U.S. Census Bureau. (2010, September 16). *Income, poverty, and health insurance coverage in the United States: 2009.* Retrieved from www.census.gov

Wilson, L. (2010, January 27). New York: Archbishop of Canterbury Visits the South Bronx. *Episcopal News Service.*

Wilson, W. J. (1987). *The truly disadvantaged.* Chicago: The University of Chicago Press.

Wilson, W. J. (1996). *When work disappears*. New York: Vintage.

Winters, M. (2006, Spring). Savage exaggerations: Worshipping the cosmology of Jonathan Kozol. *Education Next*, 71–75.

Zimmerman, C. (1996). A conversation with Jonathan Kozol. *The Plough*, 47, 1–7.

CHAPTER TWENTY-TWO

Framing Adolescents, Their Schools, and Cultures

Contested Worldviews

LINDA IRWIN-DEVITIS

How you think about adolescents is shaped by deeply held, largely subconscious worldviews about family. Worldviews about family inform our beliefs about adolescents and influence the ways we relate to adolescents in the family, school, agency, or any other setting. The argument I am making in this chapter—and the challenge for us all—is to examine our beliefs and predispositions and their foundations. I will build upon Lakoff's work on family-based worldviews and how the values privileged by a worldview inform current policies toward adolescents, their schools, and their cultures. How do our views impact our professional roles and relationships with adolescents (as well as our parenting)?

The chapter begins with an overview of historical and current lamentations on adolescents. Then the discussion focuses on the changing goals of adolescent education in America—contrasting the views shared when our nation was founded to the current stated educational purposes. With that background established, the chapter explores our understanding of adolescence and adolescent policies within the context of the theories of family worldviews, and over-arching frames that shape thinking across a wide variety of issues including adolescence and education. Finally, the chapter explores what might happen if we bring deeply held worldviews to the surface, consciously deconstruct those frames, worldviews, and values, and begin a conversation on a progressive "reframing" of adolescence and adolescent policies. Such a reframing has the potential to bring the changes many progressive educators and other professionals believe are needed. Progressive policies whose purpose it is to increase the well-being, aspirations and outcomes of all adolescents, their families and communities are possible within the American value system. These progressive policies encourage the development of students and citizens who are engaged and well-prepared for creating fulfilled, productive lives in caring communities.

Young People Are Out of Control (And So Were You!)

"What is happening to our young people? They disrespect their elders; they disobey their parents. They ignore the law. They riot in the streets inflamed with wild notions. Their morals are decaying. What is to become of them?" Plato's words are not much different from editorials, conversations in teachers' break rooms, and portrayals of teens in movies, television, print, and popular culture. With the advent of social networking, these despairing conclusions are amply illustrated with disturbing self-portraits on social networks such as Facebook and MySpace. Teen problems and pathologies are often a major portion of non-fiction bestsellers, texts, and parenting guides on adolescence: Pipher's (1995) *Reviving Ophelia: Saving the Selves of Adolescent Girls;* Simmons' (2001) *Odd Girl Out: The Hidden Culture of Aggression in Girls;* Straus' (2007) *Adolescent Girls in Crisis: Intervention and Hope;* Miller's (2008) *Getting Played: African American Girls, Urban Inequality and Gendered Violence;* Tyre's (2009) *The Trouble with Boys: A Surprising Report Card on our Sons, Their Problems at School, and What Parents and Educators Must Do;* and Savil's (2009) *The Secret Lives of Boys: Inside the Raw Emotional World of Male Teens Boys Adrift: The Five Factors Driving the Epidemic of Unmotivated Boys and Underachieving Young Men.* While there are certainly books on healthy, happy, successful adolescents, the bestsellers tend to focus on adolescent angst, surging hormones and the dangerous transition from childhood to adulthood that has the status of "common wisdom."

Adolescence was defined as a time of *sturm und drang* by G. Stanley Hall (1931/2008), the first modern psychologist to study the period between childhood and adulthood, and the impacts of wayward adolescents on the future of society. Philosophers, psychologists, parents, professionals, economists, and business elites often think of adolescence as a time of risk—and so do many adolescents and anxious parents:

> Across America today, adolescents are confronting pressures to use alcohol, cigarettes, or other drugs and to have sex at earlier ages. Many are depressed: about a third of adolescents report they have contemplated suicide. Others are growing up lacking the competence to handle interpersonal conflict without resorting to violence. By age seventeen, about a quarter of all adolescents have engaged in behaviors that are harmful or dangerous to themselves and others: getting pregnant, using drugs, taking part in antisocial activity, and failing in school. Altogether, nearly half of American adolescents are at high or moderate risk of seriously damaging their life chances. The damage may be near term and vivid, or it may be delayed, like a time bomb set in youth. (The Carnegie Council on Adolescent Development, 1995)

It is true that adolescence is a time of transition, increasing responsibility, enormous physical, social, and emotional changes, brain development, and searching for identity; however, these changes are normal, developmental, and not dissimilar from childhood transitional periods and adult transitional periods. Males (1996), Rothstein (1998), and Bracey (2009) are some of the scholars who argue against the popular hysteria of lost youth and schools in crisis. Many professionals and parents, however, are prepared to see a perilous and rocky road threatening to wreck adolescents' lives; and such views have an impact on our beliefs, behaviors, and policies.

Education as the Key to American Economic Dominance

In addition to beliefs about adolescent development, there are other, more recent additions to Americans' "common wisdom" about the purposes of adolescent education. Like the historical beliefs informing our ideas of adolescent development discussed above, current beliefs about the purposes of education are pervasive, and have recently assumed a dominance overshadowing or completely expunging historical beliefs about the purpose of American education.

Jefferson spoke often about the purposes of American education:

> No other sure foundation can be devised for the preservation of freedom and happiness . . . Preach a crusade against ignorance; establish and improve the law for educating the common people. Let our countrymen know that the people alone can protect us against the evils [of misgovernment]. (Thomas Jefferson to George Wythe, 1786)

In a similar vein, James Madison stated: "Learned institutions ought to be favorite objects with every free people. They throw that light over the public mind which is the best security against crafty and dangerous encroachments on the public liberty." George Washington Carver was also clear in his view of the purpose and power of education, "Education is the key to unlock the golden door of freedom." G. K. Chesterton added, "Education is simply the soul of a society as it passes from one generation to another." Horace Mann believed that "A human being is not attaining his full heights until he is educated." John Dewey often affirmed his strong beliefs about the purpose of education, "Education, therefore, is a process of living and not a preparation for future living." Franklin D. Roosevelt also spoke of the worth of education, "Knowledge—that is, education in its true sense— is our best protection against unreasoning prejudice and panic-making fear, whether engendered by special interest, illiberal minorities, or panic-stricken leaders." His wife Eleanor (1930) was even more specific:

> What is the purpose of education? This question agitates scholars, teachers, statesmen, every group, in fact, of thoughtful men and women. The conventional answer is the acquisition of knowledge, the reading of books, and the learning of facts. Perhaps because there are so many books and the branches of knowledge in which we can learn facts are so multitudinous today, we begin to hear more frequently that the function of education is to give children a desire to learn and to teach them how to use their minds and where to go to acquire facts when their curiosity is aroused. Even more all-embracing than this is the statement made not long ago, before a group of English headmasters, by the Archbishop of York, that 'the true purpose of education is to produce citizens.'

In these various quotes from some of our most influential leaders and thinkers, the overriding themes connected to public education are citizenship, freedom, and a path toward happiness. Then came Sputnik, a time of great fear, and a renewed focus on American education.

Adolescents: A Threat to Our National Security

Since *A Nation at Risk* (1983), there has been an increasing focus on economic rationales for education: work-force development has become the mantra from not only business interests, but also educators and education policy-makers, and it has had the greatest impact upon the shape of adolescent education. Historically, the American notion of "common schools" was to prepare a citizenry (although largely restricted to white males) who were prepared to assume their rightful roles in a democratic republic.

Linking outcomes of adolescent education to economic dominance of the nation is again in vogue. *Tough Choices or Tough Times: The Report of the New Commission on the Skills of the American Workforce* (2006) states:

"We have failed to motivate most of our students to take tough courses and work hard, thus missing one of the most important drivers of success in the best-performing nations."

Our morality, our national security, and everything in between seem to rest on the shoulders of adolescents in our society. Scholars challenge the conclusions of these recurrent exhortations with their scapegoating and over-wrought language of crisis, but their work is largely unknown to the public and ignored by the media. Therefore, progressive rebuttal has had little impact on policy or perception. There are strong rebuttals about the ability of our society to produce high-paying positions for all students even if they achieve a post-secondary education (Aronowitz & DeFazio, 1994; Gee, Hall, & Lankshear, 1996). Our census data (2009) tell us that the greatest job growth (in real numbers) in 2008–09 was in the fields of personal and home health and care aides (773,000), that require only short-term training. In fact, of the new jobs created, 52% require short to moderate on-the-job training, another 6% require an associate's or specialized post-high school training, 35% require a bachelor's degree and 7% require an advanced degree.

Perhaps adolescents are more perceptive than many pundits: they look around and see where there are jobs in their neighborhoods. Yet, we continue to hear that unless America's high school completion and college going rates improve, we will be risking our national future. As adolescents' education has taken on an increasingly vocational purpose, the notions of education as preparation for citizenship, freedom, democratic participation, fulfillment, and happiness have increasingly disappeared in educational policy and planning. The "road," or "race," to economic security through higher educational attainment has been defined by standards, high-stakes tests, fewer curricular options, tighter regulation of teaching and learning, fewer opportunities to explore beyond the basic curriculum, zero tolerance for disruptions, and teachers and principals who are increasingly focused on test scores. Educational goals of increasing adolescents' independence, democratic participation, individual exploration, and freedom of choice are few and far between in low-performing schools.

Drop-out rates escalate even as restrictions tighten. Those students who do navigate the system are prepared to follow instructions, prepare for tests, acquire facts—and in these "sanctioned" schools, it is rare to find a teacher or leader who remembers Bronowski's admonition: "It is important that students bring a certain ragamuffin, barefoot, irreverence to their studies; they are not here to worship what is known, but to question it."

As for the "declining morality" among America's adolescents, multiple sources report declining drug use, more than a decade of declining teen pregnancy rates, and little evidence of a marked increase in teen sexual activity. Urban and rural schools, where rates of violence, drug use and early sexual activity are increasing, are often the least democratic, offering little opportunity for individual exploration and the practice of freedom. These are typically schools where citizenship is defined as simply obeying the rules. They are often places where training trumps teaching. They are largely the antithesis of what one wise (anonymous) person shared, "An educational system isn't worth a great deal if it teaches young people how to make a living but doesn't teach them how to make a life."

In spite of the hysteria of national reports and the continuing critique of public education and the next generation, most 'tweens and teens survive and thrive; and the majority emulate the values and aspirations of their families and communities. There are teens, especially those who are poor or in abusive situations, who are in serious trouble. Teens whose lives, health, and future are at serious risk. Is such dysfunction endemic to adolescence or attributable to the context and climate in which adolescents live, work, and go to school? Is our overarching devotion to education as primarily a vehicle for economic survival helping or interfering with educational attainment? Is our impoverished and limited view of education partly responsible for the problems it claims to address? In some (mostly poor, often minority) communities, adolescence is pathologized; public education is vilified; and educators are denigrated. As we move further into No Child Left Behind, "Race to the Top" (the new competition among states for federal dollars to improve teaching and teacher evaluation, experiment with alternative systems for teacher salaries, implement better student data-tracking systems, and encourage charter school formation), a national curriculum, and the directions set by the Gates Foundation, the Business Roundtable and an activist U.S. Education Department, we hear less and less about the historical aims and purposes of education in our society. Indeed, the reigning "crisis" and the emphasis on public education is a major agenda item of those conservatives whose ideas are being implemented into policies from NCLB to choice issues, including charters and vouchers to accountability of schools, without any attention to societal factors that influence the students who attend. There are many and varied explanations for this conservative emphasis on education policy— and for good reason. As Kumashiro (2008) asserts: "public education has the potential to change the very conditions that have benefited certain groups. It is not surprising then, that in recent years, the Right has launched a series of policy initiatives that aim to undermine public education." He goes on to conclude, "The right is successfully reframing common sense in education" (pp. 6–7).

Some influential federal and corporate leaders and their followers attribute individual and societal problems primarily to adolescent development: lack of personal responsibility on the part of teens, their families and failing schools; the education bureaucracy; teacher incompetence; and inadequate accountability. Those ideas are "common wisdom," they shape institutional responses, and lead to divergent actions or inaction in schools, courtrooms, legislatures and think tanks. Progressive parents, educators, and citizens respond with research, statistics, issue papers, and monographs. Rarely are they influential in the debates at local, state, and federal levels.

More often, progressive educators subvert the systems to provide schools that honor democratic participation, minimize the impact of federal and state mandates, and focus on the historical values and goals of education for full, active, respectful, questioning citizenship. The opportunities for this joyful subversion are fewer as the federal and state accountability apparatus expands—and disproportionately impacts low-performing schools and districts. Progressive teachers, scholars, parents and adolescents themselves are silenced: their voices, research, and values have so little impact in shaping institutional policies toward adolescents. Why?

The shifting purpose for public education from citizenship to economic survival (or hegemony) is certainly one reason that progressive ideas are marginalized, but I suggest there is another deeper reason that is identified in George Lakoff's work on family metaphors and worldviews.

Worldviews, Adolescents, and Social Policy

How we think of adolescents, individually and collectively, is influenced by the historical and popular contexts mentioned above; but our views of teens and 'tweens are also shaped by deeper frames that shape our worldview. There are distinctive worldviews (meta-frames) that shape and divide our individual opinions, beliefs, and actions. These worldviews predispose our willingness to see young people as basically worthy of adult mentoring and second chances or to punish them as adults deserving retribution for disobedience. The tensions among worldviews and our conceptions of adolescence are reflected in dysfunctional and contradictory impulses, not only in Hall's (1931/2008) description of adolescent psyches, but also in our policies, and too often in unyielding disagreements about what is in the best interests of young people. These are the arguments that I will be making in this chapter using Lakoff's definitions of framing and metaphor from a cognitive science perspective.

When we think of an adolescent, what images and words come to mind? Those thoughts and words are evidence of the frame(s) we use to think about adolescents. The collective frames regarding adolescents are very powerful in shaping the actions of parents, teachers, and policy-makers whose decisions influence the lives and futures of young people who are within their sphere of influence. The frames defining adolescents are influenced by larger frames or worldviews, largely unconscious to the individual, held by adolescents themselves, as well as their parents, their teachers, and policy-makers. These worldviews influence and define most, if not all, aspects of a person's values, beliefs, and understandings.

Linguistic framing activates the generally unconscious mental structures that shape our understandings of a topic, a concept, a role, and a worldview. The skillful, sometimes invisible, use of frames is a key aspect of work in marketing, politics, and any type of persuasion. In order to create social change, George Lakoff (and other scientists who investigate the linguistic aspects of cognition and belief systems) indicates that social activists must "reframe" arguments. The next section of this chapter explores Lakoff's notion of family worldviews more fully, applies it to understandings of adolescence, and concludes with some suggestions for reframing our understandings of adolescence, and our social policies and practices that shape American adolescent education.

Frames, Family Metaphors, and World vews

In his most popular book exploring the ubiquity of frames, *Don't Think of an Elephant* (2004), Lakoff asks his readers to try not to think about an elephant after reading the book title. He reiterates, "Whatever you do, do **not** think of an elephant" (p. 3). As he notes, and as you are experiencing currently, once a "frame" such as "elephant" is activated, you cannot force yourself not to see the big, heavy animal with its ivory tusks, huge eyes, and long trunk. We each have our own set of frames about elephants and once those are activated, our minds fall into those frames without any conscious effort—and getting out of the frame is extremely difficult once it is activated.

Lakoff's earlier work focused on metaphors (1980) as central to our ability to make meaning. Drawing upon that work, Lakoff attempted to find the metaphors (organizing ideas, meta-narratives) that would explain the seemingly unrelated positions of American conservatives (and liberals) on key issues. Lakoff (1996) eventually began to see divergent family metaphors that could explain the seemingly incoherent pastiche of political views that unite people as conservatives (or progressives) and sometimes divide them from each other. Lakoff's primary interest in these metaphors was understanding seemingly contradictory and inconsistent political stances on issues that unite conservatives (and liberals.) "I remembered a paper that one of my students had written some years back that showed that we all have a metaphor for the nation as a family. We have Founding Fathers. The Daughters of the American Revolution. We "send our sons" to war…Given the existence of the metaphor linking the nation to the family, I asked the next question: If there are two different understandings of the nation do they come from two different understandings of family" (2004, p. 5.).

Lakoff found that divergent moral and political views could originate in the potent metaphor of nation/government as family.[1] These divergent metaphors of family (and nation/government) embody certain values and beliefs and form the basis for moral reasoning. The first of the family metaphors that provides the foundation of conservative thought is the *strict father family*. The other metaphor, the *nurturing parent family*, explains and unifies most progressive positions and understandings.[2]

The *strict father family model* is built upon the notion of a traditional family with an authoritative father supporting and protecting the family, i.e. setting and enforcing rules. The mother is responsible for the care of children and house and upholding the father's rules. Children must respect and obey their parents. Such obedience will enable children to be accountable and self-reliant. Parental love is part of the strict father model, but it never outweighs parental authority. Successful children become self-reliant and independent. Thus adolescents/young adults are to be independent and make their own way; and parents are no longer to meddle in their lives since parental work is done (Lakoff, 2002, p. 33). Moral strength and authority are primary in the patriarchal family. Nurturance and empathy are also important, but they are never allowed to interfere with the strict father's moral strength and authority. In this family metaphor, the pursuit of self-interest coming from self-discipline allows one to achieve self-reliance. Meritocracy is a central pillar of "strict father" views—one earns and gets what one deserves on the basis of individual talent and work.

In the *nurturing parent family model,* empathy, nurturance, and love are dominant and parenting is shared, not hierarchical. It is expected that being cared for, nurtured, and demonstrating and expecting empathy and respect will enable children to become responsible and self-disciplined. Nurturing families teach and model respect for those within and beyond the family. Nurturance also implies protection, support, and strength from both parents, who share responsibilities for all aspects of family life and child-rearing. Dialogue and explanations between parents and children are crucial since children need to understand parental decisions. Nurturing parenting requires understanding children as individuals, including their interests, values, and right to individuality. In this model, the moral pursuit of self-interest and fulfillment can only be realized by the practice of empathy and nurturance of others. In fact, empathy and nurturance are the basis of self-fulfillment and moral authority (Lakoff, 2002, p. 34).

Lakoff, while clearly identifying himself as a progressive, does not discuss these different family models as right or wrong, better or worse. Rather, he explores their explanatory power to make sense of a variety of outwardly contradictory positions and stances. Using Lakoff's competing views of family, one can examine the competing frames of adolescence and the resulting policies and practices regarding adolescence. These divergent family metaphors provide a theoretical base to explore the boundaries and contradictions that competing frames impose on parents, teachers, and policy-makers.

A recent example of the "strict father model" is making the news. Congress and the media are engaged in debating the abortion provisions in the health care reform bill. The "strict father model" may be seen in the statement from the Catholic Diocese of Washington, D.C., about the health care reform bill. The bishop of the Washington diocese said if the bill pays for abortion services as part of the public option,[3] the social services work of the D.C. Catholic Charities will be suspended. This is a clear example of a "strict father model," valuing obedience to church doctrine on abortion more than empathy for those in need. This position puzzles or outrages those, both Catholic and not, who value empathy in the "nurturing family model" over the obedience demanded by "the strict father."

In addition, the model of obedience to the "father" elucidates the reluctance to provide sex education or contraception. The strict father's authority also explains policies requiring parental notification for adolescents seeking abortions. Drug, alcohol, and tobacco addictions are seen as "disobedience" and a "failure of self-discipline"; and the key intervention is punishment in a "strict father" worldview. The adolescent's opinion is not sought and often ignored or cut off when offered. The failure is within the adolescent, the punishment is the father's duty, and the future is solely up to the adolescent to work out herself. While the "nurturing family" view strongly supports protecting adolescents from these destructive forces, the responses are more likely to include counseling, support, rehabilitation, and nurturance in addition to or in place of punishment. When punishment is involved, the "nurturing" model involves the adolescent in discussion and strategizing how to change behavior and collaboratively explores the kinds of support the adolescent herself identifies as important in her future success.

In education policy, we encounter some interesting examples of this conflict between worldviews. "Strict father" approaches are seen in Arne Duncan's and President Obama's words and policies, which are generally consistent with those of President George W. Bush, albeit better funded. A "strict father" worldview promotes the top-down setting of policy we are seeing in the criteria for "Race to the Top (RTTT)." RTTT affirms high-stakes testing, although with more realistic and psychometrically valid ways of measuring individual students, schools, districts, and states. There are still "report cards" which demonstrate obedience, or lack thereof, to the top-down mandates and competition in which not only schools, but also states, are winners and losers. In President Obama's controversial television speech to the nation's school children, the themes of "individual responsibility" and "personal accountability" far outweighed a more nuanced discussion of a social contract with America's young people. A social contract is based upon mutual responsibility (student, family, school, and society) and goes far beyond tests, report cards, and increasingly empty promises of "the American Dream."

Similarly, in Secretary Duncan's relentless attacks on teacher education, he plays the role of the "strict father" who is reprimanding the "mother" who is charged with carrying out his dictates obediently and without any expectation of input. There is no doubt that ardent supporters of education from both "strict father" and "nurturing family" perspectives expect high achievement and rigorous standards. The differences most often lie in choosing a set of strategies to achieve the goals and sometimes in the motives underlying the goals.

These policies are distressing at face value; more importantly, they are incompatible with what we know about successful schools. Schools that are able to educate all children, close the achievement gap, and attract and keep great teachers and leaders are nurturing schools, like those that live the values in *This We Believe* (National Middle School Association, 2003), a wonderfully written example of the nurturing family model for educating adolescents in middle schools. The vision of middle schools as nurturing places for adolescents was, at best, incompletely enacted in our nation's schools over the last several decades. That nurturing vision met vigorous opposition from the Education Department under President George W. Bush. *This We Believe* violated the "strict father" views of NCLB. NCLB emphasized teacher-centered classrooms, implementing a curriculum and standards set by the "father" (state departments and district offices), and enforced through standardization, regulation, and sanctions. NCLB mandates left little time for student-centered, democratic classrooms and schools. NCLB contains no provisions for students' exploration of their talents, roles, and place in society. *This We Believe,* rather than prescribing the outcomes, promoted team- centered schools with democratic structures that honored teachers' professionalism, collaboration, and input in school-wide policies and procedures. Schools based upon *This We Believe* and a nurturing family worldview work to ensure student success in a climate that values relationship and models responsibility and empathy while protecting students with an orderly environment. Such schools facilitate students' increasing self-governance and place less emphasis on inflexible "zero tolerance rules." The research on effective high schools highlighted the importance of commitments to strong relationships among all stakeholders (leaders, teachers, students, parents, and community), mutual respect, individualized curriculum, participatory decision-making, and high expectations. These school characteristics were associated with the highest levels of achievement and satisfaction among students, teachers, and leaders. However, these nurturing family values collide with NCLB's test-driven accountability, school report cards, and sanctions. RTT, Obama's major initiative, only affirms the top down, "strict father" model of educational reform with its emphasis on competition among the states for better tests, stricter accountability, and repetition of the perennial call for better teachers and better teacher preparation.

Family Metaphors as They Shape Views of Adolescents in Popular Culture, Education, and Social Policy

The implications of these disparate views of family are reflected in the debates that frame the views of adolescence in our culture and in policy debates:

Implications for Teachers of Adolescents

The vast majority of adolescents, in families and schools that are nurturing, navigate their 'tween and teen years without major trauma. The voices of adolescents who do not "fit the model" of expectations fare very differently, depending upon the schools and classrooms where they are expected to learn and grow. Those voices, and other research, strongly suggest that teachers of adolescents who work with their students, respect them as individuals, and provide nurturance are able to motivate students to far greater achievement, self-confidence, and increased aspirations. These voices come from school professionals (individually and, more importantly, collectively) who understand that certain students have or lack privileges that make meritocracy a dubious model and indeed a potentially dangerous one when students come from vastly different backgrounds, cultures, languages, discourses (Gee, 2008), homes, and neighborhoods. These educators are able to create "nurturing" instructional climates and educative communities that are conducive to greater learning and better social and psychological outcomes for all adolescents.

Implications for Adolescent Advocates

In many ways, this chapter reflects the assumption that you, the reader, will evaluate the research, claims, and logical consistency of the arguments I have presented, judge their merits, and, if found worthy, they may have some impact on your thinking and practice. That assumption, applied to you, may be accurate; but, increasingly, educational progressives who hold the "nurturing family" value system are finding their arguments have little impact in policy or practice.

If you responded to the ideas presented with an "ah-ha" reaction and a feeling of re-affirmation, it is likely you share many of the values of the "nurturing family." If you found yourself questioning the article, disagreeing with its assumptions, doubting the research presented and the conclusions drawn, it is likely that you do not share the "nurturing family" worldview and my argument that "nurturance" is key to good adolescent education and policy. This leads back to George Lakoff's seminal work on how we make decisions—largely on our basic worldview and the hierarchy of values that we hold as individuals and only secondarily on evidence as viewed through our worldview frames and their associated values.

In many ways, Lakoff's work on the power of values over logic, worldviews over specific issues, and the failure of progressive educators to respond effectively to the conservative educational policies of the last decade complements current work in cognitive psychology and behavioral economics (Ariely, 2009; Levitt & Dubner, 2005; Thaler & Sunstein, 2009: Brafman & Brafman, 2009);

	Strict Father Model	Nurturing Family Model
Popular culture	Supporting strict limits on alcohol and tobacco sales to minors; protecting minors from certain movies and books, including censoring print and Web access; restricting access to contraception, including parental notification in abortion; banning exposure to ideas and options inconsistent with the strict father family's values.	Negotiating rules and responsibilities; modeling and expecting democratic and respectful discussion of issues in family relations with empathy, flexibility, and active listening; emphasizing adolescent apprenticeship in decision-making and recognition of adolescent voice in decision-making.
Adolescent development	Advocating firm guidance and boundaries with strict consequences to protect adolescents from mistakes and from straying beyond their appropriate role in the strict father family—obedient and unquestioning adherence; designating LBGT as deviant behavior, as something to be corrected, a personal failing, and a practice for which an adolescent can be forced to leave the family.	Suggesting adolescents need to experiment within safe contexts, make mistakes without adult consequences, negotiate boundaries with parents and adults, and explore and challenge as they practice independent thought; honoring difference in a variety of ways, including LBGT youth.
Textbooks on adolescence and parenting guides	Discussing adolescent pathologies, the stress and turmoil of identity formation and physical change; suggesting "tough love" approaches.	Emphasizing identity development, experimentation, freedom to explore roles and new responsibilities.
Education policy	Setting standards; implementing high-stakes assessments; using graduation tests; tracking; making early decisions on vocational versus college-bound tracks; establishing a clear hierarchy with rules and enforcement in the hands of adults; enforcing zero tolerance; emphasizing top-down decision-making and curriculum mandates; emphasizing teacher-dominated classroom management with rule-dominated adult supervision rather than promoting student self-management, democratic approaches to discipline.	Practicing genuine "middle school philosophy" which values relationships and individualism; creating small schools movement; using a student-centered curriculum; practicing democratic decision-making with significant student voice in classroom management and curriculum.
Criminal justice	Trying adolescents as adults; reluctance to remove adolescents from family, even in cases of parental abuse and neglect	Emphasizing rehabilitation; welfare of the adolescent and adolescent voice as well as parental rights.

Lehrer, 2009) challenging the Enlightenment view of the rational individual operating to maximize self-interest. In this new realm of cognitive science Willingham (2009), we are far from rational, i.e., not designed to think, but rather to operate on a series of scripts, frames, and memories that shape our responses and behavior in ways that are largely unconscious. "Discourses" (Gee, 2008)—ways of believing, thinking, talking and being—are similar to the scripts and memory sequences cited by Willingham. Both Discourses and memory scripts are largely unconscious and do not require or invite "thinking." The scripts that Willingham (2009) describes are being researched though *f*MRI work; however, Discourses lend themselves to linguistic analysis both by researchers and, though less sophisticated, by teachers, other professionals, parents, and adolescents themselves. I suggest that a person's "Discourses" can be examined, reflected upon, embraced or discarded to some degree. However, these Discourses operate within the family worldview that is dominant (and largely operating below consciousness) for the individual, i.e., the dominant family metaphor is lived in specific sets of beliefs and behaviors. The power of these dominant worldviews, strict father or nurturing parent, are so strongly and deeply held that they override "rational" analysis and logical argument. Research and theories that contradict these deeply held views rarely have the impact needed to make or accept the changes advocated.

Well-written, cogent issue analysis (the forte of many progressives and academics) will not be sufficient. Critiques of conservative adolescent policies, no matter how well-argued, will only reinforce the conservative frames that dominate current policies and discussions. By arguing for a different, or more effective, type of accountability, we are using the conservative frame and reinforcing the argument that the major flaw of adolescent education is the lack of accountability. By citing the research that graduation tests disproportionately have a negative impact on high school graduation by low-income, minority students with statistics and graphs, we are not challenging the "personal responsibility," "meritocracy" and "accountability" motifs of the "strict father family. In reality, I am just pointing to results that are acceptable and deserved within that worldview. By citing recidivism rates for "boot camps" and early incarceration, we argue for more empathy, which works with other progressives, but is trumped by perceived lack of "obedience" and "personal responsibility" in the "strict father" model. By arguing for protection of LBGT adolescents and acceptance of families that are not "traditional," we are assaulting the very foundation of the "strict father family" worldview.

When these worldviews (deeply held and largely below the level of conscious and rational thought) are challenged, it is clear that the Enlightenment view of human beings as rational actors is inaccurate. The research-based argument has had modest impact upon federal education policy. When qualitative, historical, and ethnographic research contradicted the "strict father" view, it was officially ousted from recognition as valid research for guiding educational policy. The textbook example is the "scientifically-based reading instruction" (SBRI) push in Reading First. Purportedly based upon the National Reading Panel Report, a close reading of the report itself and an examination of implementation of federal and state regulations put forth in the name of the report bear little consistency and many contradictions. Adolescent literacy programs were expected to adapt to SBRI findings that were never intended for use with students who were not beginning readers, and in many cases were inconsistent with the findings of the NRP report itself. The appeal of SBRI, the avowed authority prescribing interventions for an admittedly serious problem of inadequate literacy performance, was the "answer" coming from above which merely needed consistent implementation by classroom teachers. The reality is that even many original SBRI supporters, including Grover Norquist, admitted that, though the model had robust implementation, sufficient time to demonstrate impact, and a rigorous longitudinal evaluation, Reading First failed to improve reading skills of beginning readers. The multi-billion dollar Reading First Initiative certainly made no impact on older students who lacked the literacy skills needed for success.

Current research from Harvard (Hill & Chao, 2009) on parent involvement also indicates that the NCLB requirement for parental involvement, modeled on meta-analysis largely comprised of elementary school research, has not been successful in improving adolescents' success. Hill's and Chao's findings on secondary parent involvement suggest that adolescents benefit most through parental communication of high expectations for achievement and fostering career aspirations and through linking school learning to real life. This research also indicates that the transition from middle to high school is a key time and that communication between schools, parents, and adolescents is an important factor. Again, we have a "strict father," top-down policy over-generalizing the research available from elementary school studies and tying school accountability to parent involvement without a carefully researched, nuanced understanding of what kind of involvement is most appropriate for parents, teachers, tweens, and teens.

Reframing Adolescent Education and Policy

Given current top- down accountability, high-stakes assessment and the move toward federal curriculum mandates, which are all based upon a "strict father" model, how can progressive educators be heard? If George Lakoff's (2004, 2008) work has any salience, perhaps the most important message for adolescent advocates is that we must make "nurturing family" arguments based upon American values present since the earliest days of our country. Only through consistent and ubiquitous narratives emphasizing these values will advocates find the arguments and language frames that will be persuasive, unify progressive issues in a larger vision and, at the same time, be influential in policy-making and in re-shaping "common wisdom."

By connecting individual issues, arguments, and policy positions to a common set of values, we can be more effective advocates. These values are not strictly "contested" values and are shared to some degree by almost every American. Some examples of these shared progressive values are: the American commitment to public education as necessary for an engaged and informed citizenry; protection of our children and adolescents; adolescents' ability to practice engaged citizenship by participating in democratic decision-making, collaborative goal-setting, teamwork, and reflection upon their own behaviors and understandings, needs, and wants; the understanding of our founding fathers that we find success in shared efforts and common commitments; unity and a sense of common purpose as Franklin D. Roosevelt eloquently inspired in his fireside chats; and, perhaps most importantly, the nurturance, caring and empathy that are pre-eminent in all major religious, spiritual and moral traditions.

These values, while often contested, prevailed in the Civil Rights Movement of the 1950's and 1960's, the New Deal, and Lyndon Johnson's Great Society. While all of these movements had flaws, both in conception and implementation, they were endorsed by the majority of Americans because they invoked the basic values associated with the nurturing family worldview: empathy, community, caring, an equal playing field, the right to be different (Kumashiro, 2008), safety and security through common purpose, creating engaged and active citizenry through public education, and measuring success through the growth of individuals and communities in health, happiness, and security as well as economic strength. This list is doubtlessly incomplete and in need to word-smithing. It is meant as a first step, wading into the moral issues inherent in adolescent policy in education, criminal justice, and other social issues and anchoring our arguments in values that are clear and powerful. Adolescent advocates must set a progressive agenda, a unifying narrative in which powerful research and analysis, including the variety of issues raised in this book and others, can penetrate the "strict father" worldview. This agenda includes head-on challenges to the pre-eminence of economic goals as the overriding purpose of education, educational policy and educational practice.

The "strict father" worldview has led to policies that are detrimental for many adolescents, families, communities and the professionals who work with them. The "strict father" worldview contradicts the deeply held moral convictions of many Americans who continue to fight or subvert the system. As policies become more entrenched and representative of the "strict father" worldview and more instantiated in poor and minority institutions deemed "failing," the "strict father" policies will lead many students to resist and drop out. (That dire consequence has already happened and continues to happen.) Others will learn obedience in a top-down hierarchy with little opportunity for democratic participation, little modeling of empathy and compassion, and a restricted sense of who they are and what they might become.

If this is to change, progressives must reach out to the vast majority of Americans who value both empathy and obedience. Progressives must create a narrative elevating the long tradition of progressive values in American thought and policy—empathy and compassion, freedom and engaged citizenship.

Notes

1. Lakoff does not equate *parenting* and *political views*. He also warns that individuals may vary between the views depending upon issues and may also vary over time. Even with these important caveats, Lakoff still makes a persuasive case that these guiding views of *family,* and by extension *nation,* have important explanatory power to elucidate political beliefs and values.
2. For a fascinating popular exploration of these family metaphors in American politics, read Lakoff's (2004) *Don't Think of an Elephant: Know Your Values and Frame the Debate.* For a more scholarly examination, *Moral Politics* (2002) provides a more thorough, research-based examination.
3. The Hyde Amendment already bars the use of government money for abortions.

References

Ariely, Dan. (2009). *Predictably irrational: The hidden forces that shape our decisions.* New York: Harper.

Aronowitz, S., & DeFazio, W. (1994). *Jobless future: Sci-tech and the dogma of work.* Minneapolis: University of Minnesota Press.

Bracey, Gerald W. (2009) *Education hell: Rhetoric versus reality.* Alexandria, VA: Educational Research Service.

Brafman, Ori & Rom Brafman. (2009). *Sway: The irresistible pull of Irrational behavior.* New York: Broadway Business.

Bronowski, J. (1976). *The ascent of man.* Boston: Little, Brown.

Carnegie Council on Adolescent Development (1995). *Great transitions: Preparing adolescents for a new century.* New York: Carnegie Corporation of New York.

Carver, G. W. (1991). In Kremer, G. R. (Ed.). *George Washington Carver: In his own words.* Columbia, MO: University of Missouri Press.

Chesterton, G. K. (1987). In Marlin, G. J., Rabatin, R. P., & Swan, J. L. (Eds.). *The quotable Chesterton: A topical compilation of the wit, wisdom and satire of G. K. Chesterton.* Garden City, NY: Image Books.

DeNavas, W., Carmen, B., Proctor, D., & Smith, J. C. (2009). *Income, poverty, and health insurance coverage in the United States: 2009.* Washington, DC: U. S. Census Bureau.

Dewey, J. (1897). My pedagogic creed. *School Journal, 54* (January): 77-80.

Gee, James P. (2008). *Social linguistics and literacies: Ideology in discourses, 3rd. Ed.* New York: Routledge.

Gee, J., Hall, G., & Lankshear, C. (1996). *The new work order.* Boulder, CO: Westview.

Hall, G. S. (1931/2008). *Adolescence—Its psychology and its relations to physiology, anthropology, sociology, sex, crime, and religion.* Bel Air, CA: Hesperides Press.

Hill, N. E. & Chao, R. K. (Eds.) (2009). *Families, schools, and the adolescent: Connecting research, Policy, and practice.* New York: Teachers College Press.

Jefferson, T. (1786). In B. B. Oberg (Ed.) *The papers of Thomas Jefferson,* 10:244. Princeton, NJ: Princeton University Library.

Kumashiro, Kevin K. (2008). *The seduction of common sense: How the right has framed the debate on America's schools.* New York: Teachers College Press.

Lakoff, George & Mark Johnson. (1980). *Metaphors we live by.* Chicago: University of Chicago Press.

Lakoff, George. (2002). *Moral politics: How liberals and conservatives think,* 2nd ed. Chicago: University of Chicago Press.

Lakoff, George. (2004). *Don't think of an elephant! Know your values and Frame the debate.* White River Junction, VT: Chelsea Green Publishing.

Lakoff, George and The Rockridge Institute. (2006). *Thinking points: Communicating our American values and vision.* New York: Farrar, Straus & Giroux.

Lakoff, George. (2008). *The political mind: A cognitive scientist's guide to Your brain and its politics.* New York: Penguin Books.

Lehrer, Jonah. (2009). *How we decide.* New York: Houghton Mifflin.

Levitt, Steven D. & Stephen J. Dubner. (2005). *Freakonomics: A rogue economist explores the hidden side of everything.* New York: Morrow.

Males, Mark A. (1996). *Scapegoat generation: America's war on adolescents.* Monroe, ME: Common Courage Press.

Mann, H. (1989). *On the art of teaching.* Carlisle, MA: Applewood Books.

Mann, H. (2002). In M. Engelbreit (Ed.). *Words for teachers to live by.* Kansas City, MO: Andrews McMeel.

National Commission on Excellence in Education. (1983). *A nation at risk: The imperative for educational reform.* Washington, DC: National Institute for Education.

National Institute of Child Health and Human Development. (2000). *Report of the National Reading Panel. Teaching children to read: An evidence-based assessment of the scientific research literature on reading and its implications for reading instruction* (NIH Publication No. 00–4769). Washington, DC: U.S. Government Printing Office.

National Middle School Association (2003). *This we believe: Keys to educating young adolescents.* Westerville, OH: National Middle School Association.

New Commission on the Skills of the American Workforce. (2007) *Tough choices or tough times.* Washington, DC: National Center on Education and the Economy.

Pipher, N. (1995). Reviving Ophelia: *Saving the selves of adolescent girls.* New York Riverhead Books.

Roosevelt, E. (2003). In Wigal, D. (Ed.). *The Wisdom of Eleanor Roosevelt.* New York: Citadel Press.

Rothstein, Richard. (1998). *The way we were: The myths and realities of America's student achievement.* New York: Century Foundation Press.

Rothstein, Richard. (2004). *Class and schools: Using social, economic and educational reform to close the Black-white achievement gap.* New York: Teachers College Press.

Savil, M. (2009). *The secret lives of boys: Inside the raw emotional world of male teen boys adrift: The five factors driving the epidemic of unmotivated boys and underachieving young men.* New York: Basic Books.

Simmons, R. (2001). *Odd girl out: The hidden culture of aggression in girls.* Boston: Mariner Books.

Straus, M. B. (2007). *Adolescent girls in crisis: Intervention and hope.* New York: W. W. Norton.

Thaler, Richard H. & Cass Sunstein. (2009). *Nudge: Improving our decisions about health, wealth and happiness.* New York: Penguin.

Tyre, P. (2009). *The trouble with boys: A surprising report card on our sons, their problems at school, and what parents and educators must do.* New York: Three Rivers Press

Willingham, Daniel T. (2009). *Why students don't like school: A cognitive scientist answers questions about how the mind works and what it means for the classroom.* New York: Jossey-Bass.

(This chapter is partially revised from a chapter with the same title which appeared in Joseph L. DeVitis and Linda Irwin-DeVitis, eds., *Adolescent Education: A Reader* [Peter Lang, 2010].)

CHAPTER TWENTY-THREE

Fear of Uncertainty, Control, and the Criminalizing of Youth

LYNDA STONE

As this chapter is being written, the latest American mass murderer, Jared Lochner of the recent tragedy in Tucson, is being arraigned—and a media picture of a 'crazed' individual makes most television viewers shudder. Ironically, this is also the week of the one-year anniversary of the tragic suicide of Massachusetts, formerly Irish, teenager Phoebe Prince as a result of bullying. On this occasion, her story was replaced by yet another act of violence. In the American imaginary, these two events join with Columbine and September 11 to produce a 'violent society.' No one seems to comment, by the way, on the significance that the 'criminals' are white and young. No one comments that societal conditions have contributed in part to these events. Further, that they have led directly to legal remedy is passed over as standard procedure: legislatures have rushed to enact rules that students who pose threats may be summarily excluded from schools and the majority of states now have anti-bullying laws.

The response also seems 'appropriate.' Events such as these confirm for many that the world, society today, is violent. Lochner is twenty-two years old; Prince was fifteen, further confirming that youth are central members of a violent society. What follows is not about violence per se although the theme will figure in the introduction below. It is rather about youth, about the society in which they presently live, and how they are perceived and treated within it. My thesis is that as a response to actual and perceived violence, in a society obsessed with control, youth are undergoing 'criminalizing.' In order to develop this thesis, the chapter must initially and very briefly be situated in this volume on moral and character education.

Introduction

Readers of this volume will become familiar with both negative critique and positive efforts in today's moral education. It is education, indeed often located in schools, although there are many sources and influences on morality. At the outset, it becomes difficult to say just how the young learn to be ethical. There are no simple recipes for how some persons acquire what has been called a moral compass, to live good productive lives, to share and enact fellow feeling, to contribute to a world in which there will be less and less danger for more and more people. In what follows, there will be no detailed attention to moral education, but matters of justice and ethics are central topics for concluding consideration.

The 'character' of the society does seem to matter. In a contemporary U.S. context, one wonders just how much the young are valued—especially when children and youth are 'not one's own.' Returning to the issue of violence, along with that perpetrated by and on individuals, in her writing on America's children, Valerie Polakow (2000) names violence as systemic. She writes, there exists

> the violence of poverty and homelessness, the violence of environmentally induced childhood diseases, the violence confronting children in schools and communities, the media and legislative 'criminalization' of children and a national drumbeat of 'zero-tolerance' leading to increasing confinement and incarcerating of youthful offenders. (1)

Polakow introduces one meaning of 'criminalization' concerning institutions and practices that are leading to labeling and treating youth as criminals through their entry into the juvenile—and adult—justice systems. Three points to begin: one is that the use of the active noun *criminalizing*, in the chapter title continues throughout the chapter: this is an on-going process. The second is that the 'spirit' of the justice system far exceeds its particular bounds: schools are particularly egregious participants in this criminalizing process. It might well be posited that contemporary conditions under which many youth live today are themselves 'criminal.' The third is that Polakow does not refer explicitly to the thematic of control, but surely it operates in all forms of violence, in enactment and response.

The chapter is organized into four sections and a conclusion, and texts are referenced and recommended for additional reading. The first section is a backgrounding in the present historic, societal context. Second is the definition and description of youth culture as 'in between' childhood and adulthood and its contemporary emergence as a significant social sphere. Third is a brief presentation of the U.S. justice system and its effect on youth. Fourth is an examination of school and schooling and especially how youth are being criminalized therein. A sequence of concepts appears in the title: Fear of uncertainty, the perceived need for control, and the targeted criminalizing of youth that has resulted. The events involving Jared Lochner and Phoebe Prince's bullies seem extreme, but one has to wonder what happened to their moral lives, what contributed to the violence in which they took part? The underlying but missing question concerns the presence of ethics in their lives, in society and in schools. Where is *our* ethics?

The discussion here is part of an ongoing, larger project on youth, schooling, and ethics, and much of the commentary results from years of exploration. This chapter draws on a variety of sources and recognizes its limitation in not offering a unifying theoretical approach. One could turn to Dewey or to Foucault, for instance, as a substantial and relevant philosophical lens. At this point, perhaps the best approach is a multi-disciplinary look: sources include philosophy, critical, and cultural studies, and justice studies. Three premises do operate: One is the strength of history, that lives are lived particular to space and time, to places and moments. This position is typically named 'historicist' or new historicism. The second is the centrality of language, that of 'discourse' or systemic language use: language helps determine practices and vice versa, and changes in each occur all the time. The third is that those cited in this chapter do share a strong reformist stance toward societal change and, for some, toward schooling. Finally, there are many approaches to reform. Others may believe that they have the answer, but surely contemporary society with its general problems—its youth, its justice system, and its schools—belies such a stance. I should also note that the chapter is written from a U.S./North American context but as a philosophical essay reflects a personal position.

Present Context

Given the historicist premise, neither context nor its embedded discussion is neutral, and there are many ways of presentation. A present thematic seems obvious: uncertainty in a public imagination has turned to negativity, indeed to fear, and to a particular response that calls for control. Given some obvious 'controls' over social life, for some social theorists the primary issue is what constitutes appropriate control or order.

No one today denies that the times and the society are complex. In this late modern/postmodern era, these ideas apply: an ambiguous and tentative world in which what has been taken for granted cannot be so any longer. Among 'taken-for-granteds' have been societal organization based in complications of division and hierarchy: national and international, local and global, particular and universal, individual and general. Given a multiple millennial history of haves and have-nots, change in these macro-domains might be welcomed, but most reformists concur that massive positive change—again for more people—has not happened yet. Indeed, some believe that 'things are getting worse.'

In a most direct but herein reductive sense, the present U.S. context is embedded in and contributes to a globalized, 'neo-liberal' economy largely based, both actually and rhetorically, on market capitalism. While interdependence is worldwide, an 'individualist' ethos functions in which competition dominates—the idea is to 'best the other guy.' A particular form of society, the social dimension, accompanies the economic sphere. In it, the competitive ethos has meant that the social order is an aggregate of 'individual units,' mine and ours such as family and largely localized community, are paramount; the result is a specific response to the other. The other is different from 'us,' left on its own and to be feared. There seems little compassion and generosity. Response to the economic and social spheres also appears to characterize a contemporary politics. 'Citizens' in the U.S. seem split into two camps, sometimes referred to in negative discourses toward 'the liberals' or 'the 'conservatives.' Sides may come together briefly in times of particular crisis. Everyone decried the events mentioned at the outset of this chapter, but calls for coming together in political civility soon dissipated.

The uncertain modern era is ably described by Zygmunt Bauman in two recent books, *Liquid Times: Living in an Age of Uncertainty* (2007) and *Does Ethics Have a Chance in a World of Consumers?* (2008). That he identifies 'the problem' as ethics is especially significant; however, he does name ethics as synonymous with justice, a choice that will be differentiated here at the conclusion. He operates from an initial metaphor that liquid times have turned the world into a battlefield, which picks up the sub-theme of taken-for-granteds noted above. In Bauman's sociological idiom it is widely recognized that any social form changes so rapidly that politics and justice appear fruit-less. This ubiquitous change is nowhere more present than in a divorce of power from politics and its relationship to reason. Altered in ways previously unimagined is the project of several centuries of Enlightenment hope and resolve. The understanding was to "take history under human adminis-tration and control—deploying…the most powerful among human weapons…to raise the 'is' to the level of the 'ought' (Bauman, 2008, 111). Faith in prediction and calculation has given way to fear. Here Bauman is worth quoting at length. Employing another metaphor of 'open society' for liquid-ity, gone is

> the self-determination of a society cherishing its openness, it now brings to most minds the terrifying expe-
> rience of a heteronomous, hapless, and vulnerable population confronted with, and possibly overwhelmed
> by forces it…[cannot control]….[It is] a population horrified by its own undefendability.…[and] obsessed
> by [security]…that cannot be obtained, let alone assured…[and that surely for no persons or nations is inde-
> pendent] of what happens in the rest of the world. (Bauman, 2007, 7)

Bauman connects liquid society to education. Henry Giroux locates Bauman's "negative globaliza-tion" (2007, 7) in a U.S./North American context in regard to youth.

Returning to the economic base, Giroux's villain is a government-sponsored, privatized popu-lar preoccupation with consumer acquisition, disposability, and satisfaction that absorbs everyone (see also Bauman, 2008, beginning 147). For Giroux Bauman's battlefield is comprised of a marriage of "market fundamentalism and a new authoritarianism" (Giroux, 2009, 2, 3). Now seemingly normal, elements of the 'marketplace' include privatization, deregulation, and outsourcing. All of this is facil-itated by media and electronic revolutions. Developments of several decades have been surely made worse over the last couple of years with increasing wealth disparity, Wall Street greed, and millions of American out of jobs and pushed from their homes. Further marketization has replaced democ-racy, especially after September 11. Economic fear becomes social and political fear in a set of gov-ernmental practices. Here is Giroux's list:

> militarization of everyday life, an imperial presidency (for example, think executive signing privilege
> on thousands of pieces of legislation, thwarting implementation), state-sanctioned torture, influence of
> religious extremists, and "a government draped in secrecy that was all too willing to suspend civil lib-
> erties." (5)

Hardest hit are the struggling individuals and groups that Giroux names as "disposable." Over the market-dominated decades, a social state has become a punishing state. Integral to the impact of pover-ty and class is race.

On education, a last word from Bauman, who offers still another metaphor, comparing "smart missiles" to teachers and students: survival in today's society requires new forms of learning, the abil-ity to learn as one goes, and to learn fast. But here is the most significant change: He explains, "[No] less crucial than the skill of quick learning…is the ability to instantly forget what has been learned before. Smart missiles wouldn't be smart if they were not able to 'change their mind' or revoke their previous 'decisions' with no second thoughts and regret" (Bauman, 2008, 183).

In summary, a general feeling about present life and context is characterized as uncertainty. In turn, result for many is a generalized fear. It is evident that those less fearful have relative privilege, but into each life, as the saying goes, can come misfortune and today surprisingly easily. In recent decades the state's role in managing the uncertain has been to be more and more authoritarian. A focus for authoritarian control is youth.

Youth Culture

In *Youth in a Suspect Society: Democracy or Disposability?* (2009) Giroux's emphasis is on youth as a particularly vulnerable population in our present society. They are a 'problem' in need of control. Ever since the dawn of human creation, there have been younger and older persons. If one accepts any form of developmentalism, there have always been differences between them. Moreover, it appears that the general pattern has been to socialize those young into being like their elders in order for continuation not only of the species but also of the social order they created. One imagines that these processes have never been easy; there does remain, however, nostalgia among many adults today that 'things were simpler in times past.' Who really knows?

The focus of this section is contemporary youth and the near past. Widely acknowledged is a 'youth culture,' about which much can be said. The obvious start is the ubiquitous presence of young people and their way of life. The demographical marking was the first time that the young constituted were more numerous than their elders. Youth presence is manifest in material ways such as consumerism and communications. Youth have transformed buying power in a huge market of goods just for them; for instance girls, and boys who are barely able to read know and demand the latest fashions. Youth, and adults who 'follow' the trends of youth have their own media outlets and again have changed how everyone communicates. Did anyone imagine that today's information age would look as it does? Presence, of course, is more than material; it is surely psychological. Aspects include the general condition of ambiguity and tentativeness. But the young may think little of the larger context. They are aware, however, of constant change—and in fact are 'bored' without it. Matters of place and status are just as important to them. The young want to be both individuals and members of groups and do not see the irony of protesting an individual style that looks exactly like that of their peers.

Today youth have their own social category, one that emerged out of historic and present context but is also related to categorizations of childhood and adulthood. In defining adults, for instance, think of changes since the beginning of the Enlightenment that have related to the capacity to reason. Race and gender have helped determine who is 'human' and who is not: slavery, minority status, property, franchise. A classic study on 'childhood,' by Philippe Ariès published in the 1960s sets the stage for adolescence and then youth.

Ariès's *Centuries of Childhood: A Social History of Family Life* (1960, 1962), identifies the shift in basic, broadly societal beliefs about children in Europe between the fourteenth and seventeenth centuries. He writes, "In medieval society the idea of childhood did not exist.…[As] soon as the child could live without the constant solicitude of his mother, his nanny or his cradle-rocker, he belonged to adult society.…The infant who was too fragile as yet to take part in the life of adults simply 'did not count'" (p. 128). 'Childhood' emerged by the latter centuries in two forms. One was that children were to be 'coddled' as 'toys' for adult amusement. In response to what was seen as spoiling the child, the other form was to view them as "fragile creatures of God who needed to be both safeguarded and reformed" (132, 133).

No longer viewed as theoretically definitive, Ariès nonetheless did recognize social and conceptual change. Change is also evident in the relatively recent emergence of the category of 'youth.' Prior to this there was and remains 'adolescence.' In her own classic *Act Your Age: A Cultural Construction of Adolescence*, Nancy Lesko (2001) locates the origin of the category of adolescence in the early decades of the twentieth century. Relative to the discussion of context, she writes,

> The adolescent was enormously plastic, even promiscuous…[both occupying a border and serving as a trope for complex societal issues. These included] the city as jungle, family upheaval, nation-building, political reforms, immigration, economic tumult, and international imperialism among others. (49, 50)

The focus, pan-nationally, was on wayward boys; it was then a short step to girls.

A well-intentioned response to what emerged in the early twentieth century (if not before) is the 'problem' of adolescence. It occurred in two reformist traditions, one romantic and the other scientific. Through both came 'administration' that included schools. Naming something today as 'romantic' often carries negative connotations. Early twentieth-century proposals and actual reforms produced in their best manifestations seem to be positive results: playgrounds, team sports, boy and girl scouts, compulsory schooling. These reforms are still in place today with varying evolutions and influences. Their positivity, then and now, does depend on the interpretive lens; at the least maintenance of a white, middle-class status quo with its effects requires continual interrogation. The scientific tradition had two origins, a societal 'great chain of being' derived in part from evolutionary theory, and more particularly, the psychological developmentalism of such important figures as G. Stanley Hall—the father of 'adolescence.' Interestingly, Hall's science based in recapitulation theory gave adolescence a romanticized place in the history and future of 'races' and nations. As Lesko puts this, for him "idealized adolescence…[is] the apex of human development…'before the decline of the highest powers of the soul in maturity and age.'"

> The scientific category of adolescence primarily remains today, related to, normalized, and central to a public imagination. Here are several senses of adolescence: biologically to hormones, historically to age, and sociologically, as from Coleman, to peer relations. A relatively recent addition to this conceptual panoply is research on the teenage brain that an already conditioned public easily absorbs. This last connection emphasizes the continued presence of 'adolescence,' now even more scientifically accepted. (2001, 54, 55)

The significant point about youth and their culture, or rather, cultures, is that they defy control, which contemporary society and its adults need. Without control, the general belief continues that there is no generational future. Surely one aspect of youth is what Lesko's theorization reveals: this is youth's place in time, neither children nor adults, they are the psychological 'in-between.' A pertinent historical moment is the initial identification of youth culture. Contemporary conception is symbolized in the work of James Coleman (1961) in the early sixties. His research for *The Adolescent Society: The Social Life of the Teenager and Its Impact on Education* (1961), foreshadowing subsequent focus, was conducted in schools.

Prior to "Coleman," only two large studies had been undertaken on youth social systems, one in the late forties and the other in the late fifties (Hollingshead, 1949; Gordon, 1957). Coleman's work was path-breaking because it demonstrated the strength of peer association relative to family. In the long run teens do want to fulfill parental desires for them, but at present, everyday life, peer status, and peer approval matter more. The historic thesis is that the major cause is a longer adolescence, rooted in societal changes in occupation and compulsory school attendance coupled with the centrality of the high school. Coleman writes, "[The adolescent] is 'cut-off' from the rest of society, forced inward toward his own age group, made to carry out his whole social life with others his own age. With his fellows he comes to constitute a small…[peer] society…and maintains only a few threads of connection with the…adult society" (3).

It is fifty years since the Coleman study appeared. The adult society as well as youth themselves have come to take a youth culture for granted. One wonders about recent changes within it. First, youth culture seems even more entrenched in society, perpetuated by generations of youth that have even been named, Boomers to Generation X. Second, the place of the school might well be different, not the actual site of identity formation but one of the locales in which it is played out. Media, social networks, processes of communication, and places like malls may be stronger influences. Third, as subcultures within youth culture have been and are formed, with quite a lot of internal cultural diversity, the roles of extracurricular activities, of work, of academic achievement probably have changed. Coleman's emphasis on extracurricular activities matters only to some teens today. Finally the education thesis for the study has had its own results. Coleman thought that research would indicate how schools could help direct youth into the values of the adult society, that is, act as an agency of control. One surely has to complicate control, the kinds of control utilized, along with youth response.

All too briefly, this section has introduced youth culture. What is clear in present society, indeed worldwide, is a summary understanding that a distinct youth culture exists over which adults have little control. At least in the U.S., in decades since identification and increasing societal presence, for many adults fear of youth is specific but also part of a generalized uncertainty. Two sites of control are prison and school.

Justice and Juveniles

A context and an institution stands between, arguably on a significant and increasingly influential margin, the linkage of youth in school and what constitutes criminalizing. In this chapter and this volume, attention to the justice system is necessary. In the present-day U.S., a strong and invasive justice system operates within a sub-system to deal with, to punish, youth. This section overviews the context of 'justice' and its system incorporating a racialized character, poses a brief comment on the history of the juvenile court, and looks at the impact on youth. Today it is generally acknowledged that people are criminalized within the justice system; the point is to understand extension through a vast further instantiation.

Among western nations, the U.S. stands out as a penal society. In recent decades, known since the 1970s as the era of the 'prison boom,' the numbers of incarcerated have exploded. In *Punishment and Inequality in America*, Bruce Western (2006) offers this historical context. For over a century or so

> in conception at least, and sometimes in practice, the prison sat comfortably alongside an array of welfare institutions that included not only reformatories and asylums but also public schools, hospitals, and rudimentary schemes for social insurance. Like other welfare institutions, the prison was conceived to rescue the citizenship of the unfortunate, the poor, and the deviant. (2)

Given the effects of incarceration, the rhetoric of welfare and rehabilitation often was at odds with practices that prohibited such change. Shifting for a moment, think (in today's context but with long roots) of what being in jail denies: certain employment, franchise, college loans, occupational choice, home ownership, and mental health treatment—let alone human dignity (see Marable, 2007). Those who became and become participants in the criminal justice system are 'others,' 'outsiders.' In today's societal ethos and the language employed here, they are to be feared.

To understand the penal enterprise and its impact today, it is time for some numbers. In 2003, the population involved in some way in the penal system, in jail, awaiting adjudication, on parole and probation supervision, totaled 6 percent of the entire U.S. male population, nearly seven million people. Between 1970 and 2003, the number of prisons increased sevenfold with funds diverted from social services and education. Further, in the same time period incarceration rates for young black men escalated so much that by 2004 over 12 percent of black men, ages twenty-five to twenty-nine, were in jail or prison (Western, 2006, 3). These numbers in no way reflect the impact of 'the system' on communities and the lives of family members.

Two other factors are tied to this context—and then related directly to youth. One is that in the past forty years, rates of crime, especially violent crimes, have decreased. But at the same time, and in no way causally, there has been a national war on crime. In *Governing through Crime: How the War on Crime Transformed American Democracy and Created a Culture of Fear*, Jonathan Simon (2007) writes this: "Crime has become…central to the exercise of authority in America, by everyone from the president…to the classroom teacher.…[Given the flow of information, discourse and debate that has created a culture of fear, there is] little reason to expect the civil order built around crime…to disappear anytime soon" (Simon, 2007, 4). The other factor is that the primary cause of increased incarceration has been non-violent, drug-related crimes. Targeted for illegal drug use have been inner city and poor people, especially youth. Further, regarding anti-racist criminal justice, Manning Marable (2007) reports on "the hidden 'racial paradox' in America's celebrated War on Drugs" (4). This paradox is that arrests have been overwhelmingly of young black, and less so Latino, males even as "the overwhelming majority of illegal drug abusers…[are] white" (Marable, 2007, 4.). Here are his shocking numbers: "[By 2000, for drug-use crime] black youth were 48 times more likely than white youth to be sentenced to serve time inside juvenile correctional institutions" (8).

The tragic irony is that the juvenile court was not intended nor initiated primarily as a punitive institution. The classic study is entitled *The Child Savers: The Invention of Delinquency* by Anthony M. Platt (1969, 1977, 2009). Before turning to the court's history, the book is itself interesting as it helped to alter how American social history was undertaken; it is an early revisionist account of Progressive era 'reform.' Previous interpretations of social reform, beginning in the nineteenth century, are positive and benevolent. Here is Platt: "[Historians and criminologists alike argued that the Progressive] reform impulse has its roots in the earliest ideals of modern liberalism and that it is part of a continuing struggle to overcome injustice and fulfill the promise of American life" (xli). Platt sees this history differently.

The first juvenile court was legislated in Illinois and established in Chicago in 1899 and was part of the "child savers movement." Soon other states followed, and by 1917, all but three had their own systems. As Platt explains, "[The court] was part of a general movement directed toward removing adolescents from the criminal law process and creating special programs for delinquent, dependent and neglected children" (10). Traditional commentators lauded the "noble sentiments and tireless energy of middle-class philanthropists" (10). Platt names these efforts "maternal justice" because of the leading role of women who saw their welfare efforts as natural extensions of middle-class family life. Here is Platt again: "The child savers defended the importance of the home, of family life, and of parental supervision, since it was these institutions which had traditionally given purpose to a woman's life" (83). Three leaders were Louise de Koven Bowen, Julia Lathrop, and Jane Addams. Although acknowledging the good intentions of the child savers, Platt's critique emphasizes the targeting of lower-class children and families. Rhetoric aside, the system became a strong agent of social control. The courts imposed "sanctions on premature independence and behavior unbecoming to youth" (176). Trusting government intervention, the results were "longer terms of imprisonment, long hours of labor and militaristic discipline, and the inculcation of middle-class values and lower-class skills" (83).

Much has been written about the history of the juvenile justice system. Platt's study has led this work; its presentation here is all too brief. One element of research that has followed is the study of the effect on youth who enter the system—as indicated often for a minor drug offence. The question is what it means to be treated as a 'criminal.' In the early years of the present century, Victor Rios (2007) studied what he terms the "hypercriminalization" of minority males who 'once bad, will be bad.' Central to this criminalizing are views toward youth as requiring very strong surveillance practices. The criminalizing practices include the attitudes of family and community members, those who are supposed to be supportive but who instead inflict and maintain negativity. These community members include teachers and probation officers, whose actions such as demanding continual attendance of youth at assessment meetings in schools and community centers made criminalization public.

America's justice system over the past forty years has become central to a penal state. The evidence is clear that incarceration numbers are extremely large and have targeted drug offences and, especially, minority youth. This recent history is part of a century of efforts in juvenile justice. It does seem that a principle of retributive justice operates in a system initially intended for distributive justice. These terms are taken up in the conclusion. It also seems clear that the justice system criminalizes those who enter it as control and criminalizing become central to schools.

School Today

This section examines how criminalizing moves from courts to schools that look a lot like prisons: concepts of uncertainty and fear become localized as threat; control becomes repressive and in the idiom used here, criminalizing. Virtually all schools have and produce criminalizing effects today, but some schools are worse than others. Before turning to what schools appear to have in common, attention to the underlying conditions of the worst ones is warranted. Across his career and in a recent book, Jonathan Kozol (2005) calls them and the segregated education that results, 'shameful.' Once again a specific context is salient. In the era of 'educational reform' and 'accountability,' Kozol offers elements that have become familiar to educators and non-educators alike:

> Relentless emphasis on raising test scores, rigid policies of non-promotion and nongraduation, a new empiricism…[about] named and unnamed 'outcomes'…of instruction…a fanatical insistence upon uniformity of teachers in their management of time, an openly conceded emulation of the rigorous approaches of the military…[and a frequent use of a discourse] of industry and commerce. (64)

He names this pedagogy "direct command and absolute control" (64) and makes a first point that it has especially impacted low-income, urban, most often minority, students.

Kozol's overall project has been to emphasize the role of school finance and the effects of lack of resources. In *The Shame of the Nation: The Restoration of Apartheid Schooling in America*, his thesis is that matters are actually worse than in past decades or so. He puts the situation thusly: "Schools that were already deeply segregated 25 or 30 years ago…are no less segregated now, while thousands of other schools that had been integrated either voluntarily or by force of law have been rapidly resegregating both in northern districts and in broad expanses of the South" (18).

One further comment on the issue of education finance and resources. In the larger context of neo-liberal globalization and current economic crisis, retaining present levels or increasing funding will not be easy. The issue, however, is even more complex. As Jean Anyon argues in her broad study of the relationship of the economy and schooling, *Radical Possibilities*: *Public Policy, Urban*

Education and a New Social Movement (2005), education reform is best understood relative to issues of macroeconomic policy and job availability, adequate transportation, and available housing. After an analysis of regional relationships between central cities and bands of suburbs, Anyon advocates that organizations that range from the U.S. federal government to non-governmental agencies should coordinate efforts in metropolitan reform. With such change, education reform will follow—and schools and the people who live in them will not have to bear the brunt of responsibility that now is on them alone.

The remainder of this section moves directly to school discipline and, along with accountability, the climate it creates. This does relate to moral education and a current character education emphasis that is simultaneously occurring. The point is that a set of school-based discipline practices come together in the daily lives of youth—those 'in-between,' those most threatening and feared, those in need of control to whom the only appropriate response seems 'better safe than sorry.' These practices are classroom management, rule-governed, retributive procedures named as 'fairness,' and zero-tolerance policies and practices. Here again are descriptions of context.

In *Homeroom Security: School Discipline in an Age of Fear* (Kupchik, 2010), Aaron Kupchik and Nichole L. Bracy put the position thusly:

> [In today's school policies there are] increasingly obvious parallels between schools and the criminal justice system, and the increasing likelihood that youth punished for school misbehavior are sent to the juvenile or criminal justice system....Student behaviors that once were dealt with by teachers, administrators, and counselors—such as minor fights…disruptive classroom behavior or truancy—are now outsourced. (19)

What is named 'the school-to-prison pipeline' (Ibid.) has a particular look at school in surveillance cameras, metal detectors, the presence of police officers, and drug searches with dogs. In another recent study, *Punishing Schools: Fear and Citizenship in American Public Education*, William Lyons and Julie Drew (2006) describe an actual drug search they observed in an affluent Midwest suburban high school.

> We…witnessed fifty young people being told to relinquish their property for inspection and to stand quietly against a wall. We…watched several physically intimidating men wearing military uniforms and haircuts, combat books and radios, with visible weapons and huge, eager German Shepherds…search that property for contraband. (3–4)

In this incident, a dog approached the students and touched their bodies ready to leap on culprits. The researchers report their own fear in watching this, the passivity of the entire student group that did as they were told was surprising to them. Clearly control in what they name as "punishing schools" has become acceptable.

These examples situate what are all too common practices in current school discipline. Adults in schools and classrooms have always sought order, but, as just indicated, order looks different today than in the past. The first form of control is typically classroom management, largely the purview of teachers. The old adage for each new year and new group of students was 'don't smile until Christmas.' This has given way to management systems such as a relatively recent national model of 'assertive discipline.' This discipline process incorporates rules, initial public listing of students who break them, with escalating punishments for repeated offenses. 'Management' in this system largely relies on consequences rather than causes. In its heyday, shaming worked for some and led to resistance from others as classroom 'blackboards' were filled with names. A comment about new teachers: it is not surprising that their being schooled in management systems leads to their own preoccupation with controlling students.

A principle of consequences carries over into school-wide discipline in which 'what is best for one youth' becomes 'what is best for all.' Control is rhetorically based on consistent consequences, on fairness, that probably originated in a movement named 'effective schools.' The idea is that rules are set out so that students know what is expected, and these rules are uniformly to be enforced across a school. The problem here is that implementation is virtually impossible: there is no universal approval of rules; punishments are selectively applied; inconsistency operates rather than consistency. Students learn that 'the same for all' is seldom fair. As the school-to-prison model indicates, some students receive special, often light, punishment that is denied others—the others are often minority and poor students. At the very least, it is more difficult for their parents to come to school to advocate for preference and individual welfare.

In recent decades, uniform control has been attempted through zero tolerance policies. These became 'in vogue' following school shootings such as Columbine, after September 11, and most recently in what seems an escalation of youth bullying. Safety has moved to security; punishment rather than welfare has become even more the norm. Zero tolerance begins with rules about weapons so that discovery of a penknife to cut an apple in a lunchbox carries the same penalty as bringing a gun to school. .The ludicrousness of zero tolerance is all too apparent in media reports of a little girl expelled for having a hair comb and for youth athletes suspended for tardiness after giving blood at a school drive. In events capturing media attention the result has often been 'getting around the rule.' Importantly, zero tolerance extends into drug possession and use—and laws that lead very easily to entry into the justice system.

In summary, issues of fear of uncertainty, control and criminalizing have been moved to school. No one argues that schools today have an 'easy job to do.' But also, few especially in the larger public arena are questioning practices such as zero tolerance and what seem to be very excessive surveillance practices. *A personal note here: I am outraged enough at the manner of airport patdowns and know how I would react to a menacing attack dog sniffing at my body.*

Conclusion

This discussion of youth, their culture and the conditions of their lives is appropriate for a reader on moral education. Several ideas stand out. One is that a complex society exists in which adults as well as youth seem uncertain and fearful. How to respond has become a pervasive and seemingly unending dilemma. A second is that youth do learn to be 'moral' but in contexts and conditions about which moral education has had little to say. Consider how a student suspended under a zero-tolerance policy for a scuffle he 'did not start' reacts upon his return to school and to a character education lesson on 'fairness.' Will memorizing a definition or even reading a moral tale have much relevance? Will he now be labeled a 'bad kid?' A third is focus on rule-following and procedures of compliance; control is primary in society and in school. There seems no attention beyond standardizing punishment of 'individuals' but in ways in which they are to be treated as all alike. A fourth is that 'justice' does operate but it is retributive. Gone is a principle of distributive justice, of providing safety and welfare for all but especially for those most vulnerable. Instead, in summary, fear of uncertainty has led to control and to criminalizing, especially of youth. Criminalizing has to be understood as a matter of ethics. Finally, across the society there seems little discourse on even a commonsense practice of ethics. An original working title of this chapter was 'no ethics in justice.' At times of especial crisis, people do seem to come together but this fellow feeling soon disappears. Where every day and especially in school is *our* ethics?

References

Anyon, J. (2005). *Radical possibilities: Public policy, urban education, and a new social movement*. New York: Routledge.

Ariès, P. (1960/1962). *Centuries of childhood: A social history of family life*. Trans. R. Baldick. New York: Alfred A. Knopf.

Bauman, Z. (2007). *Liquid times: Living in an age of uncertainty*. Cambridge: Polity.

Bauman, Z. (2008). *Does ethics have a chance in a world of consumers?* Cambridge, MA: Harvard University Press.

Coleman, J. S. (1961). *The adolescent society: The social life of the teenager and its impact on education*. New York: Free Press of Glencoe.

Giroux, H. A. (2009). *Youth in a suspect society: Democracy or disposability?* New York: Palgrave Macmillan.

Gordon, C. W. (1957). *The social system of the high school: A study of the sociology of adolescence*. Glencoe, IL: The Free Press.

Hollingshead, A. B. (1949). *Elmtown's youth: The impact of social classes on adolescents*. New York: John Wiley.

Kozol, J. (2005). *The shame of the nation: The restoration of apartheid schooling in America*. New York: Three Rivers.

Kupchik, A. (2010). *Homeroom security: School discipline in an age of fear*. New York: New York University Press.

Lesko, N. (2001). *Act your age! A cultural construction of adolescence*. New York: RoutledgeFalmer.

Lyons, W. and Drew, J. (2006). *Punishing schools: Fear and citizenship in American public education*. Ann Arbor: University of Michigan Press.

Marable, M. (2007). Introduction: Racializing justice, disenfranchising lives, toward an antiracist criminal justice. In M. Marable, I. Steinberg, and K. Middlemass (Eds.) *Racializing justice, disenfranchising lives: The racism, criminal justice, and law reader*.(pp. 1–14). New York: Palgrave Macmillan.

Platt, A. M. (1969, 1977, 2009). *The child savers: The invention of delinquency*. New Brunswick, NJ: Rutgers University Press. (Formerly Chicago: The University of Chicago Press).

Polakow, V. (Ed.) (2000). Introduction: Savage policies: Systemic violence and the lives of children. In *The public assault on America's children: Poverty, violence, and juvenile justice* (pp. 1–18). New York: Teachers College Press.

Rios, V. M. (2007). The hypercriminalization of black and Latino male youth in the era of mass incarceration. In M. Marable, I. Steinberg, and K. Middlemass (Eds.) *Racializing justice, disenfranchising lives: The racism, criminal justice, and law reader*. (pp. 17–33). New York: Palgrave Macmillan.

Simon, J. (2007). *Governing through crime: How the war on crime transformed American democracy and created a culture of fear*. Oxford: Oxford University Press.

Western, B. (2006). *Punishment and inequality in America*. New York: Russell Sage.

CHAPTER TWENTY-FOUR

Navigating Inequities

A Morally Rooted Pedagogy of Intentional Mentoring With Black Children and Other Youth of Color

JANIE VICTORIA WARD

> Jeff (my mentor) is really cool and all, but there are a lot of things he don't understand. He likes to act like he's down, and, I mean he is, but. He ain't Black. And he doesn't like to talk about the hard stuff about being black. Like he be happy if the race stuff wasn't there. So I guess we pretend it ain't.
>
> (JAMAL, 15 YEARS)

Development during the childhood and adolescent years is determined by biological, cognitive and socioemotional processes. Physical changes in the child's body, changes in their thinking and intelligence, and changes in the child's emotions, personality, relationships with other people, and in expanding social contexts mark this period as one of tremendous continuity and discontinuity. It has been said that adolescence begins in biology and ends in culture—meaning that the transition from childhood to adolescence begins with the onset of pubertal maturation, while the transition from adolescence to adulthood is determined by cultural standards and experiences (Santrock, 2009, p. 23). Although large numbers of adolescents show remarkable resilience and resourcefulness in the face of social, personal and societal pressures, far too many struggle with problems that restrict their ability to optimally reach adulthood. In our complex multicultural society, navigating the journey from childhood to adult maturity, particularly for children who are growing up in low-income, under-resourced, distressed homes and communities, often requires the guidance, insights, and support of proactive, reflexive, caring and committed adults. Young people who face multiple adversities hunger for adults who are purposeful in helping them to develop the competencies to overcome social and economic disadvantage, including the negative impact of gender bias, ethnic prejudice, and racial discrimination. To expect children on their own to acquire the skills needed to successfully navigate and negotiate the potential pitfalls associated with being victimized by the effects of social injustice is naïve and irresponsible. We have a moral obligation to provide all children and youth, particularly those who are growing up in environments that place them most at risk for being victimized by oppression's racial dynamics, with the appropriate attitudes, skills and values they need to assure their social and psychological well-being.

As members of a historically stigmatized and much-maligned social group, African Americans have a long, well documented history of devaluation, marginalization and discrimination. For this reason, a significant proportion of social science literature that addresses perceptions of and encounters with racism is derived from the lived experiences of people of African descent. Much of this research has documented the pervasiveness of racial discrimination in the lives of African American adults (Dovidio & Gaertner, 2005; Feagin & Sikes, 1994; Bonilla-Silva, 2003), black adolescents (Fisher, Wallace, & Fenton, 2000; Sellers, Copeland-Linder, Martin & Lewis, 2006; Wong, Eccles, & Sameroff, 2003), and other historically marginalized groups (Garcia Coll et al., 1996; Romero & Roberts, 1998; Sue, Bucceri, Lin, Nadal, & Torino, 2009; Sue et al., 2007; Tran, Lee & Burgess, 2010). All of these studies draw attention to the destructive effects of racism on psychological and social development across the lifespan. As a significant stressor racism is seen as negatively affecting individuals' emotional and physical well-being (Carter, 2007; Clark, Anderson, Clark, & Williams, 1999; Nyborg & Curry, 2003; Rosenbloom & Way, 2004; Sanders, 1997; Williams & Williams-Morris, 2000; Wong et al., 2003). Other studies have found that respondents who reported experiences with racism reported higher levels of anger, disgust, fear and heightened anxiety. Diminished personal aspirations, lowered self-esteem, increased self-doubt, and the adoption of self-defeating behaviors are some of negative outcomes associated with racial victimization.

Struggling to navigate racialized biases and the ensuing social inequities has the potential to seriously disrupt developmental trajectories over the course of one's life. Researchers argue that modern racisms (symbolic, aversive, microaggressions) are particularly difficult to predict, avoid or guard against. This is because, in contrast to old fashioned, overt, and in-your-face racism, today's racism is often subtle, normalized, and deeply embedded in our day-to-day interactions. For young people in particular, having a sense that you've been unjustly wronged, disrespected and not cared for just because of how you look or because of the faulty assumptions that others may assign to you can be quite confusing and may evoke strong feelings that are hard to understand or control. The cognitive, social, emotional and moral capacities that allow children and youth to make sense of and ultimately manage the injustices of their racial realities, develop and intensify over time. Because of this children and youth need adult mentors who can help to inculcate the appropriate attitudinal and behavioral skills to cope effectively with the stress evoked from their racial realities.

To become an effective moral mentor of a child of color adult mentors have to acquire a wide range of requisite skills. They need a deep understanding of what issues embedded within black children's moral context these children must at times struggle against, and at other times stand up for, and effective mentors must have a sense of how these struggles shape the construction of the child's race/ethnicity and gender identity. Additionally, mentors need to have an appreciation for the processes of racial socialization that parents engage in with their children that are designed to orient their offspring to the socio-political environment and protect them from the negative effects of discrimination and bias. These important lessons can be learned and adopted for use by moral mentors working with black children and other children from non-dominant groups. We begin with a focus on the moral contexts that have the potential to compromise the positive moral development of African American youth.

Racist and Discriminatory Attitudes and Behaviors
That Pervade the Moral Lives of African American Youth

Over a decade ago, members of the advisory board appointed to President Clinton's Initiative on Race, which was intended to transform the United States into a country that embraces diversity and lives as one America in the 21st century, concluded that racism in our society is alive and well and continues to be a divisive force; racial legacies of the past inform policies and practices today, which allows unfair disparities between majority and minority groups to persist; racial inequities are so deeply ingrained in American society that they are nearly invisible, and most white Americans are unaware of the advantages they enjoy in this society and of how their attitudes and actions unintentionally discriminate against people of color (Advisory Board to the President's Initiative on Race, 1998, reported in Sue, Capodilupo, Torino, Bucceri, Holder, Nadal & Esquilin, 2007). Our racial realities today are indeed more complicated, and the processes of racism are more insidious and obscure, which allows commonplace perspectives and routines to freely violate moral standards of fairness. Researchers today are investigating what are termed "modern racisms," which include Dovidio and Gaertner's (2008) theory of aversive racism, Sears and Kinder's (1985) theory of symbolic racism, and Pierce's theory of 'microaggressions' and 'microassaults', defined as those everyday, verbal and non-verbal messages intended to dismiss, demean and denigrate people of color (Pierce, 1995, Sue et al., 2007, 2009). It is important to add to this list, "horizontal racism," which occurs when members of minority groups adopt racist attitudes towards other minority groups. Together these attitudes and practices offer concrete and explicit evidence of the ways in which racism has transformed over time and is taking shape in society today.

Forty years following the civil rights era, most black children continue to reside in residentially segregated neighborhoods, separated by racial and economic difference, with less income and fewer resources in comparison to their white middle-class counterparts (Massey, 2004; Sethi & Somanathan, 2004). In addition, approximately 35% of all black children are growing up in poverty, and more than 50% of black children growing up in female headed, single family homes are living in poverty (Moore, Redd, Burkauser, Mbwana, & Collins, 2009). The lives of these black children are shaped by the broader patterns of discrimination—substandard housing, inadequate schools, constrained employment opportunities, increased violence and unsafe streets, and the hypercontrol exerted by law enforcement officers who don't always have their best interest at heart. Studies have shown that 91% of preadolescent African Americans reported experiencing at least one discriminatory experience in their lifetime (Gibbons, Gerrard, Cleveland, Wills, & Brody, 2004) and 77% of African American adolescents reported experiencing at least one discriminatory incident in the past three months (Prelow, Danoff-Burg, Swenson and Pulgiano, 2004; Seaton, 2009). In other studies, black teens report particular problems with police harassment and racial profiling and in securing employment (Swim, Hyers, Cohen, Fitzgerald & Bylsma, (2003; Seaton, 2009; Garcia Coll et al., 1996). Studies report that blacks and other youth of color have been victimized by a host of subtle verbal and non-verbal insults, snubs, dismissive looks and gestures (defined as microaggressions and microassaults) (Pierce, 1995; Sue et al., 2007, 2009). Other victim vulnerabilities associated with actual and perceived experiences of discrimination for black youth include racialized teasing and social exclusion, stereotype threat and the performance anxiety that accompanies it (Steele, 1997). Educational researchers have linked students' experiences with discrimination to their dis-identification with school and decreased achievement motivation (Eccles, Wong & Peck, 2006), and to students feeling compelled to adopt a race-less persona in order to fit in and succeed in school (Fordham & Ogbu, 1986; Fordham, 1988). Clinicians attribute depressive symptoms and conduct problems (Brody & Flor, 1998; Greene et al., 2006) to perceived victimization as well as the adoption of serious risk behaviors such as substance abuse and early sexual behavior. Add to this list the discriminatory acts experienced vicariously by youth when experiences of discrimination affecting others' (peers, siblings, or neighbors) are made known and thus become indirectly experienced by everyone in the environment. Finally, cumulative stress resulting from repeated personal experiences of discrimination can prove to be disheartening to children and teens whether the target be the child, a family member or someone from the community living in close proximity.

Along with the research uncovering the deleterious effects of racism on its victims is a growing body of literature investigating the strengths that emerge from the experience of dealing with and ultimately overcoming racism. To appreciate these strengths, it is helpful to understand the role of racial identity development and racial socialization processes, as together they establish a foundation upon which a conceptual framework for moral mentoring, i.e., mentoring practices that address these underlying moral issues of racial discrimination and inequity, can be built.

Racial Identity

In general, researchers define racial identity as a multidimensional construct, one that refers to the significance and meaning of race and ethnicity to one's self-concept (Phinney, 1996; Sellers, Smith, Shelton, Rowley, & Chavous, 1998). Researchers study the individual's psychological identification with race and ethnicity and the behavioral manifestations that stem from that identity (Cross, 1991; Helms, 1995; Phinney & Ong, 2007). Phinney's (1996) model of racial/ethnic identity development proposes that youth progress from an unawareness of race to an understanding of the role that race will play in adolescence and later in adulthood. Although racial identity development may continue across the life span, critical components of identity exploration take root in the adolescent years.

Racial identity beliefs provide important protective factors such as increasing emotional protection against psychological injury, buffering against the potential deleterious impact of racism, and providing individuals with a grounding in the meanings and knowledge derived from one's cultural history and legacy. Psychologist Howard Stevenson says, that racial identity has the potential for providing young people "with a framework to identity, evaluate, and buffer the meaning and detriment of racial tension within varied social interactions both in and out of school" (Stevenson & Arrington, 2009, p. 125), and as such the promotion of positive and purposeful racial identity can serve as an important tool for moral mentors to help youth create and discover effective strategies to resist victimization.

Researchers investigating the associations between racial identity attitudes and individual experiences with racial discrimination have found that psychological well-being will be contingent on specific racial identity beliefs (Seaton, 2009). For example, it has been suggested that understanding how society negatively views African Americans serves to buffer perceptions of discrimination on depressive symptoms and psychological well-being among African American adolescents (Sellers, Copeland-Linder, Martin, & Lewis, 2006), and that among African American girls, positive racial identity is both directly related to academic performance and indirectly related to achievement, as it serves as a barrier to the negative effects of discrimination (Thomas & Rodgers, 2009). These authors also found that in studies of ethnic identity development in Latino adolescent girls, ethnic identity is associated with psychological functioning, developmental outcomes and competencies, including academic achievement, career expectations and career self-efficacy.

Developmental processes regarding racial identity, racial attitudes and race relations are associated with age, gender, cognitive development, socioeconomic status and demographic background. Where children reside and the types of biases they are confronted with speak to the degree of salience racial stigma may have in their thinking and in their lives. Younger children learn of the salience of race largely through their interactions with peers. Social groupings become more race based in early adolescence, and children desire to spend more time with peers who are similar to themselves. As youth grow older, there is a growing awareness of racial politics and the socio-political meanings that are attributing to skin color difference. Racial stereotyping and the tensions that emerge in public spaces, particularly for young black males, make clear the stark and unrelenting reality of racial prejudice and discrimination (Ward, 2000).

Knowing that racial identity influences the ways in which children and youth experience the effects of racial bias and discrimination may be effective in providing mentors the tools needed to understand, discuss, and guide youth of color through the emotional terrain of social inequities. Similarly, information about what black parents know and teach their children about racial matters and identity that can be instructive to prospective mentors is uncovered in this brief review of relevant findings from the literature on racial socialization in African American families.

Racial Socialization

In conducting research for the book, *The Skin We're In* (Ward, 2000), I heard black parents explain that when it comes to talking about race matters—racial identity, race relations and of course racism—African Americans approach the topic from a context of shared knowledge and understanding. When talking about race among ourselves, racial difference, one of the major features that distorts or limits free and open dialogue, is removed. We tell ourselves our own stories, honestly and openly. We are free to share, construct, debate and confirm our lived experiences in the skin we're in. Researchers of racial socialization explore a variety of issues including an orientation to what black parents teach their children about the nature of racism, the negative effect racism has on the psychosocial development of family members, and suggestions for, as well as warnings against adaptive and maladaptive coping strategies (Ward, 1999, 2000).

An important function of racial socialization is what is referred to as "anticipatory socialization," "racism awareness" or "bias training." Parents can teach children to identify obstacles to development (such as racism, sexism, social class bias, etc.) and recognize how these obstacles are embedded in their cultural contexts. Working together, African American parents and adolescents build and reflect on a knowledge base of experiences around racism as a first step toward developing thoughtful and effective responses. Parental racial socialization might involve a repertoire of strategies designed to protect the emotional lives of black youth. Researchers have identified and categorized family racial socialization interactions and messages into five types; coping with antagonism, alertness to discrimination, cultural pride reinforcement, cultural legacy appreciation, and fitting into the mainstream (Stevenson et al., 2002; Stevenson & Arrington, 2009). These messages serve dual purposes—to protect and to be proactive in the face of racial antagonisms.

Different racial socialization messages have been associated with a variety of important outcomes, including more mature identity development (Barr & Neville, 2008), higher levels of self-esteem

(Neblett et al., 2008), reduced problem behaviors (Bennett, 2007), reduced acculturative stress (Thompson, Anderson, & Bakeman, 2005) and increased resilience (Brown, 2008). Children benefit academically, behaviorally and cognitively when parents are explicit in teaching them to prepare for racial hostilities and to be proud of their culture (White-Johnson, Ford, & Sellers, 2010; Bowman & Howard, 1985; Ward, 2000).

Parents speak to their children about racial matters in ways that are age and developmentally appropriate, and the content and delivery of these messages differ according to variables such as socioeconomic status and gender. For example, parents tend to focus on preparing their children and younger adolescents to face bias by promoting cultural history, traditions and pride, but as adolescents grow older, parental messages were more likely to tap their increasing cognitive capacity for understanding the more complex concepts of systemic racial inequality, group and personal racial identity processes and race relations dynamics (Cross & Fhagen-Smith, 2001; Hughes & Johnson, 2001, Quintana, 1998, Ward, 2000). Racial socialization messages are gendered as well. Bowman and Howard (1985) found that girls are more likely to receive messages about racial pride and connection, and boys receive more messages about racial barriers and egalitarian ideals.

The Case for Culturally Based Moral Mentoring

Research on racial socialization in black families suggests that the home is an important socializing setting; however, it does not have to be the only such setting. Children and adolescents can learn the lessons of resistance and resilience, cultural pride and critical consciousness from caring adults in after-school, community-based youth programs, on sports teams and in other recreational activities. Anywhere there are adults who are willing to "go there"—by being aware, honest and attentive to issues of race, power and injustice—these lessons can be taught and learned.

Many children of color are coming of age in neighborhoods, in schools, in community-based sports and recreational programs, wherever they have the opportunity to participate in mentoring programs. These programs tend to be staffed by adults of all ages, who may or may not share the racial or ethnic background of their mentees. Most of these mentors have minimal training, perhaps only during a program orientation, or if they were lucky, they might have received an occasional follow-up session over the course of their mentorship. It is assumed that it is enough to be caring, attentive, and to have free time to spend with a "disadvantaged" child in need. Despite the fact that these programs often promote and proclaim the value of diversity, the prevailing assumption is that being in a relationship is in itself enough.

Multicultural competency has emerged as a standard of care in human services delivery. To do so would mean that programs serving youth should shift away from 'colorblind' programming—particularly when it disregards cultural difference in order to maintain the illusion of sameness and equity. Intentional Mentoring is a unique mentoring model that we are starting to put in place in a select group of youth programs funded in part by the United Way of Massachusetts Bay and Merrimac Valley. Intentional Mentoring departs radically from the assumptions of the traditional model (generally characterized as a relationship in which adult mentors guide, facilitate, and transfer experiences and knowledge to children) to a more expanded understanding of mentoring as an empowering interaction among individuals (adult and child) who share processes and purposes, ambiguities and uncertainties, and learn together for the purpose of personal and social change (Mullen & Lick, 1999, p.13).

Care as a moral orientation calls attention to our fundamental connectedness with and concern for others, and from this perspective detachment in human relationships is seen as a moral problem (Gilligan, 1982). Caring as it is practiced with youth today has both cultural and political dimensions. In her discussion of what she calls "subtractive schooling practices" in U.S. schools serving U.S.–Mexican youth, Angela Valenzuela (1999) distinguishes between two very different conceptions of what it means to care about young people: one conception affirms and embraces their culture and community, and the other attempts to divorce young people from their culture and community through statements like, "it's important that you get a 'good education' so that you can get out of this neighborhood." Such statements are no doubt familiar to historically disadvantaged young people and can be heard regularly throughout youth programs. Although the adults who make such statements may mean well, their remarks can be heard as messages of disconnection and disrespect as they fail to acknowledge, honor and appreciate the sense of belonging and pride in one's heritage that can emerge from a cultural setting and which lays the groundwork for a healthy sense of self.

The culturally based model of moral mentoring that we are proposing builds on the visionary models of Silva and Tom (2001) and Benishek et al. (2004) Silva and Tom's work, focusing on the development of mentoring relationships in programs with new teachers, articulated a framework for a new vision of mentoring that includes three imperatives—embracing a moral stance, creating a caring context, and engaging in a moral pedagogy (2001, p. 51). Additionally, Benishek and her colleagues, integrating multiculturalism with feminist theory, reconceptualized multicultural feminist mentoring as an interactive process in which differences are clearly identified and explored by all parties involved to determine their relevance to the relationship. The authors urge the mentors to know, acknowledge and find ways to address and work through any gendered racial or cultural tensions to foster a more satisfying and useful mentoring relationship (p. 432).

The conceptual framework underlying our Intentional Mentoring model is based on the principle that caring, *purposeful* relationships with adults play a vital role in healthy development (Rhodes, 2002). These adults include officially assigned mentors but are also youth workers, coaches, and others who come in contact with children inside the classroom and in out-of-school environments. Research indicates that programs achieve better outcomes when they focus on fostering positive relationships between adult staff and the participating youth (Grossman & Bulle, 2006). Intentional Mentoring maintains that by being focused, purposeful and deliberate when working with boys and girls of color, staff members maximize the opportunity to build two essential psychosocial competencies related to the development of youth who must navigate the moral domain of racial inequities—resistance and resilience. Resistance as a developmental competency refers to the ability to recognize and resist the impact of negative social influences and risk behaviors—learning to stand up against those who dare to limit who or what you choose to be and to stand up for what defines the best you can be (Ward, 2000). Resilience is a dynamic process encompassing positive adaptation within the context of significant adversity. Models of resilience often include the notion of protective or promotive factors, characteristics, traits, or processes that help children to adapt to, become immune to, or overcome risks (Thomas & Rodgers, 2009, p. 119). Resistance and resilience are elements of what psychologists refer to as "moral competence"—"the knowledge, sensibilities and skills needed to assess and effectively respond to ethical, affective, or social justice dimensions of a situation" (Jagers, 2005, p. 194). These elements hold particular salience for non-dominant groups seeking to successfully negotiate dynamics of power and privilege.

Building on what we've learned from the research on racial identity and racial socialization practices in families, we promote within our intentional mentoring program the development of moral competencies encompassing three critical domains—socioemotional, cognitive, and social. The socioemotional domain (Jagers, 2001) speaks to work of self-regulation, particularly the exercise and control of moral emotions such as empathy, guilt, anger, and moral restraint. Intentional Mentors can help children develop moral self-efficacy—building facility with prosocial sensibilities such as sharing, cooperating, empathizing with others (Jagers, 2001) as well as promoting healthy emotional self-efficacy, the capacity to handle positive and negative emotional experiences (Saarni, 1998). Being able to control oneself is a critically important achievement when a teen feels that she has been disrespected, treated unfairly or has been wronged in some way. Relying on moral prescriptions and simply telling someone what to do, especially in the face of the powerful emotions that the teen feels he/she must react to, will have limited appeal to the person who is angry, confused or in pain. Intentional mentors play an important role in helping youth to develop an awareness of their emotional lives, understand the antecedents and consequences of their thoughts and behaviors, and aid in the development of responsible decision making appropriate to the situation.

Within the cognitive and social domains we urge our mentors to alert black children to their racial realities, with open and honest discussions emphasizing proactive messages and strategies, such as attendance at cultural museums and events, in order to promote cultural empowerment, cultural pride, and cultural legacy socialization (Stevenson & Arrington, 2009) as these are important elements of a strong self-concept and positive racial identity. Across the adolescent years mentors work to develop in youth the skills necessary to critically examine the sociopolitical context of race in America and the role that racism, sexism and social class bias continue to play in shaping attitudes, beliefs, values and behaviors of Americans of all colors. Learning to critically examine and decode negative media images (i.e., black men commonly depicted as "thugs" and criminals, black women commonly depicted as loud, overbearing and over-sexed) becomes important work in an Intentional Mentorship as youth can be given the tools to counter these distortions, mistruths and misinformation. Elsewhere I have argued that for people who feel they have been silenced and subjugated, a moral clarity comes from learning how to interpret one's own experience, trust one's own voice and give legitimacy to one's own perspective (Ward, 1999).

One way Intentional Mentors can help youth to develop these skills is to adopt a four-step model (Read it, Name it, Oppose it, Replace it) designed to help adults assist youth in developing the skills to effectively resist damaging racial and gendered realities (Ward, 2000). The model emphasizes the need for adults to foster in youth the capacity to generate safe, creative, effective, internal (psychological) and external (social) strategies of resistance. Briefly, "reading it" refers to analyzing a situation for the dynamics of race, gender and class—identifying the patterns, covert and overt, that make visible the routines and rituals of everyday racism and sexism. "Naming it" is the process of establishing criteria for determining if racism (or sexism) is actually at play. "Naming it" requires practical, accessible words whose meanings are shared and agreed upon by both the mentor and the mentee. Most important, this step means bringing the existence of injustice or inequity into full consciousness—"telling it like it is," a process that can be at once terrifying and empowering to both adult and child. "Opposing it" is about finding effective and appropriate ways for black youth to respond in the face of injustice. It's about knowing how and when to fight back, speak up, and assert moral authority in ways that are smart, effective and within the adolescent's control. Finally, "Replacing it" is about helping black youth to learn how to replenish the warrior spirit. Navigating injustice is hard work. Having to constantly be on guard and being responsive to negative feelings and faulty assumptions about who you are can drain and exhaust individuals. Intentional Mentors can teach youth to substitute negative attitudes with positive images, cultural knowledge, pride and self-respect (Ward, 2007, pp. 253–255). This model of decoding, discovery and discussion—"read it," "name it," "oppose it "and "replace it"—can be employed by Intentional Mentors working with youth of color as they recognize the inequalities they face in the world and search for effective resistance strategies to overcome those inequalities. The model builds on moral strengths, and it promotes resilience in the face of oppression. Most important, it is designed with an appreciation of children's real lives, challenges, and capacities in mind.

Why Is Intentional Mentoring in the Moral Domain?

Much of the literature cited in this chapter has come from studies of African American children and families. However, black families are not monolithic in their attitudes about race and racial identity or in their approaches to childrearing. Indeed, not all black families speak to their children about their racial realities. That said, there is ample evidence to suggest that, despite the diversity in parental approaches to racial matters, black children (and many other children of color) growing up in this nation report that they have been either judged, discriminated against, or treated unfairly due to the color of their skin and their perceived racial or cultural heritage. Because of this reality psychologists argue that children must be forewarned and prepared, either by their parents or by some other trusted adult who possesses the will and the skills to help youth navigate the inequities they may face. Mentors can be intentional about working with youth around these issues, especially in the absence of parents or other family members who may be unable or may choose not to do so. There are three primary reasons why this type of mentoring is needed:

First, staging an effective battle against racial inequities is hard work. As the research clearly states, the damage associated with the negative effects of racism can have annihilating effects. Forewarning children and arming them with the appropriate attitudes and skills to successfully beat back the macro and micro assaults requires the guidance of caring adults. Indeed it is our obligation to help them navigate this moral terrain, which is, after all, not of their making. Children cannot and should not do this alone.

Secondly, it is foolish to use colorblindness to silence the discourse on difference, racial politics and self-determination. Silence doesn't disrupt or interrogate existing power relationships. And it certainly doesn't urge youth to consider alternative power arrangements. We must break the silence and, despite our discomfort, talk with youth about their racial realities. To know that serious psychological damage is inevitable and then to leave kids defenseless is unjust and shows an astounding lack of care. Instead it is time for a strong, intentional, moral response to the perpetuation of the crippling discourse of colorblindness and cultural sameness that prevents black youth and other children of color from getting twhat they need to thrive.

Finally, knowledge is power. Racism creates and reproduces systems of social imbalance that have been deeply entrenched in our institutional arrangements and everyday practices. Bias training can be seen as one way to restore some sense of balance. Anticipatory socialization promotes proactive agency—it helps youth to be able to withstand and fight against systems of inequities, and resist internalizing the effects of injustice. Addressing the effects of racial inequities in the lives of children of color is a moral imperative, and in doing so, we can promote healthy moral development in all of our children.

Conclusion

The great orator Malcolm X said, "We can't teach what we don't know, and we can't lead where we won't go." Youth need adults in their lives who see themselves as part of a larger struggle for racial justice (Beauboeuf-Lafontant, 2002; Foster, 1997; Ladson-Billings, 1994). Intentional Mentoring, a culture-based, morally rooted pedagogy for helping youth navigate social inequities, requires adults who are willing to engage youth around deeply sensitive moral questions associated with discrimination and oppression and to uncover and analyze evidence of the ways in which racism and sexism become dangerously internalized in the psyche of individuals. Similarly, adults must be able to engage in discussions with youth about evolving definitions of manhood and womanhood within various cultural contexts, exploring what it means to become a responsible and productive member of a given cultural community. Lastly, Intentional Mentors must be willing to resist shying away from assisting youth as they engage in the work of exploring their cultural heritage, constructing their racial and ethnic identities, and discussing and deconstructing the experiences of discrimination related to these identities. Intentional Mentoring charts a new direction in mentoring, one that builds on positive relational connections to acknowledge the real-life experiences and psychosocial complexities of the whole child, promoting positive attitudes and values, responsible decision-making in the face of racial politics, and respectful cross-ethnic social interactions.

Note

The author wishes to thank Brian Wright and Bithia Carter for their assistance with this manuscript.

References

Advisory Board to the President's Initiative on Race. (1998). *One America in the 21st century: Forging a new future.* Washington, DC: U.S. Government Printing Office.

Alvarez, A. N., Blume, Arthur W., Cervantes, J. M., & Thomas, L. R. (2009). Tapping the wisdom tradition: Essential elements to mentoring students of color. *Research and Practice, 40* (2), 181–188.

Barr, S. C., & Neville, H. A. (2008). Examination of the link between parental racial socialization messages and racial ideology among black college students. *Journal of Black Psychology, 34*, 131–155.

Beauboeuf-Lafontant, T. (2002,). A womanist experience of caring: Understanding the pedagogy of exemplary black women teachers. *Urban Review, 34* (1), 71–86.

Benishek, L. A., Bieschke, K. J., Park, J., & Slattery, S. M. (2004). A multicultural feminist model of mentoring. *Journal of Multicultural Counseling & Development, 32*, 428–442.

Bennett, M. D. (2007). Racial socialization and ethnic identity: Do they offer protection against problem behaviors in African American youth? *Journal of Human Behavior in the Social Environment, 15*, 137–161.

Bonilla-Silva, E. (2003). *Racism without racists: Color-blind racism and the perspective of racial inequality in the United States.* Lanham, MD: Rowman and Littlefield.

Bowman, P. J., & Howard, C. (1985). Race-related socialization, motivation, and academic achievement: A study of black youths in three-generation families. *Journal of the American Academy of Child Psychiatry, 24*, 134–141.

Brody, G. H., & Flor, D. L. (1998). Maternal resources, parenting practices, and child competence in rural single-parent African American families. *Child Development, 69*, 803–816.

Brown, D. L. (2008). African American resiliency: Examining racial socialization and social support as protective factors. *Journal of Black Psychology, 34*, 32–48.

Carter, R. T. (2007). Racism and psychological and emotional injury: Recognizing and assessing race-based stress. *Counseling Psychologist, 35*, 13–105.

Clark, R., Anderson, N. B., Clark, V. R., & Williams, D. R. (1999). Racism as a stressor for African Americans: A biopsychosocial model. *American Psychologist, 54*, 805–816.

Cross, W. E. (1991). *Shades of black: Diversity in African American identity*. Philadelphia, PA: Temple University Press.

Cross, W. E., & Fhagen-Smith, P. E. (2001). Patterns of African American identity development: A life span perspective. In C. L. Wijeyesingle & B. W. Jackson (Eds.), *New perspectives on racial identity development* (pp. 243–270). New York: New York University Press.

Dovidio, J. F., & Gaertner, S. L. (2000). Aversive racism and selection decisions. *Psychological Science, 11*, 4, 315–319.

Dovidio, J. F., & Gaertner, S. L. (2005). Color blind or just plain blind? The pernicious nature of contemporary racism. *The Non-Profit Quarterly, 12* (4)

Eccles, J. S., Wong, C. A., & Peck, S. C. (2006). Ethnicity as a social context for the development of African American adolescents. *Journal of School Psychology, 44*, 407–426.

Feagin, J. R. & Sikes, M. P. (1994). *Living with racism: The Black middle class experience*. Boston, MA: Beacon.

Fisher, C. B., Wallace, S. A., & Fenton, R E. (2000). Discrimination distress during adolescence. *Journal of Youth and Adolescence, 679*–695.

Fordham, S. (1988). Racelessness as a factor in black students' school success: "Pragmatic strategy or pyrrhic victory?" *Harvard Educational Review, 58* (1), 54–84.

Fordham, S., & Ogbu, J. (1986). Black students' school success: Coping with the burden of 'acting white.' *Urban Review, 18*, 176–206.

Foster, M. (1997). *Black teachers on teaching*. New York: New Press.

Garcia Coll, C., Lamberty, G., Jenkins, R., McAdoo, H. P., Crnic, K., Wasik, B. H., et al. (1996). An integrative model for the study of developmental competencies in minority children. *Child Development, 67*, 1891–1914.

Gibbons, F. X., Gerrard, M., Cleveland, M. J., Wills, T.A., & Brody, G. (2004). Perceived discrimination and substance use in African American parents and their children: A panel study. *Journal of Personality and Social Psychology, 86*, 517–529.

Gilligan, C. (1982), *In a different voice*. Cambridge, MA: Harvard University Press.

Greene, M. L. , Way, N., & Paul, K. (2006). Trajectories of perceived adult and peer discrimination among Black, Latino and Asian American adolescents: Patterns and psychological correlates. *Developmental Psychology, 42*, 218–238.

Grossman, J. B., & Bulle, M. J. (2006). Review of what youth programs do to increase the connectedness of youth with adults. *Journal of Adolescent Health, 39*, 788–799.

Helms, J. E. (1995). An update on Helms's white and people of color racial identity models. In J.G. Ponterotto, J. M. Casas, L.A. Suzuki, and C.M. Alexander (Eds). *Handbook of multicultural counseling* (181–198). Thousand Oaks: CA: Sage.

Hughes, D., & Johnson, D. (2001). Correlates in children's experiences of parents' racial socialization behaviors. *Journal of Marriage and Family, 63*, 981–995.

Jagers, R. J. (2001). Cultural integrity and social and emotional competence promotion: Work notes on moral competence. *The Journal of Negro Education, 70* (1/2), 59–71.

Jagers, R. J. (2005). Moral competence promotion among African American children: Conceptual underpinnings and programmatic efforts. In L. Nucci (Ed.), *Conflict, contradiction and contrarian elements in moral development and education* (pp. 193–210). Mahwah, NJ: Lawrence Erlbaum.

Ladson-Billings, G. (1994). *The dreamkeepers: Successful teachers of African American children*. San Francisco, CA: Jossey-Bass Inc.

Massey, D. S. (August 2004). Segregation and stratification: A biosocial perspective. *Du Bois Review: Social Science Research on Race, 1* (1), 7–25.

Moore, K. A., Redd, Z., Burkhauser, M., Mbwana, K., & Collins, A. (2009). Children in poverty: Trends, consequences and policy options. *Child Trends, Publication #2009–11*, December 4, 2010.

Mullen, C. A., & Lick, D. W. (1999). *New directions in mentoring: Creating a culture of synergy*. London: Falmer.

Neblett, E.W., White, R. L., Ford, K. R., Philip, C. L., Nguyen, H. X., & Sellers, R. M. (2008). Patterns of racial socialization and psychological adjustment: Can parental communications about race temper the detrimental effects of racial discrimination? *Journal of Research on Adolescence, 18*, 477–515.

Nyborg, V. M., & Curry, J. F. (2003). The impact of perceived racism: Psychological symptoms among African American boys. *Journal of Clinical Child and Adolescent Psychology, 32, 258–266.*

Phinney, J. S. (Nov/Dec 1996). Understanding ethnic diversity. *American Behavioral Scientist, 40*(2), 143–153.

Phinney, J. S., & Ong, A. D. (2007). Conceptualization and measurement of ethnic identity: Current status and future directions. *Journal of Cultural Diversity, 54*, 271–281.

Pierce, C. (1995). Stress analogs of racism and sexism: Terrorism, torture and disaster. In C. Willie, P. Rieker, B. Kramer, & B. Brown (Eds.), *Mental health, racism, and sexism* (277–293). Pittsburgh, PA: University of Pittsburgh Press.

Prelow, H. M., Danoff-Burg, S., Swenson, R. R., & Pulgiano, D. (2004). The impact of ecological risk and perceived discrimination on the psychological adjustment of African American and European American youth. *Journal of Community Psychology, 32*, 375–389.

Quintana, S. M. (1998). Children's developmental understanding of ethnicity and race. *Applied and Preventive Psychology, 7*, 27–45.

Rhodes, J. E. (2002). *Stand by me: The risks and rewards of mentoring today's youth*. Cambridge, MA: Harvard University Press.

Rivas-Drake, D., Hughes, D., & Way, N. (2009). A preliminary analysis of associations among ethnic-racial socialization, ethnic socialization, and ethnic identity among urban sixth graders. *Journal of Research on Adolescence, 19* (3), 558–584.

Romero, A. J., & Roberts, R. E. (1998). Perception of discrimination and ethnocultural variables in a diverse group of adolescents. *Journal of Black Psychology, 21*, 641–656.

Rosenbloom, S. R., & Way, N. (2004). Experiences of discrimination among African American, Asian American, and Latino adolescents in an urban high school. *Youth and Society, 35*, 420–451.

Saarni, C. (1998). Issues of cultural meaningfulness in emotional development. *Developmental Psychology, 34*, 4, 647–653.

Sanders, M. G. (1997). Overcoming obstacles: Academic achievement as a response to racism and discrimination. *Journal of Negro Education, 66*, 83–93.

Santrock, J. (2009). *Adolescence* (13th ed.) New York: McGraw-Hill.

Sears, D.O., & Kinder, D. R. (1985). Whites' opposition to busing: On conceptualizing and operationalizing group conflict. *Journal of Personality and Social Psychology, 48*, 1141–1147.

Seaton, E. (2009). Perceived racial discrimination and racial identity profiles among African American adolescents. *Cultural Diversity and Ethnic Minority Psychology, 15*, 2, 137–144.

Sellers, R. M., Copeland-Linder, N., Martin, P. P., & Lewis, R. L. (2006). Racial identity matters: The relationship between racial discrimination and psychological functioning in African American adolescents. *Journal of Research on Adolescence, 16*, 187–216.

Sellers, R. M., Smith, M., Shelton, J. N., Rowley, S. J., & Chavous, T. M. (1998). Multidimensional model of racial identity: A reconceptualization of African American racial identity. *Personality and Social Psychology, 2*,1, 18–39.

Sethi, R., & Somanathan, R. (2004). Inequality and segregation. *Journal of Political Economy, 112*, 1296–1321.

Silva, D. Y., & Tom, A. R. (2001). The moral basis of mentoring. *Teacher Education Quarterly, 28*, 2, 39–52.

Steele, C. M. (1997). A threat in the air: How stereotypes shape intellectual identity and performance. *American Psychologist, 52*, 613–629.

Stevenson, H .C., & Arrington, E.G. (2009). Racial/ethnic socialization mediates perceived racism and the racial identity of African American adolescents. *Cultural Diversity and Ethnic Minority Psychology, 15*,2, 125–136.

Stevenson, H. C., Cameron, R., Herrero-Taylor, T., & Davis, G. Y. (2002). Development of the teenage experience of racial socialization scale: Correlates of race-related socialization from the perspective of Black youth. *Journal of Black Psychology, 28*, 84–106.

Sue, D. W., Bucceri, J., Lin, A.I., Nadal, K. L., & Torino, G. C. (2009). Racial microaggressions and the Asian American experience. *Asian American Journal of Psychology, 5*(1), 88–101.

Sue, D. W., Capodilupo, C. M., Torino, G. C., Bucceri, J. M., Holder, A. M. B., Nadal, K. L., & Esquilin, M. (2007). Racial microaggressions in everyday life: Implications for clinical practice. *American Psychologist, 62*,4, 271–286.

Swim, J. K., Hyers, L. L., Cohen, L. L., Fitzgerald, D. C. & Bylsma, W. H. (2003). African American college students' experiences with everyday racism: Characteristics of and responses to these incidents. *Journal of Black Psychology, 29,*1, 38–67.

Thomas, A. J., & Rodgers, C. (2009). Resilience and protective factors for African American and Latina girls. In J. E. Trimble & J. L. Chin (Ed.), *Diversity in mind and in action*. Westport, CT: Praeger.

Thompson, P. C., Anderson, L. P., & Bakeman, R. A. (2005). Effects of racial socialization and racial identity on acculturative stress in African American college students. *Cultural Diversity and Ethnic Minority Psychology, 6*, 196–210.

Tran, A. G. T. T., Lee, R. M., & Burgess, D. J. (2010). Perceived discrimination and substance use in Hispanic/Latino African-born Black, and Southeast Asian immigrants. *Cultural Diversity and Ethnic Minority Psychology, 16* (2), 226–236.

Valenzuela, A. (1999). *Subtractive schooling: U.S.–Mexican youth and the politics of caring*. Albany, NY: State University of New York Press

Ward, J. V. (2007). Uncovering truths, recovering lives: Lessons of resistance in the socialization of black girls. In B. Leadbeater, & N. Way, (Eds.), *Urban girls revisited: Building strengths* (pp. 243–260). New York: New York University Press.

Ward, J. V. (2000). *The skin we're in: Teaching our children to be emotionally strong, socially smart and spiritually connected*. New York: Free Press.

Ward, J. V., (1999) Resistance and resilience. In A. Garrod, J.V. Ward, T. L. Robinson & R. Kilkenny (Eds). *Souls looking back: Life stories of growing up Black. (173–185). New York: Routledge.*

Ward, J. V. (1995). Cultivating a morality of care in African American adolescents: A culture-based model of violence prevention. *Harvard Educational Review, 65*(2), 175–188.

White-Johnson, R. L., Ford, K. R., & Sellers, R.M. (2010). Parental racial socialization profiles: Association with demographic factors, racial discrimination, childhood socialization, and racial identity. *Cultural Diversity and Ethnic Minority Psychology, 16*(2), 237–247.

Williams, D. R., & Williams-Morris, R. (2000). Racism and mental health: The African American experience. *Ethnicity and Health, 5*, 243–268.

Wong, C. A., Eccles, J. S., & Sameroff, A. (2003). The influence of ethnic discrimination and ethnic identification on African American adolescents' school and socioemotional adjustment. *Journal of Personality, 7*, 1197–1232.

CHAPTER TWENTY-FIVE

Cultural and Subjective Operations of Ignorance and Resistance in Sexuality-Related Curricula

JENNIFER LOGUE

How has it come to be that the magnitude of pervasive and unnecessary human suffering seems so often to slip off of the radar of many good and well-meaning North American citizens? As David Purpel (1999) in *Moral Outrage in Education* has asked: where is the moral outrage in education? It is commonly assumed that social and cultural problems are rooted in ignorance and that the antidote is knowledge and moral education. But, as many of the chapters in this volume point out, the very moral education called upon to cultivate virtuous citizens who will work to create the conditions for justice and fairness are themselves complicit in the reproduction of ongoing social and global domination. Dwight Boyd (chapter 14 this volume), for example, has shown how character education fails to face up to macro moral/political problems of oppression such as racism, sexism, and classism through discursive strategies that assume a level playing field and deny the difference and conflict that permeate our culturally diverse communities. In this chapter I attempt to untangle some of the conceptual obstacles and psychic tensions involved in teaching and learning about social justice, the difficulties involved in coming to understand how each and every one of us is (albeit in different ways) complicit in ongoing social and global injustice, and, more specifically, how we often fail to see ourselves as such. I trouble common and scholarly conceptions of ignorance and resistance in social justice education so that we might begin to inspire the requisite moral outrage and action required to ameliorate and eliminate ongoing and unnecessary forms of oppression and suffering.

Given recent gay youth suicides, thinking through the barriers to teaching and learning about sexuality, especially minority sexualities, is all the more pressing. This chapter will largely engage the processes of difficult dialogue and ignorance, but the discussion has implications for thinking about how resistance functions at all levels in all areas of education. As we become more ethically engaged practitioners and continue to push ourselves as teachers to remain ethically engaged learners, we still have to push ourselves on questions about the limits of our own understanding, as well as those of our students. What are the tensions behind engaging students in difficult dialogue where they need to confront not only what they don't know about difference and structurally reproduced inequalities but also what they don't want to know? How do students respond to educational theory and practice when it is aimed at engaging them in critique of the very structures that have produced them? In other words, how do we as educators reorient our work against bias and be careful as well that we understand our own structuring biases? I suggest here that we need to think both about the psychological processes of resistance and about the structurally produced ignorance that frames our experience in education as both students and teachers.

Challenging common understandings of ignorance as a simple or innocent lack of knowledge, I examine how ignorance is productive, functioning as a strategy of both power and resistance. I outline different conceptions of ignorance to bring to the fore the tension between structures and subjectivities, complicating the problem of locating responsible agency. Exploring productive operations of ignorance on both structural and subjective levels shows just how complex notions of moral responsibility become when we consider how subjects of education are often duped by socially sanctioned forms of ignorance (masquerading as knowledge) on the one hand and their own affective investments in ignorance and self-deception on the other. I examine various ignorances and resistances we encounter, produce and live within to help us think through how we might more productively and pedagogically deal with barriers to understanding and ethicality. Part of this process will shift students (and educators) into seeing their structural habits and identities as something which renders us morally complicit in injustices with which we do not identify and as something we might collectively change. Respect, civility, and tolerance are often touted as essential virtues that we must educate our students to have,[1] and yet the commonplace bullying and violent harassment of LGBT students (and lack of teacher intervention) in schools show us that, although these virtues are lauded in theory, they are sadly lacking in practice. I argue that understanding that our own patterns of ignorance and defense often impede our ability to act ethically will help to bridge this gap.

I will first turn to psychoanalytic theory to examine both the psychological dimensions of attachment to ignorance. I then turn to an analysis of how education curricula and policy shape educational institutions into places where ignorance can take hold and indeed, play off and generate these psychological mechanisms of defense, resistance, and disavowal. To illuminate these issues more clearly, I examine sexuality education—the structuring silences of curricula that encourage students to maintain their ignorances. This sexuality-related ignorance in school not only has implications for their own and others' sexual health, it frames how they come to understand LGBT-related bias, and the same sorts of silences that attend their nascent curiosity about sexuality-related issues affect how they begin to think about LGBT people. For preservice teachers, these patterns of ignorance and disavowal have clear implications for their inability to respond ethically and educatively to ensure that LGBTQ students are able to thrive in schools. And when we examine homophobia through popular culture, it is clear they are working through their simultaneous desires to be accepting of all their students and to still hold onto their negative judgment against gay people even as they begin to problematize those beliefs. So they simultaneously desire to be better, more sensitive teachers for their students, but they also remain fearful or at least ambivalent toward gay people as they have habitually done. While this may not seem like a revolutionary step forward, it is at least a small move forward, and perhaps their own disavowals and the cultural structures that make their ignorance seem like something appealing to hold onto can now become objects for scrutiny as well. In conclusion, I show how making structural and cultural ignorances more apparent and in some ways, less threatening. By using popular culture, students can analyze how characters in "But I'm a Cheerleader" negotiate relations to ignorance in the film, and students can begin to see their own investments in maintaining ignorance as well. In the end, I argue, this beginning engagement with processes of ignorance can help to loosen their hold on students, reduce their resistance, and move them into better ethical practice.

Using Psychoanalysis to Show the Activity of Ignorance

How might we begin to uncover our affective investments in various forms of ignorance? Megan Boler argues that one important place to begin is to study the way our emotions are a site of social control since "violent practices of cruelty and injustice" are often rooted in unspoken "emotional investments in unexamined ideological beliefs."[2] Boler provides us with an account of the "effect of affect" in education and shows how our modes of seeing, the selectivity of our vision, and emotional attention have been shaped by the dominant culture.[3] She argues that by tracing genealogies of particular emotional investments one can come to recognize how the selectivity of emotion is shaped in political ways determining "how and what one chooses to see and not to see."[4] Boler's "pedagogy of discomfort" is designed to attend to the emotional discomfort critical inquiry can invite as she calls on educators and students to examine "cherished beliefs" and "constructed self-images in relation to how one has learned to perceive others."[5] However, the invitation to question cherished beliefs is not one all students readily accept.

I want to build on this important work by deepening analyses about how and why students resist and contribute to the creation of a pedagogy that seeks to stimulate in students and educators alike the desire to critically examine "inscribed habits of (in)attention."[6] I argue that key insights from psychoanalytic theory can help educators to more effectively understand and engage student resistance. Boler argues that the first sign of success for a pedagogy of discomfort is "the ability to recognize what it is one doesn't want to know, and how one has developed emotional investments to protect oneself from this knowing,"[7] and this is precisely what insight from psychoanalytic theory can help us to do.

Resistance is a topic that stimulates what I take to be a very powerful dysfunctional emotional economy circulating in both classrooms and literature. Rather than inspiring desire for both personal and social transformation, in classes that teach about homophobia and multicultural/multisexual differences, more often than not, it seems that both students and teachers experience frustration, exasperation, hostility, anger, and resentment, impeding the ability to put into practice the respect and civility that are lauded theoretically.

I suggest that student (and teacher) resistance is often misunderstood and misdiagnosed, and that part of the problem is that the conception of ignorance in much of the literature is insufficiently complex. Although there are certainly exceptions, student resistance in social justice teacher education classes tends to be viewed in very negative terms, as avoidable and blameworthy acts of belligerence and intransigence designed to absolve ignorant, privileged students from acknowledging complicity in and moral responsibility for myriad forms of domination and oppression. Those who have access to unjustifiable, institutionalized privileges are often ignorant of them as such and tenaciously resist critical examination of the way the world works to confer systemic advantage on some at the expense of others.

Without an investigation into what our concepts presuppose, open up or foreclose, we fail to see important dimensions of the current predicament we are in and fully grasp the ways in which we perform the very structures we aim to critically assess. We need to attend to the ways language produces us to think in certain categories which have built-in hierarchies in them, such that so-called neutral starting points for analysis are already loaded. Analyzing how ignorance and resistance are being deployed by students and teachers helps us to understand how using them undermines attempts to have a broader, more transformative effect.

Reading Resistance Psychoanalytically

"Resistance," writes Patrick McGee, "is a commonly used term in both psychoanalysis and pedagogy. It could be argued that, within either discipline, theory encounters practice as a kind of resistance."[8] While clearly a classroom is not the same as an analytic situation—one chooses to enter into analysis whereas students are compelled to be in a classroom, making power relations central to teaching and learning at the outset—there is much we can learn from a psychoanalytic perspective, particularly within the realm of social justice education and critical pedagogy. First of all, psychoanalysis teaches us that perceptions are passionate; knowledge is difficult, and subjectivities are split. We learn that we are in constant conflict with ourselves and the world around us, and, consequently, each of us dwells in the contradictory space between the desire to know and the desire to ignore. We learn that in the face of difficult knowledge—that is, knowledge that one experiences as upsetting, threatening, or in any way anxiety inducing—resistance is inevitable, paradoxical, and an essential dynamic in the learning process.[9] It is an important stimulus to change and a precursor to personal transformation; in fact, as we will see, Freud goes so far as to say that unless we have worked through resistance, it is unlikely that any real learning has transpired. We need to see resistance as a defense mechanism that exists in each of us; it is not just in students or particular kinds of students but in teachers, and people in general as well.

Drawing on Anna Freud, Deborah Britzman explains that before our perceptions actually become conscious, they must pass through "a kind of testing (censorship)"[10]:only when an instinct attaches to an idea that passes through the censor does it become capable of becoming conscious. This helps to explain why it is people do "not see" what is, in fact, right before them; it sheds light on the ways students were shown to hear things other than what was said and reinterpret information that they experienced as threatening. It helps us to understand, Britzman asserts that learning involves much more than the acquisition of knowledge, skills, and information, a good teacher, or a good curriculum. Learning, as Britzman contends, is a psychic event.

Shedding further light on just what it means to think of learning as a psychic event, Anna Freud contends that perceptions both pass through and constitute an ego's mechanisms of defense.[11] The term defense, she argues, "is the earliest representative of the dynamic standpoint in psychoanalytic theory," and it describes "the ego's struggle against painful or unendurable ideas or affects."[12]

Simply put, defense is the attempt to rid oneself of a perception, idea, or reality that one finds threatening, unbearable, or in some way anxiety inducing. Disturbing emotions, drives, or representations are warded off through the ego's access to a variety of defense mechanisms. In asking students to confront standpoints, situations, and ideas that are not just difficult or unfamiliar but appear to be a criticism of the learner's perspective, Anna Freud argues that we should expect denial, but we should also expect that people will surpass their initial attempts at refusing to learn. The paradoxical elements of resistance come to light when we recognize that although defense mechanisms are strategies adopted by the ego to console itself, the consolation does not come without a cost.

Freud provides us with an interesting example that clearly shows how we often resist that which is, in fact, in our own best interests. He explains, "when we undertake to restore a patient to health, to relieve him of the symptoms of his illness, he meets us with a violent and tenacious resistance, which persists throughout the whole length of the treatment."[13] In elaborating on this strange phenomenon, in typical Freudian fashion, he suggests that this is so peculiar a fact that "we cannot expect it to find much credence."[14] He explains,

> The patient, too, produces all the phenomena of this resistance without recognizing it as such, and if we can induce him to take our view of it and to reckon with its existence that already counts as a great success. Only think of it! The patient, who is suffering so much from his symptoms and is causing those about him to share his sufferings, who is ready to undertake so many sacrifices in time, money, effort and self-discipline in order to be freed from those symptoms—we are to believe that this patient puts up a struggle in the interest of his illness against the person who is helping him. How improbable such an assertion must sound! Yet it is true; and when its improbability is pointed out to us, we need only reply that it is now without analogies. A man who has gone to the dentist because of an unbearable toothache will nevertheless try to hold the dentist back when he approaches the sick tooth with a pair of forceps.[15]

This image captures quite nicely the ways in which we can and often do, quite inadvertently, resist that which is in our own best interests. Social justice educators, as I have argued earlier, too often interpret student resistance as avoidable and blameworthy. But what we learn from Freud is that resistance is a sort of knee-jerk reaction, an unconscious defensive response; even when, on a somewhat conscious level, as in the case of the dental patient, one may realize that they are thwarting the very treatment they themselves have sought and sorely require, they cannot help but resist.

In helping us realize what we might expect in classes that challenge the foundational worldviews of our students, Freud explains that resistance will always alter its intensity during the course of a treatment; "it always increases when we are approaching a new topic; it is at its most intense while we are at the climax of dealing with that topic, and it dies away when the topic has been disposed of."[16] And in helping us become aware of our own role in student resistance he emphasizes, "[n]or do we ever, unless we have been guilty of special clumsiness in our technique, have to meet the full amount of resistance of which a patient is capable."[17] In treating student resistance as a defense against knowledge that is difficult for them to bear, we might become more patient with it and less likely to mobilize our own defenses against it. Freud's description of resistance in the analytical setting is in many ways analogous to those described by social justice educators and worth quoting at length:

> We have therefore been able to convince ourselves that on countless occasions in the course of his analysis that the same man will abandon his critical attitude and take it up again. If we are on the point of bringing a specially distressing piece of unconscious material to his consciousness, he is extremely critical; he

may previously have understood and accepted a great deal, but now it is just as though those acquisitions have been swept away; in his efforts for opposition at any price, he may offer a complete picture of someone who is an emotional imbecile. But if we succeed on helping him to overcome this new resistance, he recovers his insight and understanding. Thus his critical faculty is not an independent function, to be respected as such, it is the tool of his emotional attitudes and is directed by his resistance...perhaps none of us is very different; a man who is being analyzed only reveals this dependence of intellect on emotional life so clearly because in analysis we are putting such great pressure on him.[18]

By emphasizing how our capacity to reason is dependent on affect, Freud shows that we should expect resistance, which signals that we have hit something of extreme importance; rather than feeling frustrated or affronted, we'd do better to teach, to contradict, and to provide counter examples knowing that the student finds the encounter difficult also. Overcoming and working through resistances signal that real change occurs. We need to recognize that perceptions are passionate; as Freud says, our critical capacities are not independent of emotion as the history of Western philosophy might have us believe. Although many critical educators have criticized hierarchical binary thinking, the lauding of reason over passion, it seems to me that sometimes they expect their students to respond like the Kantian subject of rational autonomy they themselves cite as worthy of critique. Sigmund and Anna Freud show that resistance is a defensive response to perceived threat and anxiety and that it holds the key to a fundamental change in perception, providing us with good reason to value and welcome it.

It might help us to become more sensitive and patient with resistance when we consider the Lacanian view that it is not just "a pathological clinging to neurosis (inertia) but the human incapacity to recognize gaps between being, wanting, and speaking. . . ."[19] In interrogating foundational beliefs, there are moments of impasse that come not necessarily from intransigence but from an incapacity to fathom or apprehend the significance of what one is confronted by. And rather than try and spell out why or how the person is stuck, a better strategy is to assist the person in naming that person's own difficulties. Lacan argues that an analyst is bound to fail if s/he attempts to point out to the analysands the nature of their problem(s); the goal for Lacan is to have the patients discover the nature of the ailment by naming their unconscious desires and recognizing the discourses to which they are subject.[20] Ellie Ragland-Sullivan demonstrates that Lacan was very critical of the "image of the analyst as an objective, scientific observer, who regards the patient's behavior as an object of study outside the analyst."[21] This posture, she says, works only to obscure psychic truths and "allows the unwary analyst to take her or his own postulates to be objective viewpoints. The analysand becomes a victim of the analyst's illusions and is unaware that Freud's discovery did not situate truth or reality in the analyst or in technique but placed truth itself in question."[22] Emphasizing that one ought not to attempt to situate resistance entirely in the analysand or attempt to read their desires, Ragland-Sullivan shows that in Lacan's view, "resistance comes from the analyst, not the analysand."[23] According to Lacan, she explains, analysts are resisting when they believe "interpretation" means demonstrating to the analysand that he or she *really* desires some object. For Lacan, the "efficacious action of an analysis occurs when the analysand is brought to the point of naming the Desire which insists beyond his or her awareness."[24] For Lacan, then, the role of the analyst is not to read a patient's desire or even to "understand" the patient; Lacanian analysts "must resist their own subjective interpretations of the analysand."[25] For Lacan, the analyst "is only a detective who can aid the analysand in finding out about the Other's discourse and Desire."[26] This insight should caution us against thinking that teachers are in a position to accurately read students' resistance; too often, for example, it seems that educators resent resistance because they read it as desire to maintain privilege, but it might be helpful to keep in mind that this reading may stem from the educator's own resistance and defense mechanisms.

In particular, I find the defense mechanism disavowal quite illuminating, and I will provide both cultural and subjective manifestations of it. Disavowal enables one to hold two contradictory beliefs together precisely because one ignores that there is a contradiction. Making an object out of these dynamics might lead us to engage students in exploration and the deep critical reflection required for transformative social justice education. But as I will explain later, we may need to come at this study of ignorance by first depersonalizing it, though to get at disavowal it will need to be repersonalized later. Exploring ignorance through images and productions that draw students into narratives can give them some sense of identification with the struggle against homophobia. From there I ask them to return to think about how those practices are reflected in the school policies that have shaped their understanding and will frame their work as teachers and find that they are more responsive to this than when we deal with difficult issues head on. It is not surprising that when we attempt to challenge students head on by bringing their structuring ignorances to their attention, they both feel comfortable expressing those ignorances that have shaped their lives and experiences and also feel defensive when we engage them directly. When I began teaching about homophobia to preservice teachers, I gave them a bias test from the Gay, Lesbian, Straight Educators' Network (GLSEN). Questions ask them to think how they would feel if a friend or family member came out to them, asks if they would see an LGBT doctor, and other similar questions.[27] The test is intended to help people recognize unconscious bias about LGBT people, but the students often fail, which doesn't endear them to the process, and some of them actually say very scary things, which is also challenging for their instructor. Because I understand the context of ignorance in which they come to these teaching tools, I know I need to find other ways to get them to think about what they don't want to know and to help them care about things they are currently ignorant about.

Structures of Ignorance in School

First, preservice teachers need to understand how their participation in social institutions and structures has gotten them to the point where ignorance can seem appealing and comfortable. It helps to look at these dynamics in particular challenges in school, so I turn to an examination of anti-bullying policy and sex education curricula to illustrate the way that ignorance functions as a socially sanctioned and culturally imposed strategy of power, which might help to explain the ongoing violence against the LGBT population as well as many teachers' ambivalent responses to discussing LGBT issues across the curricula.

In the 2009 National School Climate survey, The Gay Lesbian Straight Education Network (GLSEN) found that nearly 9 out of 10 lesbian, gay, bi and transgender (LGBT) students experienced harassment at school in the past year; nearly two-thirds reported that they felt unsafe at school because of their sexual orientation, and over a third felt unsafe due to their gender expression.[28] In September 2010 alone, there were at least 6 known suicides by openly gay, or perceived to be gay, teenagers.[29]

On September 30, 2010, the Human Right's Campaign (HRC)—the nation's largest LGBT civil rights organization—issued a nationwide action alert in response to the alarming number of bullying and harassment-related suicides across the country. The alert urged Secretary of Education Arne Duncan to speak out and push every school in the nation to implement anti-bullying policies inclusive of sexual orientation and gender identity because, although current federal education policy does offer measures to promote and support school safety, it does not comprehensively or effectively focus on issues of bullying or harassment, and in no way does it address the challenges faced by LGBT youth.[30] The Safe Schools Improvement Act—a federal anti-bullying bill introduced in the House and the Senate—is designed to amend the Safe and Drug-Free Schools and Communities Act (part of the No Child Left Behind Act) to require schools and districts receiving federal funds to adopt codes of conduct specifically prohibiting bullying and harassment, including protections on the basis of sexual orientation and gender identity/expression. This Act would also require states to report data on bullying and harassment to the Department of Education.[31] The good news is that following California, Illinois, Iowa, Maryland, New Jersey, North Carolina, Oregon, Vermont, and Washington, New York has recently become the tenth state to enact an enumerated anti-bullying law that includes sexual orientation and gender expression protections, along with those based on race, religion, etc.[32] The growing support for enumerated anti-bullying bills provides us with reasonable hope that Congress will follow suit and pass the Safe Schools Improvement Act.

The alert also asks people to take additional steps to help deal with the crisis of bullying in our schools, like, for example, writing a letter to the editor of their local newspaper as well as sending a link to the HRC's Welcoming Schools web site to school administrators. The Welcoming Schools program provides elementary school teachers, parents, and students around the country with tools to help stop the bullying and gender stereotyping that far too many students face every day.[33] Available at www.welcomingschools.org, this program offers lesson plans that depict family diversity (including LGBT families), tools with which to disrupt gender stereotyping, strategies for how to deal with "teachable moments," as when one hears the common expression, "that's so gay," as well as an overall model of best practices for elementary schools in order to teach children respect early so that the homophobic violence prevalent in middle and high schools might be prevented. As argued by the HRC, taking a proactive approach to end bullying will positively affect every student in the school, and schools have a responsibility to address the bullying epidemic that is unnecessarily affecting a vast amount of the national population.

In addition to policy efforts to pass legislation like the Safe Schools Improvement Act and programs like Welcoming Schools, Parents, Families and Friends of Lesbians and Gays (PFLAG) National have joined the Gay, Lesbian and Straight Education Network (GLSEN) to launch the Claim Your Rights campaign, an effort to empower students and their allies to report incidences of bullying, harassment, or discrimination to the Office for Civil Rights at the U.S. Education Department. The new effort to report incidents of bullying, harassment, and discrimination includes a basic toolkit and instructions on how to submit a report online that can be found on both the PFLAG National (www.pflag.org/claimyourrights) and GLSEN's websites.[34]

Noteworthy as well are grassroots programs like the Trevor Lifeline—a suicide helpline that received close to 30,000 calls from youth looking for help in 2009 alone—and a new online video channel is reaching out to teenagers who are bullied at school for being gay. The message: life really does get better after high school. The online video web site for the "It Gets Better Project," was created by the Seattle advice columnist and activist Dan Savage. The web site is a collection of videos from adults in the gay (and allied) community who share their own stories of surviving school bullying and moving on to build successful careers and happy, fulfilling lives.[35] Most recently President Obama has appeared on Savage's web site with a message of hope and future promise for youth.

These efforts offer a multi-pronged approach to changing the culture of bullying that is plaguing our schools and connected to an outrageous number of youth suicides. The end to bullying and creating a culture of respect for all isn't a one-step or one-sided effort. Studies show that when a young lesbian, gay, bisexual, transgender or questioning (LGBT) person knows there is an affirming teacher, school nurse, clergy member or parent they can trust, they are much more likely to turn to them for help when they are bullied or depressed. Similarly, when a school or community has a Gay-Straight Alliance or other affirming and accepting group, young people are less likely to feel isolated and can turn to peers and faculty advisors when they need help.

However, these antibullying programs are a contradictory response—implementing care for queer students in codes of conduct while ignoring it in curricula is not going to end fear and violence, and provides us with an example of cultural disavowal. On the one hand we demand care and civility (fundamental character traits listed in most character education programs)[36] for all students when it comes to codes of conduct while, on the other hand, we hold up heterosexual monogamous marriage as the only respectable practice of sexuality and fail to recognize or rectify the contradiction. We need to include a concept of the multi-sexual in multicultural education. Further, a look at just one small aspect of the curricula shows how cultural disavowal of the complexity of identity and desire fails to provide students with the skills and knowledge they need to act responsibly. But as teachers and pre-service teachers might start trying to act responsibly, there are a few barriers of institutionally created ignorance that frame how they and their students might take responsibility. For instance, if sexuality is not a robust part of curriculum, these "take responsibility for bullying" projects ignore or are situated in contexts that encourage sexual ignorance. Without understanding how homosexuality has been vilified and removed from official school subjects, students can't quite come to grips with why it is they don't know what they might need to know to understand the issue more fully and thus be more able to intervene. And in the one part of the curricula where it seems inarguable that different sexual identities and practices be discussed, sex education programs fail to provide students with the information they need to be empowered to make ethical decisions about their own sexuality and, instead, mandate ignorance.

I look at Illinois as one example because I happen to find myself there. The youth-created site sexetc.org explains that Illinois does not require schools to teach sexuality education. Local school boards decide which subjects this education must cover and the grade level in which topics are introduced. If sexuality education is taught, it must be age appropriate. Abstinence must be covered and stressed as the only completely effective protection against unplanned pregnancy, sexually transmitted diseases, and HIV/AIDS. Teaching about contraceptives, such as condoms, the Pill, or the Patch, is also required but does not need to be stressed. According to the Illinois School Code, "honor and respect for monogamous heterosexual marriage" must be taught. Illinois received approximately $10,001,768 in federal funds for abstinence-only-until-marriage programs in Fiscal Year 2008.[37]

Sexuality education programs are directed at solving social problems caused by sexual ignorance, but fear of school boards and parents leaves teachers fearful of answering student questions. Further, we expect students to behave well toward sexual and gender minorities but don't provide them with information that might prevent their confusion and violence. Their experiences of structural silences on sexuality, in part, explain their subjective attachment to resistance and ignorance on related topics.

Subjective Disavowal: Students Respond to "But I'm a Cheerleader!"

To show how ignorance is also productive on subjective levels, operating as a defense against difficult knowledge—knowledge that is experienced as threatening or anxiety inducing—I offer a brief analysis of preservice teachers' responses to the film "But I'm a Cheerleader." Here, as Susan Verducci and Michael Katz have argued in Chapter 29 of this volume, I suggest that bringing aspects of popular culture into the classroom can facilitate difficult dialogue and critical reflection as students seem to be more willing to dwell in the discomfort that the encounter with difference and difficult knowledge can engender. And yet, their responses reveal that that while they ascribe to egalitarian principles and beliefs, on the one hand, many of them harbor prejudice against queer folk and seem to have a desire to abdicate responsibility on the other.

Most preservice teachers want to see their students succeed, support their rights for equality of opportunity in education, and claim to want to instill in them a profound respect for diversity. They say they want to treat their students with fairness and give them the tools they need to lead happy, healthy, and successful lives. Most of them report that they feel inadequately equipped to deal with the diverse, multicultural classroom environments. Alerted to the bullying, they argue they have zero tolerance for words like fag, dyke, etc. And yet many feel that homosexuality is a sin, a bad decision, an unfortunate lot in life. Few can name more than one or two LGBT cultural heroes.

In this section I argue that popular culture can help show us that our cultural narrative is shifting; there are more images of diversity than in the past, and that bringing aspects of it into the classroom can facilitate difficult dialogue and the critical reflection on our encounter with difficult knowledge. Popular culture may help students to understand, via narrative, identification, etc. how to respect difference, but cultural representations don't always answer questions students have, and their intention may not be primarily to teach, so students are still missing out on learning in key areas that we can begin to collectively fill in by viewing and discussing aspects of it in classrooms.

Jamie Babbit's 1999 film, *But I'm a Cheerleader* depicts the experiences of youth who are sent to a sexual rehabilitation camp as a result of the homophobia of their parents, teachers, and friends. Megan (the lead character played by Natasha Leyonne) is clean cut and honest, a good student who dates the captain of the football team, and she is a cheerleader. Because she only has pictures of girls in her locker and her room, she eats tofu and doesn't enjoy kissing her boyfriend, her parents and friends conclude that she is gay and send her to sexual rehabilitation school so she can learn to how to be straight. But, not surprisingly, she learns how to come out as lesbian, and falls in love with her classmate, Graham (Clea Duvall).

I suggest that combining the kind of subtle learning that comes through popular culture seems to help students feel more comfortable asking difficult questions than they do in official classes or answering questions that they often resist when asked to think about head on. Because they are able to watch how characters work in and through ignorance, they are drawn into an examination of the processes of ignorance as they follow plot turns and begin, in some ways, to identify with characters they would usually remain distant from. Instead of dealing with their own ignorance directly, in other words, they see the process of ignorance and, of course, given the humorous bent of the movie, they also enjoy the spectacle. In the words of one of my students who had just viewed *But I'm a Cheerleader*, "I liked the fact that the movie had an underlying funny tone. I think that kept people's attention and got the message through more effectively." Although students can and do relate to the struggles of LGBT youth in popular culture, often report that they would be sad or confused if a family member, particularly their own children came out to them as gay. One even stated that they would want to send their child to a "straight camp" if they came out as gay. Most of them feel that their own sex education was limited and unhelpful and advocate implementing a more comprehensive sex education curriculum but also feel ambivalent about what the content should really be and when it's appropriate to start talking about it. And many would like to be that teacher whom troubled, anxious, students would trust and be motivated by. Many of them claim that they "don't agree with homosexuality." So, when we split the sources of moral teaching/ethics in people's lives, we might note how students can be insightful following characters in a popular narrative like *But I'm a Cheerleader* but less insightful when thinking of themselves back in the real world when conflicts with faith or fears about conflicts with parents or school boards impede their ability to act ethically.

What follows are just a few of the responses, and what I think they illuminate are fairly common forms of willful ignorance, a fairly common phenomenon of people who ascribe to egalitarian values and belief systems and yet harbor prejudices that undermine those very values but go unrecognized as such. But overall I feel my students were more open to reflection after viewing the film than they were after doing academic reading. There were several overwhelming themes that emerged in the responses. First was that the movie was funny and therefore more successful at getting its message across. One student comments, "By using humor the film doesn't turn off a person like a straightforward in your face demand would." The most common response was that people are who they are, and we all have a right to be who we are. People seem to relate to the characters, and show a desire to be open-minded, but they also seem to want to abdicate responsibility for creating the conditions for egalitarianism.

I've discussed the institutionally structured ignorance that we all work in, and I want to now return to how disavowal—holding contradictory impulses like generosity toward difference and some sense that negative consequences are eventually attached to homosexuality—shows students both moving toward respect but also tempered by disapproval. These are examples of students working through their discomforts and changing but also still in some ways denying responsibility. One way I've seen my students dwell in disavowal is by expressing an unwillingness to judge but still holding that judgment will happen: "I know that not every desire is meant to be followed. I have no definite opinion towards homosexuals, but that life is something I don't fully understand. Until that time I try to keep an open a mind as possible and pray that I make no judgments that are to be only left to God." Or "It's weird because I don't agree with homosexuality. Only because it is a sin in the Bible, but I am not interested in judging either." When students say they're happy for the lesbian characters at the end, they still express ambivalence about their own children possibly being gay, and this, in turn, makes me wonder how well some of their positive changes will translate into classroom practices. But I think that if we can talk about the dilemmas of ignorance—the way it is structurally imposed and the way it acts as a defense mechanism—we might begin to more successfully work through it.

Rethinking resistance points to ways of rethinking how students might become critical of processes of resistance in others. Clearly this will help them as they become teachers and become more active co-learners with other students. In addition, I hope that this attention to forms of resistance and ignorance also leads them into examinations of their disavowals. I intend in later classes to work in more depth through their processes of disavowal and to get them to think more about their own responses as objects of critique. We start off at a distance, thinking about structures that have led us all to embrace forms of ignorance and move closer to seeing how this works in ourselves. The larger challenge remains: being attentive enough to see when our defenses start and find new ways of living with those with whom we are not comfortable. In this way, we can begin to bridge the gap between promoting the virtues of respect, civility, and tolerance in theory to actual practices in education and our larger social and global communities.

Notes

1. See Boyd, D. (2011), Character Education from Left Field, in *Character & Moral Education: A Reader*. New York: Peter Lang; Lickona, T. (2004). *Character Matters*. New York: Touchstone; and Spring, J. (2010). *Political Agendas for Education*: *From Change We Can Believe in to Putting America First*. New York: Routledge.
2. Boler, M. (1999) *Feeling Power: Emotions and Education*. New York: Routledge, xvii.
3. Ibid., xxiv.
4. Ibid., 177.
5. Ibid.
6. This is Boler's term to describe how dominant discourses shape the selectivity or our emotional awareness. Ibid., 16.
7. Ibid., 200.
8. McGee, P. (1987). "Truth and Resistance: Teaching as a Form of Analysis" *College English* 49: 677.
9. Britzman, D. (1998). *Lost Subjects, Contested Objects. Toward a Psychoanalytic Inquiry of Learning*. Albany, NY: State University of New York Press.
10. Ibid., 138.
11. Freud, A. (1966). *The Ego and the Mechanisms of Defense*. New York: International Universities Press, Inc., 42.
12. Ibid. Interestingly, A. Freud points out that early on S. Freud had abandoned the term "defense," replacing it with that of "repression," but then later returned to it, realizing that repression was but one of many strategies the ego makes use of in dealing with conflicts that potentially lead to neurosis. She took this as her cue to delineate other mechanisms of defense, and one of her major contributions to psychoanalytic theory and practice was the development of the theory of defense and defense mechanisms, of which she named twelve.
13. Freud, S. (1966)."Resistance and Repression," *Introductory Lectures on Psychoanalysis*, ed. James Strachey. New York: Norton, 354–374.
14. Ibid., 354.
15. Ibid., 355.
16. Ibid., 362.
17. Ibid., 363.
18. Ibid.
19. Ragland-Sullivan, E. (1986). *Jacques Lacan and the Philosophy of Psychoanalysis*. Chicago: The University of Illinois Press., 121.
20. See McGee, "Truth and Resistance," for a discussion of the goals of Lacanian analysis and how they might be applied to social justice education.
21. Ragland-Sullivan, *Jacques Lacan and the Philosophy of Psychoanalysis*, 119.
22. Ibid., 121.
23. Ibid.
24. Ibid.
25. Ibid., 122.
26. Ibid., 125.
27. GLSEN (2010). Safe Space Kit, www.glsen.org/binary-data/GLSEN_ATTACHMENTS/file/000/001/1511–3.PDF, accessed Nov. 1, 2010, p. 7.
28. "2009 National School Climate Survey": nearly 9 out of LGBT students experienced harassment at school.

Available at: http://www.glsen.org/cgi-bin/iowa/all/news/record/2624.html

29. http://www.lgbtqnation.com/2010/10/education-secretary-calls-for-tolerance-in-response-to-bullying-suicides-of-gay-teens/

30. Safe Schools Improvement Act available from http://www.hrc.org/issues/12142.htm

31. http://www.glsen.org/cgi-bin/iowa/all/news/record/2429.html

32. from http://www.pridesource.com/article.html?article=42068

33. HRC Launches Alert Following Bullying-Related Suicides Around the Country available at: http://www.hrc.org/14938.htm

34. http://community.pflag.org/Page.aspx?pid=1323&frcrld=1

35. http://well.blogs.nytimes.com/2010/09/22/showing-gay-teens-a-happy-future/

36. Spring, J. (2010). *From Change We Can Believe in to Putting America First.* New York: Routledge.

37. sexetc.org, accessed Nov. 1, 2010.

CHAPTER TWENTY-SIX

Feelings of Worth
and the Moral Made Visible

BARBARA STENGEL

My jurisdiction is changed. I have abandoned jurisprudence and betaken myself to the larger sphere of mind and morals.

HORACE MANN, JULY 2, 1837[1]

An object becomes intellectually significant to us when the self reads its past experience into it. But as this past experience is not colorlessly intellectual, but is dyed through and through with interests, with feelings of worth, the emotional element is also read into the object, and made a constituent element of it....The world thus comes to be a collection of objects possessing emotional worth as well as intellectual.

JOHN DEWEY, PSYCHOLOGY

What does recognition of importance mean aside from the ascription of worth, value—that is, aside from the projection of emotional experience?

JOHN DEWEY, "THE THEORY OF EMOTION" (2)

The really good moral educators I know don't talk about themselves as *moral* educators at all. They just think of themselves as teachers and principals and parents and coaches, and they realize that everything they say and do with and in the presence of young people impacts, in perhaps predictable but not completely controllable ways, what those young people learn and how they grow. And so these (moral) educators take care to pay attention, to be responsive, to speak honestly, to elicit dialogue about difficult issues, to voice criticism (of self, other or society) constructively, to employ habits worthy of emulation, to create feelings of community and spaces for individual and shared responsibility. But they are never doing *just* that.

They know what Horace Mann knew when he left the practice of law to become the Secretary to the Board of Education in Massachusetts in 1837: that the domain of education is a "larger sphere of mind and morals," that neither mind nor morals can be neglected, that both are dimensions of the same sphere.

But they also know what John Dewey claimed from his earliest days as an educational philosopher: that any actual ascription of worth to ideas *or* actions is a projection of emotional experience, that we "read" our feeling selves into the ideas and actions we take to be worthwhile.[2]

For these really good moral educators, interactions with young people are always *about* some idea, some "subject matter," that can be represented and thought. The idea(s) might have something to do with basketball or algebra or friendship, but those interactions are never *only* about an idea. They are always also about what to do, about defending the basket or graphing a line or making a friend, and how one does it. And these good moral educators know that ideas and actions are tied to feelings, feelings that alternately stick to and slide off "objects" of thought and action, feelings that are the *experiential* measure of the value of the idea or the action. What's worth knowing and what's worth doing take shape in the recognition that worth and feeling are inextricably linked. These moral educators know that the knowing and the doing and the feeling are woven into the fabric of the world we experience, and somehow, they attend to all of it.

As I discuss in this chapter, the difference between the realm of mind and the realm of morals is not that the moral is about values and the academic is about facts. Both are about values, asking what is worthwhile—and worth and value are tied up in affective response, in emotion, as much as in reasoned judgment. The difference between mind and morals, between the academic and the moral, is an analytic rather than experiential difference; the former is about knowledge and the latter is about action. In both cases, it is emotion—energy in motion—that moves us.

Exemplary Moral Educators

Pat Wallace was my high school basketball coach more years ago than I can count. She insisted on hard work, on putting in the time to train, on doing something over and over again until you get it right, on acting with sportsmanship while striving to win, on being part of a team. It would be an understatement to say she was demanding. Nonetheless, young women lined up every year to compete for a slot on a team that was the most successful in the region. Maybe it was the tantalizing promise of athletic success that drew these young women to this challenge in the days just before Title IX. Maybe it was Pat's interest in each girl *off* the court, the fact that she could talk easily with you about your classes, your family, your boyfriends and girlfriends, your interest in music or theater. Maybe it was the way the older girls on the team carried themselves. Maybe it was the sheer enjoyment of strenuous physical activity. Maybe it was the opportunity to test oneself, to find out if you, too, were good enough to continue the tradition. Whatever it was, it was attractive. Pat wasn't perfect, yelling sometimes when a softer touch might have worked a bit better, giving a player a hard time long after the point had been made. But there was never any question that being part of this team meant becoming somebody—on the basketball court and off it.

Grace Brennan (a pseudonym) is also a basketball coach and a friend of mine, but more important, she is the mother of 12-year-old Kyle who can tell you all the cities in his home state of Vermont and who knows the distances between them and a long list of other things that you might or might not want to know but that come in handy from time to time. Kyle inhabits a space on the autism spectrum, it seems, as well as inhabiting overlapping spaces with his generally happy family in a neighborhood where adults and kids know and appreciate him even when they don't completely understand what he is up to, and in a school space where he is more and more successful every year. Kyle's mother has never treated him like he is anybody but a young man who must learn to be responsible for himself and his actions, setting limits firmly while offering him space to make a contribution to every interaction. This has not always been easy; it was never clear what Kyle could and could not do. But like his talented older brother and capable younger sister, Kyle is taken seriously but never allowed to take himself too seriously. He is one of the family, and it is his job to be as responsive to others as they are to him. When his actions make others uncomfortable, his mother points this out, taking pains to connect ideas and actions and feelings (his and those of others). When Kyle does something that might be construed as inconsiderate, she tries to show him, by explanation or example, what that means and why it matters. Noreen has always found a way to enjoy and encourage Kyle even as he stretches her day by day. And now he is able to enjoy himself—and to encourage others.

Terri McNally is a long-time mathematics teacher in a Philadelphia Catholic boys' high school, who is finally being forced to retire because the school is closing. Where other math teachers vie for the opportunity to teach the smart kids, the upper-level math, the AP courses, Terri firmly rooted herself in Algebra I, where she taught hour after hour of ninth grade boys. She will tell you that this is because she's really not that good in math, but I suspect it is because, as a mother of two boys who took a while to grow into the men they are today, she knows that 14-year-old young men are more young than men just at the point when a man is what they most want to be. Terri does not mother them, though they clearly feel safe in her care. She teaches them, asking questions, explaining mathematical moves, pushing them to confusion and then beyond to think it through and to say more, and generously allows them the time to do so. It's not clear exactly how she does it, but even a casual observer will notice that the other boys keep themselves in check while she is paying close attention to one of their mates. Maybe it is because each knows his turn will come. He will be the center of her attention. He will have the opportunity to demonstrate who he is and how he thinks and what he knows in the bright but kindly light she shines on each in turn.

Interestingly, if this were a chapter about "academic educators" rather than moral education, I could use these same three people as my exemplars. I have known a lot of basketball coaches in my time and been one myself, and Pat Wallace might well be the best I have known. She can teach basic skills, employ strategy, talk complicated Xs and Os, and move kids to more than they thought possible. Grace Brennan doesn't know as much about the towns in Vermont as Kyle does, but she knows how to draw him out, to value his inquiry, to redirect his interest to things that might fill out what he knows and likes in more useful ways. And I have honestly never seen an Algebra I teacher who drilled as near to the core of what linear equations are and are for (as well as how you can graph them) as Terri McNally does. While she might say she isn't very good at mathematics, I would say she was very good indeed at connecting algebraic ideas and ninth grade minds with real intellectual integrity.

The Moral Matters

My intuition that good moral educators often aren't focused on moral education *per se* and usually do not talk about their efforts as moral unless prompted is part of what motivated me to publish *Moral Matters* (2006) with Alan Tom several years ago. Alan and I share a concern that the moral dimensions of teaching and learning tend to get short shrift in the daily life of schools. It was not, we agreed, that there were not moral matters being negotiated constantly, only that these matters rarely garnered conscious attention in an educational climate and community overwhelmed with a whole array of apparently academic demands. This was the state of affairs even before the arrival of the second President Bush and his unholy alliance with Ted Kennedy that gave us No Child Left Behind.

Alan and I saw an artificial divide emerging between the moral and the academic dimensions of teaching and learning especially among the adherents of character education, but we saw something else as well: that many if not most educators (and policymakers and parents) acted as though the moral dimensions of work in public schools didn't exist. There seemed to be a general sense that the moral didn't matter. We called this the moral invisible position, though clearly, in some cases at least, the moral was not just invisible but denied as a legitimate purpose for public schooling.

In *Moral Matters,* we were not looking for the "best" moral educators, in part because there were no criteria that would warrant such a choice. Instead, we wanted to survey the terrain of what we called the moral visible, the kind of efforts being made to consciously and explicitly give life to the moral in teaching and learning. Maybe, we thought, we could stimulate defensible thinking about what it meant to do moral education well. And, in the process, perhaps we could encourage others to rethink their own practice.

But what of those like the "moral educators" I invoked at the start of this chapter? They don't need to rethink their practice; it is effective, even exemplary. Does it matter, nonetheless, that they don't think of themselves as moral educators? Does their failure to name their work "moral education," a move too common among accomplished contemporary educators, undercut efforts to make the moral visible? And what is actually being sidestepped when we discuss and practice education as if it were not moral? These are the questions I address here.

Enter Emotion

When educators avoid explicit acknowledgment of the moral dimensions of their work, they are sidestepping not the moral that many enact with skill, but the play of emotion that is an integral feature of valuing anything. Simply put, the moment when the moral makes its presence known is that moment when one's view of what's worth doing is called into question by a competing moral view. That is a recognizably emotional moment, a moment of sometimes profound discomfort. That discomfort gives way to another, the prejudice about admitting feeling into the domain of mind, into the realm of the academic. And so the moral is segregated, rooted out of the public domain of schooling and relegated to the private domain of family and church. But as I will develop below, it is not the moral we are banishing because it is impossible to educate without an implicit sense of what's worth doing. Rather, we are banishing the *emotional* dimensions of teaching and learning.

There is one great irony in this strategy. The play of emotion is not limited to the moral; what educators assume to be the neutral domain of the academic is as fraught with value perception and value judgment (the projection of emotion) as is the moral. It is both logically and experientially impossible to root the emotional out of either the academic or the moral. But this insight is hard to accept. The messiness it implies leaves us feeling the discomfort of doubt and uncertainty, a state of affairs integral to the process of learning, but one that schools are not structured to support or encourage. The bottom line is that the moral won't live openly in school until school becomes a place where temporary ambiguity and discomfort and the other emotions (positive and negative) associated with learning are themselves valued.

Nonetheless, and typically without attention to emotion or the origin of values, a stalwart group of moral educators has offered a wide range of efforts to pursue moral ends and make the moral visible in schools over the past several decades. Understanding these efforts was the goal of *Moral Matters* and a brief review of that work will help us to make sense of the role of emotion in the moral and academic conduct of teaching and learning and the pursuit of both moral and academic educational goals.

Making Sense of the Moral and the Academic

As suggested, some educators and policymakers actively deny the moral dimensions of educational work; others intentionally render those dimensions invisible. This may be the result of a conscious political strategy or an unconscious diversionary tactic, but neither denial nor omission is the focus here.

Consider instead those who insist that the moral ought to be an explicit educational consideration. No one advocates *replacing* the academic with the moral; rather they look to bring the moral into relation with the academic under the umbrella of education. What is the logical array of possibilities for thinking about this relationship between the moral (what's worth doing) and the academic (what's worth knowing) in educational efforts? Just what relations are at least conceptually possible?[3] We suggested five general basic possibilities, some of which had subsets: Separate, Sequential (Moral First or Academic First), Dominant (Moral Dominant or Academic Dominant), Transformative (Moral Transformative or Academic Transformative), and Integrated. These possibilities, described below, form a loose category system for analyzing one's own approach to making the moral visible in what we called a "framework for engagement" (p. 7) that would enable those who shared an interest in the moral to interact without getting tangled in preset ideological concerns.

First, one might construe the moral and the academic as two *separate* domains in educational work, viewing both as important and worthy of attention but distinctive in both effort and result. Former Secretary of Education William Bennett and others who call themselves "character educators" tend to take a Separate approach as do some versions of service learning.

Or one might understand the moral and the academic in *sequential* fashion, one preceding and clearing ground for the other. In Moral First, a typical stance among classroom teachers, one presumes that setting up rules and procedures precedes and makes possible the kind of order that is necessary for effective academic education. Mortimer Adler flips the Moral First approach on its end, arguing in his *Paideia Proposal* that it is the development of the mind that makes appreciation of the moral possible, resulting in action that might be characterized as moral.

For other educators, the moral and the academic both matter, but one matters more and dominates the educator's focus and action. The Moral Dominant perspective is readily identified in most parochial schools where mission statements and school leaders explicitly claim that a child's beliefs and way of being in the world are far more important than his or her academic achievement. An Academic Dominant educator like E. D. Hirsch articulates the value of moral education in schools, but in the end, attention to the moral is eclipsed by the focused attention Hirsch pays to the content of children's learning.

While the Separate, Sequential, and Dominant approaches to attending to both the moral and the academic tend to view the two realms as at least analytically disconnected, the final two categories, Transformative and Integrated, recognize the interconnection between the moral and the academic. Nel Noddings is a Moral Transformative educator who knows that by adopting a particular moral stance (in her case, an ethic of care), you alter the shape of the academic terrain as well. Educational reformer Ted Sizer takes a complementary approach to Noddings's. An Academic Transformative, Sizer maintains that when specific "habits of mind" ground the academic curriculum, then possibilities for moral thought and action emerge and expand. In both cases, there is a focus on the moral or the academic, but the framing of the one shapes the possibilities for the other.

The final logical possibility is that the moral dimensions of teaching and learning can be fully *integrated* in practice with the academic dimensions. While it is obviously possible for us to distinguish what's worth doing from what's worth knowing analytically, this view maintains that, in educational practice, every academic action has moral import and every moral effort has academic impact. This, I hasten to add, is my own view. For me, it is not that the moral and the academic *can be* integrated in practice; it is that they simply *are* integrated, and it is our own blindness, sometimes willed but more often a result of unconscious feeling-fueled avoidance, that renders the moral either invisible or somehow diminished.

I contend that *every* classroom interaction and *every* non-school educational interaction can be deconstructed to reveal assumptions about and instruction regarding both academic content and moral formation. The integration of the two is most obvious in those settings where the educators explicitly claim to be operating in moral and academic spheres in tandem. Deborah Meier's Central Park East High School, portrayed without commentary in Frederick Wiseman's 1994 film *High School II*, is a somewhat dated but readily available video representation of just such intentional integration. But walk into any classroom in the country today, and you can read the moral written into what is too often a narrowed and bloodless academic curriculum. What's worth doing is compliance. What's worth knowing are just those basic skills and common understandings that represent minimum qualifications for the corporate employers who value compliance as much as they value those skills and understanding.

This stereotypical NCLB-shaped (and often urban) classroom is, thank goodness, not the only model of moral/academic integration available in the United States today. In some classrooms and schools, teachers are committed to a collaborative model of intelligence and learning linked to views of conflict resolution and cooperation, all reflected in the kinds of interactions they plan and encourage and in the aspects of curriculum that are highlighted or selected for intensive instruction. In other settings, teachers view self-discipline as the *sine qua non* of learning and employ pedagogical strategies and curricular foci that develop such discipline (ironically, but correctly, employing externally imposed discipline temporarily as a tool toward internally exercised discipline). In still other environments, teachers understand themselves to be the traditional jug filling up the child's empty mug, benevolent, protective and entertaining until the mug is full. In all cases, there are moral messages offered and underscored, even when there is no mention of the moral, *and* there are academic lessons being learned even in those moments when the talk seems to be all about being good, or cooperative, or respectful.

It is worth noting that Alan Tom and I were able to find exemplars of *all* of the logical possibilities. And it is further worth noting that there was no pattern in the distribution of political spectrum views with respect to the various logical possibilities. That is, we identified both liberal and conservative exemplars occupying nearly all the possible approaches. Ways of articulating and enacting the relationship between the academic and the moral in teaching and learning are not, or at least not necessarily, politically driven, a fact that makes our category scheme useful for dialogue across ideological lines.

The alert reader will ask how I can maintain the dialogic usefulness of a set of categories when I also maintain that the moral and the academic are always integrated in experience. My response is that the positions articulated above are best understood as *advocacy positions*. To raise the banner of the moral vis-à-vis schooling as do the exemplars cited in *Moral Matters* is to call into question the conventional understanding of education that dominates schools. It is to ask whether and how schools are educative. However understood or deconstructed, "moral" and "academic" capture important intuitions about what is *desired*, what is needed in raising up the next generation.

Thus the positions articulated above are, consciously and explicitly, the views and practices of those who see a moral gap in schools and want to fill it. The question they ask and answer is how *best* to fill that gap. It is a pragmatic question with an empirical answer, one that has not been studied carefully. In an educational system that intentionally and mistakenly leaves the moral out of consideration (rhetorically and discursively if not actually), how do we make the moral visible? What are the most constructive and effective steps to take?

This is a conversation worth having—and a proposition worth testing. While I claim that we are best served by acknowledging the integrated nature of our moral and academic preconceptions and practices, by deconstructing present practice and policy to reveal the narratives that hold it in place, and by developing a new pedagogical language of responsibility that enables a more complex *and fluid* seeing of both the moral and the academic, I readily acknowledge that there is presently no empirical *evidence* that my preferred approach is the one that will result in the widespread acknowledgment of and care about the moral dimensions of educational work. I simply don't know which of these approaches will, in the long run, result in the most, the most open, and the most intelligent dialogue regarding what's worth doing in American schools and American society.

And I am forced to admit that my view does not address, any better than any of the others, why and how the moral comes to be omitted in the first place. After all, the history of American education from the first Satan Deluder Act to the explicit reflections of Horace Mann to the text of No Child Left Behind is a narrative that acknowledges the moral responsibility of teachers and schools. So the question arises, how is it that the moral *exits*? Why are these varied strategies to bring the moral back in, strategies that take every logically conceivable form, even necessary?

The answer lies in "past histories of association" (Ahmed, 2003), in complexes of idea, action, and feeling that mark our experience with respect to self, school and the meaning of "American." We *feel* that the moral is dangerous and avoid it, rendering that feeling as fear.

The Moral *Is* Dangerous but So Is the Academic

Exposing what's worth doing to the light of the potentially open forum that is public education feels dangerous when one's own preferred answer to the question is not likely to be the privileged response. But most have neither the courage nor the social trust to simply admit the feelings of discomfort and move forward to negotiate a shared understanding that accommodates all. We act fearfully by drawing physical and conceptual boundaries, separating bodies and minds, and excising the emotion intrinsic to our action from the rhetoric about it. So we talk not about how we feel and what we want, but about "objective" dangers like indoctrination, the violation of church-state separation and the loss of national identity in the face of cultural diversity—all the while accusing the other of speaking from emotion and self-interest. Each of these socially constructed dangers is rooted in overlapping American narratives that are worthy of both respect *and* skepticism.

Indoctrination

We like to think that the "American Character" is marked by individual autonomy and personal responsibility, and indoctrination undercuts the maintenance of autonomy and the preservation of responsibility. How can I be responsible as me if I do not think for myself? So a teacher who shapes my thinking about what to do and how to act threatens the integrity of that self.

True. But can there be teaching that does not shape what to do and how to act? It is difficult to imagine. Education is both necessary and dangerous.

Generally speaking, concerns about the threat of indoctrination have been applied primarily to the moral domain but not to the academic. This seems to be so because of an erroneous assumption that the academic-moral divide, such as it is, is isomorphic with the philosophically defunct fact-value divide. That is, those who worry about indoctrination tend to assume that one can be indoctrinated with respect to value(s) but not with respect to facts. This is clearly not the case. In recent years, educators have heard from those who object to the teaching of biological evolution or big bang cosmology or race and whiteness theory, exposing the value-laden quality of both processes of inquiry and the products of that inquiry that are deemed (at least tentatively) to be known.

And it is not necessarily easier to recognize value when looking through a moral lens. For example, the conservative values of order and control have remained present, if sometimes veiled, in most schools under the aegis of classroom management and discipline. Order and control are often thought of not as values, but as necessary conditions for academic learning. Instrumental, technical and/or bureaucratic language masks what are unquestionably value choices on the part of teachers and administrators. These value choices are contested by those who call for caring, relational, equitable and democratic classrooms, as well as by those who recommend constructivist pedagogical approaches. Both the fact/value split and the specific values inherent in traditional school structures can be questioned and that questioning is political, despite common protests that public schools ought not be political.

American schools *do* embody a particular moral and political agenda in both structure and curriculum. Consider the pledge of allegiance at the beginning of the each school day, the assumption that representative democracy and corporate capitalism are the best forms of polity and economy, respectively, efforts to revise the history curriculum, and the recent trend for schools to enter into "partnerships" with corporations that typically result in unequal economic gain for both entities and questionable educational value. There is, in each of these objects, a set of values operant. You can tell that something of value is at stake by your affective response—positive or negative—to the previous sentence. These values only become visible when they become objectionable to some vocal portion of the population when a person or group feels some threat and articulates opposition.

This suggests that it is not indoctrination in and of itself that we fear. There is, it seems, a fine line between indoctrination and education. For many, indoctrination is simply education that "goes too far." If students are indoctrinated into *common* values for knowledge and action (read *our* values), we think they are well taught. When students are indoctrinated into controversial values for knowledge and action (read *not our* values), we *feel* concerned. It is the feeling of concern that one's own values are under threat that prompts talk of indoctrination.

Church and State

The moral is the domain of the church; the academic is the domain of the state. At least that is how many Americans (and many educators) unhappily encapsulate the Supreme Court decisions of the early 1960s. The domain of what's worth doing cannot be permitted entrance to the public school for fear of offending some other's deeply held belief. In a nation with religious freedom at its roots, this principle is held to be inviolable.

Of course this is only part of the American story. There *is* religious freedom in our genealogy, but there is also moral control. The complicated story of the Puritans combines both. And American history is as much the framing of common religious and moral ground as it is the respect for religious—and moral—diversity. Still, when the discomfort of moral disagreement arises, Americans are as likely to choose avoidance and fear as they are to choose engagement, trust and possible resolution. It is easier to hide behind the "wall of separation" between church and state. If one wants to know what's worth doing, ask the preacher or the rabbi or the imam. And if one wants to know what's worth knowing, does one ask the teacher?

This question seems almost laughable in the light of educational policy of the past thirty years. What's worth knowing has become the proverbial political football, pitting not liberals against conservatives, but educators against the political and corporate classes. School curricula are not the purview of classroom teachers or even of the university professors who synthesize knowledge and author textbooks but are subject to the specific control of corporate and other ideology-based interests through their political surrogates. When teachers and professors stand up for what's worth knowing based on the shared findings of communities of inquiry (communities admittedly marked by values and interests) as in the case of evolution or global warming, they are beaten back by organized campaigns of rhetorical dis- and misinformation and sometimes by legal action. There is almost never intelligent engagement about the values and interests that motivate both knowledge and action on either side.

In the present educational context, the moral is the domain of the church and the academic is the domain of the state. Educators apparently have no role to play in the determination of what's worth knowing *or* what's worth doing.

Cultural Diversity and National Identity

That the United States is an immigrant culture is broadly acknowledged. That those immigrants brought (and bring) varied cultural mores with them is accepted. The point of contention is what happens after that. Does the immigrant become American by learning the language and putting on a predefined cultural mantle? And what of those who came not as immigrants but as slaves? Do they take on the cultural identity of those who enslaved them? Is there a coherent and cohesive American identity for the taking? Are Americans defined in part by their cultural diversity, by their hyphenated status? Questions of cultural diversity and national identity have stimulated political action and scholarly investigation, and both have impacted school programs through "multicultural education" and "culturally responsive pedagogy." The issue can be stated baldly: which takes precedence, cultural diversity or national identity? Which tale of America is more persuasive, the open-minded tolerance of dialogue across difference or the cohesive power of shared community? Is it necessary to choose?

That the questions above encompass emotional concerns is acknowledged even by those who consider the issues from a self-consciously intellectual standpoint. Consider Arthur Schlesinger, Jr.'s dismay at *The Disuniting of America*:

> Those intrepid Europeans who had torn up their roots to brave the wild Atlantic *wanted* to forget a horrid past and to embrace a hopeful future. They *yearned* to become Americans. Their goals were escape, deliverance, assimilation. They saw America as a transforming nation, banishing dismal memories and developing a unique national character based on common political ideas and shared experiences. The point of America was not to preserve old cultures, but to produce a new *American* culture (1998, p. 17, emphasis in the original).

Clearly, Schlesinger appreciates the link between feeling and value. The worth of ideas and the worth of actions are both wrapped up in desire. This applies to the "intrepid Europeans" of whom Schlesinger speaks, but also to American citizens and new immigrants who seek to remember and honor their past (which is sometimes but not always or only horrid) while becoming, but also reshaping what it means to be, Americans. Puerto Ricans-made-Americans unwillingly, African Americans descended from slaves, Mexican workers who send wages back home to Mexico as they try to create home in the U.S. for their American-born children, and immigrants from Southeast Asia chased here by the effects of American military intervention are just a few of the groups who *yearn* to be truly American while realizing that America can only be America, in poet Langston Hughes' idiom,[4] when the transformation goes both ways. They have feelings about America and being American, but they are not the same feelings that Schlesinger attributes to the immigrants of the earlier centuries. They value America and their feeling-framed valuing shapes their conception of both what's worth knowing and what's worth doing.

Reading Past Feelings into Present Objects

Return for a moment to Dewey's observation about the emotional quality of past experience, of thought and action:

> An object becomes intellectually significant to us when the self reads its past experience into it. But as this past experience is not colorlessly intellectual, but is dyed through and through with interests, with feelings of worth, the emotional element is also read into the object, and made a constituent element of it....The world thus comes to be a collection of objects possessing emotional worth as well as intellectual. (1887/1975, p. 239)

Dewey's point, developed at length in his *Psychology* (1887), in his "The Theory of Emotion" (1894–95), and in his understanding of *Human Nature and Conduct* (1922), is that all human experience is triadic, integrating idea, act and feeling—and this applies to experience that is characterized as academic as well as experience that is characterized as moral. Indoctrination, the wall of separation between church and state, and cultural diversity are not just intellectual and political issues and arguments. All are also "objects" which have both academic (intellectual/idea) and moral (action) facets *as well as* emotional qualities that are the basis for attributing value or worth. Americans read their individual and collective past experience with attendant strong interests and "feelings of worth" into those objects. That is, each object demarcates multiple moments in American history and aspects of American character that carry meaning and feeling and also suggest action— but not the same meaning, feeling and action for all. Negotiating the meaning and action in light of feeling might well be understood as the purpose of public (and publicly required) schooling.

Those who use indoctrination or church-state separation or national identity as tools to protest against or deny the moral dimensions of teaching and learning are responding to feelings that are not baseless. Their habitual, preferred values *will* be challenged if others who have different feelings and hold different values are permitted entrance to the conversation. Rather than engage in the direct challenge of emotion and value, most will employ the diversionary tactic of arguing socially coded positions that seem to be on the settled side of the spurious fact-value divide. But such protests and denials are also dangerous in that they deny as well felt emotions, the very feelings that move one to protest. The result is a narrowing and an impoverishment of the possibilities for education.

What Effective Moral Educators Know and Feel and Do

To talk about the moral dimensions of teaching and learning is also intellectually dangerous in that careful attention to what's worth doing breaks down both the distinction between fact and value and, even more threatening, the distinction between thought and feeling. In truth, careful and honest attention to what's worth knowing is dangerous in the same way but is typically sidestepped by those who relegate feeling to the realm of the moral. By welcoming feeling into education, by recognizing that feeling is a facet of knowledge claims as well as moral ones, we open the door to changes in power relations and changes in the privileged positions woven into systems of schooling.

But if education rather than the preservation of vested interest and power is the goal, then chances of getting there are better when emotions are acknowledged, interrogated and reconstructed with respect to ideas and action in experience. Perhaps this is why the moral educators I described at the outset are morally effective despite their disclaimers. They don't deny the moral or the academic, and they participate in rather than sidestep the emotional. How and what they value consciously permeates their efforts.

Pat Wallace loved basketball but she was also hooked on helping young men and women grow and grow up. She taught English, physical education and health. She coached basketball, softball and track, while also directing elaborate all-school musicals, drafting accomplished choreographers and musicians to assist with these efforts with remarkable success as educational efforts and artistic products. But it was basketball that turned her on, that reflected her investment of felt value in thought and action—and ultimately in us. The game of basketball provided rich ideas of technique, strategy, and purpose that brought us together and kept us moving forward in action, generating in us the same range of feelings it elicited in her—from frustration to exhilaration.

Grace Brennan loves Kyle but love for Kyle isn't enough to make her an effective moral educator. And the truth is that Kyle hasn't always been easy to love. Even as love prevails, it does not keep fear and frustration at bay. As every parent knows, our children are not in the world to make our lives easier, though we work to adopt an attitude of gratitude when our children unsettle us in constructive ways, teaching us as surely as we are teaching them. This is the attitude—the experience of integrated idea, action, and feeling—that enables Gracen to be Kyle's effective moral educator as she is his mother. It arises in part from Grace's habit—associated with if not rooted in her long experience in athletics—of facing challenge with hope and hard work. To read her journal about Kyle's development is to feel fear and frustration with her but also to recognize the play of her (acquired) knowledge and advocacy-in-action in the pattern of his growth. Recently she wrote: "All is well here. Kyle started middle school and I'm a nervous wreck (don't worry, no one can tell). He's doing well, but it's a big couple of years. Being his mom takes my breath away."

Terri McNally loves her own sons so much that there is feeling left over for the ninth grade boys she has taught for decades. Math just happens to be their shared activity. But talk to Terri long enough and you realize that if happenstance brought her to teach math, something else has kept her there. It is her recognition that math is hard and/or boring for so many students that they need a teacher who knows that math is difficult and who has mastered it anyway. Now Terri is a highly skilled teacher of algebra who intuitively and through experimentation has come to teach in a manner that reflects contemporary research about mathematical understanding and pedagogy. She's not applying research; she is teaching boys what she knows and values. Algebra is important to Terri because it is the medium for her interaction with young men, but she also perceives its importance because she has taken her students' questions seriously over the past four decades and made those answers her own. In the process of teaching algebra, she is teaching them to be open to that which is challenging and to take responsibility for themselves and their actions.

What Pat and Grace and Terri know—besides basketball and geography and algebra—is how feelings can move kids to interest. What they do is parlay specific interests into habits of mind, body and heart as well as knowledge and virtue. What they feel at any given moment is never simple, and they recognize that this is true as well for their "students." Feelings matter in valuing conceptions of knowing and doing—and they realize it. But still, they don't talk about it.

Conclusion

Too often educators and policymakers talk *and act* as if the moral should and can be excised from publicly supported education. They also talk and act as if the academic were value free and refuse to acknowledge that their own preferred academic content and pedagogy are value-laden. Even those who support attention to the moral dimensions of teaching and learning and who argue for the importance of moral education don't address or don't recognize the crucial role of emotion in the processes of valuing and values articulation and in the acquisition of virtue.

The difference between the academic and the moral is not that the moral is about values and the academic is about facts. Both ultimately convey judgments of worth and value—and worth and values are tied up in affective response, in emotion. The relevant difference is that the academic is about knowledge and thought and the moral is about action and being in the world. It is emotion that moves us both to know and to act.

Were all educators and educational policymakers as open to the play of feeling and value as those I highlight here, perhaps the moral would not be invisible in schools. But they are not; in fact, too many practice avoidance. When educators avoid the moral impact of their work, they are sidestepping their feelings. I contend that we do so at our peril. However dangerous it may be to open school doors and policy halls to the moral and its emotional complicatedness, it is far more dangerous—and self-defeating—to banish a critical experiential element from educational efforts. Until the domain of emotion is granted entrance to educational thought and action, even effective moral educators will fail to acknowledge that mission. The moral will not be made visible.

Notes

1. Quoted by Lawrence Cremin, "Horace Mann's Legacy" in Mann, 1957, p. 3. These words were written in a letter as Mann left his career in law and politics to become the first Secretary to the newly created State Board of Education in Massachusetts.
2. It is important to point out from the outset that Dewey's view is decidedly *not* a simple emotivist view in the tradition of C. L. Stevenson. Moral statements are not *merely* expressions of affective attitudes. Moral statements involve *judgments* of value, but those judgments are themselves always the complex products of experience that integrates idea, action, and affect.
3. For a full understanding of how we came to characterize moral and academic in this way and a detailed explanation of our answer to this question, see Stengel and Tom, 2006.
4. Langston Hughes, "Let America Be America Again," Available on-line at http://www.americanpoems.com/poets/Langston-Hughes/2385.

References

Ahmed, S. 2003. *The cultural politics of emotion*. New York: Routledge.

Dewey, J. 1894. "The theory of emotion. (1) Emotional attitudes." *Psychological Review* 1: 553–69.

Dewey, J. 1895. "The theory of emotion. (2) The significance of emotions." *Psychological Review* 2: 13–32.

Dewey, J. 1887/1975. *Psychology.* In John Dewey, *The early works, 1882–1898, Volume 2.* JoAnn Boydston (Ed.). Carbondale, IL: Southern Illinois University Press.

Dewey, J. 1922. *Human nature and conduct*. New York: Henry Holt.

Mann, H. 1957. *The republic and the school: Horace Mann on the education of free man*, ed. Lawrence A. Cremin. New York: Teachers College Press.

Schlesinger, A. 1998. *The disuniting of America: Reflections on a multicultural society.* New York: W. W. Norton.

Stengel, B., and Tom, A. 2006. *Moral matters: Five ways to develop the moral life of schools.* New York: Teachers College Press.

CHAPTER TWENTY-SEVEN

Teaching Themes of Care

NEL NODDINGS

Some educators today—and I include myself among them—would like to see a complete re-organization of the school curriculum. We would like to give a central place to the questions and issues that lie at the core of human existence. One possibility would be to organize the curriculum around themes of care—caring for self, for intimate others, for strangers and global others, for the natural world and its nonhuman creatures, for the human-made world, and for ideas.[1]

A realistic assessment of schooling in the present political climate makes it clear that such a plan is not likely to be implemented. However, we can use the rich vocabulary of care in educational planning and introduce themes of care into regular subject-matter classes. In this article, I will first give a brief rationale for teaching themes of care; second, I will suggest ways of choosing and organizing such themes; and, finally, I'll say a bit about the structures required to support such teaching.

Why Teach Caring?

In an age when violence among school-children is at an unprecedented level, when children are bearing children with little knowledge of how to care for them, when the society and even the schools often concentrate on materialistic messages, it may be unnecessary to argue that we should care more genuinely for our children and teach them to care. However, many otherwise reasonable people seem to believe that our educational problems consist largely of low scores on achievement tests. My contention is, first, that we should want more from our educational efforts than adequate academic achievement and, second, that we will not achieve even that meager success unless our children believe that they themselves are cared for and learn to care for others.

There is much to be gained, both academically and humanly, by including themes of care in our curriculum. First, such inclusion may well expand our students' cultural literacy. For example, as we discuss in math classes the attempts of great mathematicians to prove the existence of God or to reconcile a God who is all good with the reality of evil in the world, students will hear names, ideas, and words that are not part of the standard curriculum. Although such incidental learning cannot replace the systematic and sequential learning required by those who plan careers in mathematically oriented fields, it can be powerful in expanding students' cultural horizons and in inspiring further study.

Second, themes of care help us to connect the standard subjects. The use of literature in mathematics classes, of history in science classes, and of art and music in all classes can give students a feeling of the wholeness in their education. After all, why should they seriously study five different subjects if their teachers, who are educated people, only seem to know and appreciate one?

Third, themes of care connect our students and our subjects to great existential questions. What is the meaning of life? Are there gods? How should I live?

Fourth, sharing such themes can connect us person-to-person. When teachers discuss themes of care, they may become real persons to their students and so enable them to construct new knowledge. Mania Buber put it this way:

> Trust, trust in the world, because this human being exists—that is the most inward achievement of the relation in education. Because this human being exists, meaninglessness, however hard pressed you are by it, cannot be the real truth. Because this human being exists, in the darkness the light lies hidden, in fear salvation, and in the callousness of one's fellow-man the great love.[2]

Finally, I should emphasize that caring is not just a warm, fuzzy feeling that makes people kind and likable. Caring implies a continuous search for competence. When we care, we want to do our very best for the objects of our care. To have as our educational goal the production of caring, competent, loving, and lovable people is not anti-intellectual. Rather, it demonstrates respect for the full range of human talents. Not all human beings are good at or interested in mathematics, science, or British literature. But all humans can be helped to lead lives of deep concern for others, for the natural world and its creatures, and for the preservation of the human-made world. They can be led to develop the skills and knowledge necessary to make positive contributions, regardless of the occupation they may choose.

Choosing and Organizing Themes of Care

Care is conveyed in many ways. At the institutional level, schools can be organized to provide continuity and support for relationships of care and trust.[3] At the individual level, parents and teachers show their caring through characteristic forms of attention: by cooperating in children's activities, by sharing their own dreams and doubts, and by providing carefully for the steady growth of the children in their charge. Personal manifestations of care are probably more important in childrens' lives than any particular curriculum or pattern of pedagogy.

However, curriculum can be selected with caring in mind. That is, educators can manifest their care in the choice of curriculum, and appropriately chosen curriculum can contribute to the growth of children as carers. Within each large domain of care, many topics are suitable for thematic units: in the domain of "caring for self," for example, we might consider life stages, spiritual growth, and what it means to develop an admirable character; in exploring the topic of caring for intimate others, we might include units on love, friendship, and parenting; under the theme of caring for strangers and global others, we might study war, poverty, and tolerance; in addressing the idea of caring for the human-made world, we might encourage competence with the machines that surround us and a real appreciation for the marvels of technology. Many other examples exist. Furthermore, there are at least two different ways to approach the development of such themes: units can be constructed by interdisciplinary teams, or themes can be identified by individual teachers and addressed periodically throughout a year's or semester's work.

The interdisciplinary approach is familiar in core programs, and such programs are becoming more and more popular at the middle school level. One key to a successful interdisciplinary unit is the degree of genuinely enthusiastic support it receives from the teachers involved. Too often, arbitrary or artificial groupings are formed, and teachers are forced to make contributions that they themselves do not value highly. For example, math and science teachers are sometimes automatically lumped together, and rich humanistic possibilities may be lost. If I, as a math teacher, want to include historical, biographical, and literary topics in my math lessons, I might prefer to work with English and social studies teachers. Thus it is important to involve teachers in the initial selection of broad areas for themes, as well as in their implementation.

Such interdisciplinary arrangements also work well at the college level. I recently received a copy of the syllabus for a college course titled "The Search for Meaning," which was co-taught by an economist, a university chaplain, and a psychiatrist.[4] The course is interdisciplinary, intellectually rich, and aimed squarely at the central questions of life.

At the high school level, where students desperately need to engage in the study and practice of caring, it is harder to form interdisciplinary teams. A conflict arises as teachers acknowledge the intensity of the subject-matter preparation their students need for further education. Good teachers often wish there were time in the day to co-teach unconventional topics of great importance, and they even admit that their students are not getting what they need for full personal development. But they feel constrained by the requirements of a highly competitive world and the structures of schooling established by that world.

Is there a way out of this conflict? Imaginative, like-minded teachers might agree to emphasize a particular theme in their separate classes. Such themes as war, poverty, crime, racism, or sexism can be addressed in almost every subject area. The teachers should agree on some core ideas related to caring that will be discussed in all classes, but beyond the central commitment to address themes of care, the topics can be handled in whatever way seems suitable in a given subject.

Consider, for example, what a mathematics class might contribute to a unit on crime. Statistical information might be gathered on the location and number of crimes, on rates for various kinds of crime, on the ages of offenders, and on the cost to society; graphs and charts could be constructed. Data on changes in crime rates could be assembled. Intriguing questions could be asked: Were property crime rates lower when penalties were more severe—when, for example, even children were hanged as thieves? What does an average criminal case cost by way of lawyers' fees, police investigation, and court processing? Does it cost more to house a youth in a detention center or in an elite private school?

None of this would have to occupy a full period every day. The regular sequential work of the math class could go on at a slightly reduced rate (e.g., fewer textbook exercises as homework), and the work on crime could proceed in the form of interdisciplinary projects over a considerable period of time. Most important would be the continual reminder in all classes that the topic is part of a larger theme of caring for strangers and fellow citizens. It takes only a few minutes to talk about what it means to live in safety, to trust one's neighbors, to feel secure in greeting strangers. Students should be told that metal detectors and security guards were not part of their parents' school lives, and they should be encouraged to hope for a safer and more open future. Notice the words I've used in this paragraph: caring, trust, safety, strangers, hope. Each could be used as an organizing theme for another unit of study.

English and social studies teachers would obviously have much to contribute to a unit on crime. For example, students might read *Oliver Twist*, and they might also study and discuss the social conditions that seemed to promote crime in 19th-century England. Do similar conditions exist in our country today? The selection of materials could include both classic works and modern stories and films. Students might even be introduced to some of the mystery stories that adults read so avidly on airplanes and beaches, and teachers should be engaged in lively discussion about the comparative value of the various stories.

Science teachers might find that a unit on crime would enrich their teaching of evolution. They could bring up the topic of social Darwinism, which played such a strong role in social policy during the late 19th and early 20th centuries. To what degree are criminal tendencies inherited? Should children be tested for the genetic defects that are suspected of predisposing some people to crime? Are females less competent than males in moral reasoning? (Why did some scientists and philosophers think this was true?) Why do males commit so many more violent acts than females?

Teachers of the arts can also be involved. A unit on crime might provide a wonderful opportunity to critique "gangsta rap" and other currently popular forms of music. Students might profitably learn how the control of art contributed to national criminality during the Nazi era. These are ideas that pop into my mind. Far more various and far richer ideas will come from teachers who specialize in these subjects.

There are risks, of course, in undertaking any unit of study that focuses on matters of controversy or deep existential concern, and teachers should anticipate these risks. What if students want to compare the incomes of teachers and cocaine dealers? What if they point to contemporary personalities from politics, entertainment, business, or sports who seem to escape the law and profit from what seems to be criminal behavior? My own inclination would be to allow free discussion of these cases and to be prepared to counteract them with powerful stories of honesty, compassion, moderation, and charity.

An even more difficult problem may arise. Suppose a student discloses his or her own criminal activities? Fear of this sort of occurrence may send teachers scurrying for safer topics. But, in fact, any instructional method that uses narrative forms or encourages personal expression runs this risk. For example, students of English as a second language who write proudly about their own hard lives and new hopes may disclose that their parents are illegal immigrants. A girl may write passages that lead her teacher to suspect sexual abuse. A boy may brag about objects he has "ripped off." Clearly, as we use these powerful methods that encourage students to initiate discussion and share their experiences, we must reflect on the ethical issues involved, consider appropriate responses to such issues, and prepare teachers to handle them responsibly.

Caring teachers must help students make wise decisions about what information they will share about themselves. On the one hand, teachers want their students to express themselves, and they want their students to trust in and consult them. On the other hand, teachers have an obligation to protect immature students from making disclosures that they might later regret. There is a deep ethical problem here. Too often educators assume that only religious fundamentalists and right-wing extremists object to the discussion of emotionally and morally charged issues. In reality, there is a real danger of intrusiveness and lack of respect in methods that fail to recognize the vulnerability of students. Therefore, as teachers plan units and lessons on moral issues, they should anticipate the tough problems that may arise. I am arguing here that it is morally irresponsible to simply ignore existential questions and themes of care; we must attend to them. But it is equally irresponsible to approach these deep concerns without caution and careful preparation.

So far I have discussed two ways of organizing interdisciplinary units on themes of care. In one, teachers actually teach together in teams; in the other, teachers agree on a theme and a central focus on care, but they do what they can, when they can, in their own classrooms. A variation on this second way—which is also open to teachers who have to work alone—is to choose several themes and weave them into regular course material over an entire semester or year. The particular themes will depend on the interests and preparation of each teacher.

For example, if I were teaching high school mathematics today, I would use religious/existential questions as a pervasive theme because the biographies of mathematicians are filled with accounts of their speculations on matters of God, other dimensions, and the infinite—and because these topics fascinate me. There are so many wonderful stories to be told: Descartes' proof of the existence of God, Pascal's famous wager, Plato's world of forms, Newton's attempt to verify Biblical chronology, Leibnitz' detailed theodicy, current attempts to describe a divine domain in terms of metasystems, and mystical speculations on the infinite.[5] Some of these stories can be told as rich "asides" in five minutes or less. Others might occupy the better part of several class periods.

Other mathematics teachers might use an interest in architecture and design, art, music, or machinery as continuing themes in the domain of "caring for the human-made world." Still others might introduce the mathematics of living things. The possibilities are endless. In choosing and pursuing these themes, teachers should be aware that they are both helping their students learn to care and demonstrating their own caring by sharing interests that go well beyond the demands of textbook pedagogy.

Still another way to introduce themes of care into regular classrooms is to be prepared to respond spontaneously to events that occur in the school or in the neighborhood. Older teachers have one advantage in this area: they probably have a greater store of experience and stories on which to draw. However, younger teachers have the advantage of being closer to their students' lives and experiences; they are more likely to be familiar with the music, films, and sports figures that interest their students.

All teachers should be prepared to respond to the needs of students who are suffering from the death of friends, conflicts between groups of students, pressure to use drugs or to engage in sex, and other troubles so rampant in the lives of today's children. Too often schools rely on experts—"grief counselors" and the like—when what children really need is the continuing compassion and presence of adults who represent constancy and care in their lives. Artificially separating the emotional, academic, and moral care of children into tasks for specially designated experts contributes to the fragmentation of life in schools.

Of course, I do not mean to imply that experts are unnecessary, nor do I mean to suggest that some matters should not be reserved for parents or psychologists. But our society has gone too far in compartmentalizing the care of its children. When we ask whose job it is to teach children how to care, an appropriate initial response is "Everyone's." Having accepted universal responsibility, we can then ask about the special contributions and limitations of various individuals and groups.

Supporting Structures

What kind of schools and teacher preparation are required, if themes of care are to be taught effectively? First, and most important, care must be taken seriously as a major purpose of schools; that is, educators must recognize that caring for students is fundamental in teaching and that developing people with a strong capacity for care is a major objective of responsible education. Schools properly pursue many other objectives—developing artistic talent, promoting multicultural understanding, diversifying curriculum to meet the academic and vocational needs of all students, forging connections with community agencies and parents, and so on. Schools cannot be single-purpose institutions. Indeed, many of us would argue that it is logically and practically impossible to achieve that single academic purpose if other purposes are not recognized and accepted. This contention is confirmed in the success stories of several inner-city schools.[6]

Once it is recognized that school is a place in which students are cared for and learn to care, that recognition should be powerful in guiding policy. In the late 1950s, schools under the guidance of James Conant and others, placed the curriculum at the top of the educational priority list. Because the nation's leaders wanted schools to provide high-powered courses in mathematics and science, it was recommended that small high schools be replaced by efficient larger structures complete with sophisticated laboratories and specialist teachers. Economies of scale were anticipated, but the main argument for consolidation and regionalization centered on the curriculum. All over the country, small schools were closed, and students were herded into larger facilities with "more offerings." We did not think carefully about schools as communities and about what might be lost as we pursued a curriculum-driven ideal.

Today many educators are calling for smaller schools and more family-like groupings. These are good proposals, but teachers, parents, and students should be engaged in continuing discussion about what they are trying to achieve through the new arrangements. For example, if test scores do not immediately rise, participants should be courageous in explaining that test scores were not the main object of the changes. Most of us who argue for caring in schools are intuitively quite sure that children in such settings will in fact become more competent learners. But, if they cannot prove their academic competence in a prescribed period of time, should we give up on caring and on teaching them to care? That would be foolish. There is more to life and learning than the academic proficiency demonstrated by test scores.

In addition to steadfastness of purpose, schools must consider continuity of people and place. If we are concerned with caring and community, then we must make it possible for students and teachers to stay together for several years so that mutual trust can develop and students can feel a sense of belonging in their "school-home."[7]

More than one scheme of organization can satisfy the need for continuity. Elementary school children can stay with the same teacher for several years, or they can work with a stable team of specialist teachers for several years. In the latter arrangement, there may be program advantages; that is, children taught by subject-matter experts who get to know them well over an extended period of time may learn more about the particular subjects. At the high school level, the same specialist teachers might work with students throughout their years in high school. Or, as Theodore Sizer has suggested, one teacher might teach two subjects to a group of 30 students rather than one subject to 60 students, thereby reducing the number of different adults with whom students interact each day.[8] In all the suggested arrangements, placements should be made by mutual consent whenever possible. Teachers and students who hate or distrust one another should not be forced to stay together.

A policy of keeping students and teachers together for several years supports caring in two essential ways: it provides time for the development of caring relations, and it makes teaching themes of care more feasible. When trust has been established, teacher and students can discuss matters that would be hard for a group of strangers to approach, and classmates learn to support one another in sensitive situations.

The structural changes suggested here are not expensive. If a high school teacher must teach five classes a day, it costs no more for three of these classes to be composed of continuing students than for all five classes to comprise new students—i.e., strangers. The recommended changes come directly out of a clear-headed assessment of our major aims and purposes. We failed to suggest them earlier because we had other, too limited, goals in mind.

I have made one set of structural changes sound easy, and I do believe that they are easily made. But the curricular and pedagogical changes that are required may be more difficult. High school textbooks rarely contain the kinds of supplementary material I have described, and teachers are not formally prepared to incorporate such material. Too often, even the people we regard as strongly prepared in a liberal arts major are unprepared to discuss the history of their subject, its relation to other subjects, the biographies of its great figures, its connections to the great existential questions, and the ethical responsibilities of those who work in that discipline. To teach themes of care in an academically effective way, teachers will have to engage in projects of self-education.

At present, neither liberal arts departments nor schools of education pay much attention to connecting academic subjects with themes of care. For example, biology students may learn something of the anatomy and physiology of mammals but nothing at all about the care of living animals; they may never be asked to consider the moral issues involved in the annual euthanasia of millions of pets. Mathematics students may learn to solve quadratic equations but never study what it means to live in a mathematicized world. In enlightened history classes, students may learn something about the problems of racism and colonialism but never hear anything about the evolution of childhood, the contributions of women in both domestic and public caregiving, or the connection between the feminization of care-giving and public policy. A liberal education that neglects matters that are central to a fully human life hardly warrants the name,[9] and a professional education that confines itself to technique does nothing to close the gaps in liberal education.

The greatest structural obstacle, however, may simply be legitimizing the inclusion of themes of care in the curriculum. Teachers in the early grades have long included such themes as a regular part of their work, and middle school educators are becoming more sensitive to developmental needs involving care. But secondary schools—where violence, apathy, and alienation are most evident—do little to develop the capacity to care. Today, even elementary teachers complain that the pressure to produce high test scores inhibits the work they regard as central to their mission: the development of caring and competent people. Therefore, it would seem that the most fundamental change required is one of attitude. Teachers can be very special people in the lives of children, and it should be legitimate for them to spend time developing relations of trust, talking with students about problems that are central to their lives, and guiding them toward greater sensitivity and competence across all the domains of care.

Notes

1. For the theoretical argument, see Nel Noddings, *The Challenge to Care in Schools* (New York: Teachers College Press, 1992); for a practical example and rich documentation, see Sharon Quint, *Schooling Homeless Children* (New York: Teachers College Press, 1994).
2. Martin Buber, *Between Man and Man* (New York: Macmillan, 1965), p. 98.
3. Noddings, chap. 12.
4. See Thomas H. Naylor, William H. Willimon, and Magdalena R. Naylor, *The Search for Meaning* (Nashville, Tenn.: Abingdon Press, 1994).

5. For many more examples, see Nel Noddings, *Educating for Intelligent Belief and Unbelief* (New York: Teachers College Press, 1993).

6. See Deborah Meier, "How Our Schools Could Be," Phi Delta Kappan, January 1995, pp. 369–73; and Quint, op. cit.

7. See Jane Roland Martin, *The Schoolhome: Re-thinking Schools for Changing Families* (Cambridge, Mass.: Harvard University Press, 1992).

8. Theodore Sizer, *Horace's Compromise: The Dilemma of the American High School* (Boston: Houghton Miffiin, 1984).

9. See Bruce Wilshire, *The Moral Collapse of the University* (Albany: State University of New York Press, 1990).

(This chapter originally appeared in *Phi Delta Kappan*, Vol. 76, No. 9, 1995, pp. 675–679. Published with permission of Phi Delta Kappa International.)

CHAPTER TWENTY-EIGHT

Surveying the Soil

Building a Culture of Connectedness in School

MARCIA PECK

When I was fourteen, my parents acquired a huge plot of land that bordered on a river. Their intent, I believed at the time, was to turn us kids into farm laborers as well as to embarrass me so much that, "I would just die!" because the field was located in an area that my friends would ride by on their bikes when they were out having fun while I labored over my patch of weeds. It looked like a football field to me but was actually only half the size of a football field. My parents had decided that planting and cultivating a garden would not only yield vegetables, it would also teach us valuable life lessons about how hard work and persistence paid off in the end.

Looking back, I don't know if the "garden project" taught me much about sowing and reaping as I hated every minute of the experience. I did learn a few things, though. First, watering at the crack of dawn ensured that the water wouldn't merely evaporate in the heat and guaranteed that none of my friends would see me working in the field. Additionally, I figured out that it only takes one zucchini plant to feed a village and that I would never be able to tell a plant from a weed in its early stages. And finally, I learned about the importance of the soil.

The significance of soil isn't just about the actual stuff; it's what you do with it in order to be successful in the gardening department. No matter how carefully you select the seeds and plant them and no matter how much weeding, watering and worrying you do, they will not grow and flourish well, if at all, if you do not prepare the soil before planting. You may have a lot of soil, and you may have cultivated it well, but if it is depleted of nutrients, little will grow.

Consequently, while I may not have learned the expected lessons from gardening, I did learn about the importance of examining and then preparing the soil if you want something to take hold and grow. This lesson seems to apply to most things in life from gardens, to neighborhood watch groups, to working on a team in the office. It seems, though, that such a life lesson has not been absorbed much when it comes to schools and the variety of programs and reforms that are dumped on top of them every year in hopes one or more will take hold and improve the school. It should be noted that many of these programs are abandoned soon after implementation because they failed to produce the anticipated results.

Perhaps the programs would not work in the schools, but one will never know because too often programs are planted without scrutinizing the "soil" they are to grow in and then making adjustments if necessary. Payne (2008) mentioned this phenomenon in his study of educational reform. He noted that no matter how well organized, intentioned or capitalized it may be, a program for improvement is bound for failure when the ground it is to spring from has not been adequately prepared or is already poisoned.

I wish to advocate that this is the case with many school improvement programs touted as moral education these days. Schools ascribe to a particular program, institute it in the school, and then seem surprised when many of the students are still rude, disrespectful or lazy. Failure could be blamed on poor implementation or rotten kids who can't learn any manners, when the real culprit may be the poor soil of the school. Before blaming the program or the students, schools would do well to first analyze the soil or, in other words, the environment of the school to ascertain if a moral education program can actually grow within it. Perhaps before moving forward with this contention, it would be advantageous to briefly examine the topic of moral education.

Why Moral Education?

If you were to listen in on a conversation among teachers in the faculty lounge in most schools in America, you would think the term, "raised by wolves," would aptly describe their students. Many students are described as rude, mean, impatient, ill-mannered, crude, insensitive, reactionary, untrustworthy and unethical. Students routinely cheat on exams, curse at their teachers, and steal materials from lockers. They leave trash in the lunchroom, write graffiti on the bathroom doors and blame someone else when they are caught. In other words, according to many of the adults who work with them, today's students are greatly lacking in many of the traits deemed necessary for the proper functioning of society, both within the school and the larger community.

Due to such perceptions of incivility on the part of many students, numerous experts, educators and parents have advocated for some sort of moral education in the schools as a means to teach civility to the uncivil (Bennett, 1993; Kessler, 2000; Lickona, 1991; Noddings, 2002). Generally speaking, the term moral education refers to a systematic program to help children acquire those virtues or moral habits that will help them individually live good lives and at the same time become productive, contributing members of their communities. Such education should contribute not only to the students as individuals but also to the social cohesion of a community.

Although the necessity of teaching civility in schools has been advocated for quite a few years, the support for doing so seems to have grown exponentially over the last twenty years and seems to mirror the growth of educators' complaints regarding poor student behavior and lack of discipline. Such programs as Community of Caring, Character Counts, and Botvin LifeSkills have emerged in order to meet this perceived need, and many schools have adopted a program or two to use with their students.

For example, several years ago when I was teaching in a junior high school, our school adopted a type of moral education program. Even though we had already been designated a Community of Caring school and each month one of the Community of Caring values was highlighted on posters in the hallways, social skills training was also implemented. Each week a new skill was introduced, and students were rewarded during the week for practicing the skill. Some of the skills were, "Learning to accept, 'No.'" and "Learning to accept a compliment." The older students found such instruction tedious, most of the younger students seemed to accept it. At the very least they liked the rewards they received for practicing the skills. Additionally, many of the teachers felt the instruction was beneficial. It was common at faculty meetings to hear comments such as, "I'm glad we are teaching these social skills. I think most kids have never been taught how to accept a compliment or ask a question appropriately and now that we are teaching them these skills I've seen a real improvement in my classroom."

While not disagreeing that there very well may be a need for such moral and character education programs in schools, I believe we are putting the proverbial cart before the horse with a focus on attacking the problem of poor behavior or citizenship with one program or another. While it may be true that today's children and youth are in need of some training in these areas, it is my contention that many of the poor behaviors exhibited are a direct result of what happens *to* students within the walls of the school. Consequently, before imposing a program of moral education in a school, it may prove more fruitful to look closely at the culture of a school to ascertain if students are being treated in such a way as to encourage positive behaviors and attitudes, or, if instead, they are treated in disrespectful or disempowering ways often resulting in students exhibiting the very behaviors those in favor of moral education are trying to teach against.

Put differently, applying a program to teach students more appropriate behaviors and values within a school that routinely incites inappropriate behaviors and models a lack of respect through its treatment of students will have little, if any, effect. To borrow an analogy, teaching civility in a school context with degraded "soil" is "tantamount to bringing a lighted candle into a wind tunnel" (Payne, 2008, p. 34). Until you change the environment, lessons concerning character just aren't going to be that effective.

There are numerous structural and cultural issues both within schools and the larger society that effectively degrade the soil of a school such as the dehumanizing effect of reducing children to a number due to testing mania (Au, 2010) or the inequalities perpetuated through tracking (Oakes, 1988) as well as the harsh disciplinary measures that are disproportionally applied to children of color (McFadden & Marsh, 1992). Although these matters certainly contribute to problematic issues in schools and should be addressed as part of any comprehensive plan to improve the soil or culture of a school, this chapter is focusing primarily on the importance of building positive, democratic relationships in schools as *one* means of improving school culture. It should not be construed that such an emphasis downplays the importance of other aspects of a degraded school culture or that these other areas do not require attention as well.

Student Perspectives

My contention regarding school climate engendering poor behavior was substantiated for me while reviewing the transcript of a focus group interview I conducted with three junior high students concerning caring in schools. I came in contact with these three students as I was mentoring their first-year math teacher, Ms. Williams. The students were all in the same class and were repeatedly reprimanded in class, relegated to the hall or dispatched to the principal's office. According to their teacher, and my few observations, these students exhibited disrespectful behavior much of the time including talking back, yelling across the room, cursing under their breath and instigating rebellion in other students in the classroom. Two of them rarely completed their work in class and were failing the course. All three claimed Ms. Williams lost much of the work that they did turn in. Any observer in this class would find that these students most definitely needed to be instructed in how to interact respectfully and responsibly with adults.

For example, during one of my observations, a student would not comply with Ms. Williams's request to move to a isolated seat in the back of the room since he would not stop talking despite being told several times to be quiet. Finally, Ms. Williams told the student to either take the new seat or go to another teacher's classroom. The student stormed out angrily. Alicia, one of the focus group participants, responded by stating loudly, "How come you are always picking on him? He wasn't doing anything. God, you are so rude!"

Due to my interest in caring in schools, my mentoring work with Ms. Williams, and comments made by these students that Ms. Williams did not care about them despite the fact that she claimed she did, I decided to invite them to be part of a focus group interview on the topic of caring with particular attention on their definition of a caring teacher. All the students were in the 8th grade and could be said to come from working-class socio-economic backgrounds. Matt was a fourteen-year-old Caucasian; Alicia was a fourteen-year-old Latina, and Luis, a thirteen-year-old Latino. I did not know the two young men previous to the interview. I had taught Alicia in 7th grade for the first ten weeks of school before she moved to a different school.

The focus group interview was unstructured and lasted approximately 75 minutes. Student responses were recorded on audiotape. The students knew they were there to talk about caring teacher behaviors. There were no pre-determined questions or format because I did not want to decide what information was shared. I wanted them to feel free to say what they wanted about the topic and not be directed by my questions to particular areas of discussion. I informed the students that anything they said would be private and would not be shared with anyone else within the school. I also told them I would not identify them or the school by name in any work resulting from the interview. They all expressed disappointment in this fact as they wanted their names used. The only question that I posed was, "How do you define a caring teacher?" After that initial question, the students talked freely. During the interview, these students pointed out examples of caring and uncaring teacher behaviors as well as teachers who they believed exhibited such behaviors.

After the interview, the tape was transcribed. Excerpts from the interview are included in this chapter. It should be noted that their math teacher, Ms. Williams, had already left the school by the time the interview was conducted. A long-term substitute had taken her place, and, due to the importance the new teacher placed on building relationships with the students, was having more success with student learning and fewer struggles with student behavior. All three students stated during the interview that they were doing better academically with the new teacher.

Although the topic was caring, as I listened and later read the students' descriptions of uncaring and caring traits and their reactions to the perception that they were not cared for by some teachers and cared for by others, I began to notice that in many cases, particular teachers and school environments actually fostered the very problems educators purport they want to change through the implementation of moral education programs. Students' responses highlighted specific situations that occurred in schools, which tended to bring out the worst in them, namely, poor modeling of expected behaviors, being treated with disrespect due to their student status, and the alienating environment of certain classrooms.

Poor Modeling of Expected Behaviors

According to these students, some of their teachers failed to demonstrate the very social skills the students were being taught every day and expected to follow such as being polite, saying "please" and "thank you," and accepting a compliment. These students resented that there seemed to be a double standard for the students and the adults. If being polite was an important attribute for students to exemplify, it seemed it should be exemplified by the adults in the building as well. After all, teachers were viewed as role models for their students. Matt described this double standard in general terms when he stated,

> **Matt:** Teachers are supposed to be encouraging, tell you to get your grades up, say stuff like, "Come on; let's do it. You're going to get through school." But, some teachers will say, "Matt, you're failing and you're never going to get your grades up." That's bashing you. Teachers say no put downs, but then they go and put you down.

Speaking specifically about his math class, Matt later told of his frustration with how he and other students were treated.

> **Matt:** The big thing for me is when I raise my hand, you don't wait until the end of class to come and talk to me. When I am one of the first to raise my hand and I'm one of the last to get answered that shows that you don't care. A teacher needs to care enough about the students to help them learn. I'd say, "Ms. Williams, can I get help?" And she's like, "No, no, you're smart enough. Figure it out on your own. And that's the thing, Ms. Williams would never show anyone respect or help them. And every time I'd mouth off in her class because I was so irritated by it, she'd be like, "Matt that's disrespectful," and I'd say, "You know what, you're disrespectful to the whole class," and she'd send me off to the office for it.

Alicia and Luis both stated that they lost all respect for Ms. Williams because she insisted students exhibit certain behaviors but didn't feel these standards applied to her as well. The following is part of the transcript of Alicia and Luis talking about Ms. Williams.

> **Alicia:** I had problems with her. She expected us to say "please" when we made a request, but she would never say "please" to us.
>
> **Luis:** Yeah, she never said "please." She'd tell us to sit like a dog, she'd tell us to raise our hand like a dog; she'd never say "please."
>
> **Alicia:** And she would always yell at kids to go out in the hall when they had to blow their nose because she said it was gross to blow your nose in front of everyone. So everyone would step out in the hall, but then she would stand there in the front of the class and blow her nose.
>
> **Luis**: And you know how you are not supposed to gossip? Well, Ms. Williams would stand just outside the door towards the end of class and between classes and gossip about students with other teachers.
>
> **Alicia:** Yes, she did that a lot and right in front of the students so everyone could hear what they were talking about. I came walking out of the room one time and I heard her and another teacher talking about this one kid, and they were talking about how he had got suspended and how they were hoping he didn't come back. I was thinking how embarrassed I would be if they were talking about me and everyone heard.

According to these students, they resented being chastised for exhibiting the same poor behaviors as some teachers. They felt that if learning and demonstrating certain social skills was important, it should be important for everyone, not just young people. In such a maladaptive environment, those positive social skills lessons ran directly counter to the living lessons they saw in front of them every day. Students felt belittled and resentful within such a school environment and felt they were being treated unfairly. They reacted to such treatment by exhibiting negative behaviors. Olson (2009) explained such student reactions in *Wounded by School*. She stated, "No student I have encountered expressed absolutely no interest in doing well in school; mostly, my interviewees had been made angry and resentful by feeling poorly treated within educational environments. This, in turn, made them rebellious and difficult to deal with" (p. 43).

Being Treated as "Dirt"

In addition to the double standard for behavior noted by the focus group students, they repeatedly referred to instances where teachers, particularly Ms. Williams, treated them as less than human beings, referring to being treated as a "dog," a "wolf," and "dirt." They pointed out that some teachers felt that they did not need to treat them well because they were children and commented on being treated condescendingly. For example, Alicia stated that when she told Ms. Williams that she wanted to be a hairdresser she was ridiculed for that choice because according to Ms. Williams, "You can't support yourself on a hairdresser's salary." They also mentioned times when a teacher would scream at them or mock them with Alicia mentioning that Ms. Williams reminded them almost daily that they were "wayward children." These instances of mistreatment were perceived by students as something more than a teacher just not being "nice." They saw these actions as attacks on their actual "personhood." An example of this assertion is found the following excerpt,

> **Luis:** You got to give respect to get it. Show respect. Like, "Hi, take a seat," instead of, "Go do this; do your bell ringers." She just told us what to do like we're dogs.
>
> **Matt:** Like wolves!
>
> **Luis:** She never said please. She'd tell us to sit like a dog, she'd tell us to raise our hand like a dog; she'd never say please.

Such a sentiment was not so much an illustration that these students considered themselves on equal footing with adults but that they had experienced that children in a classroom received little respect and felt that was wrong because they were valuable people, too, even if they were young. In their eyes, being young did not mean they should be treated with disrespect. For example, the students indicated that their presence in the classroom should be valued just as much as that of an honored guest or high-status official such as the principal and be treated accordingly.

> **Matt:** You need to make students feel like they're welcome. Like if you go to a party or to a friend's house, they welcome you in ask how you doing; they want you to be there.
>
> **Luis:** Exactly! Like sometimes Mr. Tanner will meet you and shake your hand and say, "How are you?" All the good teachers know that.
>
> **Matt:** The teacher should treat you right when you come into the room, like how they would treat the principal when she walked in, like you are someone special. Cause you know, I'm a person; I'm not dirt!

When teachers treat students with disdain and disrespect, students become frustrated or angry and tend to react confrontationally as demonstrated by the behavior of the focus group students in their math class as well as in comments they made. Speaking about their interactions with disrespectful teachers Luis and Matt stated the following,

> **Matt:** Well, I wait a while before I start giving a teacher attitude. Kind of depends on the teacher. If they have an attitude, I'll give them a week, cause everyone has a bad day, but then that's it.

> **Luis:** If a teacher gives me respect, I give them respect back. Well, I'd still probably goof around, but when they'd ask me what I'm doing, I'd kind of be nice. But with Ms. Williams, I'd answer her in a tone that would freeze, because she lost my respect. She doesn't want to do anything to make the kids satisfied; it's either her way or no way.

It appears from what the students are saying that for these students how they are treated can either foster belligerence or consideration toward the adults they encountered. It should be no wonder then that student anger and frustration may spill over into the classroom and school in the form of hostility, rudeness or physical aggression.

Alienating Environment of School

While all three students reported disrespectful treatment and poor modeling of acceptable behavior, Luis and Alicia also reported feeling particularly alienated and made to feel like they did not belong in the classroom. Such feelings of alienation may have be engendered by a variety of situations such as a mismatch between the White, middle-class ethos of the teacher and these students' working-class, Latino roots. Perceptions of not fitting in could also have developed due to the fact that neither Luis nor or Alicia saw much value in education, nor were they planning on attending college. There is certainly some evidence to support such an analysis since Matt, who actually felt somewhat powerful in the classroom, was college-bound and placed great value in education; in fact, one of his biggest complaint was Ms. Williams's poor teaching as demonstrated in my first encounter with him when he stated, "I've got to get out of that class! My I.Q. is dropping by the minute!"

For whatever the reason, though, Alicia and Luis felt "pushed out" of the classroom, that there was not a place for them and that what they valued or identified with was of little import. An illustration of this concept is found in an encounter Luis spoke of between himself and Ms. Williams. Luis worked some evenings and weekends in the family construction business helping support his family and himself and earned $200 a week for his labors, a fact that he proudly shared during the interview. Speaking about this interaction he stated,

> **Luis:** I disliked everything about her. She was a…(Struggles to find a different word since he didn't want to use profanity in front of me)…witch with a "B." Like one time she tried to talk to me about what my life was going to be like if I didn't do my work in her class. She talked to me about it in front of the whole class. She told me I wasn't going to be able to support myself. I told her I already had a job working construction and made $200 a week. She just laughed at me. She said, "You can't support children on $200 a week!" I told her I wasn't going to have any kids. I don't want a kid!

In this excerpt, it appeared that Luis was not only angry about being singled out for ridicule in front of the class and being treated as if he were an immature child who didn't understand economic realities; he was also infuriated that the very thing he took pride in and provided him status in his "real" life, as opposed to his school life, was being denigrated and treated as a thing of very little value, resulting in him feeling disenfranchised in the classroom. Luis reported often choosing to resist such instances of disempowerment when he encountered them in school through negative behavior; it is little wonder, then, that when speaking of his conduct in some of his classes, Luis stated the following:

> **Luis:** A teacher tells me to do something; I'll do the exact opposite. Depends on how much they respect me. If they respect me a lot, I'll do it. They don't respect me at all, I'll do the opposite. (Pause) I'd rather have people fear me than respect me.

Luis' reaction to feelings of alienation tended to get him punished often in school which further reinforced his perception that he was not wanted. It also earned him a reputation as a troublemaker. Gassaway (2007) claimed that such alienated students often committed "educational suicide" in order to counter their marginalization. He explained this concept thusly:

> Children who seek suicide by educator deliberately act in a disruptive manner towards teachers or children, provoking confrontations, failing grades, suspensions, expulsions or arrests. They feel disconnected, uncared for, stressed, confused and angry. They lash out at school officials both verbally and physically....School personnel are not trained to deal with the level of anger they are experiencing with children; as a result, they often respond to them with punishment, suspension, failure or arrest. They say, "He is out of control. Suspend him! Fail him! Arrest him!" Rarely do public and school officials, particularly in urban, poor school districts, address the conditions that caused the children's disruptive behaviors.

Concurring with Gassaway, Page (2006) stated that children disenfranchised by school, such as Luis, are not necessarily troublemakers as much as they are troubled by what is done to them. He stated, "Teachers often fail to recognize the embarrassment, consternation, and defensiveness that is at the root of at-risk, rebellious behavior" (p. 9). Additionally, Daniels and Arapostathis (2005) noted that students who feel alienated from the mainstream of school act in resistant ways because they refuse to comply with a system that views them as lacking and has no place for them, because to conform would demonstrate acceptance of the school's appraisal of them. Therefore, a character education program designed to improve Luis's life skills would most likely not work if, as the above researchers claim, his desire to engender fear is a mechanism to help him cope in an environment that demeans him and what he is proud of, in Luis' case, his ability to earn money working in manual labor.

It is important to remember that the negative behaviors of alienated students, such as Luis, create a problem not only for the teacher and school but also affects children's life chances. Speaking of students who feel marginalized and alienated in the school environment, Payne (2008) warned of the educational consequences when he stated,

> There is a kind of mutual disinvestment going on, in which youth who are not made to feel that they are valued and welcomed members of the institution respond by disinvesting themselves in that institution and whatever it symbolizes, with ample room for misunderstanding and self-fulfilling prophecies on both sides. (p. 113)

On the Other Hand

Despite their self-reported poor behavior as well as my observations of these students behaving badly in their math class, Matt, Alicia, and Luis all noted that they tended to conduct themselves quite differently in the presence of particular teachers who they defined as "cool." As if to illustrate this fact, all three went out of their way throughout the interview process to be polite and inoffensive as illustrated by the following excerpt:

Matt: Some teachers are just out to get you in trouble. It's like they look for ways to annoy you, so they can send you to the office.

Luis: (Vehemently) Yeah. Most of the teachers in this school are awful. I hate them all! Ahhh…I don't mean you, though.

Matt: Yeah, no offense to you, though. You're cool.

Peck: None taken. Besides you guys don't really know me since you haven't been in one of my classes. (Joking) Maybe you'd feel different then.

Matt: No. I'm friends with a lot of 9th graders, and they all say you're cool. I hope I get in your class next year.

Such respectful behavior was also demonstrated by Luis during the interview when he stopped himself from using profanity and searched for a different way to convey his meaning when he stated, "She was a….witch with a B." Additionally, Luis demonstrated that he clearly recognized when student behavior crossed the line when Alicia was discussing a teacher all three of them had for social studies.

Alicia: Well, Mr. Johnson is usually pretty nice, but sometimes he gets mad and yells at us.

Luis: Well, yeah, Johnson, he was nice at the beginning of the year, and then everyone started disrespecting him, so he acted like he gave up. I can understand why he's Mr. Grumpy. Everyone gives him too much grief.

The fact that all three students knew how to conduct themselves in appropriate ways lends authenticity to the theory that perhaps something other than a lack of skills was at work when they failed to engage in a class discussion, swore at a teacher or reacted rudely, a supposition also advanced by Olson (2009) in her interviews with disruptive students. She noted, "While students who don't conform, don't hand in assignments, are oblivious to bad marks, and create havoc in school are the bane of a teacher's and a school system's life, many students who exhibit these characteristics are actually begging for perceptive, inquiring attention" (p. 43).

According to these students, then, the culture of the classroom as created by what a teacher did and said helped shape their behavior for bad or good. This notion not only is illustrated by what they said about disrespectful teachers but also about the teachers who they perceived treated them as people and actually liked having them around. The following long excerpt illustrates this point. The students are talking about teachers in general.

Matt: You have basically three ranks of teachers. You have your top level ones. The ones that are awesome. They know how to teach the kids. They're fun to talk to . . .

Luis: They're fun to hang out with. They want to know what's going on with you.…talk to you like you're a person, like they talk to another teacher.

Alicia: Like Ms. Smith, she's always interested in what is going on in my life. I told her my mom had a baby, and a couple of days later she asked if my mom would like some of the baby clothes she didn't need any more.

Luis: They are respectful.

Matt: Yeah, respectful. Meet you at the door with a smile on their face. They don't have BO. (Laughter) They shower, you know, stuff like that. Hygiene is good. That's your top ranked teacher.

Luis: Yeah, like Mr. Rehnquist. He's cool.

Matt: Then you have your middle rank of teacher and that's the one that knows what they're doing, knows their lessons fine.

Luis: They're not boring.

Matt: Yeah, they're not too boring to hang out with.

Alicia: They're not too boring; they're not too cool.

Matt: Yeah, they're like right in the middle.

Matt: Then you have your bottom rank teachers. They don't know what they're doing at all. They don't care about the kids. They can't teach their class. They can't get the kids under control. They let the kids do whatever they want.

Alicia: And then punish them for doing it.

Matt: Yeah, and punish them for doing it. And, you know, that's not cool. Those are the teachers who should be in the lowest schools, should be getting the lowest pay and everything.

Luis: Like Ms. Williams. I hate teachers like that.

Where Do We Go from Here?

Presented with the issue of a school culture which encourages poor behavior in students, a possible solution might seem to be an insistence that everyone in the school, children and adults alike, should model appropriate behavior. Everyone should say "please" when they make a request. Everyone should pay attention when someone is talking, and everyone should learn to refrain from cursing when they get angry. Perhaps the school could even purchase a life-skill education program aimed at the adults in the building and teach a new skill during faculty meetings each week. But, all these solutions forget about the importance of the "soil." Until the ground, or in the case of schools, the environment, has been analyzed, cultivated, and fertilized, very little will take root because the "soil" is depleted or in the worst cases, toxic.

Put another way, when focusing on change in schools, including improving students' character traits, too much emphasis is placed on implementing particular structures or programs while, "the need to improve culture, climate and interpersonal relationships in schools receive(s) too little attention" (Kruse, Seashore-Louis, & Bryk, 1995). And Payne (2008) reminded us, "To the extent that the problems we are trying to solve are problems of connectedness, a strictly academic approach may not take us all the way" (p. 96). Based on the student responses, and the work of other researchers, I would advocate that before adopting a program to instill better values and citizenship, schools should concentrate their efforts *first* on cultivating a culture of connectedness.

A Culture of Connectedness

In his book on school improvement, Payne (2008) consistently pointed to the importance of the social fabric of a school in the reform process. He noted that there are many problems in schools; students are unruly, teachers demoralized, and parents distrustful. But from his perspective, many of these issues could be traced to weak relationships. Speaking of troublesome issues in schools, he noted, "The problems manifest themselves in so many ways that they may obscure the fact that many of the discrete problems are either generated by or reinforced by the sheer lack of connectedness among people" (p. 24). Conversely, Payne (2008) noted that the presence of a culture of connectedness correlated with improvement when he stated, "High quality human relationships are strongly predictive of whether or not a school can gather itself together and get better" (p. 37).

Barth (1990) concurred with Payne's appraisal of the basis of problematic issues in schools. Speaking of the lack of connection in all relationships in schools he stated,

> The biggest problem besetting schools is the primitive quality of human relationships among children, parents, teachers and administrators. Many schools perpetuate infantilism....This leads to children and adults who frequently behave like infants, complying with authority from fear or dependence, waiting until someone's back is turned to do something "naughty." (p. 36)

Consequently, from my perspective, the first step in improving the soil is to purposefully and intentionally build quality relationships among everyone in the school, beginning with the adults.

Connecting Adults

Barth (1990) spoke of the importance of the adults learning to work together in *Improving Schools from Within.* He stated that building collegiality and connectedness in the adults who work in a school needs to be given top priority "because the relationships among adults in schools are the basis, the precondition, the *sine qua non* that allow, energize, and sustain all other attempts at school improvement" (p. 32), and such improvement, I would add, includes a school's attempt to implement moral education programs.

A good deal has been written concerning this issue of improving adult relationships in schools; the most promising work emphasizes building democratic interactions that value the best that each individual brings to the table, sharing power and decision making as well as highlighting the importance of the principal's role in helping to develop such a culture (Barth, 1990; Grubb & Tredway, 2010; Sparks, 2005; Terrell & Lindsey, 2009). Grubb and Tredway (2010) describe such schools as "collective." They state, "The term *collective* implies a joint and equal responsibility because the people in them are connected to each other and to a vision for change...they are based on similar values and committed to equity...and the joint responsibility of the teachers to work together for justice" (p. 13). This text, I believe provides an excellent starting point for guiding the adults in schools towards examining the relationships in their school and providing concrete ideas for enriching them in ways that will benefit the adults and help enrich the soil leading to a culture of connectedness.

Connecting Children with Adults

Along with cultivating a culture of connectedness among the adults, schools need to foster a similar culture among the adults and children. Adults need to model caring, moral behavior in their interactions with each other and with the students as opposed to having a double standard for behavior. Noddings, quoted by Smith (2004), expounded on this point when she stated, "We do not merely tell them to care and give them texts to read on the subject, we demonstrate our caring in our relations with them."

One of my graduate students stated that her middle school principal instructed the teachers at the school "to never 'write up' a student for doing something that the teacher also did." If getting angry and yelling at someone was inappropriate, it was inappropriate for children and adults. If bullying someone because you could was frowned upon, then no one should be physically or figuratively pushing someone around, including teachers. This principal felt that there should be one standard of conduct for everyone in the school and that if conducting yourself in a particular way was good for the children, it was good for the adults as well. To do otherwise was seen as an abuse of power with such abuse polluting the school "soil" thus creating the potential for student anger and rebellion.

Additionally, adults in schools need to check their perceptions and expectations of their students if they wish to foster a culture of connectedness. Terrell and Lindsey (2009) reminded us that too often adults in schools direct their attention solely to student deficits leading to impatience, anger and low expectations, all of which poison attempts to build relationships. If fostering attachments is the goal, such a focus needs to be changed. They stated, "It takes a courageous leader to be able to change the focus from 'What is wrong with the students?' to 'What is it we need to do differently to meet students' needs?'" (Terrell & Lindsey, 2009, p. 15).

Implementing Noddings' notion of "confirmation" has the potential to aid in overcoming negative views of students, for it entails looking for something positive in an individual and then endeavoring to bring that positive quality out. Noddings quoted in Smith (2004) explained confirmation thusly:

> When we confirm someone, we identify a better self and encourage its development. To do this we must know the other reasonably well. Otherwise we cannot see what the other is really striving for, what ideal he or she may long to make real. Formulas and slogans have no place in confirmation. We do not posit a single ideal for everyone and then announce "high expectations for all." Rather we recognize something admirable, or at least acceptable, struggling to emerge in each person we encounter. The goal or attribute must be seen as worthy both by the person trying to achieve it and by us. We do not confirm people in ways we judge to be wrong.

Finally, improving connectedness with students involves more than the adults no longer abusing their power or focusing on the negative; it is also tied to a classroom environment that fosters learning and collaboration. For example, the National Longitudinal Study of Adolescent Health surveyed 71,515 students in 127 schools to determine student perceptions of school connectedness. The study found that the single most important factor in students feeling connected to a school was the school climate, particularly the climate of the classroom. Results showed that school connectedness was high in schools whose classrooms were inviting places where students engaged in learning, completed schoolwork and got along with each other and with their teachers. According to the study, such a finding is significant since "this speaks to the ability of teachers to make kids feel they are important members of the school. Other research has shown that when teachers are empathetic and consistent, allow students to manage themselves, and encourage them to make decisions, the classroom is a better place—and so is the school" (Blum, McNeely, & Rinehart, 2002). It is clear that what happens in the classroom is key to whether students become connected or disenchanted with their school.

Alienated Students

When strategically planning to cultivate a culture of connectedness, special attention needs to be paid to those students who feel particularly alienated such as Alicia and Luis. Although schools are often described as alienating places for many students (Gatto, 2000), this is particularly true for poor children, English-language learners, and children of color (Fordham, 1996; Kozol, 1991; Margonis, 2006; Terrell & Lindsey, 2009). Such students are already aware that they are constituted by the larger society as well as the school as somehow less than their White, middle-class peers (Popkewitz, 1998). They often feel invisible and their culture misunderstood or even maligned, a painful proposition (Valenzuela, 1999). Consequently, alienated students have little reason to want to become connected to a place which they perceive is not interested in them. Creating connectedness for these students will therefore take more planning and concentrated efforts.

Whatever efforts are put towards building a culture of connectedness among all inhabitants of a school, it must be kept in mind that the goal is to build and enrich democratic relations of caring. If this goal is not kept in the forefront, such efforts can easily become a program of control, a way to manage the behavior of those less powerful in order to make life easier for those in control, or as a means to civilize "those kids" who don't know how to behave, a deficit view of the Other. This is the antithesis of building relationships.

Conclusion

It is understandable that schools invest large amounts of time and energy into implementing one program or another in their race to aid students in developing better behaviors and values. For many schools, student behavior is a huge problem. Teachers have a difficult time teaching and administrators are overwhelmed with discipline referrals because of it; consequently, schools often act quickly to try and alleviate the problem. But as Apple (1996) reminded us, "The problems of schools are so compelling and the urge to get in there and deal with what is happening to our children so understandably powerful we sometimes lose the capacity or do not have the time to step back and ask the critical questions…(pp. 109–110).

This chapter is advocating that despite the great need, it is imperative that educators and concerned citizens step back and ask the important questions if the goal is deep, meaningful change. In the case of moral education, instead of asking what program to implement or what positive and negative consequences work best, perhaps the critical questions should be, "How strong are the feelings of connectedness between the adults in the building and the adults and the students?" "How would students describe the environment of our school?" or "What practices do we routinely engage in that may result in students exhibiting the behavior we wish to extinguish?" Asking and answering such critical questions, holds out the possibility that any solutions will aid in repairing the school environment, as opposed to actually contaminating it, so that down the road positive programs have a chance to grow and flourish.

Once the "soil" is analyzed and then repaired and enriched, educators may find that students still need some type of formal instruction in moral education. On the other hand, they may also find that it is no longer needed as the environment does not invite students to engage in the rebellious or unethical behavior which previously was encouraged by disrespectful treatment. If a program is still deemed necessary, though, there is a very good chance that it will prove fruitful, for there is now in place a school culture to encourage the growth of positive behavior traits all because someone was wise enough to remember to survey the soil.

References

Apple, M. (1996). *Cultural politics and education*. New York: Teachers College Press.

Au, W. (2010). The idiocy of policy: The anti-democratic curriculum of high-stakes testing. *Critical Education, 1*(1). Retrieved 10/06/10 from http://m1.cust.educ.ubc.ca/journal/v1n1.

Barth, R. (1990). *Improving schools from within*. San Francisco, CA: Jossey-Bass.

Bennett, W. J. (1993). *The book of virtues: A treasury of great moral stories*. New York: Simon and Schuster.

Blum, R.W., McNeely, C.A., & Rinehart, P. M. (2002) *Improving the odds: The untapped power of schools to improve the health of teens*. Center for Adolescent Health and Development, University of Minnesota.

Botvin Life Skills. Retrieved 10/02/10 from http://www.lifeskillstraining.com/

Character Counts. Retrieved 10/11/10 from http://charactercounts.org

Community of Caring. Retrieved 10/09/20 from http://www.communityofcaring.org/

Daniels, E., & Arapostathis, M. (2005). What do they really want? : Student voices and motivation research. *Urban Education*, 40: 34–59.

Fordham, S. (1996). *Blacked out: Dilemmas of race, identity and success at Capital High*. Chicago, IL: University of Chicago Press.

Gassaway, B. (2007) *Suicide by educator*. Retrieved 10/09/10 from http://www.bernardgassaway.com/Suicide byEducator%20April%202007.pdf

Gatto, J. (2002). *A different kind of teacher: Solving the crisis of American schooling*. Albany: CA: Berkeley Hills.

Grubb, W., & Tredway, L. (2010). *Leading from the inside out: Expanded roles for teachers in equitable schools*. Boulder, CO: Paradigm.

Kessler, R. (2000). *The soul of education: Helping students find connection, compassion, and character at school*. Alexandria, VI: Association for Supervision and Curriculum Development.

Kozol, J. (1991). *Savage inequalities*. New York: HarperPerennial.

Kruse, S., Seashore-Louis, K., & Bryk, A. (1995). Teachers build professional communities. *Wisconsin Center for Educational Research Highlights, 7*(1), 6–8.

Lickona, T. (1991). *Educating for character*. New York: Bantam.

Margonis, F. (2006). Seeking openings of already closed student-teacher relationships. Daniel Vokey, ed. *Philosophy of Education*. Urbana: Philosophy of Education Society.

McFadden, A. C., & Marsh II, G. E. (1992). A study of race and gender bias in the punishment of school children. *Education & Treatment of Children, 15*(2), 140–147.

Noddings, N. (2002). *Educating moral people: A caring alternative to character education*. New York: Teachers College Press.

Oakes, J. (1988). *Keeping track: How schools structure inequality*. New Haven, CT: Yale University Press.

Olson, K. (2009). *Wounded by school: Recapturing the joy in learning and standing up to old school culture*. New York: Teachers College Press.

Page, B. (2006). *At risk students: Feeling their pain, understanding their plight, accepting their defensive ploys*. Nashville, TN: Educational Dynamics, 9.

Payne, C. (2008). *So much reform, so little change*. Cambridge, MA: Harvard Education Press.

Popkewitz, T. (1998). *Struggling for the soul: The politics of schooling and the construction of the teacher*. New York: Teachers College Press.

Smith, M. K. (2004) Nel Noddings, the ethics of care and education,' *The encyclopaedia of informal education*. Retrieved 10/23/10 from www.infed.org/thinkers/noddings.htm

Sparks, D. (2005). *Leading for results: Transforming teaching, learning and relationships in schools*. Thousand Oaks, CA: Corwin.

Terrell, R.; & Lindsey, R. (2009) *Culturally proficient leadership*. Thousand Oaks, CA: Corwin.

Valenzuela, A. (1999). *Subtractive schooling*. New York: State University of New York Press.

CHAPTER TWENTY-NINE

Doubt and the Framing of Virtue Through Film

SUSAN VERDUCCI & MICHAEL KATZ

Introduction

John Patrick Shanley, Pulitzer-Prize winning playwright and screenwriter, draws our attention to the value of doubt in a film of the same title. Exploring the tensions between certainty and doubt in the pursuit of truth, Shanley turns our gaze to the importance of questioning, and in the film, the importance of questioning one's own certainty. In this chapter, we will use Shanley's film to illustrate how teacher-facilitated viewing and discussion of films can ameliorate primary criticisms leveled at character education without relinquishing one of its strengths, its attention to virtues. We argue that the framing of virtue through film can highlight morally valuable knowledge, skills, and processes.

The method we propose is intended for use with teenagers and young adults. One criticism character education encounters is that it is best suited for young children and elementary students (see, for example, Noddings, 2002, p. 6). In important ways, character education does not come close to addressing the developmental levels and tasks of adolescents, who are, as Anne Colby (2002) writes, in an intense period of

> moral and ideological exploration, ferment, and consolidation. At this time in their lives, young people question their epistemological, moral, political, and religious assumptions, make critical career and other life choices, and rethink their sense of who they are and what is important to them. (pp. 15–16)

They question their identity, the sources of their knowledge, what makes right and wrong, religion, relationships and world around them (Mathews, 1980, 1994; Noddings, 1993; Verducci, 2002). They challenge authority and are self-reflective. Character education programs and practices seem ill suited for the quest teenagers are ready and eager to engage in.

However, character education returns moral education's attention to virtues, and this is important. Regardless of whether they are defined as traits, dispositions, or actions, virtues such as respect, honesty, integrity, humility, fair-mindedness, courage, and responsibility can engender feelings and actions that may lead to moral excellence. We propose to use film to extend the exploration of virtues to the upper grades and to do so in a way that takes into account the developmental realities of adolescents at the same time as it ameliorates many criticisms of character education.

To begin the process of showing how framing virtue through film can be morally educative, we review some major criticisms of character education's handling of virtues. We follow this with a brief discussion of the value of film for moral discourse and then articulate the sorts of conversations that teachers can engage in with students about films. We then move directly to a conversation about the film *Doubt*. Here, we focus on exploring the virtues of fair-mindedness and humility.

Criticisms of Character Education's Use of Virtues

As is evident in this volume, character education theories and practices have encountered major criticisms. Problems include deciding whose (or which) virtues warrant educational attention. In most instances, character education theorists and practitioners simply stipulate what virtues should be taught. Other programs, such as "Character Matters!," convene relevant stakeholders to determine specific lists of virtues that reflect the values of the local community. This approach, of course, assumes that the character of the community in which the virtues are inculcated is, itself, morally good.

Even if a list could be agreed upon, the virtues themselves are not clearly or sufficiently defined. Character education undermines itself in its lack of philosophical and psychological theory (Noddings, 2002). Kristjánsson (2006) makes the following trenchant point:

> despite routine appeals to the originator of a character-based take on morality, namely Aristotle, [character education] writings are disturbingly short of critical engagement with past and present philosophers. For instance, Lickona's discussion of role-modeling feeds on a narrow diet of practical examples; there is little in the way of a general rationale for this method or an explanation of what it really involves (p. 38).

A further criticism pertains to character education's lack of attention to the specific and particular contexts in which virtuous action occurs. For example, a well-known challenge to the inculcation of principled honesty asks if honesty is a virtue when a Nazi comes knocking at your door and asks if you have hidden a Jew under your bed. Although the honest answer is "yes," many have debated whether this is a moral answer. The way character education inculcates virtues rarely places them in situational and/or relational contexts. They are rarely questioned, always advocated.

Related to this point, character education does not recognize the complexity of moral situations in general and the ambiguities in which moral judgment, intuition and sensibility are called upon. It does not allow students to grapple with situations in which virtues compete and are mutually exclusive, nor does it explore the ways in which virtues might be related and connected to each other. It does not require that students think critically on complicated moral issues and dilemmas. Its critics argue that its account of the moral world is too simplistic and, some might add, too certain.

Furthermore, character education programs didactically inculcate virtues. Alfie Kohn (1998) and Nel Noddings (2002) decry the presentation of the virtues as fixed, finished and ready for adoption; this, they argue, stymies conversation and true dialogue. The narrow use of stories with inspirational "heroes" leads Kristjánsson (2006) to note that character education can lead to imitation, admiration, and unenlightened conformity but not necessarily to the development of one's ethical ideals (p. 41).

Finally, in her critique of character education, Noddings (2002) notes that this form of moral education does not deal with the possibility that the "potential for evil lies within each of us. If we are treated badly enough, we will betray our own ethical ideals, and even those we love" (p. 9). Thus, she argues,

> Teenagers need to study accounts of people gone wrong. How does it happen that some people become vicious criminals? How does it happen that "good" citizens ignore the misery around them? How does patriotism sometimes become warped into cruelty? What makes it possible for one person to torture another? Novels, biographies, poetry, films, and historical accounts are all useful here, but they cannot be chosen just for inspiration (Noddings, 2002, p. 152).

Character education has encountered problems with its content and its methods. It has come under solid attack for its lack of attention to situational and relational contexts; to the complexities and ambiguities of moral action and the moral world; to critical thinking skills necessary to identify and negotiate complex moral situations; and its lack of recognition that we all have the potential to behave badly. This list does not exhaust the weaknesses of character education; it simply highlights a few of the more important ones.

We intend in what follows to show how film, if taught effectively, can be helpful for framing conversations on virtues in ways that ameliorate these criticisms while retaining character education's use of stories. Aligned with the developmental tasks of adolescents, our method brings virtues into question, focuses on the situational and relational contexts and highlights the complexities of the moral world that teenagers are capable of perceiving. It does so in a way that retains the affective power that narrative brings to education and does so in a way that allows the potential for student self-assessment and transformation.

Film's Value for Moral Education

Most types of moral education use narratives because stories can be powerful and engaging. They can serve important pedagogical functions, such as illustrations of moral problems and action; catalysts for discussion; and a way of opening students to consider alternative realities. Not only can they serve these functions, but some argue that they do their own philosophical work and can be considered direct contributions to our thinking about ethics (Falzon, 2002; Wartenberg, 2006).

Literature and film engage and exercise the moral imagination. We come to perceive people and the world in different ways, and they are vehicles through which students come to experience alternative reality vicariously.

> To call for the imaginative capacity is to work for the ability to look at things as if they could be otherwise....To tap into imagination is to become able to break with what is supposedly fixed and finished, objectively and independently real. It is to see beyond what the imaginer has called normal or "common-sensible" and to carve out new orders in experience. Doing so, a person may become freed to glimpse what might be, to form notions of what should be and what is not yet. (Greene, 1995, p. 19).

For Maxine Greene, the imagination is released through engagement with arts such as film; they transform, deepen and liberate us. They can also lead to deep inquiry, moral reasoning and reflection as they move readers to a more embodied inquiry, one attuned to context and the particular realities of the world we experience. In the words of Martha Nussbaum (1990), "Certain truths about human life can only be fittingly and accurately stated in the language and forms characteristic of the narrative artist" (p. 5). Nussbaum assumes that literature, like life, is an exercise in moral attention; it focuses upon the moral effort required in coming to see anything, or anyone, lovingly and justly. If it succeeds, it represents a moral achievement and provides moral insights critical to living an ethical life.

Literary and visual narratives show us that moral and character issues are deeply embedded in the contexts and the lives of characters. In so doing, they dramatically reveal the complex nature of morality, and they often provide us with deeper, more nuanced and embodied insights than those which didactic teaching can provide.

Furthermore, using film for the purposes of moral education with teenagers has an advantage that literature cannot match. Film is a medium that they have grown up with; they choose it; they understand it; they are fluent in its language and symbols. All of these features make film more accessible to students than the written word in books. To derive meaning from film does not require a certain level of vocabulary and reading skills. Visual storytelling uses a common language. Although all students may not know how to analyze film, they can all "read" film.

And this, we think, helps prepare students for the critical "readiness" that John Dewey (1910/2008) writes about in *How We Think*.

> There is such as thing as readiness to consider in a thoughtful way the subjects that do come within the range of experience—a readiness that contrasts strongly with the disposition to pass judgment on the basis of mere custom, tradition, prejudice, etc., and thus shun the task of thinking. (p. 139)

In this sense films' narrative and characters open students' minds and hearts to consider seriously trenchant moral questions and pursue moral inquiry relatively unencumbered by habituated judgment. The richness in the details of life that literature and film provides can make readers and viewers "ready" to move from the comfort of the familiar into the discomfort of authentic inquiry that characterizes learning.

Film's effectiveness lies in engaging us in the details, in the context, in the lived lives of others we cannot otherwise imagine. Our multiple senses engage; we hear text through our ears and music through our bodies. We see subtext and detail through our eyes. Films create visual and visceral moods in their storytelling. All increase the potential for engaged moral inquiry. That is true, of course, only if films are properly framed and effectively taught by skilled instructors.

As easily as film opens avenues for moral education, it also contains inherent pitfalls. Marshall (2003) reminds us that, "The wary ethicist doubts that a medium that manipulates the viewer, engages the emotions, and elicits a personal connection to the characters is the best resource for ethical reflection" (p. 93). We concur with the wary ethicist and in framing virtues attempt to bring physical and emotional engagement into conversation with critical and moral reasoning.

Like Marshall, we counter that most problems can be ameliorated by the way that films are introduced, discussed and connected to teachers' curricular objectives. We contend that the framing of the film is the key to unlocking its potential for moral education, and that this opening begins with the form of the frame—conversation.

Conversation

Although there is a place for lecture, debate, direct instruction, group work, projects, papers, and other useful pedagogical strategies in framing virtue through film, conversation is a critical beginning. The qualities of conversation that we advocate are nearly antithetical to the didacticism and indoctrination characteristic of character education.

Two theorists are helpful in thinking about the general outlines of such a conversation. Noddings (2002, p. 118–147) describes three relevant types, one of which we highlight here. "Ordinary" conversation refers to conversation typically found outside academia and characteristic of our regular lives. In ordinary conversation with students, adults "try to be good, even if they do not always bring it off...[; they] have loving regard and respect for their child partners"; and for both students and teacher, "the partner is more important than the topic, the conclusion, or the argument" (Noddings, 2002, p. 128). This type of conversation prioritizes the relationship between the participants over the content of what is discussed.

Although the other types of conversation she articulates (formal argumentation and conversation on questions that have engaged human minds over time) can be used effectively to frame our understanding of particular virtues, the characteristics of the ordinary are both a prerequisite and a necessity in framing virtues through film with high school students and young adults. For students to be able to reflect in ethically useful ways—ways that carry the possibility of self-transformation—establishing classroom relationships characterized by safety and trust is necessary. Students must trust that the teacher cares and respects them and their efforts toward comprehension, expression and moral growth.

David Hansen (2001) also contributes to our thinking about the quality of the conversation in which film can frame virtues for moral education. His work on "focused" discussions extends Noddings' work. Like ordinary conversation, focused discussion includes the notion of "talking with, rather than at" (p. 80). These conversations are mutual explorations, a condition that implies that the teacher will also reflect upon and reevaluate her own thinking and actions in light of the discussion. Teachers and students begin by articulating questions and concerns they care about, and then they study and resolve them through employing the ideas, the logic, the methods and the materials of the curriculum" (p. 83). The conversation is akin to ensemble improvisation, with teacher as a part of the ensemble. The importance of listening, being in tune and responding remain critical for all participants. Unlike conversations with character educators, in these discussions students help determine the shape, content and direction of the discussion.

At the heart of Noddings' conversation and Hansen's focused discussion are questions. And in framing virtues, questions are both fundamental and critical. They act as a catalyst to inquiry. Moreover, they give our pursuit of moral knowledge and skills focus and direction. If asked genuinely, they do not prescribe answers. They do not indoctrinate. If framing virtues through film is to educate in truly moral ways, it cannot rest in the assessment of the actions of others, fictional or not. It cannot rest in the assessment of ethical frameworks; it must start with and return to the students. Although the teacher frames the film with her questions, it is the questions that students themselves want to pursue that matter. Thus, the spirit of questioning frames exploring virtue through film.

Summary of *Doubt*

Obviously, the questions that frame any filmic discussion of virtues will depend upon the content of the film.[1] To illustrate the type of questions useful for moral education, we introduce the film *Doubt* written and directed by John Patrick Shanley, and based on his Pulitzer-Prize winning play of the same title. The play has a subtitle that character educators would find attractive, "*A Parable*." Although this parable may be brief and succinctly told, this story is far from simple and its message far from one that leads us to direct knowledge of moral action. It leaves us, as the title indicates, in considerable doubt.

The story is set in a Catholic School in the Bronx during Vatican II, a time when the church underwent fundamental and controversial changes. Meryl Streep plays strict Sister Aloysius, the school's principal. Her rigid rule of the school and its students creates an environment where kindness and caring grow only in the narrow crevices her control cannot reach. The two other primary characters are the newly arrived, highly intelligent, progressive Father Flynn (Phillip Seymour Hoffman) and the young innocent Sister James (Amy Adams). In stark contrast to Sister Aloysius, they care for and nurture their students, albeit in ways muffled by "the dragon" principal.

Father Flynn opens the film with a sermon and a question: "What do you do when you are not sure?" He tells the story of a surviving sailor of a shipwreck who makes a raft and tries to use what he knows, the configuration of the stars, to guide the raft home. But fog comes in and without the stars, he can no longer tell if he is on the proper path. He is filled with doubt. "Doubt," Father Flynn says, "can be a bond as powerful and as sustaining as certainty. When you are lost, you are not alone." This story parallels that of Sister Aloysius as it launches us into the film's lean and powerful narrative. The dramatic action begins when Sister Aloysius asks Sister James to keep an eye out for one of her students, Donald Muller, the first and only African American student at the school. Aloysius plants the seed of doubt in James's mind about the relationship Flynn has to the friendless and sensitive boy, as Flynn has taken a protective interest in Donald. When Flynn calls the boy to the rectory and the boy returns upset, Sister James also becomes suspicious. Her suspicions are exacerbated when she sees Flynn leave an undershirt in Donald's locker. She reveals these incidents to Sister Aloysius, who then confronts Flynn.

Sister Aloysius' suspicions about the character of Father Flynn blossom into certainty that he is sexually abusing Donald. She begins an unwavering and unquestioning pursuit for proof to substantiate her belief. In the process, Sister Aloysius relays her belief to Donald's mother, who tragically acknowledges that her son is gay, that his father beats him for it, and that if he is returned to his last school, he would be killed. She begs Sister Aloysius to keep Donald until the end of the school year so that he can graduate. We listen in horror and sympathy as she tells Sister Aloysius that even if Donald's and Father Flynn's relationship is inappropriate, it is caring and protective and thus the best option available to her son.

Just as we might begin to conclude that Aloysius' actions are misguided, Shanley puts Flynn and Aloysius in a scene in which she reveals to Flynn her talk with Donald's mother. She demands he confess to her before he requests a transfer. He refuses. She also tells him that she contacted a nun at his last parish who confirmed her suspicions. She again demands he confess to her before he requests a transfer. Brilliantly, Shanley leaves the mystery of Father Flynn's actual relationship with Donald unsolved, but Flynn does reveal that there is *something* to the suspicions. We are left to wonder if Flynn might have acted on his vague and ambiguous acknowledgment of his sexual orientation, or if his guilt

stems simply from the fact of it. We doubt. We doubt the goodness of Flynn, and we doubt the goodness of Aloysius. We don't know the truth. The only person without doubt is Aloysius herself. She,
it seems, remains unwaveringly certain.

The final scene takes place months later. We come to understand that Flynn has been transferred;
in fact, after leaving the school he received a promotion. Sister James comes back from visiting a
sick brother and sits with Aloysius in the perennially wintry garden. It is here that Aloysius confesses that she lied about contacting the nun at Father Flynn's previous parish—the lie that pushed Flynn
into his ambiguous confession. In the final and wrenching moment of the film, Aloysius confesses
to Sister James that, "in the pursuit of wrongdoing one steps away from God. Of course there is a
price." Sister James asks, "What is it Sister?" Sister Aloysius, shaking from within and beginning
to cry, says, "I have doubts. I have *such doubts.*"

Now, it seems, we all doubt. And we are all left to form our own understanding of exactly how
Sister Aloysius has changed and what this change means.

Doubt is rife with avenues to explore for the purposes of moral education. Questions of authority, accountability, culpability, trust and responsibility are some moral topics that arise naturally from
this compelling narrative, these intriguing characters, and their troubled relationships with each other.
Given that the story concerns the nature of certainty and doubt in the human pursuit of truth, we chose
to explore the complexities of doubt and the related virtues of fair-mindedness and humility. It is likely that students will bring other virtues and moral topics into the conversation as well.

Framing a Conversation on *Doubt*

Regardless of whether the teacher intends the film to be a catalyst for discussion or an illustration
of virtues, the advance framing of the film will consist of questions that guide student viewing.
Advance framing mitigates a problem that Marshall (2003) points to: watching a film does not necessarily exercise the imagination:

> We tend to perceive a film as a pre-packaged story, ready for consumption not engagement....If we seek
> a form for ethical reflection that invites engagement...we need to acknowledge and prepare our students
> to engage a film in a way that they are unaccustomed to doing. To practice narrative as ethics...we must
> invite our students to open the package and tamper with the story. (p. 95)

Advance framing with questions and dialogue invites students to begin to "open the package" in a
way that can ameliorate the problem of students consuming a film without engaging the content. For
Doubt, such questions might include: What is involved in treating another person "fairly?" Or
"unfairly?" Is fairness compatible with compassion and caring? What does this mean for people in
positions of authority and power, such as teachers? What is the truth and how can we discover it?
Can (or under what conditions can) being mistaken about the truth lead to serious harm? What if we
cannot know the truth? What does it mean to understand our own fallibility? Is our fallibility connected to our capacity for doing evil? What is humility? What role might it play in our striving to
become moral persons? How might its absence or its opposite (i.e., arrogance or pride) present problems for treating others fairly and with compassion? What is the moral and psychological price of
being treated unfairly? And, is dishonesty in the pursuit of removing a moral danger justifiable?

Critical reflection on these questions before viewing the film helps mitigate the problem of students' relying simply on their emotional response as sufficient for understanding virtue. It moves the

film beyond mere example or illustration to catalyst for critical thinking. It can be a time when multiple ethical frameworks are introduced or it can simply provide students an opportunity to draw on their own understandings. But Kristjánsson (2006) makes the important point that,

> If…we want to fully understand the nature of the good life and the role of the particular virtues in such a life, we need objective, exemplar-independent standards to help us grasp that truth. Merely pointing to role models [or films] or other good examples is not enough. The Aristotelian educator would bring this fact home to learners, even before they were capable of understanding such exemplar-independent standards themselves, by constantly referring to moral reasons rather than merely 'good examples.' (p. 48)

Advance framing initiates the process of having students begin to identify moral reasons independently of their emotional response.

Once the film has been viewed, student response to the film can be elicited. The teacher can ask them what questions and concerns arise from their viewing. Marshall (2003) recommends that her students imagine the most disturbing moments of the film in detail and then asks them why these moments were disturbing. Teachers can elicit questions from students about the characters, their motivations and their relationships. Questions such as: Why does a specific character act as she does? What are her underlying motives (both conscious and subconscious)? To what degree does the character understand the basis of her conduct? Is she morally blind? Self-deceived? If so, how? and why? Equally important, from Noddings' perspective, is that students be asked to imagine themselves in the position of the characters, including perpetrators.

Questions about virtues can arise organically from the conversation, or they can be introduced by the teacher. What virtues do the characters display? Can you perceive any evidence of virtues in characters considered villainous? Are there virtues competing in the film? Are there virtues connecting with each other in the action of the film? How do these virtues relate to each other? Does one play a greater role than the other? Interfere with the other? Which virtue takes primacy (when, for whom or under what conditions)? Why? Which *should* take primacy and why? Under what condition might these virtues not be commendable? How, if at all, does context matter to the virtue under consideration? What challenges do the characters encounter in their pursuit of the virtue? How does the context and experience of the characters in the film play into our understanding of the virtue? Do the central characters change as a result of their experiences? If so, does change lead to new or different moral insight or understanding? Can viewers of the film arrive at different conclusions about whether and how the major character(s) have been changed as a result of their experiences? Does the complexity of motivation and situations lead to multiple sensible interpretations of what the film is trying to communicate morally?

At some point, a move from the specific film to the advance framing questions becomes necessary. The teacher should facilitate a moving back and forth, to and from the particulars of the film to the advance framing questions and principled moral thinking. And she must facilitate student exploration of the connections that the discussion of virtues and the film has to their own experience, including their own relationships. In a study of an elementary school using literary stories to teach caring, Colette Rabin (2010) found that although students were willing to explore these sorts of connections, they required prompting. Teachers will need to ask questions about how the virtue under consideration manifests itself in their experience and what meaning the discussion has for them and for their understanding of themselves as moral beings. How does the film's meaning affect how one crafts her own ethical ideal? What does it mean for one's own self-transformation? How might our biases concerning sexual orientation impact how we think about the action in the film. How, if at all, do the story and discussion fuel one's own virtuous motivations? These questions demand self-understanding and perhaps point to potential areas for self-transformation.

A skillful instructor must find ways to engage students in a meaningful, interactive dialogical conversation that weaves the discussion of the virtues to the film and to the students' interpretations both of the film and their own experiences. This artful weaving enriches the conversation and brings new meaning, clarity, and depth of understanding both of the film's content and the student's experience. The result is a deeper, richer understanding of the film, the virtues embedded in it, and the students' personal experiences. The art of weaving and leading a meaningful conversation based upon probing questioning, careful active listening, thoughtful responses to other students' comments is an art that many thoughtful teachers have been engaged in for decades. However, we do not minimize its importance in enabling film to do the ethical work we have described in this chapter.

But what specific sorts of questions about virtues can teachers use to facilitate a conversation after viewing the film *Doubt*? The questions below generate ideas that can be used to keep the conversation shifting from response to critical/moral reasoning to student experience and back again. They explore the individual virtues of fair-mindedness (the virtue necessary for treating others fairly) and humility and their intersections and connections as they are dramatized in the film. They are in list form because they are meant as aids, not as step-by-step directions.

Fair-Mindedness

- In criminal jury trials, potential witnesses are asked a final question before it is determined whether they are fit to be jurors. The question is some form of the following: Is there anything we should know that might prevent you from acting as a fair and impartial juror? What does it mean to be fair and impartial? Why are jurors not allowed to have any pre-existing relationship to those on trial? Why are they expected not to have formed any "prejudgment" about the person on trial or the facts of the case? Is such impartiality an impractical ideal for a teacher or a principal entrusted with enforcing the rules? Why? Why not? Are teachers, for example, who observe students cheating on an exam, able to be impartial in their judging what was going on? Can they be expected to give students "due process"? Is there something problematic about a person in authority playing two roles simultaneously—i.e., prosecuting attorney (gathering evidence to prove a crime was committed) and impartial judge or juror? What do your answers to these questions mean for our general ability to pursue truth?

- Have you ever been accused of something unfairly? How is being charged with a crime or a rule violation that one did not commit likely to affect the person so charged? Do you believe Father Flynn was accused unfairly? What led Sister Aloysius to be so certain about his guilt in his conduct with Donald Muller?

- Procedural fairness in jury trials—sometimes referred to as "due process"—often has multiple features; these include 1) agreed upon standards of evidence; 2) the right to an attorney; 3) the right to cross-examine witnesses; 4) the right to an impartial judge or jury; 5) and the right to appeal the verdict. But at the minimum, in schools, one has a right to "know what one is being charged with" and "the right to defend oneself" (i.e., tell one's own side of the story and be listened to with an open mind). Can Father Flynn receive due process from Sister Aloysius? If not, why not? Recall the final scene in her office when the dialogue proceeds as follows:

    Father Flynn: Why do you suspect me? What have I done?

    Sister Aloysius: You gave that boy wine and you let him take the blame.

    Father Flynn: That's completely untrue. Did you talk with Mr. McGinn?

Sister Aloysius: All he knows is that the boy drank wine; he does not know *how* he came to drink it.

Father Flynn: Then did his mother have something to add to that?

Sister Aloysius: No.

Father Flynn: So that's it.

Sister Aloysius: I am not satisfied.

Father Flynn: Ask the boy then.

Sister Aloysius: Why, he'd protect you.

Father Flynn: Why would he do that?

Sister Aloysius: Because you have seduced him.

Father Flynn (getting angry): You're insane. You've got in your head that I have corrupted this boy by giving him wine and nothing I say will change that.

Sister Aloysius: That's right.

Father Flynn: But this has nothing to do with the wine. You have had a fundamental mistrust of me before this incident. It was you who warned Sister James to be on the look out. Wasn't it?

Sister Aloysius: That's true.

Father Flynn: So you admit it.

Sister Aloysius: Certainly.

Father Flynn: Why?

Sister Aloysius: I know people.

What does this scene reveal to you about Sister Aloysius's capacity to be fair and open-minded in her dealings with Father Flynn? Have you ever found yourself completely prejudged in a negative way by someone in authority? What effect did it have on you? How do you feel about it now? Have you ever prejudged someone in a similar way? What role/s do you think our prejudices, for example, bias against homosexuals, have in judgment?

- Why do you suppose our criminal system operates on the assumption that one is innocent until proven guilty? Why do you suppose our jury system requires for punishment the criterion "guilty beyond a reasonable doubt?" What is your sense of "what a reasonable doubt" might consist of? Why do you suppose Sister Aloysius had no reasonable doubt about Father Flynn? Do most people view others charged with a crime as "innocent until proven guilty"? If not, why not?

- How important is it for the culture of a classroom (or school) that the teacher (or principal) is perceived to be fair-minded? What kinds of factors might prevent teachers from being fair-minded? What sorts of behavior might ensue from the perception that a teacher is not fair minded?

- Do you think that fairness is compatible with compassion or caring? Do you think Father Flynn was seeking to be caring when he said that he would not reveal Donald Muller's drinking of altar wine and not expel him from being an altar boy if no one found out? Was Father Flynn deceiving himself in his statements about why he did what he did? Do you think his caring for Donald was genuine? Why or why not?

- Do you aim to be as fair minded as possible in the way you treat others? Did Sister Aloysius have her own sense of fairness, one that might be different than our ordinary sense of it? Did she see herself as acting fairly when she meted out punishments to the children in the school? Why? Why not?

Humility

- What does it mean to exhibit the virtue of "humility"? What is its opposite?
- In Christian theology, we are all fundamentally sinners ("In Adam's fall, we sinned all."). Does this belief contribute to humility? Does it connect to a notion of God as an entity that loves us in spite of our moral flaws and our misdeeds? Do you believe that we are all likely to commit sins? Are some of these sins more problematic than others? Where does lying fit in? Are some lies more serious (morally) than others? How do you view Sister Aloysius's lie that she has talked to a nun in a previous parish of Father Flynn? Is it more problematic for a person entrusted with religious authority to commit serious sins than it is for others?
- Do you believe that we are all "fallible" not only in our actions but in our judgments about situations and people? What does "being fallible" mean to you? How do you view it as connected to humility?
- Do you think it is a sign of weakness to admit that you have acted badly? That you have made an important mistake that has caused harm to others? Do you believe it is hard for some people to confess to having acted badly? Have you ever (not) admitted that you have acted badly? Why? If it is hard for people to admit their faults and misdeeds, why is this the case? What kind of environment might make it easier for people to be honest and vulnerable with each other? Have you experienced such an environment? How might you cultivate this sort of environment?

Connections Between Fair-Mindedness and Humility

- Can the lack of humility interfere with a person's becoming fair-minded? If so how? Does Sister Aloysius's certainty about Father Flynn relate to her humility? Her fair-mindedness or the lack thereof? Do you believe that the ability to admit that we have mistreated others, acted badly, prejudged others unfairly, or wished harm upon others might be critical in developing our sense of fair-mindedness? Our sense of compassion? Or our general capacity to be honest with ourselves and others?
- What, if anything, has the film *Doubt* taught you about the relationship between fair-mindedness and humility?

The questions above provide ideas for the teacher to explore how *Doubt* shows the central role that "fair-mindedness" and "humility" play in one educator's efforts to act in ways that enhance students' moral and educational well-being. The film dramatizes the dangers of acting with a false sense of certainty, of not giving "doubt" its due in reaching a fair-minded decision, and of risking the abuse of one's authority in the effort to remove a potential source of wrongdoing. And its dramatization of these dangers reveals itself through the complexity of character, situation, and deep interpersonal relationships.

Conclusion

Films such as *Doubt* can draw teenagers and young adults into explorations of virtues in ways that bring moral reasoning into dialogue with affective response. *Doubt*'s depiction of the tensions inherent in the human pursuit of truth turns our attention to the importance of questioning, including the importance of questioning one's own certainty. The film, however, cannot stand on its own as a tool for moral education. Only in the hands of a skilled facilitator can the conversation engage teens and bring their minds and emotions, their own moral selves and the film's characters, into dialogue on virtues such as fair-mindedness and humility. When teachers facilitate dialogue on film through questions that challenge the absoluteness of virtues, questions that lead to thinking about the way virtues interact and compete, questions that highlight the context virtues exist in and questions that point to moral complexity, many criticisms leveled at character education dissolve.

Self-reflection is critical if self-transformation is to be a real possibility. In framing virtues, teachers encourage students to explore and examine their reasons. They suggest that students examine their own contexts, experiences and relationships that contribute to their responses and ideas. The focus on self-ethical development is what separates this sort of moral education from typical ethics classes. The nature and intent of the questions also separate this sort of moral education from character education; the conversation is not didactic, does not indoctrinate ideas.[2] This film, and others like it, can open the door to meaningful moral inquiry in young people whose developmental task centers on questioning their assumptions and the world around them. In the process of figuring out who they are, they naturally question. They naturally doubt.

This natural inclination can be advantageous to moral educators. Shanley, in an interview on National Public Radio (2008), said, "I think that certainty is a closed door. It is the end of the conversation. Doubt is an open door; it is a dynamic process." *Doubt*, in the hands of a skillful moral educator, can open the door to dynamic and meaningful conversations about the virtues of fair-mindedness and humility.

Notes

1. The controversial nature of some of the film's content might restrict its use in some (highly) conservative districts, and good judgment would be required of teachers using the film with students.
2. Of course, like most moral education pedagogies, the framing of virtue through film cannot assure the translation of moral knowledge, skills and processes to student action. Knowing about virtues is not the same as acting virtuously, and this is clearly the case with framing virtues through film. We claim, however, it is a start.

References

Colby, A. (2002). Whose Values? In W. Damon (Ed.), *Bringing in a new era in character education*. Stanford: Hoover Press.

Costas, C. (Executive Producer) & Shanley, J. P. (Director). (2008). *Doubt* [Film].

Dewey, J. (1910/2008). *John Dewey: The later works, 1925–1953, Volume 8*. Joanne Boydston, (Ed.). Carbondale, IL: Southern Illinois University Press. (Original work published in 1910)

Falzon, C. (2002). *Philosophy goes to the movies: An introduction to philosophy*. New York: Routledge.

Greene, M. (1995). *Releasing the imagination: Essays on education, the arts and social change*. San Francisco: Jossey-Bass.

Hansen, D. (2001). *Exploring the moral heart of teaching: Toward a teacher's creed*. New York: Teachers College, Columbia University Press.

John Patrick Shanley on Dogma and Doubt. (December 12, 2008). Retrieved September 14, 2010 from http://www.npr.org/templates/story/story.php?storyId=98142901

Johnson, M. (1993). *Moral imagination: Implications of cognitive science for ethics*. Chicago: University of Chicago Press.

Katz, M., & Quill, L. (May, 2008). Teaching virtue by storytelling. *British Columbia Educational Leadership Research (eJournal)*.

Kohn, A. (1998). *What to look for in a classroom . . . and other essays*. San Francisco: Jossey-Bass.

Kristjánsson, K. (March, 2006). Emulation and the use of role models in moral education. *Journal of Moral Education, 76:*1, 37–49.

Marshall, E. O. (2003). Making the most of a good story: Effective use of film as a teaching resource for ethics. *Teaching Theology and Religion. 6:*2, 93–98.

Mathews, G. (1980). *Philosophy and the young child.* Cambridge: Harvard University Press.

Matthews, G. (1994). *The philosophy of childhood.* Cambridge: Harvard University Press.

Noddings, N. (1993). *Educating for intelligent belief or unbelief.* New York: Teachers College Press.

Noddings, N. (2002). *Educating moral people: A caring alternative to character education.* New York: Teachers College Press.

Nussbaum, M. (1990). *Love's knowledge: Essays on philosophy and literature.* Oxford: Oxford University Press.

Rabin, C. (2010). Fostering dispositions through the literary-arts. *Action in Teacher Education, 31:*4, 14–27.

Verducci, S. (May/June 2002). Philosophizing with teenagers. *Knowledge Quest, 30:*5.

Wartenberg, T. E. (2006). Beyond *mere* illustration: How films can be philosophy. *Journal of Aesthetics and Art Criticism, 64:*1, 19–32.

CHAPTER THIRTY

On the Relationship of Peace Education to Moral Education

CRIS TOFFOLO & IAN HARRIS

Moral people kill. Moral, God-fearing human beings join armies and believe it is their patriotic duty to kill others in order to protect the homeland. Many support the death penalty. George W. Bush thought it was all right to invade Afghanistan in 2001 and Iraq in 2003, even though neither country, nor citizens from either country, had attacked the United States. Similarly, President Kennedy escalated U.S. aggression against Vietnam, another country that had never harmed the United States in any way.[1] Under some systems of ethics, such as just war theory, it is morally justified to retaliate if you have been attacked. But the attacks just mentioned were not justified in terms of repelling a military invasion.[2] They were outright acts of aggression that caused misery, death, displacement, and destruction to hundreds of thousands of innocent people. Bush is a very conservative United Methodist elected partially on account of his religious piety. Kennedy was a practicing Catholic. Both of them, like many other political leaders, ignored the fundamental religious command, "Thou Shall Not Kill," and still they claimed the moral high road. This lack of commitment to nonviolence among many moral people is puzzling because all religions contain strong injunctions against killing. Similar injunctions are part of many secular-rationalist systems of ethics, such as Kant's which elaborates the categorical imperative to treat others never as a means but always as ends in themselves.

Drawing upon both religious and philosophical ethical systems, moral educators teach values and attempt to inculcate abilities in individuals that will enable them to confront and resolve moral dilemmas using ethical principles embedded in their consciences, without the dictate of some outside authority or resorting to direct violence.[3] Modern moral educators also teach that people are equal.

In spite of these teachings many political leaders have relied upon violence to secure their grip over civil society, and Pax Romana[4] is still a favored way to provide security. The students who receive the above moral teachings often comply when leaders ask them to violate those principles in order to defend the homeland, acquire more resources, defeat communism or Islam, or to maintain or promote some "way of life." Why this occurs is likely related to many factors. Although some religious leaders condemn violence, many agree with political leaders who appeal for support for aggression carried out by the "motherland"; heroic deeds of violent warriors are praised within the polis and from the pulpit. People are socialized into law and order and not into egalitarian ways of interacting. History books praise military heroes and ignore the contributions of peacemakers. Violence is also condoned or overlooked in many homes, where physical and psychological assaults are the ways many people address conflict, disobedience, anger, and frustration. Violent methods of conflict resolution are celebrated in popular culture. Violent structural arrangements like poverty and homelessness are justified by cultural narratives, such as the poor are lazy (so let them suffer). Because of this wide acceptance of violent behavior, many teachers in their curricula do not question national policies that support war and forms of structural and cultural violence that condemn many people to substandard levels of existence. Likewise, they ignore environment exploitation.

These contradictions and other harms people commit are the dilemmas peace education examines. Peace educators teach about the roots of, and alternatives to, violence. While many of the first peace studies programs emerged at religious colleges and universities, and many such programs remain strongly inspired by the teachings of the prophets of the world's great religions—Buddha, Baha'u'llah, Jesus Christ, Mohammed, Moses, and Lao Tse—they primarily utilized the methodologies and tools of the social sciences to empirically examine domestic and international structural arrangements that support war systems, and the socialization and innate proclivities of human beings that support violent behavior at all levels of society. While embracing a moral framework rooted in the sacredness of all life and focusing attention on the harm and suffering endured by many, and arguing for the equality of everyone, these programs also critically examine the disparity between high moral teachings and the violent realities of the current world.

Starting from this framework, this chapter compares and contrasts peace education and moral education, and concludes with some thoughts about the efficacy of both for rearing future generations who are capable of creating a just, virtuous, and peaceful world.

History of Moral Education

The word *moral*, from the Latin *mos, moris,* means the customs and common values that hold a people together. From earliest times moral education has been seen as central to educational practices. With the rise of formal schooling, it became expected that schools should contribute to this task. Yet even before that development, every enduring community had a moral code that it worked to instill in its youth. Indigenous people passed down their moral codes through stories and in more rigorous ways, teaching virtues necessary for the survival of the group. In the Socratic tradition, virtue was taught as a way to secure social order. Confucianism ties the well-being of the state to a moral education that helps people reconcile their desires with the well-being of family and community. In Judaism the focus of education is the law enshrined in the Torah and a commitment to living according to its demands.

Moral education in the United States predates the founding of the republic, and just as today, during most of this history, it has been a contentious issue. In colonial times formal education developed most rapidly in Massachusetts, Connecticut and New Hampshire where the main religious groups were Puritans and Congregationalists. Not surprisingly, therefore, initially moral education in the United States was heavily Calvinist and carried on by the family and the church.

In addition to the Christian impulse, the founders actively promoted moral education in order to insure the success of the new republic, for they were aware that historically most political philosophers believed democracy contained within itself the seeds of its own destruction, as it easily devolves into oligarchy or tyranny (Bennett, 1995, 219). Without education, said James Madison, "popular government is but a Prologue to a Farce or a Tragedy" (quoted in Bennett, 1995, 218).

As the immigration of peasant and working-class Catholics and Jews increased throughout the 19th century, they increasingly voiced their objections to the overwhelming Protestantism of the Common School curriculum, often starting their own schools. In their turn, Protestant Americans looked upon these newcomers as lacking the skills necessary to conduct democracy and as causes of widespread crime and poverty. Horace Mann, secretary of the first state board of education ever created in Massachusetts, responded to this situation by advocating for universal, compulsory public education that could act as the "ethical leaven of society." However he understood that for this to occur, moral education had to become less sectarian, though it still should be grounded in religion. Thus by the end of the 19th century, moral education was largely a mild consensus of moral and spiritual values that appeared to be shared by all religions. The idea was that despite disagreement about creeds, it was possible to judge behavior by a common set of norms. As this mix of mild religiosity with values supportive of capitalist development mirrored the values of those with political sway as well as of middle-class parents, most Protestants remained willing to entrust the education of their children to the state.

This consensus reigned until the middle of the 20th century, when it was gradually supplemented by ideas that emerged during the Progressive Era (1890s–1920s). The ideas of Darwin, Marx, Freud, and Nietzsche, as well as the courts' increasingly strict interpretation of the doctrine of the separation of church and state, slowly impacted moral education, gradually causing public schools to pull back from moral formation, with many educators returning to the idea that moral education was the responsibility of families and churches. To the degree that moral education remained part of public schooling in the middle of the 20th century, it gradually came to embrace new themes: personal freedom, individual rights, the need for citizenship training, and the idea that rather than being wicked, children were malleable. John Dewey (1916) synthesized many of the new ideas and created a new vision of moral education. Rejecting revealed religion as its foundation, he argued the processes we witness in the natural world also apply to the social world; thus the teaching of morality should be grounded in social experience. Begin with the ideas that children already have about values and then as they are exposed to moral dilemmas teach them a mode of reasoning about making moral decisions. Learning how to respond to the world morally isn't about living according to a fixed set of principles that can always be applied in the same way. Rather it emerges contextually when one engages in activities with others in situations of free communication. For this reason schools should be organized democratically, for by growing within such institutions children's moral development will be maximized.

During the 1960s new questions about people's rights and a new awareness that different groups had conflicting values challenged educators to once again expand their approach to moral education. Excluded groups were demanding equality and access to public spaces. People began to question the individual's moral responsibility to a state that was demanding that they participate in what many considered to be an unjust war in Vietnam. To others it seemed the United States was becoming an immoral nation: the demands by African Americans, women, Native Americans, and youth to be fully included in the public sphere suggested the country was out of control. What appeared to have been lost was respect for the things that those raised in the earlier regime of moral education had been taught constituted the core of morality (i.e., faith in God, patriotism, piety, sobriety, industry, good manners, obedience to authority, etc.).

The initial response to this situation was the creation, in the late 1960s, of the "values clarification" approach. In *Values and Teaching* Louis Raths, Merrill Harmin and Sidney Simon (1966) argued that moral education had to start from an awareness of the fact that everyone has his/her own values, but given the complicity of the times, and the plethora of information about completing values and ideologies, what people needed was practice in choosing between moral alternatives. This situation required a new way of teaching that could help people make decisions and lead more coherent lives.

The Contemporary State of Moral Education

In the 1980s a conservative challenge to the values clarification approach emerged. It grew not only out of a critique of that pedagogy and the political upheavals of the 1960s, but also out of a sense of American decline which was exacerbated by such events as the 1970s oil crises, the 1979 Iranian-U.S. hostage crisis, and the economic recession of the 1980s. Facing apparent decline conservative political leaders focused on the lack of moral education in the schools that they charged liberals had encouraged with their weak values clarification curriculum and other "secular humanist" agendas that devalued faith, patriotism, respect for authority and discipline. The negative effects of this, they argued, were showing up in rising crime rates and declining academic achievement standards (Ryan, 1996).

Out of that critique came new conservative programs of moral education rooted in two different traditions that are critical of modern liberalism. "Neoclassicalists" promote "the traditional virtues of pre-modern Western civilization, especially those embodied in the cultural legacy of the ancient Greeks" (Nash, 1997, 18). They are sympathetic to Aristotle's argument that virtues, like other abilities, are acquired through practice and habit.[5] Whereas Neoclassicalists stress the timeless universality of personal virtues, "Communitarians" emphasize the importance of engaging children actively in the larger society in order to socialize them into the country's consensus on the "civic virtues" necessary to sustain a viable democratic polity. Key communitarian educational theorists are Amitai Etzioni and James Coleman. Another important actor is the Carnegie Foundation that under the leadership of Ernest Boyer (1987) conducted research in the 1970s and 1980s that convinced many that young people must be given opportunities to perform public service in order to avoid becoming excessively inward-looking. The implication for schools was that students should form stronger bonds within schools, and between the school and the surrounding community. Today typically this is done through service learning that provides the opportunity for students to practice activities in their larger communities that can contribute to the development of personal virtue and empathy (Maas Weigert & Crews, 1999).

Twenty years into experimentation with these two approaches to moral education, several criticisms have emerged. A common one is that many programs are superficial and consist of merely cosmetic changes, such as rewriting the school's mission statement. Hence the real goal is behavior modification rather than helping students develop critical thinking or skills to put their values into action. Like similar curricula in previous eras, moral education is an agenda of upper- and middle-class whites who are attempting to impose their values on other classes and/or racial groups. The difference is that in the 19th century the main goal was to create docile workers for the emerging industrial capitalist economy, whereas today the goal is to prevent the lower classes from engaging in activities (e.g., drug abuse, crime, etc.) that actually are symptoms of deindustrialization and create permanent joblessness, intergenerational poverty, and the isolation of whole communities in permanent ghettos of despair.

Robert Nash makes a related observation that: "unlike the founders of the common schools—whose main purposes in advocating 'character' education were based on an optimistic, humanitarian agenda for expanding free, state-subsidized public education to everyone . . .—contemporary character educators are 'declinists.' They believe American culture—and especially education—is in a period of 'near-catastrophic' moral decline and in desperate need of a massive virtue infusion to save them" (1997, 17). So the goal isn't to expand opportunity to more groups within the society but to prevent liberals, big government, feminists, sex educators, and various cultural relativists from sacrificing genuine learning at the altar of political correctness and diversity. The implication is that we are in a struggle between good and evil "for our culture and our children" (Bennett, 1992, 11). The schools are a key battleground in a cultural war, or as William Kilpatrick has stated, the battle for the soul of the United States is "being fought over who is going to define what is permissible and impermissible in speech, conduct, politics, music, art, literature, television and films" (Nash, 1997, 17).

History of Peace Education

Although there are no written records, throughout history human beings have employed community-based peace education strategies to preserve their knowledge of how best to promote security and peace within their group. Rather than killing each other over disputes, they employed nonviolent dispute mechanisms handed down from generation to generation through informal peace education activities. More formal peace education relies upon the written word or instruction through schooling institutions. Perhaps the earliest written guidelines come down to us through the world's great religions. Each provides a vision of peace and a goal towards which human beings should strive. (Ironically, religions also provide the rallying cry for martyrs intent on destroying the followers of other religions. This is indicative of certain ironic and contradictory aspects of moral teaching, i.e., moral values don't provide fixed proscriptions for action.)

The modern peace movement began in Europe and the United States in the nineteenth century after the Napoleonic wars. Progressive intellectuals, politicians, teachers and students formed societies to study the threat of war, the build-up of armaments, possible alternatives to war (e.g., arbitration), and to educate the public in general about the horrors and dangers of war. By the end of the nineteenth century, peace organizations were formed in nearly all European nations. Simultaneously in the United States a similar trend occurred, but the impetus came mainly from the anti-slavery and suffragette movements, Quaker and Unitarian-Universalist religious traditions, and thinkers such as Emerson and Thoreau.

The twentieth century saw considerable growth in peace education efforts and theory. In 1912 a School Peace League had chapters in nearly every U.S. state that was "promoting through the schools...the interests of international justice and fraternity" (Scanlon, 1959, 214). They had ambitious plans to acquaint over 500,000 teachers with the conditions for peace (Stomfay-Stitz, 1993). Likewise, in Europe peace societies lobbied government and held congresses to warn against the horror of modern warfare. Many of these were strong supporters of the League of Nations.

Between the First and Second World Wars, social studies teachers started teaching international relations, so their students wouldn't want to wage war against foreigners with whom they shared many things and thus shouldn't be demonized as enemies deserving of elimination. Convinced that schools had encouraged and enabled war by indoctrinating youth into nationalism, peace educators contributed to a progressive education reform where schools were seen as a means to promote social progress by providing students with an awareness of common humanity that helped break down national stereotypes that led to war. Here the emphasis was upon teaching an understanding of peoples in the world that would develop in the minds of citizens an outlook of tolerance and global awareness that, in turn, would contribute to peace.

Formal Peace Education Programs

The horrors of World War II created a new interest in "Education for World Citizenship" and also led to the creation of the world's first college-level peace studies program, established in 1948 at Manchester College in Indiana. Shortly thereafter, a few intellectuals began research projects designed to create a "science of peace" in order to counteract the science of war. A 1955 manifesto issued by Bertrand Russell and Albert Einstein and signed by other distinguished academics called upon scientists of all political persuasions to assemble to discuss the threat posed to civilization by thermonuclear weapons. These efforts became the foundation of the new academic field of peace studies that blossomed during the 1960s, an era when the world was horrified by atrocities of the U. S. war in Vietnam and very much caught up with the critiques of imperialism.

In the 1980s peace studies saw a huge growth on colleges as a result of alarm about the threatened use of nuclear weapons, raised to a fever pitch by the Cold War, especially during the presidency of Ronald Reagan, that prompted a major response by the U.S. Catholic Conference of Bishops, and grassroots peace groups, such as the Women of Greenham Common in Great Britain, and the SANE and FREEZE movements in the United States. This political climate led to the creation of new courses and programs aimed at promoting global survival, and averting international conflict and the threat of nuclear destruction (Harris & Morrison, 2003).

With the end of the Cold War in 1990, the emphasis of peace studies shifted somewhat and expanded to include formal theories of conflict resolution, the problems of post-conflict societies, and domestic issues. The curriculum of most programs has deepened to include explicit exploration of the structural and cultural roots of direct violence. After the events of September 11, 2001, attention has also been focused on the need to broaden the concept of security. Whereas "national" security once dominated the field, today academics stress the multifaceted nature of security that is operative on the international and personal as well as national level. Thus today peace studies professors are teaching about collective, common, economic, environmental, and comprehensive security and human rights. More broadly the new emphasis reflects a growing commitment to move beyond "negative peace" (i.e., the prevention and cessation of overt, direct violence), to a commitment to flesh out a more holistic conception of "positive peace," which includes the presence of justice and the elimination of all conditions that cause cultural, structural and direct violence.

At the beginning of the 21st century there are over three hundred peace studies programs in colleges and universities in the world (Harris & Shuster, 2006). Educators are now also using conflict resolution and social-emotional literacy to create positive learning climates in primary and secondary schools. Because of the vast diversity in the forms of conflicts that plague human existence, each requiring a unique strategy to address it, individuals disagree about how to achieve security and peace. Peace educators in intense conflicts highlight the costs of war and urge combatants to withdraw from warlike behavior. Peace education in regions of interethnic tension relies upon multiculturalism and awareness about the sufferings of the various groups, 'the other' involved in the conflict, to reduce hostilities. Peace educators in areas free from collective physical violence teach about oppression within that society, explain the causes of domestic and civil violence, and develop a respect for global issues, the challenge of development, environmental sustainability, and the power of nonviolence.

Divergence of Moral Education and Peace Education

Moral education and peace education have the potential to complement one another, for in a peaceful state people will behave morally, and in a moral state people will live in peace. However, the two fields have some fundamental areas of disagreement. A few of the most important differences revolve around their views of the role of the state, ideas about patriotism, conceptions of peace, and the nature of the link between ethics and the functioning of social institutions.

The neoclassicist moral education perspective tacitly assumes an important role for the state and for its authority to control behavior, grounded as it is in the ancient Greek idea that the good society is produced by the existence of the right order in the souls of its citizens, and a right order in the polis. It is virtuous citizens who ensure society will be just. They are best created and guided by strong institutions that assist them in that undertaking. In moral education this classical idea is married to the political theory of classical liberalism upon which the United States is constructed. As originally articulated by Thomas Hobbes (1914), a heavy emphasis upon the state to create peace comes from a negative view of humans as selfish creatures who are cruel and capable of great brutality. Hence we need a strong state to force us to respect the rights of all. Even in its milder forms, as articulated by John Locke (1996) and Jean-Jacques Rousseau (1997), human beings give up the freedoms they supposedly have in the state of nature in order to join civil society and benefit from the security provided by a state. This social contract amounts to an agreement to pay taxes and abide by the state's laws and policies, in exchange for police protection, a court system, and national security against an anarchic international order. Communitarian moral educators concur with this vision and seek to educate students into active and effective participation in a democratic form of this arrangement, which they think is best guaranteed by also having strong intermediary institutions (the family, civic associations, churches, etc.) that can check the state if it heads in the wrong direction.

Many peace educators start from some of the same assumptions but differ from moral educators on at least three critical counts. First, peace educators have a more optimistic view of the human potential for personal transformation and the capacity for love and forgiveness, and of our intellectual abilities to construct alternative social arrangements capable of creating a just and lasting peace. They can construct these systems, as Immanuel Kant pointed out in *Perpetual Peace,* without positing the existence of God. Those interested in promoting peace argue that the same logic that undergirds the construction of democratic national polities can also be used to construct an international legal and institutional framework that can contribute to the nonviolent resolution of conflicts globally. In this they put principles of universalism before the interests of nations, which is consistent with a universalist ethic about the sanctity of all human life, irrespective of national status. A second, and more recent development is that peace scholars, while recognizing the importance of the rule of law and state institutions in providing for the peaceful resolution of many conflicts, also view all powerful institutions, especially the state, through a lens of power and hence assume that in the process of promoting the interests of the powerful, the fate of the weak and excluded is frequently forgotten, or worse, actively and violently negated. Thus, peace educators seek to instill in their students a critical and questioning stance toward institutions of authority.

Another divergence between moral and peace education has to do with disagreements about the strategies that can be used to advance peace. People who believe that peace comes primarily from powerful institutions, are more likely to endorse "peace through strength" strategies that rely upon armed forces and police. In contrast, peace educators point out that a genuine and lasting social order and positive peace are a function of the underlying justness of social arrangements, both within nation-states and globally. Peace educators are, therefore, often critical of state-run interventions to keep the peace, a conviction that is strengthened by their research into widespread police brutality, unfairness in the court systems, problems that stem from systemic racism and sexism, and the unjustness of wars carried out by states. As a result, they advocate for "peace through justice and fairness," with the needs of all concerned parties equally considered.

These two attitudes toward the state lead to different views about the nature of patriotism and to different assessments of its importance as a civic virtue. Whereas traditional patriotism is extolled as a central and essential virtue by William Bennett and other neoclassical moral educators, peace educators are skeptical about patriotism because of its close relationship to nationalism and militarism. Historians have amply demonstrated that nationalist sentiments contributed mightily to wars. Feelings of national superiority that adhere to patriotism promote ethnocentrism and tend to divide humans into categories where those who embrace the homeland see themselves as superior to others and even use that superiority to justify violence against or even extermination of others who belong to minority groups, i.e., Jews in Germany, Tutsis in Rwanda, Blacks and Native Americans in the U.S.A., etc. Nationalist values undermine a universalistic approach to the equal moral worth of all people. A commitment to militarism, a set of attitudes and social arrangements that positively regard war as the best means to provide national security, is based upon authoritarianism and military values that help legitimize the use of force and war.

In short, many of the differences between the two literatures center around conflicting views of what people consider the essential aspects of public morality that are needed to maintain a functioning democracy, and beyond that, to differences as to how one should value the nation relative to other groups in the world. Are patriotism and nationalism virtues that require blind obedience and conformity, or do they demand critical distance and questioning? Does the importance of group solidarity give one license to do whatever is necessary to secure what the leaders say are in its interest? Is diversity something to be overcome by imposing conformity, or is it something to be embraced by learning more constructive and nonviolent methods of conflict resolution?

Finally, there is the issue of the nature of the relationship of ethics to the social structure. This is a question about whether the latter is merely the function of the behavior of individuals, which can be changed by instilling a strong moral education in children to counter their violent and selfish tendencies (which are the cause of disorder and violence in the world), or whether the root problems of violence lie rather in broader social forces and institutions which act according to the dynamics of power, unpredictable feedback loops, and complex interests that are not easily controlled by a virtuous individual acting alone? In other words, argue peace educators, the struggle to create a just and peaceful society must take place not only at the individual level but also at the level of the larger society and international levels.

Convergence of Moral Education and Peace Education

Although the above differences are very important, peace educators and moral educators agree children need to be raised in an environment that allows for the full development of their potential to become ethical, loving human beings who contribute positively to society. The two fields share a belief in the importance of providing situations that provoke an expanded view of morality, critical thinking skills and opportunities for real world problem solving.

Both schools endorse the importance of young people learning certain civic virtues that are necessary to live in harmony (courage, civility, friendship, kindness, loyalty to parent, friends and family, honesty, responsibly, obligation to help others, respect for property rights), awareness that some actions are always immoral (treachery, betrayal, stealing, violence toward the innocent), and the traditional religious virtues of prudence, justice, temperance, fortitude, faith, hope, piety, charity, and duty. Both agree we should live according to the golden rule. Peace educators also teach how to question dominant narratives and civic courage to challenge the status quo, a commitment to social justice, compassion for the suffering of others, multicultural sensitivity, and a democratic disposition.

Both would prefer children to develop moral skills in the family. Distinguished peacemaker, Elise Boulding, saw the family as a crucible in which children could learn skills that enhanced moral thinking and behavior. Women who were ignored in the marketplace and the political world had a special power in the family, where they used their caring abilities to nurture other family members. In *One Small Plot of Heaven: Reflections of Quaker Life by a Quaker Sociologist* (1989), Boulding argued families are sites where peacemaking skills like negotiating, listening, problem solving, and conflict resolution can be learned. However, it is also the case that many families are shattered or violent. In the case of dysfunctional families, children need the opportunity to learn moral behavior within a school setting.

Both peace educators and moral educators are committed to a more ambitious agenda than many other teachers in that both seek to develop not only the cognitive and theoretical abilities of their students but also their desire and ability to act in wise and moral ways to maintain and/or change society. Thus both see the need to teach formal theories of ethics and provide opportunities to practice the implication of those theories using praxis-oriented and interactive pedagogies (i.e., peer learning, service learning, case studies, study away, etc.) that give students experience in navigating the difficult waters of ethical decision making. This can be further advanced by introducing students to "moral exemplars," i.e., real people who acted out virtuously to improve their communities and by creating a sense of community within schools and between the school and the larger community. Such pedagogy and curriculum enhance students' feelings of empathy and sympathy and their prosocial skills of helping and service.

Both groups also share a belief in the importance of using stories that reinforce civil virtues. However, at times they disagree about which stories to tell, based on differences in their views about which social relations are legitimated in the stories and whose histories are highlighted or excluded, with peace educators very sensitive to stories that inadvertently continue legacies of patriarchy, colonialism, racism, and other forms of oppression. The last point is related to the fact that both groups accept the idea that there is always a "hidden curriculum" at work in all educational institutions, both in the structure of the institution and its policies, and in the materials used to teach history and the literature (i.e., the texts always convey more than mere facts and are often chosen for their more subtle lessons).

Finally, both groups agree with the views of psychological researchers of cognitive moral development that critical thinking plays an important role in moral reasoning. "In order to engage in one's own thinking on any issue it is necessary to possess as wide an understanding of that issue, and indeed, of all relevant and related issues, as it is possible to gain as a basis for a critical analysis and review of the opinions held by others" (Downey and Kelly, 1978, 17). They share an appreciation for how moral thinking develops in certain stages and understand that people spend their lives learning the skills that lead to moral and peaceful behavior. Thus, they use a developmental schema to explain the progression of moral and peaceful behavior throughout the life span. Lawrence Kohlberg's (1978) stages of moral reasoning serve as a template[6]:

STAGE	APPROXIMATE AGE	CHARACTERISTICS
Preconventional	Young children	Judgments based on own needs and perceptions and on the physical power of rule makers
Conventional	Adolescence	Judgment based on social expectations and the belief that one must be loyal to one's family, group, or nation, and maintain the social order
Postconventional	Adulthood	Judgment based on principles that go beyond specific laws or the authority of people who make the laws

The above schema has been criticized by feminists, among others, who argue it negates women's experience and the importance of caring. Carol Gilligan (1982) argues that conceptions of care become more sophisticated as a child matures, going from care of self, to care of family, friends, strangers, and ultimately to a universalized caring commitment to nonviolence. Like Kohlberg, Gilligan does not believe everybody develops the fullest moral perspectives. Some people spend their whole lives in pre-conventional stages and go through life thinking only about how fairly or unfairly they are being treated. They never reach a stage where they are concerned about the tremendous suffering of people in the war zones of Iraq, Afghanistan, Darfur, and the Congo or the kinds of suffering produced by inequality and oppression that many people experience in America's inner cities and remote rural areas. In Gilligan's work, care becomes a universal obligation because the self is understood in relational terms, not as an isolated individual. From that logic it can be argued nonviolence, involving an injunction against the hurting of all others, is elevated to a position governing all moral judgment and action. The task peace education sets for itself is to develop pedagogies and curriculum to help move as many students as possible to this kind of awareness and give them the capacity to take action.

Thus peace educators would argue Kohlberg's schema must be reconfigured to reflect a progression in how an individual develops a commitment to nonviolence:

STAGE	APPROXIMATE AGE	CHARACTERISTICS
Preconventional	Young children	Judgment based self awareness, how fairly he/she is being treated; based upon parents behavior and interpersonal relations
Conventional	Adolescence	International awareness and ecological concern. Where do I fit into a violent world?
Postconventional	Adulthood	Judgment based on empathy for others; respond nonviolently; wanting to leave a better future

The first stage is oriented toward individual survival. At this stage, morality is seen in terms of self-centered responses to sanctions imposed by society. People grow out of this stage as they move from selfishness toward responsibility, with an increased attachment to others and a growing awareness that others feel pain and can suffer injustices. The second stage involves the increased social participation of an individual toward a morality based more on shared norms and expectations and is manifested in an increased capacity for caring. The highest stage in this schema involves Carol Gilligan's morality of caring and responsibility that depends upon nonviolence and an awareness of a deep interconnectedness of all life. This is in contrast to Kohlberg's morality of justice and rights, which is based on the principle of the equality of (separate) individuals.

Conclusion

In 2007, at a PeaceJam conference in Boulder, Colorado, the Dalai Lama and Archbishop Desmond Tutu jointly made the case that in the middle of the 20th century educators undertook the research and experimentation necessary to create more effective pedagogies and curriculum materials that allowed schools to become more effective at teaching children to read, to do math, and to internalize a scientific approach to knowledge acquisition and creation. This concerted effort has paid off in many advances in science and technology from which people around the world benefit daily, through better nutrition and health care and in the development of a myriad of devices that make our lives more comfortable, productive, and interesting. They went on to argue that the challenge facing education today is to undertake serious research and experimentation that will allow us to do a better job of "educating the hearts" of the next generation. As alluded to in this chapter, serious work on this problem is now underway by psychological researchers working on processes of cognitive moral development, by moral educators who are trying to create curriculum to develop the moral sensibilities of children, and by peace scholars and educators who struggle with how to link individual moral development to the creation of more just and virtuous institutions, practices, and systems. And additional work is being done by those promoting human rights education. Each group is bringing different concerns and issues to this important discussion upon which the shape of our world's future depends. Keeping a critical dialogue going between the different approaches will accelerate progress toward this most important goal.

Notes

1. U.S. history is littered with such acts of aggression towards other people and countries that never perpetrated any aggression against this country, and in each case the act has always been justified using moral language. The same is true for other countries and warlords who have pursued resources and other advantages beyond their own borders.
2. Bush's vice president, Dick Cheney, justified these aggressions as "preventive deterrence."
3. This is a democratic perspective on morals. Some would say that values and morals come through the inspiration of divine beings and are reflected in church teaching.
4. *Pax Romana* is a Roman version of peace expressed as "if you want peace, prepare for war" as opposed to a Buddhist approach to peace of "if you want peace practice nonviolence."
5. The criticism of this neoclassicalist position is that the historically championed moral values (e.g. chastity, honesty, bravery, etc.) don't have fixed meanings because each expressed a connection to objects, relationships,

and institutions that are in flux. Thus, traditional pedagogies that demand rigid conformity and rote memorization are fundamentally flawed.

6. Lawrence Kohlberg rejected the focus on virtues valued by the neoclassicists mentioned earlier above. Instead he follows Piaget in describing moral development as a hierarchy of moral choices leading from the self-centered thinking of young children to the incorporation of more abstract or socially defined rules that ultimately result in a complex and universalistic conception of justice. These stages describe how people organize their understanding of virtues, rules, and norms and integrate these when making moral choices (Kohlberg, 1978). In addition, he rejected the relativist viewpoint promoted by the values clarification school in favor of the view that certain principles of justice and fairness represent the pinnacle of moral maturity. The morally educated person, according to Kohlberg has learned to reflect upon a moral problem that arises in a social setting, to consider alternatives, reach a conclusion based upon principles of justice, and act upon that problem.

References

Bennett, W. J. 1995. *The Moral Compass*. New York: Simon & Schuster.

Bennett, W. J. 1993. *The Book of Virtues: A Treasury of Great Moral Stories*. New York: Simon & Schuster.

Bennett, William J. ed. 1997. *Our Sacred Honor: Words of Advice from the Founders in Stories, Letters, Poems, and Speeches*. New York: Simon & Schuster.

Bennett, W. J. 1992. *The De-Valuing of America: The Fight for Our Culture and Our Children*. New York: Summit.

Bloom, A. 1997. *The Closing of the American Mind*. New York: Simon and Schuster.

Boulding, E. 1989. *One Small Plot of Heaven*: *Reflections of Quaker Life by a Quaker Sociologist*. Wallingford, PA: Pendle Hill.

Boyer, E. 1987/1983. *High School: A Report on Secondary Education in America*. New York: Harper & Row.

Dewey, J. 1916. *Democracy and Education*. New York: Macmillan.

Downey, M., & A. Kelly. 1978. *Moral Education: Theory and Practice*. London: Harper & Row.

Eisenberg, Nancy, 1998. Contemporaneous and Longitudinal Prediction of Children's Sympathy from Dispositional Regulation and Emotionality. *Developmental Psychology:* 34:5 (September) 910–924.

Gilligan, C. 1982. *In a Different Voice: Psychological Theory and Women's Development*. Cambridge: Harvard University Press.

Harris, I., & M.L. Morrison. 2003. *Peace Education,* 2nd edition. Jefferson, NC: McFarland.

Harris, I., & A. Shuster. 2006. *Global Directory of Peace Studies and Conflict Resolution Programs*. San Francisco: Peace and Justice Studies Association.

Higgins-D'Alessandro, Ann. 2005. The Importance of Evidence-based Evaluation in Character Education and a Brief History of Character and Moral Education in the United States. Talk given at the Office of Safe and Drug-Free Schools Partnerships in Character Education Program Annual Grantee Meeting Sponsored by the U.S. Department of Education, October 19.

Hobbes, T. 1914. *Leviathan*. London: Dent.

Hunter, J. D. 2000. *The Death of Character: Moral Education in an Age Without Good or Evil*. New York: Basic Books.

Kant, I. 1939. *Perpetual Peace*. New York: Columbia University Press.

Kohlberg, L. 1978. Revisions in the Theory and Practice of Moral Development. In C. S. Beck, B. Crittendon, and E. Sullivan, Eds. *New Directions for Child Development: Moral Education No 2*. San Francisco: Jossey-Bass.

Locke, J. 1996. *An Essay Concerning Human Understanding*. Indianapolis, IN : Hackett.

Maas Weigert, K., & R. Crews. 1999. *Teaching for Justice: Concepts and Models for Service Learning in Peace Studies*. Washington, DC: American Association for Higher Education.

Nash, R. J. 1997. *Answering the "Virtuecrats": A Moral Conversation on Character Education*. New York: Teachers College Press.

Raths, L., M. Harmin, & S. Simon. 1966. *Values and Teaching*. Columbus, OH: C. E. Merrill.

Rousseau, J. J. 1997. *The Social Contract and Other Later Political Writings*. Cambridge, UK: Cambridge University Press.

Ryan, Kevin. 1996. Moral Education—A Brief History of Moral Education, the Return of Character Education, Current Approaches to Moral Education—Schools, Students, and School. http://education.stateuniversity.com/pages/2246/ Moral-Education.html *Encyclopedia of Education*. The Gale Group, Inc. Retrieved 8/22/2010.

Scanlon, D. 1959. The Pioneers of International Education: 1817–1914. *Teacher's College Record* (4): 210–219.

Stomfay-Stitz, A. 1993. *Peace Education in America, 1828–1990, Source Book for Education and Research.* Metuchen, NJ: Scarecrow.

CHAPTER THIRTY-ONE

Earth's Role in Ethical Discourse and Functional Scientific Literacy

MICHAEL P. MUELLER, DANA L. ZEIDLER, & LYNDA L. JENKINS

One final paragraph of advice: Do not burn yourself out. Be…a reluctant enthusiast…a part time crusader, a half-hearted fanatic. Save the other half of yourselves and your lives for pleasure and adventure. It is not enough to fight for the land; it is even more important to enjoy it.…So get out there and mess around with your friends, ramble out yonder and explore the forests, encounter the grizz, climb the mountains. Run the rivers, breathe deep of that yet sweet and lucid air, sit quietly for a while and contemplate the precious still-ness, that lovely, mysterious and awesome space. Enjoy yourselves, keep your brain in your head and your head firmly attached to your body, the body active and alive, and I promise you this much: I promise you this one sweet victory over our enemies, over those deskbound people with their hearts in a safe deposit box and their eyes hypnotized by desk calculators. I promise you this: you will outlive the fools.

EDWARD ABBEY, 1927–1989

Introduction

Might we enjoy becoming a community of eco-activists, as Abbey suggested, by first recogniz-ing Earth's role in ethical discourse? Are there good reasons for thinking about Earth in this way? In this chapter we discuss one novel conceptualization of scientific literacy and how it relates to other conceptualizations in the science education and related research literature. We will argue why contemporary science education should include socio-scientific issues (SSI) to stimulate ethi-cal aptitude and moral inclination. Equally, if not more importantly, this chapter cultivates new ground for environmental and science education by acknowledging Earth's role in the analysis of socio-sci-entific issues. To elaborate this role for Earth more fully, as an educational context for discussion, we will address the SSI of North American pollinator decline (the loss of bees), which is a critical problem facing humanity and one of many indicators related to climate change. We have integrated ecojustice ethics through SSI to further analyze this trend.

This chapter highlights what many people take for granted in their daily lives—the natural systems. The idea of where we place our attention is significant for advancing SSI in educational theory and for influencing where teachers and students focus their attention when thinking through ethical issues situated in the environment. Sometimes, important aspects of SSI may be deemphasized or ignored and thus will be more easily obscured. But the Earth (whether it be air, water, or temperature) constantly influences our epistemological understandings of functional scientific literacy (SL). "In the realm of SSI, functional SL means that experience with social justice, tolerance for dissenting voices, mutual respect for cultural differences, and making evidence-based decisions with consideration for how those actions may impact one's community and the larger environment, must be provided for students" (Zeidler and Sadler, 2011, p. 179).

An Expanded View of Scientific Literacy

Writ large in the National Science Education Standards (National Research Council [NRC], 1996), scientific habits of mind are clearly recognized as what is necessary to become economically viable within the U.S. as well as effectively compete in a global economy (Committee on Science, Engineering, and Public Policy, 2007; Roberts, 2007; Mueller and Bentley, 2007). How much time is left for developing the kind of knowledge needed to foster happier and healthier communities and environments? How much is this school education worth? For example, within the purview of National (Science) Standards Documents (e.g., NRC), there is very little to inform an epistemological stance about moral-ethical choices in schooling. Therein lies the challenge of thinking beyond schooling and science or what has been described functional SL (Mueller and Zeidler, 2010; Zeidler and Keefer, 2006; Zeidler, Sadler, Simmons and Howes, 2005). Functional scientific literacy, put forward in a conceptual framework for SSI, considers the psychological, social and emotive growth of students and provides opportunities to understand issues from multiple perspectives. In SSI, functional SL embodies experiences with fairness, tolerance, dissenting voices, cultural differences and the enhancement of evidence-based choices, particularly within the constraints of how those decisions will impact the Earth.

An integrative or transformative (Eames, 1977) view of functional scientific literacy enables students to build on shared community and cultural ideas in their environmental using SSI as a context for evaluating emerging concerns in society. Integrative learning also resonates with the kind of practice that has been traditionally supported within science education policy. What *integrative* means for science education is that the field will become more inclusive and tolerant of an interdisciplinary venue of activities, both formal and informal, as science-learning context. Learning biological concepts such as 'ecological niche,' will have little impact on the ways that youth will need to be guided through an analysis of future choices, predicting outcomes and carrying them out in their daily lives if students' educative experiences are exclusively confined inside the classroom walls—disassociated from the world around them. When students see their own lives as indistinguishable from the shared ecological niche they occupy, they will begin to recognize the moral reciprocity with nature that becomes an ethical ideal to strive for. Through school, they develop and strive for ecological integrity concurrently.

Why begin with ethical discourse?

There is an interesting literature base for how to engage students with SSI, but there is really no explicit suggestion that ethical discourse of moral considerations might be the *most* appropriate starting point—prior to learning science content knowledge—to cultivate SSI intrigue. Consider ethical discourse as the doorway into not only SSI but a conceptual understanding of science. Think about how people quickly learn to fix cars, raise backyard chickens, or even surf! These things are learned because of an incredible desire to do them—and moral intrigue drives knowing (e.g., most who learn a martial art do so not with the expectation of facing a life-threatening fight; rather they do so with the fundamental expectation of acquiring self-knowledge). Consider youth who initiate eco-activism associated with changes in city policy (Coburn, 2006)—just imagine how sensitive young children are to even the slightest changes in environmental toxicity and particulate matter. This acute sensitivity is one way the way the Earth plays a very strong role in awakening youth from sleepwalking through community and environmental changes.

If becoming more attuned to and adapted (or adjusted) to necessary changes for human survival involves making changes that individuals would not otherwise want to make, then it follows that the Earth has already influenced significant changes in our behavior for thousands of years. Got oil? Got clean water? Some people may not be convinced until they have no choice other than to give up their way of living and consuming, especially with an increasing reliance on the market to meet basic needs. What happens when the market can no longer provide for or support all societies' needs—for example, the tragic events following Hurricane Katrina. Several preconditions are necessary for individuals to share responsibility for these things.

1. Science is something that all citizens of the world can contribute to through participatory democracy.
2. Multiple stakeholders with diverse views increase degrees of confidence in choices.
3. Youth are already part of the community.
4. Youth may be more sensitive to community and environmental changes and should therefore serve some role in community policy.
5. Youth may be attracted to exploring nature and ecosystems.
6. Youth can be trusted for their data when scientists and teachers play an active role in guiding their investigations and inquiry.
7. Diverse knowledge of the community and environment needs to be emphasized for youth, or it is highly plausible it will be eroded away without some sort of records.
8. With diverse knowledge of the community and environment, citizens are more likely to be consulted for what they know. They become community or ecological experts (motivation for learning may also become reciprocal and enhanced as the result).
9. Without this geographic (community and environmental) knowledge, citizens will not know their surroundings well enough to decipher when they are degraded or when they need to consider appropriate actions.
10. Lastly, the matter of data acquisition needs to be explained in such a way that citizens can gain meaningful knowledge and involvement (Mueller and Tippins, in press).

The "preconditions" listed above for school sciences align well with functional scientific literacy and new efforts to move schooling in the direction of civic responsibility and participatory democracy. Recently, educational research focused on academic measures such as testing priorities, civic responsibility as well as participatory democracy demonstrates overwhelmingly that testing has very little to do with whether individuals will share responsibility for the places in which they live (Kahne and

Sporte, 2008; Lleras, 2008). Unless we specifically emphasize ethical discourse in science education, it is not likely to be accepted in the vast majority of public schools in the U.S. To make this point clearer, we will now apply a case demonstrated through a focus on honeybees to argue for the practice of moral reasoning in SSI, which will then be elaborated further in terms of ecojustice, fairness and culpability for teachers.

Moral Choices and Ethical Discourse within the SSI of Declining Honeybees

In the case of bees, we can select and hybridize more aggressive bees with less aggressive bees to solve the most prevalent problems now associated with colony collapse disorder (CCD) in the news. This means taking the Africanized species of honeybee now entering the U.S. at increasing rates and crossing them with western or eastern honeybees, so they will resist harmful mites and fungi. Not too many people like this idea because they associate Africanized bees with behavior that is much too aggressive and dangerous for humans and livestock. Ask any beekeeper if they would prefer to keep the Africanized honeybees in their local hives, and the answer will surely be 'no.' Their explanation will focus on the increasing risk or liabilities that they would have to face as a consequence of keeping Africanized honeybees. In other words, we can select to hybridize aggressive bees with less aggressive bees in order to achieve the least harmful pollinators, or we might modify a plant to resist chemicals that are good for killing weeds but harm bees at the cost of interfering with a vital synchronism of dance steps used to communicate amongst eusocial insects. Thus, there are moral choices that are implicit in the ethical discourse of why we may choose to modify bees.

This question of moral choices in cases of genetically modifying or hybridizing organisms possesses interesting moral dilemmas for citizens of the world, especially when these choices are not specifically regulated by agencies such as the Environmental Protection Agency. There may be obvious consequences such as the decline of important pollinators in the U.S., but also not so obvious consequences that relate to or are analogous to pollinators worldwide. Clearly the idea of engaging youth in SSI has far-reaching influences that may resonate for young citizens later in life, when they are increasingly faced with choices which include considerations of beauty, strength, justice, fairness and humanity, to name a few (Mueller and Zeidler, 2010).

Honey has healing properties that have been well known for millennia. Bees support more than 240,000 crop species in the United States alone and many more worldwide (NRC, 2007). These crops are used for medicine, food, clothing, housing, and so forth. Bees provide billions of dollars of free services to meet human needs. This process has been described as "natural capital" or ecological services and comprises the ways in which nature is recognized to support human survival. For example, honeybees pollinate much of our food crops. When humans have tried to replace pollinators' natural services such as that of eastern honeybees, it has been at enormous cost when compared with keeping bees around for a long time (Benjamin and McCallum, 2009):

> The mountains of southern Sichuan in China are covered in pear trees. Every April, they are home to a rare sight: thousands of people holding bamboo sticks with chicken feathers attached to the end, clambering among the blossom-laden branches. Closer inspection reveals that children, parents and even grandparents are all pollinating trees by hand. It is a ritual they have been following for more than 20 years, ever since pesticides killed their honeybees. (p. 239)

As one can ascertain, a world without bees requires a very labor-intensive human endeavor equivalent with the loss of many luxury foods, products, and services which now are taken for granted on a daily basis. Benjamin and McCallum (2009) suggest honeybee services equate to a $90 billion business in the U.S. alone. In particular, many people's livelihoods and lifestyles would be significantly and adversely affected by a world without western honeybees. While wind pollination accounts for corn products that are widely used in virtually all produce we purchase at the supermarket today (even baby diapers!), bees enhance the yield. However, there is a downward trajectory of interest in honeybees, which is a moral choice affecting many. Fewer and fewer people are keeping and managing bee hives in the U.S., despite the increasing truckloads of bees shipped across the nation to serve in pollination efforts of food crops such as California almonds and southern pecans. Urban and rural people visit grocery stores and may not even know about the hidden services that western honeybees defray.

Anyone who keeps a garden will notice the buzzing noises of pollinators. If the garden is sprayed with pesticides, bees are much less likely to be present at those gardens, and there will be little 'buzz about them,' as noted environmentalist Rachel Carson (1962) reminded us. Carson imagined a world without bees long ago. She imagined the absence of spring noises along with fruitless autumn trees and the lack of fall harvests in her famous book, *Silent Spring*. She brought early nationwide attention to the loss of crucial insects that support human livelihoods. Although she was an early pioneer of moral aptitude, what has been Carson's influence in science education? The NRC (2007) suggests that pollinator declines are not a new problem. They have been monitored for some time now. Many of us, however, do not take an active interest in the things that do not seem to cause an immediate shake up of our preferred lifestyle. Will it take a significant change in the food offerings of supermarkets to stimulate some interest for colony collapse disorder, a significant problem for western honeybees? What could replace the alfalfa feed for cattle, apples, almonds, cotton, citrus fruits, soya beans, onions, broccoli, carrots, sunflowers, melons, blueberries, cherries, and pumpkins attached to so many cultural traditions, events and lifestyles that we are accustomed to now?

For now, it is enough to say that this particular topic can also be approached by reference to the students' pocketbooks—as western honeybee declines will equate with very expensive and exclusive food choices for those who can afford them. For example, with honeybee decline, honey, bacon, steak, most vegetables, cheese, milk and ice cream (with the exception of varieties of these products where alfalfa grown for cattle feed is not a consideration) could become high-status food stuffs because of the engineering needed for pollination efforts. Some coffee would not be affected, but with decreased yields by honeybees, the prevalence of coffee would decline. Only the most affluent could afford to drink coffee along with fast foods—the often vegetable-oiled White Castle or McDonald's French fries sold in the billions worldwide. This is an ironic dilemma considering the health risks associated with eating fast food cooked in greasy oil! The Earth's role in our reasoning can become quite salient when it is linked with unhealthy lifestyles.

Developing epistemic practice with ethical discourse

Benjamin and McCallum (2009) say that without the small number of apiarists (beekeepers) keeping hives across the country, western honeybees would succumb to the vulnerabilities associated with diseases, mites, pesticides and other forms of environmental degradation. Eastern honeybees and solitary pollinator species would be too few in number to handle the pollination needs (or wants) of the middle-class lifestyles enjoyed by the vast majority of people in the U.S. Beekeepers are frustrated with what seem to be insurmountable challenges in North America with genetically modified crops and urban sprawl and development encroaching on honeybee habitats. CCD is not well understood, and this disorder leaves thriving apiarists with frustration and abandoned hives for the moral decisions being made constantly by individual consumers who choose with their wallets at the grocery store. When people make choices to eat foods that are often grown with industrial agricultural practices that compound problems with CCD, consumers are directly linked to the outcomes. But think about what people could do if educated to recognize and resolve the problems associated with CCD. Do individuals now graduating from high school have enough epistemic practice with decision making to be able to recognize when honeybees decline? On the other hand, why do we need to concern ourselves with the plight of the western honeybee at all? It seems taken for granted in the increasing research on declining honeybees that the consequences are a bad thing for humans and thus should also be taken as a given within SSI. Consider also that western honeybees were imported to the U.S. with western colonization. If we emphasize the value of the services provided to us through the pollination of our food crops, then perhaps it will be simpler to focus our attention on solving this issue with technology, particularly since many people already have inherent trust in solving problems with technology.

Because we need our crops pollinated, if we cannot depend on the honeybee to do the job, then we will simply need to engineer an alternative technology. We always have and will always be able to eventually develop a technology or modify existing agricultural resources to meet our demands. Is moral reasoning needed here? The point becomes clearer when we think about whether or not to develop, say, a nano-sized technology or a robot bee to do our bidding. Is this idea too far-fetched? Already, modern technology has made possible the replacement of human arms, legs and internal organs. There is no reason to deny the development of robot bees in the near future. Flying insects are already used by the military for covert surveillance, and the possibility of flying robots for pollination could be quite an appealing prospect considering the billion dollar revenues the stakeholders would receive.

Moreover, these robot bees will be much less vulnerable to environmental chemicals, and people will not have to change the lifestyles they have grown so accustomed to. Most industrial agricultural practices based on technologies such as genetic modification of plants and animals or pesticide use would continue to flourish. But would robots be able to readily fill the niche of the western honeybee or the many other pollinators contemplated by robot creators? There are certainly other environmental benefits (such as the painful sting) that may go unnoticed by the majority of us and probably welcomed by those allergic to bee venom.

Is it ethical and responsible to dismiss the painful sting, which plays a role in shaping cultural development around living with bees and other natural organisms? While some individuals may eagerly envision the time when they can venture outdoors without worrying about hornet nests or about a honeybee sting, there are scientists who study the scientific compounds released by bee stings as a treatment for arthritis and related ailments. What about these researchers?

Today's youth seem so complacent about technology in schools that they may not even consider engaging in ethical discourse about this topic. After all, they have better things to do such as texting, sexting, email, and blissfully employing the other digital technologies that fill their lives. The harsh reality for youth is that if we continue to teach science in a decontextualized way, then they will have little to no opportunity to engage in the kind of critical discourse necessary for the evaluation of this and related topics.

Benjamin and McCallum (2009) provide a bold claim, which is supported throughout their book with extensive interviews of apiarists, pesticide companies, and farmers, that "we [sic] are the ones killing the honeybee through ignorance, unsustainable agricultural practices and dangerous use of chemicals. Urgent change is needed. But can we achieve it?" (p. 270). Maybe "we" refers to those of us who live consumed by ignorance, unsustainable agriculture and dangerous toxins. Not everyone is living with the Earth in this way. There are many moral choices that could be gleaned by just examining honeybee decline as an example of a crisis situation. But there is also something to be learned from understanding the ways in which longer-dwelling communities of people (e.g., Pima, Apache, and the Diné) have treated their lands with moral reciprocity. This is where we delve further into the Earth's role for SSI and ethical discourse.

Moral Responsibility for Educators

There is a larger, more philosophical discussion that could be engaged with regard to whether the Earth can play a role in the analysis of SSI. The Earth, obviously, is not a sentient being and cannot reason in the ways that human beings reason. But environmental philosophers such as Peter Singer (2006) and others have championed the idea of extending our moral responsibility to nonhuman animals, and the more enlarged ethical perspective is that we are embedded within ecosystems that sustain our ability to interpret Earth's natural history, which is part of our moral aptitude (Sterba, 2001). We come face to face with ethical decisions concerning the earth when we ignore nature's presence by investing in unnecessary luxury items instead of living in harmony with the Earth. One example of such a luxury item is "pesticide" that delivers a lethal toxin to "weeds." But pesticides also create disturbances in the rhythmic dances of western honeybee conversations. Some scientists have argued that CCD is a consequence of the use of industrial agricultural chemicals. If declines for the western honeybee are indeed occurring and humans play a large role in this, then it follows that we ought to act with due diligence and strive to repair our moral understanding of pesticide and industrial agricultural practices. The morals implicit within SSI ethical dialogues have a great deal to do with moral-ethical restitution and environmental resolution for the bees when guided by ethical principles (Mueller, 2009). Selecting SSI and ethical discourse constitutes a moral responsibility for science teachers.

In the field of science education, the Earth has not always played a role in ethical discourse, and with few exceptions in the educational literature, moral reasoning is not often advocated and repositioned as essential to epistemic development. But what justification exists for expanding such pursuits in schooling now? Ecojustice theory (Mueller, 2009; Mueller and Zeidler, 2010) through SSI and functional SL offers one way of demonstrating these justifications. Ecojustice theory helps us to deal with ethics and morals embedded within SSI, particularly as they connect to our environment. It strives for a holistic balance between the needs of cultural systems and the conservation of cultural diversity and the needs of environmental species and habitats. In our exemplar for this chapter, we have demonstrated some of the possible moral considerations in the case of declining western honeybees in North America and why we ought to act in a way that tends to develop the well-being of both human or cultural systems and environmental systems in an integrated manner.

Objections continue to be raised in regard to projected plans for reversing the honeybee declines. For example, because cattle for beef production are currently fed corn rather than alfalfa, why is there an emphasis on the loss of alfalfa for livestock feed? Corn is mostly wind pollinated and, although honeybees increase the yield of corn to some degree, they are not essential to corn production for cattle feed. This is where ethics and morals have to be consulted very carefully. From a scientific standpoint, cattle are ruminant grazers; they do not normally include corn in their diets. As a result of this human-induced change to their diet, they experience numerous health problems prior to being slaughtered. What would happen to our beef industry if cows were returned to a grass-based diet, but the honey bees were no longer present to pollinate the grasses?

Again, let's return to humans for a moment and focus on cultural livelihoods, traditions and practices surrounding foods that are pollinated by western honeybees. Every October, U.S. children ransack the streets in costumes searching for candy and making scary Jack-O-Lanterns. This cultural event would not be complete without the pumpkin crop that is associated with so many of our cultural memories as children trick-or-treating in the neighborhood. Consider further, all of the cultural traditions associated with gardening, seed saving, canning, and caring for cattle that would be lost with the western honeybee. These activities all save money and protect diversity. They have large-scale implications for significantly lessening our carbon footprint on the Earth. As people become more and more dependent on the market and we see exponential increases of multibillion consumer habits emerging, youth become less reliant on personal connections with their environment. In their world, and arguably the world of their parents, there is little need to understand gardening or farming because some hidden distant entity is taking care of this for them. In many ways, this lack of community reliance and dependence on the Earth to support basic needs is at the very heart of the need for ethical discourse concerning western honeybee declines.

Perhaps even a more pressing social justice concern is whether everyone will share access to basic foods. The possibility that some people will not be able to afford food when they are dependent on the market to provide for their basic needs is a serious moral concern. Is it fair that only the affluent would actually be able to purchase some products if hand pollination is needed to replace what the honey bee now does at no human or environmental cost? It is interesting to think about whether people would toil at or become happily engaged in the painstaking work associated with hand pollination. With damaging pesticides now found at twenty times their toxicity to honeybees in urban landscapes, Benjamin and McCallum (2009) suggest that perhaps the Earth is trying to tell us something here. As students in science courses do not usually have much control over which facts and subjects they study and usually take them at face value, they will feel more autonomy in investigating the moral aspects of these issues and will share some degree of responsibility for the health of their community and environment if guided by caring and morally responsive teachers.

The Changing Landscape of Moral Reasoning

If teachers want to play a role in the shaping of the health of their community and environment, then they ought to become morally culpable and not take refuge in inaction (Dewey, 1935). Let us reconsider the Edward Abbey epigraph at the beginning of the chapter. Despite the uncertainties that are implicit within science, we cannot simply end with the evidence that western honeybees are declining: what if something else takes over their ecological niche and the honeybees are about to disappear? And we cannot end with an explanation of why western honeybees matter to the environment and humans. What if the environment would be better off without humans as E.O. Wilson (2006) has asserted? We cannot defend the western honeybee without the more holistic focus that the Earth provides.

A criticism of both the NRC's (2007) report on the status of pollinators and the book referenced throughout this chapter by Benjamin and McCallum is that they do not delve deep enough into the issues of colony collapse to fully recognize the benefits of educational practices that go beyond building a garden, tending to bees, recycling, or learning about science in school. With an ecojustice perspective through socioscientific issues, we are better able to get at some of the more influential cultural skills, traditions, community events, and knowledge that need to be emphasized in school. If not, some of these traditions may eventually be lost at the same rate as the world's languages. The development of moral reasoning and critical thinking skills will provide students with the tools necessary to effectively develop their worldly understandings. Ecojustice helps to frame cultural and community decisions around rights, strengths, beauty, and what is good for the prospects of future generations. Socioscientific issues, ethical discourse, and functional scientific literacy are certainly some of the most innovative contemporary trends in education today and facilitate the development of this citizenry. Without some sort of concrete way to act upon these philosophical discussions, students are left with merely disconnected abstractions of science and inquiry twice removed from Earth. Therefore, functional scientific literacy is consonant with the acknowledgment of the role that the Earth plays in our moral reasoning and choices. As environmental toxins threaten all of us and particularly the more sensitive bodies of children worldwide, students will need to know the story of the western honeybee and its decline. They will need to know how to monitor species and habitats including their own. They will need to know how to collaborate with other schools in the pursuit of shared knowledge as they investigate these kinds of issues. It is exciting to be at the forefront of the ecojustice trends through SSI movement for science education in the name of future generations.

References

Benjamin, A., & McCallum, B. (2009). *A world without bees: The mysterious decline of the honeybee—and what it means for us.* London: Guardian.

Carson, R. (1962). *Silent spring.* New York: First Mariner.

Coburn, J. (2006). *Street science.* Cambridge, MA: The MIT Press

Committee on Science, Engineering, and Public Policy. (2007). *Rising above the gathering storm: Energizing and employing America for a brighter economic future.* Washington, DC: National Academies.

Dewey, J. (1935). The teacher and his world. *The Social Frontier, 1*(4), 7.

Diamond, J. (2005). *Collapse.* New York: Penguin.

Eames, S.M. (1977). *Pragmatic naturalism: An introduction.* Carbondale and Edwardsville: Southern Illinois University Press.

Greenberg, P.E., Kessler, R.C., Birnbaum, H.G., Leong, S.A., Lowe, S.W., Berglund, P.A., & Corey-Lisle, P.K. (2003). The economic burden of depression in the United States: How did it change between 1990 and 2000? *Journal of Clinical Psychiatry, 64*(12), 1465–1475.

Kahne, J., & Sporte, S. (2008). Developing citizens: The impact of civic learning opportunities on students' commitment to civic participation. *American Educational Research Journal, 45*(3), 738–766.

Lleras, C. (2008). Do skills and behaviors in high school matter? The contribution of noncognitive factors in explaining differences in educational attainment and earnings. *Social Science Research, 37*(3), 888–902.

Mueller, M.P. (2009). Educational reflections on the "ecological crisis": Ecojustice, environmentalism and sustainability. *Science & Education, 18*(4), 999–1012.

Mueller, M.P., & Bentley, M.L. (2007). Beyond the "decorated landscapes" of educational reform: Toward landscapes of pluralism in science education. *Science Education, 91*(2), 321–338.

Mueller, M.P., & Tippins, D.J. (In press). Citizen science, ecojustice, and science education: Rethinking an education from nowhere. In B.J. Fraser, K. Tobin, & C. McRobbie (Eds.), *Second international handbook of science education*. New York: Springer.

Mueller, M.P., & Zeidler, D.L. (2010). Moral-ethical character and science education: Ecojustice ethics through socioscientific issues (SSI). *Cultural Studies and Environmentalism, 3*(1), 105–128.

National Research Council. (1996). *National science education standards*. Washington, DC: *National Academy.*

National Research Council of the National Academies. (2007). *National Research Council of the National Academies, Status of Pollinators in North America*. Washington, D.C.: National Academy of Science.

Roberts, D.A. (2007). Scientific literacy/science literacy. In S. Abell and N. Lederman (Eds.), *Handbook of research on science education* (pp. 729–780). Mahwah: Lawrence Erlbaum.

Singer, P. (2006). *Writings on an ethical life*. New York: HarperCollins.

Sterba, J. (2001). *Three challenges for ethics: Environmentalism, feminism, and multiculturalism*. Oxford: Oxford University Press.

Wilson, E.O. (2006). *The creation: An appeal to save life on Earth*. New York: W.W Norton.

Zeidler, D.L., & Keefer, M. (2006). The role of moral reasoning and the status of socioscientific issues in science education: Philosophical, psychological and pedagogical considerations. In D.L. Zeidler (Ed.), *The role of moral reasoning on socioscientific issues and discourse in science education* (pp. 7–38). The Netherlands: Kluwer.

Zeidler, D.L., & Sadler, T. D.(2011). An inclusive view of scientific literacy: Core issues and future directions of socioscientific reasoning. In C. Linder, L. Ostman, & P. Wickman, (Eds.), *Promoting scientific literacy: Science education research in transaction* (pp. 176–192). New York: Routledge.

Zeidler, D.L., Sadler, T.D., Applebaum, S. & Callahan, B.E. (2009). Advancing reflective judgment through socioscientific issues. *Journal of Research in Science Teaching, 46*(1), 74–101.

Zeidler, D.L., Sadler, T.D., Simmons, M.L., & Howes, E.V. (2005). Beyond STS: A research-based framework for socioscientific issues education. *Science Education, 89*(3), 357–377.

CHAPTER THIRTY-TWO

Understanding Unbelief as Part of Religious Education

NEL NODDINGS

It is often recommended that courses in world religions and Bible literacy be taught in our public schools. Even Richard Dawkins (2006) approves of the latter for its contribution to the understanding of literature. However, it is rarely suggested that students should gain some understanding of deism, agnosticism, atheism, and secular humanism.

Too many adults—even supposedly well-educated adults—express scorn and contempt for unbelievers. It is widely held, and probably true, that a confessed unbeliever could not be elected president of the United States today. No matter what candidates really believe, if they hope to be elected in the United States, they had better say that they believe in God. Students are expected to learn respect, or at least tolerance, for all religions, but little is said about tolerance for unbelief.

I'll begin this paper with a discussion of terms that should be understood and their frequent misapplication. Then I'll consider briefly the intellectual and moral reasons people have offered for rejecting religion. Finally, I'll consider some possible ways to improve communication between believers and unbelievers. In all that follows, I'll speak of unbelief in the context of Christianity, although many of my comments might easily be transposed to other religions.

The Language of Unbelief

In his fascinating study of teenagers and religious belief, Christian Smith found that students sometimes declared themselves to be deists but contradicted themselves in responding to his questions: "22 percent of teen 'deists' in our survey reported feeling close or very close to God (the very God they believe is not involved in the world today). Go figure" (Smith, 2005, p. 42). Apparently, these kids had little understanding of the belief they professed.

Some confusion over the term *deism* is understandable. Over the five centuries or so that it has been used, its meaning has varied, but today it refers to belief in a God indistinguishable from nature or to a God who created the world but does not intervene in its affairs. The first interpretation is found in Spinoza and, much more recently, in Einstein. The second, differing only slightly, is reflected in the writings of the American Founding Fathers—Washington, Jefferson, Franklin, Paine, and Adams. These men spoke of a "creator" but did not believe in a God who watches over humans, hears prayers, or responds with rewards and punishments. We may quibble over whether Jefferson should be labeled an atheist and Adams a Unitarian Christian, but evidence abounds that all of them rejected the central beliefs specific to Christianity.

The deistic beliefs of the founders (and, likely, of Abraham Lincoln) are widely denied, and many Americans insist on calling them "Christians" and the United States a "Christian" nation, even though Washington explicitly denied that the nation was founded on Christian principles (Allen, 2006; Jacoby, 2004). Such false beliefs should be challenged in history courses, and at least a few brief original writings should be used to dispel them.

The term *agnostic* is, of course, derived from the Greek, but our use of the label is usually traced to Thomas H. Huxley, and Huxley's view greatly influenced Darwin. Agnostics hold that we do not know, and probably can never know, whether God exists. Their position seems both admirably humble and scientifically reasonable. Yet they are attacked from both ends of the belief spectrum. Many Christians simply lump them with atheists; atheists accuse them of fence-sitting.

Atheists think there is so little evidence (some argue there is none) for the existence of God that the only logical conclusion to draw is that there is no God. Martin Gardner, a philosophical theist, acknowledged that his faith was "unsupported by logic or science" (1983, p. 209). Indeed, he admired Bertrand Russell's definition of faith as "a firm belief in something for which there is no evidence" (quoted in Gardner, 1983, p. 209). In the writings of the theist Gardner and the atheist Russell, we see possibilities for meaningful dialogue between believers and unbelievers.

Some contemporary atheists—Dawkins, 2006; Dennett, 2006; Harris, 2004, 2006; Hitchens, 2007—make such dialogue difficult. Many of their points are well made, and one wonders why they fall on deaf ears. One wonders, that is, until one reflects on how any of us feels when her deepest convictions are not only challenged but mocked. In contrast to the heavy-handedness just mentioned, E. O. Wilson (2006) invites serious dialogue between Christians and secular humanists. I'll return to Wilson's approach in the last section of this paper.

Secular humanists (as contrasted with religious humanists) reject religion and a God-centered notion of human perfectibility. They put their efforts into improving earthly life for humans and, increasingly, into preservation of the earth and all living things. There are opponents who refer to the "religion of secular humanism," but this is wrong and adds to the confusion surrounding the language of unbelief. Most sociologists studying religion recognize that the best line of demarcation between religion and other belief systems is the inclusion or exclusion of a supreme being, God (Stark & Bainbridge, 1985). Still, this is in itself a discussion to which students should be introduced. In addition to the faulty labeling of secular humanism as a religion, some people have even called Marxism a religion because it has an eschatology—a predicted end-stage. It is indeed odd to classify a Godless ideology as a religion.

Intellectual Objections to Religion

Many thoughtful people give up (or never adopt) belief in God because they find no evidence for its acceptance. All the great attempts at logically establishing the existence of God have been demolished. Some of these proofs can be legitimately explored in math classes. In geometry, teachers might mention that a great philosopher, Immanuel Kant, used Euclidean geometry as an example of logico-mathematical certainty. Actually, at about the time of his writing, non-Euclidean geometries were being invented, and their invention proved Kant wrong in his claim of certainty. However, Kant—like many great philosophers—was also interested in religion, and he successfully destroyed all three of the traditional proofs of God's existence.

Students, unaware of these "proofs," may point at one of them intuitively. There is the world, they may say, a whole universe. Must there not have been a creator? But, then, who or what created the creator and, if the creator created himself, why could we not suppose the same of the universe? Kant answered these questions poignantly:

> We cannot put aside, and yet also cannot endure, the thought that a being, which we represent to ourselves as supreme amongst all beings, should as it were, say to itself: I am from eternity to eternity, and outside me there is nothing save what is through my will, but whence then am I? All support here fails us. (1781/1966, p. 409)

Without expecting high school students to master the details of various attempts at proof, we can induce awareness of them. An outline of Descartes' version of the ontological proof can also be engaged in math class, for example. It should, of course, be pointed out that attempts to prove that God does *not* exist have also failed, but attempts are still made (Martin & Monnier, 2003). Awareness of these logical exercises, like Bible study, can be thought of as part of religious literacy.

The argument from design has to be discussed somewhere in high school. My own preference would be to discuss creationism and intelligent design in science classes—not *as* science but as part of an ongoing challenge that scientists still face. Too often the decision to teach evolution and omit intelligent design is made by school boards, and students are left ignorant about the exciting history of the debate. Or the issue might arise briefly in social studies class—a "current events" treatment bereft of both passion and science.

In an honest discussion, students would learn that, although many scientists are secular humanists, many others retain belief in a personal God, and some provide evolutionary evidence for the existence of God. Simon Conway Morris, for example, offers powerful evidence of a pattern in evolution that leads inexorably to intelligent life. In concluding, he writes:

> None of it presupposes, let alone proves, the existence of God, but all is congruent. For some it will remain as the pointless activity of the Blind Watchmaker, but others may prefer to remove their dark glasses. The choice, of course, is yours. (2003, p. 330)

The Morris book is far too difficult for high school students, but excerpts from it could be read—so, too, the lovely lines from Kant—and readings of this sort could serve as models for generous discussion. We need not attack one another with nasty, disparaging remarks but, unfortunately, both sides have been guilty of this. Christian fundamentalists have equated atheism with evil and immorality, and some of today's atheist writers heap ridicule on believers. Educating for intelligent belief or unbelief requires a more thoughtful, considerate approach (Noddings, 1993, 2003, 2006).

Students should also learn that they may, if they wish, retain their religious affiliation even if they reject some of its beliefs. (This is not true of all religious institutions, of course, but it is of many Christian subgroups.) They should hear of cases in which priests and ministers have doubted the virgin birth, the miracles reported in the New Testament, the trinity, the existence of hell, the correctness of infant baptism, the bodily ascent of Mary into heaven, transubstantiation, and many other ideas held by some to be essential beliefs. Scholars have labeled some of these beliefs "maximally coun-terintuitive" (Slone, 2004), and they are studying how religious groups maintain such beliefs.

As a matter of fact, we cannot conclude what people actually believe from their church atten-dance or even from their public statements. We know, for example, that some of the Founding Fathers, despite their church membership, did not believe in a personal God and, although the large majority of people in the United States today claim belief in such a God, we do not know what they might say in the company of highly respected unbelievers. In such circumstances, they might well feel comfortable expressing some doubt. As Daniel Dennett (2006) has argued, many believers seem to believe in belief, not in particular beliefs.

Science fiction might be used to expand the range of students' thinking. Is it utterly impossible to imagine another dimension in which a whole world of godlike entities exist? Might some of them now and then take notice of human affairs? Why is monotheism favored over polytheism, and whose interests have been served by the elevation of monotheism?

The enduring concern about matters of spirit should be addressed. Atheists and agnostics are not devoid of a sense of wonder and spiritual awe. Bertrand Russell regarded the universe with awe, and his daughter described his life as a spiritual quest (Ryan, 1988). Believers, if they think, are assailed by doubt and unbelievers, if they accept their emotions, are deeply affected by "spirit." Miguel De Unamuno captured the conflict:

"Is there?" "Is there not?"—these are the bases of our inner life. There may be a rationalist who has never wavered in his conviction of the mortality of the soul, and there may be a vitalist who has never wavered in his faith in immortality; but at the most this would only prove that just as there are natural monstrosi-ties, so there are those who are stupid as regards heart and feeling, however great their intelligence, and those who are stupid intellectually, however great their virtue… (1954, p. 119)

Moral Objections to Belief

In the late nineteenth century, many erstwhile Christian believers turned against religion. "Declarations of unbelief often sounded more like acts of moral will than intellectual judgments," writes James Turner (1985). Oddly, Christian churches at the time had made a discernible shift from stern prac-tices toward more humane messages emphasizing the relief of suffering. The anticruelty sentiment was then turned against religion itself. Newly confessed unbelievers cited both the cruelty of nature and the cruelty of religion as reasons for their unbelief.

Darwin, for example, was certainly shaken by the cruelty and indifference of the natural world, but he was pushed even harder into agnosticism by the cruelty of Christian beliefs. He wrote:

I can indeed hardly see how anyone ought to wish Christianity to be true; for if so, the plain language of the text seems to show that the men who do not believe, and this would include my father, brother and almost all my best friends, will be everlastingly punished. And this is a damnable doctrine. (quoted in Browne, 2002, p. 432)

Today there are Christian groups that do not require belief in hell, but most still do, and thoughtful believers are likely to become unbelievers when they consider the question: What sort of God would say to his creatures, "Believe in me, or go to hell"? Karen Armstrong (1995), for example, revolted at the task she was given by the Catholic Church—to fill children with guilt and teach them doctrines through fear.

The public schools cannot speak out directly against the practices of any religious institutions (except when they violate state laws), and they should not indoctrinate either for or against religion, but they should protect children from religious cruelty by exposing them to a variety of views that may help them eventually to reject harmful beliefs such as the one on hell. I agree with Dawkins (2006) that teaching children to believe in eternal punishment in hell is a form of child abuse. In explaining why he was not a Christian, Russell, too, spoke on this: "There is one very serious defect to my mind in Christ's moral character, and that is that He believed in hell" (1957, p. 17).

An important intellectual problem arises in discussion of belief in hell. Many theologians recognize that we cannot logically hold to all three great characteristics so often attributed to God: omniscience, omnipotence, and all-goodness. Indeed, while the existence or nonexistence of God cannot be logically proved, the coexistence of these three attributes has been effectively demolished. Something has to be given up. What bewilders so many unbelievers is that few believers consider questioning God's "all-goodness"—the one attribute that is contradicted by a clear look at the natural world. When people are wiped out by tsunamis, babies are born with horrible defects, and people of all ages suffer dreadful illnesses, how can we speak of a good and merciful God? What sort of God would create a world in which its creatures must eat one another to stay alive? Even C. S. Lewis (1962) had a hard time with questions of animal pain, and he answered them badly. Indeed, although I believe that students should be exposed to Lewis as well as Russell, it might happen that, paradoxically, reading *The Problem of Pain* (1962) would convert some believers to unbelief.

Another moral objection to Christianity is its habit of placing itself above history—claiming that moral offenses by Christian groups are aberrations or misunderstandings and that Christianity is a "religion of peace." (Christianity is not alone in this, of course. Every day now we hear Moslems threatening violence when they are accused "falsely" of embracing a violent religion.) From this perspective, wrongs done in the name of Christianity are distortions, but Christians seldom ask themselves what it is in Christian doctrine that grounds such distortions, and why it is that Christian history is loaded with violence, intolerance, and cruelty. There is too little discussion of contradictions in the Bible—for example, the Prince of Peace claiming, "Think not that I come to send peace on earth: I came not to send peace, but a sword" (Matthew 10:34). The verses that follow this are not comforting, and terrible threats appear again in Matthew 11:22, 23; 12:30, 31; 13:40–42, 50. The disavowal of peace is repeated in Luke 12: 51–53.

The frustration of unbelievers is directed at the Christian God when we read Matthew 25: 35–46 where Jesus promises salvation to believers who act compassionately to "the least of these my brethren." Compassionate unbelievers want to know why God does not follow his own commands. What is he doing for the least of these my brethren?

Thoughtful readers can see what so angers Dawkins and Harris and before them Robert Ingersoll and Russell. Yet, if we mean to educate, we must find a way to communicate honestly and compassionately across the gulf of belief and unbelief.

Communicating to Educate

E. O. Wilson's *The Creation* (2006) is a model of attempted communication. Written as a letter from a secular humanist (Wilson) to a nameless southern Baptist pastor, it is "a call for help and an invitation to visit the embattled natural world in the company of a biologist." Wilson wants the pastor to join him in saving life on earth. The technique is one recommended by savvy diplomats; it was also recommended by John Dewey. The idea is to talk about something on which we might agree—to admit our differences but to join together in some significant task.

Wilson starts right out stating the differences:

> You are a literalist interpreter of Christian Holy Scripture. You reject the conclusion of science that mankind evolved from lower forms. You believe that each person's soul is immortal, making this planet a way station to a second, eternal life. Salvation is assured those who are redeemed in Christ. (2006, p. 3)

Wilson then identifies himself:

> I am a secular humanist. I think existence is what we make of it as individuals. There is no guarantee of life after death, and heaven and hell are what we create for ourselves, on this planet. There is no other home. Humanity originated here by evolution from lower forms over millions of years…

And

> For you, the glory of an unseen divinity; for me, the glory of the universe revealed at last…You have found your final truth; I am still searching. I may be wrong, you may be wrong. We may both be partly right. (p. 4)

It could hardly be said better, but we have to care enough for one another to start the conversation. In contrast to Wilson's approach, consider what Sam Harris says in his *Letter to a Christian Nation*:

> Nonbelievers like myself stand beside you, dumbstruck by the Moslem hordes who chant death to whole nations of the living. But we stand dumbstruck by you as well—by your denial of tangible reality, by the suffering you create in service to your religious myths, and by your attachment to an imaginary God. (2006, p. 91)

His letter is not an invitation to join in a mutually recognized project—saving Darfur, rescuing Katrina survivors, ending war. Rather, it is an attempt to re-educate, to show people how backward they have been and still are. I happen to agree with his main points. I, too, think beliefs should be anchored in evidence. I, too, believe religion has outlived its usefulness and does more harm than good. But if you believe in it, then—like Wilson—I would prefer to say, "You may be right; I may be right, but let's put that aside (we'll come back to it) and tackle this problem on which we can both work." And we should come back to the differences over belief; we should question and answer each other honestly but only when we have reached the point at which it is unthinkable to harm each other.

Harris claims that our schools have failed "to announce the death of God in a way that each generation can understand" (2006, p. 91). Imagine our schools trying to do this! The *New York Times* recently (Dec. 18, 2006) ran a story on a U.S. history teacher in New Jersey who told his students that evolution and the Big Bang are not scientific, that dinosaurs were aboard Noah's ark, and that only Christians have a place in heaven. "If you reject his gift of salvation, then you know where you belong…If you reject that, you belong in hell" (quoted, p. B 6). School administrators told the teacher to desist, but students and parents in the community have "mostly lined up" with the teacher. Stories like this one tempt us to join Harris and Dawkins.

Similarly, many people seem to believe it is all right—perhaps even obligatory—to say dreadful things about unbelievers. The schools can do something about this by honestly and courageously sharing the actual words of unbelievers and the undeserved epithets hurled at them. Because Thomas

Paine said, "My country is the world; to do good is my religion," did he deserve Theodore Roosevelt's condemnation as a "filthy little atheist"? Students should learn that many atheists are good people. What about Hitler and Stalin? they may ask. Well, Stalin was an atheist, but it isn't obvious that his atheism had much to do with his criminal leadership. On the other hand, it isn't clear that Hitler ever publicly rejected his Christian faith; some of his speeches appeal to Christianity to support his anti-Semitism, and many of his followers—even some in the Nazi high command—retained their Protestant affiliation (Steigmann-Gall, 2003). Much can be done in the study of history and literature to set the record straight and get students to think.

It is possible, also, to address these topics in math classes. As mentioned earlier, Descartes' version of the ontological proof and Kant's challenge to the cosmological proof could be studied. In discussion of logical puzzles and antinomies, interesting material on the life of Bertrand Russell could be introduced, including his objections to the concept of hell. Wilson is useful here, too. In a discussion of large numbers, we might share Wilson's comment on hell:

> The condemned will remain in hell…for a trillion trillion years, enough for the universe to expand to its own, entropic death, time enough for countless universes like it afterward to be born, expand, and likewise die away. And that is just the beginning of how long condemned souls will suffer in hell—all for a mistake they made in choice of religion during the infinitesimally small time they inhabited Earth. (p. 6)

Can students imagine a trillion years? A trillion trillion? Graphed against such an enormous number, what does the average human life span look like?

I am not suggesting that a special course or unit of study be organized around the topic of unbelief. That add-a-course strategy is our usual approach to new topics, but I think it is usually a mistake. Teaching explicit facts in history or special vocabulary in biology or technical details on metaphor and simile in English may actually explain the adult ignorance we so deplore in our citizens. Topics essential to human flourishing should pervade all of our subjects. It is entirely appropriate to diverge from prescribed math objectives to a discussion of the life of Descartes, Russell, Whitehead, or Erdos and to share information on their views of politics, religion, war, and nature. Similarly, science teachers should introduce students to the political issues involving evolution and creation. And in English classes, literature should be chosen for its contribution to an understanding of existential questions.

In the process of education, students should read the 23rd Psalm, but they should also read Darwin's concluding lines in *On the Origin of Species*:

> There is a grandeur in this view of life, with its several powers, having been originally breathed into a few forms or into one; and that, whilst this planet has gone cycling on according to the fixed law of gravity, from so simple a beginning endless forms most beautiful and most wonderful have been, and are being, evolved. (Darwin, 1859, p. 490)

We should, however, continue to ask questions of one another, to suggest the need for evidence and/or logical justification, to point out weaknesses in one another's positions. But we should try to limit the insults leveled at both atheists and fundamentalists. Alan Peshkin put it well in his study of a Christian fundamentalist school. Calling for civility, he wrote:

Without compassion and civility, I may too readily dismiss you and your claims for survival as a nuisance, as a barrier to progress, and thereby deny that your stripe of humanity deserves the voice, the time, and the space to be heard and acknowledged as worthy. (1986, p. 291)

We must continue to seek an avenue of communication.

Bibliography

Allen, Brooke. (2006). *Moral minority*. Chicago: Ivan R. Dee.

Armstrong, Karen. (1995). *Through the narrow gate*. New York: St. Martin's Press.

Browne, Janet. (2002). *Charles Darwin: The power of place*. New York: Alfred A. Knopf.

Darwin, Charles. (1859). *The origin of species*. London: John Murray.

Dawkins, Richard. (2006). *The God delusion*. Boston: Houghton Mifflin.

Dennett, Daniel C. (2006). *Breaking the spell*. New York: Viking.

Gardner, Martin. (1983). *The whys of a philosophical scrivener*. New York: Quill.

Harris, Sam. (2004). *The end of faith: Religion, terror, and the future of reason*. New York: W. W. Norton.

Harris, Sam. (2006). *Letter to a Christian nation*. New York: Alfred A. Knopf.

Hitchens, Christopher. (2007). *God is not great: How religion poisons everything*. New York: Twelve (Warner Books).

Jacoby, Susan. (2004). *Freethinkers*. New York: Metropolitan Books.

Kant, Immanuel. (1781/1966). *Critique of pure reason* (F. Max Muller, Trans.). Garden City, NY: Doubleday Anchor Books.

Lewis, C. S. (1962). *The problem of pain*. New York: Macmillan.

Martin, Michael & Monnier, Ricki (Eds.). (2003). *The impossibility of God*. Amherst, NY: Prometheus Books.

Morris, Simon Conway. (2003). *Life's solution: Inevitable humans in a lonely universe*. Cambridge: Cambridge University Press.

Noddings, Nel. (1993). *Educating for intelligent belief or unbelief*. New York: Teachers College Press.

Noddings, Nel. (2003). *Happiness and education*. Cambridge: Cambridge University Press.

Noddings, Nel. (2006). *Critical lessons: What our schools should teach*. Cambridge: Cambridge University Press.

Russell, Bertrand. (1957). *Why I am not a Christian, and other essays on religion and related subjects*. New York: Simon & Schuster.

Ryan, Alan. (1988). *Bertrand Russell: A political life*. New York: Hill & Wang.

Steigmann-Gall, Richard. (2003). *The holy Reich*. Cambridge: Cambridge University Press.

Slone, D. Jason. (2004). *Theological incorrectness: Why religious people believe what they shouldn't*. Oxford: Oxford University Press.

Smith, Christian. (2005). *Soul searching: The religious and spiritual lives of American teenagers*. Oxford: Oxford University Press.

Stark, Rodney, & Bainbridge, William. (1985). *The future of religion*. Berkeley: University of California Press.

Turner, James. (1985). *Without God, without creed*. Baltimore: Johns Hopkins University Press.

Unamuno, Miguel De. (1954). *Tragic sense of life* (J. E. Crawford, Trans.). New York: Dover.

Wilson, Edward O. (2006). *The creation: An appeal to save life on earth*. New York: W. W. Norton.

(This chapter originally appeared in Steven P. Jones & Eric C. Sheffield [eds.], *The Role of Religion in 21st-century Public Schools* [New York: Peter Lang, 2009].)

CHAPTER THIRTY-THREE

Moral Education for the 21st Century

A Buddhist View

DANIEL VOKEY

Human intelligence or human knowledge without proper balance of good heart, warm heart, sometimes brings more unhappiness in our fellow human beings, in other sentient beings, and in the planet itself—and in the individual person her or himself also.

H. H. THE 14TH DALAI LAMA, TENZIN GYATSO[1]

Introduction

My task in this chapter is twofold: to describe what is distinctive about moral education undertaken from a Buddhist point of view and to explain how a Buddhist approach to cultivating moral virtue is relevant to modern life in our secular, pluralistic, liberal democratic societies. Liberal democracies such as Canada and the United States are pluralistic in the sense that citizens represent a wide variety of beliefs and backgrounds and so have different moral, religious, philosophical, and political commitments. Public educational institutions are secular in the sense that morality is no longer understood according to the concepts of any one community or tradition, whether religious, philosophical, or otherwise—although the moral languages of some traditions are better represented in public life than others.[2] It is therefore not surprising that strong disagreement exists over whether moral virtue should be cultivated in public schools, colleges, and universities—and, if so, what forms of moral virtue, how, and by whom.[3] Pluralism presents a challenge, then, because even those who agree that moral education is important often disagree on what it should look like in theory and in practice.

Should public institutions refrain from undertaking moral education, if it can be such a source of conflict? As a Buddhist, and as a moral philosopher inspired by the teachings of Socrates, Plato, and Aristotle, I believe that cultivating moral virtue promotes our individual and collective well-being today as much as in classical or ancient times. Indeed, I believe that moral education is more important today than ever because, when properly understood and practiced, it can play an important role in repairing the ecological, economic, political, and social breakdowns that are reaching crisis proportions in communities across the globe. Accordingly, I think attention to moral development should be an integral part of educational initiatives across the life span, inside as well as outside formal institutions such as schools. At the same time that pluralism presents obstacles to moral education, it also presents opportunities, because the different perspectives that people have on cultivating moral virtue can be complementary to a greater or lesser degree. Ideally, sharing different perspectives upon topics such as moral education enables people to build upon the accumulated insights of each point of view. We can hope that, by comparing and contrasting different traditions of virtue ethics, those offering educational programs in public schools, colleges, and universities might identify enough common ground to collaborate effectively in promoting at least some forms of positive moral development on a socially significant scale. As our international interdependence grows, so too does our need for commitment to at least the basics of a global ethics (Goodenough 1998; Gyatso 1999).

Reaching enough agreement across religious, philosophical, political, and/or cultural differences to collaborate on moral education will not be easy. I expect that, for the foreseeable future, efforts to cultivate moral virtue within public institutions will be less comprehensive than the forms of moral education undertaken within communities whose members are united in commitment to one or another particular set of substantive moral beliefs. Still, modest goals and achievements are far better than none at all. Working together across traditions and perspectives does not require that advocates of moral education resolve *all* of their differences, and reaching even enough shared understanding to stop operating at cross purposes would itself be a positive achievement. With this in mind, my intent is not to argue that a Buddhist approach to cultivating moral virtue is superior to its alternatives. Rather, I hope to contribute to the kind of conversations across traditions through which educators inside and outside schools, colleges, and universities might reach enough of a shared understanding of moral education to bring it back onto centre stage in public life.

When discussing moral education for our modern world, I will be speaking from *a*, not *the*, Buddhist perspective. Buddhism originates in the example and words of Siddhartha Gautama (often referred to as Shakyamuni Buddha or simply "the Buddha"), who is generally considered to have lived from 566–486 B.C.E. in the place that is now Nepal. Over the many centuries since the Buddha shared his insights, a wide variety of texts, practices, institutions, and corresponding traditions have developed as Buddhist teachings have been introduced to different historical, geographical, political, linguistic, and cultural contexts.[4] When I became a Buddhist, I became part of a global community formed by all those who aspire to the enlightenment that the Buddha achieved. I did so, however, by joining a unique Buddhist tradition informed by a particular lineage of teachers.[5] What distinguishes the specific Buddhist community in which I practice is not described here in any detail. This is because, if I succeed in my intentions, my account of moral education will be general enough to be compatible with many other Buddhist traditions than my own. Still, readers should keep in mind that no one individual can speak for all other members of even one community within such long-standing and diverse social movements as Buddhism, Taoism, Judaism, Christianity, and Islam. Readers should also remember that, as a "lay practitioner," I do not speak with the authority of the senior teachers within my tradition, much less the current holder of the lineage.

When considering the Buddhist view that follows, it is also important to keep in mind that living traditions, religious and otherwise, take new forms as they adapt to new social environments and respond to the challenges of their day.[6] A perfect case in point is the ongoing transformation of Asian Buddhist teachings, practices, and institutions as they are transplanted into Western cultural contexts, and as they grapple with political, economic, and environmental issues such as global warming.[7] Again, in this context, the details of these transformations are less important than the general point: my account of moral education represents a Buddhist perspective at a particular time in history as well as a particular place. Accordingly, what I offer should be understood as an attempt, not to provide the last word on its topic, but to present core elements of a tradition in a form appropriate to the background and interests of a particular audience—a practice that dates back to the time of Siddhartha Gautama and is inspired by his example. In this case I write for those who have some degree of familiarity with one or more "western" traditions of virtue ethics, who wish to appreciate different perspectives on moral education, but who have yet to investigate what makes Buddhist views distinct.

A final introductory point: virtue means "excellence." Following Aristotle's example, human virtues or excellences are often divided into two categories according to the different ways in which they are taught and learned: Intellectual virtues are acquired principally through direct instruction and study; moral virtues (aka "virtues of character" or "moral dispositions") are acquired through habituation or practice over time (what today we might call "life experience"). Although in this chapter I focus upon more the cultivation of moral virtue, moral education must be complemented by efforts to promote all forms of human excellence if practical wisdom is our goal. To know and do the right thing at the right time requires a combination of perceptual, emotional, intuitive, intellectual, volitional, and communicative capacities (Vokey and Kerr, in press).

Achieving the Human *Telos*: Realizing "The Heart of Enlightened Mind"

> We shall not cease from exploration
> And the end of all our exploring
> Will be to arrive where we started
> And know the place for the first time.
> T. S. ELIOT "LITTLE GIDDING" (*FOUR QUARTETS*)

Buddhist virtue ethics, like its distant Aristotelian cousin, is teleological in Alasdair MacIntyre's sense of the term. As such, it describes an educational path to the realization of our full human potential, which is our final end or *telos* (MacIntyre 1988: 52–53). Like other teleological traditions, Buddhism believes that we all have the same innate human nature, including the same deep desire to reach our *telos*. We are so constituted that, when our full potential is realized, we will experience the most profound and complete form of human fulfillment possible. Conversely, we will all continue to experience some measure of restlessness and dissatisfaction unless and until our full potential is realized. It is thus not surprising that Buddhism considers it very important to describe our true nature accurately enough for us to understand how to achieve our *telos*. What is this potential that we should aspire to realize?

Mahāyāna Buddhist teachers report that our fundamental nature is *bodhicitta*, describing it as the inseparable union of unconditioned awareness, unobstructed insight, and boundless compassion.[8] *Bodhi* means "awake" and *citta* means "heart-mind," thus *bodhicitta* has various translations such as "enlightened mind," "enlightened heart," and (my favourite) "the heart of enlightened mind." One traditional Buddhist analogy likens the innate insight and compassion of *bodhicitta* to the light and warmth of the sun and compares unconditioned awareness to the boundless blue sky. Describing it as "unconditioned" means that *bodhicitta* is not the product of contingent factors but is always already there, pre-existing thought. It is thus "unconditioned" also in the sense that it is prior to and so free from all the frames of reference constructed through language, including the basic duality of *self* and *other*. It follows from this view that, contrary to what we normally assume, it is not a "self" that is aware. Rather, all thoughts, emotions, and perceptions that take the existence of "me" for granted arise within the "space" of unconditioned awareness.

Unconditioned awareness is a way of being to be experienced rather than a concept to be intellectually grasped. Words such as *bodhicitta* are thus like a finger pointing at the moon: we appreciate their meaning when we catch a glimpse of that to which they direct our attention. Because *bodhicitta* is our basic nature, we can and do experience glimpses of it on any given day, such as when something genuine touches our heart and melts our boundaries. Or, perhaps we have an experience of being "in the zone," where right action spontaneously arises as naturally and effortlessly as leaves falling from a tree. Most of the time, however, the ever-present insight and compassion of *bodhicitta* is obscured by our habits of perceiving, feeling, thinking, and acting dualistically. Experiencing is *dualistic* when what arises within the space of unconditioned awareness is interpreted through the lens of "either-or" predicates, with the result that phenomena are categorized as either "this" or "that"—either, for example, good or bad, for me or against me.[9]

The most basic form of dualism is the deeply ingrained habit of interpreting experience as the result of interaction between a "subject" (me) and "the world" (including other subjects), *each of which/whom is assumed to exist separately from the other(s)*. If we examine our experience closely, however, we will discover that "self" and "other" are relational—we could say they are two sides of the same coin. Buddhism anticipated modern science by many centuries when it taught the doctrine of dependent-origination (*pratītya-samutpāda*), which maintains that everything exits in connection with everything else. Language, which is dualistic, represents objects such as plants and animals as if they existed independently. We now appreciate that organisms and environment co-exist as a web of relationships, an exchange of energy and elements. The maple tree that I might think of as a self-existing "thing" is actually only a relatively stable, continuously changing composite of earth, air, water, and sunlight. Similarly, it is a convention of language—English, at any rate—that we each exist as separate persons. The Buddha realized, however, that this is simply a convenient fiction. Contrary to Descartes, Buddhism argues that the existence of a continuously and independently existing *thinker* cannot be validly deduced from simply observing that *thinking* is taking place. Nor can the existence of a self-existing subject be empirically confirmed, whether through introspection or otherwise.[10]

The Buddha taught that duality originates in a fundamental confusion about the true nature of phenomena, our selves included. When we do not recognize unconditioned awareness as the inexhaustible ground of being, panic arises—a kind of vertigo caused by its lack of boundaries or limits. To allay that panic we invent all manner of conceptual frameworks to establish our bearings, so to speak. Although they can be very useful, the conceptual frameworks that language creates cause further confusion to the extent we forget they are convenient fictions, rather like the grid lines and national boundaries drawn on a map. Almost invariably, we *do* forget the constructed, contingent nature of ideas and concepts because we are focusing upon *the content* of experience interpreted dualistically, while ignoring the unconditioned space in which phenomena arise. You could say that we get so caught up in the story line of the movie that we experience the images as if they were real, and give no thought to the projector and screen.

According to Buddhism, the failure to recognize *bodhicitta* as our true nature has profound consequences. Because of the panic arising from confusion, we cling tightly to our identities—our current beliefs about who we are (and are not)—and most desperately to the fundamental assumption that we exist as independent beings. In Buddhism, the term *ego* is used to designate the set of habitual patterns of self-centred perceiving, feeling, thinking, and acting that, driven by existential uncertainty, reproduce and reinforce the illusion of separate existence. All to no avail: fixation upon the content of our beliefs is at best a very temporary antidote to the imagined threat of non-existence. So long as confusion over our true nature persists, we are haunted by an underlying anxiety that, even when momentarily repressed, is never very far from the surface.

Buddhism understands our existential uncertainty, and the feelings of uneasiness and dissatisfaction that result, to be the root cause of the "three poisons" of greed, aggression, and ignorance. Desperate to distract ourselves, we become acquisitive, seeking fulfillment in material possessions and/or in more intangible assets such as sensual pleasure, emotional arousal, and intellectual stimulation. We might accumulate money, power, and fame, but again to no avail, because whatever we imagine we gain quickly becomes something that we fear to lose—and do lose, sooner or later. Our acquisitiveness thus typically gives rise to various forms of aggression, both proactive and reactive, that are intended to secure more of what we think will make us happy or to protect what we already have from perceived external threats. Thus pre-occupied with maintaining our territory and possessions, we are chronically indifferent to the well-being of others, and oblivious to the suffering that results from competition and greed.[11] According to Mahāyāna Buddhism, then, human suffering originates in anxiety over a fictional separate self that is created because we have lost sight of who we really are.

The Buddhist "good news" is this. *Bodhicitta* has not been, is not now, and never will be compromised or diminished by human confusion and neurosis, as the light and warmth of the sun remain unchanged behind the clouds that might obstruct our view of the open sky. Notwithstanding how deeply the habits of self-preoccupation are ingrained, we all have the potential to uncover wakefulness, insight, and compassion in every moment, a discovery that is likened to finding a precious jewel in "a heap of dust"—rather like the pearl of great price.[12] Because *bodhicitta* is always already there to be glimpsed through breaks in the clouds of discursive thought, we sense possibilities of a very different, more open-hearted way of being and feel pangs of remorse when we close ourselves off. Again, however, that which we long for most deeply cannot be captured in words. What it would be like to recognize *bodhicitta* as our true nature—the dawning of enlightenment—can only be suggested by analogy. Traditionally, the experience of seeing through the veil of duality is compared to being roused from a troubled sleep, since mistaking the content of dualistic thoughts and emotions for reality is like dreaming, another state in which we inhabit the worlds constructed by discursive mind (Gyamtso 1988: 87). This analogy explains why Siddhartha Gautama became known as "the Buddha" after he unravelled confusion to find the heart of enlightened mind: *buddha* is Sanskrit for *awake*.

The ever-present potential for enlightenment is good news not least because, as confusion gives rise to anxiety and fear; so insight into the true nature of things brings relaxation, contentment, and serene equanimity.

> The real glory of meditation lies not in any method but in its continual living experience of presence, in its bliss, clarity, peace, and, most important of all, complete absence of grasping. The diminishing of your grasping is a sign that you are becoming freer of yourself. And the more you experience this freedom, the clearer the sign that the ego and the hopes and fears that keep it alive are dissolving and the closer you will come

to the infinitely generous "wisdom of egolessness." When you live in that wisdom home, you'll no longer find a barrier between "I" and "you," "this" and "that," "inside" and "outside"; you'll have come, finally, to your true home, the state of non-duality. (Sogyal 1995)

What do duality and non-duality have to do with moral education? The answer lies in the connection between *bodhicitta* and the virtuous activity of a *bodhisattva*.

Right Motivation, Right Perception, Right Feeling, Right Thought, Right Action

> It is impossible for the bodhisattva to destroy or harm other people, because he embodies transcendental generosity. He has opened himself completely and so does not discriminate between this and that. He just acts in accordance with what is. From another person's point of view—if someone were observing the bodhisattva—he always appears to act correctly, always seems to do the right thing at the right time. But if we were to try to imitate him, it would be impossible to do so, because his mind is so precise, so accurate that he never makes mistakes.
>
> THE VIDYADHARA, THE VENERABLE CHÖGYAM TRUNGPA, RINPOCHÉ

For Aristotle, the right thing to do in a particular situation is what the person of practical wisdom, the *phronimos*, would do. The practically wise person possesses and exercises both the intellectual virtues and the virtues of character such as courage, temperance, and justice. To be a person of excellent character is to be "appropriately moved" by events; that is, to feel the right emotion, at the right time, to the right degree, and with respect to the right object or person. When combined with the intellectual virtues, such virtues of character enable us to apprehend what conduct would be "noble and fine" in a particular situation and to act accordingly out of love of virtue for its own sake. Moral virtues are cultivated through a process of habituation as we noted earlier. Inspired by the example and instruction of a wise teacher and with the support of a well-ordered society, we try our best to do what a genuinely virtuous person would do. By paying close attention to what results from our conduct, we can gradually learn from experience both to judge for ourselves what actions are genuinely courageous, generous, and just and to be motivated by the intrinsic rightness or goodness of virtuous action. Although it is of great individual and social benefit and a source of pleasure, virtuous conduct is experienced as its own reward by those who are truly wise.[13]

I find Buddhist and Aristotelian virtue ethics to be similar in many important respects. Both identify the right thing to do in any particular situation with what a genuinely virtuous or "fully realized" person would do, and not with what is dictated by universal principles or laws. In Mahāyāna Buddhism, the fully realized person is a *bodhisattva*, meaning a being (*sattva*) who is *awake*. Bodhisattvas manifest the six "transcendental virtues" of generosity (*dana-paramita*), discipline (*shila-paramita*), patience (*kshanti-paramita*), joyful exertion (*virya-paramita*), meditative stability (*dhyāna-pāramitā*), and intuitive insight (*prajñā-pāramitā*).[14] The virtuous activity of the *bodhisattva*, like that of the *phronimos*, is motivated by the intrinsic rightness or goodness of doing what the situation demands. Buddhism thus agrees with Socrates that "virtue is knowledge" in the sense that, once we fully appreciate how virtuous activity is its own reward—and, conversely, how acting contrary to virtue inevitably causes harm for self and others—then extrinsic motivation to do what is right, and will power to resist temptation, are both no longer required (Vokey 2007; Mukpo 2003: 204–205). Aristotelian and Buddhist virtue ethics also both acknowledge that, although it is useful to identify distinct virtues for pedagogical reasons, in actual operation they are mutually supporting—each interacts with and completes the rest (Mukpo 2003: 199–200; Trungpa 1973: 167–184). In both, one could say, practical wisdom arises when insight or clear perception is combined with the capacity to be appropriately moved. A related point is that both traditions recognize how moral virtue requires training over time, ideally with community support. Also, because both traditions believe that we become genuinely virtuous by doing what the genuinely virtuous person would do, both assign an essential role to the example and inspiration that wise elders, saints, and sages provide. In Buddhist as in Aristotelian virtue ethics, then, excellences such as generous and just activity are both *fruition* and *path,* both the fulfillment of human potential and the means to make progress toward it.

While similar to Aristotelian virtue ethics in these ways, Mahāyāna Buddhism also differs in significant respects, most conspicuously in affirming a non-dualistic worldview. The virtuous activity of the *bodhisattva* is transcendental in the sense of originating beyond ego (Trungpa 1973: 168), for the *bodhisattva* has recognized the inseparability of self-and-other. The generosity of the *bodhisattva* is thus described as perfect precisely because, from the perspective of an awakened heart and mind, the distinctions between giver, giving, and gift no longer apply.[15] This view of non-duality is reflected in the Sanskrit term translated here as "transcendental virtue," which is the word *paramita*.

> "param" means "other side" or "shore," "other side of the river"; *ita* means "arrived." "Paramita" means "arriving at the other side or shore," which indicates that the activities of the bodhisattva must have the vision, the understanding which transcends the centralized notions of ego. The bodhisattva is not trying to be good or kind, but…is spontaneously compassionate. (Trungpa 1973: 170)

Buddhist virtue ethics is also different in having maintained a kind of historical continuity that Aristotelian educational practices have not. We have no record of what answers Aristotle might have provided to important questions about *how* excellent moral virtues can be developed through the process of habituation and about *how* the intellectual and moral virtues combine in practical wisdom. In contrast, as more and more Buddhist teachers establish centers and programs in the West, we have more and more opportunities to learn from centuries of Buddhist educational experience, particularly the ongoing commitment of Mahāyāna traditions to promote the *bodhisattva* ideal. How, then, are we encouraged to unlearn habits of dualistic perception? How might we learn to "get ego out of the way" of the insight and compassion of enlightened mind, and what role does moral education play in this process?

Enlightenment One Breath at a Time

> Under the hardness there is fear
> Under the fear there is sadness
> In the sadness there is softness
> In the softness is the vast blue sky
>
> ANONYMOUS

The Buddhist path to awakening is a recursive process of hearing, contemplating, and meditating.[16] Buddhism originated at a time when teachings were communicated more by the spoken than the written word. Accordingly, the first step in learning about topics such as *bodhicitta* and *pratītya-samutpāda* is referred to as hearing or listening. While today this can mean "reading" as well, texts by contemporary Buddhist masters are often transcripts of "live" lectures to students (e.g., Gyamtso 1988; Mukpo 2002). With the rise of digital media we are coming full circle: sound and video recordings are more and more often used to replace or supplement written texts in order to preserve the nuances of oral presentation, in which the embodied presence of the teacher plays an important role. In whatever medium we encounter Buddhist teachings, what is most important is that we begin by listening (or reading) attentively, keeping an open mind, so that what we "hear" and subsequently work with is as complete and as undistorted as possible. Traditional reminders about how *not* to listen speak of the futility of pouring tea into overturned, leaky, or poisoned cups to warn against close-mindedness, forgetfulness, and arrogance: common obstacles to understanding teachings that challenge habits of dualistic fixation.

Having "heard" Buddhist teachings, the next stage is contemplating—for example, critically investigating arguments for and against the view of non-duality summarized above. Contemplating can involve one or more of (i) individual study and reflection, (ii) group discussion and debate, and (iii) question and answer sessions with a qualified teacher. Our task at this stage is to examine thoroughly what we have heard until we are confident both that we understand what was taught *and* that it holds up under dialectical cross-examination. In the case of teachings on non-duality, the process of contemplation is not complete until we can explain and defend to our own complete satisfaction the arguments that undermine naive belief in the independent existence of *self* and *other*. A classic text to support and provoke such contemplation is Nagarjuna's *Verses from the Center (Mūlamadhyamakakārikā)*, which systematically lays out dialectical arguments against fixation on the either-or thinking of dualistic views (Batchelor 2000).

Mahāyāna Buddhism has long recognized that intellectual insight, while important, can only take us so far when recognizing *bodhicitta* is our educational goal. To realize the truth of non-duality, conceptual understanding must be complemented by direct experience. For this reason, meditating is the third dimension of the process of uncovering the clarity and warmth of enlightened mind. As I have been taught, the path of meditation begins with mindfulness practice (*shamatha*), which consists essentially of maintaining a wakeful posture and returning our attention to our breath as often as we notice that our attention has strayed.[17] This sounds easy. Sooner or later, however, we become lost in thought—recollecting past events and/or imagining future scenarios—and completely forget our intention to be mindful. The instruction for such occasions is to gently and patiently label the whole excursion into discursiveness "thinking" and simply come back to the breath. Through this process we can realize that we were already "back" in the present moment by the time we "woke up" to the fact that we had been "gone." We catch a glimpse of an awareness and intelligence at work that is bigger than the deliberate actions of a self-conscious agent.

The intent to stay attentive to the breath highlights the fickleness and wildness of the untamed discursive mind. Since the time of the Buddha, practicing mindfulness meditation has typically resulted in greater awareness of the wide variety of sensations, feelings, and thoughts that arise and pass away in our experience, even when we are sitting alone in a quiet room. The non-judgmental awareness that we cultivate in meditation contrasts with our more usual day-to-day state of consciousness, in which we are so preoccupied with our internal dialogues that we fail to recognize them as self-generated interpretive commentary. In *shamatha*, the intention and practice of gently returning attention to our breath thus creates a "space" of relative relaxation in which we can witness internal dialogues without being completely captive to them. In other words, we gain some perspective on our habitual patterns by learning to dis-identify with our thinking. How does this help?

Recall that ego is driven by fear. Dismantling its constructions requires that we make friends with our fundamental existential anxiety, which means learning to sit with it, experiencing it fully, instead of running away, hiding in thoughts of the future or the past. Dis-identifying with our thoughts enables us to see precisely the strategies we use to avoid feeling uncertainty and dissatisfaction. Each time we recognize, acknowledge, and "let go" our attachments, we relax more and more into the space of intelligence and warmth that lies on the other side of fear. Eventually, enough stability, clarity, and strength of mind develop to see the "emptiness" of thoughts and emotions—how, left to themselves, they simply arise from and dissolve back into the space of unconditioned awareness. With enough practice, we would see clearly that all phenomena arising in experience are nothing other than expressions of our true nature, causing difficulty only when their empty nature is not appreciated. Meditation gradually becomes less and less a matter of struggling with the products of discursive mind and more and more a process of recognizing their transparency.

S*hamatha* is only one form of meditation, and meditation is only one part of the Buddhist "curriculum" or path. The art and science of education are to create specialized environments (classrooms, meditation halls) and to design progressive activities (math drills, meditation exercises) to support the development of capabilities and dispositions that are meant to be applied in everyday life. I have emphasized here the formal practice of sitting meditation because it plays two key roles in cultivating moral virtue, which is essential to realizing our full human potential. First, as we have seen, *shamatha* helps us make friends with fear. To the extent that habits of self-centred perceiving, feeling, thinking, and acting are relaxed, we can respond to situations with the spontaneous wisdom of an open heart and mind. Second, until we are able to get ourselves enough out of the way to let *bodhicitta* shine through, it remains important to continue trying to do what the genuinely virtuous person would do. Mahāyāna Buddhism offers a variety of contemplative exercises to remind us that actions shape character.[18] In particular, teachings on *karma* underline the importance of replacing unwholesome with wholesome activities of body, speech, and mind when we leave the meditation cushion for the street (Patrul 1998). Developing good habits to replace bad ones requires that we recognize when we are operating on the "me" plan, which involves both discernment and presence of mind. Meditation develops both. By retuning again and again to the breath, we cultivate the capacity to be attentive to the present moment; by watching the movement of discursive mind in meditation *we learn to recognize the operations and deceptions of ego during daily life.* In this sense, the injunction to "know thyself" remains as important as ever to the path of moral virtue.

Moral Education for the 21st Century

Expertise in teaching mindfulness meditation is one example of what Mahāyāna Buddhism has to offer the kind of moral education initiatives that would be appropriate within modern, pluralistic, secular societies. Buddhism is, of course, only one of many "wisdom traditions" that offers time-tested teachings and practices through which to cultivate an open heart and mind (Walker 1987). Given the state of the world, we can hardly afford to ignore any source of practical wisdom! Accordingly, I am ready to endorse any tradition or community, religious or otherwise, that manifests the qualities and characteristics of Buddhism that I admire. In what follows, I will consider those positive features of traditions that I believe will be essential to collaboration on moral education in a pluralistic world.

When true to its origins, Aristotelian virtue ethics is practical, not simply theoretical: "We are inquiring not in order to know what virtue is but in order to become good since otherwise our inquiry would have been of no use" (*Nicomachean Ethics* II.2). Similarly, Buddhist teachings and practices are meant to deliver results. Siddhartha Gautama is referred to as "the Great Mendicant" because, like a doctor, he sought to end suffering—you could say he wished to help us return to a state of original health. Perhaps because of this pragmatic orientation, the Buddha admonished his students not to accept what he taught simply because of his reputation. When true to its origins, then, Buddhism is *non-dogmatic*, insisting that its claims are tested through a dialectic of experience and reflection. A corollary of this is that Buddhism is prepared to re-think what it takes to be true, useful, and good in light of new information and new arguments. Through the centuries, Buddhist traditions have demonstrated that they are willing and able to learn from what is unfamiliar, and this *adaptability* is essential if we are to benefit from the opportunities of pluralism.

Two important cases of Buddhist adaptability come to mind. One is the willingness to enter into dialogue with science (Gyatso 2005). Notwithstanding postmodern and other misgivings, natural science remains the paradigm of reliable knowledge in the modern world. Ways of conceiving and promoting moral education must therefore be perceived to be compatible with science in order to be credible. By exhibiting a willingness to engage with science, Buddhism both reaps the rewards of empirical research *and* demonstrates that there is no necessary link between cultivating moral virtue and accepting the dictates of tradition and custom uncritically.

Another example of Buddhism's adaptability is the way in which it is developing teachings and practices of social responsibility and critique—inspired, I suspect, by the prophetic traditions of Judaism, Christianity, and Islam (Glassman 1998). This brings Buddhism even closer into alignment with Aristotle, for whom a concern with ethics naturally leads into a concern with politics and governance: "…even if the good of the community coincides with that of the individual, it is clearly a greater and more perfect thing to achieve and preserve that of a community; for while it is desirable to secure what is good in the case of an individual, to do so in the case of a people or a state is something finer and more sublime" (*Nicomachean Ethics* I.2). I was attracted to the particular lineage I joined and have become more and more convinced of its relevance to modern challenges because of the way in which it attends to culture and politics as well as to individual self-cultivation.[19] I have also been impressed by the ways in which Buddhist teachings are taking up analyses of the forms of systemic oppression that are based upon socially constructed categories of class, race, gender, sexual orientation, ability, and more. There is learning both ways. Rita Gross (1993) considers what feminists have to offer Buddhism as well as the reverse, for some elements of Buddhist tradition re-inscribe patriarchy while others undermine it. Similarly, while Buddhism is not immune to the hazards of "spiritual materialism" (Trungpa 1973)—"new age" magazines are full of glossy ads for products and programs to enhance your prospects for enlightenment—David Loy (2003) has also shown how a Buddhist social theory can diagnose and treat our self-destructive pursuit of profit. The importance of cultivating moral virtue is underlined when poverty, disease, pollution, consumerism, and militarism are recognized as symptoms of confusion; that is, the institutionalization of passion, aggression and ignorance.

In addition to being pragmatic, non-dogmatic, and willing to learn, Buddhism has three additional features I believe are important to 21st century moral education. (The term might sound old-fashioned, but moral education includes those versions of environmental education, transformative education, anti-racist education, and critical pedagogy that undertake to promote commitment to one or more moral values.) One, Buddhism is non-anthropocentric as demonstrated by the bodhisattva vow to achieve enlightenment for the benefit of *all* sentient beings. This corrects the tendency of mainstream Western ethical traditions to assume that only humans have intrinsic value and must be treated with respect. In this way, Buddhism has a natural affinity to many indigenous traditions, particularly those forms of Buddhism that retain a living connection to the sacredness of the earth and its elements.[20] Two, when true to its origins, Buddhism is committed to non-aggression. No less (and perhaps more) than in other times and places, we in the modern West need to be reminded again and again that violence engenders more violence, not peace or justice. This reminder connects to my final point: in working directly with fear, Buddhism can help us close the gap between knowing and actually doing what is right, good, and true. History shows that we often fail to live up to our highest ideals, and this applies as much to moral educators as anyone else, including those located within institutions of "higher" education. Perhaps my colleagues in other faculties of education would agree that joining critical theories with emancipatory practices is not our *forté*. If my own observations are accurate, our success in teaching others to embrace the cause of social justice, while limited, is greater than our success in addressing the relationships of greater and lesser privilege that are endemic to, and perpetuated by, the current structures of the academy. Buddhism reminds us that moral education should not be only, or even primarily, something that adults provide for children and youth. As Parker Palmer (1998: 10) observes, "*Good teaching cannot be reduced to technique; good teaching comes from the identity and integrity of the teacher.*" In this view, our primary responsibility as educators is to look to our own ability to know and do what the genuinely virtuous person would do. The least we could say is that it will be very difficult to teach others to love virtue for its own sake if we do not.

Notes

1. "Balancing Educating the Mind with Educating the Heart" was the theme of a Roundtable Dialogue at the University of British Columbia (UBC) Chan Centre for the Performing Arts on Tuesday, April 20, 2004. The discussion was moderated by Bishop Michael Ingham; the participants were the Dalai Lama, Dr. Jo-Ann Archibald from the Stó:lo Nation, Professor Shirin Ebadi, Rabbi Schachter-Shalomi and Archbishop Desmond Tutu. For a web cast of the dialogue see http://www.iar.ubc.ca/programs/tibet/DalaiLamaVancouver /dlv/events/roundtable.html.

2. As a member of the Faculty of Education at UBC, I work on the traditional, ancestral, and unceded territories of the Musqueum and Coast Salish First Nations. I mention this not only to express gratitude to the Musqueum people who have made me welcome, but also to emphasize that the different perspectives people bring to moral matters (reflecting their different geographical, historical, social, and theoretical locations) are not politically neutral. That some moral languages enjoy a more prominent place in public discourse than others must be understood in part with reference to ongoing relationships of conquest, colonization, and oppression.

3. The essays in the collection by Kiss and Euben (2010) provide a recent overview of the debate in the U.S. over proposals to return virtue ethics to public universities and colleges.

4. Entries in the *Shambhala Dictionary of Buddhism and Zen* (Fischer-Schreiber, Ehrhard, and Diener 1991) such as those under "Siddhartha," "Buddha," "Buddhism," "Theravāda" "Hinayāna" and "Mahāyāna" provide excellent, concise descriptions both of (a) the historical development and geographical expansion of Gautama's teachings and (b) technical Buddhist terms. Williams's (1989) "Introduction" also provides a good overview. The "BuddhaNet" website provides another kind of global overview of Buddhist traditions, teachers, and texts: http://www.buddhanet.net/.

5. My academic study of Buddhism began in the 1970s, my meditation practice began in 1985, and I formally became a Buddhist in 1989. The more I practice and study Buddhism, the more I realize how much I have yet to learn about its many and diverse traditions. What I present here is drawn principally from the Karma Kagyü lineage within Tibetan Mahāyāna Buddhism, particularly as taught to Western audiences by one of its modern lineage-holders, Chögyam Trungpa Rinpoché, and by his eldest son and successor, Sakyong Mipham Rinpoché. For more background on these teachers and their lineage please see http://www.shambhala.org/buddhism.php.

6. See Slater (1978) for an insightful account of how religious traditions can maintain continuity through change.
7. For an introduction to the intersection of political, economic, and environmental issues see *The Story of Stuff: How Things Work* (http://www.youtube.com/watch?v=gLBE5QAYXp8) narrated by Annie Leonard. On "green dharma" see Kaza and Kraft (2000).
8. For philosophical discussions of this view, see Gyamtso (1988) and Thrangu (1996). I am here using *bodhicitta* as essentially synonymous with "buddha-nature" or *tathagatagarbha*.
9. For a detailed explanation and defence of the view that subject-object experiencing is the result of the superimposition of dualistic conceptual frameworks upon what is prior to discursive thought, see Loy (1988: 39–95, 138–150); also Wilber (1985).
10. For elaboration of these points and references to other texts, see Vokey (2001: 214–227).
11. For an audio-visual presentation of this point, see "What about me" http://www.youtube.com/watch?v=FDSAAlrqAHM.
12. Matthew 13:45–46. The precious gem comparison is in Shantideva's *The Way of the Bodhisattva* (*Bodhicharyavatara*). See Chödrön (2005: 71); also Trungpa (1991: 130).
13. This is, in barest outline, the interpretation of Aristotle's *Nicomachean Ethics* that I find persuasive. I am indebted to MacIntyre's (1988) discussion of practical judgment although I disagree on some key points (Vokey 2001: 109–283).
14. Chödrön (2005: xv) expounds Shantideva's teachings on the *paramitas*; see also Trungpa (1991: 108–131).
15. On this point, see Williams (1989: 44–45; cf. Kongtrül 1992: 64–65) on the notion of three-fold purity.
16. See Vokey (2007) for more detail on specific applications of "hearing, contemplating, and meditation" to working with confused thoughts and conflicting emotions, two fundamental forms of the dualism that obscures enlightened mind.
17. On the importance of posture to practice of as well as on the meditation cushion, see Johnson (1996).
18. Perhaps the best example is *The Four Reminders*, a practice of contemplating the preciousness of being born human, the inevitability of death, the unavoidable functioning of karmic cause and effect, and the fruitlessness of ego-centric pursuits (Mukpo 2002).
19. For more on this point, please see remarks by Mipham Rinpoché on the Shambhalian Buddhist view of enlightened society (http://www.shambhala.org/teachers/sakyong_talk01.php).
20. See Wangyal (2002); cf. the discussion at http://buryingthebones.com/about/buddhism-and-indigenous-traditions/.

Bibliography

Aristotle. *Nicomachean ethics.* (2009). (trans D. Ross; revised with an introduction and commentary by L. Brown. New York: Oxford University Press.

Batchelor, Stephen. (2000). *Verses from the centre: A Buddhist vision of the sublime.* New York: Riverhead.

Chödrön, Pema. (2005). *No time to lose: A timely guide to the Way of the Bodhisattva.* Boston: Shambhala.

Fischer-Schreiber, Ingrid; Ehrhard, Franz-Kark; and Diener, Michael S. (1991). *The Shambhala dictionary of Buddhism and Zen* (trans. M. H. Kohn). Boston: Shambhala.

Glassman, Bernie. (1998). *Bearing witness: A Zen master's lessons in making peace.* New York: Bell Tower.

Goodenough, Ursula. (1998). *The sacred depths of nature.* New York: Oxford University Press.

Gross, Rita M. (1993). *Buddhism after patriarchy: A feminist history, analysis, and reconstruction of Buddhism.* New York: SUNY.

Gyamtso, Tsultrim. (1988). *Progressive stages of meditation on emptiness* (2nd. ed). Oxford: Longchen Foundation.

Gyatso, Tenzin (His Holiness the XIV Dalai Lama). (1999). *Ancient wisdom, modern world: Ethics for a new millennium.* London: Little, Brown.

Gyatso, Tenzin (His Holiness the XIV Dalai Lama). (2005). *The universe in a single atom: The convergence of science and spirituality.* New York: Morgan Road.

Johnson, Will. (1996). *The posture of meditation: A practical guide for meditators of all traditions.* Boston: Shambhala.

Kaza, Stephanie, and Kraft, Kenneth. (2000). *Dharma rain: Sources of Buddhist environmentalism.* Boston: Shambhala.

Kiss, Elizabeth and Euben, J. Peter. (2010). *Debating moral education: Rethinking the role of the modern university.* Durham: Duke University Press.

Kongtrül, Jamgon the Third. (1992). *Cloudless sky: The mahamudra path of the Tibetan Buddhist Kagyu School* (trans. R. Gravel). Boston: Shambhala.

Loy, David. (1988). *Nonduality: A study in comparative philosophy.* New Haven: Yale University Press.

Loy, David. (2003). *The great awakening: A Buddhist social theory.* Boston: Wisdom.

MacIntyre, Alasdair. (1988.) *Whose justice? Which rationality?* Notre Dame: University of Notre Dame Press.

Mukpo, Mipham J. (Sakyong Mipham Rinpoché). (2002). *Taming the mind and walking the bodhisattva path.* Halifax: Vajradhatu.

Mukpo, Mipham J. (Sakyong Mipham Rinpoché). (2003). *Turning the mind into an ally.* New York: Penguin Putnam.

Palmer, Parker. (1998). *The courage to teach: Exploring the inner landscape of a teacher's life.* San Francisco: Jossey-Bass.

Patrul Rinpoché. (1998). *The words of my perfect teacher* (rev. ed.; Padmakara Translation Group). Boston: Shambhala.

Slater, Peter. (1978). *The dynamics of religion.* San Francisco: Harper and Row.

Sogyal Rinpoché. (1995). *Glimpse after glimpse.* San Francisco: HarperCollins.

Thrangu Rinpoché, Khenchen. (1996). *The Uttara Tantra: A treatise on Buddha Nature* (rev. ed.). Boulder: Namo Buddha Seminar.

Trungpa, Chögyam. (1973). *Cutting through spiritual materialism.* Boston: Shambhala.

Trungpa, Chögyam. (1991). *The heart of the Buddha.* Boston: Shambhala.

Vokey, Daniel. (2001). *Moral discourse in a pluralistic world.* Notre Dame: University of Notre Dame Press.

Vokey, Daniel. (2007). Hearing, contemplating, meditating: In search of the transformative integration of heart and mind. In C. Eppert and H. Wang (Eds), *Cross-cultural studies in curriculum: Eastern thought, educational insights* (pp. 287–312). New York: Routledge.

Vokey, Daniel, and Kerr, Jeannie. (in press). Intuition and professional judgment: Can we teach *moral discernment?* In L. Bondi, D. Carr, C. Clark, and C. Clegg (Eds.), *Towards professional wisdom: Practical deliberation in the 'people professions.'* London: Ashgate.

Walker, Susan. (Ed.). (1987). *Speaking of silence: Christians and Buddhists on the contemplative way.* New York: Paulist.

Wangyal, Tenzin (Rinpoché). (2002). *Healing with form, energy, and light: The five elements in Tibetan Shamanism, Tantra, and Dzogchen.* Ithaca: Snow Lion.

Wilber, Ken. (1985). *No boundary: Eastern and western approaches to personal growth.* Boston: Shambhala.

Williams, Paul. (1989). *Mahayana Buddhism: The doctrinal foundations.* London: Routledge.

Contributors

Bennett, William J. William J. Bennett has written widely on character education for several decades. He is currently a CNN political analyst and host of *Morning in America,* a nationally syndicated radio program. He was director of the National Endowment for the Humanities and Secretary of Education under President Ronald W. Reagan and director of National Drug Control Policy under President George H. W. Bush. He has also been affiliated with Empower America, the Heritage Foundation, and the Claremont Foundation. His most recent books are *The American Patriot's Almanac: Daily Readings on America,* with John Chubb (Thomas Nelson, 2008) and *A Century of Turns: New Hopes, New Fears* (Thomas Nelson, 2010).

Benninga, Jacques S. Jacques S. Benninga is professor of educational psychology and early childhood education in the Department of Curriculum and Instruction, California State University, Fresno, where he also directs the Bonner Center for Character Education and Citizenship. His primary research interests are moral development, character education, and the civic education of young children. He has published extensively in those areas.

Berkowitz, Marvin W. Marvin W. Berkowitz is the Sanford N. McDonnell Professor of Character Education at the University of Missouri—St. Louis. A developmental psychologist, he directs the McDonnell Leadership Academy in Character Education for school principals. He has written widely on character education, moral development, and prevention of risky behaviors. He is on the editorial board of *Merrill-Palmer Quarterly* and has served on the board of directors of the Association for Moral Education, the Character Education Partnership, and the Jean Piaget Society.

Boyd, Dwight. Dwight Boyd is a professor emeritus of philosophy of education in the Department of Theory and Policy Studies at the University of Toronto, where he taught from 1975 to 2008. His research focuses on moral and political issues in the context of moral education, gender and education, and cultural and racial differences in education. He has published in such journals as the *Journal of Moral Education, Harvard Educational Review*, and *Educational Theory.* He has also served as President of the Ontario Morals/Values Education Association, the Philosophy of

Education Society, and the Association of Moral Education, which honored him with the Kuhmerker Award for distinguished contributions and service to the field of moral education.

Boyles, Deron. Deron Boyles is a professor of educational policy studies at Georgia State University, where he teaches philosophy of education and social foundations of education. He was president of the American Educational Studies Association in 2010. His scholarly interests include school/corporate connections, epistemology, pragmatism and John Dewey, and critical theory. His recent books are *Schools or Markets? Commercialism, Privatization, and School/Business Partnerships* (Routledge, 2004); *The Corporate Assault on Youth: Commercialism, Exploitation, and the End of Innocence* (Peter Lang, 2008); and *The Politics of Inquiry: Education Research and the 'Culture of Science,'* co-authored with Benjamin Baez (State University of New York Press, 2009).

Cooley, Aaron. Aaron Cooley teaches in the Master of Arts in Public Policy program at New England College in Henniker, New Hampshire. He formerly worked at the North Carolina General Assembly and the North Carolina Governor's Office of Education Policy. His research interests focus on democracy, education, and public policy. His articles and reviews have appeared in *Educational Research Quarterly, Educational Studies, Southern California Interdisciplinary Law Journal, Journal of Educational Policy, International Journal of Philosophical Studies, Journal of Popular Culture,* and *Political Science Review.*

Covaleskie, John F. John F. Covaleskie is an associate professor of educational studies at the University of Oklahoma. He taught kindergarten, elementary school, middle school, and high school, as well as serving as a principal and curriculum coordinator in public schools, before becoming a college professor. His published work focuses on the meaning of democratic life and the moral nature of democratic education and citizenship. He has published in *The Journal of Thought, Educational Studies,* and *The Journal of Educational Controversy.*

Delattre, Edwin J. Edwin J. Delattre is a professor emeritus of philosophy at Boston University's College of Arts and Sciences and dean emeritus of its School of Education. He is also president emeritus of St. John's College in Annapolis, Maryland, and Santa Fe, New Mexico. He is a former vice chair of the National Council of the National Endowment for the Humanities and a member of the State Board of Education of the Commonwealth of Massachusetts. He has been affiliated with the American Enterprise Institute and the Heritage Foundation. His most recent book is *Character and Cops: Ethics in Policing,* 5th ed. (AEI, 2006).

DeNicola, Daniel R. Daniel R. DeNicola is a professor of philosophy at Gettysburg College, where he served for over a decade as provost. Previously, he held a parallel title at Rollins College. Past president of the Southeast Philosophy of Education Society, he has published on moral theory, applied ethics, and the moral psychology of Adam Smith. Recently, he has been exploring the philosophy of place, modes of learning, and liberal education.

DeVitis, Joseph L. Joseph L. DeVitis is a visiting professor of educational foundations at Old Dominion University in Norfolk, Virginia. Recipient of the Distinguished Alumnus Award from the College of Education, University of Illinois at Urbana-Champaign, he is past president of the American Educational Studies Association, the Council of Learned Societies in Education, and the Society of Professors of Education. He has written books on moral development, the helping professions, teacher education, school reform, competition in education, the success ethic, and higher education. His most recent books are *Critical Civic Literacy: A Reader* (Peter Lang, 2011) and *Adolescent Education: A Reader* (Peter Lang, 2010), edited with Linda Irwin-DeVitis.

Fletcher, Scott. Scott Fletcher is a professor of education and dean of the Graduate School of Education and Counseling at Lewis and Clark College in Portland, Oregon. His scholarship addresses issues in the philosophy of education, curriculum theory, and teacher education. He has worked in a number of states on teacher preparation policy and with a variety of national school reform initiatives, including the Annenberg Institute for School Reform and the Coalition of Essential Schools. His books include *Education and Emancipation: Theory and Practice in a New Constellation* (Teachers College Press, 2000) and *Philosophy of Education, 2004* (Philosophy of Education Society, 2005).

Glass, Ronald David. Ronald David Glass is an associate professor of philosophy of education at the University of California, Santa Cruz, and director of the University of California multi-campus research program, the Center for Collaborative Research for an Equitable California. He focuses on education as a practice of freedom, issues of ideology and justice, and democratic reform in low-income, racially, culturally, and linguistically diverse communities. His book, co-edited with Pia Lindquist Wong, *Prioritizing Urban Children, Teachers, and Schools Through Professional Development Schools* (State University of New York Press, 2009) examines a six-year Freirean project, The Equity Network, to transform urban schools and the teaching profession.

Harris, Ian. Ian Harris is a professor emeritus in the Department of Educational Policy and Community Studies, University of Wisconsin—Milwaukee. A leading scholar in the field of peace education, he has written *Peacebuilding for Adolescents: Strategies for Educators and Community Leaders,* co-edited with Linda Rennie Forcey (Peter Lang, 1999); *Peace Education,* 2nd ed., co-authored with Mary Lee Morrison (McFarland, 2003); and *Books Not Bombs: Teaching Peace Since the Dawn of the Republic,* co-authored with Charles F. Howlett (Information Age, 2010).

Hudd, Suzanne S. Suzanne S. Hudd is a professor of sociology at Quinnipiac University in Hamden, Connecticut. She teaches courses in social stratification and studies social and cultural influences on education and other institutions. She has written on such topics as character education in American life, middle school students' perceptions of character education, and creating a culture of integrity in higher education.

Irwin-DeVitis, Linda. Linda Irwin-DeVitis is a professor and dean of the Darden College of Education at Old Dominion University, Norfolk, Virginia. She specializes in reading, language arts, adolescent literacy, and the critique of political constructions of literacy. She has had extensive teaching experience in New Orleans and Jacksonville-area middle and high schools. She has written in such journals as *ALAN Review, Educational Studies,* and *Educational Theory.* Her most recent book (edited with Joseph L. DeVitis) is *Adolescent Education: A Reader* (Peter Lang, 2010).

Jenkins, Lynda L. . Lynda L. Jenkins teaches biology and environmental studies at Dalton State College in Georgia and is a doctoral candidate as the University of Georgia. Her doctoral research focuses on the use of citizen science as an educational context in science and environmental education.

Katz, Michael S. Michael S. Katz is a professor emeritus of philosophy and education at San Jose State University. His recent research has focused on ethical issues in teacher-student relationships. A past president of the North American Philosophy of Education Society, he is the lead editor (with Nel Noddings and Kenneth Strike) of *Justice and Caring: A Search for Common Ground in Education* (Teachers College Press, 1999) and the lead editor (with Susan Verducci and Gert Biesta) of *Education, Democracy and the Moral Life* (Springer, 2009).

Kohn, Alfie. Alfie Kohn is a popular writer and speaker on progressive educational issues. He has challenged many conventional school practices and authored incisive critiques of them. His most recent books include *What Does It Mean to Be Well Educated? And More Essays on Standards, Grading, and Other Follies* (Beacon, 2004); *Unconditional Parenting: Moving from Rewards and*

Punishments to Love and Reason (Atria, 2005); *The Homework Myth: Why Our Kids Get Too Much of a Bad Thing* (Da Capo, 2006); *Beyond Discipline: From Compliance to Community* (Association for Supervision and Curriculum Development, 2006); and *Feel-Bad Education: Contrarian Essays on Children and Schooling* (Beacon, 2011).

Kuehn, Phyllis. Phyllis Kuehn is director of the Doctoral Research Center in the Kremen School of Education and Human Development at California State University, Fresno. She also teaches graduate research methods courses for its Department of Educational Research and Administration. Her research area is the effects of low academic language skills in student achievement.

Lewis, Catherine. Catherine Lewis is a senior research scientist in the School of Education at Mills College in Oakland, California. She has published numerous articles and book chapters on character education, Japanese primary education, and social, emotional, and intellectual patterns in childhood and adolescence. She is the author of *Educating Hearts and Minds: Reflections on Japanese Preschool and Elementary Education* (Cambridge University Press, 1995).

Lickona, Thomas. Thomas Lickona is a professor of education at the State University of New York at Cortland. He is past president of the Association for Moral Education and serves on the board of directors of the Character Education Partnership and the advisory council of the Character Counts Coalition. He lectures widely on fostering character education in the home and school. A prolific author of popular books on character education, his most recent texts include *Sex, Love and You: Making the Right Decision,* co-authored with Judith Lickona and M. D. Boudreau (Ave Maria, 2003) and *Character Matters: How to Help Our Children Develop Good Judgment, Integrity, and Other Essential Virtues* (Touchstone, 2004).

Logue, Jennifer. Jennifer Logue is an assistant professor of educational foundations at Southern Illinois University, Edwardsville. She specializes in philosophy of education, gender, and women's studies. She has published in *Philosophy of Education, Philosophical Studies in Education, and Discourse: Theoretical Studies in Media and Culture.*

Mueller, Michael P. Michael P. Mueller is an assistant professor of science education at the University of Georgia. His environmental philosophy focuses on how thinking frames one's relations with others, including nonhuman species. Through community activism and teacher preparation, he emphasizes that we should share responsibility for cultural diversity, biodiversity, natural habitats, and nature's harmony.

Nelsen, Peter J. Peter J. Nelsen is an assistant professor of philosophical foundations of education in the Department of Leadership and Educational Studies at Appalachian State University in Boone, North Carolina. His research interests include moral, political, and epistemological issues in educational philosophy and teacher education. He has published articles in *Philosophy of Education, Education and Culture, the Journal of Curriculum Theorizing*, and the *Journal of Teacher Education.*

Noddings, Nel. Nel Noddings is Lee L. Jacks Professor Emerita at Stanford University. She is a past president of the National Academy of Education, the Philosophy of Education Society, and the John Dewey Society. She has written extensively on caring, ethics and education, spirituality, feminist issues, constructivism, school reform, and the concepts of evil and happiness. Her most recent books include *Happiness and Education* (Cambridge University Press, 2004); *Educating Citizens for Global Awareness* (Teachers College Press, 2005); *Philosophy of Education,* 2nd ed. (Westview, 2006); *Critical Lessons: What Our Schools Should Teach* (Cambridge University Press, 2007); *When School Reform Goes Wrong* (Teachers College Press, 2007); and *The Maternal Factor: Two Paths to Morality* (University of California Press, 2010).

Ognibene, Richard. Richard Ognibene is a professor emeritus of education at Siena College in Loudonville, New York. His teaching career in academe spanned four decades at four institutions, three of which he served as dean of education. His current research areas include school choice and charter schools and the history of 19th-century higher education in New York State's Capital District.

Peck, Marcia. Marcia Peck is an assistant professor of educational foundations and secondary education at Georgia College & State University in Milledgeville. Her academic interests include teacher research, teacher empowerment, and school improvement. She is the co-author (with Andrew Gitlin) of *Educational Poetics: Inquiry, Freedom, and Innovative Necessity* (Peter Lang, 2005). Her most recent publication is a book chapter in *Adolescent Education: A Reader*, co-edited by Joseph L. DeVitis and Linda Irwin-DeVitis (Peter Lang, 2010).

Purpel, David E. David E. Purpel was a professor emeritus of curriculum and educational foundations at the University of North Carolina at Greensboro. He was passionately committed to fostering informed public discourse on education. He enriched those he touched in such works as *The Moral & Spiritual Crisis in Education: A Curriculum for Justice and Compassion in Education* (Bergin & Garvey, 1988); *Beyond Liberalism and Excellence: Reconstructing the Public Discourse on Education,* co-edited with H. Svi Shapiro (Praeger, 1995); *Critical Issues in American Education: Democracy and Meaning in a Globalizing World,* co-edited with H. Svi Shapiro (Routledge, 2004); and *Reflections on the Moral and Spiritual Crisis in Education,* co-authored with William M. McLaurin (Peter Lang, 2004).

Romanowski, Michael H. Michael H. Romanowski is currently a professor of education in the Middle East. He was formerly a professor in the Center for Teacher Education at Ohio Northern University in Ada, Ohio, and has taught in China, Russia, Africa, and Afghanistan. His articles have appeared in numerous scholarly journals as well as the popular media. His most recent book (with Teri McCarthy) is *Teaching in a Distant Classroom* (IVP, 2009).

Schaps, Eric. Eric Schaps is founder and director of the Developmental Studies Center in Oakland, California, which produces and disseminates literacy, character education, and community-building programs for elementary and middle schools. His published work focuses on education, program evaluation, and the prevention of problem behaviors in children. He has received the Science to Practice Award from the Society for Prevention Research and the Sandy Award for Lifetime Achievement in Character Education from the Character Education Partnership.

Simpson, Douglas J. Douglas J. Simpson is the Helen DeVitt Jones Chair in Teacher Education in the Department of Curriculum and Instruction, Texas Tech University. He is a past president of the American Educational Studies Association, the Society of Professors of Education, and the Council of Learned Societies in Education. His recent books include *John Dewey and the Art of Teaching: Toward a Reflective and Imaginative Practice* (Sage, 2005), co-authored with Michael B. Jackson and Judy C. Aycock; *John Dewey: Primer* (Peter Lang, 2006); *Ethical Decision Making in School Administration: Leadership as Moral Architecture* (Sage, 2008), co-authored with Paul A. Wagner; and *Teachers, Leaders, and Schools: Essays by John Dewey* (Southern Illinois University Press, 2010), co-edited with Sam F. Stack, Jr.

Smith, Karen. Karen Smith is a doctoral candidate in the Department of Educational Leadership at the University of Missouri—St. Louis and principal of Mark Twain Elementary School in Brentwood, Missouri. Her school is one of Missouri's "Schools of Character." Her academic interest is character education, especially in primary schools.

Stengel, Barbara. Barbara Stengel is a professor of the practice of education at Peabody College, Vanderbilt University, where she also serves as director of secondary education. Her major interest is in the moral and relational dimensions of teaching, learning, and leadership. Her current focus is the role of emotion, especially fear, in teaching/learning interaction. She is the co-author (with Alan R. Tom) of *Moral Matters: Five Ways to Develop the Moral Life of Schools* (Teachers College Press, 2006) and the editor of *Philosophy of Education, 2007* (Philosophy of Education Society, 2008).

Stone, Lynda. Lynda Stone is a professor of philosophy of education and chair of the research area in Culture, Curriculum, and Change at the University of North Carolina at Chapel Hill. She is currently President of the John Dewey Society and Vice President of the American Educational Studies Association. Her academic interests include philosophy of education, social theory and foundations of education, and democratic education. She has published internationally and nationally for over 25 years. Her contribution to this volume continues a philosophical project on problematic discourses of adult and youth ethics and schooling.

Thayer-Bacon, Barbara J. Barbara J. Thayer-Bacon is a professor of education in the College of Education, Health, and Human Services at The University of Tennessee, Knoxville. Her primary research areas are philosophy of education, pragmatism, feminist theory and pedagogy, and cultural studies in education. She has published widely in such journals as *The Journal of Thought, Educational Theory, Studies in Philosophy and Education, Inquiry, Educational Foundations,* and *Educational Studies.* Her most recent books are *Transforming Critical Thinking: Constructive Thinking* (Teachers College Press, 2000)*; Relational "(e)pistemologies"* (Peter Lang, 2003); and *Beyond Liberal Democracy in Schools: The Power of Pluralism* (Teachers College Press, 2008).

Toffolo, Cris. Cris Toffolo is a professor and chair of the Department of Justice Studies at Northeastern Illinois University in Chicago. She has extensive teaching and research experience in Guatemala, Ghana, Bangladesh, Pakistan, Northern Ireland, Nigeria, and South Africa. She currently serves as co-chair of the Board of the Peace and Justice Studies Association (PJSA) and is a member of the editorial board of *Peace and Change.* Since 1991, she has served as Amnesty International (USA's) Pakistan Country Specialist. Her research areas are conflict resolution, human rights, theories of justice, social movements, peace education, and third world politics. She is the editor of *Emancipating Cultural Pluralism* (State University of New York Press, 2003) and the co-author (with Peggy Khan) of *The Arab League* (Chelsea, 2007).

Verducci, Susan. Susan Verducci is a professor of humanities and coordinator of an undergraduate teacher preparation program at San Jose State University. Her fields of interest include educational philosophy, ethics, moral development, philanthropy studies, and professional education. She is the co-editor (with William Damon) of *Taking Philanthropy Seriously: Beyond Noble Intentions to Responsible Giving* (Indiana University Press, 2006) and the co-editor (with Michael S. Katz and Gert Biesta) of *Education, Democracy and the Moral Life* (Teachers College Press, 2009).

Vokey, Daniel. Daniel Vokey is an associate professor of educational studies at the University of British Columbia. His research areas are moral philosophy and professional ethics, with a focus on the role of spirituality in promoting just, sustainable, and fulfilling ways of life through education. He is a past president of the Canadian Philosophy of Education Society and currently serves as chair of the North American Philosophy of Education's Ethics SIG. He is the author of *Moral Discourse in a Pluralistic World* (University of Notre Dame Press, 2001).

Ward, Janie Victoria. Janie Victoria Ward is a professor of education and chair of the Africana Studies Department at Simmons College in Boston. Her professional work and research interests have focused on the development of African American adolescents, especially their identity formation and moral growth. Along with her teaching responsibilities, she works with youth counselors, secondary school educators, and other practitioners in a variety of settings. Her most recent books are *The Skin*

We're In: Teaching Our Children to Be Emotionally Strong, Socially Smart, and Spiritually Connected (Free Press/Simon and Schuster, 2000) and *Gender and Teaching*, co-authored with Frances Maher (Lawrence Erlbaum, 2001).

Winton, Sue. Sue Winton is an assistant professor of educational leadership and policy at the State University of New York at Buffalo. Her research areas are critical policy analysis and democratic education; and her teaching foci are politics of education and critical study of Canadian and U.S. educational policy. She has written in such journals as the *Journal of Educational Policy, Comparative Education,* and *Changing Perspectives.*

Wynne, Edward A. The late Edward A. Wynne was a professor of education emeritus at the University of Illinois, Chicago, and a prominent advocate for character education for several decades. His work is especially notable for its application to classroom settings, as in the case of one of his last books (co-authored with Kevin Ryan) *Reclaiming Our Schools: Teaching Character, Academics and Discipline,* 2nd ed. (Prentice Hall, 1996).

Yu, Tianlong. Tianlong Yu is an associate professor of educational foundations at Southern Illinois University, Edwardsville, and a visiting "Taishan Scholar" professor of education at Shandong Normal University, China. Born and raised in China and educated in both China and the United States, he writes on the social foundations of education with a keen interest in issues of moral education and multicultural education. He is the author of *In the Name of Morality: Character Education and Political Control* (Peter Lang, 2004) and a number of articles in such journals as *Equity and Excellence in Education, Multicultural Education, Asia Pacific Journal of Education,* and *Discourse: Studies in the Cultural Politics of Education.*

Zeidler, Dana L. Dana L. Zeidler is a professor and program coordinator of science education at the University of South Florida. He is a past president of the National Association for Research in Science Teaching and has served on the executive board of the Association for Science Teacher Education. His research focuses on developing a theoretical framework for theory and practice related to socio-scientific issues in science education.